For Reference

Not to be taken from this room

REF 980.003 ENC V.1

Encyclopedia of Latin America

Encyclopedia of
Latin America

⇥| VOLUME I |⇤

Amerindians through Foreign Colonization
(Prehistory to 1560)

Encyclopedia of
Latin America

⤜❙ VOLUME I ❙⤛

Amerindians through Foreign Colonization
(Prehistory to 1560)

J. MICHAEL FRANCIS
VOLUME EDITOR

THOMAS M. LEONARD
GENERAL EDITOR

☑ Facts On File
An imprint of Infobase Publishing

Encyclopedia of Latin America
Volume I: Amerindians through Foreign Colonization

Copyright © 2010 by J. Michael Francis

Facts On File, Inc.
An imprint of Infobase Publishing
132 West 31st Street
New York NY 10001

Library of Congress Cataloging-in-Publication Data
Encyclopedia of Latin America / Thomas M. Leonard, general editor.
p. cm.
Includes bibliographical references and index.
ISBN 978-0-8160-7359-7
1. Latin America—History—Encyclopedias. I. Leonard, Thomas M., 1937–
II. Francis, J. Michael (John Michael) III. Burkholder, Mark A., 1943–   IV. Rankin, Monica.
F1406.E5155 2010
980'.01303—dc22   2009014594

Text design and composition by Lina Farinella
Cover printed by Sheridan Books, Ann Arbor, MI
Book printed and bound by Sheridan Books, Ann Arbor, MI
Date printed: May 2010
Illustrations by Patricia Meschino
Printed in the United States of America

10 9 8 7 6 5 4 3 2 1

This book is printed on acid-free paper.

CONTENTS

❧ EDITORS AND CONTRIBUTORS ❧

EDITORS

Volume editor **J. Michael Francis, Ph.D.**, associate professor of Latin American history at the University of North Florida, earned a Ph.D. in history from the University of Cambridge. He serves as book review editor for the journal *Ethnohistory* and has published several books on Latin American history, including *Invading Colombia* (Penn State UP) and *Politics, Murder, and Martyrdom in Spanish Florida* (American Museum of Natural History).

General editor **Thomas M. Leonard, Ph.D.**, is distinguished professor and director of the International Studies Program at the University of North Florida. Leonard received a bachelor's degree from Mt. St. Mary's University, an M.A. from Georgetown University, and a Ph.D. from American University. Among Leonard's several publications on U.S.–Latin American relations are *The United States and Central America* (Georgia), *Panama, the Canal and the United States* (Regina), and *Latin America during World War II* (Rowman and Littlefield). He also edited the three-volume *Encyclopedia of the Developing World* (Taylor & Francis), *Encyclopedia of United States–Cuban Relations* (MacFarland), *Day by Day: The Seventies* (Facts On File), and *Day by Day: The Forties* (Facts On File).

CONTRIBUTORS

Altman, Ida. Ida Altman taught at the University of New Orleans for 24 years and joined the University of Florida history department in 2006. She is author of *Emigrants and Society: Extremadura and Spanish America in the Sixteenth Century* and *Transatlantic Ties in the Spanish Empire: Brihuega, Spain, and Puebla, Mexico, 1560–1620* and coauthor, with Sarah Cline and Juan Javier Pescador, of *The Early History of Greater Mexico*. She is completing a book entitled *The War for Mexico's West: Indians and Spaniards in New Galicia, 1524–1550.*

Andrien, Kenneth J. Kenneth J. Andrien is Humanities Distinguished Professor in History at Ohio State University. He received a B.A. at Trinity College and M.A. and Ph.D. degrees at Duke University. Andrien is the author or editor of several books and of numerous articles in scholarly journals and book chapters.

Benton, Bradley Thomas. Bradley Thomas Benton is a doctoral candidate in the Department of History at the University of California, Los Angeles. His dissertation focuses on the 16th-century indigenous nobility of Texcoco, New Spain.

Berger, Eugene C. Eugene C. Berger is an assistant professor of Latin American history at Missouri Southern State University. He has made research trips to Spain, Chile, and Peru. He earned a Ph.D. from Vanderbilt University in 2006. Berger's dissertation is entitled "Peru's Periphery: Frontier Identity and the Politics of Conflict in Seventeenth-Century Chile."

Blanton, Justin. Justin Blanton is a graduate student at the University of North Florida with a focus on colonial Latin American history. His current research focuses on the 17th-century mission system of Spanish Florida.

Borrero, Roberto Múkaro. Roberto Múkaro Borrero is on staff at the American Museum of Natural History's Department of Education. He currently serves as president and chairman of the United Confederation of Taíno People and as chairman of the NGO Committee on the United Nations International Decade of the World's Indigenous Peoples, a special committee of the Conference of NGOs in Consultative Relationship with the United Nations (CONGO).

Browman, David L. Dr. David L. Browman is the director of the Interdisciplinary Program in Archaeology at Washington University in St. Louis. A good deal of his research has investigated the origins of complex society in the puna and altiplano of the Central and South-Central Andes. Recently, he has also devoted significant time to the intellectual history of Americanist archaeology.

Brown, Clifford T. Dr. Clifford T. Brown holds degrees in archaeology and anthropology from Yale and Tulane. He has conducted archaeological fieldwork in various parts of Mexico and northern Central America. He has published extensively on the archaeology and ethnohistory of the region. He is currently assistant professor of anthropology at Florida Atlantic University.

Brown, Kendall. Kendall Brown, a professor of Latin American history at Brigham Young University, is a specialist in the colonial history of the Andes and the political economy of the Spanish Empire. He is currently researching the history of Latin American mining.

Buechler, Jeff. Jeff Buechler is a Ph.D. candidate in anthropology at the University of Illinois at Chicago. His research involves ancient Maya archaeology and hieroglyphic writing, focusing on the Petexbatún region of Guatemala.

Carvajal Contreras, Diana Rocío. Diana Rocío Carvajal Contreras is a Ph.D. candidate in archaeology at the University of Calgary. Her area of expertise is the analysis of animal remains, especially fish and mollusks. She has worked in Colombia, Panama, and Nicaragua.

Christensen, Mark. Mark Christensen is a Ph.D. candidate at the Pennsylvania State University. His dissertation is devoted to Nahua and Maya interpretations of Catholicism.

Christie, Jessica. Jessica Christie is associate professor in the School of Art and Design at East Carolina University and teaches about native North American, Mesoamerican, and Andean pre- and postcontact visual culture. Her research and writing interests center on the Maya and Incas. She has published about Maya palaces and elite residences, indigenous landscapes of origin, and a book about Inca sculpted outcrops is forthcoming.

Chuchiak IV, John F. John F. Chuchiak IV obtained his doctorate from Tulane University in 2000 with a dissertation entitled "The Indian Inquisition and the Extirpation of Idolatry: The Process of Punishment in the *Provisorato de Indios* in the Colonial Diocese of Yucatán, 1569–1812." He is currently associate professor of colonial Latin American history and the director of the Latin American, Caribbean and Hispanic Studies Program at Missouri State University in Springfield, Missouri. His research specialty is in colonial Latin American history with specific research interests in the conquest and colonial history of Mexico and Yucatán, and in colonial Maya ethnohistory. He is also the author of several dozen other articles and chapters published in edited volumes and anthologies. He is presently completing a book manuscript entitled *Battling for the Heavens: Religious Conflicts and Maya Resistance on a Colonial Mexican Frontier, 1563–1721.*

Coe, Michael. Michael Coe is a master's candidate in Latin American studies from Georgetown University. He has traveled extensively throughout the Southern Cone of South America. Coe obtained his bachelor's degree in international affairs from the University of Colorado at Boulder.

Cole, Michael S. Michael S. Cole is assistant professor of history at Florida Gulf Coast University and was awarded a Ph.D. in history by the University of Florida in 2003. He is currently preparing a book-length manuscript on the history of native witchcraft trials in colonial Honduras.

Conway, Richard. Richard Conway is a doctoral candidate in Latin American history at Tulane University. His research focuses on the social history of cross-cultural relations between Native Americans and Spaniards in colonial Mexico. He earned an M.A. from the University of Southern Mississippi and a B.A. from the University of Wales, Swansea.

Cook, Karoline P. Karoline P. Cook is currently a postdoctoral fellow at the USC-Huntington Early Modern Studies Institute in Los Angeles. She received her Ph.D. from Princeton University in 2008. Her dissertation was entitled "Forbidden Crossings: Morisco Emigration to Spanish America, 1492–1650." She recently published the article "Navigating Identities: The Case of a Morisco Slave in 17th-Century New Spain" in *The Americas* 65, no. 1 (July 2008).

Delbridge, Spencer. Spencer Delbridge is a Ph.D. candidate in Latin American history at Pennsylvania State University. He is currently working on a biographically driven doctoral dissertation reexamining Maya and Spanish leadership in the conquest and colonization of Mexico's Yucatán Peninsula.

Diaz, Rosalina. Dr. Rosalina Diaz is a native of Arecibo, Puerto Rico. She is an educational anthropologist specializing in gender and ethnicity issues in the Spanish-speaking Caribbean. At present, she is an associate professor of education at Medgar Evers College of the City University of New York.

Donahue-Wallace, Kelly. Kelly Donahue-Wallace is the author of *Art and Architecture of Viceregal Latin America, 1521–1821* (University of New Mexico Press) and coeditor of *Teaching Art History with New Technologies: Reflections and Case Studies* (Cambridge Scholars Publishing). She is currently associate professor of art history and chair of the Department of Art Education and Art History at the University of North Texas.

FitzPatrick, Elena. Elena FitzPatrick is a graduate of Oberlin College and a Ph.D. student in art history at the City University of New York. She studies Latin

American art, focusing on the material culture of ritual and pageantry in colonial Mexico and Central America.

Goforth, Sean H. Sean H. Goforth is an instructor of world politics at Coastal Carolina University. He was educated at the University of North Carolina–Chapel Hill and the School of Foreign Service at Georgetown University.

González, Francisco J. Francisco J. González received a B.A. in history from the University of Puerto Rico–Mayaguez, an M.A. in history from Minnesota State University–Mankato, and a J.D. from Hamline University School of Law. He is an independent researcher on Caribbean pre-Columbian and colonial history and on Taino ethnic and cultural survival in Puerto Rico.

Gorman, Rebecca D. Rebecca D. Gorman is a Ph.D. candidate in the Department of Anthropology at the University of Florida. Her research interests include American historical archaeology, the early contact period of the Southeastern United States and the circum-Caribbean region, the Spanish mission period of the Southeastern United States, intersocietal interaction, and historic period aboriginal and European ceramic studies. Her current work at the Mission San Juan del Puerto in Jacksonville, Florida, focuses on indigenous issues of materiality, interaction, social constructions based on practice, and cultural continuity and change spanning the early contact period through the end of the mission period in Florida.

Granum, Angela. Angela Granum is an M.A. candidate in Latin American studies at Georgetown University. She is focused on economic development in Latin America and hopes to work on grassroots development projects upon graduation.

Gray, Saber. Saber Gray is a senior Honors History and English major at the University of North Florida. She is currently writing a thesis on Spanish-Indian relations in early colonial Spanish Florida.

Hawkins, Christina. Christina Hawkins graduated magna cum laude with a B.A. from the University of Maryland, Baltimore County. She is currently pursuing an M.A. at Georgetown School of Foreign Service in Latin American studies, with a concentration in political economy and government.

Hidalgo, Alex. Alex Hidalgo is a doctoral student in history at the University of Arizona, where he specializes in colonial Latin America and early Europe. His main interests include visual culture, ethnohistory, and intellectual activity in the Atlantic world. His dissertation will focus on native and Spanish-American cartography in Oaxaca during the 17th and 18th centuries.

Horswell, Michael J. Michael J. Horswell is an associate professor of Spanish and Latin American literature at Florida Atlantic University, where he chairs the Department of Languages, Linguistics, and Comparative Literature. He is author of *Decolonizing the Sodomite: Queer Tropes of Sexuality in Colonial Andean Culture* (University of Texas Press), as well as of articles and book chapters on colonial literary figures such as Sor Juana Inés de la Cruz, Felipe Guamán Poma de Ayala, and the Inca Garcilaso de la Vega.

Kashanipour, R. A. R. A. Kashanipour is a social historian and historical anthropologist of indigenous Mesoamerica. He has conducted historical research on Yucatecan ethnohistory and the colonial frontier and ethnographic studies on native healing practices and Maya identity formation. Bridging social history and medical anthropology, his recent work examines the role of healing and medical practices in forming material and intellectual connections between indigenous peoples, Africans, and Europeans in late colonial Yucatán.

Kole, Kathleen M. Kathleen M. Kole is a graduate student at the University of North Florida, specializing in colonial Latin American history. She is currently preparing a coauthored manuscript on the 1597 Guale uprising in Spanish Florida.

Kyle, Chris. Dr. Chris Kyle is an associate professor of anthropology at the University of Alabama at Birmingham. He is the author of *Feeding Chilapa: The Birth, Life, and Death of a Mexican Region* (University of Oklahoma Press), the coeditor (with Rani T. Alexander) of "Beyond the Hacienda: Agrarian Relations and Socioeconomic Change in Rural Mesoamerica" (special theme issue of *Ethnohistory*, 2003), and the author of several articles on economic and political aspects of rural Mexico.

Lane, Kris E. Kris E. Lane is professor of history at the College of William and Mary in Virginia. He is author of *Quito 1599: City and Colony in Transition* (University of New Mexico Press) and *Pillaging the Empire: Piracy in the Americas, 1500–1750* (M. E. Sharpe). He also coauthored *The Atlantic World* (Harlan Davidson) and edited *The Indian Militia and Description of the Indies* (Duke University Press). Lane has published articles on slavery, mining, witchcraft, and piracy and is currently working on a history of Colombian emeralds in the early modern world.

Loebel, Thomas J. Thomas J. Loebel currently directs CAGIS Archaeological Consulting Services based out of the Department of Anthropology at the University of Illinois at Chicago. His research interests focus on the archaeology of late Pleistocene/early Holocene hunter-gatherers in North America, with a specialization in lithic analysis and high-powered microwear studies of stone tools.

Lozano, Stephanie. Stephanie Lozano, a graduate student of Latin American studies and anthropology at California State University, Los Angeles, is working as a museum educator for the Los Angeles County Museum of Art. Her research interests are ancient Maya funerary practices, trade among the Maya and Aztecs, Mayan hieroglyphic decipherment, and Kaqchikel Mayan language.

Mangan, Jane. Jane Mangan is Malcolm Overstreet Partin Associate Professor of History at Davidson College. Mangan specializes in colonial social history and is the author of *Trading Roles: Gender, Ethnicity, and the Urban Economy in Colonial Potosí* (Duke University Press). At present, she is researching a project focused on Peru and Spain entitled "Transatlantic Obligations: Legal and Cultural Constructions of Family in the Sixteenth-Century Iberian World."

Mann, Kristin Dutcher. Kristin Dutcher Mann is associate professor of history and coordinator of the Social Studies Education Program at the University of Arkansas at Little Rock. Her research focuses on music and dance in the indigenous and mission communities of northern New Spain.

Marte, Lidia. Lidia Marte is a Caribbeanist with research interests in the Hispanic Caribbean (particularly Dominican Republic). She holds a Ph.D. in cultural anthropology and is currently a lecturer in the Department of Anthropology at the University of Texas at Austin.

Matthew, Laura. Laura Matthew received a Ph.D. in Latin American history from the University of Pennsylvania and currently teaches at Marquette University. She is the coeditor of *Indian Conquistadors: Indigenous Allies in the Conquest of Mesoamerica* (University of Oklahoma Press) and has published articles on the concept of ladinos and ladinization in colonial Guatemala.

Mendoza, Rubén G. Rubén G. Mendoza received an M.A. and Ph.D. in anthropological archaeology from the University of Arizona, Tucson. In addition to being an active member of the Register of Professional Archaeologists, Mendoza is a professor of social and behavioral sciences and the director of the Institute for Archaeological Science, Technology and Visualization at California State University, Monterey Bay. A Mesoamerican archaeologist by training, Mendoza is widely published as both a scholar and photographer and has undertaken archaeological field investigations in both Mexico (Puebla and Guanajuato) and the United States (Colorado, Arizona, and California). His current anthropological endeavors center on the historical archaeology and ethnohistory of the Spanish colonial missions of California and the Southwest.

Morell, Tyler. Tyler Morell is a student at Georgetown University, where he is pursuing a master's degree in Latin American studies. He is a graduate of Kenyon College, where his interests in development, government, and literature began. These interests led him to study abroad in Cuba, Ecuador, and Mexico. A current resident of Washington, D.C., he intends to work in international relations, with an emphasis on education.

Myrup, Erik. A specialist on colonial Brazil and the larger Luso-Brazilian world, Erik Myrup earned his Ph.D. from Yale University in 2006. He is currently an assistant professor at the University of Kentucky. He has also worked as a missionary in western Brazil and as a writer and editor in Taiwan.

Nash, Donna. Donna Nash, Ph.D., is adjunct curator of South American archaeology at the Field Museum in Chicago. She studies the Wari Empire and has been leading excavations in southern Peru for 10 years. Her research endeavors to understand how bureaucratic governments developed, and she is particularly interested in the role women played in state politics.

Netherly, Patricia J. Patricia J. Netherly is an anthropologist covering the fields of pre-European archaeology, ethnohistory, and ethnology of the Andes and Amazon. She has more than 20 years' field experience, working on the north coast of Peru, coastal Ecuador (El Oro Province), and in Amazonian Ecuador. Her interests include political anthropology, complex society, and cultural ecology. She is presently at work on a book on the western Amazon.

O'Toole, Rachel Sarah. Rachel Sarah O'Toole is currently assistant professor of the early modern Atlantic world and colonial Latin America in the Department of History at the University of California, Irvine. Her publications include "From the Rivers of Guinea to the Valleys of Peru: Becoming a *Bran* Diaspora within Spanish Slavery," *Social Text* (Fall 2007); "Danger in the Convent: Colonial Demons, Idolatrous *Indias*, and Bewitching *Negras* in Santa Clara (Trujillo del Perú)," *Journal of Colonialism and Colonial History* (Spring 2006); and "'In a War against the Spanish': Andean Defense and African Resistance on the Northern Peruvian Coast," *The Americas* (July 2006).

Palka, Joel. Joel Palka is associate professor of anthropology and Latin American and Latino studies at the University of Illinois at Chicago. His research interests include ancient Maya culture, Mayan hieroglyphic writing, historic Maya culture change, and Lacandon Maya society.

Plummer, Kathryn. Kathryn Plummer received a B.A. in Latin American studies, with a minor in Spanish from Willamette University in Salem, Oregon. She has worked at the National Center for Refugee and Immigrant Children and Refugees International and currently is serving as the president of the Latin American Graduate Organization. In addition to obtaining an M.A., she will graduate with a certificate in refugees and humanitarian emergencies from the Institute for the Study of International Migration. She is passionate about migration studies, with a primary interest in protection of the displaced in complex emergencies.

Restall, Matthew. Matthew Restall is Edwin Erle Sparks Professor of Latin American History at the Pennsylvania State University. His 10 books focus on various aspects of Spanish-American, Afro-Mexican, and Maya history during the colonial period.

Roa-de-la-Carrera, Cristián A. Cristián A. Roa-de-la-Carrera is associate professor of Spanish and Latin American studies at the University of Illinois at Chicago. He is the author of *Histories of Infamy: Francisco López de Gómara and the Ethics of Spanish Imperialism* (University Press of Colorado) and various articles published in journals such as *Hispanic Review, Colonial Latin American Review*, and *Revista Chilena de Literatura*.

Rugeley, Terry. Terry Rugeley is professor of Mexican and Latin American history at the University of Oklahoma. He is the author of four books dealing with the history of 19th-century Mexico, including *Of Wonders and Wise Men: Religion and Popular Cultures in Southeast Mexico, 1800–1876* (University of Texas Press), and more recently, his translation of a German-language travel memoir, *Alone in Mexico: The Astonishing Travels of Karl Heller, 1845–1848* (University of Alabama Press). His latest work, *Rebellion Now and Forever: Mayas, Hispanics, and Caste War Violence in Yucatán, 1800–1880*, published in May 2009 by Stanford University Press.

Sandweiss, Dan. Dan Sandweiss is dean and associate provost for graduate studies and professor of anthropology and quaternary and climate studies at the University of Maine. He is an archaeologist who researches past climate change and cultural development, and ancient maritime adaptations, primarily in Peru. Sandweiss's work has appeared in *Science, Nature, Proceedings of the National Academy of Sciences*, Geology, *Latin American Antiquity, Journal of Field Archaeology*, and other journals and volumes. A past Sigma Xi Distinguished Lecturerer, he is founding editor of *Andean Past* and a member of the editorial boards of *Latin American Antiquity* and *Chungará*.

Scher, Sarahh E. M. Sarahh E. M. Scher has a B.F.A. from Washington University and an M.F.A. in printmaking and M.A. in art history from New Mexico State University. She is currently a doctoral candidate at Emory University, working on her dissertation "States of Dress: Gender, Role and Status in Moche Art." Her most recent article, "Held in the Balance: Shamanism and Gender Roles in Ancient and Modern Practice," appeared in *Acta Americana: Journal of the Swedish Americanist Society*.

Scholl, Jonathan. Jonathan Scholl is pursuing his Ph.D. in colonial Latin American history at the University of Florida. His research interests include intercultural interaction in the early colonial Andes and the functioning of the early-modern European empires.

Schuett, Jennifer. Jennifer Schuett is a graduate student at Edmund A. Walsh School of Foreign Service at Georgetown University in the Latin American Studies Program, specializing in foreign policy and security issues. Schuett is also an associate of the Cuba Program at the Center for International Policy in Washington, D.C., and has worked for Common Hope, a development organization in rural Guatemala. In addition, Schuett has traveled extensively in the hemisphere for research purposes, focusing on social movements and political institutions.

Schwaller, John F. John F. Schwaller is currently professor of history and president of the State University of New York at Potsdam. His academic and administrative career includes appointments at five universities over the last 30 years. He is a specialist in the history of early colonial Latin America and has written several books and scores of articles on the topic.

Schwaller, Robert. Robert Schwaller is a Ph.D. candidate in history at the Pennsylvania State University. His research focuses on the development of racial terminology and ideologies in 16th-century Mexico. He is currently completing his dissertation, entitled "Defining Difference in Early New Spain."

Sell, Barry D. Barry D. Sell is an independent scholar currently residing in Glendale, California. He graduated from the University of California at Los Angeles (UCLA) with a Ph.D. in early Latin American history. He is currently working on a comparative project that looks at Jesuits and Franciscans in early Latin America and Asia, with an emphasis on European interaction with the Nahuatl-speaking peoples of colonial Mexico and with the peoples of Japan and China during the same period.

Sheehy, James. James Sheehy received a Ph.D. in anthropology in 1992 from Pennsylvania State University. He specializes in Mesoamerican archaeology and ceramic analysis.

Shih, Tien-Ann. Tien-Ann Shih is a doctoral candidate in the Department of Anthropology at the University of Chicago. Her dissertation focuses on the production of citizens, subjects, and sacred space in the highland Andes during the 16th and 17th centuries.

Stross, Brian. Brian Stross, professor of anthropology at the University of Texas at Austin, received B.A. and Ph.D. degrees from the University of California at Berkeley. He has done extensive field research in Mexico, Guatemala, and Belize. As a linguistic anthropologist, he has a special interest in languages and cultures of indigenous Mesoamerica, focusing particularly on Mesoamerican iconography and epigraphy of the Classic Maya. Additionally, he is particularly interested in ethnobotany and the anthropology of food.

Tavárez, David. David Tavárez, assistant professor of anthropology at Vassar College, is an ethnohistorian and linguistic anthropologist. His publications on colonial evangelization projects and Nahua and Zapotec indigenous religious practices include nine journal articles and eight book chapters. A forthcoming book on these topics is tentatively entitled *Invisible Wars: Clandestine Indigenous Devotions in Central Mexico.* He is also the coauthor of a forthcoming translation and critical edition of Chimalpahin's modified version of López de Gómara's *Conquista de México.*

Townsend, Camilla. Camilla Townsend is professor of history at Rutgers University in New Brunswick. She is the author of *Malintzin's Choices: An Indian Woman in the Conquest of Mexico* (2006), *Pocahontas and the Powhatan Dilemma* (2004), and *Tales of Two Cities* (2000), as well as numerous articles in such journals as the *American Historical Review, The Americas, Colonial Latin American Review,* and the *Journal of Women's History.* She has been the recipient of grants from the Fulbright Office, the American Association of University Women, the American Philosophical Society, and the National Endowment for the Humanities.

Tyce, Spencer. Spencer Tyce is a native of Pensacola, Florida, and is a graduate student at the University of North Florida. His current research focuses on the German conquistadors and the conquest of Venezuela in the early 16th century.

Van Cleve, Janice. Janice Van Cleve is a writer, world traveler, and Maya researcher with a degree in medieval history and minors in languages. She is author of *Eighteen Rabbit: The Intimate Life and Tragic Death of a Maya God-King,* as well as several research papers focusing on Copán, Honduras. Her next book focuses on the founder of the Copán dynasty and its connection to the "Entrada" at Tikal in 378 C.E.

Von Nagy, Christopher. Christopher Von Nagy was educated at Berkeley (A.B. with honors) and Tulane (Ph.D.). Since the 1990s he has undertaken field research into the Olmec and related cultures on the Tabasco coastal plain of Mexico. More recently, he participated in a milestone climate science project, writing a database backbone system to handle and help analyze data from a multiyear investigation into the carbon sequestration potential of the prairie ecosystem under elevated global temperatures. He is currently involved in designing the humanities and science curricula for a Montessori adolescent program in Reno, Nevada.

Weeks, John M. John M. Weeks is librarian and contributing scholar, American Section, at the University of Pennsylvania Museum of Archaeology and Anthropology. His research interests include the late prehistory and early history of southern Mesoamerica, especially the Maya, and the Caribbean.

Whittington, Stephen L. Stephen L. Whittington has been director of the Museum of Anthropology and adjunct associate professor of anthropology at Wake Forest University since 2002 and was director of the Hudson Museum at the University of Maine from 1991 until 2002. He earned a Ph.D. in anthropology at the Pennsylvania State University in 1989. A bioarchaeologist who has directed archaeological projects in Honduras and Mexico and has analyzed ancient human skeletal remains in Honduras and Guatemala, he is coeditor, with David Reed, of *Bones of the Maya: Studies of Ancient Skeletons* (Smithsonian Institution Press) and coauthor, with Roger Nance and Barbara Borg, of *Archaeology and Ethnohistory of Iximché* (University Press of Florida).

Witschey, Walter R. T. Dr. Walter R. T. Witschey, a Maya archaeologist and geographic information system (GIS) consultant, is professor of anthropology and science education at Longwood University. He is director emeritus of the Science Museum of Virginia, where he served for 15 years as its second director; past president of the Virginia Academy of Science; science columnist; and former CEO of a computer services enterprise. He is coauthor of the Electronic Atlas of Ancient Maya Sites, a 5,800-site registry.

Woodruff, Erin. Erin Woodruff received a bachelor's degree in Spanish and international studies from the University of Miami in 2004 and received her master's in history from the University of North Florida in 2007. Currently, she is working toward a Ph.D. in Latin American history at Vanderbilt University, where her focus is the history of colonial Spanish Florida.

Zborover, Danny. Danny Zborover began his studies in archaeology at the Hebrew University in Jerusalem. He completed a B.A. in archaeology and Latin American studies at the University of Calgary, Canada, and a master's degree at Leiden University, The Netherlands, where he focused on Mesoamerican archaeology and indigenous historical documents. He is currently a Ph.D. candidate in the Department of Archaeology at Calgary, where his research focuses on the Chontalpa Historical Archaeology Project, in Oaxaca, Mexico.

❧ LIST OF ENTRIES ❦

List of Illustrations, Maps, and Tables in This Volume

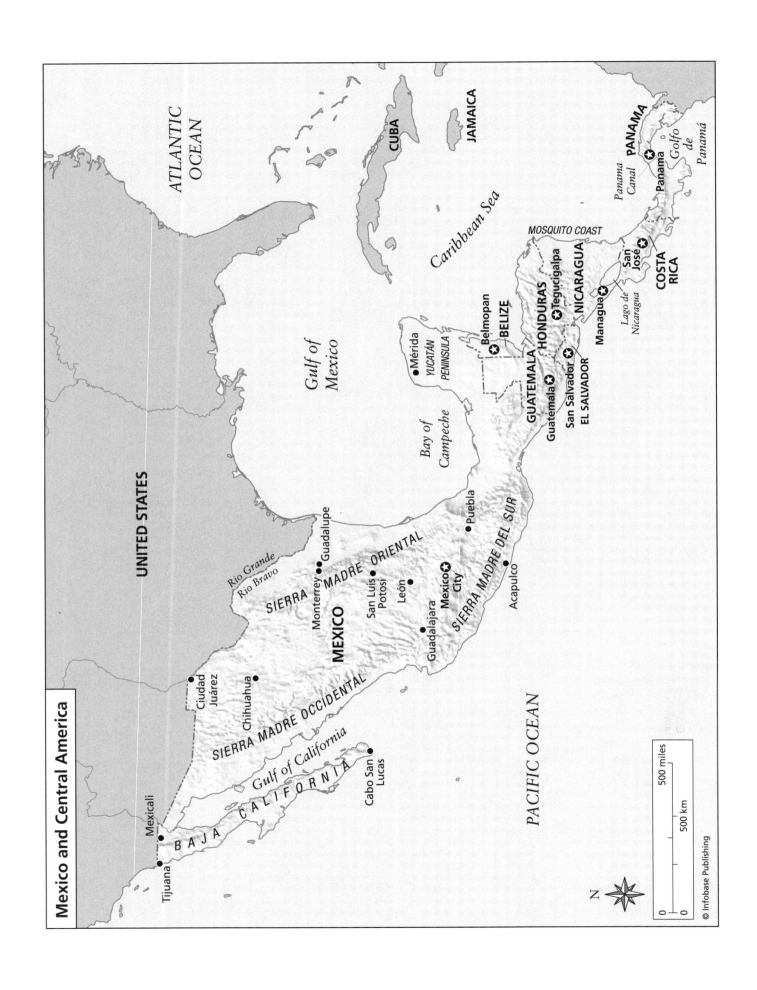

Mexico and Central America

UNITED STATES

ATLANTIC OCEAN

CUBA

JAMAICA

PANAMA

Golfo de Panamá

Panama Canal

Panama

MOSQUITO COAST

Caribbean Sea

San José

COSTA RICA

Tegucigalpa

NICARAGUA

Lago de Nicaragua

Managua

HONDURAS

Belmopan

BELIZE

Mérida

YUCATÁN PENINSULA

GUATEMALA

Guatemala

San Salvador

EL SALVADOR

Gulf of Mexico

Bay of Campeche

Puebla

Guadalupe

Rio Grande
Rio Bravo

Monterrey

SIERRA MADRE ORIENTAL

San Luis Potosí

León

Guadalajara

Mexico City

SIERRA MADRE DEL SUR

Acapulco

MEXICO

Ciudad Juárez

Chihuahua

SIERRA MADRE OCCIDENTAL

Gulf of California

Cabo San Lucas

BAJA CALIFORNIA

Mexicali

Tijuana

PACIFIC OCEAN

N

500 miles

500 km

0

0

© Infobase Publishing

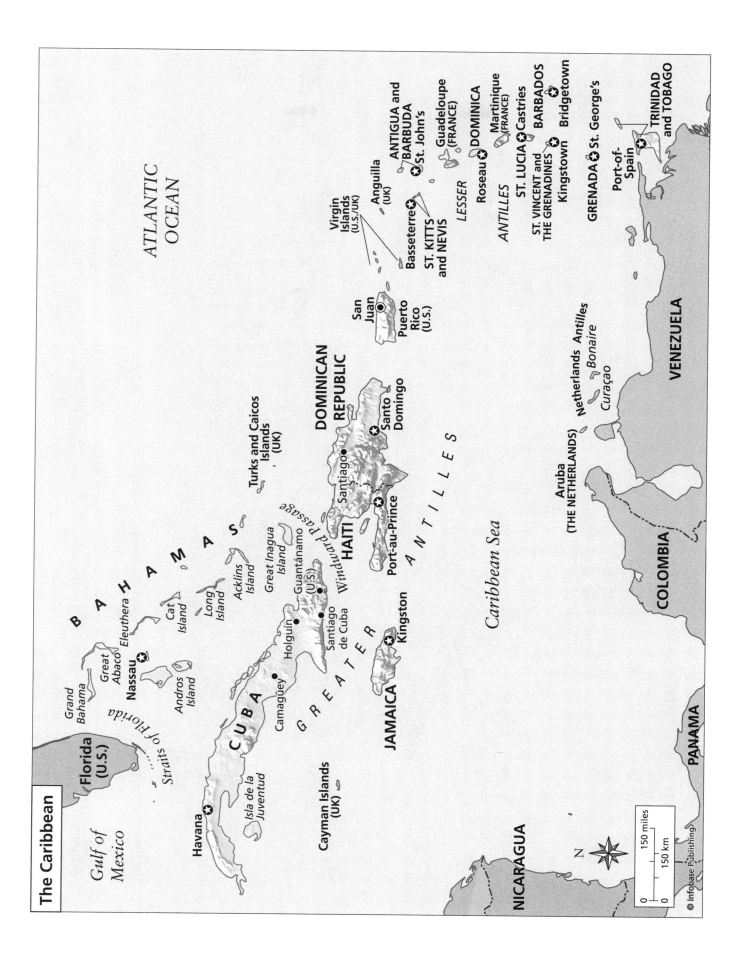

The Caribbean

ATLANTIC OCEAN

Gulf of Mexico

Florida (U.S.)

Straits of Florida

Grand Bahama

Great Abaco

Nassau

Andros Island

Eleuthera

Cat Island

Long Island

Acklins Island

B A H A M A S

Great Inagua Island

Turks and Caicos Islands (UK)

Havana

Isla de la Juventud

C U B A

Camagüey

Holguín

Santiago de Cuba

Guantánamo (U.S.)

Windward Passage

Cayman Islands (UK)

JAMAICA

Kingston

G R E A T E R

HAITI

Port-au-Prince

Santiago

DOMINICAN REPUBLIC

Santo Domingo

A N T I L L E S

Caribbean Sea

San Juan

Puerto Rico (U.S.)

Virgin Islands (U.S./UK)

Anguilla (UK)

Basseterre

ST. KITTS and NEVIS

ANTIGUA and BARBUDA

St. John's

Guadeloupe (FRANCE)

DOMINICA

Roseau

Martinique (FRANCE)

Castries

ST. LUCIA

ST. VINCENT and THE GRENADINES

Kingstown

BARBADOS

Bridgetown

LESSER

ANTILLES

GRENADA

St. George's

Port-of-Spain

TRINIDAD and TOBAGO

Netherlands Antilles

Bonaire

Curaçao

Aruba (THE NETHERLANDS)

VENEZUELA

COLOMBIA

PANAMA

NICARAGUA

N

0   150 miles
0   150 km

© Infobase Publishing

South America

ATLANTIC OCEAN

CUBA

DOMINICAN REPUBLIC

HAITI

Caribbean Sea

HONDURAS

NICARAGUA

COSTA RICA

PANAMA

Cartagena

Caracas

VENEZUELA

Orinoco R.

Georgetown

Paramaribo

Cayenne

Medellín

COLOMBIA

Bogotá

GUYANA

SURINAME

French Guiana
(FRANCE)

Cali

Quito

ECUADOR

Putumayo R.

AMAZON

Manaus

Amazon R.

Belém

Fortaleza

Guayaquil

BASIN

Madeira R.

Recife

Trujillo

A
N
D
E
S
M
T
S.

PERU

BRAZIL

BRAZILIAN

Tocantins R.

São Francisco R.

Lima

Cuzco

Salvador

Lake
Titicaca

La Paz

Cochabamba

BOLIVIA

Sucre

Brasília

Goiânia

HIGHLANDS

Belo Horizonte

PACIFIC
OCEAN

PARAGUAY

São
Paulo

Santos

Rio de
Janeiro

CHILE

Asunción

ARGENTINA

Pôrto
Alegre

Paraná R.

ATLANTIC
OCEAN

URUGUAY

Cerro Aconcagua
22,834 ft.

Cordoba

Santa
Fe

Valparaíso

Santiago

Buenos
Aires

Montevideo

Concepción

P
A
M
P
A
S

Falkland Is.
(Islas Malvinas)
(UK)

South
Georgia I.
(UK)

N

Punta Arenas

TIERRA DEL
FUEGO

Cape Horn

0   500 miles

0   500 km

❧ PREFACE TO THE SET ❧

How does one define Latin America? Geographically, Latin America stretches from the Rio Grande River on the U.S.-Mexican border and Cuba, bordering the Caribbean Sea and the Atlantic Ocean, to Tierra del Fuego at the southern tip of South America. The area is two and one-half times the size of the United States. Brazil alone is slightly larger than the continental United States. Within this vast geographic region there is enormous human and physical variety.

In historical terms, Latin America includes those parts of the Americas that at one time were linked to the Spanish, Portuguese, and French Empires and whose people speak a Romance language (a language derived from Latin, such as Spanish, Portuguese, French, and the derivative Creole). When Napoleon III popularized the term *Latin America* in the 1860s, he implied a cultural relationship between France and those countries of the Western Hemisphere where these language traditions existed: Mexico, most of Central and South America, Cuba, the Dominican Republic, Puerto Rico, Haiti, Martinique, Guadeloupe, and French Guiana. A literal interpretation of Napoleon III's definition would also include portions of the Southwest United States, Florida, and Louisiana; Quebec in Canada; and the islands of St. Pierre and Miquelon off of Newfoundland's coast. English is the first language of most Caribbean islands, and Papiamento, a form of Creole, is predominant in the Netherlands Antilles and Aruba. Amerindian dialects remain the primary languages in parts of Mexico, Guatemala, Ecuador, Peru, and Bolivia.

The mixture of languages illustrates the diversity of race and culture across Latin America. The Amerindians, or Native Americans, dominated the pre-Columbian time period. In the 21st century, their descendants are still prevalent in Mexico, Guatemala, Ecuador, Peru, Bolivia, and the upper reaches of the Amazon River in the Andes Mountains. Latin America was colonized primarily by the Spanish and to a lesser degree by the Portuguese, first and foremost in Brazil. British, French, and Dutch interlopers followed, and in the 20th century,

the United States had a profound impact across the region. For economic reasons, slavery was practiced most notably in Brazil, along the Ecuadoran coast, and in the Caribbean Islands. Each of these ethnic groups—and the descendants of interracial relationships—produced its own culture with unique religious traditions, family life, dress styles, food, art, music, and architecture. With accelerated globalization throughout the 20th century, Western ideas and culture have had a significant impact upon Latin America.

Geography and climatic conditions also play a major role in the development of societies, their cultures, and economies. Latin America is no exception. For example, the Andes Mountains that traverse the west coast of South America served as the centerpiece of the Inca Empire in the pre-Columbian period, the source of gems and ores during the Spanish colonial period, and the ores and petroleum essential for modern-day industries. The Andes westward slopes and coastal plains provided agricultural products since the earliest of times. The rolling plains, or pampas, of north-central Argentina, southern Brazil, and Uruguay coupled with a Mediterranean-type climate turned those areas into highly productive cattle and grain centers. In contrast, the Amazon rain forest in Brazil, while still home to undiscovered Native American groups, offered little economic advantage until the 20th century, when the logging industry and land clearing for agricultural expansion cut deep into the rain forest's expanse. The tropical climate of the Caribbean and the coastal areas of Central America offered fertile ground for sugar, tobacco, and tropical fruits.

People, geography, language and culture, and economic pursuits transformed Latin America into one of the world's most diverse regions. Yet, the 41 countries and foreign dependencies that make up Latin America share four distinguishable historical time periods: the pre-Columbian period, followed by nearly three centuries of colonial rule; the struggle for national identity during the 19th century; and the quest for modernity since 1900.

The *Encyclopedia of Latin America* takes a chronological approach to the examination of the Latin American experience. Divided into four volumes, each devoted to one of the four time periods that define Latin American history, this unique reference work contrasts sharply with traditional encyclopedias. It provides students and general readers the opportunity to examine the complexity and vastness of the region's development and culture within a given time period and to compare the time periods.

Volume I, *Amerindians through Foreign Colonization*, focuses on the pre-Columbian period from the earliest Native American societies through the arrival of the Spanish conquistadores. Scholars continue to debate the number of Native Americans, or "Indians" as Christopher Columbus labeled them, who resided in the Americas when Columbus first reached the region in 1492. Estimates range from a low of 10 million to a high of slightly more than 100 million. While most scholars agree that the earliest waves of migrants came to the Americas across the Bering Straits land bridge as early as 40,000 years ago, there is continued debate over both the dates of settlement and descent of the earliest settlers. More recent scholarship in Chile and Brazil place the earliest New World migrants to 33,000 B.C.E. and suggest them to be of South Asian and Pacific Islander—rather than Eurasian—descent.

By the time of the European arrival on Latin America's mainland in the early 1500s, three highly organized Native American societies existed: Aztec, Maya, and Inca. Mexico's central valley was home to the rigidly stratified Aztec society, which by the time of the conquest reached southward and eastward to the Caribbean coast. The Aztecs had earned a reputation for their military prowess, for the brutal exploitation of the peoples brought into the empire, and for ceremonial city building, evidenced by its capital, Tenochtitlán, the site of contemporary Mexico City. From Peru's Cuzco Valley, the Inca Empire in South America stretched 3,000 miles (4,287 km) through the Andes mountain chain and inland to the east from Ecuador, in the north, to Chile, in the south. Through a tightly controlled bureaucracy, the Incas exercised control of the conquered communities. The Maya civilization began approximately in 1000 B.C.E. and, through a system of independent city-states, extended from Mexico's Yucatán Peninsula through Guatemala. For reasons not yet fully understood, Classic Maya civilization began its political collapse around 900 C.E., but Mayan society and culture remained intact. Aside from the three major groups, many other Native American societies existed throughout Latin America, such as the Arawaks and Tainos in the Caribbean and the Mapuche and the Guaraní in Argentina, Paraguay, and Chile.

Marked differences separated groups within the larger society and each group from the other. For example, even today, the Mexican government reports nearly 200 different linguistic groups; Guatemala, 26 different Mayan dialects; and an estimated 10 million Native Americans speak some form of the Quechua language in the high Andes along South America's Pacific coast. Elaborate ceremonies that included human sacrifice characterized the Aztec, Inca, and Maya religions. Agriculture was the primary economic pursuit of all Native American groups, while hunting and fishing were pursued by some groups. Textiles and metalwork usually contained designs peculiar to each indigenous group.

Volume II, *From Colonies to Independent Nations*, focuses on the Spanish colonial period, from the early 16th century through the early 19th century. At the beginning of this time period, the Spanish explored the South and North American continents, laying out an empire in the name of the king and queen of Spain and the Roman Catholic Church. Despite the vastness of the empire, which stretched from Tierra del Fuego at the southern tip of South America to the far reaches of the northwest Pacific Coast, eastward to the Mississippi River and into the Floridas, the Spanish attention focused on the areas of modern-day Mexico and Peru. Both were home to significant Native American societies and rich in mineral wealth, particularly gold and silver. The colonies existed for the benefit of Spain, and the application of mercantilist economic policies led to the exploitation of natural resources, regulation of manufacturing and agriculture, and control of international trade, all of which contributed to a pattern of large land holdings and abuse of labor. In effect, the system drained the colonies of its specie and other wealth and negated economic development and the emergence of a significant entrepreneurial class in the colonies. The Spanish imposed their political and cultural systems on the colonies, including the Native Americans. A highly centralized governmental structure provided little opportunity for political participation by the Spanish colonial residents, except in matters at the local level. The colonial laws and rules were made in Spain and enforced in the New World by officials appointed by the Crown. During the colonial period, the Catholic Church became an entity unto itself. It administered education, hospitals, social services, and its own court system. It tithed its followers and charged fees for religious services. Because the church was exempt from taxes to the Spanish Crown, it emerged as a colonial banker and a benefactor of the Spanish colonial system. The church, therefore, was not anxious to see the system change.

In theory, the Brazilian colonial experience paralleled the Spanish model, but in application, the Brazilian model was much different. The states established on Brazil's Atlantic coast were administered like personal fiefdoms by the king of Portugal's appointed authorities. Because the colony lacked natural resources for mass exploitation and a Native American population to convert to Catholicism, Portugal gave little attention to its New World colony.

Latecomers to the New World, the British, French, and Dutch colonization schemes were confined to the Caribbean region. As with the Spanish and Portuguese, each island fell victim to the political system of the mother country. Over time, the local governments of the British became more representative of the resident population. The economic focus on sugar production caused the importation of slave labor from Africa.

New World discontent in the mid-17th century led to reforms in the Spanish colonial system, but it took European events in the early 19th century to bring about Latin America's independence by 1826. Only Cuba and Puerto Rico remained under Spanish rule, and the British, French, and Dutch maintained control over their Caribbean island positions. Brazil received its independence on September 7, 1822, but continued to be governed by a member of the royal Portuguese family until November 15, 1889.

The legacies of colonial rule became evident immediately following independence. The establishment of governmental institutions and the place of each nation in the growing global economy that characterized 19th-century Latin America are the subject of volume III, *The Search for National Identity*. In addressing these issues, political and religious leaders, intellectuals, and foreigners who came to Latin America were confronted by the legacies of Spanish colonial rule.

The New World's Spanish descendants, the creoles, replaced the Spanish peninsulars at the apex of the rigid social structure and sought to keep political power confined to themselves. Only conflicting ideologies separated the elite. One group, the Conservatives, remained tied to the Spanish tradition of a highly centralized government, a privileged Catholic Church, and a hesitancy to reach out to the world. In contrast, the Liberals argued in favor of a greater decentralization of political power, the curtailment of church privileges, and greater participation in world affairs, particularly trade. Liberals and Conservatives, however, did not want to share political power or wealth with the laboring classes, made up of mestizos, Native Americans, or blacks. The dispute over the authority of central governments played out in different ways. In Argentina and Chile, for example, Conservatives Juan Manuel de Rosas and Diego Portales produced constitutions entrenching the Spanish traditions. In Central America, it signified the disintegration of the United Provinces by 1839 and the establishment of Conservative-led governments. The contestants for Mexican political power took to the battlefield, and the struggle produced 41 presidents from 1822 through 1848.

The Latin American world began to change in the 1860s with the emergence of Liberal leaders. It increasingly contributed raw materials to industrialized Europe. The heads of state welcomed foreign investment for the harvesting and processing of primary products and for constructing the supportive infrastructure. And, while the Liberals struck against church privileges, as in Chile during the 1880s, they still retained political power and continued to discriminate against the working classes.

Brazil and the colonized Caribbean Islands fell within the same purview as Spanish America. Although Brazil peacefully achieved independence in 1822, it continued its monarchial form of government until 1889. During that same time period, Brazil participated in the world economy through the exportation of sugar, followed by rubber and coffee. Meanwhile, the Caribbean Islands from Cuba southward to Trinidad and Tobago continued to be administered as part of European colonial empires. Administrators from Spain, Great Britain, France, and the Netherlands arrived to govern the island and to oversee the exportation of primary products, usually sugar, tobacco, and tropical fruits.

Latin America's participation in the global economy accelerated in the 20th century, but the new era also brought new players in the region's economic and political arena—the United States and Latin America's lower socioeconomic groups. These concepts form the basis for the entries in volume IV, *The Age of Globalization*.

The U.S. entry into Latin American affairs was prompted by the Cuban struggle for independence from 1895 to 1898 and the U.S. determination to construct a trans-isthmian canal. The U.S. three-month participation in the Cuban-Spanish War in 1898 and its role in securing Panama's independence in 1903 also confirmed long-standing assumptions regarding the backwardness of Latin American societies, owing to the legacies of the Spanish colonial system. More obvious was the need to secure the Panama Canal from foreign interlopers. U.S. policymakers combined the two issues—political and financial irresponsibility and canal security—to justify U.S. intervention throughout the circum-Caribbean region well into the 1920s. U.S. private investment followed the government's interventions and together led to the charge of "Yankee imperialism."

The entrance or attempted entrance into the national political arena by the middle and lower socioeconomic groups remained an internal affair until after World War II, when they were considered to be part of an international communist movement and again brought the United States into Latin America's internal affairs. Argentina and Chile provide early 20th-century examples of the middle sector entering the political arena while the governments continued to suppress labor. The results of the Mexican Revolution (1911–17) provided the first example of a Latin American social revolution addressing the needs of the lower socioeconomic class at the expense of the elite. In the 1920s and 1930s, small Communist or communist-like political parties or groups emerged in several countries, including Costa Rica, Chile, Brazil, and Peru. While of concern at the time, the presence of communism took on greater importance with the emergence of the cold war in 1945, when the "generation of rising expectations" fused with the Communists in their call for a complete overhaul of the socioeconomic and political structures rooted in Spanish colonialism. In the ambience of the cold war, however, the 1954 presidential election of Jacobo Arbenz in Guatemala, Fidel Castro's actions in Cuba in 1959 and 1960, the 1963–65 political crisis in the Dominican Republic, the administration of Chilean president Salvadore Allende from 1970 to 1973, and the Central American wars during the 1980s were intertwined into the greater context: struggles of freedom against international communism based in Moscow. To "save" these countries from communism, the United States intervened but in so doing restored and propped the old order. The struggle against communism also resulted in a generation of military governments across South America.

Beginning in the 1980s, democratic governments replaced military regimes across Latin America, and each of the countries experienced the growth of new political parties, mostly left of center. The new democratic governments also accepted and implemented the neoliberal, or free-market, economic model in vogue at the time. By the mid-1990s, many of the free-market reforms were in place, and Latin America's macroeconomic picture had vastly improved. Still, the promised benefits failed to reach the working classes: Half of all Latin Americans remained poverty stricken. In response to their personal crisis, beginning in 1998 with the election of Hugo Chávez as president of Venezuela, the Latin American people started placing so-called leftists in their presidential palaces. Latin America may be at the precipice of another change.

HOW TO USE THIS ENCYCLOPEDIA

The *Encyclopedia of Latin America* explores broad historical developments within the context of four time periods that together make up the complete Latin American historical experience. For example, the student or general reader can learn about a given country, when it was a "location" during the pre-Columbian period (volume I), a part of the Spanish colonial empire (volume II), a new nation struggling for its identity (volume III), or in its search for modernity (volume IV). The same can be done with political ideas and practices, economic pursuits, intellectual ideas, and culture patterns, to mention just a few of the themes that are explored across the four volumes. To locate topics in each of the four volumes, the reader should utilize the list of entries in the front matter of each volume. Words set in SMALL CAPITAL LETTERS in the body of a text indicate that an entry on this topic can be found in the same volume. At the conclusion of each entry are cross-references to related entries in other volumes in the set. For further help with locating information, the reader should turn to the comprehensive set index that appears at the end of volume IV.

Within each volume, the entries focus on the time period at hand. Each volume begins with an introduction providing a historical overview of the time period, followed by a chronology. A glossary of terms can be found in the back matter of the book. Each entry is followed by a list of the most salient works on the subject, providing the reader the opportunity to further examine the subject. The suggested readings at the end of each entry are augmented by the select bibliography appended to each volume, which offers a listing of the most important works for the time period. The further readings for each entry and selected readings for the volume together form a comprehensive list of Latin America's most important historical literature.

Each volume also includes a collection of documents and excerpts to illustrate the major themes of the time period under consideration. Offering eyewitness accounts of significant historical events and personages, they perhaps will encourage the user to further explore historical documentation.

ACKNOWLEDGMENTS FOR THIS VOLUME

Collaborative works of this nature are extremely rewarding endeavors, both personally and intellectually, and I am grateful for the opportunity to contribute to this ambitious and important collection. To that end, I would like to express my sincere gratitude to my friend and colleague Thomas M. Leonard, who invited me to edit volume I of this four-volume encyclopedia. As series editor, Tom assumed the unenviable task of coordinating and overseeing the entire project, which he did with great skill, enthusiasm, and, perhaps most important, good humor.

This project never would have come to fruition had it not been for the generous contributions and enthusiastic support of dozens of friends and colleagues. More than 60 scholars from a wide range of academic disciplines and backgrounds submitted entries for this volume. I wish to thank each one of them for graciously sharing his or her time and expertise; the volume is far richer for it. Danny Zborover, Kendall Brown, Patricia Netherly, R. A. Kashanipour, Sean H. Goforth, John F. Chuchiak IV, and Mark Christensen deserve special thanks for the outstanding contributions they made to this volume.

I would like to thank James Lockhart, Camilla Townsend, and Allen J. Christenson for kindly sharing their wonderful translations of a small corpus of remarkable colonial indigenous texts. Likewise, I am grateful to Janice Van Cleve, Donna Nash, Joel Palka, Danny Zborover, Kristin Dutcher Mann, Sarahh E. M. Scher, Jessica Christie, Dan Sandweiss, Frances F. Berdan, and the staff at the Michael C. Carlos Museum of Emory University for sharing so many wonderful photographs and illustrations that fill this volume.

I am privileged to work closely with a large number of gifted, motivated, and engaging students at the University of North Florida. I am particularly pleased that four of them contributed entries to the volume. Justin Blanton, Kathleen M. Kole, Spencer Tyce, and Saber Gray are all exceptional students, and all four are going to develop into fine historians. Kathleen and Saber, in particular, merit special thanks. In the early stages of this project, Kathleen worked tirelessly, gathering bibliographical references, ordering rare books and articles, and helping to secure copyright permissions. As the volume approached completion, Saber provided invaluable assistance, without which the volume's production would have been delayed many months. Saber read the entire manuscript carefully, and she offered important editorial suggestions and identified numerous factual errors. Moreover, she helped to secure the final copyright permissions. I am most grateful for her professionalism and her friendship.

It has been an absolute delight to work with the entire staff at Facts On File. From its inception, Claudia Schaab has guided this project with professionalism and patience. Moreover, the editorial staff did an outstanding job with the original manuscript, and I am grateful for all of their recommendations. I hope to have an opportunity to work with them again.

Lastly, I would like to express my sincere gratitude and eternal admiration to my wife, Annie, and my dear friend Bill David.

—J. Michael Francis

≫❦ INTRODUCTION ❦≪ TO THIS VOLUME

The past few decades have witnessed a remarkable transformation in our understanding of the pre-Columbian world and the history of its inhabitants. Scholars from across academic disciplines have joined in an effort to shed light on a region long overlooked and poorly understood. These collaborative and multidisciplinary efforts have forced scholars to reevaluate much of what was previously "known" about the pre-Columbian period, from basic categories of periodization to interpretations of Native American political institutions, religious beliefs, economic organization, warfare, and demography.

Once considered a "people without a history," Latin America's pre-Columbian inhabitants are now beginning to recover their long-muted voices as well as the richness of that region's past. In fact, contrary to popular belief, the "written" history of the peoples of the Americas did not begin with the arrival of Christopher Columbus. Rather, more than a thousand years before Columbus embarked on his famous voyage, Maya scribes in Mexico and Central America had created a system of writing that was capable of recording any aspect of Maya speech. Remarkably, only in the past five decades have scholars managed to "crack" the Mayan code, in what some have characterized as one of the greatest code-breaking feats in human history. As a result of this accomplishment, our understanding of the Maya world has been dramatically transformed.

The Maya were not alone in recording their history. Other Mesoamerican cultures recorded information on stone sculptures, ceramics, cave walls, and in screen-folded books called codices. In South America, current scholarship on pre-Incaic and Incan *quipus* (an Andean device consisting of a series of placed knotted cords) has begun to challenge the notion that *quipus* served only as mnemonic devices used to record such information as census data, troop numbers, and the contents of storehouses. A growing number of scholars now suggest that

quipus could be used to record sophisticated grammatical constructions; in other words, *quipus* could record language and therefore could be "read."

Efforts to recover indigenous voices have not been limited to the scholarship on the pre-Columbian period. In recent years, historians of the conquest and early colonial period have devoted much more attention to the rich corpus of written and pictographic materials from the early colonial period recorded in native languages such as Nahuatl, Mixtec, and Maya, among others. A closer examination of these sources has challenged much of the previous scholarship on the conquest era, revealing that the encounter between the peoples of the New World and the Old was not simply a tale of victors and vanquished.

New discoveries are reported frequently, as scholars from across disciplines work to reconstruct the pre-Columbian and early colonial histories of the Americas. The purpose of this volume is to offer readers a broad synthesis of the new scholarship of the past few decades. It represents one of few general reference works that offer broad geographical and topical coverage of the pre-Columbian period as well as the early decades of conquest and colonization; here, individual entries cover topics ranging from art and architecture to music, politics, and warfare. Moreover, many topics are approached from a thematic perspective, allowing readers to follow similar themes across regions and chronological periods. Entries such as religion, economy, trade, family, women, food, literature, migration, and agriculture (among many others) trace these topics across different cultures, from Mesoamerica to the Caribbean and South America; furthermore, they move chronologically from the early pre-Columbian settlements through the dramatic decades of the conquest period.

Collectively, these entries reveal the remarkable diversity of the peoples and cultures of Latin America before 1492, as well as their varied responses to the early

Spanish and Portuguese colonial effort. Nevertheless, it is important to acknowledge the limitations inherent in a work of this nature. For one, not every ethnic group is represented in the pages that follow. Also, readers will note that much more attention is given to the period between ca. 250 C.E. and 1560 than to the long history of the earliest settlements in Latin America. The limited coverage of the period from the initial human migrations across the Bering land bridge more than 40,000 years ago to the earliest settlements in Latin America is the result of a relative paucity of information, especially compared to the tremendous volume of material for the period 250–1560.

Lastly, certain regions, such as Central Mexico, the Yucatán Peninsula, and the central and southern Andes receive more attention than other parts of Latin America. This is because those regions supported populations under the Aztec, the Maya, and the Inca that have attracted a great deal of scholarly interest. Moreover, because these regions also attracted larger numbers of European settlers (who wrote extensively about them), we simply have more information for these areas than for other parts of Latin America where there were few, if any, Europeans in the early colonial period.

CHALLENGES IN EDITING THIS VOLUME
Orthography

In preparing this volume for publication, J. Michael Francis was faced with a series of challenges, among the most significant of which related to the current debate regarding orthography. In recent years, scholars working throughout Latin America have introduced a new lexicon, with distinct spellings to reflect pre-Columbian indigenous languages and meanings, as opposed to the colonial terminology (and understandings) introduced by Europeans. To further complicate this matter, it should be noted that the colonial documents themselves are rarely uniform and do not always follow the same orthographic conventions. For example, consider the most commonly accepted spelling in English for the Aztec ruler Montezuma, which reflects the old Spanish pronunciation of the Nahuatl name; however, 16th-century Nahuatl-language sources offer different spellings, including *Motecçuma*, *Motecuçuma*, and even *Moteuhçoma*. Further, in modern Mexico, his name is often rendered *Moctezuma* or *Motecuhzoma*. Likewise, recent scholarship on the Incas reflects consideration of Quechua orthography: *Inca* becomes *Inka*, *quipu* changes to *khipu*, and *chasqui* becomes *chaski*, to cite just a few examples.

Today, a growing body of scholarship has adopted this new orthography, but its usage remains uneven and highly inconsistent. Therefore, in order to limit confusion and thus reach the broadest audience possible, we have decided to use traditional spellings for most of the entries in this volume. Nevertheless, in some cases (such as Tiwanaku, Wari, and *kuraka*), the new orthography has been so widely adopted that it made little sense to adopt

the old spellings (Tiahuanaco, Huari, and *curaca*). At any rate, where possible, we have included alternate spellings in parentheses to reflect the new orthography and, thus, help guide readers to additional sources.

Organization and Coverage

A second challenge involved general organization and coverage. In order to maintain certain common threads through all four volumes in this series, the authors agreed that certain topics should be addressed in each volume. This standardization required that some terms be applied anachronistically in the early volumes. For example, in this volume (as well as the two that follow), readers will find that individual country entries are based on modern political boundaries, many of which were created following the independence movements of the early 19th century. This organization allows readers to follow the historical trajectory of one particular country from its pre-Columbian past through to the present. Of course, this decision is somewhat problematic for the earlier volumes because the political boundaries of Latin America's modern nation-states did not exist in the pre-Columbian period or in the early colonial era. The Inca Empire, for example, extended through much of modern Peru, as well as much of Ecuador, Bolivia, southern Colombia, northwestern Argentina, and northern Chile. Conversely, the Aztec Empire never encompassed the entirety of the modern state of Mexico, while Maya territory extended through the territory of modern Guatemala and Belize, as well as some parts of Mexico, Honduras, and El Salvador. Readers should therefore approach the individual country entries with some caution, recognizing that modern political boundaries were not a reality in the period covered in this volume.

Chronological Scope

Finally, the chronological scope of this volume also merits explanation. Readers will note that this volume does not end abruptly with Christopher Columbus's arrival in the Caribbean in 1492. While this might seem a logical point to transition from one volume to the next, the year 1492 did not represent such a dramatic break in the history of Latin America, especially outside the Caribbean. It was another three decades before Hernando Cortés initiated the conquest of Mexico, and the conquest of the Inca Empire did not begin until 40 years after Columbus's maiden voyage. Coverage in this volume therefore continues roughly to 1560. By then, the "age of conquest" was drawing to an end; Europeans had toppled the great empires of the Aztecs and the Incas, and new settlements had been established across two continents, from the Spanish borderlands of Florida and what is now the U.S. Southwest to the southern cone of South America.

Undoubtedly, the arrival of Europeans initiated a series of sweeping and often devastating changes for Latin America's indigenous peoples. By 1560, European diseases such as smallpox, measles, and influenza had caused unprecedented demographic loss among native populations throughout the Americas, though the effects were not uniform. Few regions were spared the ravages of disease, some did not return to preconquest population figures until the 19th century, and several never recovered. Yet, despite the changes that began with Columbus's arrival in the Caribbean, the pre-Columbian world did not simply disappear.

The aim of this volume, then, is to depart from the tendency to view 1492 as a single event that represented a complete rupture from the pre-Columbian past. The early conquest period did not bring about the total destruction or final conquest of Latin America's indigenous peoples. Rather, it should be viewed as the beginning of a complex and protracted process, with legacies that survive well into the present. As readers will see in this volume, the conquest of Latin America was an uneven process in which Europeans, Africans, and Native Americans all played important and lasting roles.

The entries that appear in this volume also explore the many changes that occurred during the transformative decades of the early conquest period. They highlight the diverse and uneven responses and adaptations of Latin America's indigenous to the arrival of the first waves of European conquistadores, revealing a story we are only just beginning to understand. It is our hope that this approach will help readers appreciate the richness, complexity, and diversity of Latin America's pre-Columbian past and how that past continues to shape the course of Latin American history.

LATIN AMERICA BEFORE 1492: A BRIEF OVERVIEW

The history of early human occupation in the Americas remains a hotly contested subject; future findings using DNA analysis to trace genetic links between pre-Columbian populations in the Americas and their Old World ancestors will reveal a great deal more about the earliest Americans. Archaeologists and linguists continue to add new information to our understanding of the first human settlers in North and South America, and future findings may well revise the chronology of the Americas' distant past. Nevertheless, at present, most scholars maintain that the earliest Americans journeyed across the ice-free Bering land bridge in a series of migrations that began as early as 40,000–50,000 B.C.E. These migrations likely continued until ca. 9000 B.C.E., when sea levels rose and the land bridge became impassable. By that time, bands of hunters and gatherers (and fishers) had spread across North America and into Central and South America. In fact, by 10,000 B.C.E., bands of hunter-gatherers occupied sites scattered throughout the Americas, from Alaska to Tierra del Fuego.

Between 8000 and 2000 B.C.E. (the Archaic period), a series of important changes led to a dramatic growth in the number of sedentary villages throughout Latin America. A general rise in temperatures, beginning ca.

8000 B.C.E., separated the Archaic period from the earlier Paleo-Indian era (12,000–8000 B.C.E.). It is precisely at this time, when temperatures began to increase, that plants were first domesticated in the Americas, including squash in Mesoamerica, manioc in Brazil, and the potato in Peru. By 5000 B.C.E., inhabitants in Mexico had domesticated maize, a crop that eventually spread throughout the Americas and became a staple in many pre-Columbian diets. When the Archaic period ended, ca. 2000 B.C.E., a variety of beans, chili peppers, and other crops had been added to a growing list of domesticated plants. Cotton, too, had been domesticated by at least 2500 B.C.E. Of course, the domestication of various plant species was not the only important innovation of the Archaic period. As early as 5500 B.C.E., settlers in Amazonia began to produce pottery, a tradition that spread first through northern South America and then into Central America and Mexico.

From the end of the Archaic to 250 C.E., dramatic changes began to unfold throughout Latin America. This long period saw the rise of complex public architecture, glyph writing, and the emergence of expansionist states. By 1500 B.C.E., the Andean peoples of South America were producing kiln-fired ceramics, working in copper and gold, and supporting large populations. At the same time, settlement in the Caribbean increased dramatically, with Arawak migrants moving up the Orinoco River and into the islands; several hundred years later, Ciboney Indians began to arrive in Cuba.

Significant changes occurred elsewhere as well. By 250 C.E., a series of large complex chiefdoms had emerged throughout the Amazon region. In Mesoamerica, this period witnessed the early rise of the Zapotec and Mixtec peoples in Mexico, the rise and fall of Olmec civilization along Mexico's gulf coast, and early Maya settlements in southern Mexico, Guatemala, Belize, and Honduras. This period also witnessed several innovations that would become the cornerstones of Mesoamerican civilizations. For example, evidence for writing in glyphs and the use of the 260-day sacred calendar date back at least to 600 B.C.E.

Throughout the pre-Columbian period, Mesoamerica was home to a variety of different groups, such as the Olmecs, the Maya, the Zapotecs, Mixtecs, and, much later, the Aztecs (Nahuas). Yet, despite their differences, these disparate groups shared a number of traits unique to Mesoamerican peoples, such as the use of glyphic writing, the production of bark paper or deerskin books called codices, and a complex calendrical system (with a 260-day sacred calendar and 365-day solar calendar); they also played a ball game (the precise rules of which are still poorly understood). Many of these characteristics continued well into the colonial period.

By 100 C.E., Mesoamerica boasted a number of large urban centers. The Maya site of El Mirador dominated much of northern Guatemala, and Central Mexico's Teotihuacán already supported dense urban populations; over the next several centuries, Teotihuacán came to exert its influence over much of Mesoamerica. At the same time, dozens of Maya cities emerged out of the jungles of Mexico, Guatemala, and Belize, and by 250 C.E., the Maya had created a complex glyphic writing system.

During the Classic period (250–900), Mesoamerican populations created urban centers as large as any found elsewhere in the world. A thousand years before Columbus set sail for the New World, Teotihuacán's urban core had as many as 200,000 inhabitants. At the same time in the Maya lowlands, Tikal boasted a population that likely reached 60,000–80,000. Nevertheless, most of these cities were destroyed or abandoned centuries before the first Europeans arrived in Mesoamerica. Internecine warfare, drought, environmental degradation, overpopulation, loss of faith in rulers, and disease all contributed to the end of the Classic period.

Large urban centers dominated northern Yucatán for much of the Postclassic period (900–1519), with Maya cities such as Uxmal, Chichén Itzá, Cobá, and Mayapán exerting influence at various times. By the early 16th century, however, these cities, too, had been largely abandoned, and thus the first Europeans encountered a Maya population that was highly decentralized. Central Mexico, on the other hand, presented a different story. Beginning in the early 13th century, waves of Nahuatl-speaking migrants began to arrive in the Valley of Mexico, filling a power vacuum left after the fall of the Toltecs and their capital city of Tula. Among these early migrants was a small band known as the Mexica. Eventually, in the year 1325, the Mexica settled on an island in the valley and began constructing the city of Tenochtitlán. A century later, the Mexica would establish a military and political alliance with two other city-states; this Triple Alliance became the Aztec Empire. From 1428 until 1519, the Aztec Empire expanded over much of central and southern Mexico, forging what was perhaps the largest empire in pre-Columbian Mesoamerica. When Hernando Cortés reached the Aztec capital in 1519, he encountered a city of more than 100,000 residents, far larger than its European contemporaries of Paris, London, or Seville. Within two years, the Aztec Empire had crumbled, and Tenochtitlán's ruins became the site of the Spanish capital, Mexico City.

In contrast to Mesoamerica, South America was inhabited by a veritable kaleidoscope of ethnic groups, with diverse cultures, languages, traditions, and histories. South America's Andean region saw the flourish of a series of advanced civilizations, such as the Nazca, Moche, Tiwanaku, and Wari; less-known civilizations such as San Agustín and the Muisca dominated much of Colombia; and around 1000 C.E., the first Incas began to settle the Valley of Cuzco. However, it was not until the 15th century that the Incas began to expand their empire, a process that began in earnest after 1438. Thus, like the Aztec Empire in Mexico, the Inca Empire was relatively new when the first Europeans arrived. In November 1532, when Francisco Pizarro and his band of 168 Spanish conquistadores first encountered the Inca ruler Atahualpa, the empire, known as Tawantinsuyu (Four Parts Together), extended over 380,000 square miles (984,200 km²).

Thus, by the period of European contact and conquest, Latin America was a highly diverse region, made up of disparate groups with distinct cultures, political organizations and institutions, languages, and traditions. Some of these groups lived in small sedentary villages, while others were organized into complex chiefdoms. Still others, such as the Aztecs and the Incas, had forged large empires with millions of subjects.

THE ATLANTIC WORLD IN THE AGE OF CONQUEST, 1492–1560: A BRIEF OVERVIEW

Columbus's 1492 voyage initiated a period of unprecedented European expansion into the continents surrounding the Atlantic Ocean; this "age of conquest" was led by Spain and Portugal. Even before Columbus's historic Atlantic crossing, the Portuguese had made landfall on the Atlantic islands of Madeira (1419), the Azores (1427), and the Cape Verdes (1456), and the Spaniards had begun the conquest of the Canary Islands (between 1478 and 1493). All of these Atlantic voyages by the two Iberian powers served as a base and proving ground for the invasion and conquest of what became Spanish America, known then as the Indies, and Portuguese Brazil.

After 1492, Spain's possessions expanded from a few isolated Caribbean outposts to include Aztec territories in Mexico, Maya domains in southern Mexico and Central America, and, within a decade, the extensive human and mineral resources of the Inca Empire in South America. The original conquistadores, followed by Crown bureaucrats and Catholic clergymen, firmly consolidated Spanish sovereignty over the central regions of Mexico and Peru. Collectively, the new possessions served as the foundation of the Spanish Atlantic empire, which encompassed a vast region, extending from the current south of the United States to the southern tip of South America.

Well before the Spanish conquests, Portuguese explorers had made their way along the coast of Africa, founding an outpost in Ceuta (1415); and between 1450 and 1505, they had established at least 14 trading posts in Guiné, where they exchanged European goods with local African polities for slaves. These slaves were shipped from Guiné to the Cape Verde Islands and then sent to Portugal, which served as the center for the growing European slave trade. At the same time, Portuguese settlers had transformed the Madeira Islands into a prosperous producer of sugarcane, which was sold throughout the Mediterranean and northern Europe. Portuguese merchants also explored the coast of Africa, and in 1488, Bartholomeu Dias rounded the Cape of Good Hope, demonstrating that seagoing vessels could gain entry into the rich markets of the Indian Ocean. This route was then exploited in 1497 when Vasco da

Gama left Lisbon and entered the Indian Ocean via the Cape of Good Hope, reaching the Indian city of Calicut on May 20, 1498. Two years later, the discovery of Brazil by Pedro Álvares Cabral seemed insignificant compared to the immensely profitable African and Eastern trading outposts established by the Portuguese. After Portuguese control over the Far Eastern spice trade weakened a century later, Brazil would become the "crown jewel" of Portugal's overseas possessions.

THE SPANISH ATLANTIC IN THE AGE OF CONQUEST

The Spanish invasion of the New World consisted first of the Caribbean islands and next moved to Mexico and Central America and then to Peru, as expeditions incorporated new lands into the Crown's domain. The major expeditions of Hernando Cortés in Mexico and Francisco Pizarro in Peru both benefited from having large numbers of Amerindian allies, and their victories resulted from small, highly mobile, and technologically superior Spanish forces leading indigenous uprisings against the unpopular, divided Aztec and Inca states. Restive ethnic groups, such as the Tlaxcalans in Mexico and the Cañari in the Andes, were valuable allies to the Spanish conquistadores in overthrowing the Aztec and Inca states. Nonetheless, the position of the conquistadores was hardly secure after the overthrow of the major indigenous polities. The Spanish consolidated their newly acquired wealth, status, and power by making strategic alliances with powerful Amerindian ethnic groups, often marrying or taking as concubines the daughters of local indigenous elites. In Peru, the Spaniards even put a seemingly docile member of the Inca royal family, Manco Inca, on the throne to legitimize their rule in the Andes. Manco eventually rebelled in 1536 and almost succeeded in driving the Europeans out of the Andes; ultimately, he established a rival Inca kingdom in the remote jungle region of Vilcabamba, where his successors remained until the Spaniards captured the fortress in 1571.

To divide the spoils of conquest, the conquistadores gave out *encomiendas*, grants that allowed them to collect taxes and labor services from a designated group of indigenous towns in return for military protection and religious instruction. These grants gave the Spanish holder, the *encomendero*, social status and a source of capital and labor to buy property, engage in mining, or pursue commercial opportunities. The *encomienda* allowed the conquistadores to drain resources from the already existing Amerindian economies and invest them in emerging colonial enterprises.

By the middle of the 16th century, the Crown had slowly phased out the *encomienda* in wealthy, densely populated central areas of the Indies, although it persisted along the fringes of the empire. Squabbles among the conquistadores led to disorder, particularly in Peru, and the onset of European epidemic diseases dramatically reduced the Amerindian population in the central zones

of the Spanish Indies. Moreover, Crown authorities feared creating a New World nobility of *encomenderos*, while churchmen wanted direct control over evangelizing the indigenous peoples. Furthermore, the rise of new colonial cities and the discovery of fabulously rich gold and silver mines attracted a new influx of migrants from Spain, who resented the political, social, and economic dominance of the *encomiendas* system.

To replace the *encomenderos*, the Crown sent bureaucrats, clergy, and other settlers to rule, convert, and populate the newly acquired lands. In Spain, the Crown established the Board of Trade, or Casa de Contratación (1503), to control colonial commerce and the Council of the Indies (1524) to serve as a court of appeals in civil cases, a legislative body, and an executive authority to enforce laws for the Indies. In the Americas, the Crown set up an extensive bureaucracy to rule the newly conquered lands, headed by a viceroy in each of the two major political units, the Viceroyalties of New Spain and Peru. Within these two viceroyalties, the metropolitan government founded a series of high courts, called *audiencias* (six in Peru and four in New Spain), to hear civil and criminal cases. These justices worked with the viceroys to enforce legislation sent from Spain and to issue laws dealing with local matters. To limit the regional power of the *encomenderos*, authorities in Spain created a network of rural magistrates to regulate contact between Spaniards and Amerindians, to collect the head tax or tribute, and to assign forced (corvée) labor service for state projects.

Roman Catholic clergymen took firm control of converting the Amerindians to Catholicism in the two viceroyalties. At first, the religious orders—primarily the Franciscans, Dominicans, Augustinians, Mercedarians, and, later, the Jesuits—played a leading role in evangelizing the indigenous peoples. Over time, members of the secular clergy established parishes under the overall supervision of a series of bishops appointed by the Crown (seven in New Spain and eight in Peru) and shared evangelization duties with the regular orders.

THE PORTUGUESE SEABORNE EMPIRE

During the 60 years after Cabral's landing in Brazil in 1500, the Portuguese continued expanding their trading activities throughout the Atlantic Basin and beyond, to the Far East. Portuguese traders controlled the slave trade in the Atlantic world, and in the Far East, they seized most of the spice trade to Europe. The Portuguese established only small overseas fortresses and warehouses and enforced their commercial prominence with their navy rather than by establishing settler colonies like their rival, Spain. The center of Portugal's empire in this early period was its outpost at Goa, in India, and the only Crown agency supervising the empire was the India House, established in Lisbon in 1503. Through this agency, the Crown exercised a monopoly over this seaborne commerce, licensing Portuguese nobles and merchants to engage in foreign trade for a share of the profits.

The Portuguese exploration and settlement of Brazil proceeded more slowly, as the local indigenous peoples had no densely populated, organized states capable of funneling trade goods to Portuguese coastal outposts. After Cabral's initial explorations, the Crown licensed a few small coastal dyewood trading posts or factories to open a barter trade with the indigenous Tupí-Guaraní peoples for brazilwood. Within a few decades, this barter system began to break down as many Amerindian groups balked at cutting dyewoods for the Portuguese and the inroads of French traders placed increased demands on the semisedentary Tupí-Guaraní peoples, which emboldened them to demand more valuable goods (including firearms) in payment for cutting and hauling dyewoods. As a result, the Portuguese began systematically enslaving the native Brazilian peoples, which led to periodic wars.

The Portuguese monarchy later promoted full-scale colonization in Brazil by granting charters to wealthy notables, called *donatários* (proprietors), who would bankroll and govern the first settlements. The Crown gave these proprietors the authority to control the distribution of land, dispense justice, grant town charters, oversee commerce with the Amerindians, and force indigenous people to work for the colony. The Crown also granted the proprietors large personal tracts of land. Although the king authorized the trade in dyewoods, he made the business a royal monopoly, ensuring the monarchy a large share of the profits. Nonetheless, only the colonies at Pernambuco, Bahia, Rio de Janeiro, and São Vicente managed to survive and prosper. Hostile relations with the indigenous peoples, chronic shortages of capital, and hostility between settlers and the proprietors led other colonies to wither.

In 1549, the Crown dispatched the first governor-general of Brazil, Tomé de Sousa, to fight the French and hostile Amerindian groups, and Sousa later founded the city of Salvador as the capital of Brazil. The economic success of Portuguese Brazil was not ensured, however, until profitable sugar plantations emerged in the northeast, around Olinda and Salvador da Bahia. The Portuguese colonists continued exploiting and enslaving the Tupí-Guaraní peoples, until their near extinction from disease and overwork (in some coastal regions) encouraged the introduction of African slaves to work on the plantations. The colonial enterprise in Brazil required permanent settlements, ongoing relations with indigenous peoples, and commercial agriculture, which required outlays much greater than the Portuguese had expended to build their trading outposts in Africa and Asia.

The institutional influence of the Roman Catholic Church in Brazil was minimal in the first half of the 16th century, and the first bishopric in Salvador da Bahia was not established until 1551. Most of the evangelization of the indigenous peoples fell to the Society of Jesus (Jesuits), whose first representatives arrived in 1549. They soon set up religious houses to convert and care for the indigenous communities of the interior. Although the Jesuits remained influential in the educational, spiritual, and economic life of Brazil, they often engaged in conflicts with settlers over the welfare of indigenous peoples. The colonists viewed the missions as an impediment to the enslavement of Amerindians to work on the sugar plantations. The Jesuits maintained that many Portuguese settlers acted immorally and abusively toward the Amerindians. The Jesuits even ran afoul of the first bishop of Bahia, Pedro Fernandes Sardinha, who argued that the society's first responsibility lay in ministering to Portuguese settlers, not converting Amerindians. With such divisions within the church and between the order and civil society, the Catholic Church in Brazil had less influence in the evolution of colonial society than it did in the Spanish Indies.

By 1560, the Spanish and Portuguese Atlantic empires were an immensely varied agglomeration of landscapes, climates, disease environments, cultures, languages, and customs. Despite its diversity, this Atlantic world also had unifying networks of political, economic, and social cohesion. The encounters between the Spanish and Portuguese and the native peoples of America and Africa altered preexisting modes of production, technology, commerce, politics, social hierarchies, patterns of diet and disease, and religion. At the same time, African and Amerindian peoples managed to incorporate these changes into their political, social, and religious practices, producing a constantly evolving mixture that was not entirely European, indigenous, or African, particularly in the Americas. Spanish and Portuguese notions of wealth, for example, led to intensive mining of precious metals and commercial agriculture, and the introduction of new foodstuffs and animals set in motion changes that transformed Africa, Brazil, and the Indies in significant ways. At the same time, indigenous food products (such as chocolate, maize, potatoes, and tobacco) and cultural practices reshaped European lifeways. In this sense, the Spanish Indies and Brazil represented a new world, indeed, tied to Europe and the wider Atlantic Basin.

—Kenneth J. Andrien
J. Michael Francis

◆ TIME LINE ◆
(PREHISTORY TO 1560)

50,000 B.C.E.– 40,000 B.C.E.

- Earliest waves of human migrants cross the Bering land bridge, initiating settlement in the Americas.

12,500

- Evidence of human settlement at Monte Verde, Chile, and Taima Taima, Venezuela

12,000–8000

- Paleo-Indian period in Mesoamerica

ca. 10,000

- Earliest evidence of human settlement in the Amazonian regions of Brazil, Peru, Ecuador, and Colombia
- Early human occupation sites in Bolivia, Venezuela, Argentina, and other regions of South America
- Earliest evidence of textile production in South America

9500

- Earliest evidence of human occupation in Panama, at La Yeguada and Lake Alajuela

9000

- Rising sea levels make the Bering land bridge impassable.

8000–2000

- Archaic period in Mesoamerica, characterized by a rise in temperatures and the domestication of various plants

ca. 8000

- Earliest evidence for the domestication of squash in Mesoamerica, potato in Peru, manioc in Brazil
- Evidence of early textile production in Mesoamerica

5500

- Earliest examples of pottery in Amazonia, representing the earliest ceramic tradition in the Americas

ca. 5200

- Earliest evidence for the domestication of maize in Tabasco, Mexico

ca. 5000

- Evidence for maize domestication in South America

4600

- Earliest evidence for the domestication of manioc in Mesoamerica

4500

- Early hunter-gatherers settle near future site of Lima, Peru.

4000

- Earliest human occupation of the island of Hispaniola

3500–1800

- Valdivia culture flourishes in Ecuador.

3000

- Local development of pottery in Panama, at sites such as Monagrillo
- Significant monumental architecture appears in Peru, at sites such as Caral.

2700

- Earliest evidence for the domestication of chilies in Mesoamerica

2500

- Cotton is domesticated in the Mexican lowlands.

2000–1000

- Early Preclassic period (or Early Formative period) in Mesoamerica
- Complex public architecture emerges in Mesoamerica.

2000

- Settled farming villages appear throughout Mesoamerica.
- Formative period in the South American Andes sees formation of sedentary villages in Peru and Bolivia.
- Construction begins at Peruvian site of El Paraíso.

1800–1400

- Ocós culture on the coast of Guatemala and in Chiapas

1800

- Evidence of kiln-fired ceramics in South America

1500

- Arawak populations move up the Orinoco River and eventually into the Caribbean.
- Evidence of sheet-metalworking in copper and gold in the southern Andes of South America
- Zapotec peoples first settle in the Valley of Oaxaca.
- Mixtec peoples first settle in region that corresponds to the modern Mexican states of Oaxaca, Puebla, and Guerrero.

1400–200

- Chavín culture in Peru

1200–1000

- Early settlement at the Maya site of Kaminaljuyú, near the modern capital of Guatemala

1200–500

- Olmec civilization flourishes in Mexico's Gulf Coast region.

1000–400

- Middle Preclassic period (or Middle Formative period) in Mesoamerica

1000

- Ciboney Indians arrive on the island of Cuba.

600

- Earliest evidence of glyphic writing and the sacred calendar anywhere in Mesoamerica, found at the Zapotec village of San José Mogote in the Valley of Oaxaca

500

- Zapotec chiefdoms establish the city of Monte Albán.

400 B.C.E.–1 C.E.

- Early Horizon period in Peru

400 B.C.E.–250 C.E.

- Late Preclassic period (or Late Formative period) in Mesoamerica
- City of El Mirador dominates the Maya lowlands region.
- City of Teotihuacán begins its rapid growth and domination over much of Central Mexico.
- Large, complex villages emerge throughout the Amazon region.

200 B.C.E.

- Early construction begins at Maya site of Tikal.

200 B.C.E.–700 C.E.

- Nazca culture flourishes in southern Peru.

1–600 C.E.

- Early Intermediate period in Peru

50–800

- Moche culture dominates Peru's north coast.

100

- Evidence of widespread farming and agriculture in the Caribbean

- Taino migrants arrive in the Leeward Islands.
- Evidence of kiln-fired ceramics in Mesoamerica

100–1200

- San Agustín culture in Colombia

ca. 150

- City of Cuicuilco, located at the southern edge of the Valley of Mexico, is partially destroyed by a volcanic eruption.

250–900

- Classic period in Mesoamerica
- Teotihuacán exerts influence over much of Mesoamerica, until its dramatic fall in the seventh century.
- Zapotecs dominate much of the Oaxaca region of Mexico.
- Mixtec peoples occupy parts of Oaxaca, Puebla, and Guerrero.
- Period of flourish in much of the Maya lowlands, with the dramatic growth of Maya centers such as Tikal, Calakmul, Yaxchilán, Caracol, Palenque, and Copán
- Maya have a fully developed glyphic writing system.

300–1100

- Much of Bolivia is dominated by Tiwanaku culture.

378

- Siyaj K'ak, perhaps on orders from the ruler of Teotihuacán, leads a military conquest of several Maya lowland sites, including Tikal. A new dynastic order begins at Tikal, with close ties to Teotihuacán.

426

- K'inich Yax K'uk' Mo' establishes Copán dynasty, which lasts almost 400 years.

500

- Evidence of tobacco cultivation at the site of Cerén in modern El Salvador

500–900

- City of Monte Albán dominates Mexico's Oaxaca region.

562–594

- El Niño triggers drought conditions in Peru.

600–1000

- Middle Horizon period in Peru
- Wari culture flourishes in Peru.

650

- Construction of Maya city of Chichén Itzá begins.

738

- Copán's king, Waxaklajun Ub'aah K'awil, is captured and executed at Quiriguá.

800

- Major construction ends at Monte Albán.

800–1200

- Las Ánimas period in Chile

800–1537

- Muisca peoples flourish in Colombia's eastern highlands.

822

- Copán dynasty ends.

900–ca. 1200

- Central Mexico dominated by the Toltecs, from their capital city Tula.

900–1519

- Postclassic period in Mesoamerica
- Rise and fall of numerous northern Yucatán Maya cities such as Uxmal, Sayil, Chichén Itzá, Cobá, and Mayapán

909

- The last recorded long-count calendar date appears on a Maya monument at Toniná.

1000

- Colombia's Muisca Indians mine emeralds at Muzo.
- Incas begin to settle around the Valley of Cuzco.
- Maya city of Chichén Itzá falls into decline.
- Evidence of earliest human occupation on the island of Tenochtitlán, future capital of the Aztecs

1000–1450

• Late Intermediate period in Peru

1050

• Arawaks and their descendants, the Taino, have settled on Cuba.

1200

• Acolhua, Tepaneca, Culhua, Chalca, and Xochimilca migrants arrive in the Valley of Mexico.

ca. 1250

• Mexica (Aztecs) arrive in the Valley of Mexico.

1325

• Mexica (Aztecs) establish their capital city, Tenochtitlán.

1372

• Acamapichtli, son of a Mexica noble and a Culhua princess, becomes the first Mexica king, or *tlatoani*. He rules until 1391.

1391

• Huitzilíhuitl becomes Mexica king, ruling until 1417.

1400

• Incas dominate the Cuzco valley region.

1417

• Chimalpopoca becomes Mexica king, ruling until 1427.

1427

• Itzcóatl becomes Mexica king, ruling until 1440.

1428

• The Triple Alliance between the Mexica, Texcoco, and Tlacopán is established, forming the Aztec Empire, which will quickly expand.

1438

• The Chancas launch an assault on the Inca capital of Cuzco. Following a successful defense, the Incas begin process of rapid imperial expansion.

• Pachacuti Inca Yupanqui becomes Inca ruler, governing the empire until 1471.

1440

• Montezuma Ilhuicamina (Montezuma I) rules Aztec Empire until 1468.

1441

• Violent collapse of Maya city of Mayapán in Yucatán Peninsula.

1450–1455

• Severe drought and famine in Central Mexico

1450–1533

• Late Horizon period in Peru

1451

• Christopher Columbus is born in Genoa, Italy.

1450s

• Inca emperor Pachacuti Inca Yupanqui establishes Machu Picchu as a royal estate.

ca. 1460

• Incas conquer the Chimú of northern Peru.

1468

• Axayácatl rules Aztec Empire until 1481.

1470–1480

• The Kaqchikel Maya establish their highland capital at Iximché.

1471

• Topa Inca Yupanqui becomes Inca ruler and governs for 22 years.

1478

• Aztec army suffers devastating defeat in campaign against the Tarascans. As many as 20,000 Aztecs are killed during the battle.

1479

• On September 4, the monarchs of Spain and Portugal sign the Treaty of Alcaçovas.

ca. 1480

- Incas initiate conquest campaigns in northwest Argentina.

1481

- Tizoc rules Aztec Empire until 1486.

1484

- Hernando Cortés is born in Medellín, Spain.

1486

- Ahuitzotl rules Aztec Empire until 1502.

1487

- Thousands of captives are sacrificed at the dedication ceremony of the Templo Mayor in the Mexica (Aztec) capital city of Tenochtitlán.

1492

- On January 2, the Catholic monarchs, Isabella and Ferdinand, defeat the last Muslim kingdom in Spain and triumphantly enter the city of Granada.
- Edict of Expulsion forces Spain's Jewish population to either convert to Christianity or leave Spain; many Spanish Jews flee to neighboring Portugal.
- On April 17, Isabella and Ferdinand draft an agreement with Christopher Columbus. The Capitulations of Santa Fe include certain promises to Columbus if his venture proves successful.
- On August 4, three vessels—the *Niña*, *Pinta*, and *Santa María*—depart from the Spanish city of Palos, under the command of Columbus. On September 9, the three ships leave the Canary Islands, and one month later, on October 12, Columbus and his men sight land.
- On December 25, the *Santa María* strikes a reef and sinks. With the assistance of a local chieftain (cacique) named Guacanagarí, the crew salvages most of the ship's cargo.
- Europeans first learn about the use of tobacco when the Taino Indians show them the leaves.

1493

- Papal bulls issued by Pope Alexander VI grant Castile title to the lands Christopher Columbus has discovered and charge the monarchy with Christianizing the inhabitants of those lands.
- Columbus embarks on his second of four voyages to the Americas. Outfitted to establish a European colony, Columbus's ships carry a wide variety of Old World grains, grasses, vegetables, and livestock. Sugar is introduced to Hispaniola.

- Columbus returns to Hispaniola to find that the fortress he established at La Navidad has been destroyed, and the Spanish garrison killed.
- Huayna Cápac becomes Inca king, governing the expansive empire until his death in 1527.

1494

- On June 7, following negotiations between Portugal and Castile, the Treaty of Tordesillas is signed; the treaty establishes a designated line 370 leagues west of Cape Verde. Spain is permitted to claim territories to the west of that line, and Portugal receives authority to claim territories to the east of the boundary.
- During his second voyage, Christopher Columbus discovers the island of Jamaica.

1496

- Portugal's king, Dom Manuel, issues an expulsion order for all Jews who do not convert to Christianity.
- Christopher Columbus builds the first American caravel on the island of Hispaniola.

1498

- Christopher Columbus departs on his third voyage to the New World, charged with carrying colonists and supplies to Hispaniola as well as conducting further exploration. Among the colonists are 30 women.

1499

- Spanish explorer Alonso de Ojeda sets out from Spain to conquer and explore the northeastern coast of South America.

1500

- Pedro Álvares Cabral claims Brazil for the Portuguese Crown.

1501

- Gaspar Corte Real explores the northeast coast of Newfoundland and the coast of Labrador. Reports of rich fish stocks in the Great Banks encourage Iberian fishermen, mainly Basques, to establish small processing plants in villages that still bear Portuguese and Spanish names.
- Muslims, Jews, and other heretics, as well as their children, are henceforth forbidden to travel to the New World.

1502

- Montezuma Xocoyotzin (Montezuma II) rules Aztec Empire until 1520.

- Nicolás de Ovando arrives as governor of Hispaniola.
- Explorer Amerigo Vespucci maps the northeastern coastline of the Southern Cone.
- Christopher Columbus embarks on his fourth and final voyage to the New World.

1503

- House of Trade (Casa de Contratación) is established in Seville; it is charged with supervising and regulating the traffic of goods and peoples between Spain and Spanish America.

1504

- Queen Isabella dies, leaving Ferdinand king of Aragon and regent of Castile.

1506

- On May 20, Christopher Columbus dies at the age of 55.

1508

- Pope Julius II grants the privilege of *patronato real* (royal patronage) to the Spanish monarchy, giving the Crown the right to appoint bishops and parish priests in the New World.

1511

- The first American *audiencia* (high court) is established at Santo Domingo.
- The Spanish conquest of Cuba begins.

1512

- Laws of Burgos are issued by King Ferdinand of Spain to regulate relations between Spaniards and the indigenous inhabitants of Hispaniola.
- Hatuey, the Indian cacique who led the first indigenous revolt against colonial rule in Cuba, is captured and burned at the stake.

1513

- Juan Ponce de León becomes the first Spaniard to explore La Florida; he will return to colonize the region in 1521 but will die during the campaign.
- Blasco Núñez de Balboa informs the Spanish Crown of the existence of the Pacific Ocean, which he claims for Castile.
- King Ferdinand names Pedro Arias de Ávila as governor of the new colony of Darién.
- Pope Leo X authorizes the creation of the New World's first ecclesiastical see at Santo Domingo.

1514

- Alessandro Geraldini, the first bishop in the Americas, oversees the construction of the cathedral of Santo Domingo.

1515

- The city of Havana is founded.

1516

- Juan Díaz de Solís lands briefly in what is now Argentina.
- The archbishop of Toledo, Francisco Jiménez de Cisneros, awards the Dominican friar Bartolomé de Las Casas the title of "universal defender and protector of the Indians."

1517

- Diego Velásquez de Cuéllar, the governor of Cuba, authorizes Francisco Hernández de Córdoba to lead a voyage of exploration of the Yucatán Peninsula.
- Charles I becomes king of Aragon and Castile.
- Alfonso Manso, the bishop of Puerto Rico, becomes the first inquisitor in the New World.

1518

- A smallpox epidemic devastates the Indian population on Hispaniola.
- First *asientos* are issued to transport slaves to the Americas.

1519

- Cuba's governor, Diego Velásquez de Cuéllar, commissions Hernando Cortés to lead an expedition west, building on the previous expeditions of Francisco Hernández de Córdoba (1517) and Juan de Grijalva (1518).
- Governor Velásquez's efforts to remove Cortés from command come too late, and on February 18, Cortés sets sail from Cuba, with more than 500 men, 11 ships, 16 horses, and some artillery.
- Scuttling all but one of his ships (which he dispatches to Spain), Cortés and his forces march inland, initiating the conquest of the Aztec Empire.
- Pedro Arias de Ávila is appointed governor of Panama; he immediately relocates the capital to the Pacific side, near present-day Panama City.
- Vasco Núñez de Balboa is arrested, tried, and beheaded.
- Ferdinand Magellan anchors in the bay of what is now Montevideo, Uruguay; he then sails past the entire region and through the straits that today bear his name.
- King Charles I is elected Holy Roman Emperor Charles V.

1520

- On June 30, Hernando Cortés and 450 of his men escape from Tenochtitlán during the Noche Triste. More than 900 Spaniards are captured and killed, as are 1,000 of Cortés's Tlaxcalan allies.
- On the same day, the Aztec ruler, Montezuma, dies after being struck by a stone.
- Cuauhtémoc becomes the last Aztec king, ruling until 1525.
- A major smallpox epidemic ravages Central Mexico.

1521

- Hernando Cortés launches a direct assault on the Aztec capital of Tenochtitlán, with the assistance of 20,000–30,000 Indian allies. Tenochtitlán falls to Cortés's forces, ending 93 years of Aztec imperial domination. Mexico City is founded on the ruins of the Aztec capital.
- On the island of Hispaniola, Wolof slaves lead the first recorded slave revolt in the Americas.

1522

- A Spanish law restricts immigration to the New World to Castilian Old Christians.
- Gil González Dávila leads the Spanish conquest of Nicaraguan territory.
- French pirate Jean Fluery attacks and seizes three Spanish treasure ships.

1523

- Pedro de Alvarado, a lieutenant of Hernando Cortés, arrives in Central America with a force of 400 Spaniards and hundreds of Tlaxcalan allies to conquer the Maya of highland Guatemala.

1524

- The Council of the Indies is established to administer Spain's imperial affairs.
- Twelve Franciscan friars arrive in Mexico City to begin the "spiritual conquest" of Mexico's indigenous population.
- Alvarado founds the colonial capital of Santiago de los Caballeros de Guatemala (Tecpán), located near Iximché, the Kaqchikel Maya capital.

1525

- During a conquest campaign in Guatemala, Hernando Cortés orders the execution of Cuauhtémoc, the last Aztec ruler.

1526

- In order to protect ships and regulate trade, Spanish vessels are required to travel in fleets; over the next few decades, a system will develop that dispatches an annual convoy to Mexico (la flota) and another to Panama for Peru (los galeones).
- Disgruntled Spanish conquistadores burn much of the Kaqchikel Maya city of Iximché.

1527

- Pánfilo de Narváez leads an expedition of 400 men and 40 horses into northwestern Florida. Only four men will survive, including Álvar Núñez Cabeza de Vaca, who will later record his eight-year ordeal as a captive among the Indians and his remarkable overland journey from east Texas (near modern-day Galveston) to New Spain (Mexico).
- The Inca Huayna Cápac, ruler of the vast Inca empire, and his chosen heir both die unexpectedly, sparking a violent civil war between two half brothers, Huáscar and Atahualpa.

1528

- Second audiencia (high court) in the Americas is established in Mexico City.

1529

- A special ceremonial bullfight is celebrated in Mexico City to mark the anniversary of Hernando Cortés's conquest of Tenochtitlán eight years earlier.
- The Caribbean city of Santa Marta (Colombia) is founded.
- Francisco Pizarro obtains royal authorization to launch an expedition of exploration and conquest in Peru.

1531

- Francisco Pizarro founds the city of San Miguel de Piura on the northern coast of Peru, commencing the invasion of Inca territory.
- The Indian Juan Diego sees a vision, the Virgin of Guadalupe.

1532

- On November 16, Francisco Pizarro captures the Inca ruler Atahualpa and holds him hostage in the city of Cajamarca.

1533

- Caribbean city of Cartagena de Indias (Colombia) is founded.

- On August 29, after collecting a rich ransom for the Inca's release, Pizarro orders Atahualpa's execution.

1534

- Jauja, the first capital of Spanish Peru, is formally founded; the capital is later moved to Lima, the "City of Kings."
- Sebastián de Benalcázar founds the city of San Francisco de Quito amid the smoldering ruins of the conquered Inca city.

1535

- The legendary Inca general Rumiñahui is captured and executed.
- Sebastián de Benalcázar establishes the port city of Guayaquil.
- The first viceroyalty in the Americas is established in New Spain (Mexico).
- Diego de Almagro, a veteran of the conquest of Peru and a former partner of Francisco Pizarro, organizes his own expedition to move south to conquer Chile. Not finding any gold, a disgruntled Almagro and his men will return to Cuzco in 1537.
- Vasco de Quiroga, the Franciscan bishop of Michoacán, argues that because the Indians failed to establish a civil society (as defined by Europeans), the lands of the New World were unoccupied and therefore available to peoples capable of creating such a society.
- Gonzalo Fernández de Oviedo y Valdés, King Charles I's official chronicler of the Indies, publishes his *Historia general y natural de las Indias.*

1536

- Manco Inca assembles an army of 100,000 and lays siege to the city of Cuzco. In early 1537, with his forces dwindling, Manco withdraws northward to Vilcabamba.
- Spanish conquistador Gonzalo Jiménez de Quesada leads an expedition into Colombia's eastern highlands, resulting in the conquest of the Muisca Indians and the establishment of the New Kingdom of Granada.
- In Mexico City, the Franciscans open a college for Indian students called Santa Cruz of Tlatelolco; there, young Indian nobles study Spanish, Latin, rhetoric, logic, theology, music, and medicine.
- With the papal bull Cum ad nil magis, the Portuguese Inquisition is formally established to police the behavior and the beliefs of subjects of the Portuguese Crown.

1537

- Pope Paul III, in Sublimis Deus, confirms the basic humanity of the Indians, meaning that they are capable of becoming Christians; he forbids their enslavement and the seizure of their lands or property.
- The port of Guayaquil (modern Ecuador) is formally founded.

1538

- Christopher Columbus's son Fernando publishes his *Historia del almirante*, a biography of his father.
- The *audiencia* (high court) of Panama is established.
- The Battle of Las Salinas is fought near Cuzco, Peru.
- King Charles I issues a royal decree allowing the establishment of the first brothel in Mexico City.

1539

- Hernando de Soto undertakes the first extensive land exploration of La Florida. Three years later, de Soto will fall ill and die on the west bank of the Mississippi River.
- The first printing press in the Americas begins operation in Mexico City.

1540

- Pedro de Valdivia is granted permission to conquer Chile. He sets out with 1,000 Peruvian Indians and roughly 150 Spaniards. In February of the following year, he will found the city of Santiago del Nuevo Extremo.
- The Society of Jesus (Jesuit order) is founded.
- The Mixtón War begins.
- Francisco Vásquez de Coronado leads an expedition into New Mexico and Arizona.

1541

- Francisco Pizarro is murdered.

1542

- The New Laws of 1542 prohibit further *encomiendas* and order the reversion to the Spanish Crown of all *encomiendas* upon the death of the current *encomendero*. The New Laws also ban the enslavement of Indians. Widespread resistance to the laws will lead to some revisions, restoring the right to pass *encomiendas* to an heir; nevertheless, the ban on personal service will be preserved.
- Bartolomé de Las Casas's influential and highly controversial text, the *Brevísima relación de la destrucción de las Indias* (*Very Brief Account of the Destruction of the Indies*), is published.
- Spanish explorer Juan Rodríguez Cabrillo becomes the first Spaniard to explore the territory that will later become California.

- Francisco de Orellana completes navigation of the Amazon River.

- Viceroy Antonio de Mendoza leads a force of 500 Spaniards and 50,000 Indian allies to defeat the Mixtón Indians, ending the Mixtón War.

- Hernán Pérez de Quesada leads an ill-fated expedition in search of El Dorado.

- Francisco de Montejo leads the conquest of the Yucatán Peninsula.

1543

- The Consulado (Merchant Guild) of Seville is established to help organize fleets to the New World and supervise the loading and unloading of vessels.

1544

- The Viceroyalty of Peru is established; the first viceroy, Blasco Núñez Vela, arrives with orders to enforce the New Laws of 1542. Two years later, when Núñez Vela attempts to impose his authority by force, Gonzalo Pizarro will have the viceroy captured and executed.

1545

- Pope Paul III convokes a general council of the Catholic Church to respond to the challenges of the Protestant Reformation and initiate reforms within the church. The council meets in the northern Italian city of Trent, and in 1563, the Council of Trent will promulgate its decrees, which will profoundly influence Catholicism in Iberia and the Americas.

- The rich silver mines of Potosí are discovered, sparking a boom in silver mining in the Viceroyalty of Peru.

1547

- Santo Domingo becomes the metropolitan see of the Indies.

1548

- Silver is discovered in Zacatecas, Mexico.

- Gonzalo Pizarro is captured and executed.

1549

- The Portuguese Crown appoints Tomé de Sousa as Brazil's first governor general.

- The first Jesuit missionaries arrive in Brazil, as do Brazil's first paid troops, known as the *tropas de primeira linha*.

- The city of La Paz is founded in present-day Bolivia.

1550

- The *audiencia* (high court) of Santa Fe is established, with jurisdiction over most of present-day Colombia and Venezuela.

- Silver mining begins in Guanajuato, Mexico.

1551

- Brazil's first diocese, centered in Salvador, is established.

- The University of San Marcos is founded in Lima, Peru.

1552

- Francisco López de Gómara's *Historia general de las Indias* (General history of the Indies) is published in Zaragoza, Spain.

- Aztec healer Martín de la Cruz produces his Codex Badianus, an illustrated manuscript that describes indigenous botanical medicine; the work is translated into Latin by his collaborator, Juan Badiano.

- The University of La Plata is founded in Sucre, in modern Bolivia.

1553

- Mexico's Royal and Pontifical University opens, with a curriculum based on that of the University of Salamanca in Spain.

- The Hospital Real de Naturales (Royal Indian Hospital) is founded in Mexico City.

1554

- Pedro de Cieza de León's *Descubrimiento y conquista del Perú* (*Discovery and Conquest of Peru*) is published.

- Peruvian rebel Francisco Hernández Girón is captured and executed by viceregal forces.

1555

- Bartolomé de Medina invents a method of refining silver ores through amalgamation, a process that makes it possible to refine lower-grade ores. The new technology quickly spreads throughout Spanish America.

1556

- King Charles I (Holy Roman Emperor Charles V) abdicates the Spanish throne in favor of his son, Philip II.

- The Augustinians found the University of San Fulgencio in Quito.

1558

- The Jesuit order founds its first university in the Americas, the Universidad de Santiago de la Paz in Santo Domingo.

1559

- A royal decree of June 12 creates the *audiencia* (high court) of Charcas (Upper Peru), with jurisdiction over much of the territory of modern Bolivia.

1560

- Lope de Aguirre joins Pedor de Ursúa's ill-fated expedition in search of El Dorado.

Entries A to Z

A

aclla (aqlla) *Aclla* is a Quechua word that means "chosen woman." The *acllas*, or *aqllakuna*, were the only women under Inca rule who received a formal education, and they played a critical role in the expansion of the Inca Empire (see INCAS). The *acllas* were rumored to have been among the Inca state's most beautiful women and were supposed to remain virgins throughout their lives, or at least until they were awarded in marriage. Removed from their families from about the age of 10, the girls were taken to various parts of the realm, where they were sequestered in one of the many state *acllawasi*, or "houses of the chosen women." According to one Spanish observer, the largest *acllawasi* housed as many as 200 women of different ages.

Long overlooked by scholars of Inca imperial expansion, the *acllas* played important roles in the social, political, religious, and economic organization of the Inca state (see ECONOMY). They wove rich TEXTILES used in religious and political ceremonies; these textiles were also distributed by the state as compensation for services rendered and as payment to the Inca's burgeoning army. The *acllas* also brewed great quantities of maize beer, or *CHICHA*, which was central to political and religious life in the Inca realm (see RELIGION).

The fate of the *acllas* varied. After four years of specialized training, they were qualified to serve as *mamak-una*, or priestesses; however, not all became priestesses. Some *acllas* were removed from the *acllawasi* and were given in marriage to men whom the Inca ruler wished to reward for their services to the state.

See also WOMEN (Vols. II, III, IV).

—J. Michael Francis

Further reading:
Terence N. D'Altroy. *The Incas* (Malden, Mass.: Blackwell Publishing, 2003).

agriculture Native Americans developed a variety of agricultural methods to suit local conditions. In the temperate highland areas of Mesoamerica and the Andes, people practiced permanent agriculture. Intensive cultivation provided sufficient harvests to support both the Aztec and Inca Empires. In low-lying and tropical areas and in arid regions, Native Americans relied on hunting and gathering to supplement shifting agriculture. Whichever type of agriculture was practiced, Native Americans had long-standing traditions of horticulture, irrigation, and shaping the landscape to serve their needs. This is seen in the *CHINAMPA*, or aquatic garden, of the Valley of Mexico and other places.

CARIBBEAN BEFORE 1492
The first evidence of widespread farming and agriculture in the Caribbean dates from around 100 C.E. and corresponds with the arrival of the Igneri or Saladoid, Arawak-speaking migrants from northern South America. The TAINO, descendants of the Saladoid, introduced new farming techniques that led to increased yields capable of supporting large populations.

Although the Taino hunted, fished, and collected wild plants for FOOD and other uses, their society depended mainly on the cultivation of root crops typical of Amazonian cultures: These included MANIOC, or cassava (*Manihot esculenta*), sweet POTATO (*Ipomea batatas*), yautia (*Xanthosoma sagittifolium*), and arrowroot or *lirén* (*Calathea allouia*). Of these, manioc was by far the most important.

Manioc plants have yields per acre comparable to those of rice or plantains; additionally, they provide all the calories and carbohydrates needed by a typical adult. Nevertheless, the root requires careful preparation because its sap, when exposed to air, turns into prussic or hydrocyanic acid, a powerful poison. The Taino and other indigenous cultures developed a process to extract this sap and render the root into flour suitable for baking and for use in stews.

MAIZE (from the Taino *mais*) was also cultivated but was less important than manioc as a food staple. The Taino cultivated several varieties of maize, generally with softer shells than those cultivated in Mesoamerica. The Taino did not make corn flour but rather roasted the grains or used them in soups and stews. The CARIB, another group with South American origins that settled the islands of the eastern Caribbean, used maize (*anasi* in their language), as well as fermented manioc and sweet potatoes, to make a potent alcoholic drink that was consumed during religious festivities (see ALCOHOL).

To supplement their diets, the Taino and Carib also grew several varieties of beans, which provided additional proteins and complemented their otherwise starchy diets. Peanuts or groundnuts (*maní* in Taino) were also cultivated and formed an important part of the indigenous diet.

Several species of gourds, squashes, and pumpkins were cultivated; these were used both as food and as containers. Pineapples (*ananas*) were also grown across the regions. Used as flavoring and as an irritant or poison for their arrows, chili peppers (known as *ají* by the Taino) were also widely grown.

Nonfood crops constituted another important aspect of indigenous Caribbean agricultural production. COTTON, the fibers of which were used to make TEXTILES and cords, was both cultivated and collected from wild varieties. Farmed cotton plants, however, produced higher yields and stronger threads. Fibers from cultivated and naturally occurring species of agave and maguey plants were used to make cordage for fishing lines and bowstrings and to weave hammocks. The crushed seeds from the *bija* shrub (*Bixa orellana*), which was grown around village huts, provided a vivid red dye that was used in textiles and as body paint (see DYES AND DYEWOOD).

TOBACCO (from the Taino *tabaco*) was cultivated to use as medicine and during religious ceremonies (see RELIGION). The Taino smoked dried tobacco leaves in pipes and cigars; the leaves were also finely ground and inhaled through a hollow tube.

The tools used by the indigenous peoples of the Caribbean to plant and tend their crops were simple but effective. The main farming implement was a planting stick (known as a *coa* among the Taino) about five feet long with a sharp, fire-hardened point. Petal-shaped axes made from polished hard stones were also common.

The indigenous peoples developed sophisticated farming practices that improved on the technologies imported from their Amazonian ancestral lands. The Taino and Carib, limited to the narrow bands of fertile land on their generally mountainous islands, practiced intensive agriculture, while their relatives in mainland South America, with exponentially more cultivable land available, relied on extensive agriculture. The last involved using fires to clear and fertilize plots of land (slash-and-burn farming) that could yield crops for three to five years before the soil was exhausted and the farmers were forced to repeat the process elsewhere, thus allowing the previously farmed plot to lay fallow. By contrast, the Caribbean indigenous peoples limited the use of slash-and-burn farming to certain types of soils and perhaps also crops, such as maize. In the Caribbean, mound farming was the most common way of growing the staple manioc root plant. Farmers built low mounds of earth, typically about three feet high and nine feet across, in rows several feet apart. About 10 pieces of manioc root were planted on each mound. By planting on a mound, the roots received more water and air. This technique also facilitated harvest when the root matured.

Irrigation was practiced among the Taino on the island of HISPANIOLA. Spanish chroniclers described large-scale irrigation canals on the relatively flat lands of the Xaraguá valley, a somewhat arid part of the island, watering fields of cotton.

MESOAMERICA BEFORE 1492

Agriculture emerged independently in a small number of regions around the world in the millennia following the last ice age. Mesoamerica was one of the most significant of those key regions. The civilizations of Mesoamerica developed a complex agricultural economy, which produced the economic surplus necessary for the growth of large populations and societies. By the time of the Spanish conquest, Mesoamerica's native inhabitants had developed elaborate and intensive systems of cultivation that fed millions of people and provided commodities for both local and long-distance trade. After the conquest, Mesoamerican foods spread rapidly around the world and today are a vital part the global diet and ECONOMY.

Domestication of Plants

The domestication of plants represents one of the most significant technological and economic innovations in human history. True domestication implies the modification of a plant through manipulation of its reproduction, thus replacing natural selection, at least partially, with artificial selection. Domestication is usually visible archaeologically through an increase in the size of the edible portion of the plant, typically the seed or fruit. In addition, humans often modify a plant's natural seed dispersal mechanisms, facilitating the harvesting of seeds to eat. Archaeologists who excavate plant remains are able to trace such changes and map plants' domestication.

Plant Domestication in Mesoamerica

Mesoamerican farmers grew many different crops. The most productive and economically important was maize

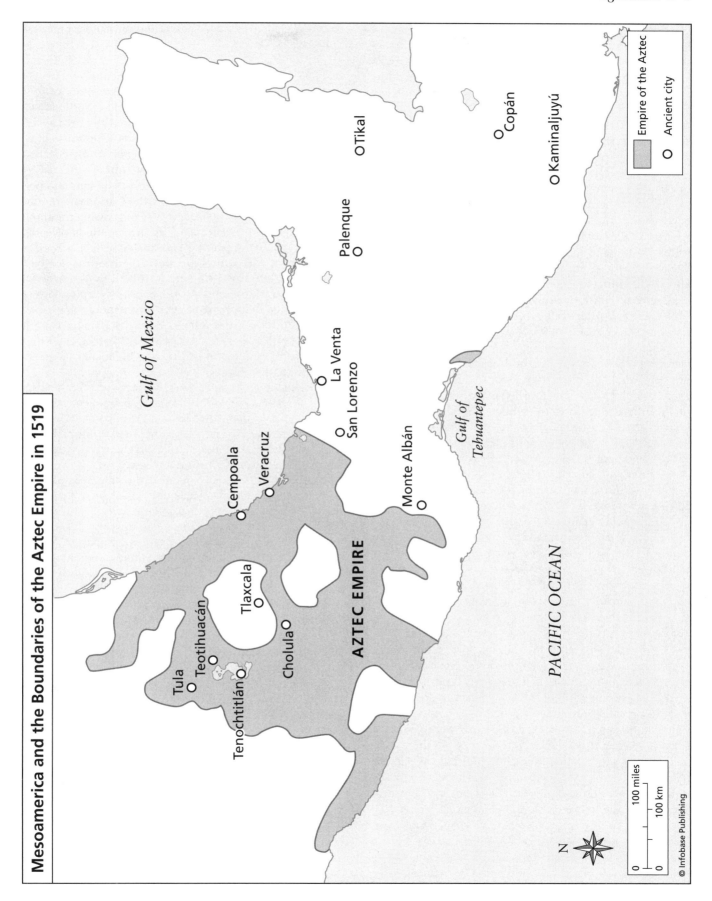

Mesoamerica and the Boundaries of the Aztec Empire in 1519

Gulf of Mexico

Tula

Teotihuacán

Tlaxcala

Tenochtitlán

Cholula

Cempoala

Veracruz

La Venta

San Lorenzo

Monte Albán

Palenque

Tikal

Copán

Kaminaljuyú

AZTEC EMPIRE

Gulf of Tehuantepec

PACIFIC OCEAN

Empire of the Aztec
Ancient city

N

100 miles
100 km

© Infobase Publishing

("Indian corn," or *Zea mays*). Historically, Mesoamerica has boasted many varieties of maize, grown in different regions, at different altitudes, and for diverse purposes. Today, maize, or corn, is one of the world's staple crops. The origins of maize remain poorly understood. For many years, the wild ancestor of maize was unknown, and some researchers thought it was long extinct. Modern genetic research has demonstrated through DNA analysis that an annual variety of a Central Mexico grass called teosinte is the wild progenitor of maize. Nevertheless, the history of the domestication process remains murky. Recent research suggests that maize was domesticated in the central Balsas River area of the highlands of southwestern MEXICO, but the earliest physical evidence of domesticated maize comes from the lowland archaeological site of San Andrés in Tabasco, Mexico, and dates from about 7,300 years ago. This is far from the native range of teosinte and must represent the cultivation of an already domesticated plant. Molecular and paleoecological data imply an initial date for domestication at least 9,000 years ago.

The next most important plants to be domesticated were squash (*Cucurbita pepo*) and beans. Evidence of the domestication of squash dates from some 10,000 years ago. It is also likely to have been domesticated in the dry southern and western Mexican highlands. Less is known about the domestication of beans, which may have occurred somewhat later, perhaps about 2000 B.C.E. In combination with corn and squash, beans formed the foundation of Mesoamerican agriculture. Grown together in the same plots, these plants revitalize the soil and offer a nutritionally balanced diet.

Many other plants were also cultivated. Manioc, a lowland root crop, appeared by 4600 B.C.E., although its domestication probably took place in South America. Sunflower (*Helianthus annuus*) appears in the archaeological record by about 2700 B.C.E. Chilies (*Capsicum*) have a long history in Mesoamerican agriculture and cuisine. Although several species of peppers were probably domesticated in South America, one (*C. annuum*) may have been domesticated in Mesoamerica. Chia (*Salvia hispanica* L.) was a staple food, possibly rivaling maize in importance among AZTECS. Today, it is used mainly for medicinal purposes and to make a refreshing drink; however, in pre-Hispanic times, the seeds were ground into flour. Tomatoes (*Lycopersicon esculentum*) were grown in Mexico before the conquest, but how they got there—the wild species are South American—is unknown. Cotton (*Gossypium*), although not a food, was as economically significant in Mesoamerica as it is today worldwide. It appeared in the lowlands around 2500 B.C.E.

A wide variety of tree crops were farmed and managed in Mesoamerica. CACAO (*Theobroma cacao* L.) was a major crop. Cacao beans were used as currency and to make a savory drink. Cacao cultivation was concentrated in ecologically propitious environments, most notably in Tabasco, Chiapas, and NICARAGUA. Other important tree crops included avocado, anona (custard apple), papaya, and *guayaba* (guava).

Agricultural Systems

The varied systems of cultivation developed in Mesoamerica represent significant social and technological accomplishments, while the intensification of agriculture is usually essential to the growth of complex societies. Traditional agriculture in Mesoamerica employed a slash-and-burn system, whereby a plot, or MILPA, was prepared by cutting the natural vegetation, letting it dry, and burning it. The ash and carbon from the burning added nutrients to the soil. Corn and squash were planted in the fields at the beginning of the rainy season, with beans perhaps planted later.

Ancient Mesoamericans developed several methods of agricultural intensification, some highly original. Irrigation was developed by the earliest complex society: A dam at the Olmec site of Teopantecuanitlán dates from about 1200 B.C.E. (see OLMECS). Other dams existed in Puebla and Oaxaca. Most known archaeological irrigation systems are found in the arid highlands of central and southern Mexico.

Raised aquatic fields, or *chinampas*, were constructed by excavating a network of canals in swamps or wetlands and then piling up the dredge spoil to build islands between the canals. The islands were supremely productive: Not only was the swamp mud fertile, but the water percolated through the sides of the canals where it was drawn up by the plant roots. Farmers dredged the canals periodically and dumped the spoil on the fields, which were thus refertilized. In addition, the canals supported aquatic species, such as fish, for consumption. *Chinampas* are still used for cultivation in the southern part of the Valley of Mexico (Xochimilco), where they are sometimes incorrectly called "floating gardens." The remains of ancient *chinampas* are found throughout Mesoamerica, with the largest concentrations in Central Mexico, especially the Valley of Mexico; the southern MAYA lowlands, especially northern BELIZE and adjacent areas; and along the coast of Veracruz. *Chinampa* agriculture clearly made a major contribution to the Aztecs diet at their capital of TENOCHTITLÁN in the Valley of Mexico, and possibly to the economy of the earlier, nearby city of TEOTIHUACÁN. The archaeological *chinampas* of the Maya lowlands are also extensive. Modern agronomists have been experimenting with *chinampas* to increase agricultural production in the developing world.

SOUTH AMERICA BEFORE 1492

Agricultural development in South America naturally stems from the earliest human settlements in the region. The MONTE VERDE archaeological site in CHILE as well as the El Abra site in COLOMBIA are widely believed to be the oldest human settlements in the Americas, each occupied some 14,500 years ago. Some evidence also exists of food cultivation practices in the AMAZON Basin at about the same time. Archaeologists have uncovered berries, more than three dozen edible plants, and nuts at these early sites. From these origins, agriculture in South America was developed and adapted to the continent's varied geography. The rudimentary practices of the earliest settlements gave way to complex terraced fielding and irrigation techniques in successive civilizations of pre-Columbian South America. Using these techniques, several civilizations were able to create vast and reliable harvests of numerous crops, which was oftentimes a momentous feat given the unaccommodating South American terrain.

The earliest civilizations in South America included the Valdivia community in ECUADOR, from ca. 3500 to 1800 B.C.E., and the Norte Chico culture, which occupied several hubs in PERU from roughly 3000 to 1800 B.C.E. Over the course of their existence, these communities cultivated beans, manioc, hot peppers, maize, and squash, as well as cotton for clothing. While domesticated maize was grown in Mexico from around 3500 B.C.E., it was not until a millennium later that the staple first appeared in South America. In South America, and particularly the Andes, the most important domesticate was the potato. By 2000 B.C.E., a handful of communities in South America were cultivating a variety of vegetables and harvesting nuts, which led to permanent settlements.

Building on the knowledge of their predecessors, the INCAS adapted technology and created an agricultural system that spanned some of the world's most diverse environments. Because of a lack of flat land in many parts of the Andean highlands, the Incas created terraced fields to facilitate the production of crops. By cutting rivets and tiers into the steep terrain, they were able to create a series of shelflike plateaus that permitted the cultivation of staple crops, the most widely grown being potatoes. The Incas relied heavily on *andenes* and *camellones*, both artificial terraces but distinct in terms of application, to create soil suitable for agriculture. To aid harvests, the Incas created *cochas*, which were essentially artificial lagoons, along the coasts. The Incas' terracing techniques, advanced irrigation techniques, sophisticated aqueducts, and extensive road systems enabled them to eat a wide variety of vegetables and fruits.

An assortment of beans and squash were cultivated from the time of the earliest human settlement in the Americas. Cotton was also one of the first products to be cultivated. Eventually, maize made its way from Mexico to become a staple of many South American diets. These staple crops continued to be cultivated throughout South America and remain the chief sources of nutrition to this day in many parts of the Andes and the Amazon Basin. Agricultural refinements over the millennia enabled the Inca to feed more than 12 million inhabitants in the 15th century. Indeed, the Incas' agricultural system was so efficacious that many experts assert that if it were readopted today, it would solve the food shortages experienced in many Andean nations. Even so, the Incas' agricultural sophistication is perhaps best appreciated in the light of discoveries made by a series of societies that existed prior to the rise of the Inca.

EARLY COLONIAL LATIN AMERICA

While the arrival of Spaniards and Portuguese brought considerable changes to agriculture and the environment, many aspects of Native American agriculture endured long into the colonial period. Before the conquest, agriculture in the Americas differed from that in Europe in terms of technology, cultivation practices, and types of crops. Because of the resilience and adaptability of maize, Native Americans harvested it throughout many regions. Maize was the most widespread staple and was supplemented with foods such as avocados, tomatoes, beans, and chilies. In the Andes, potatoes and the grain called quinoa were also cultivated, as was COCA. In lowland areas, the Tupí, Maya, and others grew maize or manioc as a staple, as well as sweet potatoes and other vegetables such as squash.

People in tropical, forested regions cultivated the land on a shifting or rotational basis throughout the colonial era. They cleared land for cultivation by felling trees and burning the undergrowth, although certain plants were left to maintain fertility and retain water in

Felipe Guamán Poma de Ayala's illustration of the eighth month, or August; this was the Chacra Yapuy Killa, the month to turn the soil. *(The Royal Library, Copenhagen, Denmark)*

the soil. This farming technique of slash and burn, or swidden agriculture, proved well suited to wet and warm conditions. Fields typically yielded significant crops for two or three years. The land would then be left fallow for a decade or so, with the farmers moving to new locations where the cycle would begin again. In areas of permanent agriculture, such as the Andes, Native Americans prepared soils by using fertilizers and weeding plots of land. They also relied on irrigation systems such as terracing to capture and retain rainwater. In wetland areas such as the lakes of the Valley of Mexico, irrigation involved the use of dams, dikes, and canals. In the case of *chinampa* agriculture, plots of land were constructed above the water level by using soil dredged from lakes. These fertile *chinampas* generated bountiful harvests and survived through the colonial period until today.

Native Americans often appropriated Spanish and Portuguese farming techniques. Native Americans had typically tilled land using a *coa*, or digging stick, whereas Europeans used plows that were pulled by draft animals. While many Native American groups readily adopted European implements such as axes, hoes, and, at times, plows, they did not necessarily replace their established agricultural practices. For example, Native Americans continued to plant seeds in an individual fashion, in contrast to the European method of broadcast sowing. The endurance of traditional cultivation practices was related to the preservation of existing systems of land tenure. While colonialism threatened the integrity of Native American landholdings, *milpas* (household plots of land) remained vital to village subsistence. Most lands were owned by individual families, although communal lands were allocated to nobles and some land was held in common by communities. In many areas, the greatest threat to Native American landholdings came from the interrelated processes of population decline and the rise of large landed estates, or haciendas.

In the early colonial period, Latin American agriculture underwent its most widespread change through the introduction of Old World DISEASES and flora and fauna as part of what is known as the COLUMBIAN EXCHANGE. Early generations of Spanish and Portuguese settlers preferred foods to which they were accustomed. Accordingly, they brought numerous new food species to the Americas. WHEAT, olives, grapes, citrus fruits, and other plants from the Mediterranean became common foodstuffs in some parts of the Americas, depending on the suitability of the crop to local conditions. Wheat and grapes, for instance, fared poorly in parts of Mexico because of the climate (see WINE). Similarly, African imports such as bananas, millet, okra, rice, and sorghum, followed the forced migration of slaves across the Atlantic (see SLAVERY).

The Columbian Exchange also involved the importation of new pathogens, pests, and animals that significantly altered agriculture. With catastrophic population collapse, lands were left fallow, facilitating the rise of Spanish estates, particularly ranches. Lacking natural predators, populations of cattle, goats, pigs, and sheep grew rapidly. Sheep proved a particular menace to Native American agriculture by roaming freely across lands and trampling crops. In some areas, sheep brought widespread environmental change, denuding the land of plants and, in the case of the Mezquital Valley in Mexico, transforming land that had been used for intensive irrigation agriculture into desert.

The arrival of the Portuguese and Spanish led to the rise of new forms of commercial agriculture. Some imported crops, such as SUGAR, were cultivated for European markets. Spaniards also sought to harness Native American LABOR to obtain brazilwood, cacao, cochineal, cotton, and indigo for commercial markets. Not all of these ventures were successful, as with the case with silk. Of greater success were haciendas. These commercial enterprises, which were run either by elite Europeans or monastic orders such as the Jesuits, supplied urban and Spanish markets and became crucial in the production of wheat, barley, and maize. While the extent of haciendas' development varied considerably from one region to the next, in some areas they became extensive enterprises that alienated Native American lands, altered labor relations, and disrupted local agriculture.

See also AGRICULTURE (Vols. II, III, IV); CACAO (Vols. II, III); COCA (Vols. II, III).

—Clifford T. Brown
Richard Conway
J. Michael Francis
Sean H. Goforth
Francisco J. González

Further reading:
Fatima Becht, et al., eds. *Taino, Pre-columbian Art and Culture from the Caribbean* (New York: Monacelli Press-Museo del Barrio, 1997).

Alfred W. Crosby. *The Columbian Exchange: Biological and Cultural Consequences of 1492* (Westport, CT: Greenwood, 1972).

Scott L. Fedick, ed. *The Managed Mosaic: Ancient Maya Agriculture and Resource Use* (Salt Lake City: University of Utah Press, 1996).

Thomas Killion, ed. *Gardens of Prehistory: The Archaeology of Settlement Agricultura in Greater Mesoamerica* (Tuscaloosa: University of Alabama Press, 1992).

Kim MacQuarrie. *The Last Days of the Incas* (New York: Simon & Schuster, 2007).

Charles C. Mann. *1491: New Revelations of the Americas before Columbus* (New York: Knopf, 2005).

Elinor G. K. Melville. *A Plague of Sheep: Environmental Consequences of the Conquest of Mexico* (New York: Cambridge University Press, 1994).

John C. Super. *Food, Conquest, and Colonization in Sixteenth-Century Spanish America* (Albuquerque: University of New Mexico Press, 1988).

Ernesto E. Tabío. *Agricultura aborigen antillana* (Havana: Editorial de Ciencians Sociales, 1989).

Aguilar, Gerónimo de (b. ca. 1489–d. 1531) *Spaniard shipwrecked along Yucatán's coast; he lived for eight years among the Yucatec Maya before being rescued in 1519 by Hernando Cortés*

Gerónimo de Aguilar has gained much fame for his role as translator in the Spanish CONQUEST of the Aztec empire (see AZTECS). Born in Écija, Spain, Aguilar was trained as a priest and took minor orders before departing for the New World, perhaps in 1510. In the spring of 1511, while en route from PANAMA to Santo Domingo (see HISPANIOLA), Aguilar's ship struck shoals near Jamaica; Aguilar and roughly 20 other Spaniards set off in a small lifeboat, which was blown west toward the Yucatán Peninsula. By the time they reached Yucatán, more than half of the men had died from hunger and exposure; the survivors, including Aguilar, were immediately taken captive by the local MAYA. Five Spaniards were sacrificed; however, Aguilar and several others managed to escape and were received by another Maya ruler, who kept them as slaves. For the next eight years, Aguilar lived among the Yucatec Maya and learned to speak their language. When HERNANDO CORTÉS reached Yucatán in 1519, Aguilar was one of two Spaniards from the 1511 shipwreck still alive (Gonzalo Guerrero was the other). When Cortés learned of Aguilar's presence, he went to great lengths to rescue him; Cortés needed a translator as he prepared to move his forces against the Aztec Empire. Aguilar played a significant role as interpreter between the Maya and Cortés; nevertheless, his long-term value proved to be limited because he did not know how to speak NAHUATL, the Aztec language. Increasingly, Cortés began to rely on a young native woman, one of 20 women whom the Maya had given Cortés as a peace offering. Her name was LA MALINCHE, and she spoke both Maya and Nahuatl. Over time, as Malinche learned more Spanish, Aguilar's role as interpreter became less important.

—J. Michael Francis

Further reading:

Matthew Restall. *Seven Myths of the Spanish Conquest* (Oxford: Oxford University Press, 2003).

Hugh Thomas. *Conquest: Montezuma, Cortés, and the Fall of Old Mexico* (New York: Simon & Schuster, 1995).

Aguirre, Lope de (b. ca. 1514–d. 1561) *Spanish conquistador who led a failed rebellion against the Spanish Crown*

Born in the Basque town of Oñate ca. 1514, Lope de Aguirre was one of thousands of early 16th-century Spaniards who journeyed to the Americas in search of fame and fortune. Aguirre's story, however, is one of frustration, bitterness, and anger. He has been portrayed both as a tragic hero and as a cruel tyrant. Immortalized in Werner Herzog's 1972 classic film, *Aguirre, the Wrath of God*, Lope de Aguirre has acquired international fame, but Herzog's imaginative representation of the conquistador bears little resemblance to the historical Aguirre.

The paucity of documentary evidence makes it very difficult to reconstruct a detailed picture of Aguirre's early life in the New World. It appears that he left Spain in 1534. For the next two decades, spent mainly in PERU, Aguirre seems to have been a loyal servant to the Crown. He earned his living by breaking horses and as a soldier. In 1555, he fought with Crown loyalists in the Battle of Chuquinga against the rebel forces under Francisco Hernández Girón. Aguirre was left with a permanent limp and few lasting rewards for his services.

Then, in 1560, an aging Aguirre joined Pedro de Ursúa's ill-fated expedition to search for the land of EL DORADO, a kingdom east of Peru, rumored to be filled with unimaginable riches. Aguirre joined a force of more than 300 Spaniards and scores of African slaves and Indian carriers (see SLAVERY). After months of suffering in the AMAZON's blistering heat, the party found no evidence of El Dorado. Then, on New Year's Day of 1561, as frustrations mounted, Aguirre joined with a dozen other armed men and murdered the leader of the expedition. Aguirre's revolt against the Crown had begun, and over the next six months, another 60 members of the expedition were killed. The survivors sailed down the Amazon River, eventually reaching the island of Margarita on July 20, 1561. There, Aguirre and his close followers plotted to return to Peru and conquer it for themselves.

Aguirre never reached Peru. With his rebellion collapsing from within and Spanish forces closing in, Aguirre drafted a remarkable letter to King Phillip II, in which he denounced the Spanish ruler for failing to recognize and reward those who had suffered so greatly in service to the Crown and never received their due compensation. Shortly before his death, Aguirre murdered his mestiza daughter, Elvira, an act he justified as merciful to spare her from the abuse she would endure as the daughter of a rebel. On October 27, 1561, Aguirre was shot; his corpse was beheaded, quartered, and put on public display as a warning to others.

—J. Michael Francis

Further reading:

Thomas Holloway. "Whose Conquest Is This Anyway? *Aguirre, the Wrath of God.*" In *Based on a True Story: Latin American History at the Movies*, edited by Donald F. Stevens, 29–46 (Lanham, Md.: SR Books, 2005).

Stephen Minta. *Aguirre: The Re-Creation of a Sixteenth-Century Journey across South America* (London: Jonathan Cape, 1993).

alcabala The *alcabala* was a sales tax collected in Spain and eventually extended to the American colonies. As with many Spanish commercial and fiscal terms, *alcabala* is of Hispano-Muslim origin (*al-qabāla*), from the period when the Moors ruled much of the Iberian Peninsula. As the Christian monarchies reconquered Iberia, they imposed the *alcabala*. In 1342, the Castilian Cortes (national legislative body) granted King Alfonso XI permission to make the *alcabala* a royal tax.

When establishing the Board of Trade (CASA DE CONTRATACIÓN) in 1503 to regulate commerce with the new American colonies, Queen Isabella apparently discussed imposing the *alcabala* in the New World; however, the tax had yet to be implemented when she died the following year. Her successors generally granted new colonies a temporary exemption from the *alcabala*. Consequently, several decades passed before the colonies began to pay it: Philip II imposed the *alcabala* in MEXICO in 1574, GUATEMALA in 1575, and PERU in 1591. Whereas the *alcabala* rate in Spain was 10 percent (on merchandise going both to and coming from the Americas), it was a much lighter 2 percent in the Americas during the 16th century. Basic foodstuffs and indigenous goods were generally exempt, along with a number of other items, such as books, medicines, paintings, and weapons. The seller was required to pay the tax on the first and each succeeding sale of a good.

During the 16th century, the royal treasury lacked the manpower and other resources to collect the *alcabala* itself and so tended to farm out its collection to private individuals or groups, such as merchant guilds (*consulados*) in CITIES.

See also ALCABALA (Vol. II); ALMOJARIFAZGO (Vol. II); QUINTO (Vol. II).

—Kendall Brown

Further reading:
Clarence H. Haring. *The Spanish Empire in America* (San Diego: Harcourt Brace Jovanovich, 1985).

Alcaçovas, Treaty of (1479)

On September 4, 1479, the Catholic monarchs of Castile and Aragon signed this accord with the Catholic king of Portugal (see MONARCHS OF PORTUGAL; MONARCHS OF SPAIN). Sometimes referred to as the Peace of Alcaçovas, this treaty effectively ended the war of succession for the Castilian Crown, which had erupted five years earlier. In addition to confirming Queen Isabella as the legitimate ruler of the kingdom of Castile, the agreement established some important foundations for future Atlantic explorations of discovery and conquest. In return for ceding to Portugal all rights to establish outposts along the African coast, the Treaty of Alcaçovas confirmed the Canary Islands as a Castilian possession. It granted to Portugal the islands of the Azores, Madeira, and Cape Verde and made it illegal for any Spaniard to sail to these Portuguese possessions without license from the Portuguese Crown. In January 1492, when Ferdinand and Isabella captured Granada, the last Moorish stronghold on the Iberian Peninsula, the stage was set for the

Spanish monarchs to turn their attention toward the west. It was then that they agreed to help fund a Genoese sailor named CHRISTOPHER COLUMBUS, who claimed he could find a route to Asia by sailing west and thus avoid having to compete against the Portuguese. In this endeavor, Castilian sovereignty over the Canary Islands proved central to Columbus's successful first voyage, and the islands remained important to Spain's Atlantic empire throughout the colonial period.

—J. Michael Francis

alcohol

Latin America's pre-Columbian inhabitants made fermented beverages from various plant and animal products. With an ethylene alcohol content of between 1 and 5 percent, these drinks were both nutritious and inebriating. For millennia, they played significant roles in the religious lives and curing practices of those who used them, whether by drinking, taking as an enema, or pouring off in sacrifice to deities or in communion with the departed (see RELIGION). The Spaniards who colonized much of Latin America shortly after 1492 introduced grape WINE and hard liquor, the latter made through the distillation of fermented products. These European beverages had a significantly greater alcohol content and less nutritional value than their American counterparts. Europeans also brought with them a different set of attitudes concerning the consumption and regulation of alcohol.

Alcohol acts on the central nervous system, reducing attention, inducing relaxation, and slowing reaction time, with varying effects on the personality, including a general lessening of social inhibitions. With a significant blood alcohol level, one becomes drunk, causing slurred speech, clumsiness, and a form of euphoria. Indigenous groups generally experienced these effects communally and sporadically, expressing them primarily in the shared context of group religious ceremonies, abandoning themselves fully to the limits of inebriation allowed by the generally low alcohol content of their beverages, and viewing their temporary inebriation as a state of contact with the sacred. WOMEN participated less in drinking activities, if at all. Curers and diviners also employed alcohol as a necessary component of their calling.

The Spaniards imbibed too, but generally more individually and in private. They also drank more frequently and with greater attention to self-control. They thus viewed the communal abandon of indigenous drinking occasions with disapproval and disparagement.

Depending on the region, fermented beverages in Latin America were generally based on fruits, roots, or grains, though some indigenous groups used honey, tree sap, or the fluid from a century plant (agave cactus). In Central MEXICO, the AZTECS brewed *octli* from the latter. Later called PULQUE in Spanish, *octli* is still made by fermenting juice collected after cutting off the flowering stem of an agave. Evidence from Classic Mayan (250–900 C.E.) writing and images indicates that this drink was also consumed much earlier by MAYA peoples; however, by the time that Spaniards arrived in Maya territory in the early 16th century, the lowland Maya were more noted for a honey-based fermented drink they called *balché*, which contained strips of bark from the *Lonchocarpus* tree. Maya in highland Chiapas drink a fermented beverage made from freshly squeezed sugarcane juice and called CHICHA in Spanish, a name originally given by highland GUATEMALA Maya to a fermented MAIZE drink.

The Spanish term *chicha* is applied from Mexico to ARGENTINA to any kind of fermented beverage. It may have been borrowed from an Aztec term for "bitter water" or possibly from a Kuna word for maize. In PERU, *chicha* is usually made from maize, either sprouted or ground before germination and then moistened in the manufacturer's mouth to break down the starches into maltose; regional variants use quinoa, amaranth, barley, garbanzos, and/or seeds from the pepper berry tree (*Schinus molle*) instead of maize. In the eastern Andean lowlands, *chicha* is more frequently made from cassava root (MANIOC) that is chewed by specially selected women and then spat into a fermentation container. In the Peruvian highlands, during the Inca Empire, women were schooled in chewing and brewing ground maize for *chicha*, and recent excavations have uncovered the ruins of a brewery staffed and run by women with gracefully sloping foreheads, belonging to the Peruvian WARI Empire a millennium before the INCAS, who made maize beer with pepper berry seeds. This *chicha* is thought to have been central to Wari religious activities.

Even more recent excavations in HONDURAS suggest that the local elite were making a fermented CACAO pulp drink more than a thousand years prior to the current era and that this practice may have led to the discovery that fermenting, roasting, and grinding cacao seeds could produce an even tastier, if bitter and nonalcoholic, drink that was beaten to a froth and sometimes spiced with chilies. Eventually, processing fermented cacao beans gave rise to the chocolate industry.

Numerous fermented drinks have been produced in Latin America using regionally specific fruits. For example, in northwest Mexico, saguaro and *pitahaya* cactus fruits supplied the sugar base for the drinks. In the north-central region, the fruit of the nopal, or prickly pear cactus, was used. On the western coast, it was the fruit of the hog plum, or *jocote*. *Tepache* is a common fermented drink in Mexico. Weakly alcoholic, it is of colonial origin and made mainly from various fruits. Pineapple-based *tepache* is a popular beverage in many parts of Mexico.

In northwest Mexico, sprouted maize was, and continues to be, ground and fermented in water to make a beer of great cultural importance, called *tesgüino*. In the central region, in addition to the consumption of *pulque*, green cornstalks were squeezed for their sugary liquid as a fermented drink base. Mesquite (*Prosopis*) seedpods were chewed along with the seeds in northern Mexico, put in hot water, and left to ferment to produce a mildly alcoholic beverage. In South America, *algarrobo* (*Prosopis*) pods were processed the same way.

In Central America, sap from the *coyol* palm was drained from a felled tree and fermented to make a mildly alcoholic drink with enzymes that interact with sunlight to produce a unique kind of inebriation. The Shuar of Ecuador used the fruit of the *chonta* palm to produce their traditional alcoholic beverage.

Alcohol use in indigenous Latin America prior to European contact was mostly communal, public, and religious. Beverages were based on fermentation. Spaniards brought distillation techniques and different attitudes toward drinking. By 1560, colonists and indigenous groups were beginning to influence each other, and this exchange continued throughout the colonial period. The broad dissemination of cane liquors did not occur until later in the colonial period, when Caribbean rum emerged as one of the most widely consumed alcoholic beverages in the Atlantic world.

See also AGUARDIENTE DE CAÑA (Vol. II); PULQUE (Vol. II).

—Brian Stross

Further reading:
Henry Bruman. *Alcohol in Ancient Mexico* (Salt Lake City: University of Utah Press, 2000).

Almagro, Diego de (b. ca. 1475–d. 1538) *Spanish conquistador in Peru and first conqueror of Chile* Born ca. 1475 in the Extremaduran town of Almagro, Diego de Almagro was the illegitimate son of Juan de Montenegro and Elvira Gutiérrez, who were both from lower-class families. In 1514, he traveled to the fledging Spanish colony in PANAMA with the new governor, PEDRO ARIAS DE ÁVILA. Active in the establishment of the colony, Almagro befriended fellow Extremaduran FRANCISCO PIZARRO during an expedition they led in 1515. Entering a three-way partnership with Pizarro and the clergyman Hernando de Luque, Almagro took part in the first two scouting expeditions along the southern coast of South America from 1524 to 1528. On one of these expeditions, Almagro lost his left eye and several fingers during a battle with the Indians. While Pizarro continued to lead expeditions to the south, Almagro remained in Panama to recruit men and outfit ships for a third major expedition.

Setting out before Almagro, Pizarro and his men arrived first at Tumbez along the coast of ECUADOR and in 1532 apprehended and held the Inca emperor ATAHUALPA for ransom (see INCAS). Extorting from the Inca a large amount of GOLD and SILVER, Pizarro began the CONQUEST of PERU. Almagro and his men did not arrive on the Peruvian coast until April 1533, several months after Pizarro had acquired the Atahualpa ransom.

Almagro demanded his share of the treasure, but Pizarro refused to part with any of it, instead sending Almagro and his men south to conquer Cuzco, the Inca capital, and its surrounding region. In early December 1534, Almagro was named governor of Cuzco and southern Peru. A few months later, the Spanish Crown named him governor of the new territory of Chile to the south, which he was instructed to conquer and colonize. Facing many hardships in crossing the Andes Mountains and the Atacama Desert, Almagro's expedition eventually made it to Chile and during two brutal years conquered much of the northern part of the region. However, in 1537, on learning that civil war had broken out between Pizarro and other conquistadores in Peru (see CIVIL WARS-PERU), Almagro quickly returned with an army to defend his claim to Cuzco. Reaching Cuzco in early 1537, Almagro's army defeated the local Inca leader and took possession of the city. Almagro proclaimed himself governor, but his claim was immediately disputed by Pizarro. The two men declared war on each other, and on April 26, 1538, their armies met at the BATTLE OF LAS SALINAS outside Cuzco. Almagro, ill from disease, was captured by HERNANDO PIZARRO during the battle. Diego de Almagro was tried and executed on July 8, 1538.

—John F. Chuchiak IV

Further reading:
John Hemming. *The Conquest of the Incas* (New York: Harcourt Brace Jovanovich, 1970).

altepetl   The *altepetl* was the largest Nahua sociopolitical unit in Mesoamerica to survive Spanish conquest and colonization. (The Nahuas were and are an ethnic indigenous group in Mesoamerica that included the Mexica, or AZTECS.) It was also the fundamental building block of what some scholars refer to as preconquest empires. The term itself is a quasi-compound in NAHUATL of the words *atl* (water) and *tepetl* (hill, mountain), alluding to two fundamentals of community life. When used in more formal contexts, such as Nahua petitions to the viceroy of Mexico or the monarch of Spain, native scribes would separate its components and write it as *in atl in tepetl* (the water, the mountain).

During the colonial period, the term *altepetl* was often translated into Spanish as *ciudad* (city) and *pueblo* (people, settlement). The latter meaning is more accurate than Spanish or English terms that emphasize European-style urban entities, so scholars have turned increasingly to using the Nahuatl term to describe these ethnic city-states of greatly varying size. Nahua writers themselves would apply the term to describe small communities in Mexico and Spain as well as to areas as large as Peru, Japan, and Africa. The *altepetl* was composed of named subunits called *CALPULLI*, or *tlaxilacalli*.

The defining characteristics of the *altepetl* include a TLATOANI (ruler), a central marketplace (*tianquiztli*, borrowed into Mexican Spanish as *tianguis*), and the main temple of its patron deity (almost always a foundational figure), often literally replaced by a large single-nave church that is named after the community's current Christian patron saint.

By far the most famous *altepetl* today is MEXICO CITY–TENOCHTITLÁN, once the home of the ill-fated Aztec "emperor" MONTEZUMA, then the site of Mexico City. *Mexico* literally means "place of the Mexica," the ethnic grouping or subgrouping to which Montezuma belonged. The name would also be applied to the colonial region and the later independent nation.

—Barry D. Sell

Further reading:
James Lockhart. *The Nahuas after the Conquest: A Social and Cultural History of the Indians of Central Mexico, Sixteenth through Eighteenth Centuries* (Stanford, Calif.: Stanford University Press, 1992).

Alvarado, Pedro de (b. ca. 1495–d. 1541) *"conqueror" of Guatemala*   Born in Badajoz, Spain, Pedro de Alvarado first reached the New World in about 1510. He joined his uncle on HISPANIOLA, moved to CUBA, and participated in JUAN DE GRIJALVA DE CUÉLLAR's expedition to the Yucatán coast in 1518. The following year, he returned to the mainland as a leading captain in HERNANDO CORTÉS's conquest of the Mexica (Aztec) capital, TENOCHTITLÁN. During that campaign (1519–21), Alvarado gained a reputation for ambition and brutality; for example, he was blamed for the 1520 massacre of unarmed AZTECS in the city.

In 1523, encouraged by Kaqchikel MAYA envoys, Alvarado convinced Cortés to back a campaign into highland GUATEMALA. The invading force of 250 Spaniards, several dozen Africans, some 3,000 Central Mexico Nahuas, and thousands of allies from Oaxaca encountered a fractured political landscape. Exploiting the rivalry between the K'iche' (Quiché) and the Kaqchikel, Alvarado aligned with the latter, establishing a foothold in the Kaqchikel capital of IXIMCHÉ (renamed Santiago) in 1524. However, Spanish control in Guatemala was tenuous, and exorbitant tribute and labor demands backed by excessive violence led to the Kaqchikel Rebellion (1524–30). Alvarado left the highlands in 1526, returning to Spain. While Pedro de Alvarado has long been viewed as the conqueror of Guatemala, in fact, it was thousands of Mesoamerican indigenous allies—aided by indigenous disunity and the spread of epidemic DISEASE—and the 1527–29 military campaign by Pedro's brother, Jorge de Alvarado, that made a permanent Spanish presence possible.

Pedro de Alvarado was said to be handsome, a fine horseman, garrulous, sometimes cruel, vain about his clothing and appearance, and in love with his common-law

Nahua wife, Luisa (a daughter of the ruler of TLAXCALA), with whom he had two children. He later married, one after the other, two of the sisters of the duke of Albuquerque.

Alvarado spent the first half of the 1530s traveling between Guatemala, HONDURAS, and PERU, attempting to capitalize on conquest opportunities. In 1537, he traveled back to Spain to secure the governorships of Honduras and Guatemala. Charles I initially granted him both posts for the next seven years. After returning to MEXICO, Alvarado was helping to suppress the MIXTÓN WAR in New Galicia (western Mexico) when he was trampled by his own horse. He died several days later, on July 4, 1541.

—Spencer Delbridge
Matthew Restall

Further reading:
Ross Hassig. *Mexico and the Spanish Conquest*, 2d ed. (Norman: University of Oklahoma Press, 2006).

Matthew Restall and Florine Asselbergs. *Invading Guatemala: Spanish, Nahua, and Maya Accounts of the Conquest Wars* (University Park: Pennsylvania State University Press, 2007).

amauta   According to one 16th-century chronicler, the sixth ruler of the INCAS, Inca Roca, founded a number of schools in the capital city of CUZCO. There, young noblemen were trained in a variety of disciplines, such as poetry, music, philosophy, history, and astrology. They were also taught how to "read" and record information using a sophisticated system of woven, colored knots known as QUIPUS. The men who taught at these advanced schools were *amautas* (philosophers, wise men). In Cuzco, *amautas* were celebrated orators and storytellers. This specialized and highly venerated group of poet-historians crafted a wide range of works, which they recited both publically and in private ceremonies for the Inca elite. Because these works were transmitted orally (perhaps with the assistance of the *quipus* as mnemonic devices), most of these works were lost after the Spanish conquest. Nevertheless, in their efforts to record the history of the Inca Empire, some Spanish chroniclers turned to the *amautas* for their accounts of the preconquest past. For example, the 16th-century work of the Jesuit priest Blas Valera offers a unique view of Inca history based largely on the testimonies of the *amautas* who served under the Inca ruler ATAHUALPA.

—J. Michael Francis

Further reading:
Sabine Hyland. *The Jesuit and the Incas: The Extraordinary Life of Padre Blas Valera, S.J.* (Ann Arbor: University of Michigan Press, 2003).

Amazon   The geographic and cultural area known as Greater Amazonia (Amazon Basin) includes the watershed of the Amazon River, the watershed of the Orinoco River, the Guiana Highlands, and most of the Brazilian Highlands and northeastern BRAZIL, and extends westward to the foot of the Andes. It encompasses tropical rain forest, dry forest, thorn scrublands, and savanna. In contrast to the Andes or the Pacific coast, the prehistory of Greater Amazonia is not well known. It is clear, however, that the inhabitants of the area mastered a difficult environment and developed a sustainable agriculture. Indeed, food surpluses supported population growth.

When Europeans arrived in the 16th century, as many as 5 million people may have inhabited Greater Amazonia, with some societies organized as stratified chiefdoms. The Omagua, whose settlements were located along the Amazon River and the lower Napo River, may have reached this level of complexity but did not leave monumental remains. Other groups, in the Venezuelan Llanos of the central Orinoco and to the south of the Amazon River, built towns linked by causeways and roads in both the forests and on the savannas. In the south, towns were surrounded by baulks and ditches, areas of raised fields, and artificial fish ponds (see VENEZUELA). Settlements in the north had large and small mound complexes, as well as causeways and raised field complexes, but were designed somewhat differently.

While the generally accepted archaeological record begins about 12,000 years ago, with evidence of human occupation in southern and eastern Brazil and the western Amazon region in modern COLOMBIA and ECUADOR, human entry into Greater Amazonia may have been considerably earlier. During the Pleistocene period, which lasted until the onset of the warm Holocene about 10,000 years ago, the climate was as much as 41° Fahrenheit (5°C) cooler, and there was less rainfall. The forest that covered the heart of the Amazon watershed included trees adapted to cooler weather; these species today are found in the cloud forests of the eastern slopes of the Andes in the west and on the high peaks of the Guiana and Brazilian Highlands in the east. Until the end of the Pleistocene, the northern shore of South America and some distance inland was semiarid savanna with dry forest. Gallery forests fringed the rivers. This more humid environment supported trees and other plants found in the humid rain forest and offered access to important resources not found on the savanna. Thus, this semiarid environment offered many more food resources, both plants and animals, than was originally believed. To the east of the Guiana and Brazilian Highlands, a corridor of dry forest terrain extended south and west along the southern edge of the rain forest. This may have offered familiar resources to migrating populations, and archaeologists believe that one major route of entry into the Amazon region was along this arc of dry forest and savanna.

The Pleistocene period ended abruptly. Within decades, the average temperature increased and rainfall patterns changed, with the northern savannas and north coast of South America now receiving more rain. Increased rainfall and water from melting glaciers in turn

A man and a young boy paddle across the Amazon River near Iquitos, Peru. *(Courtesy of J. Michael Francis)*

increased the discharge from the headwater rivers into the main stream of the Amazon River. The sea level rose, and flooding now occurred in the lower valleys of the eastern Amazon and its tributaries. The rivers of central and western Amazonia were also affected, flooded by the backed-up water; they are still reexcavating the sediment deposited in their beds today. Around the central rain forest of Greater Amazonia, with a new assortment of species, lay the dry forest and savanna zones of the Llanos of Colombia and Venezuela, the *cerrado* of eastern and southern Brazil, and the Llanos de Mojos in BOLIVIA. Despite the rapid environmental changes, however, archaeologists have discovered numerous sites dating back 10,000 years that indicate human adaptation to the changing weather patterns. The appearance of sites at about 10,000 years ago also reflects an increase in the population, which may have first entered Greater Amazonia several thousand years earlier.

The dry forest region of eastern and southern Brazil included many wild rhizomes and tubers that stored starch over the dry season. Many of these plants may have been gathered by foraging peoples. At the beginning of the Holocene period, crops such as *llerén*, taro, sweet POTATO, and MANIOC (cassava) began to be cultivated. In time, manioc was being processed into a dry meal that could be both stored and easily transported. Peanuts, which probably grew wild on riverbanks, were also cultivated over time, as were hot peppers. In the rain forest, root crops were supplemented by tree fruits and palm nuts and shoots. Some 7,000 years ago, MAIZE, which had been domesticated in MEXICO, was being grown in the forested lowlands of eastern Ecuador. Amazonian foragers also gathered plants with medicinal or hallucinogenic properties (see MEDICINE) and constructed their dwellings from trees using palm fronds and grasses for thatch.

The inhabitants of Greater Amazonia prospered, with increased food production leading to larger populations and greater social and political complexity. These peoples both modified and extended their environment. On the savannas of the Llanos of the central Orinoco and the Llanos de Mojos of Bolivia, where sheet flooding left the ground under water for months at a time, indigenous peoples constructed settlements on low artificial mounds and sometimes the remains of earlier villages. These were connected by raised causeways. They also constructed fields on platforms that raised their crops above the waters of the seasonal floods. Artificial fish ponds and weirs also stabilized food production. Forest resources were brought closer by creating artificial islands above floodwater levels and planting them with forest trees and plants. The forest-dwelling societies that lived near the upper Xingú River in southern Brazil surrounded their settlements with moats and berms. These villages were also linked by raised causeways. Settlements were not isolated; rather, they appear to have been grouped into regional polities of varying size without a central authority.

The Omagua and related societies along the Amazon River westward to the Napo and Ucayali Rivers had access to a greater range of resources along the main rivers and fertile *várzea* land on which annual floods deposited silt, as well as higher land for longer-term cultivation. Omagua societies were highly militaristic; their chiefs had hundreds of warriors at their disposal, as well as huge war canoes. Although not centrally organized, the Omagua were expansionistic, moving westward and conquering new territory until the arrival of Europeans.

The Spanish initiated the settlement of the Amazonian lowlands at the foot of the Andes immediately after the CONQUEST of the INCAS. CITIES such as Sevilla de Oro and Ávila were founded in order to mine GOLD. In 1534, Fray Gaspar de Carvajal took part in FRANCISCO DE ORELLANA's expedition down the Napo and Amazon Rivers, observing that in some places, indigenous settlements lined the banks of the Amazon for leagues. These were ruled by chiefs, and there were priests and temples. The inhabitants produced and stored enormous quantities of FOOD.

On the Atlantic coast, Sir Walter Raleigh, who sought EL DORADO as the Spanish had, extolled the wealth and fertility of the lower Orinoco, where he hoped to establish settlements. Nineteenth-century European naturalists were keenly interested in the many forms of life found in the Amazonian rain forest, while others saw it as a source of riches including gold, hardwoods, and rubber. By the early 20th century, however, the rain forest was viewed more negatively by many Europeans because it did not easily lend itself to Western-style exploitation.

See also SERTÃO (Vol. II).

—Patricia J. Netherly

Further reading:
William Balée and Clark Erickson, eds. *Time and Complexity in Historical Ecology: Studies in the Neotropical Lowlands* (New York: Columbia University Press, 2006).
William M. Denevan. *Cultivated Landscapes of Native Amazonia and the Andes* (New York: Oxford University Press, 2001).

Amazon women Legends and myths of Amazon WOMEN are nearly universal, appearing from Asia Minor to India to the post-CONQUEST Americas. Although their origin is debatable, most scholars trace these female warriors back to the ancient Greeks, where they surface as antagonists in epic poems and are memorialized on tombs and shrines and represented in ART and iconography. The etymology of the word *Amazon* is disputed, but popularly

the word is understood to mean "breastless," derived from the combination of the negating prefix *a-* and *maza* (breast), and related to the myths that the warrior women cut out their right breasts to facilitate javelin throwing in battle. An inversion of hegemonic Greek gender roles, the Amazons appear in many legendary accounts as living independently from men at the edges of civilization, controlling important resources, and occasionally battling men, but also using them for procreation.

Many of these characteristics of the Amazons are recorded in Caribbean and South American chronicles, letters, and histories from the first 50 years after conquest. While the geography and details related to the women are varied, all of the early reports have one thing in common: They seem to be products of European imagination, results of misinterpretation of indigenous testimonies, and, in some cases, purposeful deployment of the legendary figures by authors eager to inspire further exploration, conquest, and pillage. Their first appearance in a European text written in the Americas can be attributed to CHRISTOPHER COLUMBUS, who reports in his diary and in his letter to Luis de Santángel (1493) of armed and solitary women who inhabit Martinique, an island in the Caribbean.

Some of the more literate CHRONICLERS would have known of the Amazons' celebrated attributes and deeds from classic literature and early modern sources, such as the popular sequel to the novel *Amadis of Gaul*, the *Deeds of Esplandian* (1510), in which the Amazons are said to inhabit the "islands of California" led by a queen, Calafia, whence came the name of the state of California. Other early accounts appear in Peter Martyr's *Decades* (1516), in a Spanish translation of Sir John Mandeville's *Travels* (1521), and soon after in Antonio Pigafetta's account of FERDINAND MAGELLAN's voyage around the globe (1522).

In his Fourth Letter (October 15, 1524), HERNANDO CORTÉS mentions that one of his captains reported testimonies from "the lords of the province of Ciguatán, who affirm that there is an island inhabited only by women, without a single man, and that at certain times men go over from the mainland and have intercourse with them; the females born to those who conceive are kept, but the males are sent away." DIEGO VELÁZQUEZ DE CUÉLLAR had charged Cortés with looking for the Amazons, and as Cortés's captain details, this Amazon-inhabited island "was very rich in pearls and gold." These kinds of accounts, in which wealthy Amazons are rumored to exist, proliferate as the conquistadores turn their attention to South America. The mythic women are found in letters written to King Charles I during the conquest of New Granada (COLOMBIA), led by GONZALO JIMÉNEZ DE QUESADA, and further south reports came in from modern-day PARAGUAY, ARGENTINA, CHILE, PERU, and ECUADOR.

The most elaborate account of the Amazons in the Indies is featured in Fray Gaspar de Carvajal's narrative of FRANCISCO DE ORELLANA's expedition down the river that now bears the infamous warrior women's name: *Relación del nuevo descubrimiento del famoso río grande de las Amazonas.* In 1541, Orellana, under the command of GONZALO PIZARRO, set out to find the renowned "Land of the Cinnamon." After encountering many hardships that forced them to break off from Pizarro's group to find provisions, Orellana and Carvajal, along with 50 men, navigated farther down the Napo River and what is now known as the Amazon River; eventually, they reached the Atlantic Ocean. On Saint John the Baptist day, June 14, 1542, Carvajal reported encountering hostile Indians who "intended to take us to the Amazons," of whom they had heard rumors since the beginning of the journey. Indeed, the expedition was attacked by the Amazons; these "tall," "white," "long-haired," "muscular" women fought naked, with the "strength of ten Indians," wielding bows and arrows and rallying their male subjects to nearly defeat the Spanish. Later, Orellana questions an Indian captive, who answers all of his leading questions about the female warriors affirmatively. Most of the well-known characteristics of the mythic Amazons are confirmed: They lived apart from men; they procreated through captive men, raising the female offspring and banishing or killing the males; and they controlled fabulous wealth. The witness even named their leader, Coñori, an Amazon queen who resided in a splendid palace whose walls were lined with silver and whose ceiling was decorated with parrot feathers. Of course, Orellana was unable to capture an Amazon, and the women remained elusively inscribed in oral accounts and written chronicles well into the 18th century, forming part of the "invented" America that still inspires historians, novelists, and artists.

—Michael J. Horswell

Further reading:

Fray Gaspar de Carvajal. *"Relación del nuevo descubrimiento del famoso río grande de las Amazonas."* In *La aventura del Amazonas,* edited by Rafael Díaz Maderuelo (Madrid: Dastin, 2002).

Hernando Cortés. "The Fourth Letter." *Hernando Cortés: Letters from Mexico,* translated and edited by Anthony Pagden (New Haven, Conn.: Yale University Press, 1986).

J. Michael Francis. *Invading Colombia: Spanish Accounts of the Gonzalo Jiménez de Quesada Expedition of Conquest* (University Park: Pennsylvania State University Press, 2007).

Irving A. Leonard. *Books of the Brave: Being an Account of Books and of Men in the Spanish Conquest and Settlement of the Sixteenth-Century New World* (Berkeley: University of California Press, 1992).

architecture

MESOAMERICA BEFORE 1492

The iconic image of Mesoamerican antiquity is a temple atop a step pyramid. Temple pyramids, along with ball courts and certain other architectural elements, are among the defining characteristics of Mesoamerican culture. Although style and engineering varied across Mesoamerica, the architecture shared essential attributes that unified it as an expression of culture. The stylistic canon included buildings such as temples, palaces, step pyramids, and ball courts. Common architectural elements included supporting substructures and platforms, moldings of various kinds, roof combs, and mosaic sculpture, as well as certain decorative motifs that were found over a wide geographical area. Thus, Mesoamerican architecture is a stylistically coherent marker of cultural patterns.

The earliest substantial architecture in Mesoamerica coincides with the first appearance of social complexity. At the site of Paso de la Amada, in coastal Chiapas, the inhabitants built a number of substantial buildings in the Early Formative period (ca. 1900–1000 B.C.E.). Mound 6 was a large dwelling, much bigger than other houses at the site. Apparently, it was the principal residence. Nearby, archaeologists have excavated a ball court that dates to about 1600 B.C.E. It is about 260 feet (79 m) long and 100 feet (30 m) wide, making it the largest construction known for Mesoamerica in this early period; it also highlights the centrality of the ball game in Mesoamerican culture. Only a few centuries later, Mesoamerica's first kings, living across the Isthmus of Tehuantepec at Olmec sites (see OLMECS), are shown in their colossal head portraits wearing ball game helmets. We also know from the POPOL VUH that MAYA religion and mythology ascribed a central role to the ball game in the development of social relations. Other Early Formative period ball courts have been discovered at both Maya and central Mexican sites.

Other early public buildings are known from Formative Mesoamerica at sites such as San Lorenzo Tenochtitlán, Veracruz, and Chalcatzingo, Morelos. The earliest buildings, from San Lorenzo Tenochtitlán and Paso de la Amada, are made of clay, earth, or adobe, with perishable superstructures built of wood and covered in wattle and daub. Massive earthen construction took place at San Lorenzo Tenochtitlán, an Olmec site, during the Early and Middle Formative periods. Early platforms at Chalcatzingo, also an Olmec site, are faced with rough field stones and date from the Early Formative Amate phase (ca. 1500–1100 B.C.E.).

From the Middle Formative period onward, regional traditions of architecture developed in Mesoamerica. The two most important regional traditions were that of the Maya culture of eastern and southern Mesoamerica and that of the central Mexican highlands. Other traditions existed, such as those in Oaxaca, Veracruz, and west Mexico.

Maya Architecture

In the Maya lowlands, the earliest well-dated architecture is found at the site of Cuello in northern BELIZE. The structures, which date from approximately 1000 B.C.E.,

Final phase of Copán's ball court as commissioned by the city's ruler, Waxaklajuun Ub'aah K'awiil, in 738 C.E., looking south. The tarpaulin in the background protects the famous hieroglyphic stairway, the longest stone carved inscription in the entire Maya realm. *(Courtesy of Janice Van Cleve)*

consist of low (10-inch [25.4 cm]) platforms of earth and stone, covered with plaster floors and supporting perishable wooden structures apparently apsidal in form. Apsidal houses, still built by the Yucatec Maya, have a plan consisting of two long parallel walls enclosed at the ends by semicircular walls. Similar buildings from the Formative and Classic periods are found at other locations in the Maya area.

The earliest large and complex sites in the Maya lowlands are found in the Mirador Basin of what is today the north-central department of Petén, GUATEMALA. These sites evolved into giant monumental ceremonial centers during the Middle and Late Formative periods (1000 B.C.E.–250 C.E.). The sites include EL MIRADOR, the largest, as well as Nakbé, Tintal, and Wakna. Residential architecture is known from both El Mirador and Nakbé. At Nakbé, early Middle Formative (ca. 800–600 B.C.E.) residential architecture includes stone-faced platforms up to six and a half feet high, with vertical walls constructed of roughly shaped slabs of limestone and topped with floors made of limestone marl or plaster. By the end of the Middle Formative period at Nakbé (600–400 B.C.E.), massive platforms, measuring 10 to 26 feet (3 to 7.9 m) in height and covering 430,000 square feet (39,947 m²),

were being constructed. In one case, a structure 60 feet (18.2 m) tall was built.

Some early Maya ceremonial structures are massive constructions. The largest structures of El Mirador, the Danta and El Tigre complexes, were among the largest buildings ever built by the ancient Maya. Other substantial Formative architecture existed at sites throughout the Maya lowlands, including Lamanai, Belize; Yaxuná, Yucatán; and TIKAL, Guatemala. This architecture clearly foreshadows the styles and forms of later Classic period Maya architecture but also possesses interesting peculiarities of its own.

Architectural complexes called "E-groups" appear in the late part of the Middle Formative period at Nakbé and were also constructed early in the architectural history of other sites in the Petén, such as Uaxactún and Tikal. An E-group is composed of a pyramidal structure—usually a radial pyramid with four stairways—facing a long building to its east. The buildings are juxtaposed so that a person standing on the platform will see the Sun rise over the middle of the long building on the equinoxes and over the north and south corners of the building on the solstices. In some cases, rather than one long building, three smaller ones were built and similarly aligned. These complexes clearly constitute a particular type of architectural arrangement with ritual meaning.

Radial pyramids, mentioned above, also appear at this time. They are a widespread and persistent architectural form. These are square step pyramids with approximate quadrilateral symmetry, usually having four stairways, one ascending each side. They may or may not have inset corners and a stone temple on top. They occur in the "twin-pyramid complexes" of Tikal and Yaxhá. Some of the latest Maya pyramids are radial in form, such as the Temples of Kukulkán at CHICHÉN ITZÁ and MAYAPÁN, dating to the Terminal Classic and Postclassic periods, respectively. Round structures, although rare in Classic Maya architecture, also appear in the late Middle Formative in the Maya lowlands. They, too, continue into the Postclassic period. Maya roads, called *sacbés* (Yucatec Maya for "white road"), also seem to date from the late Middle Formative period. They formed an integral element of Maya architecture and cityscapes for many centuries, until the arrival of the Spanish. These causeways represent a significant engineering achievement. They were often wide, tall, and graded and ran straight for great distances, connecting either different parts of a city or sometimes linking distant CITIES with each other.

Toward the end of the Middle Formative period and during the succeeding Late Formative, carefully cut and squared stones began to be used in lowland Maya architecture. Advances in quarrying and masonry apparently led to the development of more elaborate architectural motifs, such as apron moldings and rounded corners on pyramids and platforms, both of which became enduring elements of the Classic architectural repertoire.

One distinctive attribute of Formative period Maya architecture is the construction of massive triadic temple pyramids. These consist of a huge stepped substructure, usually with inset corners, crowned by three smaller temple pyramids facing a small plaza atop the base. The largest of the three temple pyramids is set back on the substructure, while the two smaller constructions sit in front, facing each other and flanking the court. Stucco began to be used to adorn Maya building facades during the Late Formative period. Thick layers of stucco were modeled into elaborate and complex designs including monumental faces of deities. The tradition of architectural stuccos continued throughout the pre-Columbian period.

The Classic period (250–900 C.E.) represents the apogee and flourish of Maya high ART, including architecture. During the Classic period, corbelled vaulting was widely used to roof buildings. Inscriptions, low-relief sculpture, and modeled stucco adorned buildings. Many buildings were elaborately painted as well.

Regional styles of architecture developed in the Early Classic period. For example, in the northern lowlands of Yucatán, megalithic masonry is found at sites such as Izamal, Aké, Ikil, and Tepich. Some TEOTIHUACÁN influence is seen in the architecture of several important sites, including Tikal, COPÁN, and Dzibilchaltún. This influence often takes the form of *talud-tablero* terrace faces (see below under "Central Mexican Architecture").

Distinctive regional styles flourished during the later Classic period. Scholars draw different geographic boundaries between the various regional styles, but most agree that the following stylistic areas can be recognized.

The Southern style includes at least Copán, in HONDURAS, and Quiriguá, in Guatemala. The style is distinguished by the particularly elegant and well-executed facade sculptures, as well as a tendency toward sculpture in the round, which is unusual in the Classic Maya canon.

The Central, or Petén, style is found at the major sites in the heart of the Maya lowlands, in the department of Petén in Guatemala, adjacent areas of western Belize, and southern Quintana Roo and southern Campeche in Mexico. Sites exhibiting this style include Tikal, Uaxactún, CALAKMUL, Xunantunich, and many others. The buildings are constructed of carefully coursed, well-squared limestone blocks. One outstanding characteristic of the style is the construction of towering temple pyramids. These have a square or rectangular plan, ascend steeply, and culminate in a small temple set back on the tall substructure. The temple roofs often bear large roof combs that increase their overall height. Typically, a single, steeply inclined staircase ascends the pyramid on the principal side. Some are funerary pyramids and

A fine example of a corbelled arch on the east flank of the Copán ball court. The Classic Maya never learned the art of the true arch, and thus interior rooms of stone structures were often small and narrow. *(Courtesy of Janice Van Cleve)*

Built ca. 750 C.E., Tikal's Temple 5 measures 190 feet (57.7 m) in height, making it the site's second tallest temple. To date, no tomb has been found inside this temple. The picture, taken in 2008, shows the newly completed restorations to Temple 5. *(Courtesy of J. Michael Francis)*

contain tombs, while others may have been dedicated to particular gods.

The Western style includes Mexican sites such as Palenque in Chiapas and Comalcalco in Tabasco and, arguably, the major sites of the Usumacinta river valley, such as Piedras Negras and Yaxchilán. The Western style is most easily recognized by the use of mansard roofs that convey a lightness and grace not often achieved elsewhere in the Maya area. Comalcalco is the westernmost major Maya site. Located on the alluvial plains of Tabasco where stone was not available, the buildings were constructed of fired brick.

The Río Bec style extends from the northern border of the Petén (at Naachtún) to the northwest and includes the site Río Bec, as well as Xpuhil and Becan, among others. The Río Bec style is defined by the presence of false towers that seem to imitate the giant funerary pyramids of the Petén. To the north of the Río Bec style, but overlapping it, is the Chenes style. The Chenes style is related to the Río Bec style but lacks the false towers. Chenes architecture is typified by complex geometric mosaic sculptures on the facades of buildings, including "monster-mouth doorways" in which the iconography

of the facade sculpture turns the principal doorway of a building into the symbolic mouth of a deity.

The culmination of northern Maya architecture is the Puuc style, centered in the region of the Puuc hills in southern Yucatán. It overlaps with Chenes architecture, both geographically and stylistically. The Puuc style also carries complex mosaic sculpture on the facade, but usually only above the medial molding. The masonry is quite remarkable: Walls were built with a rubble core strongly cemented with lime mortar. The core was then covered with a veneer of thin and beautifully squared stones with shallow tenons. The veneer was not load bearing but created a finely finished exterior. The engineering of these buildings is superb, and many remain well preserved. The most famous Puuc sites are located in the Puuc Hills, including Uxmal, Labná, Sayil, Nohpat, Oxkintok, Chacmultún, Xkichmook, Kiuik, and many others; however, the style extends over the entire northern plains and east to the border of Quintana Roo.

In the Late and Terminal Classic periods (ca. 800–1100 C.E.) in Yucatán, a unique manifestation of Maya architecture emerged at the famous site of Chichén Itzá. The style combines Puuc stylistic elements with central

Mexican motifs, such as serpent columns, warrior columns, *tzompantli* (sacrificial "skull racks"), I-shaped ball courts, and extensive colonnades. The central Mexico elements were once seen as evidence of a Toltec invasion from that region, but current thought emphasizes the eclectic sources of these influences (see TOLTECS).

The last flowering of Maya architecture took place during the Postclassic at Mayapán in central Yucatán and at many smaller sites along the Caribbean coast of the peninsula. This type of architecture was not well engineered; stones were frequently not well squared, and coursing and bonding were casual at best. Aesthetically, the style recapitulates earlier Maya elements, including radial pyramids, corbelled vaults, and stelae, but also features "Mexican" elements such as serpent temples, round temples, and colonnades. A related style emerged in the Guatemala Highlands, where double temples, an Aztec building type, occur with some frequency and ball courts proliferated.

Cityscapes and Settlement Patterns

Maya buildings, both public and residential, were arranged in complex patterns. Major public and ritual structures were often arranged in relation to astronomical phenomena and physiographic features of apparent religious significance, such as caves and hills. In combination with the historical idiosyncrasies of the builders, these factors led to intricate and attractive juxtapositions of different building types.

Domestic buildings, including residences, kitchens, storage structures, and other ancillary constructions, were arranged into patio groups, or *plazuelas*, of varying sizes in which multiple buildings faced on to one or more shared courtyards. The patio groups in turn usually formed clusters that may have constituted wards or neighborhoods. The complicated patterning of residential settlement is widely believed to reflect the structure of the kinship system. The density of Maya settlement, although not high, clearly qualifies as a type of urbanism. Intensive studies of Maya settlement indicate that populations of sites were often in the tens of thousands.

Central Mexican Architecture

Central Mexican architecture employed distinctive motifs throughout its history. For example, round temples and the use of columns tend to distinguish Mexican from Maya architecture. Also, central Mexican peoples constructed raised lines of masonry bordering both sides of stairways. Called *alfardas*, these vaguely resemble balustrades and are rare in the Maya area.

One of the most notable early architectural monuments of Central Mexico is the pyramid at Cuicuilco in the Valley of Mexico. In the Late Formative period, Cuicuilco grew to be a large community with a population perhaps as large as 20,000. The pyramid is round and faced with cobbles. The site was abandoned at the end of the Formative period, possibly because of the eruption of the nearby volcano, Xitle.

At the beginning of the Classic period (ca. 1 C.E.), the site of Teotihuacán began to grow rapidly and soon became the largest city in Mesoamerica, as well as one of the largest cities in the world at the time. Its sphere of influence eventually encompassed most of Mesoamerica. The city was a carefully planned metropolis, with streets laid out in a grid pattern, creating uniform square blocks. The principal avenues ran north-south and east-west and met in the ceremonial heart of the city, at the Ciudadela, which encloses the Pyramid of QUETZALCÓATL (the Plumed, or Feathered, Serpent).

The architectural style includes several distinctive motifs. The pyramids were rectangular in plan, with several terraces and, usually, a single staircase on the principal side. The biggest structures are the Pyramids of the Sun and the Moon, which are among the largest pyramids of the ancient world. The iconic motif of Teotihuacán architecture is the "*talud-tablero*," in which each terrace of a step pyramid was formed of a lower sloping *talud* (sloped) surmounted by a vertical *tablero* (board, panel) with a rectangular inset. The *tablero* typically projected out beyond the top of the *talud*. The combination of slopes, angles, and insets created a complex juxtaposition of planes and volumes that was visually appealing.

Residential architecture was distinctive too. The city blocks were filled with large multiroom apartment complexes built around courtyards that must have housed sizable extended families. More elaborate apartments boasted relief carvings and wall paintings, while more modest dwellings contained warrens of small rooms.

The Toltec culture of the Early Postclassic period developed in the northern reaches of Mesoamerica, but its influence and contact spread as far as the U.S. Southwest to the north and the Maya region to the south. The architecture featured extensive colonnades sometimes with anthropomorphic columns or columns with relief carving. I-shaped ball courts are associated with the Toltecs, although not uniquely so.

The AZTECS were the last significant pre-Columbian culture of Central Mexico. Their architecture continued the Central Mexico tradition but with new variations on the basic themes. For example, the Aztecs built double temples in which a single step pyramid supported two temples dedicated to different gods. The best-known example of a double temple is the Templo Mayor (Great Temple) of their capital, TENOCHTITLÁN, today MEXICO CITY. The Aztecs also built round temples dedicated to the wind god, Ehécatl, a version of Quetzalcóatl.

With the arrival of the Spaniards in the 16th century, many aspects of the formal architecture of pre-Columbian Mesoamerica were suppressed. Some elements survived, however, particularly in the vernacular architecture of more remote areas.

SOUTH AMERICA BEFORE 1492

Architecture is important in the study of pre-Columbian South America, not only because it may be beautiful or monumental, but also because it imparts information about the societies that created it. Architecture covers structures of all kinds, singly, in groups, or on a regional scale. Besides buildings, it can include free-standing walls, fortresses, aqueducts, flights of terraces, roads, and the like. Particularly for societies without written records, architecture provides information about its function, as well as social and political organization, ideology, and RELIGION. The relationship between social organization and architecture may be evident in design or layout, or it may be hidden in the fabric of the structure.

The reasons why people are motivated to build public monuments cannot always be determined from the monument alone. For example, while religion and ideology are powerful motivators, they do not necessarily muster a large number of workers at a time. Nevertheless, many scholars have assumed that large architectural complexes of antiquity were built by state-level societies. This is certainly correct in the case of the INCAS and the WARI of the Andean highlands, as well as the CHIMÚ of the Pacific coast. The architecture of these societies had a recognizable state style, both in the major centers and in the hinterlands. The structures and monuments that remain today were built of materials that have withstood the passage of time. They are found for the most part on the Pacific coast and in the Andean highlands. Some societies of northern South America and parts of the AMAZON Basin built elaborate, multistoried structures of perishable materials, which have been lost except for their footprint, which can be recovered through archaeological excavation.

Architecture is often associated with groups of related or complementary structures or cities. Indeed, the Western mind associates civilization with cities and architectural style. The pre-European societies of South America produced civilizations, not all of which were fully urban but which, nonetheless, built spectacular architectural monuments.

The earliest domestic structures were found in the upper Jequetepeque and Nanchoc Valleys and are 10,000 years old. These buildings were so small they were probably used only for sleeping. A couple of thousand years later in the same area, the houses were somewhat larger and were grouped with several within eyesight. By 6,700 years ago, in the nearby Nanchoc Valley, foragers and incipient farmers had built a pair of low mounds on three levels, which functioned as the only public structures in the valley. This ceremonial center was in use for some 2,400 years, after which the mounds were covered with fresh soil and abandoned.

By this time, populations were farming full time, and ceremonial complexes in different architectural styles began to appear up and down the Pacific coast and in the adjacent highlands. At Huaricoto in the Callejón de Huaylas, a highland valley with links to the coast, 13 superimposed ritual structures with architectural features associated with the Kotosh tradition in the form of circular, sunken hearths with ventilation shafts were found. The earliest is 4,200 years old. In the Supe Valley on the north-central coast of PERU, there may have been a long agricultural tradition perhaps similar in its early stages to the Nanchoc and Jequetepeque Valleys. By 4,200 years ago, farming populations had begun to build large platform mounds around open plazas at a site now called Caral, which was occupied for six centuries. The design reflected not only the monumentality of the mounds but also the sunken circular plazas between them. The mounds appear to have been built in two major construction phases by all the inhabitants of this part of the valley. Cut masonry retaining walls were filled with stones from the river packed in reed carrying bags. The walls were then faced with stone and plastered. There were residential areas with small houses and domestic trash near the mounds and in a large area to the southwest. The architecture of Caral indicates a number of things: First, the valley's population had made an early transition to irrigated AGRICULTURE, which supported a larger population; and second, their ideology led people to expend time and energy in erecting large mounds. Caral is not unique; there are numerous sites with large mounds in both the Supe and Pativilca Valleys. Nonetheless, Caral predates the better-known styles of ceremonial architecture by some 2,000 years.

The tradition of building large, impressive platform mounds as temples and tombs for royal individuals continued on the Pacific coast. As at Caral, autonomous groups controlling a portion of a valley but sharing a larger religious tradition built ceremonial centers in particular architectural styles. On the central coast, ceremonial centers consisted of platform mounds in a U-shaped configuration, as seen in the valleys from Huaura to Lurín—a style also evident at CHAVÍN de Huántar in the highlands and the Caballo Muerto complex in the Moche Valley. Farther north, in Supe, Casma, and Nepeña, mounds were rectangular with circular forecourts. At this time on the north coast, from the Virú Valley to Lambayeque, ceremonial platform mounds were low, with inset central stairways and rectangular forecourts. Colonnades topped each mound, and painted, molded adobe sculpture decorated the walls. The central mound was flanked by low lateral mounds, giving a U shape that antedates the U-shaped mounds at Chavín by several centuries. The orientation of the U-shaped mounds is toward the mountains, the source of water. The lateral wings may be related to the dual social organization of the society, as is the case with Mapuche U-shaped mounds and ceremonial fields today.

The culmination of the tradition of constructing large mounds of adobe occurred during the Early Intermediate period, when the religious tradition and art style known as MOCHE dominated the northern valleys. It was thought that the area in which the Moche style in CERAMICS and architecture was prominent indicated an expansionist state, or possibly two such states, one centered in the Moche Valley at the Huaca de la Luna and Huaca del Sol (see HUACA). However, the Moche style is now understood to have been adopted by the elites and priests of regional polities that controlled a valley or part of a valley. Nonetheless, it is probable that the largest constructions, such as the Huaca del Sol or Huaca Fortaleza, drew on larger populations for their construction. The Huaca del Sol originally was a platform mound 380 yards (347 m) long, 175 yards (160 m) wide, and 45 yards (41 m) high. It was the largest structure built in the Americas at that time. Two-thirds of the structure was washed away by Spanish treasure hunters, who diverted the Moche River to "mine" the mound for GOLD. It appears that the function of the Huaca del Sol was primarily administrative. The religious center was at the Huaca de la Luna, which lay about half a mile to the south. It was a platform mound that measured 318 yards (290 m) from north to south and 230 yards (210 m) from east to west, and was about 100 feet (30.4 m) high. The walls of the terraces were plastered and decorated with polychrome friezes, representing the faces of divinities and other religious symbols. Between the two *huacas* was a large settlement.

In the next valley to the north of the Moche, the Chicama Valley, there were two large platform mounds at opposite ends of a relict terrace above the sea at the valley's western edge. Known today as Huaca Cao and Huaca El Brujo, both were built during the Moche period. Huaca Cao has been excavated and friezes covering the walls of the forecourt and the faces of the terraces have been uncovered. These structures would have been awe-inspiring at the time of their use. It is not known whether Huaca El Brujo had a religious or administrative function. Cao was a ceremonial site. Nevertheless, it is probable that in many cases administrative and ceremonial functions were carried out in different areas of the complex. At Huaca del Sol and at Huaca Cao, archaeologists have found that many of the adobes carry marks that are believed to represent markings on the quota of bricks contributed by different groups in the valley.

After about 750 C.E., there were major changes in Andean society. Ceremonial centers were always important, but individual mounds were relatively smaller; however, as polities became larger, particularly on the coast and in the highlands, new architectural forms emerged. Compounds, palaces, and larger urban concentrations replaced the great ceremonial platforms and relatively modest settlements of the Moche.

On the North Coast a new society, the CHIMU, emerged some 300 years after the heyday of the Moche. Over the course of some 300 to 400 years, the Chimu, centered in the Moche Valley, conquered the coastal valleys from Tumbes in the north to Casma in the south. Their influence extended farther south almost to LIMA. Instead of building large, lavishly decorated platform mounds, this society constructed large walled palaces, which served as administrative centers as well as the residence of the rulers. This pattern was first seen at the site of Galindo in the upper Moche Valley. This architectural form was developed most elaborately at the Chimu capital of CHAN CHAN. Here, over a period of three or four centuries at least 10 large compounds were built, each one associated with a particular ruler and his cohort.

These compounds varied in size and plan, but all were immense, roughly rectangular areas enclosed by massive walls of rammed earth (*tapia*). The tallest of these walls measured 29 feet (9 m) in height. The architectural plan of these compounds, called *ciudadelas* by archaeologists, was tripartite. Entry into the compounds was restricted, with the principal entrance on the north side leading into an immense enclosed courtyard. There were raised benches along the sides. The southern end was closed off by the walls of rooms that filled the width of the compound. There were one or more entrances into the rooms behind and likely a roof over the platform area. Apparently, this served as a proscenium, or stage, for the presentation of ritual enactments or for the ruler himself. The northern courtyard could have held an audience of hundreds of people who could then witness these rituals at a distance.

The central section of the *ciudadela* was a honeycomb of rooms and room complexes with restricted access. Some were surely the private apartments of the ruler and his family. Others had administrative functions, which are not fully understood. There were three-sided open rooms with niched walls that may have been points of administrative or ritual control. Archaeologists refer to these as *audiencias*. Despite all the investigation of the past 40 years, archaeologists are still not sure of their function. The *audiencia* complexes appear not only at Chan Chan but also in other Chimu administrative centers in the outlying valleys of the Chimu Empire. The southern third of the *ciudadela* compounds held a platform mound within which lay the tomb of the resident ruler. There was also a deep open well dug down to the water table to supply water to the palace. The remains of wattle-and-daub structures indicate that low-status people, probably retainers serving the palace, lived here. The walls of the northern and central sections of the *ciudadela* and the burial platform were decorated with modeled friezes with marine and abstract motifs in the characteristic Chimu style. There were at least four free-standing platform mounds, which were probably temples, which were located outside the area of the *ciudadelas*. These platform mounds were undoubtedly ritual centers. However, they are so heavily looted that it is difficult to say much about their architectural style. They were dwarfed by the sheer size and extent of the palace compounds and were rivaled in size by several of the burial platforms. Among the Chimu, architecture was associated with political power and the ability to command human energy.

The architecture of the INCA Empire, centered at Cuzco in the southern highlands of Peru, is the best-known of the pre-Columbian period in the Andean region. While much of Inca Cuzco has been lost to almost five centuries of European influence, there are many intact sites, such as Pisac and Ollantaytombo, in its hinterland. MACHU PICCHU has become both a cultural icon and a tourist destination. There are a number of features that characterize all Inca architecture: Building complexes were generally laid out around enclosed courtyards called *cancha*; doorways and wall niches were trapezoidal; and roofs were steeply pitched and elaborately thatched. There was usually a wall with one or two entries around the complex. Around the courtyard were four or more buildings, one to a side, with entries facing the *cancha*. The highest status buildings, those intended for the Inca ruler, his representatives, and high members of his administration, were built of the famed Inca pillow masonry. In this stoneworking technique, each stone was individually fitted without mortar, and the outer surface of the stone was finished with the center of the stone slightly raised and the edges slightly recessed, giving a pillowed effect. This stonework was sometimes used to frame trapezoidal doorways in buildings where the rest of the walling was of roughly shaped double-faced masonry with a rubble fill. The most utilitarian buildings, such as storehouses, were built of single-course stone walls. Other buildings were of adobe resting on a stone foundation. Low thatched roofs protected these buildings from the effect of rain.

Inca architects planned high-status buildings so that there would be long sight lines through multiple trapezoidal doorways or through trapezoidal windows. Sometimes the sight line ended in a trapezoidal niche in an inner wall. The stone used was carefully chosen and frequently brought from distant quarries. At the great administrative site of Huanuco Pampa, the length of an immense plaza was lined with enormous rectangular buildings with multiple trapezoidal doors opening on the plaza. It has been suggested that such buildings were used to house large groups of transient persons, such as soldiers. Within the plaza was a small, stepped platform, the *ushnu*, which was faced with fancy stonework. This was apparently intended as a kind of artificial mountain. From its summit, the Inca himself, or his representative, would officiate at ceremonies in the sight of the populace who filled the plaza.

Inca architects also worked on landscape. They designed great flights of terraces, used to grow prized crops such as maize, and walls, in conjunction with smaller structures. In some cases even the Inca roads were incorporated symbolically into settlement design. The sources of important rivers or canals were often marked by elaborately carved stone *pacchas* through which water was made to flow, replicating the landscape. At Huanuco Pampa, the two main roads entered and exited at opposite corners, creating an X-like pattern and dividing the plaza into halves and fourths, both symbolically important to the Inca. The architecture of the Inca was deliberately intended to impress the observer and reflect the extent and power of their vast empire.

EARLY COLONIAL ARCHITECTURE

Architecture played an important role in the creation of Spain's empire in the Americas. The destruction of indigenous temples and the construction of churches and administrative buildings symbolized the change in political, religious, and social order. The reinvention of native communities as the cities and towns of the Spanish Empire became a vivid visual reminder of the radical transformation of Latin America during the early colonial era.

The effect of the CONQUEST on Latin American architecture differed across indigenous communities. Many saw little immediate effect, and buildings continued to be constructed as before. Soon, however, mission complexes populated by Franciscan, Dominican, and Augustinian friars and civic buildings for colonial bureaucrats appeared in native villages (see RELIGIOUS ORDERS). Other native communities were forcibly relocated from widely dispersed locations into single, centralized towns known as *reducciones*, or *congregaciones*, to facilitate conversion and administration (see CONGREGACIÓN). Some of these *reducciones* were located on existing settlement sites; others were newly built. Many came to assume a similar appearance, with an open plaza surrounded by civic buildings and a nearby mission complex.

Cities such as the Aztec capital of Tenochtitlán and the Inca capital city of CUZCO were heavily damaged during the conquest. HERNANDO CORTÉS admired the beauty of Tenochtitlán but explained in a letter to the Spanish king that he had to destroy it in order to defeat and humiliate his enemy. In Cuzco, the long siege held the Spaniards in the city as the Inca army pelted them with boulders from above damaged buildings, while others were intentionally demolished by the conquerors. Nevertheless, the colonizers soon rebuilt the imperial cities, now suitable for viceregal courts (see VICEROY/VICEROYALTY). Their practices were codified in King Philip II's 1573 ordinances for town planning. The king's rules reflected the ideal of urban planning, inherited from ancient Roman cities and their Renaissance humanist champions.

In Mexico, Cortés moved into MONTEZUMA's palace, while Alonso García Bravo redrew the city plan, incorporating existing roads, canals, and secular buildings on a reticulated grid. García's plan, however, used only a quarter of Tenochtitlán's massive sacred precinct for the new central plaza, or *plaza mayor*. The rebuilding of Cuzco was similarly dependent on existing structures. The walls of Cuzco's Coricancha (Golden Temple) became the foundations of the new church and convent of the Dominican order. The round wall beneath the church apse supported a balcony for religious services.

The Church of Santo Domingo in Cuzco, Peru, built on top of the Inca temple Coricancha *(Courtesy of Kelly Donahue-Wallace)*

Palaces for Cuzco's Spanish inhabitants were built using the masonry from the homes of the Inca nobility. Early colonial city architecture consequently combined European Renaissance characteristics, indigenous foundations and construction techniques, and even Moorish decoration, as many churches and palaces included gilded and polychromed wood ceilings and repeated geometric or vegetal motifs.

Churches in the early colonial era were first built in the urban centers, as each of the missionary religious orders constructed a church and monastery for itself. Like the Dominican monastery in Cuzco, the Franciscan monastery in Mexico City took into account its responsibility for converting the local native population in its construction plans. An early structure at the site was an open-air chapel known as San José de los Naturales. In Peru, a similar phenomenon occurred, and urban churches included a *capilla de indios* (chapel for Indians) to segregate the churches' two populations. The Jesuit church in Cuzco, built on the ruins of the palace of the Inca HUAYNA CÁPAC, retains its Indian chapel.

Soon after the conquest, urban centers also saw the construction of cathedrals ministered by local bishops and archbishops. Cuzco's cathedral was built on the site of Inca Viracocha's palace using materials from the Inca city's buildings and massive main square. Mexico City's first cathedral employed stones from the ruined Templo Mayor. These earliest cathedrals in the Viceroyalties of New Spain and Peru—including the one in Lima—were roundly criticized by colonists as soon as they were completed. To many colonists, the humble early colonial cathedrals were too small and plain to pay proper homage to their faith. By 1562, architect Claudio de Arciniega had completed a new plan for the Mexico City cathedral, with three aisles, side chapels, and a projecting polygonal apse; construction on the massive stone building began in 1572 and ended more than two centuries later. Lima and Cuzco also undertook the construction of newer and larger cathedrals after mid-century; Cuzco's cathedral was under way by 1560 and Lima's soon after. The Peruvian structures employed the same floor plan, with slight modifications, as the cathedral in Mexico City.

The hybrid quality of many early colonial cities was repeated in the missions erected to convert indigenous peoples to Christianity. Although generally based on the European monastery plan, with a church located within a walled atrium and a convent surrounding a cloister, missions in Latin America were adapted to the needs of the new context. It was common in both viceroyalties, for example, for mission complexes to rest on the foundations of indigenous temples, a solution that was not only practical but also a potent symbol of religious imposition.

Open chapels may have been another adaptation to the evangelical context. These structures provided a covered balcony or chamber to protect a consecrated altar but otherwise opened on to the mission atrium. The specific form of an open chapel varied from site to site; the most elaborate structures had rib vaulting and multiple chambers, resembling the hypostyle mosques of southern Spain. Although open-air masses were not unknown in Europe, the popularity of these structures in early colonial Latin America suggests that they were concessions to the outdoor rituals characteristic of indigenous religions. Similarly, the ornamentation on many churches in New Spain employed Renaissance architectural features alongside the glyphlike relief carvings of the so-called *tequitqui*, or Indo-Christian style. Other sites appear to reflect the tastes of the Moorish-influenced, or Mudejar, art of southern Spain. The architecture of missions constructed at the end of the 16th century in Peru, on the other hand, displays a consistently classicizing architectural vocabulary, with round arched entrances located on the sides of the church nave.

The architecture of the early colonial period was constructed principally by indigenous craftsmen, who employed familiar building techniques including coursed masonry, rubble-core walls with stone revetment, and wood-beamed ceilings. The building plans reflected native traditions and European sources and models. Between 1520 and 1570, however, European craftsmen began arriving in the Americas in ever greater numbers, and architecture in urban centers came to be dominated by guilds. These organizations of carpenters, bricklayers, stone masons, and others controlled the professions through their ordinances. The rules addressed everything from the ethnicity of members—some guilds excluded native practitioners—to training and contracts.

See also ARCHITECTURE (Vols. II, III, IV); ART (Vols. II, III, IV).

—Clifford T. Brown
Kelly Donahue-Wallace
Patricia J. Netherly

Further reading:

Gauvin Bailey. *Art of Colonial Latin America* (London: Phaidon, 2005).

Kelly Donahue-Wallace. *Art and Architecture of Viceregal Latin America, 1521–1821* (Albuquerque: University of New Mexico Press, 2008).

Mary Miller. *Maya Art and Architecture* (London: Thames & Hudson, 1999).

Jerry D. Moore. *Architecture and Power in the Ancient Andes* (Cambridge: Cambridge University Press, 1996).

Adriana Von Hagen and Craig Morris. *The Cities of the Ancient Andes* (London/New York: Thames & Hudson, 1998).

Argentina The name *Argentina* is derived from the Latin word for SILVER, *argentum*, and was popularized by Spanish poets during the Renaissance. Myths about Argentina's great silver wealth began almost immediately after the arrival of the Spanish and also are responsible for the name of Argentina's principal river, the Río de la Plata, or "river of silver." For most of its early history however, *Argentina* was not the term used to describe the colony; instead, it was referred to as a collection of provinces, with the Río de la Plata Province as its default head. Argentina covers most of South America's Southern Cone. It is bordered by the Atlantic Ocean on the east and the Andes Mountains (and CHILE) on the west. The Paraná-Pilcomayo river system marks much of its northern border with PARAGUAY and BOLIVIA, while it extends to South America's southeasternmost tip. It is separated from URUGUAY by the River Plate Estuary, where its modern capital and largest city, BUENOS AIRES, is located.

Argentina's northwest was home to nearly two-thirds of Argentina's pre-Columbian population. Most groups were agriculturalists who irrigated high-yield crops, allowing towns and villages to develop (see AGRICULTURE). The most advanced and largest of the groups were the Diaguitas. The Diaguitas' villages were not large but were organized enough to provide LABOR to build dams and wind walls. The INCAS conquered some Diaguita villages, while others kept Inca expansion at bay; nonetheless, most Diaguita settlements showed some traces of Inca influence in their ART, language, and RELIGION. The Diaguita were often polygamous. Most wore wool CLOTHING from guanacos and llamas, and many developed tools and ornaments made of copper, GOLD, and silver. Less advanced neighbors of the Diaguita included the Comechingone, who resided near modern Córdoba, and the Juríes (Tonocontés), who practiced flood farming in the flatter saline plains farther away from the Andes.

Many of Argentina's pre-Columbian inhabitants were nomadic hunters, as the open grasslands of the Pampas, Patagonia, and Tierra del Fuego fed an abundance of wandering rhea and guanaco. The most prominent of these groups were the Querandí, who inhabited the Pampas southwest of the River Plate, and their southern neighbors, the Tehuelche Guenakén. Even though the Pampas are vast and Tehuelche villages consisted of transportable tents, each Tehuelche village had well-established hunting grounds. Entering a neighbor's grounds without permission was a serious offense, which at times led to violent clashes. Tehuelche leadership was usually hereditary, but ineffective leaders were abandoned by villagers.

Their proximity to the sea meant that the Chanik Tehuelche and the Ona of Tierra del Fuego often hunted smaller game and fished. Each nuclear FAMILY usually owned a canoe, and each member had a task while aboard it. Killing a seal meant that several families could eat for weeks at a time. Smaller prey included penguins, cormorants, herring, and mussels. These societies were egalitarian and patrilineal. The supreme being Watavineva was life maker, life taker, and creator.

The Alcaluf, Yahgan (Yagán), and Chonos inhabited Argentina's extreme south. Like the Tehuelche Guenakén, these groups were nomadic but had territorial divisions and even their own waters. During part of the year, the Yahgan lived in conical dwellings made from sticks and covered with animal skins, which they also used for clothing. The Chonos more frequently wore cloth that they crafted from dog fur and tree bark fiber.

The Huarpes resided on Argentina's eastern Andean slope. These agriculturalists possessed llamas and used irrigation techniques to grow quinoa, maize, and beans. In the 15th century, the Huarpes were incorporated into the Inca Empire. The Puelche-Guanakén and the Pehuenche were nomadic hunter-gatherers whose territory straddled the Andes. Both groups were multilingual and traded animal skins in Chile and Argentina. The Pehuenche reliance on the nut from the Araucaria pine was the primary feature that distinguished them from their Puelche neighbors.

The CONQUEST of Argentina began largely as an extension of Spain's conquest of the Inca Empire in PERU. By pushing south from Peru, and from the Atlantic into the Río de la Plata, the Spanish hoped to find more precious metals and ways to more efficiently ship the silver and gold they continued to seize from the Inca (see MINING).

Juan Díaz de Solís discovered the mouth of the River Plate in 1516, but soon after stepping ashore, he and his men were killed by local Querandí Indians. FERDINAND MAGELLAN explored the estuary as well, in 1520, but avoided the Querandí and continued along his southerly route to the Pacific. Sebastian Cabot explored the Atlantic coast in 1527 before founding the soon-to-be-abandoned town of Sancti Spiritus along the Paraná River. Cabot returned safely to Spain, and Charles I decided to fund an impressive force of 1,600 to accompany PEDRO DE MENDOZA in his attempt to settle Argentina's east coast. Mendoza founded Buenos Aires in 1536, but such a large contingent proved difficult to feed. Spanish desperation at a lack of food and supplies provoked new hostilities with the Querandí, and Mendoza soon abandoned his men. He later died on his return voyage to Spain. In the meantime, Mendoza's subordinates had followed the Paraná upriver; they founded Asunción in 1537.

The development of Argentina's northwest was also deeply affected by the rise and fall of the Inca Empire. DIEGO DE ALMAGRO, fresh from his conquest of the Inca in partnership with the Pizarro brothers, passed through the northwest on his way to Chile's central valley in 1535. Diego de Rojas led a longer incursion from Peru in 1547, eventually reaching the Paraná but not making contact with Asunción.

New expeditions from Chile focused on settling the Tucumán region, which was thought to be both a good source of indigenous labor and a more direct route to Upper Peru. In 1553, Francisco de Aguirre founded the first permanent Spanish settlement in the region, Santiago del Estero. During the same decade, other towns developed in the region but were soon abandoned after local indigenous groups attacked them. By 1560, Chile's colonists had quickly depleted Santiago's local indigenous workforce, and its *encomenderos* sought new sources of labor (see ENCOMIENDA). This led to the founding of Mendoza in Huarpe territory in 1561. Although the mountain pass from Santiago to Mendoza was closed by snow for much of the year, the trek took only eight days.

See also ARGENTINA (Vols. II, III, IV); BUENOS AIRES (Vols. II, III, IV).

—Eugene C. Berger

Further reading:

Jorge Hidalgo. "The Indians of Southern South America in the Middle of the Sixteenth Century." In *The Cambridge History of Latin America*, Vol. 1: *Colonial Latin America*, edited by Leslie Bethell, 91–118 (Cambridge: Cambridge University Press, 1984).

Mario A. Rivera. "Prehistory of the Southern Cone." In *The Cambridge History of the Native Peoples of the Americas*, Vol. 3, Part 1: *South America*, edited by Frank Salomon and Stuart B. Schwartz, 734–768 (Cambridge: Cambridge University Press, 1999).

David Rock. *Argentina 1516–1987: From Spanish Colonization to Alfonsín* (Berkeley: University of California Press, 1987).

Arias de Ávila, Pedro (Pedrarias Dávila, Pedrarias)

(b. ca. 1440–d. 1531) *Spanish conquistador, governor of Panama, and conqueror and governor of Nicaragua* Born in Segovia ca. 1440 into the lesser nobility, Pedro Arias de Ávila, or Pedrarias, as he was later known, served as a soldier in many of the European wars of the early 16th century. He married Isabel de Bobadilla y Peñalosa, from a wealthy and prominent FAMILY whose influence helped him gain entry to the court of King Ferdinand. In 1513, Ferdinand named Arias de Ávila to the position of governor of the new colony of Darién, which had been founded in 1511 by VASCO NÚÑEZ DE BALBOA.

Along with his wife and family, Pedrarias sailed to the isthmus of PANAMA in early 1514 as captain general and governor of the region of Castilla de Oro, making him the first royal-appointed permanent Spanish governor on the mainland Americas. Authorized to conduct the formal investigation, or *residencia* trial, of Balboa, whom he believed to be a dangerous obstacle to his governorship, Pedrarias suspended the investigation and made a pact with Balboa to ensure his support and that of other colonists, even arranging for the marriage of Balboa to one of his older daughters who had remained in Spain. Nevertheless, the men remained rivals, and Balboa planned to launch a new expedition of discovery to explore the Pacific Ocean, which he had discovered the year before (1513). Known for his ruthlessness and violent temper, Pedrarias tricked Balboa and seized his ships and supplies. He then had Balboa arrested and resumed his *residencia*. Fearing reprisals from Balboa's many supporters, Pedrarias accused Balboa and several of his leading captains of treason. They were executed by beheading in early January 1519.

Pedrarias then began to send out conquest expeditions both northward and southward from Panama City, which he founded in 1519. However, a new governor arrived in 1520 to relieve Pedrarias of his governorship and conduct his own *residencia* trial. The new governor's quick death from natural causes and his replacement's weakness allowed Pedrarias to emerge exonerated from the charges against him of cruelty and abuse of power in office.

From the end of 1520 until 1527, Pedrarias moved northward and began the CONQUEST and occupation of modern-day NICARAGUA, founding the town of León and ruling the region with an iron hand. Executing many of his rivals, including several of his own lieutenants, such as GIL GONZÁLEZ DÁVILA, Pedro Arias de Ávila died on May 30, 1531, in León.

—John F. Chuchiak IV

Further reading:

Eduardo Tejeira-Davis. "Pedrarías Davila and His Cities in Panama, 1513–1522: New Facts on Early Spanish Settlements in America." *Jahrbuch für Geschichte von Staat, Wirtschaft und Gesellschaft Lateinamerikas* 33 (1996): 27–61.

arms   See WARFARE.

art

MESOAMERICA BEFORE 1492

Mesoamerican material culture is divided into four major periods: the hunter-gatherer societies of the Archaic period (8000–1600 B.C.E.); the socially stratified farming communities with early ceremonial centers of the Formative period (1600 B.C.E.–C.E. 200); the Classic period (200–850 C.E.), characterized by the construction of major ceremonial centers associated with urban centers; and the Postclassic period (850–1519), which began with the collapse of major ceremonial centers and ended with the creation of relatively militarized states and the emergence of the Aztec Empire (see AZTECS).

A division between public spaces used for ceremonial practices and as open-air markets and private spaces, which often correspond to the archaeologically identifiable living spaces of local elites, emerged in the ceremonial sites built in the Early (1600–900 B.C.E.) and Middle (900–400 B.C.E.) Formative periods. For example, the Paso de la Amada site in Chiapas (ca. 1600 B.C.E.) and La Venta in Veracruz (ca. 800 B.C.E.) both feature a central axis of orientation and are composed in part by platforms that surround a large, open plaza. Moreover, La Venta includes two major architectural features that

recur in Mesoamerican ceremonial centers throughout the Classic and Postclassic periods: a ball court (usually I shaped) and a pyramid (see ARCHITECTURE).

The first pan-Mesoamerican artistic style, usually called the "Olmec style," also emerged during the Formative period (see OLMECS). The Olmec style may have originated in or been adopted relatively early in the Gulf Coast centers of San Lorenzo, La Venta, and Tres Zapotes, or in the Central Mexico site of Chalcatzingo, from where it spread to other regions. Some of its central motifs are human figures with flaring upper lips (which may represent jaguar-human hybrids), the use of flame-shaped eyebrows, and clefts atop human heads. Other motifs include "baby-faced" figurines with cranial deformation, and carved monumental heads with helmet-shaped headdresses, which may depict actual rulers and might have served as thrones.

The emergence of a calendrical system native to Mesoamerica—composed of a 260-day divinatory count, a 365-day count, and among the MAYA, the Long Count with a mythohistorical starting point—provided a key cultural context for the development of regional artistic styles on many media: stone, frescoes, portable ceramic objects, and CODICES. The Maya and the ZAPOTECS are two Classic period societies notable for their development of a complex iconographic tradition that merges naturalistic and abstract depictions of humans, animals, and natural forces with the calendrical system described above and a writing system. Each Classic Maya ceremonial site had its own accretive building program, which was controlled by local rulers. One of the main purposes of this program was to celebrate the life and warfare exploits of the *k'uhul ajaw* (divine ruler), who ruled over a specific polity designated with an emblematic glyph. Maya artists erected stelae and carved lintels depicting these rulers as they assumed office, performed public rituals, communicated with their ancestors, conducted warfare, and commemorated the ending of a *k'atun* (20-year period). Although Maya artists did not depict an individual's facial features, they replicated elite dress with great care, including details such as embroidered motifs on the robes of elite WOMEN. Rulers were often depicted in stereotypical poses wearing elaborate feather headdresses and holding a wide bar decorated with celestial motifs. Each successive ruler attempted to expand on his predecessor's architectural and iconographic plan. Elites also commissioned and exchanged polychrome pottery, figurines, and engravings carved in costly materials, such as jade and OBSIDIAN.

The epitome of Classic Zapotec material culture is found at MONTE ALBÁN, which featured monumental architecture, elite tombs and living quarters, and a large assembly of stone carvings, some of which were recycled from other sites in the Valley of Oaxaca. Perhaps the most striking set of depictions of the human figure from this site are the so-called Danzantes, a large group of slabs, each showing an individual often accompanied by a name glyph. Although these individuals were originally thought to be sacrificial victims, a recent reconstruction of the building to which the engravings were attached suggests they are individuals ordered by age and social rank. Other large engravings on stone slabs include groups of ball players at other sites in the Valley of Oaxaca, such as at Dainzú.

Zapotec tombs located throughout Oaxaca often contained large ceramic effigy vessels depicting specialists dressed as supernatural beings and/or deity complexes, including the rain deity Cocijo, the MAIZE deity, and other entities that may have been deified ancestors. The iconographic system exemplified by these vessels is closely related to Zapotec epigraphic writing and the day signs in the divinatory calendar. While Zapotec glyphic writing is not yet fully understood, it has been proposed that a number of public monuments contain information similar to that depicted on Maya stelae, such as names of rulers, actions performed, and dates of public ceremonies.

In contrast, although the Central Mexico site of TEOTIHUACÁN generated a number of influential forms of symbolic and material expression, it possessed no systematic writing system, and its architectural program does not appear to emphasize the actions of individual rulers. At its height, around 500 C.E., Teotihuacán was the most densely populated urban center in Mesoamerica (with about 200,000 inhabitants), and artisans and workers from the Gulf Coast, Oaxaca, and Maya regions coexisted there. Teotihuacán's characteristic *talud-tablero* building style, which features a slope–flat step progression, influenced building styles as far away as the Maya sites of COPÁN and CHICHÉN ITZÁ. The city's iconography for a rain deity (featuring fangs and circular eye ornaments) and a plumed serpent deity, on display in the Temple of QUETZALCÓATL, was diffused widely throughout Mesoamerica, along with tripod ceramic vessels and stylized flat masks in jade and other precious materials. Various locations in the city featured fresco paintings of water-giving deities, aquatic motifs, jaguars, and dancing warriors bearing hearts attached to spears; some of these images are also depicted on small pottery vessels. The standing of the city as a locus for craft production, trade, and iconography is attested by the depiction of a Teotihuacán envoy meeting a Zapotec noble on the Lápida de Bazán; moreover, various texts and stelae attest to the links between Teotihuacán and K'inich Yax K'uk' Mo, a ruler of Copán.

Throughout Mesoamerica, a major transition in architectural and material culture began in the Early Postclassic period. Some sites, such as the Classic Maya–influenced murals of Cacaxtla, Puebla, and the Mexican-style regalia of Maya nobles depicted in Terminal Classic stelae at Seibal, attest to cross-regional influences. Northern Yucatán witnessed the emergence of the Puuc style, characterized by tall ornamental combs placed atop structures, and the building of shallow, fake temple facades atop pyramid structures. The site of Chichén Itzá,

which began as a Classic-period center, was expanded in the Postclassic with the construction of a new district featuring a pyramid, a columned hall, and monumental stone sculptures depicting eagle warriors, jaguar warriors, and skull racks (*tzompantli*) that appear to be strongly influenced by similar structures in the Postclassic Central Mexico site of TULA. Although earlier scholars interpreted these similarities as evidence of a military conquest of Maya sites by Central Mexico armies, more recent work suggests a more complex set of trade, diplomatic, and/or political interaction among elites.

Postclassic and early colonial Mesoamerican codices—texts painted on tree bark paper featuring the pictographic writing system of Central Mexico and the syllabic glyph writing in the Maya region—contain a wealth of information about Mesoamerican cosmology, calendars, sociopolitical history, and elite genealogies. While very few extant codices date from before the Spanish CONQUEST, those produced shortly after 1521 share many stylistic and structural elements with their pre-Columbian counterparts. There exist four pre-Columbian Mayan texts that contain, among other elements, calendrical calculations and cosmological events associated with specific dates, as well as data on lunar phases and eclipses.

Central Mexico codices can be divided into three broad pictographic traditions. The Mixtec tradition is represented by four pre-Columbian texts—Bodley, Colombino-Becker, Zouche-Nuttall, and Vienna—and four early colonial works—Becker II, Egerton/Sánchez Solís, Muro, and Selden. These works provide a narrative about the emergence of the MIXTECS from a mythical tree at Apoala and the creation of the world; they also contain detailed accounts about the life and deeds of specific Postclassic Mixtec rulers, such as Lady Six Monkey and Lord Eight Deer. The Mexica (Aztec) tradition is represented by the bark-paper texts now known as Borbonicus, Tonalamatl Aubin, Telleriano-Remensis-Vaticanus A-Ríos, and Tudela. Finally, the Borgia Group, all made of hide, consists of texts known as Aubin 20, Borgia, Cospi, Fejérváry-Mayer, Laud, Porfirio Díaz Reverse, and Vaticanus B. It is unlikely that the Borgia and the Mexica texts were painted before 1521 but rather were produced shortly after the Spanish conquest; together, they contain about 102 pictorial almanacs focusing on the cosmological order and the 260-day divinatory count. Many of the elements employed in the Mixtec, Mexica, and Borgia traditions resemble one another, and authors trained in this "international style" were probably able to decode them, regardless of which Mesoamerican language(s) they spoke.

Finally, in their capital of TENOCHTITLÁN, the Mexica people built characteristic structures such as the Templo Mayor, which was constructed in seven stages (each associated with specific Mexica rulers) and has two temples on its summit. The Templo Mayor contains multiple iconographic references to the emergence of the tutelar deity Huitzilopochtli. One of the major original Mexica contributions to Mesoamerican art was the production of public stone sculptures on various scales. Some of these, such as the Teocalli of the Holy War, refer to both former Mexica rulers and to Mexica deities. Others, such as Tizoc's Stone, depict military victories over other Mesoamerican communities. The Mexica stone calendar, discovered in the 18th century, refers to the four previous ages of the world and depicts the 20 day signs in the divinatory count. Other statues depict a variety of Mexica deities, such as Xipe Totec, Xochipilli, and Coatlicue, or the specialists who represented them in public ceremonies. In spite of major changes and discontinuities, there exist many common iconographic and calendrical traditions that would have rendered some of the Late Postclassic material culture familiar to Mesoamerican artisans from the Late Formative period.

SOUTH AMERICA BEFORE 1492

In the ancient Americas, art was a part of life. The finest art objects were made for the elite of society, but beautifully made CERAMICS or colorful beaded necklaces are often found in otherwise simple graves. South America can be broadly divided into two main cultural areas: the Andes and the AMAZON. While the arts of the Andes are fairly well known, those of the Amazon are not. Other than some ceramic figurines, not much has survived the wet, warm climate of the jungle. It can be speculated, however, that early Amazonian arts were similar to those of today, which are characterized by elaborate featherwork, wood carvings, and ceramics.

Artwork in the Andes consisted primarily of TEXTILES, metalwork, ceramics, and stone sculpture supplemented with feathers, animal skins, and exotic hardwoods from the Amazon. While most exotic items came from the Amazon region, spiny oyster shells were brought in from the warm coastal waters of ECUADOR. While all of these materials were used to make items of beauty and importance, textiles were the supreme and most valuable art form. They were used not just for CLOTHING but as ritual gifts to the spirit forces and expressions of cultural belonging and prestige. Both men and women wove, and young and old were put to work preparing and spinning the thread to be used in weaving. On the coast, COTTON was commonly used to make textiles, while in the mountains alpaca wool was most often used. Coastal and mountain communities traded fibers, thus alpaca wool is found in textiles on the coast and cotton in those made in the mountains. High-status garments often showed off alpaca fibers dyed with rare or difficult-to-use colors, such as red and blue. Sometimes entire tunics were covered in bright feathers from tropical birds, which were cut and tied to the fabric to form a design. The massive quantity of feathers required for such costumes, and the need to import them from the far-off jungles, made feather tunics both rare and high-status garments.

The artistry of most Andean textiles is in the fineness of the thread and weaving techniques. Some textiles are as closely woven as modern machine-made fabrics, and the Spanish favorably compared Inca cloth to European velvet (see INCAS). Andean weavers developed a remarkable number of techniques, some of which were found nowhere else. These allowed the artists to produce textiles that not only looked attractive but embodied spiritual ideas of essence and wholeness. Most garments were formed as an entire piece on the loom, not cut and sewn from pieces of cloth. It was felt that the creation of a textile on the loom gave it a spiritual existence of its own, and cutting the cloth would kill this spirit. Elite textiles frequently featured spiritually important motifs, sometimes highly abstracted. Gauzelike fabrics were created with designs that could be seen only while the fabric was on the loom. It was not particularly important for people to be able to perceive these images; rather, the fact that they were there imparted their spiritual essence to the cloth and helped give it a life and spiritual power of its own. Cloth was a common gift to the ancestors and other spirits, and other important offerings such as ears of MAIZE were made more sacred by wrapping them in cloth. Rich textiles were sometimes further decorated with embroidery, appliqués, and three-dimensional borders.

Metalwork traditions in the Andes tended to center on casting GOLD alloy in the north (modern-day Ecuador and COLOMBIA) and forming sheets of gold, SILVER, or copper in the central and southern areas. The northern casting tradition strongly influenced the artistic culture of Central America, where it reached its greatest elaboration as an art form. Cast forms in Colombia include those of the MUISCAS (1000–1550), which feature flattened, angular human figures, and the Tolima (900–1500), which are dominated by abstract images of supernatural beings. Intricate nose, ear, and mouth ornaments were also created by casting metal. Some of this jewelry included hollow forms with small pieces of metal inside so that they would make a noise as the wearer moved. Most of these items were made from a gold-copper alloy called *tumbaga*.

Artists to the south preferred to work with sheets of metal that were cut, shaped, and pieced together. Moving elements were sometimes attached with wires, which allowed the ornaments to reflect light as the wearer moved. Hollow objects that could make a noise were also a part of the southern tradition, and bells and rattles were made to adorn elite personages. The most startling innovation of southern Andean metalworkers was creating a surface of pure silver or gold on an alloy body. This allowed the artists to use only a small amount of precious metal to create a piece that looked as though it were made of pure silver or gold, taking advantage of copper's superior strength while maintaining the important surface color. Silver was associated with the Moon and gold with the Sun in many Andean cultures, thus the appearance of metal ornaments was spiritually important for religious and political leaders. In most Andean cultures, men wore more jewelry and ornamentation than women

These large gold alloy ear ornaments would have been worn by a member of the Chimú nobility. They depict divers collecting brightly colored *Spondylus* shells in lands hundreds of miles to the north, symbolizing the elite's access to luxury goods. *(Courtesy of the Michael C. Carlos Museum of Emory University/Photo by Michael McKelvey)*

This miniature fruit formed part of an elite Inca burial offering, which also included a bed and a set of panpipes. It is made from thin sheets of silver, carefully shaped and crimped together. *(Courtesy of the Michael C. Carlos Museum of Emory University/Photo by Michael McKelvey)*

wore. Many men wore ornaments in their ears and noses as well as on their heads, necks, and wrists.

The technique of firing ceramics in South America was first developed in the northern Andes, in modern-day Ecuador. Ceramic production ran the gamut from simple undecorated vessels used to cook and serve daily food to elaborate, finely crafted and decorated pieces used for ceremonial purposes or as grave goods. Figurines, whistles, and even drums were made from fired clay. There is archaeological evidence that fine ceramic wares were imported or traded among cultures. Ceramics could be decorated in any number of ways. Designs could be pressed or cut into the surface of the clay before firing, making a textural decoration, or the surface could be painted. Some cultures, such as the Paracas of southern PERU, used mineral pigments mixed with plant resin to decorate important ceremonial wares. They were not heat-resistant and so could not be used as cooking and serving vessels. Slip, a fine suspension of clay particles, was more often used to decorate ceramics. The thin layers would be painted on using a brush of hair or plant fibers, then rubbed with a smooth stone to make the surface shiny after firing.

The Valdivia culture of present-day Ecuador (3500–1800 B.C.E.) produced thousands of small ceramic figurines depicting women and men. These figures changed over time from simple, flattened forms decorated with incised lines to rounded bodies with elaborate hairdos. The later Jama-Coaque culture (350 B.C.E.–600 C.E.) is well known for its ceramic sculptures of men and women, which are often large, with elaborate hairstyles and ornaments. These sculptures were often made using molds, which allowed artists to create multiples of the same figure. The use of mold-made ceramics spread rapidly, and the technique found some of its greatest expression among the Moche, who produced dozens of ceramic objects from a single mold. The use of molds was almost always combined with some hand building, and pieces from the same mold usually have different surface decoration. The Nazca (200 B.C.E.–700 C.E.) of the southern coast of Peru reached the pinnacle of color decoration in their slip-painted ceramics, using more colors than any other culture, including cream, black, red, yellow, several shades of brown, and a rich purple. Inca artists created many types of vessels decorated with geometric designs, including *urpus*, which were large storage vessels with pointed bottoms that could be more than two feet tall.

Large blocks of stone suitable for carving are not found on the coast, and so it is in the mountains that stone carving developed as an art form. The San Agustín culture of present-day Colombia (100–1200 C.E.) is known for monumental statues carved from stone. These depict fanged heads and human figures, some holding weapons. The styles range from somewhat representational to flattened and abstracted. Fangs are an important feature of Andean iconography, denoting supernatural status and perhaps referring to the powerful jaguar of the Amazonian lowlands. The same fanged motif was important to the people of Chavín de Huántar in the Peruvian highlands (900–200 B.C.E.). They carved flat stone panels with elaborate linear figures, combining aspects of different animals to depict supernatural beings and religious leaders transforming into spirit animals. These carvings were made with finely chiseled lines on a flat surface, creating a shadow line that confused the eye and created a sense of wonder that communicated the spiritual message of the Chavín cult. Near Lake Titicaca in the central Andes, the Tiwanaku culture (which reached its apex 500–800 C.E.) created monumental stone sculptures that showed elites wearing intricately decorated tunics and holding ceremonial objects. These imposing monoliths represent the power of the Tiwanaku elite and their possession of other fine art forms, such as textiles and ceramics.

EARLY COLONIAL

Art in early colonial South America and Mesoamerica displayed a plurality of forms, techniques, processes, influences, and contexts. While Spanish soldiers and missionaries infamously destroyed many examples of indigenous art, including Andean HUACAS and Mesoamerican CODICES, the arrival of Europeans in the 1520s and 1530s had little immediate impact on the art of other native communities. Ceremonial and utilitarian textiles, ceramics, metal figurines, manuscripts, and other objects continued to be made according to traditional techniques and bore familiar symbols and decoration. Over time, art

changed as indigenous artists responded to new demands from native and European patrons and traditional avenues for professional training were replaced by monastic schools and guild apprenticeships based on European models. Artists from Spain further altered artistic expression in the Americas.

In the early colonial period several traditional arts flourished in the Andean region of South America, the most robust artistic center in the new Viceroyalty of Peru (see VICEROY/VICEROYALTY). Andean silversmiths continued to produce utilitarian accessories for wardrobes and figurines of precious metals, selling them to both native and European customers. They likewise expanded their repertoire of products to include liturgical instruments, altar frontals, and tablewares. Andean textile artists continued to create *uncu* tunics, with geometric *tocapu* patterns denoting authority. These garments were purchased by elite indigenous patrons and appeared in portraits painted from the 17th to the late 18th century. With the introduction of European decorative motifs, the *uncus* and other textiles incorporated new forms, including European-inspired lacelike designs, scrolls, grotesques, and figures. The artists also made new types of goods, such as wall hangings, and adopted imported manufacturing techniques and materials, including cochineal dye from Mesoamerica and sheep's wool. Ceremonial cup production was also transformed in the early colonial era. Given in pairs to commemorate political and social relationships, these vessels bear geometric motifs incised into their walls. Sometime around the 1530s, wooden *queros* began to be painted, and by the 1570s artists depicted figures and more descriptive motifs using an inlaid polychrome technique.

In addition to traditional arts, South American indigenous artists were trained in urban settings to use European materials, techniques, and models. In 1536, Fray Jodoco Ricke established the Colegio de San Andrés in Quito to train students in carpentry, painting, sculpture, and other arts and crafts. The school's students received high praise from colonial authorities for their use of Renaissance naturalism. This new, European-influenced approach to art was particularly visible in the paintings created for the South American missions in the late 16th and early 17th centuries.

In Mesoamerica, soon to be called the Viceroyalty of New Spain, many traditional arts flourished in the early colonial period, particularly manuscript painting, mural painting, feather mosaics, sculpture, and metalwork. These arts flourished largely because they were embraced by the missionaries and colonial authorities for the evangelization and administration of indigenous peoples (see RELIGION; RELIGIOUS ORDERS). They similarly served native patrons negotiating the new colonial context.

Soon after MEXICO CITY (on the ruins of Tenochtitlán) was established as the capital of Spain's colony in Mesoamerica, missionaries established schools where native peoples received religious instruction as well as education in artistic practices. The first and most important school was San José de los Naturales at the Franciscan convent. Founded by Fray Pedro de Gante, it assumed responsibility for transforming the work of Aztec *tlacuilos* (painters), *amantecas* (feather mosaicists), and other indigenous artists into objects that would serve the evangelical effort. Gante embraced these arts for their beauty as well as for their ability to teach the stories of the Catholic faith. Like the artists at Ricke's school in Quito, the Mexican artists learned from European prints and paintings and soon adopted a more European style in their work, frequently merging the imported forms and iconography with local tastes and symbols. Some of the art of the early colonial era in New Spain consequently has a hybrid appearance, which has been labeled Indo-Christian, or *tequitqui*.

Sculpture and murals created by native artists trained at the monastic schools and in less formal contexts are located throughout the earliest surviving mission complexes in New Spain. The paintings and sculpted images illustrate the life and death of Christ, the Virgin Mary, and the saints. A famous example appears in the Church of San Francisco in Tecamachalco, where 28 narrative scenes on bark paper are glued between the ribs of the choir loft. Executed in 1562 by the indigenous painter Juan Gerson, the paintings tell stories from the Old and New Testaments to address the theme of sin and judgment.

Sculpture on outdoor chapels, known as *posas*, and on stone crosses erected in the churchyard, on the other hand, use a short-hand, almost glyphic, array of symbols to embody the tenets of the Christian faith. Seen during outdoor services, these images were intended to help convert the indigenous people to Christianity by using a symbolic and ornamental vocabulary that recalled pre-Columbian pictographs.

Manuscript painting also thrived in New Spain during the early colonial era, serving missionaries, colonial authorities, and indigenous communities. In a few very early examples, only experts can distinguish the materials and appearance of the early colonial paintings from pre-Columbian Late Postclassic objects. In most extant examples, however, European paper and the bound book format replaced skin or bark paper screenfolds, helping to date the work to the early colonial era. Artists also developed a new collection of pictographic signs to account for the Spaniards' arrival and the new historical context and incorporated elements of European-style naturalism into their images. The painted manuscripts, however, continued to offer much the same content as before the conquest, recording history and genealogy, measuring time and the complex ritual calendar of indigenous faiths, and mapping territories (see MAPS). In some cases, the manuscripts were made for native patrons; indigenous maps and other bureaucratic manuscripts were even accepted in Spanish courts as legal documents. Other paintings copied earlier codices for curious Europeans. The 1541 Codex Mendoza, for example, included pages

reproducing the tribute that subject peoples sent to Aztec rulers. Religious codices that survived the flames of evangelization were copied for missionaries who hoped to banish pagan practices; annotations in Spanish identify the deities and rituals of the past.

Feather mosaics were perhaps the most beautiful examples of indigenous art to persist into the early colonial era. Employing the traditional technique of gluing single barbs from the feathers of brightly colored birds onto plant fiber paper, colonial *amantecas* created shimmering visions of Christian themes. The iridescent barbs shift as the light moves, creating an almost electrical effect. Church officials admired these luxury goods for their beauty and commissioned artists to create miters, copes, and other vestments. The artists also created small wall hangings, including the famous 1539 image of the Mystic Mass of St. Gregory, commissioned by a native patron and sent to Pope Paul III, perhaps in recognition of his decree on the humanity of Indians.

In addition to traditional media, new types of objects were introduced during the early colonial era. Painting on cloth was widely practiced in the new viceroyalties soon after the conquest. The most famous example of this type of art is the image of the VIRGIN OF GUADALUPE. According to the legend, the Virgin's image appeared miraculously on the cape of Juan Diego, an Indian, in 1531. The painting has been attributed to an indigenous painter, Marcos Cipac. Other European artistic media to gain popularity during the early colonial era include wood sculpture painted in lifelike colors, carved and gilded altar screens, and printed woodcuts.

See also ART (Vols. II, III, IV); MURALISTS, MEXICAN (Vol. IV).

—Kelly Donahue-Wallace
Sarahh E. M. Scher
David Tavárez

Further reading:
Gauvin Bailey. *Art of Colonial Latin America* (London: Phaidon, 2005).
Kelly Donahue-Wallace. *Art and Architecture of Viceregal Latin America, 1521–1821* (Albuquerque: University of New Mexico Press, 2008).
Margaret A. Jackson. *Moche Art and Visual Culture in Ancient Peru* (Albuquerque: University of New Mexico Press, 2009).
Rebecca Stone-Miller. *Art of the Andes: From Chavin to Inca* (New York: Thames & Hudson, 2002).

asiento An *asiento* was a contract or license to import African slaves to the Spanish-American colonies (see SLAVERY). For a price, the Spanish Crown awarded an *asiento* to individuals or companies to bring a specific number of captives over a number of years to designated ports in the Americas. The royal trading house, or CASA DE

CONTRATACIÓN, oversaw the contracts and collected the fees related to the transatlantic slave trade, ensuring that the Crown profited from it. The first *asientos* were issued in 1518 to don Jorge de Portugal to import 400 slaves and to Lorenzo de Gouvenot o Gavorrod to import 4,000 slaves.

The Spaniards were the first European colonizers in the Americas who could afford the high costs associated with enslaved African labor. In the late 15th and early 16th centuries, both enslaved and free African men took part in the first military ventures into the Caribbean, and later into MEXICO and PERU (see CONQUEST). Serving in Spanish armies as well as newly established households, enslaved men were in high demand among the wealthy conquistadores. The early Spanish settlers on HISPANIOLA perceived the native TAINO as too weak to labor in the GOLD mines. Moreover, the Taino resisted this work. In response to the colonists' demands, King Ferdinand and Queen Isabella allowed Spanish merchants to import captives in 1501 but prohibited the enslavement of Muslims, Jews, and those newly converted to Catholicism (see MORISCO). In 1502, the governor of HISPANIOLA, Nicolás Obando, privately introduced 16 slaves to the Spanish Caribbean. Other merchants and migrants followed suit, bringing their own and other slaves from Spain to the Americas.

After 1510, the Crown taxed each slave brought to the Americas, which quickly led to the establishment of the *asiento*. By institutionalizing the commercial slave trade to its colonies, the Spanish Crown profited from the slave trade, if not its actual transactions. By 1518, colonists in the Caribbean specifically requested blacks who did not speak Spanish because they were considered easier to control. Portuguese merchants acquired captives from local contacts and established agents along the Upper Senegambian coast and other parts of "Guinea," or Atlantic Africa (especially West Central Africa). Indeed, the *asiento* allowed contracted merchants to transport slaves directly from the Atlantic African coast to the Americas. Before 1518, the Spanish Crown required that Africans bound for the colonies first be brought to Europe to be baptized and indoctrinated as Catholics.

The *asiento* trade (and its illegal counterparts) supplied the growing colonies of Mexico and Peru, in particular. By the mid-1550s there were approximately 3,000 slaves in the Viceroyalty of Peru (see VICEROY/ VICEROYALTY). The distance from the Caribbean port of Cartagena increased the prices for captives destined for urban areas, especially the coastal city of LIMA and gold-mining towns such as Carabaya in the southern Andes.

See also *ASIENTO* (Vol. II).

—Rachel Sarah O'Toole

Further reading:

Herbert Klein and Ben Vinson III. *African Slavery in Latin America and the Caribbean*, 2d ed. (New York: Oxford University Press, 2007).

Atahualpa (Atawallpa, Atahuallpa) (b. ca. 1502– d. 1533) *last independent Inca emperor* Born ca. 1502 to one of the Inca emperor HUAYNA CÁPAC's concubines from the region of ECUADOR, Atahualpa soon came to be one of his father's favorite sons and his trusted general in his northern wars. His legitimate half brother HUÁSCAR ruled over the southern part of the empire from the capital of CUZCO as regent for his father, who was campaigning in the north.

On the death of their father in 1527 from a DISEASE that may have been smallpox, Huáscar proclaimed himself Inca ruler, or Sapa Inca (see INCAS). The Inca elite in Cuzco considered him the rightful heir to the throne since he was the legitimate son of Huayna Cápac and his sister queen. They demanded that Atahualpa swear allegiance to him.

Atahualpa did not immediately rebel against his brother. For five years after Huayna Cápac's death, Atahualpa ruled almost undisturbed by his brother in the north. Then, in the year 1532, assured of his army's loyalty and the support of some of the nobility, Atahualpa rose up in rebellion against Huáscar. Atahualpa became known for his ruthlessness. In early 1532, he slaughtered all of the inhabitants of several towns that supported his brother as both a lesson and a warning. The two brothers waged a brutal civil war that cost the lives of thousands and depleted much of the empire's wealth and food supplies.

Also in early 1532, Spanish conquistadores, under the leadership of FRANCISCO PIZARRO, landed at Tumbes on the northern coast of PERU. Becoming aware of the civil war, Pizarro sent word to both opposing camps and asked Atahualpa's faction for a meeting with Atahualpa. The Inca emperor agreed to a meeting, and on November 16, 1532, Pizarro and his band of conquistadores kidnapped Atahualpa in the northern Andean town of Cajamarca. There, they held him captive, promising to release him in exchange for a ransom in GOLD and SILVER. Although the ransom was paid, Pizarro betrayed his promise, and Atahualpa remained imprisoned.

Before his own capture by the Spaniards, Atahualpa had received word that his brother had been defeated and that Atahualpa's armies had managed to take Cuzco and capture Huáscar. While imprisoned, Atahualpa sent the order to have Huáscar murdered. Even after his death in 1532, however, Huáscar's allies continued to fight Atahualpa's army.

Using the murder of Huáscar as an excuse, Pizarro ordered Atahualpa's execution by strangulation on August 29, 1533. Pizarro soon realized that this was a mistake, however. He quickly named Topa Huallpa, whom he believed would appeal to both sides in the civil war, as the new Inca emperor. Nevertheless, the war continued. Topa Huallpa allied himself with Huáscar's faction, and he and the Spaniards were soon under attack from Atahualpa's followers. Topa Huallpa died within a few months, whereupon the Spaniards reaffirmed their alliance with Huáscar's faction by placing Huáscar's brother MANCO INCA on the throne. Manco Inca helped the Spaniards destroy the remnants of Atahualpa's army—and thus helped to bring about the final CONQUEST of Peru in 1536—before he, too, rebelled against the Spanish.

See also ATAHUALPA, JUAN SANTOS (Vol. II).

—John F. Chuchiak IV

Further reading:

Juan de Betanzos. *Narrative of the Incas*, translated and edited by Roland Hamilton and Dana Buchanan (Austin: University of Texas Press, 1996).

audiencia   The *audiencia* (high court) was the most important and powerful colonial institution in Spanish America. It was created to address both criminal and legal matters, yet it also enjoyed extensive legislative and administrative functions. In 1511, less than two decades after CHRISTOPHER COLUMBUS's 1492 voyage, the Spanish Crown authorized the establishment of the New World's first *audiencia*, located on Santo Domingo (see HISPANIOLA). The Audiencia of Santo Domingo was in part created to counter the power of the island's viceroy, Diego Columbus.

As Spain's colonial possessions in the New World increased, additional *audiencias* were created to facilitate their governance. The first mainland *audiencia* was established in MEXICO (New Spain) in 1527, just six years after the conquest of the Aztec Empire (see AZTECS). Later, *audiencias* appeared in PANAMA (1538, abolished in 1543 but reinstated in 1564), PERU (1543), GUATEMALA (1543), New Galicia (1547), BOGOTÁ (Santa Fé de Bogotá, 1549), La Plata (modern BOLIVIA, 1559), and Quito (modern ECUADOR, 1563). By the end of the 16th century, a total of 11 *audiencias* had been established in Spanish America. Most of Spanish America's 16th-century *audiencias* consisted of a president, four judges (*oidores*), and a crown attorney (*fiscal*) Only the *oidores* voted on judicial matters.

See also *AUDIENCIA* (Vol. II); *OIDOR* (Vol. II); *REGIDOR* (Vol. II); *RESIDENCIA* (Vol. II); *VISITA* (Vol. II).

—J. Michael Francis

ayllu   In the central Andean region, the QUECHUA term *ayllu* refers to the basic kinship unit that regulated social, religious, and economic relations. Governed by a hereditary ruler, or KURAKA, each *ayllu* consisted of extended FAMILY lineages whose members traced their descent to a common ancestor, often mythical. *Ayllu* members also shared a sacred place of origin, such as a mountain peak, cave, stream, or lake. The precise historical origins of the *ayllu* are unclear; however, archaeological and ethnohistorical evidence suggests that Andean communities organized into *ayllus* hundreds of years before the 15th-century expansion of the Inca Empire.

The emergence of the *ayllu* likely represented a long-term adaptation strategy to the region's diverse natural environment. Under this system, *ayllu* members did not reside in the same nuclear settlement; instead, members were disbursed to various ecological zones at different altitudes, where they were able to exploit vastly different resources. For example, mid-elevation settlements cultivated MAIZE, quinoa, and various tubers; meanwhile, members of the same *ayllu* who settled at lower elevations harvested various fruits, peppers, and COCA leaves. The highest elevations were ideal for herding llamas and alpacas. All of these goods were then circulated among members of the same *ayllu*, thus making it virtually self-sufficient and guaranteeing each member access to a full complement of goods and resources. Lands were held in common and were allocated to different families based on their numbers and status. *Ayllus* were governed by the principles of reciprocity and redistribution and were typically divided into two opposing parts, known as *hanan* (upper) and *hurin* (lower).

In a land characterized by dramatic local variations in temperatures, rainfall, soils, and elevations, this "vertical economy" helped Andeans mitigate the risks posed by drought, flood, or frost. A crop failure in one ecological zone could be balanced by a surplus in another, thus this "archipelago" settlement pattern protected *ayllu* members from potentially devastating local conditions. Not surprisingly, the system required a high level of political organization and communal cooperation. Major work projects, such as the maintenance of irrigation canals, the construction of roads and bridges, and the organization and celebration of religious festivals, all required the participation of the entire *ayllu*. Men and WOMEN shared most tasks, and both contributed to the political, economic, and spiritual welfare of the community. In theory, the *ayllu* was endogamous, with members taking spouses from within the extended family networks of the same *ayllu*.

Both Inca imperial expansion (see INCAS) and the Spanish CONQUEST threatened local *ayllu* autonomy. While the *ayllu* did experience some important changes as a result of these external pressures, many Andean *ayllus* survived, and the *ayllu* continues to govern a large number of rural highland communities in modern Peru.

—J. Michael Francis

Further reading:

Terence N. D'Altroy. *The Incas* (Malden, Mass.: Blackwell, 2003).

Aztecs   The term *Aztec* generally refers to the Mexica people, who dominated large portions of Mesoamerica from their great capital in the Valley of MEXICO and who flourished for nearly two centuries before their violent clash with the Spaniards in 1521. Of all pre-Columbian cultures of Mesoamerica, the Aztecs are probably the best known to modern scholars since their history and achievements were recorded in great detail by the early colonial Spanish and indigenous CHRONICLERS. Though the encounter with

Europeans produced much valuable information regarding their rapid demise, very little is known about their early beginnings. No pre-Columbian Aztec CODICES have survived, thus most historical reconstructions come from later retrospective accounts. Furthermore, archaeology at their capital, TENOCHTITLÁN, is hindered because the majority of the remains are buried under the contemporary urban sprawl of MEXICO CITY.

Although the designation *Aztec* has been used in the literature in multiple ways, none of the NAHUATL-speaking people (Nahuas, who included the Mexicas) in fact referred to themselves as "Aztecs"; rather, their identities were based on the kingdom or ethnic group to which they belonged. The modern appellation *Aztec* derives from the toponym *Aztlán* (Place of the Herons, in Nahuatl), perhaps an island in a lake somewhere in the northern lands of the Chichimec tribes. According to the Mexicas' own histories, *Aztlán* was their place of origin. Oppressed by other groups or forced to relocate due to environmental stress, these particular inhabitants of Aztlán (there were in fact several groups who claimed descent from there) started on their long migration probably as early as the 11th century C.E.

Other origin myths tell of Chicomoztoc, or "Place of the Seven Caves," where each of the caverns housed a different ethnic group who left for Central Mexico, the Mexica ancestors being the last to depart. They left under the command of their patron deity, Huitzilopochtli (Hummingbird to the South), traveling in eight groups called the *calpultin*, each of which numbered between seven and 20 people. These *calpultin* were headed by three men and a woman, who carried their patron gods and sacred bundles on their backs. After a long journey, which overall might have lasted for almost two centuries and encompassed some 20 stops along the way, they were among the last Nahuas to arrive in the Valley of Mexico. On arrival, some of the *calpultin* members insisted on settling in a place called Coatepec (Serpent Hill); however, according to the myth, Huitzilopochtli objected and sacrificed the dissidents. It was only after these events that Huitzilopochtli bestowed on them the tribal name by which they would become known throughout Mesoamerica, the *Mexica*. Among their stops might have been the Toltec capital of Tollan (TULA), where they could have gained important skills as builders, artisans, and warriors and acquired a taste for a more sophisticated urban lifestyle (see TOLTECS).

With the new knowledge and dress they adopted along the way, the Mexicas continued to push toward the center of the valley, which they found already densely populated. They settled first in Chapultepec, from which they moved to an isolated hill at Tizapán and became subjects of the king of Culhuacán. Although he had successfully employed the seemingly barbaric Mexica warriors to defeat his Xochimilca enemies, he soon expelled the Mexicas from his land after they sacrificed his daughter and flayed her. Following their expulsion

from Tizapán, the Mexicas continued their migration. Finally, in 1325, their long voyage came to an end when they established a settlement on a small island in Lake Texcoco, which was under the domain of the Tepanec king Tezozómoc from Azcapotzalco. According to their own myths, it was here that the Mexicas witnessed the vision that Huitzilopochtli had prophesied—an eagle perched on top of a cactus near a spring—as a sign of their promised homeland. This would be the place where the Mexicas would establish their mighty capital city, Tenochtitlán (literally "Among the Stone-Cactus Fruit," while the name has also been associated with an early Mexica leader named *Tenoch*).

The choice of settling this desolate island might have been in part due to its defensible location; additionally, these were originally "water people" (*atlaca Chichimeca*) who drew their subsistence from lacustrine environments (such as in Aztlán). Alternatively, the site might have been chosen simply because it was one of the few unoccupied places in Mexico's central valley. Regardless, the Mexicas made the most of their newly founded home. Their early ECONOMY was based on the exploitation of local resources, namely intensive fishing, hunting, and gathering. Lacking most natural resources, they traded duck and fish for stone and wood from the mainland and started to construct their houses and temples. Soon, they expanded the available agricultural land by building up CHINAMPA, or fertile plots of cultivated raised fields in the shallow lake bed, which provided high yields of MAIZE, beans, squash, and chilies (see AGRICULTURE). Over the years, they continued to reshape their immediate surroundings. Among other public works, the Mexicas built a long dike to control the lake's water level and prevent the severe flooding that periodically damaged the city. They constructed several long causeways that connected the island to the mainland and an aqueduct to transport water from the springs at Chapultepec on the mainland back to the city. Thirteen years after initial settlement, a territorial conflict had forced one group to leave and establish the twin city of Tlatelolco on a smaller island to the north, thus creating two distinct groups: the Mexica-Tenochca and the Mexica-Tlatelolca. Soon, however, Tenochtitlán and Tlatelolco formed a single urban island, connected by various avenues and canals. Before long, their city was as strong and impressive as any other in the Valley of Mexico.

AZTEC RULERS AND IMPERIAL EXPANSION

In return for this granted land, the Mexicas became the mercenaries and subjects of the Tepanec king of Azcapotzalco, the most powerful ruler in the valley at the time. Under Tepanec rule, the Mexicas participated in various wars against Azcapotzalco's enemies. Despite their subordinate position in valley politics, the Mexicas continued to seek connections to local royal dynasties in order to achieve the coveted *tlatocayotl* status that would entitle them to establish and rule over their own dynastic kingdom. The Tenochcas soon crowned their first ruler,

Acamapichtli (r. 1372–91), son of a Mexica noble and a princess from Culhuacán, Tula's ancient ally. Similarly, in an effort to tie their emerging lineage to a powerful royal house, the Tlatelolcas chose Cuacuauhpitzahuac, son of Tezozómoc, king of Azcapotzalco, as their ruler. In 1383, the Mexicas assisted the Tepanecs in conquering the cities of Xochimilco, Mixquic, and Cuitláhuac at the southern part of Lake Texcoco; and in 1395, they took over the Otomí city of Xaltocán. Acamapichtli's son and successor, Huitzilíhuitl (r. 1391–1415), also married a Tepanec princess of Azcapotzalco, thus reducing the Mexicas' tribute load.

Huitzilíhuitl and Cuacuauhpitzahuac were succeeded by Chimalpopoca (r. 1415–26) of Tenochtitlán and Tlacateotl of Tlatelolco, to whom the Tepanecs granted the city of Texcoco as their first tribute; shortly thereafter, however, both rulers were killed during a revolt in the Tepanec kingdom. It was then left for Itzcóatl (r. 1427–40), the new Tenochca king, to centralize Aztec authority and rewrite Aztec history. Itzcóatl burned the early CODICES available to other religious leaders of competing groups and established the important office of the *cihuacóatl* adviser. In 1428, Itzcóatl took on Texcoco and defeated Maxtla, Tezozómoc's son and the current Tepanec king. Following this critical overthrow, known as the Tepanec War, Itzcóatl seized Azcapotzalco's kingdom and established the TRIPLE ALLIANCE between his ally rebel rulers Totoquihuaztli of Tlacopan and Nezahualcóyotl of Texcoco (the town of Huexotzinco also took part in the rebellion but withdrew soon after). The alliance entailed a mutual peace agreement and the unequal distribution of tribute among the three conquering towns; however, due to its prominent military role in these events, Tenochtitlán soon became the strongest entity in the Triple Alliance. At the same time, the Tlatelolcas were denied a place in this new political order, and the rift between them and the Tenochcas grew even further.

Itzcóatl was succeeded by his nephew Montezuma (Moctezuma) Ilhuicamina (Montezuma I; r. 1440–68), who is often credited as being the true founder of the Aztec Empire. Under Montezuma's rule, the Aztecs subjugated the southern lake towns of Xochimilco, Culhuacán, and Coyoacán and embarked on an imperial expansion beyond the valley into the modern states of Morelos and Guerrero. Montezuma's reign also survived a severe drought that struck the Valley of Mexico between 1450 and 1455, and the capital's economy nearly collapsed.

Axayácatl (r. 1468–81), Montezuma's grandson and successor, followed his predecessor's example and continued to strengthen Aztec hegemony through more conquests; however, he was not always successful. For example, in 1478, Aztec forces suffered a disastrous defeat at the hands of the Tarascans, who killed more than 20,000 Aztec soldiers in a single battle. Still, as the empire grew larger and stronger, tribute began to flow to the capital's treasure houses, and exotic goods filled its markets; although each Aztec city had its own market,

the most renowned was that of Tlatelolco. By the time the Spaniards saw it in 1519, Tlatelolco was visited by 60,000 people a day and was supervised meticulously by the POCHTECA long-distance merchants. Even in 1473, this in itself was a strong motive for Axayácatl to conquer and annex Tlatelolco to Tenochtitlán's already existing quarters and replace its rulers with Tenochca governors.

Tizoc (r. 1481–86), Axayácatl's brother and heir to the throne, failed to follow his predecessors' success on the battlefield; as a consequence, his reign was short-lived. In fact, it has been suggested that Tizoc was poisoned by members of his own council. He was replaced by yet another of Axayácatl's brothers, Ahuitzotl (r. 1486–1502), who embarked on an aggressive expansion campaign, reaching all the way to the Valley of Oaxaca and the Soconusco, a coastal region that was known for its CACAO and quetzal feathers. Montezuma (Moctezuma) Xocoyotzin (Montezuma II; r. 1502–20) son of Axayácatl, was next in line (see MONTEZUMA). He conquered additional parts of Oaxaca; however, for the most part, he was occupied with consolidating a vast empire that had already reached a critical size for indirect control.

According to Aztec historical sources, written several decades after the Spanish CONQUEST, a series of menacing omens appeared early in Montezuma's reign. These omens, eight in total, prophesied the empire's doom and destruction. Indeed, it fell to this ill-fated emperor to meet HERNANDO CORTÉS and his soldiers in Tenochtitlán on November 8, 1519, after which he curiously submitted to their outrageous demands to hold him as captive in his own city. Although it is unlikely that Montezuma thought of Cortés as a reincarnation of the Toltec king-god QUETZALCÓATL, returning now to the valley to claim his throne, it does appear that Cortés himself gained his trust and manipulated him into a submissive attitude. Considered a traitor by his own council and subjects, Montezuma died on June 30, 1520, from a stone hurled at him when the Aztecs attacked the palace. After his untimely death, his brother Cuitláhuac (r. 1520) took the throne and expelled the Spaniards from the city. His rule was also cut short, however, when he died in a smallpox epidemic that had spread among the defenseless indigenous peoples (see DISEASE). The last Aztec king was CUAUHTÉMOC (r. 1520–25), Cuitláhuac's cousin, who attempted to defend Tenochtitlán from the invading Spaniards and their allies, but he was eventually captured in 1521. Four years later, in February 1525, Cuauhtémoc was executed in GUATEMALA under Cortés's orders. Thus ended the proud lineage of Aztec kings.

AZTEC EMPIRE

On the eve of the Spanish conquest, the Aztec Empire extended over much of the territory of today's Mexico, stretching from the Pacific coast to the Gulf coast and from the north of the Valley of Mexico to the Soconusco region on the Guatemalan border. This was never a homogenous territorial sovereignty; rather, the Aztec

Stone statues rest against one of the stairways from several construction phases of the Templo Mayor in the Aztec capital. The final stage of the construction was completed in 1487, just three decades before Europeans first entered Tenochtitlán in 1519. *(Courtesy of J. Michael Francis)*

Empire embraced pockets of independent kingdoms populated by diverse ethnic groups. Still, by 1519, the joint forces of the Triple Alliance controlled an empire with 5 to 6 million people living in more than 300 indigenous communities, in a territory meticulously divided into 38 provinces. Since these provinces encompassed numerous ethnic groups and diverse languages, the Aztecs imposed their own language, Nahuatl, as the lingua franca among the conquered elite and even renamed their communities. This was the largest indigenous political entity ever to arise on Mesoamerican soil and the second largest in the New World, after the INCAS of PERU.

The driving force behind this imperial expansion was the Aztec army. From their humble beginnings as mercenaries of Azcapotzalco, the Aztecs emphasized militarism and warfare in their iconography and sacred ART, much of which echoed that of the earlier Toltecs of Tula. Every young man in Aztec society had to join the army and further prove himself as an adult by capturing an enemy on the battlefield. This achievement was publicly demonstrated by a particular haircut, and the number of captives was indicated by the length of one's cloak and the right to wear a lip plug. The army included special units maintained by the state and made up of nobles and oth-

ers who proved themselves worthy in battle; among the most prestigious were the orders of the Jaguar and the Eagle Knights. However, since the majority of the army was in fact composed of commoners who also farmed the empire's land, warfare had to be limited to the wintertime, when agricultural activity was at a hiatus.

Nevertheless, the enterprise of territorial conquest mostly began diplomatically, with Aztec emissaries sent to negotiate with local rulers. If these rulers did not join the empire voluntarily, the marching armies soon followed. With their tens of thousands of swords and spears edged with sharp OBSIDIAN blades, colorful yet fearsome costumes, and tall feathered banners, they were likely a terrifying sight for any nonconforming town. For the most part, the Aztecs left the existing social, political, and religious order intact if the conquered province provided no further resistance. In cases where military confrontation was inevitable, the armies often laid waste to the place and people and replaced the local government with an Aztec governor or a tribute collector. On rare occasions, the Aztecs even mobilized large groups of migrants from the Valley of Mexico into distant provinces, where enclaves were established among the local people. In some unstable areas, it was necessary to set up a permanent military garrison, such as the one in the Valley of Oaxaca.

Once political relations were cemented between subject towns and the Triple Alliance, the region was reorganized as a tributary province. Although tribute depended largely on the wealth of the local rulers and the natural resources available to them, those who rebelled were required to pay higher amounts than those who joined the empire peacefully. These taxes were carefully recorded in the Aztec codices as in the early colonial manuscripts *Matrícula de tributos* and the Codex Mendoza. The tribute that flowed to Tenochtitlán, Texcoco, and Tlacopán included food supplies, raw materials, COTTON cloths, and CACAO beans, with the last two also serving as monetary units. At the same time, Aztec imperial expansion stimulated specialization in the provinces, since a great deal of the tribute that flowed to the capital was in the form of finished luxury goods such as jewelry and costumes for the Aztec nobility. Subject towns were further committed to participate in the long-distance trading economy of the *pochteca*; moreover, they were to allow free passage to Triple Alliance armies and provide resources and supplies to Aztec soldiers. At times, they were forced to offer victims for sacrifices in Aztec ceremonies.

In addition to the tributary provinces, the Aztecs established several strategic provinces that bordered unstable areas and important trade routes. Instead of tribute, their rulers provided "gifts" to the Aztec Empire, although once the empire expanded past a strategic province, this agreement would transform into a tributary arrangement. Other important towns, such as Cholula in Puebla, were able to remain independent from the Aztecs without developing a hostile relationship, while keeping an open economic network with the empire. Even where no direct conquest could be achieved, the Aztecs encouraged secondary liaisons through marital alliances among the royal lineages. Still, due largely to its ethnic and political diversity, the Aztec Empire was never a stable entity; rebellions were quite common throughout its short history. Even among the Tenochca political leaders there were strong disagreements, which came forcefully into play in the matter of the Spaniards' march inland from Veracruz and their subsequent presence in Tenochtitlán. Furthermore, the Aztecs were never able to conquer resilient groups such as the Tlaxcalans or the Tarascans, and the battles with these enemies were occasionally disastrous for Triple Alliance troops. Indeed, the eventual downfall of the Aztec Empire would largely be due to these resentful conquered and unconquered groups who willingly joining the Spanish conquistadores as allies.

AZTEC SOCIETY

Aztec society was divided along strictly defined class lines, with the *huetlatoani* (he who speaks) as supreme ruler at the top of the social structure. The ruler was elected from among the males of the previous ruler's FAMILY and controlled his vast empire from his palace in Tenochtitlán. His closest adviser was the *cihuacóatl* (snake woman), an office occupied by a male. The *cihuacóatl* was similarly chosen from the members of a special lineage. The position was formally established in the 1420s and outlasted even the Aztec royal lineage when a *cihuacóatl* served as the last Aztec *tlatoani* from 1525 to 1526. While the *huetlatoani* was considered a divine incarnation of the celestial authority, the *cihuacóatl* represented the terrestrial aspects of the rule. Together, they embodied the Aztec concept of cosmic duality in both the social and political realms. Under them were the jurisdictional, administrative, military, and religious councils, whose members were chosen from among the *tetecutin*, nobles and the king's relatives. Below these were the rest of the nobles by birth (*PIPILTIN*), who functioned as administrators, priests, and war chiefs. Under the Aztecs, all members of the nobility were exempted from tribute payment. Another highly regarded position was that of the *calpixqui*, an Aztec administrator who ruled over a town where the local dynasty had been replaced by the *huetlatoani*. Despite the fact that most of these positions were occupied by men, noblewomen also had strong influence on decision making in the political sphere, and several were chosen as lesser rulers in the city-states around the lake. The nobility could practice polygamy, and the *huetlatoani* himself had numerous wives and concubines.

The relatively small nobility ruled over the majority of the population, known as the *macehualtin*, or commoners (see MACEHUAL). They included general workers, artisans, soldiers, farmers, and fisherman, all of whom had to pay tribute in goods and LABOR, such as helping to construct public works. At the same time, Aztec (Mexica) commoners seemed to have fared better than others in the realm, as household excavations have revealed that they had access to imported goods such as polychrome CERAMICS and obsidian. In early Aztec history, commoners could occasionally be granted the noble rank of a *quauhpilli* (eagle lord) on account of their military achievements; however, this practice was eliminated under Montezuma Xocoyotzin's reign, when the number of nobles was becoming too large to support. Still, upward social mobility remained possible through the "intermediate" level between the elite and the commoners, which was mostly composed of rich *pochteca* merchants and luxury goods artisans.

Below the *macehualtin* were the *mayeque*, rural farmers who did not live in a CALPULLI but worked the lands of the nobility. At the bottom of the social hierarchy were the slaves (*tlacotin*), who were bought at the market to provide hard labor at nobles' households (see SLAVERY). For the most part, the *tlacotin* consisted of people who had unpaid debts or criminal records and thus had the opportunity to buy their freedom (see CRIME AND PUNISHMENT). At the same time, slaves might have been easily used as sacrificial victims or purchased to serve that purpose.

The Aztecs maintained their primordial tribal organization even in their great city. The bulk of the population lived in *calpultin* (great houses), loose corporate kin groups unified by a common ancestor (*calpulteotl*) and a specialized profession. Each *calpulli* occupied a neighborhood, where land was divided among the respective families. Although most land was considered communal, there is evidence to suggest that in the early 16th century, there was a trend toward privatization and capitalization of territorial properties. The *calpultin* were ruled by a traditional government of elders and a government of nobles, the latter mediating between the *calpulli* and the central government of the king and managing the tribute obligations of each group. Noble boys attended the *calmecac* schools, where they learned religious, political, military, artistic, and administrative skills, while the commoners went to the *telpochcalli*, where they were trained as warriors. Girls helped with household chores such as grinding maize and weaving cloth, although noble girls could have been trained as priestesses. Both boys and girls participated in the *cuicacalli* (house of song), where they learned ceremonial songs and dances.

AZTEC RELIGION

According to Aztec mythology, the Earth was formed from a crocodilian monster that floated on a great disc of water in the center of the universe. The Aztec universe was divided into quadrants oriented to the cardinal directions, with the center serving as the fifth direction. Space was further divided vertically into nine layers below the Earth's surface and 13 above it. At the uppermost level resided the two primordial creator deities, Ometecuhtli and Omecihuatl, the Lord and Lady of Duality. They had four sons, who ranked among the most important deities in the Aztec pantheon: Quetzalcóatl, Huitzilopochtli, Xipe Totec, and Tezcatlipoca. Each was associated with a cardinal direction, color, animal, tree, and other aspects and possessed a divine-human personality; Tezcatlipoca, for example, was as omnipotent as he was capricious, characteristics that often associated him with the Aztec sorcerers.

Before the current world was created, it had passed through four destructive phases, each dominated by a different "sun." Within each sun, different types of people were created but then destroyed in a major catastrophe

This photograph shows the so-called Aztec calendar stone, on display at Mexico City's National Museum of Anthropology and History. The figure in the center of the calendar represents Tonatiuh, the sun deity who presided over the Fifth Age in which the Aztecs lived. Tonatiuh is surrounded by the four previous ages of creation and destruction. (*Courtesy of J. Michael Francis*)

(as depicted in the so-called Aztec calendar stone). In the fifth and current sun, Quetzalcóatl created humanity from the previous era's bones and ashes, which he had acquired from the god of the underworld, Mictlantecuhtli; Quetzalcóatl gave life to these bones and ashes by mixing them with his own blood. This benevolent deity also provided humans with the first maize and invented the calendar and fine arts. In order to prevent this world from being destroyed before the cycle's natural end by an earthquake, the sun was to be constantly fed with human blood in honor of the sacred covenant between the gods and humans. For this reason, HUMAN SACRIFICE was a paramount component in Aztec religious rituals, and bloodletting was an important ceremonial activity among most nobles, who used sharp objects to draw blood from their earlobes, tongues, limbs, and genitals.

The Aztecs are perhaps best known for their ostentatious sacrifices on top of the Templo Mayor, where hundreds of thousands of victims' hearts were cut and torn from their chest with obsidian knives, then offered as divine sustenance to the gods by priests. Since the majority of these victims were caught during the so-called FLOWER WARS, the death toll might not have been higher than in most European wars at the time, which aimed to slay the enemies in the battlefield rather than capture them alive. Undoubtedly, however, these gory and public spectacles had the additional propagandistic purpose of frightening any potential opponents of Aztec dominion.

Other important deities in the Aztec pantheon were Tlaloc and Chalchiuhtlicue, who were the principal water and storm deities. Aztec kings would conduct annual pilgrimages during the dry season to honor the water deities and ensure the renewal of the rains. Xipe Totec was the god of fertility, and festivities in his honor involved flaying a sacrificial victim, which was then worn by a priest. The Sun God, Tonatiuh, was equally important to this agriculture-based society and was further associated with warriors who died in battle. Even so, the one and true war god was Huitzilopochtli, the Mexica patron god who led the people out of Aztlán; human sacrifices were offered to him regularly. According to Aztec mythology, Coyolxauhqui, the Moon Goddess and older sister of Huitzilopochtli, attempted to kill their mother, Coatlicue, but was hindered and defeated by the heroic Huitzilopochtli. A gigantic carved image of the dismembered Coyolxauhqui was found at the foot of Templo Mayor, indicating that these myths were commemorated and reenacted in the sacred geography of Tenochtitlán. There were numerous other gods, goddesses, and lesser deities, and the Aztecs even incorporated the sacred idols

A serpent head at the base of one of the staircases of the Templo Mayor, located in the ceremonial precinct of the Aztec capital city of Tenochtitlán, modern-day Mexico City *(Courtesy of J. Michael Francis)*

of conquered peoples into the pantheon; these were housed in a special temple in Tenochtitlán. To accommodate and maintain all these supernatural beings, full-time priests and priestesses occupied the different shrines; according to one chronicler, the Templo Mayor was served by 5,000 people. Not surprisingly, religious ceremonies were common throughout the year, and besides human sacrifice, these included activities such as song, music, dance, and ball games.

AZTEC CALENDARS, SCIENCE, AND ARTS

For the Aztecs, time was cyclical and repetitive, and their complex calendric system reflected this notion. The solar calendar consisted of 365 days, divided into 18 groups of 20 days each, with the addition of five "unlucky" days. This particular calendar was associated with the agricultural cycle of planting and harvesting, as well as the rotating market system. Each of the 18 "months" featured a particular ceremony, mostly related to themes of agricultural fertility and dedicated to a different deity. Like most Mesoamerican cultures, the Aztecs also observed a ritual calendar (*tonalpohualli*) of 260 days, which combined 20 days names with a rotating cycle of 13 numbers; this sacred calendar might have been derived from the length of the human gestation period. Perhaps for this reason, the *tonalpohualli* was also the basis of the Mesoamerican personal identification system, by which individuals would be named after the day on which they were born (for example, 1 Alligator or 7 Flower), with an additional personalized name often derived from the natural world. Each of these different 260 name-number combinations were further associated with a patron deity and carried a specific set of fortunes, which could be favorable, ominous, or indifferent. These prognostications were recorded in a sacred book called the *tonalamatl* and were used by specialists to divine the fates of every newborn, to determine an auspicious day for a temple inauguration or a king's coronation, and even to foretell the final fate of an empire.

The two calendars of 365 and 260 days meshed together to form a longer cycle of 52 years, known as the "calendar round." The calendar round served the purpose of measuring longer periods of time and distinguished the solar years by their specific position in the calendar. However, unlike the MAYA, who used what is known as the Long Count, the Aztecs did not tie their calendar rounds to a fixed starting date, so determining the exact position of any recorded event can often be confusing. To commemorate the end of a calendar round and the beginning of a new one, every 52 years the Aztec celebrated the New Fire Ceremony on top of Mount Citlaltépec, which was dedicated to Xiuhtecuhtli, the "Old God." The entire city of Tenochtitlán was cast in darkness and silence, and old idols and cooking pots were discarded. Then, a fire was lit in the chest of a sacrificial victim on top of the mountain, and this flame was brought down back to the city to light the hearths in the temples and households. The Aztecs believed that if the priests failed to light the new fire, the end of the world would arrive in the horrific form of *tzizimime*, or "devouring monsters."

The Aztecs practiced naked-eye astronomical observations for the purpose of adjusting their calendars and agricultural activities, mostly by looking at cyclical celestial phenomena such as solar, lunar, and planetary movements. Rather than applying this knowledge for scientific ends, they used it as the basis for their intricate mythology and cosmogony, while unique celestial events such as eclipses and comets were considered as divine omens that could foretell destruction (such as those observed before the arrival of the Spaniards). In addition, the Aztecs possessed vast medical and anatomical knowledge (see MEDICINE), as well as a detailed geographical record of their empire whereby MAPS and kingdoms' territorial extent were recorded on large cloth sheets.

Aztec craftsmen and artisans were renowned for their magnificent work in feathers, semiprecious stones, and GOLD; the last might have been taught by Mixtec artisans who were brought from Oaxaca to reside in the valley (see MIXTECS). Above all, the Aztecs excelled in sculpting large stone monuments with intricate designs, which for the most part depicted religious motifs such as deities and gods. Other monuments were dedicated to Aztec emperors, and these usually contained historical details such as coronation dates and the names of conquered city-states. In addition, the Aztecs carefully recorded their historical and mythical narratives, as well as poetry and other LITERATURE. One of the greatest Aztec poets was Nezahualcóyotl, the influential king of Texcoco. All of these literary genres were most likely kept in screenfold codices and other documents written with the Aztec glyphic writing system, which employed pictographs, ideographs, and phonetic elements. Although the early colonial chronicles tell of extensive archives of recorded knowledge that had existed in Tenochtitlán before the Spaniards' arrival, none of these has survived, and all the Aztec codices we know of today postdate the Spanish conquest.

—Danny Zborover

Further reading:
Michael E. Smith. *The Aztecs* (Oxford: Blackwell Publishing, 2003).

B

Balboa, Vasco Núñez de (b. ca. 1475–d. 1519)
Spanish conquistador, founder of first permanent Spanish settlement in Central America and first European to sight Pacific Ocean
Vasco Núñez de Balboa was born ca. 1475 in the town of Jerez de los Caballeros, in Extremadura, Spain. In 1499, he joined the expedition of Rodrigo de Bastidas to the northern coast of South America. After a failed attempt at colonization, Bastidas's expedition returned to the island of Hispaniola. Balboa decided to stay behind in Santo Domingo to become a farmer, borrowing money to purchase a small parcel of land.

Unsuccessful at farming, Balboa accumulated many debts. In an effort to escape his creditors, he sealed himself in a barrel and stowed away on a ship under the command of Martín Fernández de Enciso headed for a struggling Spanish colony in northern Colombia. On arrival, Balboa used the knowledge of the area he had gained on the Bastidas expedition and persuaded the remaining colonists to transplant their township across the Gulf of Uraba to the site of Darién, on the coast of present-day Panama.

Following Balboa's lead, the colonists founded the new town of Santa María de la Antigua, which was the first permanent Spanish settlement in Central America. Elected as a town magistrate, Balboa quickly rose to be the leader of the new colony. By December 1511, Balboa had received royal recognition to serve as the interim governor and captain general of the area.

Balboa then led various expeditions into the interior and ultimately subjugated most of the local indigenous population; indeed, many native people were enslaved and granted in *encomienda* to the colonists. During his expeditions, Balboa learned of the apparent existence of a culture rich in gold to the south. During an expedition to find this golden kingdom, on September 25, 1513, Balboa became the first European to sight the Pacific Ocean, which he named the "Great South Sea." Although he claimed the region and the sea for the king of Spain, he later received only the title of governor of the South Sea with a small coastal territory to be placed under the jurisdiction of the new governor, Pedro Arias de Ávila, who had been sent from Spain in 1514.

Resenting his loss of prestige, Balboa and the new governor soon became rivals. Balboa retreated to the Pacific side of Panama and began to build a small fleet of ships to explore the South Sea. Arias de Ávila, however, thwarted this attempt, having learned of Balboa's efforts to discredit him at the Spanish court. Under the pretense of wishing to consult with Balboa, Arias de Ávila had him arrested on arrival and put on trial for treason. In early January 1519, after a rapid trial, Vasco Núñez de Balboa and four of his captains who had been named as accomplices were beheaded.

—John F. Chuchiak IV

Further reading:
Charles L. G. Anderson. *Life and Letters of Vasco Núñez de Balboa* (New York: Fleming H. Revell Co., 1941).
Kathleen Romoli. *Balboa of Darién: Discoverer of the Pacific* (Garden City, N.Y.: Doubleday, 1953).

Bastidas, Rodrigo de (b. ca. 1468–d. 1527) *founder and governor of the coastal city of Santa Marta, Colombia*
A native of Seville, Spain, Rodrigo de Bastidas was among the first Europeans to sail to the New World, joining Christopher Columbus on his second voyage in 1494. In

42

1500, the Spanish Crown authorized Bastidas to organize his own expedition in search of new territories to conquer. That same year, Bastidas first explored the coast of Santa Marta, where he and the Spaniards with him bartered with local native people for GOLD and pearls. However, fierce resistance from the region's indigenous population and limited evidence of mineral wealth delayed the establishment of permanent Spanish settlements along COLOMBIA's northern coastline. In fact, another 25 years passed before Bastidas returned to the region and founded Spain's first town in Colombia, which was called Santa Marta. Bastidas served as Santa Marta's first governor. During the first decades of the 16th century, Santa Marta attracted few Spaniards; those who did venture along Colombia's Caribbean coast did so in search of slaves, gold, and, on occasion, pearls. Despite the fact that the region fell loosely under governor PEDRO ARIAS DE ÁVILA's jurisdiction in PANAMA, there was no permanent Spanish presence in Santa Marta until the mid-1520s.

In November 1524, the Crown reached an agreement (*capitulación*) with Bastidas, entrusting the new governor with the conquest and settlement of the province and port of Santa Marta. Bastidas was to take at least 50 Spaniards to settle the new town, 15 of whom were supposed to be accompanied by their wives. Bastidas's tenure as governor did not last long; upset that the governor refused to distribute all the gold they had acquired, Bastidas's lieutenant, Pedro de Villafuerte, and several of his supporters stormed the governor's house late one night and attacked him. Bastidas survived but was critically wounded. Fearing that he would be murdered if he remained in Santa Marta, he was taken to Santo Domingo to seek medical attention but never reached HISPANIOLA. Rodrigo de Bastidas died from his wounds in CUBA in January 1527.

—J. Michael Francis

Further reading:

J. Michael Francis. *Invading Colombia: Spanish Accounts of the Gonzalo Jiménez de Quesada Expedition of Conquest* (University Park: Pennsylvania State University Press, 2007).

batab   The term *batab* (plural, *batabo'ob*) referred to the headman of a Yucatec MAYA village. The origins and usage of the term are both pre-Columbian. *Baat* means "hatchet," while *-ab* adds the concept of instrumentality, thus producing "by means of the hatchet," or more idiomatically, "he who wields the hatchet." In all probability, this referred to the use of a ceremonial hatchet designed to denote authority.

Prior to the Spanish CONQUEST in the region (1526–44), the Yucatec Maya were divided into a complex political patchwork. *Batabs* governed individual villages, while above them were the *jalach wíinik*, or "true men," who ruled regions. While at first the Spanish failed to recognize the former, during their campaign to concentrate Indian populations in settled villages, they reinforced the authority of the *batab*, who became the point of access for virtually all matters of village governance, including tribute, LABOR, and the teaching of Spanish Catholicism (see RELIGION). The *batab*, in association with a council of elders known as the REPÚBLICA DE INDÍGENAS, administered petty justice and guarded the village land title. *Batabs* and *repúblicas* survived into the early national period, and despite legal decrees limiting their power, the *batabs* continued to perform similar functions to those of earlier times.

—Terry Rugeley

Belize   The area that is today Belize was one of the cradles of MAYA civilization. The site of Cuello, located in the north of the country, almost two miles (3 km) west of the town of Orange Walk, is possibly the oldest Maya ceremonial center, dating to at least as early as 400 B.C.E. Early structures consisted of little more than raised earthen mounds that sustained huts made from perishable materials. As Maya society became more complex and diversified, ceremonial structures such as pyramids, plazas, and causeways emerged. Several factors encouraged the growth of civilization here: The hot climate with regular rain aided AGRICULTURE, while Belize's multiple river systems facilitated trade both within the region and without. By the end of the late pre-Classic period (300 B.C.E.–250 C.E.), the city of Lamanai (submerged crocodile) was already in full bloom along the New River. Lamanai (along with a few other CITIES in western Belize and northern GUATEMALA) survived into the early 17th century, considerably reduced in size but still a vital community.

While the Classic period (250–900) is most commonly associated with the Petén and southern Campeche sites, numerous Belizean Maya sites shared in the overall dynamism of the region. CARACOL was the largest of these centers and managed to hold its own against its aggressive neighbor TIKAL. Farther to the north, but also on the Mopan River, Xunantunich (stone woman) prospered until its eventual collapse around 900. Altún Ha (heavy stones beside water) also stood out in the same time. In 1968, archaeologists working in this northeastern Belizean zone discovered the largest jade carving of the Maya world, a 9.75-pound (4.43-kg) representation of the sun god K'inich Ahau. Meanwhile, numerous other centers emerged in southern Belize. These include Lubaantún, famous for its carefully cut, mortarless stones, and Nim Li Punit, site of the country's largest stela.

The first Spanish attempts to conquer the Belize region produced little result. Alonso Dávila entered the region as part of FRANCISCO DE MONTEJO's initial attempt to subdue the Yucatán Peninsula but was forced to withdraw owing to stiff Maya resistance. In 1543–44 Gaspar Pacheco, his son Melchor, and his nephew Alonso succeeded in establishing the first semipermanent Spanish presence near present-day Bacalar. They gathered tribute from the northern Belize region for a time, but key Maya cities maintained their independence and eventually forced out the Spanish in the early 1600s.

See also BELIZE (Vols. II. III. IV).

—Terry Rugeley

Benavente, Toribio de (Motolinía) (b. ca. 1482/ 1491–d. 1569) *Franciscan friar famous for his ministry among Central Mexico's indigenous peoples*

While there is a great deal of uncertainty regarding the early history of Toribio de Benavente's life in Spain (born ca. 1482–91), there is much less when it comes to his last 45 years, which he spent in MEXICO (1524–69). That is because like his fellow Franciscan BERNARDINO DE SAHAGÚN, Benavente was a foundational member of the Mexican church and an important figure in the fledgling colony of New Spain.

He reached the Gulf coast of Mexico in May 1524 in the company of 11 other Franciscans (see RELIGIOUS ORDERS). Although preceded by other clerics, this was the first official delegation of priests to reach the newly conquered territory. They became known later as "the Twelve." The number was no accident, for these friars viewed themselves as following in the footsteps of the Apostles. While they slowly made their way from the coast to MEXICO CITY, Benavente discovered that the Indians began to refer to the friars as *motolinía*, a NAHUATL term that translates as "poor, afflicted one[s]." Benavente considered this a divine sign and made it part of his name. It stuck so firmly that it has been his primary designation ever since.

During his long tenure in the New World, Motolinía served in many capacities. He was a parish priest, administrator, Franciscan representative before the civil and royal authorities, and writer. At a time when travel was slow going by foot, horse, or ship, he was posted all over colonial Mexico; he also traveled as far as GUATEMALA and NICARAGUA, where he visited the famous Masaya Volcano. In the 1550s, he engaged in public disputations with the famed Dominican friar BARTOLOMÉ DE LAS CASAS, the "Defender of the Indians." While few of Motolinía's writings survive, those that do bear witness to many of the church's early successes in converting, baptizing, and indoctrinating the indigenous peoples of Mexico. Motolinía outlived all the other members of "the Twelve," dying in Mexico City in 1569.

See also FRANCISCANS (Vol. II).

—Barry D. Sell

Further reading:
Motolinía (Benavente), fray Toribio de. *Historia de los indios de la Nueva Espana* (Madrid: Alianza, 1988).
Robert Ricard. *The Spiritual Conquest of Mexico*, translated by Lesley Byrd Simpson (Berkeley: University of California Press, 1966).

Bobadilla, Francisco de (d. 1502) *Christopher Columbus's successor as governor of West Indies*

By 1500, rumors were circulating throughout Spain of CHRISTOPHER COLUMBUS and his brothers' incompetence in ruling the island of HISPANIOLA. As a result, the Spanish monarchs, King Ferdinand and Queen Isabella, sent Francisco de Bobadilla to replace Columbus as governor of the colony. The powers bestowed on Bobadilla far outreached those given to his predecessor. In all likelihood, Bobadilla was given such leverage because he was both a nobleman and a knight.

Bobadilla was a religious knight of the Order of Calatrava. He chronicled the brutal nature of Columbus's regime in the Americas (see CHRONICLERS). According to his 48-page document, Columbus was harshest on his own followers. Bobadilla reported that a man who stole corn out of hunger had his nose and ears cut off before being auctioned off as a slave and that a woman who slandered Columbus's nobility was stripped naked and forced to ride through town on a mule.

In 1500, with his orders from the king and queen, and a crew of 500 men and a handful of slaves, Bobadilla took his place as the new governor of the Indies. He sent Columbus and his brothers back to Spain in shackles. However, Bobadilla's tenure as governor was even more disastrous than that of his predecessor. Under his rule, the conditions of indigenous slaves grew to be subhuman. Bobadilla also demonstrated clear favoritism toward his followers, to whom he gave gifts of land and franchises.

Bobadilla governed until 1502, when he was replaced by Nicolás de Ovando. During the return voyage to Spain, Francisco de Bobadilla's ship was struck by a hurricane and Bobadilla drowned.

—Christina Hawkins

Further reading:
Pedro L. San Miguel. *The Imagined Island: History, Identity and Utopia in Hispaniola* (Chapel Hill: University of North Carolina Press, 2005).

Bogotá

The city of Bogotá is located in the fertile plains of COLOMBIA's eastern highlands. Its name derives from a powerful MUISCA ruler (sometimes called Bacatá) who governed this densely populated region when the first expedition of Spanish conquistadores arrived in 1537 (see CONQUEST). Led by GONZALO JIMÉNEZ DE QUESADA, this small expeditionary force of 179 Spaniards spent almost two years exploring Muisca territory before they founded the city. Eventually, Jiménez de Quesada's decision to establish a formal settlement was based on the unexpected arrival of two other expeditions. In February 1539, NIKOLAUS FEDERMANN's (Nicolás Federmán) expeditionary force arrived from VENEZUELA, and less than two months later, another Spanish force, this one led by Sebastián de Belalcázar, arrived from Quito (ECUADOR). Both Belalcázar and Federmann attempted to lay claim to the region. While the region had no GOLD or SILVER mines, its fertile soils, dense indigenous population, and EMERALD and salt mines were highly attractive to the Spanish conquistadores. Thus, in an effort to help legitimize his own claim to the conquest, Jiménez ordered the foundation of the region's first three Spanish towns, Santafé de Bogotá, Tunja, and Vélez. Bogotá's foundation date is April 27, 1539.

During the initial years of Spanish settlement, Bogotá maintained much of its pre-Columbian character. The city's early European inhabitants lived in Indian houses, or *bohíos*, which were constructed from dried mud and thatch. It was not until after 1542 that Bogotá's municipal authorities issued orders to build residences with brick or stone. In 1549, just a decade after its humble foundation, the Spanish Crown officially recognized the region's growing importance and authorized the establishment of an *AUDIENCIA* at the site of Colombia's modern capital city. Still, by 1560, the region remained dominated by the surrounding population of Muisca Indians, which likely exceeded 200,000. By contrast, Bogotá's Spanish population at the time numbered less than a few thousand.

See also BOGOTÁ (Vols. II, III, IV).

—J. Michael Francis

Further reading:

J. Michael Francis. *Invading Colombia: Spanish Accounts of the Gonzalo Jiménez de Quesada Expedition of Conquest* (University Park: Pennsylvania State University Press, 2007).

Frank Safford and Marco Palacios. *Colombia: Fragmented Land, Divided Society* (New York: Oxford University Press, 2002).

Bolivia Bolivia has three major environmental zones: the altiplano, the mid-elevation valleys, and the Amazonian jungle (see AMAZON). Accordingly, the patterns of the early inhabitants of Bolivia followed different trajectories. The altiplano is a high-altitude (12,000–15,000 feet [3,658–4,572 m]), essentially treeless grassland in a plateaulike basin bounded on the east and west by two parallel ranges of the Andes. The environment is semiarid, with annual rainfall decreasing from the north to south from 24 inches (609 mm) to four inches (101 mm), respectively. The eastern slopes of the Andes broaden into two major valleys in the Cochabamba and Chuquisaca areas, which have wetter, milder climates. The Amazonian jungle area includes major drainages of the Amazon River and has an annual rainfall of about 118 inches (2,997 mm).

The earliest evidence of human habitation in the altiplano and central valley areas dates back to about 11,000–12,000 years ago. At sites such as Mina Avaroca in the altiplano, hunter-gatherer populations exploited wild guanaco and vicuña herds and apparently colonized the area from the Pacific coast. In the mid-valley to the east in present-day Cochabamba, at sites such as Jaihuayco, Mayra Pampa, and Ñuapua, there is evidence of the killing of late Pleistocene megafauna such as *Equus* and *Mylodon* dating from approximately 11,000 years ago. The Bolivian Amazonian area has not yet yielded sites of comparable age; however, in the Brazilian Amazonia across the border, sites associated with extinct fauna dating to 11,500–13,000 years ago indicate that the Bolivian Amazon region was also inhabited this early.

While the earliest altiplano inhabitants may have moved between the Pacific coast and Bolivian zones on a seasonal basis, by 10,000 years ago, there is clear evidence of year-round altiplano occupation. These ancestors of the TIWANAKU and INCAS began an agropastoral lifestyle, herding camelids and cultivating plants, around 8,000 years ago (see AGRICULTURE). While initially it was supposed that llama and alpaca were domesticated prior to plants and were first domesticated in the central highlands of PERU, there is new evidence of a possible second center of camelid domestication in the central Bolivian altiplano. In the wetter areas near Lake Titicaca, several varieties of POTATO and other root crops and various types of native grains (Chenopod family) were being cultivated by the Late Archaic period, 4,000–5,000 years ago. In the drier southern areas, due to a lack of adequate precipitation to grow crops, a more complete animal-based type of pastoral nomadism evolved.

In the mid-elevation eastern valleys, with their milder climates, a much more robust collecting and gathering ECONOMY evolved during the Archaic period. Preliminary evidence indicates this also occurred in the Amazonian lowlands.

The Formative period began around 4,000 years ago in Bolivia. In the altiplano, this period saw the development of settled villages, as well as a local religious tradition, Pajano, which originated in the Lake Titicaca area (and a variant of which spread to southern Peru, where it was called Yaya-Mama). The Pajano tradition was first characterized by fish, amphibian, and reptilian motifs but later included a dyadic component of wet-dry, male-female, and so on. Typically, subterranean rectangular temples were constructed; these were adorned with stone stelae and panels and, later, were also usually associated with mounds and U-shaped complexes. Copper, SILVER, and GOLD artifacts were considered items of wealth, and in the later part of the period, the first metal alloys were produced. The production of pottery is one of the hallmarks of the Formative period. Among the items that began to appear in the altiplano, some were part of a "hallucinogenic complex" that included such material artifacts as incense burners, snuff tablets, and inhaling tubes, which are believed to have been introduced from the valleys or lowlands, as the hallucinogenic substances that were used derive from those areas.

Agricultural villages began appearing in the mid-valley at the same time as they appeared on the altiplano. Initially assumed to be the result of diffusion from the altiplano, CERAMICS inventories for the mid-valley show clear relationships with Amazonian groups as well as altiplano influences. Therefore, one can parse a kind of two-pronged spread of sociocultural complexity into Bolivia: one emanating from the Pacific coast and Peru and a second coming from Amazonia into the Bolivian lowlands and spreading up the Amazon tributaries.

The second great Andean empire, the Tiwanaku, emerged during the first millennium C.E., from ca. 300 to 1100. During this time, the polygonal architectural style that became the hallmark of the Incas was developed, as were the tin-copper and tin-nickel-copper binary and ternary alloy bronzes, elaborately decorated ceramic ritual corn beer (CHICHA) drinking cups (called *keros*), and the string-knot counting system (see *QUIPU*). The vibrant, independent, but closely allied Cochabamba federation emerged in the mid-valley as an important trade partner for Tiwanaku, while further east the large Mojocoya chiefdom evolved. In northern Bolivian Amazonia, in the Llanos de Mojos region of the lowlands, this period also appears to have seen the initial development of the immense complex of canals, causeways, and mounds.

After the demise of the Tiwanaku Empire, the Bolivian altiplano was marked by an era of political balkanization. The highland altiplano was re-formed into a dozen or more autonomous polities. Conflict seems to have characterized the political sphere (evidenced by the remains of elaborate fortresses, or *pucarás*), as different groups vied for dominance or simply for survival. Ultimately, all were to be conquered by a group evolving in similar circumstances farther north, the Incas.

Although less studied, a similar pattern of fractionation appears to have characterized the mid-valley polities and the Amazonian area. Although the Incas conquered and incorporated the mid-valley and altiplano into their empire in the 1400s, the Spanish CONQUEST followed so closely that during the postconquest colonial period, the disparate *señoríos* (or chiefdoms) that characterized Bolivia up until the 19th-century establishment of the republic generally reverted back to the kingdoms that had emerged following the decline of the Tiwanaku.

See also BOLIVIA (Vols. II, III, IV).

—David L. Browman

Further reading:

William L. Balee and Clark L. Erickson. *Time and Complexity in Historical Ecology: Studies in the Neotropical Lowlands* (New York: Columbia University Press, 2006).
John W. Janusek. *Ancient Tiwanaku: Civilization in the High Andes* (Cambridge: Cambridge University Press, 2008).

Brazil   The early history of Brazil is part of the larger story of Portuguese expansion. Portugal, located on the edge of western Europe, was in many ways a bridge between the Mediterranean and the Atlantic during the early modern era. The origins of Portugal's expansionism can be traced to the invasion of Ceuta in North Africa in 1415. In the decades that followed, Portuguese mariners explored the coasts of western Africa and moved into the Atlantic, colonizing Madeira, the Azores, the Cape Verde Islands, and São Tomé. In 1488, Bartholomeu Dias rounded the Cape of Good Hope and sailed up the coast of eastern Africa, laying the groundwork for Vasco da Gama's epic voyage to Calicut (in modern-day India) a decade later. In 1510, Afonso de Albuquerque defeated the Muslim rulers of Bijapur, effectively gaining control of Goa. In the years that followed, his compatriots would extend Portugal's reach all the way to Macau (near modern-day Hong Kong). First discovered in 1500 in the midst of Portugal's drive to reach Asia, Brazil would eventually become the largest and most important component of Portugal's overseas empire. In this regard, the social, political, and economic foundations of Brazilian history are firmly rooted in the larger context of Portuguese expansion and in the encounters between Europeans and other peoples during the 15th and 16th centuries.

The early colonization of Brazil built on Portugal's experiences during the preceding decades. In Africa, Portuguese mariners had confronted a number of large, complex societies whose inhabitants had developed immunity to European DISEASES over centuries of intermittent contact. Unlike the Spanish in MEXICO or PERU, the Portuguese in Africa had neither the manpower nor the unexpected epidemiological advantages to create an inland empire. Instead, they created coastal factories or fortified trading posts in order to barter with local allies for GOLD and slaves (see SLAVERY; TRADE). Portugal's Atlantic islands, on the other hand, were largely uninhabited upon the Europeans' arrival, enabling more permanent settlements to be established. On Madeira and São Tomé, the Portuguese established plantation-based economies that produced large quantities of SUGAR for European markets (see ECONOMY). Significantly, both of these patterns of development would be used in Brazil over the course of the 16th century.

During the first three decades after the discovery of Brazil in 1500, Portuguese attempts to colonize the new land were limited. Brazil was used primarily as a convenient stopover for the far more lucrative voyages to India. The only commodity found to be of value in the new land during these years was brazilwood, a form of dyewood that would eventually give the new land its name (see DYES AND DYEWOOD). As fortified trading posts were established along the coast of Brazil in order to barter with indigenous groups for dyewood and fresh supplies, other Europeans, especially the French, began to compete for control of the new land. In response, the Portuguese Crown implemented a series of reforms, including the establishment of DONATARY CAPTAINCIES and the subsequent creation of a colonial bureaucracy, and the use of large-scale military expeditions. By the end of the 1560s, Portugal had successfully expelled the French from Brazil and had consolidated its control over indigenous groups along the coast.

Although the demographic data is imprecise, scholars estimate that Brazil's pre-Columbian population ranged between 2 and 5 million people. The Portuguese divided Brazilian indigenous peoples into two distinct groups based on language. The Tupí (sometimes referred to as Tupí-GUARANÍ) inhabited the coast from Ceará in the northeast to São Paulo in the south and then inland into the Paraná and Paraguay river basins (see TUPINAMBÁ). The Tapuya (a generic Tupí term that referred to non-Tupí speakers) were found north of Ceará and interspersed at different points along the coast. The Portuguese were most familiar with Tupí society, and much of what we know about pre-Columbian Brazil is based on this diverse group. As the Portuguese CHRONICLER Pêro de Magalhães Gândavo wrote in 1570, "It is impossible to either enumerate or comprehend the multitude of barbarous heathen that Nature has planted throughout this land of Brazil." Modern scholars believe that there were in fact between 40 and 100 distinct language families spoken in 16th-century Brazil. Many, but not all, are now classified under three general headings: the Tupí and the Gê (corresponding, in part, to the Tapuya), as well as Arawak/Carib speakers in the north.

Native civilizations in Brazil were very different from what the Spanish encountered in Mexico and Peru. Unlike their counterparts in Mesoamerica and the Andes, the Brazilian indigenous consisted largely of seminomadic peoples who practiced slash-and-burn forms of AGRICULTURE, with subsistence-based economies. In addition to hunting, fishing, and gathering fruit, for example, Tupí society cultivated beans, MAIZE, squash, and MANIOC and migrated to new areas when the soil gave out. Contact and trade between different groups was limited, even among those who spoke similar tongues. WARFARE was common, and many groups practiced ritualistic CANNIBALISM. Aside from LABOR, Brazil's indigenous people offered little in the way of wealth for early colonists, and initial interactions centered mainly on the dyewood trade as well as formal and informal sexual liaisons. In this regard, by the middle of the 16th century, the *mameluco* offspring of Luso-indigenous unions formed a significant segment of Brazilian society, particularly in São Paulo and Pernambuco.

As was the case throughout the Americas, the discovery of indigenous peoples in Brazil raised important questions about how New World populations should be understood and treated. In both Spain and Portugal, the debate pitted church and state against local settlers, who sought to make use of indigenous peoples for tribute and labor. In the case of Brazil, the Portuguese Crown generally maintained that Brazil's indigenous groups should not be enslaved but rather converted to Christianity. Significantly, Jesuit missionaries first arrived in Brazil in 1549 with the country's first governor general (see RELIGIOUS ORDERS). In time, the Society of Jesus would become the most important institutional force in the new colony with the possible exception of the Portuguese state itself. The Jesuits and other missionaries established a system of *aldeias*, or mission villages, in which they housed and tutored native people who agreed to give up the practices of cannibalism and polygamy or who otherwise sought protection from local settlers. *Aldeias* would subsequently become a standard mode of European-indigenous interaction in Brazil through the mid-18th century, when the Jesuits were expelled from the Portuguese Empire.

Like the Jesuit missionaries, local colonists had designs on the New World native population. During the three decades after the discovery of Brazil, indigenous labor was limited mainly to the dyewood trade. By the mid-16th century, however, native slaves were sought for a variety of other work, including to labor on sugar plantations, which were becoming increasingly important in the northeast. In this regard, in spite of royal and religious efforts to prevent indigenous slavery, the enslavement of natives by local settlers would play an important role in the colony's economic development through the mid-17th century. For Brazil's indigenous, the shift from barter to a plantation-based slave economy came at a critical demographic moment. Although Brazil's indigenous population steadily decreased over the course of the 16th century, this was especially the case in the 1560s, when a series of severe epidemics devastated native populations. Thereafter, Portuguese-indigenous relations would be fundamentally changed, as indigenous labor was less available and increasingly expensive. Additionally, Portuguese planters came to believe that the land's seminomadic native population had little aptitude for the intense and highly skilled labor required on the sugar plantations.

In order to solve the labor shortage, mill owners drew on Portugal's history in Madeira and São Tomé, importing large numbers of African slaves to work on the sugar plantations. Although the transition from indigenous to mainly African labor would not be complete until the 1630s, by the end of the 16th century, the Portuguese had clearly staked the future of the colony on the African slave trade. As the first nation in the Western Hemisphere in which African slavery was instituted on a large scale, Brazil would also be the last to give it up. Whether laboring on rural plantations along the coast, in mining districts in the interior, or in urban centers, African slaves were a fundamental reason for Brazil's future economic success. Although Asia would remain an imperial priority for Portugal for the next century, by the late 1560s, all of the major factors were in place for Brazil to become the most dynamic and dominant component of Portugal's overseas empire.

See also BRAZIL (Vols. II, III, IV); COLÔNIA DO SACRAMENTO (Vol. II); MARANHÃO (Vol. II); MINAS GERAIS (Vol. II); PERNAMBUCO (Vol. II); RIO DE JANEIRO (Vols. III, IV); SÃO PAULO (Vols. II, III, IV).

—Erik Myrup

Further reading:
Leslie Bethel, ed. *Colonial Brazil* (New York: Cambridge University Press, 1987).

brazilwood   See DYES AND DYEWOOD.

Buenos Aires   Unlike other colonial urban centers such as MEXICO CITY, BOGOTÁ, or CUZCO, the city of Buenos Aires, in modern-day ARGENTINA, was not constructed on the site of a pre-Columbian native settlement. In fact, Buenos Aires began as a temporary Spanish encampment on the banks of a remote estuary in southeastern South America.

In 1534, in response to growing competition between the crowns of Spain and Portugal over jurisdiction in eastern South America, Castile's monarch, King Charles I, reached an accord with a Spanish nobleman named PEDRO DE MENDOZA. The agreement, or *capitulación*, authorized Mendoza to prepare a large expedition to settle the region around the Río de la Plata (River Plate, or literally, "Silver River"). In exchange, Mendoza was appointed governor of the new lands, from which he was entitled to receive a handsome share of their riches. Mendoza prepared an armada of 16 ships carrying 1,600 men, as well as cattle, horses, and other accoutrements necessary for the establishment of a permanent settlement. In February 1536, Mendoza's armada arrived at the River Plate, where they founded an encampment that they named Puerto Nuestra Señora Santa María del Buen Aire.

The new settlement did not last long. Persistent attacks from nearby indigenous groups, combined with starvation and DISEASE, devastated the European settlers. Within 18 months of their arrival, Mendoza's force had fallen by two-thirds. The settlement was finally abandoned in 1541, its survivors transferring to Asunción (PARAGUAY). It was not until 1580 that a permanent Spanish settlement was established on the site of modern Buenos Aires; the Spaniards christened the new town Ciudad de Santa María de la Santísima y Puerto de Santa María de los Buenos Ayres. More than a century would pass before Buenos Aires began to emerge as one of South America's most important urban centers.

See also ARGENTINA (Vols. II, III, IV); BUENOS AIRES (Vols. II, III, IV).

—J. Michael Francis

Further reading:
David Rock. *Argentina, 1516–1987: From Spanish Colonization to Alfonsín* (Berkeley: University of California Press, 1987).

Burgos, Laws of   See LAWS OF BURGOS.

C

Cabeza de Vaca, Álvar Núñez (b. ca. 1485/1492– d. 1559) *survivor of the failed expedition to Florida, later wrote famous account of his eight-year journey across North America* After successful service in the military (1511–21), Álvar Núñez Cabeza de Vaca received a royal appointment to serve as treasurer on Pánfilo de Narváez's 1527 expedition to Florida. The Spanish Crown had authorized Narváez to lead an expedition to conquer and settle the lands from the Río de las Palmas (northeast Mexico) to Florida; however, the expedition ended in disaster, and most of its participants, including Narváez, were killed. In 1528, a hurricane redirected the expedition from its intended destination off the western coast of the Gulf of Mexico to the eastern gulf coast. By raft and foot, the surviving conquistadores traveled westward along the shore. On the east Texas coast, Cabeza de Vaca was separated from the others and taken captive by Native Americans he encountered there. Five years later, in 1533, Cabeza de Vaca was reunited with the only three survivors of the Narváez expedition, out of more than 500. The four continued down the coast, crossing through south Texas and eventually reaching northwest Mexico. As they headed south in 1536, down Mexico's western coast, they encountered Spanish soldiers and thus began their journey home.

Though Cabeza de Vaca returned to Europe in 1537, it took five years for his account, *La relación* (later known as *Naufragios*), to be published. It was written as a *probanza de mérito*, or "proof-of-merit petition," to request royal compensation for his services and sufferings. In the account, Cabeza de Vaca expressed his interest in returning to the Americas under royal commission. In 1540, he was given the title of *adelantado* and appointed governor of the Río de la Plata province of South America. However, Cabeza de Vaca's governorship was cut short when, in 1544, he was arrested and escorted back to Spain. Tried seven years later, he was at first stripped of his titles and charged with crimes such as misconduct in office and abuse of native populations; however, the penalties were drastically reduced, and his reputation was eventually restored.

Cabeza de Vaca's 1542 *Relación* offers one of the first geographic and ethnographic accounts of the landscapes and peoples of North America. He recounts the harsh treatment he received by some Indians he encountered, as well as the trust and respect he found among others. Essentially living the life of a native—even posing as a powerful shaman—Cabeza de Vaca urged his fellow Spaniards to treat the indigenous people well and proposed peaceful pacification over violent conquest. Later expeditions, such as those under Hernando de Soto and Francisco Vásquez de Coronado, would consult Cabeza de Vaca's *Relación* in the hopes of locating and conquering rich new kingdoms in North America.

—Saber Gray

Further reading:
Rolena Adorno and Patrick Pautz. *Álvar Núñez Cabeza de Vaca: His Account, His Life, and the Expedition of Pánfilo de Narváez,* 3 vols. (Lincoln: University of Nebraska Press, 1999).

cabildo The *cabildo* was the city council in colonial Latin America. Spanish political theory of the Middle Ages and early modern period held that in the absence of other governmental units, the city council was the most elemental governmental institution. As a result, in order to both claim and incorporate new territory into the Spanish Crown, conquistadores would frequently first establish a city and a city council for its governance.

The *cabildo* consisted of as many as 24 *regidores* (see *REGIDOR*). Initially in the New World, these city councilmen were elected by the citizens of the city. Eventually, however, they fell under the royal patrimony, and the Crown began to appoint important personages of the colony to these seats. By the late 16th century, the Crown had begun the practice of selling seats on the city councils at public auction. The winning bidder received not only the right to enjoy the office throughout his life but, on payment of a bonus, could name a successor.

The *regidores* governed CITIES in accordance with Spanish law and tradition. They generally received no salary for their service, although occasionally they would allocate small sums to themselves for certain activities. They regulated local government, including allocating land for houses and garden plots, monitoring the city's supply of FOOD and water, seeing to public safety, and managing the municipal courts. The authority of the colonial Spanish city extended into the hinterland until it came under the authority of another city or other governmental unit. Consequently, city councils also controlled farming and ranching in the hinterland.

The *cabildo* also included two municipal court judges (*alcaldes*). They were elected annually by the *regidores*. Normally, one judge supervised the municipal courts, while the other served the farmers' and ranchers' court.

See also *CABILDO ABIERTO* (Vol. II).

—John F. Schwaller

Further reading:
John Preston Moore. *The Cabildo in Peru under the Hapsburgs* (Durham, N.C.: Duke University Press, 1954).

Cabral, Pedro Álvares (b. ca. 1467–d. ca. 1520)
Portuguese discoverer of Brazil A native of Belmonte, Portugal, Pedro Álvares Cabral was born into a well-connected aristocratic FAMILY. His father, Fernão Cabral, was a councilor to King John II, and his mother, Isabel de Gouveia, was descended from a prominent family in the Beira region. As a young nobleman, Cabral benefited from royal patronage, studying literature, cosmography, and the arts with other young peers at court.

Following Vasco da Gama's epic voyage to India (1497–99), the now adult Cabral was awarded command of a follow-up expedition. He set sail in early March 1500, with 13 ships and more than 1,200 men. In the weeks that followed, the expedition passed the Canary Islands and the Cape Verde Islands before veering southwest in order to avoid the doldrums and catch the trade winds that would carry the ships around the Cape of Good Hope. In the process, the Portuguese fleet swung wide, stumbling upon the coast of northeastern BRAZIL.

On April 22, Cabral's scouts spotted a distant mountaintop near modern-day Porto Seguro. The following day, Cabral sent a small party ashore. Altogether, the fleet remained in this vicinity for nine days, replenishing supplies and attempting to TRADE with the region's indigenous in order to facilitate future voyages.

Cabral eventually weighed anchor in early May, sending one ship back to Portugal with news of the discovery, while the remainder continued the voyage to India. Cabral finally reached Calicut in September 1500. There, he engaged in heavy fighting with Muslim traders before being forced to retreat to Cochin, where he was better received. During the months that followed, the expedition suffered a number of setbacks. By the time Cabral sailed up the Tagus in late July 1501, only five of his ships remained.

Although the discoverer of Brazil was initially well received by the Crown, Cabral would subsequently fall from royal favor; in fact, his journey to India would be his first and last voyage. Two years later, he married Isabel de Castro. Together they raised six children on a small estate near Santarém. Although the exact date of Cabral's death is not known, probate records indicate that he died sometime before late 1520, when his remaining possessions were divided among his heirs.

—Erik Myrup

Further reading:
William Brooks Greenlee, ed. *The Voyage of Pedro Álvares Cabral to Brazil and India* (London: Hakluyt Society, 1938).

cacao Described as the "food of the gods" by the 18th-century botanist Carl Linnaeus, cacao has a long and complex history in the Americas. From the Classic period (250–900 C.E.) and through the early colonial period, the TRADE and consumption of cacao beans served as a symbol of wealth and power in Mesoamerica. Under Spanish rule, political and religious leaders attempted to control both its production and consumption by the indigenous population.

Growing only in the tropics, cacao (*Theobromba cacao*) was domesticated in the Central American rain forests during the 15th century B.C.E. (see AGRICULTURE). Archaeological records from the Classic period indicate that cacao was a high-value commodity that symbolized noble status and prestige. Epigraphers deciphered the term *kakawa* (the origin of the modern term) on drinking vessels associated with royal MAYA burials. Large-scale glyphics texts from the period describe the consumption of cacao-based drinks during rituals associated with marriage and succession. Although production was limited to a few subtropical regions, during the Postclassic, cacao was used throughout MEXICO, Central America, and the AMAZON. For the Mexica (AZTECS) of Central Mexico, cacao served as both a commodity and a form of currency.

In TENOCHTITLÁN, imbibing cacao, which was mixed with MAIZE and chilies, was a luxury open only to Mexica nobles. In Chiapas, tribute payments were largely made in cacao, a practice that continued through the early colonial period.

Sixteenth-century Europeans viewed cacao with trepidation. While CHRONICLERS and explorers struggled to define its physical properties, religious officials challenged its use in rituals (see RELIGION). Religious officials in GUATEMALA, for example, equated the production of cacao beverages by indigenous women with WITCHCRAFT and sorcery. Chocolate arrived in Europe in 1544 with a group of Maya elites who displayed it before the future king of Spain, Philip II. It was not, however, until the 17th century that the importation and use of cacao by Europeans became acceptable.

See also AGRICULTURE (Vols. II, III, IV); CACAO (Vols. II, III).

—R. A. Kashanipour

Further reading:
Sophie D. Coe and Michael D. Coe. *The True History of Chocolate* (London: Thames & Hudson, 1996).

cacique   The term *cacique* was a TAINO or Arawak word used to indicate a ruler or chief. A *cacicazgo*, or chiefdom, from which the term *cacique* derives, refers to a type of society that is territorially based, possesses an incipient bureaucracy, and is ruled by a chief who retains arbitrary but limited power. Certain goods and services are concentrated in a permanent centralized authority, which performs a redistribution function. Tribute, gifts, or surplus production are used as a way of manipulating the distribution of goods and services throughout the entire society. Most *cacicazgos* were found in the Greater Antilles, northern coastal South America, the northern Andes, eastern Bolivia, lower Central America, and parts of Mesoamerica.

The Spaniards adopted the concept, and it came to replace the local indigenous terms of leadership throughout the entire colonial system. After the CONQUEST, caciques served as cultural brokers, or buffers, in dealings with Spaniards and, in doing so, often prevented exploitation and cultural disorganization. In return for their services, caciques received tribute from properties worked by dependent laborers and, in regions with a market system, taxes from the local marketplace. They engaged in such commercial enterprises as sheep and cattle ranching and the raising of silkworms.

Caciques also acquired privileges such as the right to carry swords or firearms and to ride horses or mules. They adopted prestigious Spanish surnames and honorific titles, such as *don*. When the Spaniards first introduced municipal councils, the cacique in the first postconquest generation usually filled the highest office of governor and typically served for life, a reflection of the hereditary nature of indigenous rulership (see ALTEPETL; CAH). Caciques actively sought the confirmation and protection of rights associated with rulership from Spanish authorities and increasingly claimed their landholdings as private property.

By the 16th century, the term cacique referred to the heir of a preconquest ruler and the single possessor of a *cacicazgo*. The affluence and influence of the cacique, however, deteriorated rapidly during later colonial times. Epidemics led to the loss of population and thus tribute (see DISEASE). Spanish authorities further limited income by progressively eliminating exempt tribute categories. The decay of the missionary system, the ineffectual efforts of the government to control exploitation of the Indians, the inability of Indian towns to preserve their lands and status, and the subordination of Indians to systems of hacienda and peonage contributed further to the decline of the cacique.

See also CACIQUE (Vol. II).

—John M. Weeks

Further reading:
Robert Kern, ed. *The Caciques: Oligarchical Politics and the System of Caciquismo in the Luso-Hispanic World* (Albuquerque: University of New Mexico Press, 1973).

cah   The term *cah* (plural, *cahob*) is a MAYA word used to describe the organizational unit of the pre-Columbian and colonial Maya. Although *cah* can be loosely translated as "town," it meant much more to the Maya. The *cah* was the central unit of Maya culture and society and served a conceptual, geographical, and sociopolitical role. Each individual was considered a *cahnal*, or "*cah* member," and lived on a *cah* house plot among a *chibal*, or "patronym group," made up of relatives and close associates. A Maya's relationship to his or her *cah* was so strong that it served as the context for self-identity. Indeed, the Maya lacked a term of ethnic designation, such as "Indian," a generic term used by Spaniards for all the indigenous inhabitants of the Americas. Instead, their self-identity centered around the *cah*, creating an "us-and-them" distinction, with the members of the *cah* being "us," and all others, including other Maya from different *cahob*, being "them."

As a geographical entity, each *cah* had specific boundaries that included both the house plots of the community and land located outside the *cah* that was used or owned by its members. All *cahob* had a plaza surrounded by administrative and religious buildings and the homes of the *cah*'s important families. Politically, the *cah* was organized with a BATAB, or "governor," and other administrative positions filled by nobles. Also, the *chibal* largely determined the economic and sociopolitical organization of the *cah*, creating units and subunits of varying class and status.

After the arrival of the Spaniards, the *cah* continued to serve its central role in the lives of the Maya, largely functioning in the same way as it had before. Indeed, although the *cah* began to exhibit elements of Spanish culture—such as cathedrals, CABILDOS (town councils), and Spanish goods—it absorbed such elements within existing frameworks. In nearly all of the extant colonial Maya documentation—especially that of the 16th century—individual Mayas continued to identify themselves not as Indians but rather as members of a particular *cah*.

—Mark Christensen

Further reading:
Matthew Restall. *The Maya World: Yucatec Culture and Society, 1550–1850* (Stanford, Calif.: Stanford University Press, 1997).

Calakmul The pre-Columbian MAYA center of Calakmul (Kaan) flourished in what is today southern Campeche state, MEXICO. It lay midway between the Gulf of Mexico and the Caribbean coast and probably mediated much of the transcoastal TRADE, working through a network of smaller, nearby centers such as Dzibanché and Kohunlich.

Around 500 C.E., Calakmul began a long rivalry with its southern neighbor, TIKAL. Initially, the upstart city got the better of the contest: Calakmul defeated Tikal in a major battle in 562, although the city of Tikal itself survived. In 679, Calakmul's leaders compelled Bajal Chan Kawiil, lord of the vassal city of Dos Pilas, to launch a ferocious attack on Tikal. The latter was subdued, but two decades later a new ruler revitalized Tikal and launched a new offensive. This time the northern rival was defeated, bringing an end to Calakmul's expansion. Much like the Peloponnesian War in Greece, the protracted struggle ultimately sapped the entire region and led to its generalized collapse from about 600 onward. Both Tikal and Calakmul shared in this decline, and by 900, the two supercenters were largely abandoned.

—Terry Rugeley

Further reading:
Simon Martin and Nicolai Grube. *Chronicle of the Maya Kings and Queens: Deciphering the Dynasties of the Ancient Maya* (London: Thames & Hudson, 2000).

***calpulli* (calpolli)** *Calpulli* in NAHUATL means literally "big house" and is the preferred word in sources such as the FLORENTINE CODEX for the named subunits of the ALTEPETL. Nevertheless, indigenous scribes more frequently referred to these subunits as *tlaxilacalli* (the etymology is uncertain; however, the last element is apparently *calli*, meaning "house" or "structure"). Their closely shared meaning when glossed in Spanish was

barrio (neighborhood, district); nonetheless, the *calpulli* were not identical to the subdivisions of European sociopolitical units.

Rather than a hierarchically organized center with dependencies, each *altepetl* had its own *tlaxilacalli/calpulli*, organized in a cellular or modular structure. Ideally in pairs, fours, or eights (although the numbers greatly varied), each *altepetl* subunit was the equal of the others, at least in theory. A microcosm of the whole, each was also potentially the basis of a new *altepetl*. Community tasks and responsibilities rotated in a fixed order (usually based on perceived seniority and importance) between the subunits. This sort of less linear framework can also be found in other areas of Nahua life, such as the household compound, monumental art, song/poetry, and traditional rhetoric.

Counterparts of the *tlaxilacalli/calpulli* can be found in some Mesoamerican areas and not in others. The *siqui, siña,* and *dzini,* as they were called in various Mixtec dialects, are comparable to the central Mexican subunits (see MIXTECS); on the other hand, the MAYA equivalent of the *altepetl,* the *CAH,* apparently did not contain similar subunits.

As central as the *tlaxilacalli/calpulli* were to community life, the *altepetl* remained the foremost expression of unit identity. *Altepetl* names were often unique or uncommon, while those of *tlaxilacalli/calpulli* were repeated over and over. When native record-keepers ascribed an affiliation to individuals or families, their membership in an *altepetl* (with or without mention of the specific subunit) was the most common way to indicate group affiliation.

—Barry D. Sell

Further reading:
Rebecca Horn. *Postconquest Coyoacan: Nahua-Spanish Relations in Central Mexico, 1519–1650* (Stanford, Calif.: Stanford University Press, 1997).
Kevin Terraciano. *The Mixtecs of Colonial Oaxaca: Ñudzahui History, Sixteenth through Eighteenth Centuries* (Stanford, Calif.: Stanford University Press, 2001).

cannibalism In 1493, soon after landing in the New World on his second voyage, CHRISTOPHER COLUMBUS sent a report to the Spanish monarchs, Isabella and Ferdinand, offering his initial impressions of the Caribbean islands. In the letter, Columbus claimed that one of the islands was inhabited by bald people, another by Amazons, one by people with tails, and still another by cannibals (see AMAZON WOMEN). The letter contains the first reference to New World cannibals. Indeed, the word *cannibal* originated from Columbus's men, who heard the Caribbean natives refer to a nearby indigenous culture of feared, cannibalistic warriors (the CARIB) as the "Caniba." Tales of monstrous, semihuman, or subhuman beings existed in Europe prior to Columbus's arrival and thus facilitated the perception of barbarous, morally perverse New World peoples that required and deserved conquering. In the 16th-century words of Francisco López de Gómara, "Long live, then, the name and memory of [HERNANDO CORTÉS], who conquered so vast a land . . . and put an end to so much sacrifice and the eating of human flesh!"

Similar to López de Gómara, many 16th-century narrators used, and often exaggerated, the existence of cannibalism in the New World to define a type of "Other" who could only stand to benefit from the social and religious reforms of the conquerors. Ecclesiastics were especially disturbed by cannibalism. To them, it represented the devil's attempt to copy and mock the Eucharist (see DIABOLISM IN THE NEW WORLD). Indeed, the cannibalistic scenes the friars witnessed helped them to justify their need to administer the gospel to the indigenous people. Fray TORIBIO DE BENAVENTE (Motolinía) described a Nahua sacrificial ceremony in which the victims' hearts were removed, and then the Indians "dragged [the victims] away, slashed their throats, cut off their heads, and gave the heads to the minister of the idols, while the bodies they carried, like mutton, to the lords and chiefs for food." The Dominican friar Diego Durán provides perhaps the most extravagant 16th-century account of New World cannibalism. Describing the precontact Nahuas, he states, "In those days, the bellies of the lords were gorged with that human flesh. It is said of that king that not a day passed . . . that he did not eat human flesh. For this he had many slaves and each day had one killed so he could eat that flesh, or so his guests could, or those who usually shared his meals."

However, not all the ecclesiastics' reports of cannibalism had such an exaggerative or condemning tone. As a Protestant missionary sent to BRAZIL in 1556, the Frenchman Jean de Léry lived among the TUPINAMBÁ and witnessed firsthand many aspects of their culture, including cannibalism. Although he disapproved of cannibalism, he noted that whereas the Tupinambá eat their enemies out of vengeance, at times Europeans are guilty of worse. He asks the reader of his narrative, "have we not found people in these regions over here, even among those who bear the name of Christian . . . who, not content with having cruelly put to death their enemies, have been unable to slake their bloodthirst except by eating their livers and their hearts?" He then goes on to cite various examples, including the St. Bartholomew's Day massacre. Thus, for Léry, the Tupinambá practiced cannibalism as a part of a meaningful cultural ritual, while Europeans senselessly engaged in similar brutalities.

With few exceptions, however, most of the conquistadores' and friars' accounts of cannibalism were exaggerations of small-scale rituals that they themselves never witnessed. Nevertheless, cannibalism did exist among the precontact cultures of the New World. Some scholars have suggested that indigenous groups practiced it on a massive scale as a means to add protein to their diets. Such theories, however, lack convincing data. More recently, anthropological findings and ethnohistorical records have led scholars to discover that in most pre-

contact settled societies, human flesh was eaten only occasionally and only during strictly monitored rituals.

Out of all the New World cultures that practiced cannibalism, scholars know the most about the Nahuas (see AZTECS). The Nahua worldview was based on a cosmic balance and order that required constant maintenance through rituals, including human sacrifice. Although human sacrifice regularly occurred, not all victims were eaten. On the contrary, only during select rituals, such as the Feast of the Flaying of Men, were victims consumed, and then, only the most important captives were selected. In such cases, the captors and their kin were allowed to participate in the rituals surrounding the sacrifice, including the reverent, postmortem consumption of the victim's flesh, which was prepared in a MAIZE stew. Interestingly, because a warrior knew that one day he, too, might be captured, sacrificed, and consumed, he did not participate in the eating of his captive saying, "Shall I perchance eat my very self?"

In the semisettled cultures of Brazil's Tupí-speaking nations, cannibalism was less restricted. The various Tupí nations engaged in constant warfare, not for territory, but for captives and vengeance. Captives were killed with a single blow to the head, cooked, and eaten by the community as reparations for those they had lost in battle to other Tupí nations. Although cannibalism arguably occurred more frequently among the Tupí than other groups, human flesh was not a staple of the Tupí diet and was consumed sparingly. Overall, although cannibalism was practiced in the New World prior to the arrival of Europeans, it was selective and not on a large scale and was imbued with cultural and supernatural meaning.

—Mark Christensen

Further reading:

Diego Durán. *The History of the Indies of New Spain* (Norman: University of Oklahoma Press, 1994).

Jean de Léry. *History of a Voyage to the Land of Brazil, Otherwise Called America*, translated and introduction by Janet Whatley (Berkeley: University of California Press, 1990).

Capitulations of Santa Fe (April 17, 1492)

The Capitulations de Santa Fe initiated the commercial relationship between CHRISTOPHER COLUMBUS and the MONARCHS OF SPAIN, Ferdinand and Isabella. Competing with the Portuguese for Asian markets, the monarchs sought a route to the East Indies that did not conflict with the papal bull Romanus Pontifex, issued in 1455, which granted the Portuguese exclusive rights to the southern trade routes along the African coast. Columbus's proposal to sail west to reach Asia intrigued Ferdinand and Isabella, whose support of his venture is enshrined in the Capitulations. On the condition that Columbus was successful, the monarchs were to grant him the hereditary title of admiral and the commissions of viceroy and governor general. These titles invested Columbus with royal authority to establish and administer trading posts on behalf of the Spanish Crown. The Capitulations also specified that he receive one-tenth of the profits from the merchandise gained during his voyages, jurisdiction over lawsuits resulting from his enterprise, and the right to invest one-eighth of the costs of outfitting his ships and one-eighth of the resulting profits.

Because the Capitulations offered benefits that were contingent on the voyage's success, they created legal disputes between the royal court, Columbus, and his heirs. Columbus had to prove to the Crown that his voyages were indeed successful, and he wrote a number of letters to this effect. His descriptions of the indigenous peoples and natural world of the Caribbean islands reflected this need for self-promotion. However, his inability to administer soon became evident, and the Crown attempted to strip away the privileges they had bestowed in the Capitulations. For years, Columbus and his heirs lobbied the royal court to fulfill the original terms of the agreement.

—Karoline P. Cook

Further reading:
Helen Nader, ed. *The Book of Privileges Issued to Christopher Columbus by King Fernando and Queen Isabel, 1492–1502* (Los Angeles: UCLA Center for Medieval and Renaissance Studies, 1996).

Caracol　Caracol is an enormous archaeological site located on BELIZE's western border. The name means "snail" or "conch" and refers to the enormous number of conch shells discovered there. The center's pre-Columbian name is unknown. Caracol was a Classic-era MAYA center, and it lay in the heartland of that era's civilization in the web of rivers that branch inland from the Belizean and Tabascan coasts. Long growing seasons, abundant water, and easy river travel allowed the inhabitants of the city to grow wealthy through extensive regional TRADE, while they fed themselves through a combination of slash-and-burn MILPA farming and other systems of AGRICULTURE. Construction at Caracol dates from 70 C.E., but the city did not reach its apogee until at least half a millennium later. Its strategic advantage was its location near tributaries of the Macal River, which in turn connected it with the Belize River. At its height, Caracol's population may have been as high as 150,000. It was an archenemy of the powerful city of TIKAL, located west-northwest in what is today GUATEMALA's Petén district. Caracol glyphs record that its people defeated Tikal in a battle in 562 and that they dealt a similar defeat to the nearby city of Naranjo in 631. However, Caracol succumbed to the same stresses that scourged other Classic-era CITIES: overpopulation, maldistribution of resources, soil erosion, and collapse of older trade systems. The last recorded date here is 859; the center appears to have been abandoned within 200 years.

Today the site of Caracol lies some three hours from the main roads in Belize's Cayo District. While it includes a series of impressive temples and ball courts, as well as several *aguadas*, or "artificial water reservoirs," its most astonishing structure is the *Caana*, or "sky building," a 136-foot temple that is the tallest in Belize and one of the largest in the Maya world.

—Terry Rugeley

Further reading:
Arlen F. Chase and Diane Z. Chase. *Investigations at the Classic Maya City of Caracol, Belize: 1985–1987*. Monograph 3 (San Francisco: Pre-Columbian Art Institute, 1987).

Carib　The Carib, or Kalinago, inhabited the Lesser Antilles or the Leeward Islands of the eastern Caribbean, arriving from South America around 1000 C.E. The Carib homeland, to the west and south of the Orinoco river delta, is located next to that of the Arawak-speaking ancestors of the Saladoid, who had settled the islands of the Caribbean centuries earlier. The Carib, skilled sailors and aggressive warriors, slowly but steadily moved from island to island, conquering the local Saladoid. By 1500, the Carib had reached the Virgin Islands and perhaps even PUERTO RICO.

Carib society was loosely egalitarian, although only for men. There were no established chieftains or elite classes, and all Carib males were expected to be warriors, with those excelling in combat and taking many captives obtaining wealth and prestige. Particularly successful men might be recognized as *ubutu*, or leaders, although their authority was more symbolic than real. WOMEN, both Carib and enslaved TAINO-Saladoid, were responsible for tending the crops (mainly MANIOC and MAIZE), cooking, manufacturing household articles such as CERAMICS and baskets, and raising children (see FAMILY). Since only men could participate in most religious and social activities, Carib society developed distinct male and female subcultures, with women even speaking a separate language based on the Arawak spoken by Taino female captives.

The Carib had a fearsome reputation not only because of their constant raids on their neighbors but also because they practiced CANNIBALISM. Usually, male captives were selected to be eaten as part of victory celebrations. Nevertheless, the Carib also peacefully traded and intermarried with their neighbors and developed a vast TRADE network that connected the Caribbean islands with northern South America.

Carib spirituality was based on the belief of the duality of the spirit beings that ruled nature. Bakamo, the great Sky Serpent (star constellation), guided and protected seafaring canoes but could also cause harm if offerings were not made. Likewise, the spirits of deceased ancestors could turn *maboya*, or evil, if neglected. The *boyez*, or shaman, could summon these spirits to heal the sick or interpret dreams.

The Carib fiercely resisted European encroachment on their islands for several centuries. They also intermarried with runaway African slaves and Taino refugees (see SLAVERY).

—Francisco J. González

Further reading:
David Harris. *Plants, Animals and Plants in the Outer Leeward Islands, West Indies* (Berkeley: University of California Press, 1965).

Casa de Contratación (1503–1790)

A centralized board of TRADE, the Casa de Contratación was originally the only authorized trading house and provisioning agency for Spain's mercantile trade with its colonies in the Indies. Eventually, the Casa de Contratación came to control all trade as well as navigational training and served as the chief commercial court of the Spanish Empire.

With CHRISTOPHER COLUMBUS's discovery of the New World in 1492, Spain needed to create a system of trade with its new colonies. While developing the first trading fleets, the Crown realized that controlling and regulating interoceanic trade with the New World would become necessary. Between 1494 and 1502, Queen Isabella's confessor and council, Bishop Juan Rodríguez de Fonseca, controlled virtually all aspects of Spain's trade with the Indies. By late 1502, however, it had become apparent that the Crown needed to create new institutions in order to control both the governmental and the fiscal/mercantile aspects of their New World colonies. Accordingly, in 1503, the Catholic monarchs determined to relieve Bishop Fonseca of his economic and trading obligations by creating the Casa de Contratación.

On January 20, 1503, the Crown formally established the Casa de Contratación. The new institution was located in the Royal Alcázares in Seville until 1598, when it moved into what is now known as the Casa Lonja (which also houses the Archivo General de las Indias).

Initially, the Casa de Contratación was made up of a treasurer (*tesorero*), a chief accountant (*contador*), and a business and trading manager (*factor*). Other posts were added as it took more control over maritime trade and transoceanic TRANSPORTATION and then also regulated the immigration of Castilians to the New World. In 1508, the Italian AMERIGO VESPUCCI was appointed as the first chief pilot, serving from 1508 to 1514. By 1514 a postmaster general had been appointed and eventually a large number of lawyers, notaries, and other officials were added to the bureaucracy.

By the end of the 16th century, the Casa de Contratación operated as a board of trade, a supreme commercial court, and a clearinghouse for all merchant traffic and oversaw certain immigration issues. In essence, its operations were divided into three distinct divisions. The treasury functions came under the authority of the treasurer. The chief duties of the treasurer and his officials were to receive and safeguard the GOLD and SILVER bullion and precious stones that were owed to the royal treasury as payment of the *quinto real*, or royal fifth tax.

The *factor*, as business manager of the Casa de Contratación, focused on outfitting and provisioning ships and purchasing supplies, armaments, and all kinds of merchandise from Europe for shipping to the Indies. His office also had the responsibility of administering all of the nonprecious metal merchandise that arrived from the Indies. The *factor* and his subordinates also oversaw all trade regulations, as well as the annual merchant fleets that sailed between Spain and the Indies.

The *contador*, or chief accountant, had the difficult task of registering all persons and merchandise carried by outgoing or incoming vessels. His office also controlled the fiscal review and accounting of other overseas Crown officials.

The Casa de Contratación in Seville functioned and ensured a royal monopoly on trade with the New World colonies from 1503 until it was moved to Cádiz in 1717. As the Spanish Bourbon monarchs reformed the colonial trading system in the late 1700s, it gradually lost its importance until it was finally abolished by decree in 1790.

See also CASA DE CONTRATACIÓN (Vol. II).

—John F. Chuchiak IV

Further reading:
Clarence Henry Haring. *Trade and Navigation between Spain and the Indies in the Time of the Hapsburgs* (Cambridge, Mass.: Harvard University Press, 1918).

cassava See MANIOC.

Catholic Church

BRAZIL

The early history of the Catholic Church in BRAZIL was dominated by one religious order, the Jesuits. In 1549, a group of six Jesuits, under the leadership of Manuel de Nóbrega, arrived in Salvador do Bahia, along with the region's first governor general, Tomé de Souza. By 1550, a second group of four Jesuits arrived; in the subsequent years, others followed. The Jesuits enjoyed a close relationship with the representatives of the royal government. While they focused their efforts largely on the conversion of indigenous peoples, they also played an important role in the general life of the colony. Although eventually many RELIGIOUS ORDERS participated in evangelization, in Brazil, the Jesuits took the lead, their influence expanding steadily throughout the early colonial period. Starting in Bahía, they spread Christianity along the Brazilian coast. The indigenous people, who relied on some AGRICULTURE and hunting and gathering, lived in small settlements that were widely dispersed in the interior. They frequently moved their villages to take advantage of new land and shifts in wild animals and plants. The Jesuits attempted to move the natives into larger villages and settlements to ease the process of conversion, thus beginning a practice (CONGREGACIÓN) that would continue throughout the colonial period. This also meant that the Jesuits had more control over the native peoples, who were also sought after by colonists as a source of LABOR. The Crown and local governors had established mixed decrees regarding Indian SLAVERY. Some royal laws and local traditions allowed for the enslavement of indigenous people, while in general the Crown discouraged it. The Jesuits fought to keep the natives free and under their immediate supervision.

While focusing their efforts mainly on the coastal indigenous population, the Jesuits also set out for the interior, to what would become the city of São Paulo. There, the order not only founded a settlement but also a school for local native children (see EDUCATION). They also learned local languages in order to better evangelize. José de Anchieta developed the first grammar of the local language, Tupí, and translated Christian teachings into that language. The Jesuits used a modified form of the language that was somewhat intelligible to a broad number of tribes; it became the native lingua franca of the region. Although the Jesuits forcefully opposed the enslavement of both Africans and indigenous people, they were successful only in the latter case. Colonists increasingly imported African slaves to work on SUGAR plantations and at other ventures, and, indeed, as the demand for labor increased, the Jesuits themselves came to be some of the largest owners of African slaves in the colony.

The secular, or diocesan, clergy was slow to emerge in Brazil (see CLERGY, SECULAR). The first diocese was created in 1552 in Salvador do Bahia. The secular clergy tended to concentrate their efforts among the Portuguese residents of the colony and generally served coastal villages. The Portuguese Crown claimed control over the church in Brazil as part of the *Padroado Real* (royal patronage). Under this, in return for early support of missionary activity, the Portuguese Crown retained the right to nominate persons to high ecclesiastical office, such as bishop, or to clerical benefices. The Crown also retained the right to control papal communications with Brazil by requiring royal permission for papal decrees and letters to be promulgated there.

SPANISH AMERICA

The Catholic Church played a central role in the pacification and settlement of the Spanish New World. Following CHRISTOPHER COLUMBUS's initial voyage to the West Indies, nearly every voyage and expedition counted a member of the Catholic clergy among its members. Because it based its possession of the New World in part on grants from the pope in recognition of its evangelization efforts, Spain needed to actively support missionaries and the spread of Christianity in order to defend its rights to the region. This was the basis for the royal

patronage (*patronato real*), a set of rights and privileges granted by the pope to the Spanish monarchs in recognition of their support for the conversion to Catholicism of non-Christian peoples.

The priests of the Catholic Church fell into two large categories. Priests and other clergy who belonged to organized religious orders were called "regular" clerics. The term *regular* comes from the Latin *regula* meaning "rule," signifying that these clerics had to follow a special set of rules in their daily lives, such as the Rule of St. Francis or the Rule of St. Benedict. They might be members of orders such as the Franciscans, Dominicans, or Jesuits. The normal parish priest, who reported directly to a bishop or archbishop, was referred to as a "secular" cleric, from the Latin word *saeculum*, meaning the "spirit of the world," signifying that they lived out in the world rather than within a cloister.

The earliest missionaries to the Americas were members of religious orders, specifically the Jeronimites, Mercedarians, and the Franciscans. The basic pattern of evangelization was to have at least one priest accompany each major expedition. In the case of HERNANDO CORTÉS's expedition to MEXICO, the designated missionary was a Mercedarian; in the CONQUEST of PERU, FRANCISCO PIZARRO brought a Dominican. Frequently, other priests also joined the early expeditions but as regular members of the company. In the case of the Cortés expedition to Mexico, there were probably as many as three other priests, the most famous of whom was the secular priest Juan Díaz.

In the aftermath of Spain's military conquest of the Americas, small groups of missionaries began to arrive to engage in the ongoing process of evangelization. For example, in Mexico shortly after the formal defeat of the AZTECS, three Franciscan friars arrived, and within a matter of months another larger group of 12 joined them. The Dominicans were the first order to send missionaries to Peru after the nominal defeat of the INCAS. Two small expeditions, one consisting of six and another of eight friars, embarked for Peru. Because of the distance and the dangers of the journey, only about 10 arrived.

The first missionaries had great difficulty communicating with the indigenous peoples. Only a very few Spaniards could speak native languages. The missionaries had to confront the problem of either teaching the indigenous Spanish, or Latin, or learning the indigenous languages themselves. They opted to do the latter. Because of the multiplicity of native languages, the missionaries first learned the languages of the dominant cultures, namely, NAHUATL for the areas conquered from the Aztecs, QUECHUA for the regions of the Incas, and MAYA for the Yucatán and Central America. The Spanish then used these three languages as the common native languages for each area, regardless of what language an individual might speak. These languages thus became linguas franca in each of their territories. The missionaries then set about making grammars of the native languages, translating catechisms into them, and learning about local customs in order to begin to teach Christianity.

The missionaries wrestled with how best to communicate the essentials of the Christian faith to the Indians. The two options were either to find words in the native languages that approximated Christian ideas or to simply incorporate the Christian concept and Spanish word into the native language. For example, among the Aztecs, the missionaries referred to God either with the Spanish word *dios* or the Nahuatl word *téotl*. In general, for central concepts, they opted to continue to use the Spanish word. Other notions, such as sin, were somewhat alien to the Indians. The missionaries decided to use a native word, *tlatlacolli*, meaning "something damaged." This resulted in what one scholar has characterized as the "double mistaken identity." The Spaniards thought that the native word meant roughly the same as the Spanish word and did not grasp that it might have various meanings and refer to a broad spectrum of cultural understandings (see SYNCRETISM). Similarly, indigenous people thought that the Spanish word must mean roughly the same as their word and thus did not understand its Spanish cultural context.

In general, secular clerics arrived later than the religious orders, although, as noted, some seculars participated in the conquest expeditions, such as Juan Díaz in Mexico. Secular priests functioned under the authority of their bishop. It was not until the early decades of the 1500s that the first bishops were appointed to govern the church in the New World. The first diocese was that of Santo Domingo, created in 1511 under the supervision of the archbishop of Seville. In 1546, it became an independent archdiocese. In Mexico, the first diocese, Puebla de los Ángeles, was created shortly after the conquest of that country in 1525. Nevertheless, the diocese of Mexico, with its capital in MEXICO CITY, later became the see of the archdiocese of Mexico, erected first as a diocese in 1530 and elevated to an archdiocese in 1546. In South America, LIMA was the first diocese, erected in 1541 and also elevated to an archdiocese in 1546.

As a result of the royal patronage, the bishops of the New World were appointed by the Spanish king. The main church of a diocese was called a cathedral because it housed the bishop's throne, or cathedra. The cathedral was governed by a body of clerics, called the cathedral chapter (*cabildo eclesiástico*). Appointed by the king, it served the cathedral of the diocese and also as an administrative council for the bishop. Each chapter had 27 members. Local parish priests generally were appointed by the local bishop, although the king retained the right to appoint them if he so desired. They were called curates (*curas*). By the 1570s, the Crown had begun to guarantee the wage of the curates, thus converting the curacies into beneficed curacies. A beneficed curate enjoyed certain privileges, including what constituted a lifetime appointment. Some local curates also served as judges in the ecclesiastical court system. These priests were called *vicarios* (vicars) since they enjoyed the powers of judge vicariously through the local bishop.

The religious orders were largely self-governing and organized around their convents. The great majority of religious orders were mendicant, meaning they supported themselves through alms. Their members were generically known as friars. The Society of Jesus, or the Jesuits, supported itself through both alms and farms, ranches, sugar mills, and other money-making endeavors. Each convent elected its abbot or leader, along with a council of friars, to assist the abbot. In turn, orders were divided into provinces. The leadership of the various convents elected one friar, known as the provincial, to govern the province. Similarly, councils of friars assisted the provincial. The provincial and his aides assigned individual priests to the various parishes served by the order. These parishes were called *doctrinas*, and the priests who served in them were known as *doctrineros*.

The daily routine in a parish did not differ greatly between curacies and *doctrinas*. Part of each day was spent teaching Christian doctrine to children and then to groups of adults, who were normally separated by gender. The priests taught in the native languages they had learned and sometimes used comic book–like pictures to aid their teaching. The latter are called Testerian catechisms, after Jacobo de Tastera, an early Franciscan missionary. The parish priest also had to prepare couples for marriage, listen to confessions, visit the sick, and perform burial rituals. Because the indigenous population completely overwhelmed the available priests, there was far greater demand for services than the priests could accommodate. They trained Indian assistants to take over some duties, such as teaching doctrine, caring for the church itself, and organizing the service MUSIC.

See also AUGUSTINIANS (Vol. II); *AUTO DE FE* (Vol. II); CATHEDRAL CHAPTER (Vol. II); CATHOLIC CHURCH (Vols. II, III, IV); *COFRADÍAS* (Vol. II); DOMINICANS (Vol. II); FRANCISCANS (Vol. II); INQUISITION (Vol. II); JESUITS (Vol. II); MISSIONS (Vol. II); MERCEDARIANS (Vol. II); RELIGION (Vols. II, III, IV).

—John F. Schwaller

Further reading:
Charles R. Boxer. *The Church Militant and Iberian Expansion, 1440–1770* (Baltimore, Md.: Johns Hopkins, 1978).

Robert Ricard. *The Spiritual Conquest of Mexico*, translated by Leslie Byrd Simpson (Berkeley: University of California Press, 1966).

John F. Schwaller. *Church and Clergy in Sixteenth-Century Mexico* (Albuquerque: University of New Mexico Press, 1987).

ceque   See *ZEQUE* SYSTEM.

ceramics In general, pre-Columbian pottery consisted of earthenware vessels and other objects manufactured from various clays. Pottery is an ancient tradition in the Americas, with multiple centers of development and elaboration. In many regions, pottery became a prominent component of the material cultural tradition. The production of pottery was strongly associated with the emergence and continuity of settled cultures based on horticultural and agricultural economic systems (see AGRICULTURE; ECONOMY). Potting became a feature of life throughout Mesoamerica, the Intermediate Area (between Mesoamerica and northern South America), Amazonia (see AMAZON), and the Andean region, where its manufacture was associated with the processing, cooking, and storage of various tubers, MAIZE, and grains and with the feasting, political, ritual, burial, and symbolic needs of society (see FOOD). Largely earthenware, pre-Hispanic pottery was highly diverse and included storage and cooking jars in a wide range of shapes and sizes; service plates and bowls; fermentation jars; drinking cups; zoomorphic, phytomorphic, and anthropomorphic vessels; and burial vessels (large vessels in which the dead were placed and then buried). Other objects made of pottery in various regions included incense burners, stools, snuff spoons and drug containers, jewelry, pubic covers for women, spinning tools, paint palettes, net sinks, MANIOC graters, musical instruments, printing devices, beads, and figurines (see ART; MUSIC; RELIGION). Pottery use and manufacture was associated with both the household and larger regional and imperial political economies.

TECHNOLOGY

Throughout the Americas, low to moderate temperature-fired ceramics were produced at the household level. However, in both Mesoamerica and the Andes, kiln-fired production was widespread by 100 C.E. In the southern Gulf lowlands of Mesoamerica, fine paste orange wares were produced in updraft kilns. The glossy, black-smudged ceramic wares of the CHIMÚ kingdom in coastal PERU were also produced in kilns. Except in a very limited sense, high-temperature firing suitable for the application of vitrified glazes was not a feature of pre-Columbian ceramic traditions. Glazelike surface treatment did develop in a small border region along the Pacific coast frontiers of GUATEMALA and MEXICO, where pottery of the Plumbate tradition was manufactured and subsequently traded throughout large areas of Early Postclassic Mesoamerica (see TRADE). Except in the MAYA area and Andes, where precursors of the pottery wheel developed, pots were assembled from coils, slabs, and mold-made parts without the benefit of a rotating base. Mass manufacturing developed in Mesoamerica, the Andes, Amazonia, and, likely, the Intermediate Area, where different techniques were employed to maintain manufacturing efficiencies and standardization. In Mesoamerica, molds were often employed, for instance, in the manufacture of *incensarios* (incense burners) at the large Classic-period city of TEOTIHUACÁN. There, too, figurines were systematically manufactured using molds. Later, large workshops in Central Mexico serviced the needs of a massive rural, town-, and city-dwelling population. Within the Andes, low-value objects, such as the mass-manufactured Inca *kero* and *paccha*, vessel forms related to the consumption and offering of CHICHA beer, and serving and storage vessels, were mass manufactured along with more specialized components, such as spouts (see INCAS). By 400 B.C.E., slip casting was employed along the southern coast of Peru to make bottle spouts to systematic standards.

Medium- to large-scale production of pottery in pre-Hispanic contexts is often indicated by the presence of quantities of production-damaged fragments, waster sherds, and highly standardized forms. Major production facilities were located at Aztec sites in the Basin of Mexico (see AZTECS), Inca CITIES such as Huánuco Pampa, and earlier Andean cities such as TIWANAKU. Elsewhere in Amazonia and the Intermediate Area, pottery production was limited to the household level, with part-time and full-time specialization characteristic of some regions, for instance the Chibcha culture of lower Central America and northern COLOMBIA (see MUISCA). Ornate polychromes of the Nicoya Peninsula of COSTA RICA, produced between 600 and 1100 C.E., are among the most elaborate examples of this tradition and are likely to have been manufactured by full-time specialists.

Pottery was decorated in a wide range of styles, from simple incision and punctuation to more complex excision, carving, stamping, and modeling. Color schemes were created through choice of clay, manipulation of the firing environment, and application of clay slips, sometimes in conjunction with the application of resin employed in resist ceramics such as the Usulután wares of the Maya region. Postfiring painting was also employed. At Teotihuacán, the true fresco technique was used on elaborate tripod vessels to create scenes representing priests dressed as deities similar to those depicted on murals found on apartment walls. During the Mesoamerican Preclassic, differential firing techniques, such as smudging or refiring, were employed to produce service vessels such as plates and bowls with precisely differentiated, and later mottled, areas of cream and dark grays.

POLITICAL ECONOMY

Pottery served numerous functions in the Americas, from the quotidian to the hegemonic; in fact, pottery became an important tool for the communication and negotiation of prestige and power. Cooking and service containers are more often than not associated with the daily needs of the household, but they also served the needs of the elite. Large cooking and service vessels signal the emergence of feasting within corporate groups or communities, which were often tied to factional politics. Workshops and industrial-scale manufacture of pottery are associated with emergent complex polities and empires, where redistribution, gifting, and the provisioning of large populations were necessary.

In the Inca Empire, for example, pottery production was partially controlled by the state. Specialists were recruited and relocated to new settlements throughout the empire to produce pottery storage and service vessels, both in local styles and in the geometrically decorated imperial style; this imperial style included the double-handled, flared-mouth storage vessel, or *aryballos*. Workshops within such new cities as Huánuco Pampa in Peru produced large quantities of quotidian ceramics to service the needs of both the rotating population of MITA LABOR tax workers and permanent residents.

SYMBOLIC ASPECTS

Pottery is a semiotically loaded technology that communicates status, esteem, and meaning via symbols applied through a variety of techniques, ranging from modeling to plastic decoration to painting and fresco techniques. Value and, hence, status and esteem related to the complexity and sophistication of the ceramic product. In the Classic Maya world, ornate pottery vases with polychrome scenes containing text and signed by the artists formed part of the elite gifting system. Mythological representations depicted significant aspects of the Maya creation epic, the POPOL VUH. The images painted on the vases mirrored murals and, presumably, illustrations painted on the now lost Classic period CODICES.

In Peru, elaborate polychrome pottery manufactured during the Early Intermediate period and later in such regions as the Nazca river valley served to communicate religious precepts and encode representations of daily life (see NAZCA LINES). There, pottery phytomorphs, zoomorphs, and anthromorphs reproduce fruits, MAIZE, fish, and humans, from WOMEN to warriors (see WARFARE). The iconography on these ceramics reduplicates the iconography on similarly important COTTON TEXTILES and that associated with the geoglyphs of the adjacent pampa. This representational tradition is widespread in the coastal region where houses, ritual scenes, and aspects of daily life, such as the manufacture of *chichi*, were encoded in three-dimensional representations. The depiction of ritual and daily life in modeled pottery vases was also seen in western Mesoamerica during the Preclassic period.

In Peru, too, pottery was used to encode social and sexual concepts of gender, submission, eroticism, and male homoeroticism. Various stirrup spout, bridge and spout, and wide-mouthed vases depict sexual scenes ranging from intercourse to oral and anal sex. These sexualized images co-occur with a tradition of the modeled and painted representation of prisoners, sacrificial heads, and ritual scenes (see HUMAN SACRIFICE). Farther to the north, along the coastal lowlands of ECUADOR and Colombia, a similar interest in the ceramic representation of the phallus is present in the Andean-influenced ceramic traditions of the region.

Pottery miniatures were produced in a number of areas. Among the OLMECS of Mesoamerica, small cooking *ollas* and service bowls and platters were produced to scale with the most common figurine type. These 1–2 inch (2.5–5 cm) miniatures were presumably used to create ritual or didactic scenes in conjunction with fired clay figurines. Alternatively, they may be among the few examples of pottery toys.

Pottery figurines were among the most important elements of material culture that could be used to infer aspects of gender construction in the pre-Hispanic world, where ethnohistoric records are nonexistent or too far removed in time. Quotidian aspects such as dress and hairstyles may be inferred (see CLOTHING). Often small, less well made figurines depict pregnancy, suggesting that the symbolic concerns of common households in regions such as Mesoamerica were different than those of the elites, who sought and displayed finely made pottery.

EARLY DEVELOPMENT

The earliest well-documented pottery in the Americas comes from Amazonia and the Santa Elena Peninsula of southwest Ecuador. Early pottery use in the Santarém region of the lower Amazon precedes that of Ecuador by at least 2,000 years. There, simple, decorated red-brown pottery bowls appeared as early as 5500 B.C.E. in shell midden sites. In Ecuador, Early Valdivia culture ceramics have been dated between 3300 and 1850 B.C.E. There, pottery is associated with the precocious development of circular or U-shaped villages, similar to those of the Tropical Forest culture of the Amazon Basin; for the Amazon Basin, there is evidence of increasingly dispersed settlements, as maize and legume farming populations expanded to make use of river margin alluvial soils. However, it remains unclear whether the early development of pottery technology in Amazonia and coastal Ecuador played a part in the subsequent emergence of potting traditions in Mesoamerica and the Andes, or whether they were isolated developments.

REGIONAL TRADITIONS

The earliest pottery tradition of Mesoamerica emerged during the second millennium B.C.E. along the Pacific coastal margin of the Mexican state of Chiapas and appears not to have local antecedents. This early tradition was characterized by the production of large service *tecomates*, or gourdlike, narrow-mouthed jars without necks; these jars are considered elements of a beverage service associated with feasting and the development of incipient political systems. They may have been used to ferment and serve maize or other alcoholic beverages. Local pottery traditions were well entrenched in Mesoamerica by the last centuries of the second millennium B.C.E., concurrent with the emergence of large-scale maize-based farming communities. Cylindrical seals, early printing devices, were part of this early Mesoamerican tradition.

Ceramics emerged as a feature of settled Andean communities by 1800 B.C.E. Ceramic musical instruments were particularly important in the Andean world, where mold- and slip-casting techniques were used to manufacture tuned panpipes, trumpets, and drums. Special whistle containers were also manufactured; these produced a sound when liquid was poured out.

The precocious use of pottery in the lowlands of the lower Amazonia laid the foundation for a technological tradition that continued until the arrival of Europeans. Pottery is strongly associated with lowland sites along the Amazon and its affluents, as well as the rolling savanna plains, the Llanos de Mojos, in Bolivia, where extensive populations built complex earthworks. The highly modified, nutrient-rich soils of Amazonian sites, known as *terra preta*, which were essentially massive middens that were widespread by 1 C.E. in Amazonia, were especially well suited for pottery making. Amazonian potters provided containers for daily use and ritual and burial needs, as well as furniture and clothing in the form of women's pubic covers. Most elaborate in the Marajoara phase of Marajó Island at the mouth of the Amazon (ca. 400–1300 C.E.), pottery was used to signal social identity and rank through the use of elaborate polychrome modeled anthropomorphic funerary urns. This tradition of polychrome funerary and ceremonial ware has been found across the lowlands in Amazonia, Colombia, Ecuador, and Peru by 1000 C.E.

Throughout the Americas, ceramics served a variety of pragmatic material and cultural needs while simultaneously communicating social position. Ceramics were a focal point of pre-Hispanic technological innovation through the development of kilns, specialized paints, and other manufacturing techniques. Most important, they served as a canvas that gave shape to a variety of artistic traditions, from the depiction of royal and mythological scenes to the modeling of daily life.

—Christopher Von Nagy

Further reading:

Steve Bourget. *Sex, Death, and Sacrifice in Moche Religion and Visual Culture* (Austin: University of Texas Press, 2006).

Dorie Reents-Budet and Joseph W. Ball. *Painting the Maya Universe: Royal Ceramics of the Classic Period* (Durham, N.C.: Duke University Press/Duke University Museum of Art, 1994).

Helaine Silverman. *The Nazca* (Malden, Mass: Blackwell, 2002).

Chanca wars The Incan idea of past events was very different from the European concept of history. Events may or may not have taken place; a narrative may have been edited. Nevertheless, whether called history or myth, the accounts of Inca political consolidation, like those of the origin of the Inca rulers, were important political statements intended to validate Inca rule and expansion (see Incas). The account of the Chanca wars is found in many of the early chronicles. It was clearly an important statement, aimed at justifying a major shift in political strategy from that of a small, regional polity to that of an expansive, imperial state.

The narrative states that during the reign of Viracocha Inca, a peace-loving ruler, an ethnic group from the west, the Chancas, conquered Andahuaylas. The Chanca ruler then decided to conquer the Inca capital city of Cuzco. He divided his army into three parts, each under a pair of generals, and sent messengers to Viracocha Inca demanding submission. After consultation with his lords in council, Viracocha Inca decided to submit; he fled the city with his family and followers, including his first-born son and heir apparent, Inca Urqon. A younger son, Inca Yupanqui, decided to defend Cuzco to the death. He was joined by three young nobles, among others, but they were still far outnumbered by the Chanca forces. Each night Inca Yupanqui prayed to the god Viracocha, who told him in a dream that he would send help. When the Chanca army attacked Cuzco, unknown warriors rose up as if from the ground and defeated the Chanca. These warriors were called *purun auca*, or "warriors from the wilderness"; some believed that they had been transformed from stones. The other two Chanca armies were easily vanquished. Inca Yupanqui's power and prestige were greatly enhanced; he later became the Inca ruler, assuming the name Pachacuti Inca Yupanqui (He Who Overturns the World).

—Patricia J. Netherly

Further reading:

Terence N. D'Altroy. *The Incas* (Malden, Mass.: Blackwell, 2003).

Chan Chan Chan Chan was the capital city of the Chimú Empire, founded in the early 14th century on the north coast of Peru. At its height, the city spanned nearly eight square miles (20.7 km³) and housed some 30,000 people. Chan Chan was built of adobe and made up of monumental elite residences, called *ciudadelas*, as well as scattered intermediate and commoner dwellings. Because of the north coast's desert climate, the city resorted to the use of forced labor programs for canal construction and agriculture. Using this system, Chimú elites were able to prosper and accumulate large amounts of luxury items, particularly metalwork. Each *ciudadela* compound was dedicated to an individual ruler. The structures were made up of high, thick walls laid out in a rectangular formation with a single entrance. After his death, the ruler was buried within the compound, and his family, charged with its upkeep. Within the *ciudadela*, leading families set up residences, stored luxury goods, and administered the estate. The interiors of these *ciudadelas* had a repetitive mazelike organization, which may have served as a deterrent to thieves. Interior walls were ornamented with adobe reliefs, which contained no reference to rulers, history, or daily life. Instead, they combined geometric shapes (diamonds and lines are the most common), as well as natural creatures (particularly fish and birds). These repetitive design elements align with the Chimú practice of accumulation, a unique penchant for collecting goods in large, guarded storage rooms. U-shaped rooms called *audencias* line the labyrinthine passages and were probably used as administrative offices that also restricted access to elite residences and storerooms. Sometime between 1462 and 1470, the INCAS conquered Chan Chan, at which point the Chimú leader and his court were captured and exiled to the Inca capital of CUZCO. It is believed that the Incas may have organized their empire of tribute labor and storage according to Chimú models.

—Elena FitzPatrick

Further reading:
Richard W. Keathinge. "Socio-Economic Organization of the Moche Valley, Peru, during the Chimú Occupation of Chan Chan." *Journal of Anthropological Research* 29, no. 4 (Winter 1973): 275–295.
Rebecca Stone-Miller. *Art of the Andes: From Chavín to Inca* (London: Thames & Hudson, 2002).

chasqui (chaski)   The QUECHUA word *chasqui* refers to the highly trained Inca runners, or couriers, who delivered messages (either orally or written on QUIPUS), royal decrees and orders, and transported goods and perishable packages for Inca emperors by means of a relay system. The system was reportedly developed by the 10th emperor of the INCAS, Tupa Inca Yupanqui (r. 1471–93).

Chasqui runners were trained from childhood, with only the most physically fit and fastest finally being chosen for service. The young men who served as runners played an important role in ensuring the Incas' control over their far-flung empire, which spanned from ECUADOR in the north to CHILE and parts of ARGENTINA in the south. Runners were dispatched from local *chasquiwasi* (houses of the *chasquis*), which were set several miles apart. Father Bernabé Cobo, a Spanish eyewitness, wrote that each station consisted of two buildings facing each other on either side of the road. At each house were two young men, ready to deliver messages in either direction. While one rested, the other was ready to run out and receive an incoming message. Throughout the Inca period, *chasqui* stations were manned 24 hours a day. Those who fell asleep while on *chasqui* duty or failed to deliver a message received the death penalty (see CRIME AND PUNISHMENT).

Each messenger carried a conch shell trumpet, which he used to announce his arrival at the next relay post, or *tambo*. *Tambos*, similarly manned with two runners, were set at regular intervals along the highways, in between the larger *chasquiwasi*. When a *chasqui* arrived at the next station, he passed his message or cargo (which he carried in a small pack strapped to his back called a *qipi*) to the next runner. He then rested and received food and drink before returning to his original station.

The *chasqui* ran at high speeds along the more than 14,000 miles (22,526 km) of interconnected Inca roadways, which were spread throughout PERU, Ecuador,

BOLIVIA, and parts of COLOMBIA, Argentina, and Chile. It was reported that a message from the coast to the Inca capital of CUZCO would arrive within two days, while a message from Cuzco to Quito in the northern reaches of the empire would arrive within a few days. In most cases, the messages or goods traveled about 50 leagues a day.

—John F. Chuchiak IV

Further reading:
Bernabé Cobo. *Inca Religion and Customs* (Austin: University of Texas Press, 1990).
John Hyslop. *The Inka Road System* (Orlando, Fla.: Academic Press, 1984).

Chavín   *Chavín* is the name associated with the earliest major Andean culture and artistic style. The term itself comes from Chavín de Huántar, an archaeological site in the Ancash Department of modern PERU. The Chavín period began around 1400 B.C.E. and lasted for about a thousand years. Archaeologists have advanced several theories regarding the culture's origins: Max Uhle saw Mesoamerican influence; Julio C. Tello, who conducted the early excavations at Chavín de Huántar, thought its roots lay eastward in the AMAZON Basin, given the depiction of Amazonian animals such as the cayman and the jaguar in the site's religious iconography. Others have pointed to influences from coastal and maritime cultures that predated the settlement of Chavín de Huántar. Sites influenced by the Chavín culture often include U-shaped temples and stone sculpture using kennings, double-profile heads, and reversible imagery to depict deities and tropical animals.

Although it has not been proven that the culture originated at Chavín de Huántar, that site was an important administrative and pilgrimage center. Highland agriculture there sustained several thousand people by the end of the Chavín period (ca. 300 B.C.E.), and social stratification had emerged (see AGRICULTURE), though little is known about the site's political organization. The most impressive ruins are the temple complexes, which have subterranean passages where some of the principal ritual objects were located. The most famous of these still at the site is the Lanzón, a large elongated granite shaft carved to depict an anthropomorphic deity. Probably the most famous Chavín artifact is the Raimondi Stone, an elaborately carved monolith, which has been on display in Lima's National Museum of Anthropology since 1874. Chavín de Huántar is a UNESCO World Heritage site.

The Chavín culture had religious and artistic influence over a region stretching from Cupisnique in the north to Ica and Ayacucho in the south. After the Chavín period ended, local and regional cultures showing some Chavín characteristics eventually emerged; these included groups such as the WARI and MOCHE.

—Kendall Brown

Further reading:
Richard L. Burger. *Chavín and the Origins of Andean Civilization* (New York: Thames & Hudson, 1992).

Chibcha   See MUISCA.

chicha   *Chicha* is the Spanish word for the mildly alcoholic beverages fermented from MAIZE, fruits, seeds, and other plants that are consumed today from MEXICO to South America. *Chicha*'s fame derives from its use in the pre-Columbian Inca Empire, where it was the beverage of choice at ceremonies, political events, feasts, and funeral rituals (see INCAS). The Inca emperor and local lords provided *chicha* to commoners in exchange for LABOR. Elite *aqllakuna* women (see ACLLA) brewed *chicha* on a large scale in multiroom buildings (such as that excavated at the Inca city of Huánuco Pampa in northern PERU).

Chicha was also produced in households and consumed as a daily staple. Pre-Inca evidence of *chicha* production from the MOCHE, Recuay, WARI, TIWANAKU, and CHIMÚ cultures spans the time from the Early Intermediate period (200 B.C.E.–650 C.E.) to the Spanish CONQUEST. *Chicha* use is evidenced by large jars with narrow necks that were used for cooking, fermentation, and storage and by decorated drinking vessels (see ARCHITECTURE; CERAMICS). The jars are associated with linear floor depressions, as well as grinding stones that were used to process malted corn kernels. A ceramic vessel from the Moche culture depicts individu-

als brewing *chicha*. Storage bins of uniformed-size corn kernels at Pampa Grande (Moche culture), dregs resulting from household *chicha* brewing at Manchan (Chimú culture), and pepper-tree berries recovered in a large brewery at Cerro Baúl (Wari culture) provide organic evidence of *chicha* production. Iconographic representations of the plant *Anadenanthera colubrina* on TEXTILES, pottery, and stone in Moche and Wari cultures suggests it was used as a hallucinogenic additive to *chicha*, as it is by shamans today. The earliest but tenuous evidence of *chicha* consumption in the Andes are ritual vessels decorated with corn motifs, which date from the Initial-period (1500–800 B.C.E.) site of Kotosh and the Early Horizon (800–200 B.C.E.) CHAVÍN site of Chavín de Huántar.

—James Sheehy

Chichén Itzá   The center of Chichén Itzá dominated the political landscape of the northern Yucatán for most of the Early Postclassic period. The name Chichén Itzá means "by the mouth of the well of the Itzá" and refers to the MAYA city's ninth-century conquest by peoples of the southern Gulf coast.

The city had a long and complicated history. It began as a minor settlement between 600 and 750 C.E., drawing on the elegant Puuc architectural style of centers such as Uxmal. But the Itzá invasion brought momentous changes. These aggressive peoples quickly extended their power throughout the north and east of the peninsula,

A glass of *chicha* (maize beer) and a basket of maize kernels. *Chicha* production is widespread though the Andean region. *(Courtesy of J. Michael Francis)*

eliminating the rival Yaxuná-Cobá group and establishing firm control over the economically critical salt deposits of Emal. By the late 800s, Chichén Itzá had displaced all other northern plains centers in terms of power and wealth. The Itzá operated a lucrative salt-for-OBSIDIAN TRADE. They also superimposed on their city an array of features commonly associated with Central MEXICO, including warriors, the Feathered Serpent god (QUETZALCÓATL), phalluses, and the reclining figures known as Chac Mool that were probably used as receptacles for ceremonial offerings. The long-supposed transfer of styles from the Toltec city of TULA to Chichén Itzá has recently come into question, however, given evidence that the latter actually predated the former (see TOLTECS).

Through their control of coastal waterways, Chichén's rulers also supervised a vast trade network; CACAO, seashells, feathers, and precious stones were all sought-after commodities. The city began to decline sometime after 1000, possibly as a result of the commercial and political disruptions occurring throughout Mesoamerica. The remaining Itzá relocated to the area of GUATEMALA's Petén, and the first Spanish conquistadores found only abandoned ruins where the mighty kingdom had once stood.

Despite its importance in Postclassic Mesoamerica, considerably less is known about Chichén's political and dynastic history than about the far older Maya centers of the southern lowlands. The increasing use of paper during the Postclassic period meant that few stone inscriptions survived in Chichén. Virtually all of these inscriptions date from the reign of K'ak'upakal K'awiil and his brother K'inil Kopol (ca. 900).

In death, Chichén Itzá has retained its powerful allure. Indeed, so many people visit the site every year that Mexico's National Institute for Archaeology and History has restricted access to temples such as the iconic Castillo. Regardless, Chichén Itzá seems destined to remain one of the most visited archaeological zones in the world.

—Terry Rugeley

Further reading:
Jeff Karl Kowalski and Cynthia Kristan-Graham, eds. *Twin Tollans: Chichén Itzá, Tula, and the Epiclassic to Early Postclassic Mesoamerican World* (Washington, D.C.: Dumbarton Oaks Research Library & Collection, 2007).

Susan Kepecs and Rani T. Alexander, eds. *The Postclassic to Spanish-Era Transition in Mesoamerica: Archaeological Perspectives* (Albuquerque: University of New Mexico Press, 2005).

childhood See FAMILY.

Chile
Early Spanish explorers picked up the word *Chile* from the INCAS, who used it to describe territory to the south of PERU. There are a number of theories regarding the origin of the word; likely, it derived from the QUECHUA, Mapuche, or Aymara language.

Modern Chile stretches along South America's Pacific coast from roughly 17° S latitude to the tip of the continent. Its eastern boundary follows the Andes mountain chain down the spine of South America. Chile also has a territorial claim in Antarctica, directly south of the continent, and governs Easter Island. Chile's length means that it incorporates a wide variety of climatic zones, from the arid north to the deciduous forests of the south.

There is evidence that human activity began in Chile 30,000 years ago, and a number of archaeological sites reveal that both big-game hunting and some cultivation began to take place between 10,000 and 9000 B.C.E. On the eve of Spanish CONQUEST, Chile's indigenous cultures included the Diaguita in the desert to the north, the Picunche in the central valley, the Mapuche (Araucanians) in the southern forests, the seminomadic Pehuenche and Puelche in the Andes and the Patagonia in the fjords of the far south, and the Chono on and near the island of Chiloé.

Although indigenous groups in central Chile lived in close proximity to one another, they maintained important ethno-linguistic differences. For example, the Pehuenche were racially, culturally, and linguistically distinct from both the Mapuche of the plains and the Patagonians to the south. Generally, it is believed that the Mapuche developed culturally on the western side of the Andes and the mountain groups on the eastern side.

Most of these groups in central and southern Chile were divided into small, kin-based settlements but engaged in intergroup contact through the region's well-developed TRADE network. The intermediaries of this network were the Pehuenche and Puelche, hunter-gatherers who moved through different regions in pursuit of guanacos, *ñandú* (rhea), and pumas, which brought them into frequent contact with other ethnic groups. Contact and mobility were further increased almost immediately after the arrival of Europeans and, in particular, after the introduction of Spanish horses.

During the early period of the Spanish conquest, intertribal alliances were dynamic and complex. The Pehuenche and Puelche were neighbors and culturally similar, yet despite their proximity, they developed a political antipathy through their alliances with the Mapuche and the Huilliche peoples, respectively. The relationship was further complicated when the Pehuenche entered into multiple and fleeting alliances with Hispanic creole settlers.

DIEGO DE ALMAGRO led the first Spanish exploration of Chile from Peru in 1535. With the help of Prince Paullu, the Inca MANCO CÁPAC's brother, Almagro conquered the Andean provinces known to the Inca as Purumauca, Antalli, Pincu, Cauqui, and Araucu. At the eastern entrance to the Aconcagua Valley, which later became the gateway to Chile's capital, Almagro decided to turn back to Peru. However, before he left, Almagro waited for reports from the several expeditions he had sent ahead. One of these expeditions reached (and named) the port of Valparaiso, while another, led by Gómez de Alvarado, went southward. Gómez de Alvarado reported to Almagro that the farther he traveled, the worse the terrain became. As he moved south, Chile's climate became increasingly cold, and the land, barren and full of large, muddy rivers. Alvarado added that he came across a number of indigenous groups, whom he characterized in a negative light. Alvarado was unimpressed with one group (thought to be the Huarpes), in particular, who, he said, dressed in pelts and ate only roots.

Alvarado's group met armed resistance. The Spanish fought off an attack at the Maule River and fought the "skirmish" of Reinoguelén at the junction of the Ñuble and Itata Rivers. This battle was the first contact between the Spanish and the Mapuche and resulted in the death of two Spaniards and the capture of scores of Mapuches. Nevertheless, Alvarado's disappointment did not prevent others from trying their luck in Chile; in 1541, PEDRO DE VALDIVIA led an expedition from Peru into Chile's Aconcagua Valley. Valdivia founded Santiago de la Nueva Extremadura, was named Chile's first governor, and sent his lieutenants south and east into what would eventually become the Argentine province of Cuyo (see ARGENTINA).

After founding the city of Santiago, Valdivia led an expedition south in 1546, which met with strong Mapuche resistance near the Bío-Bío River. Conflicts only increased when the Spanish presence grew after 1549 in response to the discovery of GOLD in the region. Valdivia's expedition established Spain's grip on much of Chile, but the conquest stopped short when Valdivia was killed by the Mapuche in 1553. Valdivia's former Mapuche groom, Lautaro, set an ambush for the governor as he rode to the aid of the Spanish fort of Tucapél.

Lautaro's knowledge of the Spanish had made him an indispensable military leader for the Mapuche. Armed with the euphoria of the victory over Valdivia and the knowledge that the Spanish would return to the south if not driven out of Chile, Lautaro led a Mapuche counteroffensive in 1557. After months of marching, he was nearing Santiago when he was intercepted by Spanish forces and killed in a battle with Chile's new Spanish governor, Francisco de Villagra.

This turn of events quickly evolved into the Arauco War, a seemingly eternal conflict between the Spanish (and later Chilean) soldiers and the Mapuches. The failures in these campaigns became an important conundrum for Spanish governors, writers, and soldiers alike, who were accustomed to quick conquests. An important literary representation of the Arauco War can be found in the "first American epic," *La Araucana* by Alonso de Ercilla y Zúñiga, originally published in 1569. As a soldier, Ercilla saw few victories for the Spanish during his brief stay in Chile, where he had arrived in 1557. Not surprisingly, his epic reflected the voice of a frustrated adventurer.

See also ARAUCANIANS (Vol. II); CHILE (Vols. II, III, IV); SANTIAGO DE CHILE (Vols. II, III, IV).

—Eugene Berger

Further reading:
H. R. S. Pocock. *The Conquest of Chile* (New York: Sten & Day, 1967).
Mario A. Rivera. "Prehistory of the Southern Cone." In *The Cambridge History of the Native Peoples of the Americas*, vol. 3, part 1: *South America*, edited by Frank Salomon and Stuart B. Schwartz, 734–768 (Cambridge: Cambridge University Press, 1999).

Chimú   The Chimú were an Andean ethnic group that ruled an empire the Spaniards later called Chimor. Living along the northern coast of PERU, the Chimú flourished from 900 to 1460, when their kingdom was conquered by the INCAS. The great adobe coastal city of CHAN CHAN, founded around 900 c.e., was the capital of the Chimú Empire. At its height, Chimú territory stretched from Tumbes in the south over 600 miles (965 km) to Huaura, near the site of modern LIMA. The earlier MOCHE had inhabited part of that region, and the Chimú perpetuated some Moche traits but were also influenced by the WARI culture that expanded into northern Peru several centuries prior to their emergence.

Life in the arid coastal desert challenged the Chimú. Their AGRICULTURE required irrigation, and they built and maintained the most elaborate system of canals in the ancient Andes. Such projects demanded complex social and bureaucratic organization. Fish and shellfish taken from the coastal waters provided an important supplement to their diet. A powerful aristocracy dominated Chimú society, and the Chimú believed their king was a god. Much of the GOLD initially plundered by the Spanish conquistadores probably came from the Chimú region, for they had focused much of their craftsmanship on metallurgy and excelled as goldsmiths. They were also well known as weavers (see TEXTILES).

The Spaniards were able to obtain information about Chimú history and mythology as the Chimú had only recently been conquered by the Incas. Inquiries revealed that Tacaynamo had arrived by sea on a raft and established himself as ruler and high priest of the Moche Valley. Later Chimú kings claimed descent from Tacaynamo. In the mid-14th century, Tacaynamo's grandson Ñançenpinco led the first Chimú expansion, conquering the Santa and Jequetepeque Valleys to the south and north, respectively. A century later, the Chimú king Minchançaman carried out the last phase of Chimú imperial expansion, extending their rule over Tumbes near the present-day Peru-ECUADOR border and southward to the Chillón Valley. Minchançaman was still ruling when the Incas conquered the Chimú around 1460. They took him to CUZCO as a hostage in an attempt to ensure the cooperation of the Chimú.

—Kendall Brown

Further reading:

Michael Edward Moseley and Alana Cordy-Collins, eds. *The Northern Dynasties: Kingship and Statecraft in Chimor* (Washington, D.C.: Dumbarton Oaks Research Library & Collection, 1990).

John H. Rowe. "The Kingdom of Chimor." *Acta Americana* 6 (1948): 26–59.

chinampas   Sometimes mistakenly called "floating gardens," *chinampas* are a Mesoamerican intensive agricultural system of high fertility, high yields, and multiple annual crops (see AGRICULTURE). Cultivators modified boggy areas by digging drainage canals and forming raised fields of rich canal mud piled between them. They also piled layers of mud and decaying vegetation on shallow lake bottoms until fields rose above the water level. Field margins were stabilized with wooden piles or wattle retaining walls, and trees were planted along the edges. Construction of *chinampas* was LABOR intensive and beyond the capabilities of FAMILY groups. The centralized authority of a chiefdom or state was required to mobilize sufficient labor to undertake the project.

Generally found surrounding or adjacent to urban settlements, *chinampas* were important resources for supporting large populations. *Chinampas* were constructed throughout Mesoamerica, appearing as early as the Late Formative period between the city of TEOTIHUACÁN and Lake Texcoco. Raised fields were not restricted to lake margins in arid highland areas; the MAYA built them in the wet lowlands. Extensive tracts of *chinampa*s in Lakes Chalco and Xochimilco and surrounding the Aztec metropolis of TENOCHTITLÁN-Tlatelolco produced much of the food needed to support the capital of the empire (see AZTECS).

The canals permitted easy canoe transport of the crops to markets, maintained constant soil moisture, provided mud and floating plants to renew soil fertility, and were home to edible fish and lake animals. Aztec nobles sometimes became owners of these valuable resources after they were captured from other groups; they then rented them to farmers. Colonial documents reveal that many cultivators built their houses on the *chinampas* they farmed. Following the CONQUEST OF MEXICO, Spaniards began to drain the Basin of Mexico's lakes and divert springs for drinking water. As a result, over time most of the pre-Columbian *chinampas* disappeared, and today only Xochimilco maintains a small area of them.

—Stephen L. Whittington

Further reading:

Edward E. Calnek. "Settlement Pattern and Chinampa Agriculture at Tenochtitlán." *American Antiquity* 37 (January 1972): 104–115.

chroniclers   The chroniclers (*cronistas*, in Spanish), as understood in the 16th century, wrote about the lives and deeds of rulers and those who excelled because of their virtue, military skill, or intellect. Since their inception in the Middle Ages, chroniclers had a strong pedagogical orientation. The Castilian-Leonese legal code contained in the Siete Partidas (proclaimed as law in 1348) instructed the MONARCHS OF SPAIN to read or listen to the accounts of the lives of their predecessors and use them as guides for their own conduct. However, the moral, political, and military instruction of rulers was not the chroniclers' only job. They were also to describe the times. Epistemological standards, therefore, were key to the development and transformation of the tradition, perhaps being more important than a writer's literary or rhetorical ability. Chroniclers thus were expected to use reliable information (obtained from key participants, official documents, or, less commonly, those who witnessed events) and to speak from a position of social and intellectual authority.

Spanish expansion into the Americas brought about intense writing and publication of narratives about exploration, CONQUEST, indigenous life and history, and evangelization. While letters written by CHRISTOPHER COLUMBUS, AMERIGO VESPUCCI, and HERNANDO CORTÉS were often included as part of the historiographical corpus on Iberian colonial expansion, the chronicling of Spanish colonialism truly began with Peter Martyr d'Anghiera (1457–1526), who produced the first historical narratives about the Spaniards' conquest of the Americas. As reports from conquerors and explorers reached Spain, Martyr made sense of the news for a courtly audience familiar with classical and humanist traditions. The first Latin edition of Martyr's *Decades de orbe novo* (Decades of the New World) appeared in 1511; the work covered only the first decade of the colonial era, from Columbus's first voyage of 1492 to Vicente Yañez Pinzón's voyage to BRAZIL in 1499.

It was not until 1530 that Miguel de Eguía, the publisher in Alcalá de Henares, issued a complete edition with all of Martyr's "decades" (chapters). In 1520, King Charles I appointed Martyr royal chronicler, thus officially recognizing his endeavors as historian of Spanish colonization. Martyr's work contained the first authoritative representations of Amerindian populations and the colonization process. His descriptions of the inhabitants of the Antilles provided a lens through which his contemporaries tended to look at Amerindian populations as a whole; moreover, his criticism of some Spanish conduct in the Indies shaped future reflections on the colonial project.

After Martyr's death, the Crown made provisions to have Antonio de Guevara continue his work. A 1526 royal decree (*cédula*) ordered that all of Martyr's papers be put in Guevara's possession; however, Guevara never fulfilled his commission. Only with the 1532 appointment of Gonzalo Fernándo de Oviedo (1478–1557) as a royal chronicler was the effort to write the history of Spanish expansion reinvigorated. Acting under the authority and supervision of the COUNCIL OF THE INDIES, Oviedo set out to correct the work of Martyr, whom he had criticized for having indiscriminately recorded what his informants told him. Oviedo relied on his own lived experiences, published accounts, original documents, and interviews. He also made use of his power of attorney granted by the Crown to summon depositions from all royal officers in the Indies. Published in 1535, the first part of Oviedo's *Historia general y natural de las Indias* (General and natural history of the Indies) was the first major account of Spanish colonization published in the Spanish language.

Oviedo's work presents a complex view of Spanish colonization. While extolling the merits and accomplishments of the conquistadores, he also harshly criticizes the greed and destructive behavior of some of their most outstanding leaders. Harboring no doubt about the political and economic significance of conquest and colonization, Oviedo sets out to defend the legitimacy of Spanish claims to sovereignty in the Indies and justifies the destruction of indigenous populations based on derogatory views on their morals and nature. These themes proved to be of critical importance in subsequent histories of the Spanish conquest. Oviedo's *Historia* defined the course for future historians, whose accounts revolved around the interpretation of events relevant to the great debates on colonial policy. It also set the general tone of the discussion for chroniclers and historians such as Fray BARTOLOMÉ DE LAS CASAS, Francisco López de Gómara (1511–ca. 1566), and BERNAL DÍAZ DEL CASTILLO.

Prior to the publication of Oviedo's *Historia general y natural*, FRANCISCO DE XEREZ had published a brief account of the conquest of PERU. Xerez's contemporaries were astonished to read about the treasure ATAHUALPA had paid FRANCISCO PIZARRO in ransom for his freedom and about the subsequent execution of the indigenous ruler in spite of his compliance with the Spaniard's demands. Xerez's account helped undermine the legitimacy of the conquest, as FRANCISCO DE VITORIA's remarks morally rejecting the conquest of Peru made clear. Subsequent news about the civil wars among Spaniards in the New World caused outrage in Spain and helped undermine the conquistadores' reputation at court (see CIVIL WARS IN PERU). It was partly because of these accounts that the Crown moved to issue the NEW LAWS OF 1542, which sought to reform colonial administration, protect indigenous rights, and curb the power of the conquistadores in the colonies. In the proceedings before the Council of the Indies, Las Casas read from one of the earliest versions of the *Brevísima relación de la destrucción de las Indias* (*A Very Brief Account of the Destruction of the Indies*), a work that denounced the offenses committed by the conquistadores against the Indians. Las Casas's account played a critical role in shaping the course of reform drafted in the new legislation; at the same time, it cast a shadow on the historical meaning of the conquest and the merits of the conquistadores.

The political and ideological struggles of the 1540s and 1550s informed the production of two of the most important works of the 16th-century Spanish historiographical canon, Las Casas's *Brevísima relación* and López de Gómara's *Historia general de las Indias* (General history of the Indies), both published in 1552. Both Las Casas and Gómara openly condemned the evils of the conquest, although they had very different views on the legitimacy and desirability of conquest as a means for subjugating indigenous populations. Their works played a crucial role in supporting a negative perception of Spanish imperialism throughout Europe. Based on previous accounts, reports from the Indies, and interviews, the narratives provoked strong reactions among those who had participated in the conquest. Most notably, Díaz del Castillo, a veteran of the conquest of MEXICO, wrote a passionate reply from the eyewitness perspective. He aimed to counter the damage that López de Gómara and Las Casas had done to the public image of the conquistador.

In addition to the political debates, another key source of controversy was that of the writer's authority, as the transatlantic development of the genre had caused chroniclers to rely more heavily on empirical information to authorize their writings. Oviedo was the first to insist on the critical importance of eyewitness testimony and direct knowledge, and later PEDRO CIEZA DE LEÓN's *Crónica del Perú*, whose first part was published in 1553, relied on his own eyewitness experiences and extensive fieldwork throughout Peru, which included interviews with indigenous informants. Like Bernal Díaz, Cieza saw himself as an outsider to the world of highly educated chroniclers, but both writers ended up consolidating new standards of truth and authority developed in accordance with their lived experiences.

See also LÓPEZ DE GÓMARA, FRANCISCO (Vol. II); OVIEDO, GONZALO FERNÁNDEZ DE (Vol. II).

—Cristián A. Roa-de-la-Carrera

Further reading:
David A. Brading. *The First America* (Cambridge: Cambridge University Press, 1991).

Cieza de León, Pedro de (b. ca. 1520–d. 1554)
Spanish chronicler of Peru Pedro de Cieza de León, known by the end of his life as the "prince of Peruvian CHRONICLERS" for writing the first history of the Andes, was born in the Spanish town of Llerena, Extremadura, around 1520 into a family of minor merchants, notaries, and clergy. As a youth, he witnessed HERNANDO PIZARRO unload a treasure-laden ship in Seville in 1534; the treasure was part of the Inca ATAHUALPA's ransom. Thus inspired, on June 3, 1535, Cieza de León soon set sail for the Indies. He arrived first in HISPANIOLA and then departed for Cartagena. Cieza de León spent the next decade participating in expeditions throughout the

region under the leadership of Captain Jorge Robledo. The future chronicler took careful notes of his observations; these would eventually constitute his ethnographic accounts of the flora, fauna, and diverse peoples of South America and the momentous events he encountered firsthand.

A true soldier-chronicler, Cieza made frequent references to his balancing of both occupations as he helped to found CITIES in what is present-day southern COLOMBIA. He acquired modest wealth from the spoils of CONQUEST and eventually received an *ENCOMIENDA* at Arma near the Cauca River. When Sebastián de Belalcázar murdered his patron, Robledo, in October 1546 and sacked Cieza's *encomienda*, the chronicler left the region, turning up later that year in Popayán to join the loyalist forces, ironically under Belalcázar's leadership, in order to pursue the rebel GONZALO PIZARRO in PERU. Cieza's shift in alliances allowed him a firsthand view not only of the epic retaking of Peru by PEDRO DE LA GASCA's royalist forces but of the remarkable trek through the former Inca Empire, from Pasto to CUZCO (see INCAS).

Cieza had the uncanny ability to gain the trust of his informants, whether they were indigenous people or Spanish captains and governors. Soon after Pizarro's defeat, Gasca recognized Cieza's abilities as a chronicler and gave him access and perhaps resources to compile materials for his chronicles and histories. Though never the official chronicler of the Gasca administration, Cieza traveled widely under Gasca's authority and interviewed a wide range of officials, clergymen, indigenous CACIQUES, and, famously, some of the remaining Inca *quipucamayocs* (*QUIPU* "readers") in Cuzco. His writings are clear and informative and reflect more than an immediate witnessing of events; Cieza transcended the genre and wrote a work that put the Incas into universal history. His work became the crucial source for many historians who followed, especially for the Inca Garcilaso de la Vega, who quoted liberally from Cieza in his *Comentarios reales de los Incas (Royal Commentaries of Peru)*. Cieza finished part 1 of his four-part masterpiece in September 1550, in LIMA, and soon thereafter began the return journey to Spain, where he had arranged to marry Isabel López de Abreu, the daughter of a merchant in Seville. He presented part 1 of his *Chronicle of Peru* to Prince Philip at Toledo in 1552, and it was approved for publication by the COUNCIL OF THE INDIES the same year. The work quickly became popular, with multiple printings throughout Europe.

Cieza did not live to see the publication of parts 2, 3, and 4 (all of which remained unpublished until the late 19th and 20th centuries). Nevertheless, he left instructions in his will to have the manuscripts, which circulated widely in the 16th century, published or sent to his much-admired fellow historian the Dominican friar BARTOLOMÉ DE LAS CASAS.

See also GARCILASO DE LA VEGA (Vol. II); PERU (Vols. I, II, III, IV).

—Michael J. Horswell

Further reading:
Alexandra Parma Cook and Noble David Cook. Introduction to *The Discovery and Conquest of Peru: Chronicles of the New Word Encounter* (Durham, N.C.: Duke University Press, 1998).

cities

MESOAMERICA BEFORE 1492

The earliest cities in Mesoamerica were a cluster of settlements established in the Mirador Basin of GUATEMALA's northern Petén region and adjacent areas of BELIZE. A number of sprawling cities, including EL MIRADOR and Nakbé, emerged in the basin no later than the Late Formative period (400 B.C.E.–200 C.E.). At the center of these settlements were enormous elite residential and ceremonial compounds, many of which were connected to other such centers by elevated causeways. The ceremonial precincts were surrounded by residential areas that became progressively less dense as one moved away from the city center. El Mirador, for example, covered an area of 10 square miles (26 km²) and supported a population some estimate to have been as high as 80,000, a settlement density of about 30 persons per acre. If accurate, this would place El Mirador among the most densely populated cities ever to arise in Mesoamerica's lowlands, though the number of inhabitants was still well below that of cities elsewhere in Mesoamerica, particularly the highlands of Central MEXICO.

The most notable cluster of early settlements in the highlands was situated in the Valley of MEXICO, where contemporary MEXICO CITY is located. There, urban development dates to the Late Formative and Early Classic (200–600 C.E.) periods. Cuicuilco, on the southern edge of the valley, was the largest of several evolving settlements until it was partially destroyed by a volcanic eruption in about 150 C.E.; it was abandoned by 200 C.E. It is estimated that at its peak, Cuicuilco had a population of about 20,000, which would have made it the largest settlement in Mesoamerica outside of the Mirador Basin. Although the site has been obscured by lava, Cuicuilco was clearly a compact city and among the first to have had the sort of internally differentiated ECONOMY associated with urbanization, something that was not seen in the Mirador Basin cities.

TEOTIHUACÁN, located in the northeast portion of the Valley of Mexico, was initially a contemporary of Cuicuilco. It, too, grew rapidly after its founding in about 200 B.C.E. Teotihuacán's growth accelerated after the destruction of Cuicuilco, with the population reaching 60,000 to 80,000 by 200 C.E. By 300, most of the city's signature architectural features had been constructed, including the monumental Avenue of the Dead, the Pyramids of the Sun and the Moon, and the Ciudadela, a vast ceremonial and residential precinct situated near the city center (see ARCHITECTURE). Before its collapse in 650, Teotihuacán covered some eight square miles (8 km²) and was home to 125,000 to 200,000 people. Throughout the

Early Classic period, Teotihuacán was easily the largest settlement in Mesoamerica (and in the Americas) and among the largest on earth.

Archaeological excavations of areas outside the central ceremonial precincts have shown that Teotihuacán had an economically and ethnically diverse population. Residential compounds inhabited by peoples from the Gulf coast, modern-day Oaxaca, Yucatán, and Guatemala have been identified. Archaeologists have discovered more than 500 workshops in which CERAMICS, OBSIDIAN, and ground stone were manufactured. Workshops devoted to the production of perishable goods, though not identifiable through surface surveys, are likely to have been common as well. The most important occupational specialty appears to have been the manufacture of tools and other goods made of obsidian.

Teotihuacán also shows clear indications of centralized planning. The cruciform design is created by the three-mile-long (5-km) north-south running Avenue of the Dead, which bisects the city and establishes the general alignment of nearly all of its thousands of residential compounds, palaces, temples, and plazas. Though streets and structures in the city's four quarters were not arranged into a symmetrical rectilinear grid, they are aligned in a common orientation. The San Juan River, which flows through the city, was rechanneled to conform to the orientation of streets and structures, and drainage systems were built to direct runoff into the river. By 300 C.E., Teotihuacán had become the center of Mesoamerica's first true empire. For the next 300 years, the city's political influence extended throughout central and southern Mexico, reaching as far south as contemporary Guatemala. The city's political concerns seem to have been focused particularly on controlling the production, manufacture, and distribution of obsidian. Sometime around 650, Teotihuacán experienced a violent collapse. Its palaces and central ceremonial structures were defaced or destroyed, and the city was largely abandoned thereafter.

Other regions of Mesoamerica witnessed similar processes of population concentration and urban growth at roughly the same time as occurred in the Valley of Mexico. In the Valley of Oaxaca, for example, a city known today as MONTE ALBÁN was built atop a barren hill that rises from the valley floor. The hilltop forms a linear ridge on which massive temples, palaces, and plazas were constructed. Residential areas of the city were located on terraces built on adjacent hillsides. At its peak, from 500 to 900 C.E., the city covered about three square miles (7.7 km²) and was home to a population of 15,000 to 20,000. Unlike Teotihuacán, Monte Albán does not show evidence of central planning other than the elite residential and ceremonial complex found on the hilltop. Monte Albán was similar to Teotihuacán, however, in having a commercial urban economy, with a substantial portion of the population involved in nonagricultural production.

Substantial population and settlement growth in the Early Classic period occurred in the area surrounding the Mirador Basin in the northern Petén region of Guatemala

and adjacent areas of Mexico, Belize, and Honduras. Although the earlier Mirador Basin cities had declined or disappeared by the Classic period, a multitude of others, including TIKAL, CALAKMUL, CARACOL, Uaxactún, Palenque, and COPÁN arose and continued the lowland urban tradition. Lowland cities differed significantly in physical layout from the patterns seen in Teotihuacán and Monte Albán. Maya cities of the Classic period were more similar to the earlier pattern found at El Mirador, with ceremonial and elite residential precincts surrounded by densely settled but economically rural areas. Indeed, few Classic Maya cities achieved the population density of the earlier Mirador Basin sites. Calakmul, for example, had a population estimated at 50,000 people spread over an area of 27 square miles (70 km²). Caracol was larger, with some 120,000 to 180,000 people spread over 65 square miles (168 km²). Both Calakmul and Caracol had a settlement density of 10 or fewer persons per acre, far below the density of 100 persons per acre that has been estimated for Teotihuacán and the residential areas of Monte Albán. Likewise, the density was significantly lower than the 30 persons per acre estimated for El Mirador. As at El Mirador, specialized craft production was much more limited in Classic Maya cities, as was the commercialization of urban economies. Most residents of Maya cities (including those in the Mirador Basin) remained agricultural in their economic orientation (see AGRICULTURE). For this reason, many scholars question the extent to which Maya settlements, even the largest, are properly classified as urban settlements.

The collapse of Teotihuacán in the late seventh century was followed by similar declines in Monte Albán and, most spectacularly, in the Maya lowlands. In the Valley of Oaxaca, Monte Albán had been abandoned by 1000, to be replaced by numerous smaller settlements dispersed throughout the valley. The collapse of cities in the Maya lowlands occurred in the eighth and ninth centuries. Unlike the central Mexican highlands, where the collapse or decline of urban centers was accompanied by population dispersal and the growth of new urban centers in the same general vicinity, the Maya region experienced a sharp drop in overall population. Some refugees from declining centers likely moved into adjacent highland regions of Guatemala and the Mexican state of Chiapas, while others moved north on the Yucatán Peninsula, where they were apparently absorbed into local groups and fed the growth of cities that emerged in the Late Classic (600–900 C.E.) and Postclassic (900–1519 C.E.) periods. The northern Yucatán Peninsula witnessed the most notable urban growth, at centers such as Cobá, CHICHÉN ITZÁ, Sayil, Uxmal, and MAYAPÁN. Nevertheless, these cities never attained the size nor exhibited the splendor of the earlier lowland Maya centers.

In the highlands of Central Mexico, the collapse of Teotihuacán was followed by a long period of political fragmentation. Local regions came to be dominated by regional centers, many of which had begun to form during Teotihuacán's dominance. Cholula and Cacaxtla in the

Valley of Puebla, Xochicalco in the Valley of Morelos, and El Tajín in coastal Veracruz are among the best known, but small cities of 10,000 or more dotted the landscape of the central and southern highlands. Many were built in defensible locations, reflecting the acute political competition and the high incidence of WARFARE that characterized the period. Xochicalco, for example, was built on a low hill ringed by terraces that formed defensive ramparts.

In the Early Postclassic period, in the 11th and 12th centuries, the city of TULA, situated just north of the Valley of Mexico, partially reintegrated many local regions, creating the short-lived Toltec Empire (see TOLTECS). At its peak, Tula covered an area of about five square miles (13 km²) and had a population that might have approached 60,000. Though much of the site has been damaged or destroyed, Tula appears to have resembled Teotihuacán in the uniform orientation of its residential and ceremonial structures and in its overall cruciform design, indicators of central planning in the city's initial construction and subsequent growth. Also like Teotihuacán, Tula was a highly diversified manufacturing center.

With the fall of Tula in the late 13th century, Mesoamerica entered a period of political fragmentation that lasted into the early 15th century. By this time, however, urban centers were common throughout Mesoamerica. During these periods of political fragmentation, the characteristic political form was the city-state, known in NAHUATL as an *ALTEPETL*, which consisted of an administrative center and a number of subordinate outlying settlements. The geographic and demographic scale of the *altepetl* varied, as did the form of the settlements found within them. Commonly, the administrative center of an *altepetl* was an urban settlement, where some combination of manufacturing, commercial, ecclesiastical, and administrative specialists were concentrated. Throughout the Postclassic period, and perhaps also in the Classic period, political competition pitted *altepetl* against *altepetl*. The subjugation of one by another regularly led to the creation of small and generally fragile "empires." In so far as *altepetl*s were fairly evenly matched demographically and economically, it proved difficult for any to obtain a lasting advantage that could translate into sustained political domination. Teotihuacán had been able to achieve a striking measure of hegemony through much of Mesoamerica because its initial expansion predated the maturation of the *altepetl* organization in outlying regions. Following the destruction of Cuicuilco, Teotihuacán had emerged as an unrivaled power that was able to expand into a vacuum where it lacked meaningful competitors. It was a vacuum that quickly filled with regional centers, however, and thus Teotihuacán likely faced localized but progressively strengthening opposition in the years leading up to its final collapse. The Toltec expansion occurred in this more mature and hostile political climate, which goes some distance in explaining its lighter footprint and the shorter duration of its political dominion.

What most constrained urban growth and ensured that nearby *altepetl*s were in rough parity were the primitive systems of TRANSPORTATION in pre-Columbian Mesoamerica. Lacking draft animals and wheeled vehicles, most goods were moved from their point of production to the point of consumption by human porters, known as *tlamemes*. This greatly limited the distances over which low-value commodities, including basic foodstuffs, could be moved before the cost of transportation overtook the value of the goods themselves (see FOOD). Because of this, urban development was sharply constrained.

In both the Valley of Mexico and the Pátzcuaro Basin (in the contemporary Mexican state of Michoacán), the canoe offered lakeside settlements opportunities to draw supplies from a much larger territory than was practical for landlocked communities. In the Late Postclassic period, Tzintzuntzán, on the shore of Lake Pátzcuaro and the center of the Tarascan Empire, grew into a three-square-mile (7.7-km²) settlement populated by 25,000 to 30,000 people.

The preeminent example of a lakeshore settlement was TENOCHTITLÁN, the most important of three cities that ruled the Aztec Empire (see AZTECS). Tenochtitlán was situated on an island in Lake Texcoco in the Valley of Mexico. From this position, the city was able to draw supplies from a multitude of smaller cities that through the Postclassic period had grown up along the lakeshore. Like Teotihuacán and Tula, Tenochtitlán was a planned settlement, divided into four quarters with a ceremonial precinct at the center. Much of the city was in fact built on land created through land reclamation, by dredging silt from the lake bottom and expanding what had begun as a small rocky outcrop into a sizable island. According to Aztec accounts, the city was founded in 1325. By the time it reached its full extent, it covered an area of more than five square miles (13 km²) and had a population estimated at well above 200,000 people. At a density of more than 150 persons per acre, Tenochtitlán was the most densely settled city, as well as the largest ever to arise, in Mesoamerica. Smaller ceremonial precincts were located in each of the four quarters of the city, and numerous open plazas that formed meeting places for periodic markets were scattered throughout the city. There were three main avenues, leading north, south, and west, each linking up with a broad causeway that connected the island to the mainland. The city itself was crisscrossed by canals, which allowed cargo-laden canoes to supply neighborhood markets. Freshwater was piped into the city from a spring at Chapultepec, located several miles west of the city on the mainland.

Finally, several Postclassic cities in the central Mexican highlands were known for their specialized functions. For example, in the Valley of Puebla, the city Cholula, which had some 100,000 inhabitants and was the second-largest city in Mesoamerica at the time of the Spanish CONQUEST, was an important religious center and pilgrimage site (see RELIGION). Texcoco, on the east side of the Valley of Mexico, was renowned as a center of learning. Azcapotzalco, on the western shore of Lake Texcoco, had a famous slave market (see SLAVERY). Otumba, near the earlier city of Teotihuacán, produced TEXTILES, particularly ones made of maguey fiber. Though they varied in size, internal organization, and settlement density, when Spaniards arrived in Mesoamerica, they found a landscape dominated by scores of urban settlements.

SOUTH AMERICA BEFORE 1492

The trajectory to complex society and what is usually termed *civilization* in South America differs somewhat from that of the Old World. In the traditional definition, civilized societies had centralized rulers who lived in palaces located in cities; these centers had specialized administrators, writing, stratified social classes, and a large resident population, and TRADE was conducted by a class of merchants who ventured their own money. These civilizations also often had a distinctive ARCHITECTURE and a high ART style.

The artistic achievements of Andean peoples in textile production or metallurgy cannot be denied. Likewise, their architectural monuments were impressive and are a tribute to a sociopolitical organization that enabled their societies to mobilize human energy on a large scale. Andean cities, however, continue to puzzle scholars because they appear to have lacked some of the above-mentioned characteristics of civilizations.

While there were large settlements in other areas of South America, the Andean region was most notable for its cities before the arrival of Europeans. Andean societies in both the highlands and the coast had overcome severe environmental challenges to produce a secure food supply; this, in turn, supported a larger population and led to more complex social and political organization. In the Andes, both on the coast and in the highlands, people lived in landholding descent groups from which they took their primary identity. These descent groups, called *AYLLU* in the highlands, were organized in an ascending series of ranked, dual levels, by means of which the larger society ensured access to agricultural products, marine resources, and the meat and fiber of llamas and alpacas. At the lowest levels, each descent group had a headman; at higher levels, these rulers were lords, called *KURAKA* in the highlands. Artisans and traders appear to have been organized into similar descent groups subject to a higher-level lord. At its apex, the whole polity was governed by two ranked rulers. This was true of the Inca Empire and all the societies that preceded it (see INCAS).

By 5,000 years ago, some Andean descent groups on the Pacific coast and in the highlands were living in larger settlements, while others were scattered across the countryside in homesteads and hamlets. These groups came together for religious festivals; the corporate nature of the society made it possible to organize the LABOR to erect large ceremonial centers. Most of the labor for these projects was not permanent but rather on a cyclical basis. Moxeque in the Casma Valley is a ceremonial com-

plex built and occupied between 3,500 and 3,000 years ago that exemplifies the beginnings of Andean urbanism. Two very large, and very different, adobe platform mounds were constructed in stages, each at the end of an esplanade made up of five large plazas aligned 41° east of north. The northern mound was ceremonial in function. The southern mound, of a different architectural design, appears to have functioned as a center of political administration and ceremony. The site has been partly destroyed through cultivation, but along either side of the esplanade of linked plazas were aligned small mounds and walled compounds that appear to have housed the elites associated with the corporate groups (*ayllu*-like). It is not known whether the two areas of domestic habitation or elite compounds were inhabited full time or whether these corporate groups resided on their lands most of the time and left a skeleton caretaker population at Moxeque between ceremonial occasions.

Tiwanaku lay just south of Lake Titicaca. It was located near agricultural land suitable for high-altitude crops, such as POTATO, and high-altitude pastures that were ideal for raising llamas and alpacas for fiber, transport, and meat (see TRANSPORTATION). Agricultural land was expanded through the construction of raised fields in wetlands and along the lakeshore. The lake also provided important aquatic resources, particularly fish and birds, and plants such as reeds. Before about 500 C.E., Tiwanaku was one of several small communities that served as ritual centers for the corporate groups living in the hinterland. By 500, it was linked to other groups by trade routes that brought meat and fiber from the herding groups in the high puna and products such as MAIZE, peppers, and salt from the warm valleys of the Pacific and COCA from the warm valleys of the eastern slopes of the Andean cordillera.

The exchange appears to have taken place in the context of repeated pilgrimages to the ritual center at Tiwanaku. Some corporate groups may have sent part of their group to live in these areas as colonists. By 800, the Tiwanaku divinities had become preeminent in the region, commanding devotion from different groups over a wide area. They were represented in a widely diffused art style, which was used on high-status and common CERAMICS, woven into textiles, and carved on the walls of temples. The ritual devotion brought wide access to human energy, which was used to bring red sandstone and blue andesite from distant quarries for the construction of monumental places of worship and ritual feasting. There were several immense temples: the Akapana with a seven-tiered pyramid, the Kalasasaya, and Pumapunku. All of these pyramids were enclosed within immense plazas, usually with a raised area where rituals could be performed before a large number of worshippers. The entire ritual area was set off from the rest of the city by a moat. To the east, within the moat and just beyond it, were enclosed compounds that housed the elite. To the south of the monumental area was an area of wetland, which provided grazing and water during the dry season. Beyond this area to the south was an area of lower-status domestic occupation.

Neighborhoods were made up of groups of walled compounds. Within each compound were a number of houses, each with a kitchen area, a storage area, and trash pits. In some cases, there was evidence of weaving and other craft production. It has been suggested that the residents in these compounds may have been members of the same *ayllu*-like group. What is lacking at Tiwanaku from a Western point of view are districts of artisans and merchants, evidence for a standing military force or bureaucracy, and large palaces for rulers. Goods were circulated and exchanged, it would appear, during religious festivals.

The CHIMÚ Empire was an expansive polity that arose in the Moche Valley on the north coast of PERU about 900 C.E. The preeminent urban center was moved from the up-valley site of Galindo to uncultivated land on the littoral, signaling a major ideological shift. This new capital was CHAN CHAN, which served as the seat of the Chimú state until it was conquered by the Incas in the first third of the 15th century. Unlike Tiwanaku, Chan Chan was a new city that evidenced a certain amount of urban planning. At its apogee, the city covered some eight square miles (20.7 km²). The monumental core contained approximately 10 immense walled compounds, presumed to be the palaces of rulers and inhabited by their descendants after their death. On the eastern and northern sides of the core area were four large platform mounds, which may have been temples. However, with the Chimú Empire there is a change in Andean religion, with the rise of sacralized political rulers who were themselves the principal protagonists in religious rituals.

None of the 10 compounds are exactly alike, but in general, these great rectangular compounds, called *ciudadelas* by some scholars, are aligned with the entrance on the north side in two roughly north-south columns. The internal divisions in most are tripartite, with about a third of the area at the entrance given over to an immense enclosed plaza. At the southern end was a raised area, which could have served as a proscenium for politico-religious rituals. The central area of the compound was made up of reception rooms and living quarters for the ruling elite. There were also large areas of what have been called storerooms, associated with U-shaped, niched structures, called *audiencias*; however, their precise function remains unknown. Finally, there was a large platform mound, which served as the burial place of the ruler. It probably was a center of ritual before and after his death. The final sector of the compound, between one-third and one-fourth of the total area, contained low-status housing, presumably for retainers, and a walk-in well, dug down to the water table, which provided water for everyday purposes and perhaps also to support limited gardens.

Between the great compounds were different kinds of structures, some evidently used by high Chimú authorities below the ruler. Others were the residences of provincial lords of different ranks, who may not have occupied them

full time. Finally, there appear to have been compounds associated with high-status craft production. To the west and south of the compounds associated with the rulers were cemeteries and extensive areas of walk-in wells and sunken gardens. There were also extensive areas of low-status, agglutinated structures within compound walls, which appear to have been the dwellings of common folk, grouped by their *ayllu*-like corporate groups. On the north coast, artisans and exchange specialists were grouped within such fictive descent groups that were subject to the higher-status lords. It is not known whether the population of Chan Chan was maintained by the stores of the ruler, supported by provincial lords, or if lands to the north of the city were assigned for cultivation. It is probable that all three modalities were used. Exchange appears not to have been institutionalized in markets, and most goods were probably redistributed by the rulers or the lower lords.

While the Chimú replicated elements of the architecture found at Chan Chan in their provincial centers, it was not always systematic. In contrast, the Incas, whose state expanded swiftly between the 13th and 15th centuries, used urban planning as a systematic part of their governing strategy. The city of CUZCO, which lies in a highland valley of the south-central Andes, was the capital and the cosmological center of the Inca Empire. The Inca state was divided into two moieties: the *hanansaya*, or upper moiety, and the *hurinsaya*, or lower moiety. This division was also found in the urban plan of Cuzco. Further, two of the four quarters (*suyus*) of the realm, Chinchaysuyu and Antisuyu, made up the *hanansaya*, while Cuntisuyu and Collasuyu were in the *hurinsaya*. This division extended outward from the city core to the surrounding valley and beyond, to the whole realm.

The core of Cuzco contained the compounds of each of the rulers, occupied by the ruler in his lifetime and by his descendants thereafter. There were temples and the *aqllawasi*, or "houses of the chosen women" (see ACLLA). Near the center of the city were two large contiguous plazas, the Aucaypata and the Kusipata, where ceremonies were held. These plazas were separated by one of the two rivers that delimited the city. The Temple of the Sun, or Coricancha, was the largest religious complex, but in general, buildings in Cuzco lack the monumentality of the temples of Tiwanaku or the compounds of Chan Chan. The one monumental construction associated with Cuzco is Sacsayhuamán, three immense zigzag walls on the hill above Cuzco, crowned with two towers. This was a sacred place and may also have served as a fortress. The blocks of stone that make up the walls are cyclopean and fitted together without mortar.

High-status Inca buildings within the city core were made of exquisitely fitted "pillow" masonry. They were built as walled compounds, or *cancha*, usually two to a city block. Streets were paved but narrow, with a drainage conduit down the middle; the Spanish complained that only two could ride abreast on one of these streets. The roads to the different *suyus* came together at the Aucaypata. From the Temple of the Sun, the Inca conceived of 42 sight lines, or ZEQUES, that extended outward into the valley. Along these were *huacas* (shrines), natural features or artificial ones, such as houses or canals. Some of these shrines commemorated points in the Inca politico-religious mythology; others denoted boundaries between different social groups. Important mountain peaks or passes and sources of water for irrigation canals were significant points on the *zeques*. Non-Inca social groups, whether closely tied to the Inca or recently conquered provincial lords, were assigned lands for cultivation and house sites in the valley following the logic of the *zeques*.

Inca ECONOMY and society were highly planned and controlled. Large numbers of people were brought together, perhaps several times a year, but they may not have lived in the city permanently. The Inca state provisioned workshops and artisans; the *agllawasi* produced fine textiles as well as CHICHA. Inca armies were provisioned from the storehouses. Independent trade and exchange were not found here, nor was independent craft production; nonetheless, in Andean terms, Cuzco was an important and symbolic urban center.

EARLY COLONIAL

The Spanish conquerors and colonists who ventured to the Americas after 1492 brought with them the notion that the city was the ideal form of human settlement. Cities were believed to offer inhabitants a more dignified and intellectually refined existence than villages, towns, or rural homesteads. Likewise, moral rectitude and virtue were associated with urban life. These positive attributes were held to be reflected in the physical layout and the general presentation of settlements: A well-designed and well-swept city was seen as an outward manifestation of the inner intellectual, spiritual, and moral virtues of its inhabitants. Spaniards differed from the Portuguese in this respect. The Portuguese, like British, French, and Dutch colonists elsewhere in the Americas, were much more inclined to live in villages and on rural homesteads. Alone among European colonizers of the Americas, Spaniards sought to use their colonial possessions as a palate upon which to construct cities that reflected Renaissance notions of ideal town planning and Christian ideas of virtue. While this was the intent, bringing it to fruition in the colonies often proved a difficult task.

The earliest Spanish settlements in the Americas, established on HISPANIOLA in the 1490s, were fortified centers with irregular internal plans. Setting aside the short-lived and ill-fated LA NAVIDAD established during CHRISTOPHER COLUMBUS's first voyage, the first efforts to create settlements began in 1493 with the founding of Isabela on the north coast of Hispaniola and a string of smaller outposts in the island's interior. It quickly became apparent that Hispaniola's southern coast was the more suitable for maintaining contact with Spain. By 1500, Isabela had been largely abandoned, and the center of

Spanish operations had moved to Santo Domingo on the southern coast. In an effort to remedy what was seen in Spain as a disorderly attempt at founding a colony by early administrators, in 1502, the Crown dispatched 2,500 settlers to Santo Domingo under the command of Nicolás de Ovando, the newly appointed governor of Hispaniola. Ovando arrived with orders to create settlements inhabited only by Spaniards, a precedent that in later years was applied in an attempt to segregate Spaniards and Indians into physically and administratively separate entities: the *república de españoles* and REPÚBLICA DE INDIOS. Shortly after Ovando's arrival in Santo Domingo, a hurricane destroyed the original settlement. This provided the governor the opportunity to resite the settlement and to create the first city in the Americas with a grid configuration, formed by aligning streets at right angles to create square or rectangular blocks around an open central plaza.

For the next seven years, Ovando presided over the founding of a network of settlements on Hispaniola, all apparently built in the grid design. By the time Ovando was recalled to Spain in 1509, roughly 8,000 to 10,000 Spaniards inhabited Santo Domingo and its satellites. The numbers increased further with the conquest and settlement of CUBA, where governor DIEGO VELÁZQUEZ DE CUÉLLAR established seven urban sites between 1511 and 1515. In 1513, the Crown issued a new and detailed set of instructions on the founding of settlements. These were given to PEDRO ARIAS DE ÁVILA to guide his efforts in establishing settlements on the mainland in the newly created province of Castilla del Oro in Central America. The 1513 document is the first to specifically mention and describe features of the grid design, apparently enshrining Ovando's earlier improvisations into official Crown policy. From this point forward, the Crown's instructions repeated or, in a few cases, refined and elaborated on the same general idea.

By 1519, there were perhaps 25,000 Spaniards in the Caribbean and Castilla del Oro, scattered among a couple of dozen settlements, most of them built in an approximation of the grid pattern favored by Ovando and the Crown. Nevertheless, the shifting and generally bleak economic outcomes of MINING and AGRICULTURE, combined with the catastrophic decline in the indigenous LABOR force, made it next to impossible for the Spaniards to construct stable and lasting settlements in the first decades of the 16th century. This came only later, following the Spanish penetration into Mesoamerica and the Andean region. Native societies in both Mesoamerica and the Andean region differed substantially from those of the Caribbean islands and the Central American lowlands, where the indigenous population was comparatively small and the main settlements were no more than large villages. Mesoamerica and the Andes, on the other hand, were both densely populated and had preexisting urban settlements. The premier example of a native urban center was the island city of Tenochtitlán, which was conquered by HERNANDO CORTÉS in 1521. On the eve of the conquest, Tenochtitlán was home to some 200,000 inhabitants, a far larger population than that of any contemporary European city west of Constantinople. Though not configured in a tidy grid design, Tenochtitlán nevertheless induced awestruck commentary from the Spaniards, who witnessed it as a functioning indigenous city.

As it turned out, Tenochtitlán also provided the Spaniards with their first opportunity to faithfully implement the Crown's instructions on the founding of new cities. During the course of the conquest, Cortés and his allies reduced Tenochtitlán to ruins. Once the conquest was complete, Cortés set about reconstructing the city. An open plaza, or *zócalo*, was built in a location that overlapped the south side of the earlier ceremonial precinct. A church, built from the stones of the Aztec Templo Mayor, faced south onto the open square. On the square's remaining sides were government buildings and prominent commercial establishments. Streets extended outward at right angles from the four corners of the square, and other streets were set at right angles to these to form a grid. Residential (and dual residential-commercial) blocks were interrupted by smaller open plazas and church, convent, and hospital complexes. Following the Crown's guidelines, the city's most prominent residents, including government and ecclesiastical officials, nobles, and elite merchants, were granted residential lots nearest to the city center and along the principal arterials that intersected with the *zócalo*. Petty merchants, craftsmen, and others of more modest means were accorded residential lots elsewhere. Though the city was not walled, it was racially segregated, and no Indians were allowed to live within the planned portion of the settlement. Instead, beyond the grid, were irregularly organized indigenous residential areas.

The basic design of the refurbished Tenochtitlán, today's Mexico City, was thereafter replicated wherever circumstances permitted. Outside Mexico City, urban settlements in Mesoamerica and the Andes generally survived the conquest intact, making it difficult or impossible to impose a grid design. Ceremonial precincts were frequently converted into plazas, and churches were built from the stones of earlier pyramids and temples; however, the general configuration of streets and neighborhoods in most pre-Columbian cities was left intact. The grid pattern was instead replicated in two basic types of settlements: cities newly built to house Spanish immigrants (see MIGRATION) and towns formed as part of the 16th-century indigenous resettlement programs (see CONGREGACIÓN).

In furtherance of the policy of maintaining segregation between Spanish and Indian elements of colonial society, Crown officials set about constructing a series of new settlements intended to be inhabited only by Spaniards. In Mesoamerica, examples of provincial cities built mainly or exclusively to house Spaniards include Acámbaro (1526), Villa Rica de Chiapas (1528), Antequera (1529), Puebla (1531), and Valladolid (1541). A similar process occurred following the Spanish conquest of the Andean region. Administrative centers were built throughout South America, including the cities of Cartagena (1533), Quito (1534), LIMA (1535), Asunción (1537), Popayán (1537), BOGOTÁ (1538), Santiago (1541), La Paz (1548), and Caracas (1567).

Through much of Mesoamerica and the Andes, and everywhere in Latin America outside of these regions, indigenous populations of the early colonial period lived in small towns or villages, or on rural homesteads. The steep decline in the native population following the arrival of Spaniards only accentuated the dispersal, changing the countryside from an initial thick carpet of indigenous peoples to a lightly settled landscape most notable for its emptiness. Ecclesiastical authorities made modest efforts to assemble dispersed populations into nucleated settlements that were modeled after the cities built for Spaniards. This was most common at early convent sites in Central Mexico, such as Huejotzingo (1529), Chilapa (1534), Santa Fe de la Laguna (1534), and Tiripitío (1537). The major effort to resettle the indigenous population came later, however, when government authorities became involved in the last quarter of the 16th century. Colonial administrators throughout Latin America were ordered to gather together the dispersed survivors in the countryside and to concentrate them in thousands of newly formed settlements. These *congregaciones*, as both the program and the resulting settlements were called, were modeled on the grid pattern that had by this time become predictable and formulaic. Indeed, the basic pattern was established long before 1573, when King Philip II issued the Crown's final and most comprehensive set of instructions on urban design. These instructions were issued in time for the final *congregaciones* of the late 16th century but were little more than a summary of the practices that had been refined over the preceding 70 years.

See also CITIES (Vol. II).

—Chris Kyle
Patricia J. Netherly

Further reading:

René Millon. "Teotihuacán: Completion of Map of Giant Ancient City in the Valley of Mexico." *Science* 170, no. 3,962 (1970), 1,077–1,082.

Richard M. Morse. "Urban Development." In *Colonial Spanish America*, edited by Leslie Bethell, 165–202 (Cambridge: Cambridge University Press, 1987).

William T. Sanders and David Webster. "The Mesoamerican Urban Tradition." *American Anthropologist* 90, no. 3 (1988): 521–546.

Michael E. Smith. "City Size in Late Postclassic Mesoamerica." *Journal of Urban History* 31, no. 4 (2005): 403–434.

Robert C. Smith. "Colonial Towns of Spanish and Portuguese America." *Journal of the Society of Architectural Historians* 14, no. 4 (1955): 3–12.

Adriana Von Hagen and Craig Morris. *The Cities of the Ancient Andes* (London: Thames & Hudson, 1998).

civil wars in Peru

civil wars in Peru The Spanish CONQUEST of PERU was an era of great turmoil, heightened by civil war. Civil war among the INCAS facilitated the conquest. In the aftermath of the Spaniards' defeat of the Incas, the conquistadores fell to fighting among themselves over the spoils. Attempts by the monarchy to limit Spanish abuse and exploitation of the indigenous population led to yet more civil war.

When FRANCISCO PIZARRO and his band of Spanish soldiers and adventurers invaded Peru in 1532, they arrived at Tumbés to find the city ruined by war. Informants told them that in the wake of ruler HUAYNA CÁPAC's death, war had broken out between factions headed by two of the Inca's sons, HUÁSCAR and ATAHUALPA. They represented rival *PANAQAS*, or royal lineages, and to some extent different regions of the Inca Empire, with Huáscar's power centered at CUZCO and Atahualpa's around Quito. In the struggle, Atahualpa's forces defeated and captured Huáscar, whose followers saw in the Spaniards a way of reversing the war's outcome. Following Atahualpa's capture by Pizarro, Huáscar's *panaqa* cooperated with the Spaniards. One of its members, MANCO INCA, temporarily became a puppet ruler.

As for the Spaniards, following the capture and execution of Atahualpa and their occupation of Cuzco, they divided into two principal factions, headed by the four Pizarro brothers on the one hand, and DIEGO DE ALMAGRO on the other. Almagro and Francisco Pizarro had received a royal contract, or *capitulación*, to undertake the conquest, but Almagro felt cheated of his fair share of the plunder and political authority. King Charles I ordered that Pizarro govern northern Peru, and Almagro, the south, but the precise boundaries remained unclear. Pizarro managed to mollify his partner somewhat by helping fund a large Almagro-headed expedition into CHILE, which departed in July 1535.

By the time Almagro returned in 1537, discouraged and angered by his failure to find anything but hardship on his trek, Manco Inca had launched a massive rebellion against the Spaniards. Still threatened, the Spaniards in Cuzco, led by HERNANDO PIZARRO and GONZALO PIZARRO, had survived a ferocious siege. Almagro seized the city on April 18, 1537, and imprisoned the Pizarros. He also defeated a relief expedition under Alonso de Alvarado on July 13 near Abancay. Through his Chilean trek and seizure of Cuzco, Almagro was supported by Paullu Inca, one of Manco's half brothers. From his new capital of LIMA, founded in 1535, Francisco Pizarro sent emissaries to negotiate with Almagro, who as a sign of goodwill freed Hernando Pizarro, Gonzalo already having escaped. Hernando then led a force that on April 6, 1538, defeated Almagro at the BATTLE OF LAS SALINAS. The opportunistic Paullu switched sides before Almagro's imminent defeat. His refusal to join Manco meant that the division among the Indians continued. In fact, Manco continued to launch attacks against both the Spaniards and the indigenous groups who cooperated with them. Taken prisoner,

Almagro was executed on Hernando's orders, a decision that contributed to Pizarro's 20-year imprisonment in La Mota castle in Spain, when he returned there in 1539 to defend the Pizarrist cause against Almagrist accusations. In Peru, Almagrists took a bloodier revenge when on July 26, 1541, they broke into Francisco Pizarro's Lima mansion and murdered the conquistador. In the ensuing chaos, Diego de Almagro the Younger seized power and dominated Peru for a year until defeated at the Battle of Chupas (September 16, 1542) by a force commanded by Cristóbal Vaca de Castro, recently sent to Peru by the king to impose peace on the warring Spaniards.

Even the deaths of Pizarro and Almagro and the arrival of Vaca de Castro did not bring lasting peace, however. A new civil war erupted in 1544 when Blasco Núñez de Vela arrived as VICEROY and attempted to enforce the NEW LAWS OF 1542, by which Charles I tried to eliminate the abusive *ENCOMIENDA* system. Led by Gonzalo Pizarro, the *encomenderos*, who consisted largely of the early conquistadores and their supporters, took up arms against the viceroy. By October 1544, Núñez de Vela was driven from Lima; and on January 16, 1546, the viceroy was defeated and killed by Pizarro's forces at the Battle of Añaquito. Although encouraged by some of his followers to declare Peru independent and make himself king, Gonzalo declined. Massive resistance throughout the Americas compelled Charles I to rescind the New Laws. A new royal official, PEDRO DE LA GASCA, gradually weaned support from Pizarro by offering pardons and other rewards to rebels. At Jaquijahuana (April 9, 1548) Gasca's forces defeated Pizarro, who was abandoned by most of his army. The captured Gonzalo was executed the following day.

Pizarro's execution at first seemed to bring the civil wars to an end, but this, ultimately, was not the case. In 1552, the Crown again tried to curb Spanish abuse of the Andeans. Charles I demanded enforcement of earlier decrees that outlawed coercion of indigenous LABOR and required that Indian workers be paid adequate wages. Limits were also to be set on the amount of tribute that *encomenderos* could demand. As in the case of the New Laws of 1542, this threatened the interests of colonials who lived by exploiting the indigenous population. They needed workers particularly at the SILVER mines and on COCA plantations, where Indians were unlikely to work voluntarily (see MINING). A new war broke out on November 13, 1553, when Spaniards in Cuzco, led by Francisco Hernández Girón, rebelled. From Cuzco, the revolt spread to Huamanga and Arequipa. Royal power had been weakened somewhat by the 1552 defeat of Viceroy ANTONIO DE MENDOZA, although the interim viceroy, Melchor Bravo Saravia y Sotomayor, president of the Lima AUDIENCIA (high court), managed to gather royalist forces. In October 1554, the viceroy's forces defeated the rebels at the Battle of Pucará, near Lake Titicaca. This ended the period of civil wars in Peru, although one of the root causes—conflict over the exploitation of the Indians—was not entirely resolved. Nonetheless, royal power was established in Peru and would be more thoroughly institutionalized in the following decades, particularly during the rule of Viceroy Francisco de Toledo (1569–81).

—Kendall Brown

Further reading:
Pedro de Cieza de León. *The Discovery and Conquest of Peru: Chronicle of the New World Encounter,* edited and translated by Alexandra Parma Cook and Noble David Cook (Durham, N.C.: Duke University Press, 1998).
John Hemming. *The Conquest of the Incas* (New York: Harcourt, 1970).
Rafael Varón Gabai. *Francisco Pizarro and His Brothers: The Illusion of Power in Sixteenth-Century Peru* (Norman: University of Oklahoma Press, 1997).

clergy, secular The evangelization of MEXICO was carried out by two main groups: the regular clergy, who followed the *regula,* or "rule" (Franciscans, Dominicans, Augustinians, and Jesuits; see RELIGIOUS ORDERS), and the secular clergy, who lived in the *saeculum,* or "world." Although the regular clergy are most often cited for their role in the early religious history of New Spain, the secular clergy also played a significant role. Secular priests joined HERNANDO CORTÉS's expedition to TENOCHTITLÁN, baptizing indigenous people and administering the sacraments along the way. After the initial wars of the CONQUEST, those conquistador-priests who did not receive royal appointments entered into contractual agreements with individual *encomenderos* (see ENCOMIENDA), who were obliged to care for the spiritual well-being of the native population assigned to them. However, because the secular clergy had a reputation for being ignorant, slothful, and immoral, Cortés suggested to King Charles I that only regular clergy, who were thought to live purer lives, be sent to New Spain.

Despite such requests, the number of secular clergy continued to grow, although not as rapidly as that of the regular clergy. Competition for provinces and parochial jurisdiction, nevertheless, frequently contributed to strained relationships between secular and regular clergy in the 16th century. In addition, the regular clergy traditionally served as an adjunct to the usual ecclesiastical hierarchy, which was composed exclusively of secular clerics. Typically, a secular clergyman would take precedence over a regular clergyman of the same rank, and regular clergy were also subject to the authority of the local bishop. Yet, due to unusual circumstances, regular clerics in colonial Latin America were allowed a larger role than they had in Europe. Seeing conversion as a solution to Spanish-indigenous relations, the monarch and the pope authorized regular clerics to administer the sacraments, fulfill various parochial duties, and, in many instances, function beyond episcopal control to convert the native population to Christianity. However, as the native population declined, so did the missionary

program; this, coupled with other changes in the late 16th century, eventually led the Spanish Crown to favor the secular over the regular clergy and begin the secularization of New Spain with the Ordenanza del Patronazgo (1574).

Unlike regular clergy, the secular clergy did not take vows of poverty and could own property. Indeed, secular priests actively participated in the colonial ECONOMY. Many secular clerics pursued additional economic endeavors to supplement their church salaries and the fees they earned from administering the sacraments. Some occupations were associated with their clerical careers, such as employment with the Holy Office of the Inquisition, or professorships in universities. Others' financial endeavors were more commercial, and included trading in livestock, CLOTHING, slaves, CACAO, and other commodities (see SLAVERY; TRADE). For the most part, secular clerics concentrated on administering to Spanish populations and preferred appointments in CITIES, especially MEXICO CITY, leaving the regular clerics to attend to the indigenous population. The Spanish population and the potential wealth from mines and ports also attracted a large number of secular clerics. Not all priests looked for ways to increase or supplement their incomes, however. Some engaged in a variety of charitable works, founding colleges, convents, and chantries.

The complex ecclesiastical organization of the CATHOLIC CHURCH provided the secular clergy with a variety of positions, some of which (mainly the lower ones) were not filled until the late 16th century because of financial constraints. Bishops in New Spain enjoyed many administrative, legislative, and judicial privileges and commonly created staffs of numerous assistants to help them attend to their duties. Frequently, when a bishop died or was absent for an extended period, the cathedral chapter with its dignitaries and assistants would oversee the administration of the cathedral and diocese. Ideally, the bishop, episcopal staff, and cathedral chapter provided an organizational and administrative hierarchy for the parishes, which were made up of priests and their assistants. Finally, chaplains who served colleges, hospitals, monasteries, and other institutions, were also part of the secular clergy.

As a social unit, the secular clergy was divided into upper and lower categories of prestige and wealth. The bishop, his staff, and those priests who served on cathedral chapters made up the upper clergy. Parish priests, chaplains, and all other clerics lacking high ecclesiastical appointments made up the lower clergy. Because of the prestige and financial benefits allotted to the upper clergy, such clerics came mainly from the higher levels of society, while the lower clergy came from the middle to lower stratum. No indigenous or African individual entered the clergy in the 16th century.

See also CATHEDRAL CHAPTER (Vol. II); CATHOLIC CHURCH (Vols. II, III, IV); *COFRADÍA* (Vol. II); RELIGION (Vols. II, III, IV).

—Mark Christensen

Further reading:
John Frederick Schwaller. *The Church and Clergy in Sixteenth-Century Mexico* (Albuquerque: University of New Mexico Press, 1987).

clothing Depending on the climate and culture of an area, clothing in the pre-Columbian Americas consisted of a vast array of items. Animal skins, TEXTILES made from plant and animal fibers, and feathers all served to cover the body. Clothing not only kept people warm and dry but also indicated status and social affiliation; for example, because it was less LABOR-intensive than COTTON or wool textiles and was not as soft, clothing made from maguey-plant fibers was considered an indication of lower status. The AZTECS had strict rules governing clothing, including who was allowed to wear cotton and who must wear maguey. The INCAS referred to maguey-wearing peoples as "naked" because they did not wear "proper" clothing. Inca nobles felt their brightly colored and finely woven textiles marked them not only as Inca but as civilized.

In most of the cultures from Mesoamerica to South America, textiles were prized as status items because of the tremendous amount of time and resources that could go into their making. The more elaborately woven a textile was, the more valuable it was. MAYA stone carvings depict royal WOMEN wearing dresses and capes with complex geometric designs, and thousands of miles south in TIWANAKU, massive stone sculptures represent elite males wearing highly patterned clothing. While the methods of decoration and form varied, there were some nearly universal types of clothing. One was the tunic, a basic shirt form. Tunics sometimes had sleeves, which could be sewn on from separate pieces or formed from extra width on the shoulder falling down the arm. The length of a tunic could vary from just below the navel to ground length. Like most clothing in the Americas, tunics were not fitted; rather, they fell loosely around the figure. A belt could be added to fasten the tunic more tightly to the body. Tunics could be worn by men or women. Men frequently also wore a loincloth, a length of material that passed between the legs and then fastened around the waist, usually with ties. Loincloths could be decorated or plain and could have long flaps of material that fell over and covered the ties. Like other kinds of clothing, elaborate loincloth flaps could indicate social status, with more sophisticated designs indicating higher status.

ART from COSTA RICA depicts both men and women wearing loincloth-like garments. The women sometimes added a band around the breasts. Men could also wear a skirt of material that wrapped around the waist and fell to the knees. Maya rulers are frequently shown wearing a textile skirt, covered by a net of jade beads. This jade-bead skirt was associated with the MAIZE god and indicated the ruler's role in keeping the favor of the gods of AGRICULTURE. Jade ensembles worn by Maya rulers could

The geometric bird design in this delicately woven headcloth from the Chancay culture (1100–1440) is only visible when the textile is extended flat. When worn, the design would have disappeared, although it remained a part of the spiritual value of the cloth. *(Courtesy of the Michael C. Carlos Museum of Emory University/Photo by Michael McKelvey)*

weigh more than 10 pounds (4.5 kg). Women sometimes wore skirts that left their breasts bare, as depicted in some west Mexican figures from Nayarit and Colima. More often, they wore some sort of dress. Dresses could be nothing more than long tunics, or they could be wrapped and pinned rectangles of fabric, as the Incas and other highland Andean women wore. The pins could be plain or elaborate and were also an indicator of social status. Over these dresses, many South American women wore a shawl, which could be used to carry children as well as cover the body. In many cultures, differences in color, pattern, and weaving could announce not only social status but also one's social affiliation. Different patterns could belong to kin groups, and different cultures might prefer one kind of weave over another. People from the same area would be able to tell a person's culture, village, and even FAMILY from their clothing. Similar to the Incas' attitude toward maguey wearers, some modern QUECHUA speakers in the Andes referred to foreigners as *qualas* (naked), because while they wore clothing, it did not communicate much about the wearer.

Animal skins were also incorporated into indigenous dress. Some skins were coveted not only for their beauty but for spiritual reasons. The pelt of the jaguar, the largest wildcat in the Americas, was an important marker of status in many cultures. The jaguar, a night hunter that can swim as well as climb trees, was seen as a powerful spirit. Jaguars became closely connected with shamans and other spiritual specialists, and wearing their spotted

This female figure from Costa Rica's Florescent period (300–800) shows several forms of body adornment: a *tanga* (a thonglike loincloth), earrings, and elaborate body paint. Intricate knot patterns would have been applied to the body with ceramic stamps. *(Courtesy of the Michael C. Carlos Museum of Emory University/Photo by Michael McKelvey)*

skin may have symbolized the transformation of the shaman from human to spirit form. The strength and ferocity of the jaguar made it difficult to hunt, adding another level of prestige to wearing the skins. Dancers wearing jaguar skins are depicted on Maya ceramic cylinder vessels. Other animals that were hunted for their skins included foxes, pumas, and ocelots. Animal pelts were frequently used as headdress items in the Andes region. Wearing the animal's skin may have been associated with a clan's spirit founder or may have indicated the wearer's social role. It is also known that fox skins were worn by some coastal Andean men who protected fields of grain from hungry animals; perhaps they believed the fox's agility and hunting skill was thus transferred to them.

Many cultures of the Americas made sandals from plant fibers and/or leather. The footbed of a sandal could be made of leather or tightly woven grasses. This was held to the foot with leather straps or twine and in fancy cases with textile, as seen on rulers depicted on Maya stone monuments. Their sandals have enclosed heels and

ornaments attached to them. Miniature versions of fancy sandals have been found in Andean graves as offerings. These elaborate sandals have silver footbeds, held by red wool textile adorned with silver plaques. While these would have been impractical for walking, it is possible that similar sandals were worn by members of the elite during certain ceremonies.

Feathers were also an important aspect of clothing, adorning headdresses, capes, and shirts. They were also used to make fans. The status value of feathers lay in their color and scarcity. Perhaps the most difficult feathers of all to obtain were the tail feathers of the male quetzal bird. These feathers are exceptionally long (up to 25 inches [63.5 cm]) and a rich emerald-green color. The birds' natural habitat is in tropical areas that stretch from modern-day MEXICO into PANAMA. Naturally shy, quetzals spend most of their time high in the rain forest canopy. Compounding the difficulty of finding the birds was the fact that the males have only two tail feathers, so many birds had to be killed or trapped and plucked to produce just one item of clothing. One surviving Aztec headdress includes dozens of quetzal feathers in an extravagant display of wealth. Maya portrayals of kings in their royal regalia feature plumes of nodding quetzal feathers. The deep green color of quetzal feathers, like that of jade, was associated with growing plants and the earth's fertility.

Other colored feathers were used to decorate headdresses and ceremonial shields. Cultures on the western coast of South America traded with the jungle cultures of the east to procure feathers. The bright jewel tones of macaw, parrot, and even hummingbird feathers are found in coastal tunics, capes, and headdresses. Headdresses were important symbols of prestige and power. Many of them are depicted in ART as large, elaborate creations, which would have been difficult to wear. It is possible that a ruler only rarely wore very large headdresses.

Along with everyday clothing, people wore specific outfits for special occasions or certain tasks. Ball game players throughout Mesoamerica wore padded belts and other gear to protect themselves against the heavy rubber ball, which could weigh as much as a bowling ball. Warriors from Mesoamerica to the Andes frequently wore headdresses that announced their military status. They also carried shields, which could be elaborately decorated while still being functional defense mechanisms. Priests, priestesses, and other participants in religious activities often wore clothing designed for ritual (see RELIGION). Sometimes the clothing was a costume that allowed the person to act in place of a god; sometimes it carried symbolic references to the powers that were being called upon.

Another important aspect of body decoration was tattooing and body painting. Mummified remains with tattooed designs have been found in PERU and CHILE. People also painted and stamped themselves with more temporary designs. In Central America, cultures produced stamps with designs that could be dipped in colorant and pressed onto the body. They also produced cylindrical forms with designs that could be rolled onto the body in a long strip. The materials used to make these designs could be colored clays, which came in a variety of shades from yellow to deep red; other dyes came from plant extracts. For example, the juice from the unripened jungle fruit *Genipa americana* will turn black and can stain the skin for up to two weeks. People could create designs on the body that could be as temporary or as permanent as they wanted, to fit in with the way they dressed themselves.

See also CLOTHING (Vol. III).

—Sarahh E. M. Scher

Further reading:
Patricia Anawalt. *Indian Clothing before Cortés: Mesoamerican Costumes from the Codices* (Norman: University of Oklahoma Press, 1981).

Margaret Young-Sánchez and Fronia W. Simpson. *Andean Textile Traditions: Papers from the 2001 Mayer Center Symposium* (Denver, Colo.: Denver Art Museum: 2006).

Clovis culture   First identified at the site of Blackwater Draw in 1936 near the town of Clovis, New Mexico, and best known for the distinctive fluted Clovis spear point, the Clovis culture remains the earliest accepted evidence of humans in the New World. Prior to the 1926 discovery of similar, but smaller and less robust fluted points found with extinct forms of bison at the Folsom site in New Mexico, considerable debate raged surrounding the antiquity of human occupation in the New World. The discovery of unmistakable human artifacts found in direct association with extinct bison at the Folsom site confirmed that humans had indeed occupied North America at the end of the last ice age. In 1936, evidence for human occupation was pushed back even further, when larger and more robust Clovis fluted spear points were found in association with several species of extinct Ice Age animals, particularly mammoths, below a level containing Folsom points and bison bones. Although these artifacts were suspected to be exceptionally old at the time, it was not until the advent of radiocarbon dating in the 1950s that an age of circa 11,000 radiocarbon years before the present was confirmed, verifying the Late Pleistocene age of the Clovis culture. Recent redating of many previously investigated sites now suggests a minimum time range of circa 11,050 to 10,800 radiocarbon years ago for the Clovis culture, equivalent to some 13,250 to 12,800 calendar years ago.

In the years since their initial discovery at the Blackwater Draw site, Clovis points and related forms have been recognized and found across the entire continental United States and portions of Central and South America. Originally thought to represent a colonizing population that entered North America across the Bering land bridge through an ice-free corridor, the Clovis culture rapidly spread across the continent during the same period in which nearly 35 species of Ice Age megafauna went extinct, prompting many researchers to hypothesize that the Clovis people were responsible for hunting many of these species to extinction. This has become known as the "overkill theory," a fiercely debated hypothesis that states the Clovis culture possessed a highly specialized method of hunting large game that allowed them to rapidly spread across and adapt to new landscapes. As they entered new areas and hunted local game to extinction, they were forced to move on to new areas, continuing the expanding "wave" of both colonization and extinctions across the New World.

An opposing hypothesis suggests that the Clovis culture represents the spread of a new and innovative technology across a preexisting population. Current research continues to refine our understanding of the Clovis culture with data suggesting that multiple migrations along coastlines as well as overland routes were highly likely and that the Clovis people relied on a wide range of resources, not just large game. Whether Clovis represents a colonizing population or the spread of a new technology continues to be debated, but what remains remarkable is the rapid spread of the Clovis culture across the vastness of the New World.

—Thomas J. Loebel

Further reading:
Nina Jablonski, ed. *The First Americans: The Pleistocene Colonization of the New World* (San Francisco: California Academy of Sciences, 2002).

coca   For thousands of years, the leaves of domesticated coca have played an important role in the cultures of South American indigenous peoples. The principal varieties were cultivated from the Caribbean coast to BOLIVIA. Indigenous cultivation and use of coca continues today in the Andes of PERU and Bolivia, where Aymara and QUECHUA Indians chew coca leaves with lime to release a mild stimulant that alleviates fatigue and hunger; coca is also widely used in ritual offerings. Coca leaves also contain important nutrients and vitamins, which make them nutritionally important in regions where the diet is high in carbohydrates. Archaeological evidence shows that the domestication of coca occurred in tandem with that of early FOOD crops such as squash and beans (see AGRICULTURE). Some 200 wild species of coca are found in the humid forests of the eastern slopes of the Andes in Bolivia and Peru.

The first variety of coca to be domesticated, *Erythroxylum coca* var. *coca*, comes from this region, with the other three domesticated varieties descending from it. The leaves of this species have the highest levels of cocaine alkaloid, although it is still very low. Limited quantities of coca are legally sold for this use in ECUADOR and Peru. Nevertheless, it is this variety of *Erythroxylum* that is used in the production of cocaine. The second variety of *E. coca*, *E. coca* var. *ipadu*, is found in the western AMAZON region. The leaves are powdered and mixed with ash, which acts like lime. The powder is formed into balls, which are held in the cheek. This variety is probably pre-Columbian in origin.

The other species of domesticated coca is *Erythroxylum novogranatense*, of which there are two distinct varieties. *E. novogranatense* var. *truxillense* was the preferred coca in pre-Columbian times, prized for its superior flavor. It was grown along the coast of Peru in the warm zone on the lower western slopes of the Andes, called the *chaupiyunga*. There are two known sites where this coca was grown for the INCAS: Quibi in the Chillón Valley and Collambay in a tributary valley to the Moche River. It was undoubtedly also grown in Ecuador. This variety is legally grown today, inland from the Peruvian city of Trujillo; its aromatic oils were used to flavor Coca-Cola. The domestication of the Trujillo variety of coca is very old. Evidence for the preparation of lime dating to 7,000 years ago has been found at the Cementerio de Nanchoc ceremonial site on Peru's northern coast. The domestication of *E. coca* var. *coca* must have begun on the eastern slopes of the Andes at a still earlier date. Trujillo coca is intermediate in morphology between the coca of the eastern slopes of the Andes and the other variety, *E. novogranatense* var. *novogranatense*, called Colombian coca because it was found in COLOMBIA and VENEZUELA.

See also AGRICULTURE (Vols. II, III, IV); COCA (Vols. II, III); DRUGS (Vols. III, IV).

—Patricia J. Netherly

codices An indigenous manuscript format once common throughout Mesoamerica, codices are rightfully considered one of the great literary traditions of the world. The first archaeological evidence for the use of codices dates back to 600 C.E., though this consists only of small fragments that were found in MAYA tombs. The best-preserved examples are the Maya, Mixtec, and Borgia group codices from the Postclassic period (about 15 codices), and the Aztec and other codices from the early colonial period (more than 500 examples) (see AZTECS; MIXTECS). It is likely, though, that most Mesoamerican indigenous groups produced and used these documents for more than a millennium.

Although in relation to Mesoamerica the term *codices* generally refers to the various forms of indigenous manuscripts, it is also used to describe documents that were folded into an accordion-like (or screen-fold) shape. The paper was commonly made from *amatl* (fig-tree bark), maguey fibers, or deer hide. After the Spanish CONQUEST, European paper, which was often coated with a thin layer of white plaster, was used. A specialized painter-scribe,

or *tlacuilo*, applied the pictographic content and hieroglyphic text in vivid colors, frequently on both sides of the page. Its unique format made it possible to spread the codex so a large audience could view it, while still being easily portable in its folded state.

The subject matter of codices was diverse, covering themes such as RELIGION and myth, history and genealogy, politics and ECONOMY, cartography (see MAPS) and astronomy, or anything else that needed recording. As with modern-day books, it is common to find several of these themes combined together in a single codex. The narrative could range from epic tales of rulers (as in the Mixtec Codex Nuttall) to the daily life of commoners (the Aztec Codex Mendoza) (see LITERATURE). Codices were used by the literate nobility, priests and priestesses, and government officials, although the schematized pictographic style would have been comprehensible to the majority of the population, even to those who spoke different languages. These painted narratives were often performed orally and theatrically at feasts and other public events.

Although extant codices have been extremely useful in understanding Mesoamerican culture history, many of their pictographic qualities are still poorly understood, our knowledge being limited because so few survived the Spanish conquest. Several European CHRONICLERS described vast libraries housing codices, none of which were preserved. For the most part, it was the Spanish conquistadores and zealous priests who destroyed pre-Columbian codices, on account of their depictions of indigenous religious themes and the fact that the codices themselves were often considered sacred objects. Bishop DIEGO DE LANDA, for example, is reported to have burned at least dozens of Maya codices. After the conquest, several pre-Columbian codices were brought back to Europe as trophies; some of these texts survive today. Many of the colonial codices were created with the encouragement of European friars, who soon realized that the information they contained could be used to better understand and so convert Mesoamerica's indigenous groups. Perhaps the best-known example in this regard is the FLORENTINE CODEX, an encyclopedic manuscript composed by Aztec scribes under the careful supervision of the Franciscan friar BERNARDINO DE SAHAGÚN; this remarkable text includes both pictorial and alphabetic writing.

—Danny Zborover

Further reading:
Elizabeth Hill Boone. *Stories in Red and Black: Pictorial Histories of the Aztec and the Mixtec* (Austin: University of Texas Press, 2000).

Colombia Few countries in the world boast a geography as diverse as the modern republic of Colombia. The 440,000 square miles (1.139 million km²) that make up its territory equal the combined areas of France, Spain, and Portugal. It boasts two extensive coastlines, one that borders the Pacific and another to the north that runs along the Caribbean. To the east, the upper and lower llanos (plains) extend over an area that covers almost one-fifth of Colombia's total territory, with part of the AMAZON Basin filling in the southeastern corner of the country. To the southwest, just beyond Colombia's southern border with ECUADOR, the Andes Mountains narrow to a width of less than 125 miles (200 km). There, they split and fan out to form three separate ranges, the Cordillera Occidental, the Cordillera Central, and the Cordillera Oriental. The western and central ranges, dissected by the Cauca River, run vertical, almost parallel courses through the country. The Cordillera Oriental, by contrast, breaks from the central range just north of Pasto, where it rises sharply from the eastern banks of the mighty Magdalena River and then veers slightly to the northeast toward the Venezuelan border (see VENEZUELA). All three mountain ranges have innumerable mountain valleys, dominated by mountain lakes and rivers, and vast plains with fertile soils.

Colombia's unique topography and its location, with ties to the Amazon Basin, the vast Llanos, the Andes, and Central America (with its modern border with PANAMA), helped to make Colombia a natural conduit for the flow of peoples, goods, and knowledge. It is likely that MAIZE from Mesoamerica first made its way into South America via Colombia; likewise, it appears that MANIOC, first cultivated in BRAZIL, moved up to Mesoamerica through Colombia. The same appears to be true for the spread of pottery, which appears to have developed first in Colombia (see CERAMICS). Thus, for millennia, Colombia served as a veritable gateway between South America, Central America, and the Caribbean, leaving Colombia with one of the New World's richest and most complex pre-Columbian histories. Even within Colombian territory, the Cauca and Magdalena Rivers linked the north and the south, facilitating the movement of goods and peoples.

Compared to Mesoamerica and the central and southern Andes, Colombian archaeology is still in its infancy. Nevertheless, it has become increasingly clear that before the Spanish CONQUEST, the region supported a diverse mix of cultures and ethnicities, dispersed throughout most of the country. Large numbers of pre-Columbian settlements have been located along the Caribbean coast, as well as the Cauca river valley, and the highland plains of the Cordillera Oriental (which was home to the MUISCA Indians when Europeans first arrived in late 1530s). Unfortunately, little is known about the earliest human settlements in Colombia. Archaeologists have found only scant evidence for the Paleoindian and Archaic periods. Sites such as La Tebaida and La Elvira, both in the Cauca Valley, as well as El Espinal in Tolima, and the eastern highland sites of El Abra, Tequendama, and Tibitó, all appear to date back more than 11,000 years. At Tibitó, archaeologists found bones of extinct mastodons and horses. Likewise, in eastern Colombia's Llanos, there is little evidence of preceramic sites; archaeologists hypothesize that the earliest human settlements in the Llanos date back to 15,000–5,000 B.C.E., with small populations that supported themselves largely by hunting large mammals.

Colombia's Caribbean zone also has a long history of human settlement. For example, beginning as early as the ninth century B.C.E., the Zenú (Sinú) peoples of the Caribbean lowlands began to construct a series of canals in the lower San Jorge River; eventually, this canal system developed into the largest hydraulic project in South America, covering an area of more than 1 million acres. By 2000 B.C.E., large numbers of coastal settlements existed along the northern coastline, with populations with mixed economies that relied on both marine goods and the cultivation of root crops such as manioc. Zenú society appears to have been highly stratified, with local rulers able to mobilize large numbers of laborers for communal projects.

Colombia's Caribbean region was also occupied by the Tairona, a Chibcha-speaking group that dominated the northeastern coastline around the foothills of the Sierra Nevada of Santa Marta. There, archaeologists have located numerous Tairona sites, some consisting of dozens of round wooden buildings and fine masonry platforms.

Perhaps the best known of Colombia's preconquest inhabitants were the Muisca (sometimes referred to as the Chibcha), who occupied the fertile plains of Colombia's eastern highlands. The Muisca were relatively late arrivals to Colombia's eastern highlands, having migrated to the region from northern Colombia and Venezuela at the beginning of the ninth century C.E. The Early Muisca period (800–1200) saw the emergence of ceremonial centers, a significant growth in interregional TRADE, the introduction of goldwork, and an intensification in WARFARE. The transition to the Late Muisca period (1200–1537) was not marked by dramatic changes; the eastern highlands experienced further population growth, a proliferation of different forms of pottery, and an increase in long-distance trade. Muisca markets were filled with goods obtained both within and outside Muisca territory. COTTON cloth, dye tints, COCA leaves, fish, TOBACCO, palm wine, and CHICHA, barbasco for fish poison, cabuya for ropes and cord, calabashes and gourds, fruits, animal skins, honey, wax, vegetables, spices, oils, and maize were all exchanged. Muisca merchants also traded salt and EMERALDS for GOLD, seashells, and other luxury goods not found in the eastern highlands. Precise trade routes remain unclear, but long-distance exchanges likely occurred through a series of intermediary towns.

The Muisca did not congregate in large urban centers; rather, they resided in dispersed homesteads, ranging in size from several dozen inhabitants to a few thousand. These settlements were spread throughout the entire territory, allowing the Muisca to take advantage of the resources and conditions of different ecological zones. On the eve of the Spanish conquest, Muisca territory corresponded roughly to the modern Colombian departments of Cundinamarca and Boyacá, covering a territory of more than 1,000 square miles (2,590 km²), with a population that likely exceeded 500,000 inhabitants. Some scholars have suggested that when the first Spanish expedition arrived in 1537, Muisca territory was divided into two separate kingdoms, one ruled by the Zipa of BOGOTÁ, and the other governed by the Zaque of Tunja. However, recent studies suggest that Muisca territory was far more decentralized, with powerful chiefdoms centered not only around Bogotá and Tunja but also at Turmequé, Cocuy, Duitama, and Sogamoso, among other independent chiefdoms.

When the first band of Spanish conquistadores arrived in Muisca territory, led by GONZALO JIMÉNEZ DE QUESADA, the region quickly emerged as the most important in Colombia. Attracted by its welcoming climate, fertile soils, dense indigenous population, and nearby access to gold and emerald mines, Europeans quickly moved in to settle the region's first three Spanish towns, Santafé de Bogotá, Tunja, and Vélez. Within a decade, the region had experienced significant change. By the time the AUDIENCIA (high court) was formally established in Santafé de Bogotá in 1550, European settlers had successfully introduced Old World crops such as WHEAT, barley, and sugarcane (see SUGAR), a variety of fruits and vegetables, and flax to make linen. Horses, cattle, pigs, goats, mules, and sheep also adapted quickly and easily to their new environment (see COLUMBIAN EXCHANGE; FOOD), and Spanish *encomenderos* (see ENCOMIENDA) reaped enormous profits through the collection of indigenous tribute and LABOR services.

Compared to the Spanish conquests of MEXICO, PERU, or GUATEMALA, the Spanish conquest of Muisca territory involved relatively little bloodshed; nevertheless, the arrival of Europeans and Africans still proved devastating to the Muisca population. Between 1558 and 1560, the entire eastern highlands was struck by a series of epidemics, which swept through Muisca territory (see DISEASE). In the province of Tunja alone, the Indian population fell by more than 30 percent in just a few years. By 1636, just a century after the conquest, Colombia's Muisca population had declined by as much as 80 percent.

While the majority of Spanish colonists in early colonial Colombia chose to settle within Muisca territory, other regions in Colombia also attracted Europeans. The location of pre-Columbian gold mines played an important role in determining the locations of Colombia's earliest European towns: Popayán (1537), Santa Fe de Antioquia (1541; reestablished in 1546), Tocaima (1545), Pamplona (1549), Ibagué (1550), Mariquita (1551), La Victoria (1557), and La Palma (1560) were all located near pre-Columbian gold-mining sites. Still, despite the fact that Colombia attracted significant numbers of European settlers, by 1560, most of Colombian territory remained far removed from Spanish control.

See also BOGOTÁ (Vols. II, III, IV); CARTAGENA DE INDIAS (Vol. II); COLOMBIA (Vols. II, III, IV); GRAN COLOMBIA (Vol. III); NEW GRANADA, VICEROYALTY OF (Vol. II).

—J. Michael Francis

Further reading:
J. Michael Francis. *Invading Colombia: Spanish Accounts of the Gonzalo Jiménez de Quesada Expedition of Conquest* (University Park: Pennsylvania State University Press, 2007).

Armand Labbé, ed. *Shamans, Gods, and Mythic Beasts: Colombian Gold and Ceramics in Antiquity* (Washington, D.C.: American Federation of Arts, 1998).

Frank Safford and Marco Palacios. *Colombia: Fragmented Land, Divided Society* (New York: Oxford University Press, 2002).

Frank Salomon and Stuart B. Schwartz, eds. *The Cambridge History of the Native Peoples of the Americas*, vol. 3, part 1: *South America* (Cambridge: Cambridge University Press, 1999).

Columbian Exchange

"Among the extraordinary though quite natural circumstances of my life," wrote the 16th-century Italian Girolamo Cardano, "the first and most unusual is that I was born in this century in which the whole world became known." The late 15th-century arrival of Europeans in the Western Hemisphere initiated a series of long-term and wide-reaching exchanges. People, animals, DISEASE, crops, commodities, and ideas flowed into new areas and in new directions. The biological and cultural exchange between the Old and New Worlds—labeled the *Columbian Exchange* by the historian Alfred Crosby—transformed diverse landscapes and disparate lives across the globe.

When CHRISTOPHER COLUMBUS reached American shores, he found a land that lacked the principal crops of the Old World, such as WHEAT, barley, and rye, and free of beasts of burden, such as horses and cattle. In the Americas, there were no European, Asian, or African domesticates, and conversely, in Europe, Asia, and Africa, there were no American plants or animals. The FOODS that today are often associated with countries' so-called traditional cuisines were not found in those places before 1492. Italians ate no tomatoes and the Irish no POTATOES; Indians (from India) consumed no chilies and Ethiopians no peanuts; Argentines ate no beef and Jamaicans no chicken. Only Old World elites drank coffee and tea, while the New World nobility enjoyed TOBACCO and chocolate.

The Old World emigrants of the 16th century immediately recognized the bounty of the Americas. Staple crops such as MAIZE, MANIOC, and potatoes, as well as other vegetables and seeds, spices, beans, chilies, and tomatoes provided rich sustenance. New World domesticates included amaranth (*Amaranthus*), avocados (*Persea americana*), beans (*Phaseolus vulgaris*), cashews (*Anacardium curatellifolium*), CACAO (*Theobromba cacao*), chilies (*Capiscum*), COTTON (*Gossypium*), guava (*Psidium*), maize (*Zea mays*), manioc (*Manihot esculenta*), papayas (*Carica papaya*), peanuts (*Arachis hypogaea*), pineapples (*Ananas comosus*), potatoes (*Solanum tuberosom*), squashes (*Cucurbita*), sunflowers (*Helianthus annunus*), tobacco (*Nicantia rustica*), and tomatoes (*Solanum lycopersicum*).

Guinea pigs roam freely in a private residence in Ollantaytambo, Peru. *(Courtesy of J. Michael Francis)*

The more modest list of New World faunal domesticates included alpacas (*Vicugna pacos*), GUINEA PIGS (*Cavia porcellus*), llamas (*Llama glama*), and turkeys (*Meleagris*).

While Europeans were quick to identify the richness of the Americas, they also recognized that Old World crops, particularly geographically limited ones, such as SUGAR, could thrive in tropical environments. During his 1492 encounter with the Caribbean, Columbus collected samples of exotic and useful New World crops, including maize and cotton. During his second voyage of 1493, he and his settlers brought a wide variety of Old World plants and animals, including wheat, barley, grapes, chickpeas, olives, onions, horses, and cattle. Unbeknownst to both the Europeans and Americans, other living organisms, including bugs and diseases, also made the journey. From the Americas, a variety of syphilis arrived in the Old World. From Europe, a host of lethal pathogens, including smallpox, yellow fever, and influenza, invaded the New World. These first encounters typified important aspects of the Columbian Exchange. For one, they demonstrate that material exchanges moved both to and from the Old and New Worlds. They also illustrate that these exchanges were not always benign in nature. While the New World lacked the main Old World domesticated animals, it also lacked the pathogens of smallpox, bubonic plague, typhoid, influenza, malaria, and yellow fever, all of which stemmed from human-animal interaction. Furthermore, the exchange of goods came with important cultural components.

The Columbian Exchange did not simply involve trading valued commodities between Europe and the Americas; rather, the history of the biological and cultural exchanges during the early colonial period is a rich and truly global story. The American staples of manioc, potatoes, and maize became important global staples by the close of the 16th century. Manioc, a South American root crop also known as cassava, became an important component in West African AGRICULTURE as early as the 16th century. In 1593, for example, Sir Richard Hawkins, an important adviser to the English monarch, detailed the seizure of a Portuguese ship leaving Angola loaded with manioc. Nearly a century later, the Fulani and Hausa peoples of the kingdoms of the Kongo and Angola cultivated the crop.

Potatoes, which were once exclusively the food of Andeans, disseminated widely during the 16th century. While the Spaniards who first encountered them found them unusual, by the close of the century, potatoes were being cultivated in many parts of Europe and Asia. In 1600, the French botanist Olivier de Serres provided a detailed history of the tuber and described the crop's cultivation in North America, England, Switzerland, Spain, and France. Similarly, Chinese accounts from late in the century identified potatoes among a collection of new foreign domesticates that also included tomatoes, peanuts, and guava.

No staple spread the globe as quickly and widely as maize. By the close of the 16th century, it was cultivated in Europe, the Middle East, Southeast Asia, Africa, and throughout the Americas. Leonard Rauwolf, an explorer and amateur botanist who collected seed samples from the Middle East, noted evidence of this distribution. In 1574, he found that maize was cultivated throughout the Ottoman Empire, particularly from modern-day Turkey to Jerusalem.

The movement and distribution of domesticates was not simply from the New to the Old World. Old World commodities arrived with the initial waves of European conquerors. The introduction of Old World commodities and LABOR systems altered the biological and cultural composition of the New World.

Sugarcane, a geographically limited Old World commodity that required tropical environs and massive labor, was a driving force behind European expansion in the Americas. Before the 16th century, sugar was almost exclusively cultivated in the East Indies and was available on the global market in only very limited amounts. Universally appealing and limited in quantity, sugar was more valuable than GOLD on the world market. By the mid-16th century, however, American sugar production dominated. In 1501, Columbus created the first sugar plantation in the New World, and in 1516, the first shipment of New World sugar arrived in Europe. The story of sugar production, however, was not a sweet tale. Rather, the rise of sugar was fundamentally linked to the rise of New World SLAVERY and the decline of indigenous peoples in the Caribbean and BRAZIL. On the island of HISPANIOLA (present-day Dominican Republic and Haiti), by 1600, the native population was nearly extinguished under the disastrous combination of labor exploitation and disease. In the absence of indigenous labor, Europeans imported massive numbers of enslaved Africans. By 1600, for example, some 15,000 African slaves were working on Brazil's 150 sugar plantations. In the century that followed, the number of African slaves increased tenfold.

Europeans took domesticated animals into the areas to which they moved. Early European voyagers introduced horses, cattle, pigs, chickens, and sheep, but the arrival of these animals did not come without costs. Sheep, for example, extracted a considerable toll on the physical landscape and so, also, the human landscape. In valleys north of present-day MEXICO CITY, widespread sheep production transformed the forest and farmland of the 1530s into the unfertile prairies of the 1560s. The native inhabitants of the areas, who subsisted mainly on slash-and-burn horticulture, were no longer able to feed themselves. As a result, more than 90 percent of the population was extinguished.

The demographic shifts associated with the Columbian Exchange were monumental. During the 16th century, Europe's population increased by nearly 20 percent and Asian populations by nearly 10 percent due to the new sources of food and wealth. The Americas, on the other hand, suffered the worst demographic collapse in human history. One of the most important biological exchanges between the Old and New Worlds took place at the microscopic level. From the first decades of contact with Europeans, smallpox, typhus, influenza, and measles inundated susceptible American populations. The rapid spread of Old World diseases, described by scholars as "virgin-soil epidemics," affected entire communities, from the young to the old, the weak to the fit. Combined with European abuse and exploitation, Old World diseases disabled every indigenous group they touched.

The first recorded account of epidemic smallpox in the New World comes from the coast of MEXICO in 1517. By 1520, the disease had spread to the densely populated Valley of Mexico. In 1526, ahead of the Europeans themselves, the disease spread into Central America. By the end of the 16th century, the native population of Mexico City had been reduced to no more than 30 percent of its precontact strength. The 16th-century historian and polemicist BARTOLOMÉ DE LAS CASAS reported that the 6 million pre-Hispanic indigenous inhabitants of Hispaniola had been reduced to 30,000 by the 1550s.

While estimates of the Amerindian population before the arrival of Europeans vary considerably, it is likely that it was as high as 60 million. There is little scholarly debate on the significance of the rapid decline of native populations across the hemisphere, however. By the close of the 16th century, fewer than 10 million native inhabitants lived in the Americas. After a century of the Columbian Exchange, the human makeup of the Americas had changed dramatically. The populations of the Caribbean had virtually disappeared. Major population centers such as those in the Valley of Mexico and the Andes were exponentially reduced. Even in frontier areas, such as the AMAZON Basin, where Europeans rarely ventured, native populations fell victim to Old World diseases. Given the overwhelming decline of indigenous peoples, virtually everyone in the New World was directly affected by the Columbian Exchange.

The exchange of crops and commodities was accompanied by the exchange of cultural components such as ideas and institutions. The creation of sugar plantations, for example, came with the exploitive labor practice of slavery. During the 16th century, Europeans created the foundations for subsequent labor practices, particularly the transatlantic slave trade. With the dramatic decline in native labor, Europeans imported African slaves. Across this period an estimated 350,000 slaves were shipped to the Americas, with the vast majority winding up on Caribbean and Brazilian sugar plantations.

European cultural and ideological systems often served to justify the cruel and exploitive aspects of the Columbian Exchange. Early modern European political systems struggled to consolidate wealth and authority. Expansion into the Americas, hastened by debilitated local populations, provided new opportunities for Europeans to bolster their regional and global positions. While it is true that Europeans often lamented the abuse of Americans and Africans, this exploitation was justified and even bolstered by Old World, and particularly European, philosophical and religious traditions. For example, by citing classical philosophy, religious interpretations, and medieval political thought, European monarchs defended the destruction of indigenous societies and the enslavement of Africans as aspects of a "just war" in the name of society and civilization.

After only a century, the Columbian Exchange had transformed the biological and cultural character of people around the world, and the effects were both uneven and complex. On the one hand, the introduction of valuable new sources of food fed population explosions in Europe and Asia. Europe, once a somewhat unimportant and fractured region of the Old World, found itself a controlling force in a global system of TRADE and exploitation. On the other hand, the introduction of Old World diseases and colonial systems of exploitation led to the demographic collapse, the most significant in human history, of indigenous Americans. The New World, once a chain of independent economic and social systems, became a colonized and subjugated source for the world's wealth. Furthermore, the exploitive social and economic systems that formed during the earliest parts of the Columbian Exchange were limiting and lasting forces.

See also CATTLE (Vol. II); COLUMBIAN EXCHANGE (Vol. II); EPIDEMICS (Vol. II); SHEEP (Vol. II); SUGAR (Vols. II, III).

—R. A. Kashanipour

Further reading:

Noble David Cook. *Born to Die: Disease and the Conquest of the New World, 1492–1650* (New York: Cambridge University Press, 1998).
Alfred Crosby. *The Columbian Exchange: Biological and Cultural Consequences of 1492* (Westport, Conn.: Greenwood Press, 1972).
Elinor Melville. *A Plague of Sheep: Environmental Consequences of the Conquest of Mexico* (New York: Cambridge University Press, 1994).

Columbus, Christopher (b. 1451–d. 1506) *navigator and explorer credited with "discovering" the Americas*

Christopher Columbus was born between August and October of 1451 in Genoa, Italy. At age 14, he attended Prince Henry's school of navigation in Sagres, Portugal. His formative business endeavors included trips to Greece, Ireland, and possibly Iceland. Columbus's taste for travel came at a unique nexus in European history. Access to prized silks, spices, and other goods from Asia and India were becoming increasingly difficult to procure. The seizure of Constantinople by Ottoman Turks in 1453 resulted in a geopolitical crisis for Europe, as the gateway land routes to the Asian markets were no longer considered reliable. Columbus, along with his brothers, devised a strategy for reaching Asia by sailing west across the Atlantic Ocean. Despite modernity's widespread and erroneous belief that most 15th-century people believed the world was flat (propagated by Washington Irving's

1828 biography of Columbus), most Europeans in fact accepted Arab, Greek, and Roman conjectures that the world was spherical. Hence, in theory, Columbus's notion of sailing west to arrive at an eastern landmass was not at all revolutionary in the 1480s. Opposition to Columbus's plan regarded the circumference of the globe, not its shape.

Columbus's calculations of the distance between Europe and Asia via westward navigation were rife with errors. He drew on highly flawed works that miscalculated the proportion of the world's landmass compared to its sea mass. Furthermore, he mistakenly calculated distances based on an Arabic model but did not recalculate his model to take into account the lengthier measure of an Arab mile, which was roughly 1,830 meters (about 1.14 miles) as compared to the Italian mile, which measured about 1,238 meters (about 0.77 miles). Columbus found it difficult to secure funding for his expedition because experts at the time recognized the faulty logic in his plan. He proposed an expedition of three ships to King John II of Portugal, whose advisers vetoed it because Columbus's calculated distance to Asia was far too short. Columbus then turned to the Italian city-states of Genoa and Venice; neither expressed interest. His brother made overtures to King Henry VII of England, who warmed to the idea too late.

Columbus first approached the MONARCHS OF SPAIN, Ferdinand and Isabella, in 1486. They rebuffed his offer but sagely offered him an annual salary and free lodging and food throughout the country in order to keep him from gaining support elsewhere. After finally driving the Moors from Iberia in 1492, Columbus pressed his luck with a much more receptive Spanish Crown. Isabella dismissed him, but as he was leaving Córdoba, dejected, he was stopped by Ferdinand's guards. The king of Spain was ready to defy royal advice and fund Columbus's voyage. Indeed, the king would later claim credit for being "the principal cause why those islands were discovered." Half of Columbus's trip would be financed by private Italian investors and half by the Spanish Crown. The Crown offered him the title of "admiral of the seas," as well as generous funding and terms of discovery and colonization (see CAPITULATIONS OF SANTA FE).

Columbus departed Spain with three ships—the *Santa Clara* (nicknamed the *Niña*), *Pinta*, and *Santa María*—on August 3, 1492. After replenishing supplies at the Canary Islands, the convoy began one of the world's most famous treks, a five-week journey across the Atlantic Ocean. At roughly 2:00 A.M. on October 12, 1492, Rodrigo de Triana aboard the *Pinta* spotted land. Columbus named the island San Salvador, though exactly which island he first encountered is a source of debate. He soon met the native population, members of the Arawak or TAINO tribes. Columbus's journal entries concerning this initial meeting recount his belief that the locals "would make good servants" and could be easily conquered and Christianized. From San Salvador,

The Franciscan monastery at La Rábida, famous for its association with Christopher Columbus. It has been suggested that Columbus first visited the monastery in 1485; however, it was not until 1491 that Columbus turned to the friars at the monastery to help him prepare his petition to the Spanish monarchs to support his voyage across the Atlantic. *(Courtesy of J. Michael Francis)*

Columbus ventured north to CUBA and HISPANIOLA, where the *Santa María* ran aground on Christmas morning. Dubbed LA NAVIDAD colony, Columbus left a crew of 39 men in what is now Haiti, hoping to return a year later to a thriving Spanish outpost. He finally docked in Spain on March 15, 1493, igniting a maelstrom of interest in his discovery.

Columbus returned to the Americas three more times. His second voyage led to the discovery of the Lesser and Greater Antilles and ultimately docked at Hispaniola, where La Navidad colony was found destroyed. Columbus instituted a brutal set of policies that devastated the Taino population; they were killed or enslaved in large numbers. On his third voyage in 1498, Columbus focused his travels on the northern crest of South America, exploring the coast of VENEZUELA and Trinidad. This voyage also highlighted his firm stance against Spanish dissent; discontent and disobedience among the settlers provoked harsh reprisals, including hangings. The dark side of Columbus's rule in the Americas was partially chronicled by the Dominican friar BARTOLOMÉ DE LAS CASAS, who accompanied him on his third voyage. In 1502, Columbus launched a fourth voyage in search of the Strait of Malacca to the Indian Ocean, which led him to explore the coastline of Central America, including HONDURAS, NICARAGUA, COSTA RICA, and PANAMA. He was stranded in Jamaica for a year before returning to Spain on November 7, 1504.

Columbus's final years were marked by renewed piety and quarrels with the Spanish Crown over the pecuniary provisions of his initial contract. He died a wealthy man at the age of 55 on May 20, 1506, in Valladolid, Spain, unwavering in his belief that he had discovered a sea route to the Asian coast. His remains were originally interred in Valladolid, but over the succeeding centuries, they were scuttled from Spain to Santo Domingo, Dominican Republic, to Havana, Cuba, and finally back to Seville, Spain.

—Sean H. Goforth

Further reading:

Christopher Columbus. *The Log of Christopher Columbus* (Camden, Me.: International Marine Publishing Co., 1987).

Bartolomé de Las Casas. *The Devastation of the Indies: A Brief Account* (New York: Seabury Press, 1984).

Samuel Eliot Morison. *Admiral of the Ocean Sea: A Life of Christopher Columbus* (Boston: Little, Brown & Co., 1942).

This late 19th-century mausoleum-monument, housed in Seville's cathedral, is believed to hold Christopher Columbus's remains. The few bone fragments in the tomb were subjected to DNA testing in 2003; however, the findings were inconclusive. The four heralds carrying Columbus's tomb represent the kingdoms of Castile, León, Aragon, and Navarre. *(Courtesy of J. Michael Francis)*

congregación A *congregación* was a nucleated settlement of indigenous people, typically consisting of a *cabecera*, or "head town," and several nearby politically subordinate towns (*sujetos*); it was created under the Spanish colonial policy of forcibly consolidating scattered native populations. *Congregación* (the process of relocation, also known as *reducción*) was intended to facilitate acculturation to Spanish norms of civilized living and improve Spanish access to Native Americans for the purposes of governance, tax collection, distribution of LABOR, and religious indoctrination (see RELIGION).

In 1511, the protests of the Dominican order over the mistreatment of Indian laborers at the hands of Spanish *encomenderos* (recipients of labor grants) on the island of HISPANIOLA convinced the Crown that it was in danger of losing its only colony of any importance at the time in the Americas. The native population was dying off at an alarming rate due to overwork, malnutrition, physical abuse, and the introduction of Old World DISEASES. The dwindling supply of indigenous labor made it difficult to retain Spanish settlers or attract new settlers. In response, the Crown surmised that these problems could be solved by standardizing and limiting the largely unregulated institution of the *ENCOMIENDA*, which it did through the promulgation of the LAWS OF BURGOS in 1512.

While the Laws of Burgos failed to slow the population decline, they set a number of precedents for royal policies on the Indians, including *congregación*. The first article mandated that indigenous people living scattered throughout the countryside should be relocated to settlements near the Spaniards they served, the latter initially providing for the Indians' basic necessities and later ordering them to begin raising their own provisions. The old dwellings were to be burned to prevent the native people from returning to them. The second article mandated that the Indians were not to be harmed during relocation, and the remaining articles regulated various aspects of their lives and relations with their Spanish overseers. The first two articles became the blueprint for subsequent resettlement programs throughout Spanish America, under the direction of either civil or ecclesiastical authorities.

In New Spain (MEXICO), *congregación* began in the mid-16th century and was often carried out by the RELIGIOUS ORDERS. The first major effort at resettlement by civil authorities was completed between 1550 and 1564, and most of the native communities of later centuries were products of this initial series of *congregaciones*. The same could be said of GUATEMALA, where the Dominicans and Mercedarians created numerous *congregaciones* in the late 1540s and 1550s. While many of these settlements endured, sometimes even into the present day under modern political configurations, others declined as their residents returned piecemeal to their ancestral lands. Some disappeared altogether within a few decades. The Mercedarians carried out a series of *congregaciones* in HONDURAS, beginning around 1540, although less is known about the stability of these settlements. In PERU, the process of *congregación* was implemented in the mid-1560s but did not have much momentum until it was stepped up under the administration of Peru's fifth viceroy, Francisco de Toledo.

Under a similar policy (*redução*) implemented by the Portuguese in BRAZIL, indigenous people were gathered into Jesuit mission villages (*aldeias*). Begun in 1550, the *aldeia* system was less ambitious than its Spanish counterparts and after peaking in the late 1550s and early 1560s, went into a period of decline, succumbing to the effects of WARFARE and Old World diseases.

See also *CONGREGACIÓN* (Vol. II); *REDUCCIÓN* (Vol. II).

—Michael S. Cole

conquest

BRAZIL

The initial encounter between Portuguese sailors and Amerindian set the tone for subsequent encounters and eventual Portuguese colonization. When PEDRO ÁLVARES CABRAL first stumbled upon the coast of BRAZIL in April 1500, he did not immediately begin settlement; rather, he replenished the supplies of his fleet, using Brazil as a convenient stopover point on his journey to India. Leaving behind a handful of convicts to establish an outpost and learn indigenous tongues, Cabral and his men were following a pattern that the Portuguese had previously employed in Africa: establishing a series of factories, or trading posts, with little attempt at controlling inland territory (see TRADE). Neither the new land nor its inhabitants were viewed as an imperial priority at this point. In many ways, this was a reflection of Portuguese reaction to the indigenous societies initially encountered in Brazil. Unlike the native civilizations in MEXICO and PERU, with dense urban populations and highly developed systems of AGRICULTURE and tribute, Brazil's indigenous population consisted largely of semisedentary peoples who practiced slash-and-burn agriculture and had subsistence economies (see ECONOMY). Accordingly, Brazilian Indians appeared to offer little in the way of wealth to early Europeans.

Brazil's indigenous population at the time of the conquest was highly diverse. Although demographic information is imprecise, scholars estimate that the new land was peopled by 2 to 5 million native inhabitants prior to the arrival of the Portuguese. Brazil's indigenous population during this period can be divided into three distinct groups. Tupí-GUARANÍ speakers, including the TUPINAMBÁ, were found along the coasts of Brazil from modern-day Ceará in the northeast to São Paulo in the south, then inland to the Paraná and Paraguay river basins. Non-Tupí speak-

ers, or Tapuya, lived in the north above Ceará and interspersed at different points along the coast, and included those who spoke Gê as well as other isolated languages. Finally, Arawak- and Carib-speaking peoples lived in the north (although the Portuguese would not have sustained contact with this last group until the late 17th century). Contact between different indigenous groups—including those who spoke similar languages—was limited mainly to trade, though military alliances were not uncommon. In this regard, there was a great deal of fighting among different indigenous groups, and WARFARE and the capture of enemies were extremely important.

Initial interaction between Europeans and indigenous groups in Brazil was based mainly on trade with both the Portuguese and French, who had also begun sailing to Brazil in the early 16th century. French and Portuguese merchants provided axes and other metal tools to the Amerindians in exchange for dyewood, the only resource that Europeans initially found to be of worth in the new land (see DYES AND DYEWOOD). Both Portuguese and French merchants attempted to exploit native rivalries—establishing alliances with competing indigenous groups—just as the natives themselves played one European side against the other. In this regard, the conquest of Brazil can in many ways be understood as a story of Luso-French rivalry.

In a juridical sense, the Portuguese traced their claim to Brazil through the TREATY OF TORDESILLAS (1494), which had divided the world between the Catholic kingdoms of Portugal and Castile. And yet, a generation after the discovery of Brazil, the Portuguese had done little to systematically colonize the new land; instead, it was the French who were making steady gains. In response to this threat, Portugal's King John III sent an expedition to Brazil in 1530. Accompanied by more than 400 colonists, Martim Afonso de Sousa was instructed to keep French ships away from the coasts of Brazil. Four years later, the Crown reinforced these actions by establishing a system of DONATARY CAPTAINCIES, geographic jurisdictions that were awarded to a lord proprietor; in exchange for these grants, recipients were responsible for settling the land. Based on grants of feudal lordship in medieval Portugal, the captaincy system had previously been used with varying degrees of success in Madeira, the Azores, and the Cape Verde Islands. In the case of Brazil, however, the attempt to use private initiative and resources for imperial aims for the most part failed. Only two of Brazil's original 15 captaincies were successful: Pernambuco and São Vicente. Significantly, both enjoyed relatively peaceful relations with local Amerindians. Additionally, the Portuguese colonists in Pernambuco began to cultivate sugarcane, establishing a plantation-based economy that initially relied on indigenous LABOR (see SUGAR). However, following the great epidemics that devastated Brazil's indigenous population in the mid-16th century, the Portuguese began to import large numbers of African slaves (see DISEASE; SLAVERY).

Following the failure of the donatary captaincies, the Portuguese Crown sought to reassert its control of the new land. In 1549, John III sent Tomé de Sousa to serve as Brazil's first governor general. Accompanied by a fleet of five ships, six Jesuit priests, and more than a thousand other men, the new governor would go on to found the city of Salvador da Bahia, Brazil's first colonial capital. Nevertheless, Luso-French rivalry in Brazil did not come to an end. In 1555, Nicolas Durand de Villegagnon, a French naval officer, led a band of soldiers and religious outcasts—mainly French Huguenots and Swiss Calvinists—to establish France Antarctique, a small colony and fort near modern-day Rio de Janeiro. Although the Portuguese initially did little to drive the French from their new colony, France Antarctique was subsequently weakened after the arrival of more French colonists, including Catholics who bickered with their Protestant counterparts over church doctrine. Following a series of Portuguese raids between 1565 and 1567, France Antarctique was abandoned, thus assuring Portuguese dominion of the new lands. In effect, by this point, all of the major factors in Brazil's first stage of history were complete: the decline of Brazil's indigenous population, the consolidation of Portuguese sovereignty, the beginnings of a plantation-based economy, the arrival of African slaves, and the founding of Brazil's major colonial CITIES.

THE CARIBBEAN

Spain's first military conquests in the New World occurred in the Caribbean region and were based on general patterns established during the 800 years of Reconquista against the Moors, as well as the subsequent conquest and colonization of the Canary Islands. From CHRISTOPHER COLUMBUS's second voyage in 1493 until the final conquest of the major Caribbean islands and the advance toward the Central American mainland, the conquest of the Caribbean established the basic pattern of Spanish conquest and colonization of the rest of the New World.

The initial Spanish conquest of the Caribbean can be dated to the second voyage of Columbus to the island of HISPANIOLA in 1493. Returning to the New World with more than 1,500 Europeans, Columbus discovered that his first established colony at LA NAVIDAD had been destroyed, and all those he had left there, killed. To avenge the destruction of Columbus's first settlement, the Europeans who accompanied the explorer launched a war against the island's TAINO peoples; the conflict eventually led to the creation of Spain's first base of operations in a series of conquests. Soon, all of the major islands of the Caribbean fell under the control of the Spanish Crown.

In 1493, Columbus established a new settlement named Isabella on the eastern part of the island of Hispaniola, and the Spanish colony of Santo Domingo quickly became the first of a series of Spanish settlements that would serve as staging posts and launching points for the conquest of the rest of the Caribbean. However, in 1500, Columbus was removed as Santo Domingo's

governor; his replacement, Nicolás de Ovando, began the systematic conquest of the rest of the island of Hispaniola, launching two major wars in 1500 and 1504 in the hopes of discovering and exploiting more wealthy resources for Spain. When early expectations that GOLD and precious metals would be found in abundance on the island vanished, new groups of Spanish immigrants began to look to other islands for sources of quick wealth (see MIGRATION).

Hispaniola (Santo Domingo)

Despite its paucity of mineral wealth, Santo Domingo remained an important colonial administrative center, with its own AUDIENCIA, or high court, which served throughout the 16th century as a major launching point for all subsequent conquest expeditions. It was also on the island of Hispaniola that the Spanish Crown introduced the *repartimiento* system, which divided the conquered indigenous populations into labor drafts for use by Spaniards. Similarly, following the promulgation of the 1512 LAWS OF BURGOS, Santo Domingo witnessed for the first time in the New World the creation of the ENCOMIENDA system in the Indies. Both systems proved devastating for the island's Amerindian population.

The Taino inhabitants of Santo Domingo did not survive long under Spanish rule. Various sources reported the initial Taino population of Santo Domingo to be anywhere from 4 million to slightly more than 100,000 people before the conquest. Regardless, according to all colonial accounts, by 1550, less than 200 native Tainos remained on the island.

Puerto Rico

Using Santo Domingo as a base of operations, in late August 1508, the Spanish conquistador JUAN PONCE DE LEÓN, who had traveled with Columbus on his return voyage in 1493, began the conquest of the island of PUERTO RICO. Arriving with a small army of soldiers, Ponce de León established the settlement of Caparra as the first Spanish town, located at San Juan Bay. The island's small Taino population (estimated to have numbered fewer than 50,000) was unable to resist the Spanish conquest. The Spaniards quickly conquered and enslaved those Taino who fought them, forcing the native population to work in the few small gold mines discovered on the island (see MINING). A series of bloody rebellions occurred shortly after the initial conquest, led by the Taino leader Agueybana. These revolts ultimately led to the defeat of the natives and the deaths or flight of most of the island's remaining Taino residents. The lack of slave labor on the island resulted in the importation of some of the first African slaves into the Caribbean and the organization of slaving expeditions to the other larger islands; these efforts to procure additional slaves for the island also inspired early expeditions to the newly discovered mainland of South and Central America. By 1514, no more than a few thousand Tainos remained on the island.

Jamaica

During his second voyage, Columbus encountered the island of Jamaica in 1494. After defeating the Taínos, Columbus claimed the island for Spain. Nevertheless, no effective attempts at conquest and colonization occurred until 1509, when Juan de Esquivel was sent from Santo Domingo to conquer the island and establish the first settlement. Esquivel's new town, called Sevilla la Nueva, located on the northern part of Jamaica, became the island's first administrative center. A series of small-scale wars with the Taíno eventually led to the conquest of the island and the creation in 1523 of the town of Santiago de la Vega on its southern side. Once the Spanish discovered that Jamaica did not have any easily accessible gold mines or other mineral wealth, it dwindled to the status of a minor outpost; the island supported a small population that included a few Spanish ranchers. Eventually, Jamaica fell under the administration of the Columbus family, who received it in perpetuity as a type of personal fiefdom in compensation for the loss of many of their promised privileges.

Cuba

The conquest of CUBA, the largest of the Caribbean islands and one of the last to become subject to Spanish rule, did not occur until 1511; in that year, the viceroy of the Indies, Diego Columbus, commissioned DIEGO VELÁZQUEZ DE CUÉLLAR to organize an expedition from Santo Domingo. The governor led a force of more than 300 men to conquer the island (alternately called the Isla Fernandina). Landing on Cuba's southern coast, Velázquez established the first permanent settlement on August 15, 1511, at the site of Baracoa. Over the next several months, Velázquez and his expedition subdued the eastern part of the island, leaving the western part of the island untouched for several years.

Taíno resistance on the island of Cuba was actually led by the CACIQUE Hatuey, a Taíno leader from Hispaniola, who had fled to Cuba to lead guerrilla warfare against the Spanish. Hatuey received significant support from Cuba's native inhabitants. For almost a year, the Taíno resisted, pinning down the Spanish at their fortified town of Baracoa. Eventually betrayed by one of his own followers, Hatuey was later captured and executed by the Spanish; he was burned at the stake on February 2, 1512.

After 1512, the Taíno of eastern Cuba offered only slight resistance to Spanish expansion, yet the Spaniards on Cuba committed many atrocities in their subjugation of the western side of the island, which was not complete until 1516. By 1517, Cuba was also experiencing a shortage of indigenous labor, and the small number of African slaves imported to the island still necessitated the enslavement of Amerindians from other regions. Several important slave-raiding expeditions were then sent out from Cuba in 1517 and 1518 under the command of FRANCISCO HERNÁNDEZ DE CÓRDOBA (1517) and JUAN DE GRIJALVA (1518). During these two expeditions, Spaniards from Cuba discovered the Yucatán Peninsula and the existence of large populated empires of indigenous peoples on the Mexican mainland (see AZTECS; MAYAS). Cuba eventually became the staging ground for the later conquest of MEXICO and its mainland.

Other Islands

From the earliest voyages of Columbus and other Spanish explorers, Spain claimed control over all the islands of the Caribbean, including the Lesser Antilles. However, once they discovered that most of these islands, especially those in the Bahamas and the Lesser Antilles, did not contain rich gold mines or other mineral resources, the Spanish effectively abandoned their efforts to colonize or settle them. With the exception of early settlements on the islands of Dominica and Guadalupe (Guadeloupe), both considered important weigh stations in the provisioning of voyages to and from the Indies, Spain effectively counted the costs of subduing the more warlike CARIB Indians on these islands as too high for such a low return.

The gradual eradication of the Taíno inhabitants of the Caribbean islands and their replacement with African slaves eventually led to the establishment of Spanish colonies on the Caribbean's larger and wealthier islands. As the need for slave labor for the mines and early plantations increased, Spanish expeditions began to look to more distant lands to conquer and Amerindians natives to enslave. Although the first decade of the 16th century witnessed the creation of a few short-lived settlements on the Caribbean coasts of South and Central America, the first attempt at permanent conquest and colonization on the Caribbean mainland did not occur until 1514, with the expedition of PEDRO ARIAS DE ÁVILA. Nevertheless, even this expedition failed to find quick wealth or other mineral resources, and the colony was abandoned shortly afterward.

Early Spanish colonists on the larger Caribbean islands found vast tracts of available land but soon realized that the labor to mine the gold they discovered as their only valuable export product was quickly disappearing. European epidemic diseases initially devastated the indigenous population, and subsequent slave labor and forced *encomienda* service likewise took their toll on the already weakened native groups. Thus, ready access to large populations of Amerindians as forced laborers was essential to keep the colonists' early economy running. From 1492 to 1515, the need to discover more Indian labor served as the spur to the exploration and conquest of one island after another. The depletion of each region's native labor population led to the subsequent conquest of the next region; thus, the conquest of Puerto Rico, Jamaica, and Cuba ultimately resulted from the depletion of native laborers available on Santo Domingo. Similarly, the conquest of Mexico and the initial expeditions into North and Central America began with the depletion of native laborers on the island of Cuba. The experience gained in conquering and administering their Caribbean island possessions, then, set in place the basic pattern of the Spaniards' conquest and colonization of the rest of the New World.

CENTRAL AMERICA

Early explorations in the Caribbean set the stage for the conquest of Central America. On his fourth voyage in 1502–04, Columbus explored the Atlantic coasts of HONDURAS, NICARAGUA, COSTA RICA, and PANAMA. Near one of the Bay Islands, he encountered seagoing canoes laden with trade goods and finely dressed people. This was the first evidence of wealthy and powerful Mesoamerican cultures; however, apart from the early attempts to settle Panama, the conquests of Central America did not begin in earnest until after 1521 and the conquest of Mexico.

Panama, Costa Rica, and Nicaragua

Spaniards founded early settlements in Central and South America between 1504 and 1506. FRANCISCO PIZARRO initially established a settlement in COLOMBIA, but conflicts with local Indians forced him to relocate to Darién, in Castillo del Oro (Panama). In 1513, VASCO NÚÑEZ DE BALBOA crossed the Isthmus of Panama to the Pacific Ocean in his search for gold, pearls, and slaves. Arias de Ávila (known as Pedrarias) became governor in 1515 and dispatched various expeditions throughout the region.

In 1522–23, soon after the city of Panama was founded, GIL GONZÁLEZ DÁVILA and Andrés Niño received royal authority to sail and explore north along the Pacific coast. They traveled to western Nicaragua and Lake Nicaragua, where they encountered a large, wealthy, and culturally advanced Amerindian population. They eventually reached the Bay of Fonseca.

Pedrarias knew that the Crown planned to replace him as governor as part of its efforts to bring the Indies under direct royal control, so he decided to take over Nicaragua. He sent an expedition to the Pacific coast under the command of Francisco Hernández de Córdoba (not the explorer of the Yucatán), who founded the cities of Bruselas on the Gulf of Nicoya in present-day Costa Rica, Granada on the western shore of Lake Nicaragua, and León to the north.

Hernández de Córdoba decided to terminate Pedrarias's authority in Nicaragua. From León, he sent expeditions north into territory between Nicaragua and Honduras, where HERNANDO CORTÉS had claimed authority. Harassed indigenous groups called on Cortés for protection, and his forces blocked the forces of Hernández de Córdoba, who now feared Pedrarias's wrath. He invited Cortés to take control of Nicaragua. Cortés was organizing an expedition to Nicaragua when he decided to return to New Spain. Pedrarias arrived from Panama, took over, executed Hernández de Córdoba, and sent expeditions into Honduras, which he claimed.

In mid-1526, Pedro de los Ríos replaced Pedrarias as royal governor of Castillo del Oro and claimed jurisdiction over Nicaragua. Meanwhile, Diego López de Salcedo arrived as royal governor of Honduras and also claimed Nicaragua. He led an expedition to León in 1527. Unfortunately for him, the Crown decided to detach Nicaragua from Castillo del Oro and named Pedrarias governor of the new province. Pedrarias arrived in León and imprisoned López de Salcedo, only releasing him in 1529 after he renounced his claims to much territory, an act that finally settled questions about jurisdiction of Nicaragua and Honduras.

Guatemala and El Salvador

Spanish efforts to explore and conquer GUATEMALA and EL SALVADOR began in earnest after the conquest of Mexico. Their arrival was not a surprise to the local MAYA populations. In 1519, Aztec emperor MONTEZUMA had sent word to the K'iche' and Kaqchikel Maya that invaders had arrived from the east; and despite the fact that almost five years would pass before the first Spanish expedition arrived in the region, epidemic diseases had reached southern Guatemala as early as 1519–20. K'iche' and Kaqchikel emissaries met with Cortés in 1521 and 1522 and offered their alliances (see IXIMCHÉ).

PEDRO DE ALVARADO met with Kaqchikel ambassadors in Soconusco, which encouraged him to leave Mexico in late 1523 to invade Guatemala with an army of a few hundred Spaniards on foot and horseback, African slaves and freemen, and thousands of Nahuas and other indigenous allies. The captains were Alvarado, his brothers (Jorge, Gonzalo, and Gómez), their cousins, and Pedro Portocarrero. Alvarado (as did Jorge later) had married a royal Tlaxcalan woman, doña Luisa, shortly before the invasion, which helped him recruit native allies (see TLAXCALA).

Alvarado's forces crossed the K'iche' frontier early in 1524. The first battle at the Samalá River ended in Spanish victory. The second battle of El Pinar resulted in defeat for the K'iche's and the death of their ruler, Tecún Umán, now a Guatemalan national hero. After a third defeat in the Quezaltenango Valley, the K'iche's invited the invaders to their capital, Utatlán. Believing the invitation to be a trap, Alvarado destroyed the city.

Alvarado demanded reinforcements from the Kaqchikels. With fresh troops, the invaders continued to eliminate K'iche' resistance; they destroyed the Tz'utujil army at Lake Atitlán and headed into present-day El Salvador. At Acajutla, they engaged but could not defeat a Pipil force and turned back.

In mid-1524, Alvarado founded his colonial capital, Santiago de los Caballeros de Guatemala (Tecpán), near Iximché, the Kaqchikel capital. Demands for tribute, supplies, and labor soon strained the Spanish-Kaqchikel alliance and drove the Kaqchikels into the mountains, where they began a guerrilla war against the Spaniards that lasted six years. The Spaniards abandoned Iximché.

Cortés, who was in Honduras to quell Cristóbal de Olid's rebellion, sent for Alvarado. Some soldiers did not wish to go and took refuge in Iximché. In early 1526, the city was burned when Alvarado and his allies defeated the rebels in battle. He marched with troops to Honduras, aided Cortés, and returned to Guatemala later that year with survivors from Cortés's army. One of these men was the conquistador BERNAL DÍAZ DEL CASTILLO, who later wrote *The True History of the Conquest of New Spain*.

In 1527, Jorge, Gonzalo, Gómez, and their cousins left for Mexico; they returned to Guatemala with 200 Spaniards and 5,000–10,000 Mexican allies for a massive assault against the Kaqchikels. Late in 1527, while Pedro de Alvarado was on his way to Spain, Jorge founded the colony's second capital at Bulbux-ya (Almolongo/Ciudad Vieja), near the base of the Volcán de Agua. Through the spring of 1529, Jorge campaigned as far as San Salvador and against the K'iche's and other Maya groups. He settled San Salvador, Chiapa, and San Miguel.

In 1530, Pedro de Alvarado returned to Guatemala, and the Kaqchikels finally surrendered. They were saddled with heavy tribute and labor obligations. Pedro left Guatemala again in 1535 for Spain via Honduras to avoid Alonso de Maldonado, who had been sent by the Audiencia of New Spain (see AUDIENCIA) to investigate charges of brutality (the Dominican friar BARTOLOMÉ DE LAS CASAS estimated that between the years of 1524 and 1540 Pedro de Alvarado and his brothers caused the deaths of 4 million Guatemalan natives). Maldonado quickly reduced the burdens imposed on the indigenous population when he took control in 1536. He retained power until 1539, when Pedro, exonerated by the Crown, returned. He brought with him a new wife, doña Beatriz de la Cueva.

Alvarado died in 1541 after being crushed by his horse during a battle in Jalisco. The CABILDO (town council) of Santiago de Guatemala named his widow, doña Beatriz, as governor. Her one-day rule ended with her death; an earthquake caused a torrent of water from the top of the Volcán de Agua to destroy the capital, which was subsequently moved to its third location, known today as Antigua.

Honduras and Higueras

Conflict and competition between Spanish captains, governors, and *audiencias* made the conquest of Honduras-Higueras exceedingly complex. The province of Higueras e Cabo de Honduras united two regions: Honduras included the eastern districts, territory west from Cabo Camarón to a point west of Trujillo and the Valley of Olancho; Higueras extended along the Atlantic coast west and north to the Golfo Dulce region and toward the boundaries of Guatemala and Yucatán, and included all territory from the Caribbean coast south to Nicaragua and San Salvador.

Honduras-Higueras was heavily populated when Spaniards arrived. Large towns existed in the valleys of Comayagua and Naco, and along the Ulúa River. The most complex cultures were in the rich Ulúa and Comayagua Valleys, while less complex ones characterized the Atlantic coast.

Indigenous resistance to the Spanish presence varied. Coastal native populations were easily subdued. Amerindians of the mountainous interior of Higueras and the valleys of Comayagua and Olancho strongly resisted colonial campaigns. The inhabitants of Naco and Ulúa quickly accepted early Spanish presence but resisted permanent colonization.

Vicente Yáñez Pinzón and Juan Díaz de Solís explored the coast of Honduras in 1508, but conquest did not begin until 1524, when Gil González Dávila sailed to the northern coast. He had to throw many horses overboard in a storm at what became known as Puerto de Caballos. Afterward, he sailed west and founded San Gil de Buenavista. He sailed back along the coast, landed, and journeyed inland toward Nicaragua. The San Gil colonists soon moved to the indigenous town of Nito. Hernández de Córdoba in Nicaragua learned of the Spaniards to the north and sent HERNANDO DE SOTO and a company of men to engage them. González Dávila's force won the battle and returned to Puerto de Caballos, where González learned that other Spaniards had arrived.

Cortés sent Cristóbal de Olid and his forces to Honduras in 1524. Olid arrived at Puerto de Caballos, founded Triunfo de la Cruz, renounced Cortés's authority, and announced his intention to rule the province. When Cortés learned of Olid's rebellion, he sent Francisco de Las Casas in command of 150 men. They arrived off Triunfo de la Cruz just as Olid prepared to battle González Dávila. A storm destroyed Las Casas's ships, and Olid captured the survivors and defeated González. Las Casas and González eventually wounded their captor. They tried and executed him and reasserted Cortés's authority.

Unaware of Olid's defeat, in late 1524, Cortés organized an expedition of 140 Spaniards and 3,000 indigenous allies. This company was beset by starvation and disease as it marched through the tropical forests of Tabasco, Campeche, and Petén. In early 1525, they encountered the remnants of the Nito colonists. Cortés and about 40 Spaniards and some native fighters sailed to the Golfo Dulce, fought the inhabitants of Chacujal, and sent food back to Nito. Eventually, Cortés abandoned Nito and moved to Puerto de Caballos, where he founded Natividad de Nuestra Señora.

Rumors of the death of Cortés and his men reached New Spain and eventually his enemies gained control of Mexico City. He planned to sail back immediately, but only in 1526 did he finally do so, at the urging of supporters who had regained control. By the time Cortés departed, he controlled heavily populated districts inland, and indigenous leaders from a wide area had offered their allegiance to him.

Late in 1525, the Crown appointed Diego López de Salcedo as royal governor of Honduras as part of its plan to bring the governance of the Indies under direct royal control. López de Salcedo arrived in late 1526, after Cortés had departed, and led his forces to Nicaragua, where he claimed authority. He imposed such heavy burdens on the native population along the way that they abandoned their towns and became hostile. López was imprisoned in Nicaragua until 1529 and was never able to reassert his authority as governor.

Andrés de Cerezeda became acting governor after the unpopular administrator died in early 1530. Cerezeda's rule was a period of anarchy and conflict; however, it also marked the beginnings of permanent colonization in Honduras and delimitation and occupation of Higueras.

From 1532 until 1544, the Crown authorized governors of Guatemala, Honduras-Higueras, and Yucatán to colonize the same general territory virtually simultaneously. This caused renewed confusion and conflict. The Crown appointed Francisco de Montejo, *adelantado* of Yucatán, as governor of Honduras-Higueras in 1535 and united the two provinces. Montejo renounced the governorship later that year because of his failure in colonizing Yucatán and precarious personal finances, but the Crown required him to take office.

Meanwhile, Pedro de Alvarado was asked to make the province part of Guatemala and intervened in Higueras, instituting important reforms. He sent his brother, Gonzalo, to found Gracias a Dios and then sailed for Spain in 1536. Despite misgivings, Montejo felt constrained to assume governorship. He established ambitious development plans and undertook the conquest of Higueras. By 1537, only small areas were truly pacified, and Lempira, a powerful indigenous leader of a territory in Higueras and neighboring San Miguel, led a general revolt centered on Peñol de Cerquín. The Spaniards under Montejo laid siege for months but could not breach the stronghold. Finally, they invited Lempira to negotiate, shot him in the forehead when he arrived, and entered the fortress as indigenous defenders stood by, stunned by their leader's death. Campaigns that continued through the spring of 1539 finally ended Amerindian resistance.

Five years of chaos followed Montejo's conquest of Higueras once Pedro de Alvarado had returned from Spain in 1539. Both men felt justified in claiming leadership. Eventually, the Crown decided Alvarado was more likely than Montejo to bring security and order to Honduras-Higueras. In exchange, Montejo received authority over Chiapas, which he claimed as part of Yucatán.

Therefore, in 1539, Honduras-Higueras became a province subordinate to Guatemala. However, after Alvarado's death, the union was dissolved, and at the end of 1541, Montejo was recalled to the governorship because of his administrative wisdom and military achievements. Nevertheless, his right to rule was soon disputed. The viceroy and Audiencia of New Spain attempted to reunite Honduras-Higueras with Guatemala in spring 1542. Unaware of Montejo's return, the Audiencia of Santo Domingo appointed Juan Pérez de Cabrera governor during that summer. By the end of the year, the viceroy had taken power from Montejo on behalf of New Spain. In response, Santo Domingo removed Pérez and reappointed Montejo as governor.

The New Laws of 1542, promulgated by the Crown to institute better government for the Indies, finally resolved this complex situation. In 1543, the Crown created the Audiencia de Los Confines, with jurisdiction and complete control over Honduras-Higueras, Guatemala, San Salvador, Nicaragua, Costa Rica, Chiapas, and Tabasco, and legal jurisdiction over Yucatán. Its members took office in 1544 and designated Gracias a Dios as the capital. With the imposition of firm royal authority, Honduras-Higueras finally entered a period of calm and order.

COLOMBIA

The first Europeans to explore Colombian territory arrived less than a decade after Columbus's initial voyage to the New World. In 1499, Alonso de Ojeda led a voyage to the Guajira Peninsula, along the Caribbean coastline. A year later, Rodrigo de Bastidas also explored Colombia's northern coast, where he and his companions bartered with local Amerindians for gold and pearls. However, fierce resistance from the region's indigenous population and limited evidence of mineral wealth delayed the establishment of permanent Spanish settlements along Colombia's northern coast. In fact, more than two decades passed before Bastidas returned to the region and founded Spain's first town in Colombia, which he named Santa Marta; Bastidas served as Santa Marta's first governor. During the first decades of the 16th century, Santa Marta attracted few Spanish settlers; those who did venture along Colombia's Caribbean coast did so in search of slaves to sell on Hispaniola or to barter with local Indians for gold or pearls. It was not until the mid-1520s that the Spanish Crown negotiated a formal agreement with Bastidas, entrusting the new governor with the conquest and permanent settlement of the province and port of Santa Marta. In 1533, Pedro de Heredia founded the Spanish town of Cartagena. From these two Caribbean outposts, Spanish expeditions began to explore Colombia's vast interior.

No single event influenced the exploration of Colombia more than the news of Francisco Pizarro's 1532 discovery of the Inca Empire in Peru. When reports of the fabulous riches to be had in Peru reached Santa Marta, many of the city's disgruntled residents abandoned Colombia for Peru. By early 1535, only nine horsemen and 40 foot soldiers remained. That year, fearful of losing its foothold in northern South America, the Spanish Crown negotiated a contract with Pedro Fernández de Lugo, granting him the governorship of Santa Marta and authorizing him to explore Colombia's interior. In November 1535, Fernández departed from the Canary Islands with a fleet of 10 ships and more than 1,200 passengers. Within three months of his arrival in Santa Marta, Fernández authorized his lieutenant, a 27-year-old lawyer named Gonzalo Jiménez de Quesada, to lead a military expedition from the coastal city of Santa Marta into Colombia's interior.

In early April 1536, Jiménez departed with a force of roughly 800 Spaniards and a large number of indigenous carriers and African slaves; the Jiménez expedition was more numerous than the combined forces under Cortés in Mexico and Pizarro in Peru. Jiménez's men were divided into two separate groups, with 500–600 Spaniards marching overland, supported by more than 200 others who boarded five brigantines and sailed up the Magdalena River. The official purpose of the expedition was twofold: to find an overland route from Colombia's Caribbean coast to newly conquered Peru and to follow the Magdalena River to discover its source, which some believed would

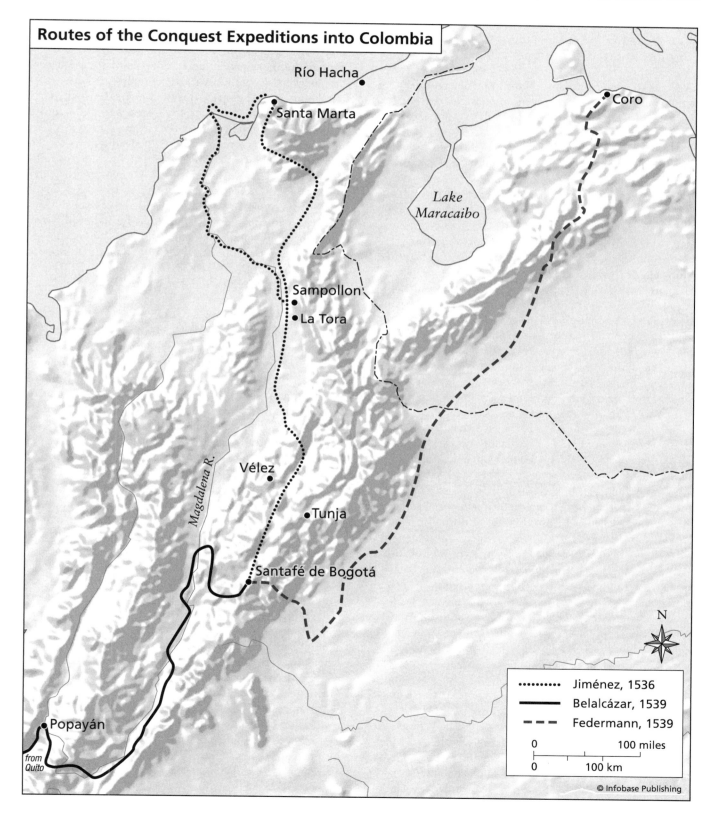

Routes of the Conquest Expeditions into Colombia

Río Hacha

Coro

Santa Marta

Lake Maracaibo

Sampollon

La Tora

Magdalena R.

Vélez

Tunja

Santafé de Bogotá

N

Popayán

from Quito

.... Jiménez, 1536
———— Belalcázar, 1539
– – – – Federmann, 1539

0   100 miles
0   100 km

© Infobase Publishing

lead the expedition to the South Sea (Pacific Ocean). It found neither. Instead, nearly three-quarters of Jiménez's men perished, most from illness, hunger, and malnutrition. Some Spaniards fell victims to jaguar or cayman attacks or to mortal wounds from Indian arrows laced with a deadly 24-hour poison. Others, too exhausted or too injured to continue, limped back to the brigantines and returned to Santa Marta. Yet despite the high casualty rate, for the 179 survivors of the 12-month venture, the expedition proved to be one of the most profitable campaigns of the 16th century. In early March 1537, almost a year after they had set out from Santa Marta, Jiménez and his men successfully crossed the Opón Mountains and reached the densely populated and fertile plains of Colombia's eastern highlands, home to the Muisca.

Jiménez recognized the importance of his discovery immediately. The dense population, rich agricultural lands, pleasant climate, splendid public architecture, and, perhaps most important, evidence of nearby sources of gold and emeralds were unlike anything they had seen elsewhere in the province of Santa Marta. Nevertheless, instead of returning to the coast to report their discovery to the man who had organized and funded the expedition, Santa Marta's governor, Fernández de Lugo, Jiménez and his followers chose to delay their return. Perhaps they did not want to risk losing the spoils of their hard labor and suffering to the many newcomers who would flood the region on hearing news of its riches. For the next two years, with no contact or correspondence with any other Europeans, the entire expedition remained in Muisca territory. From roaming base camps, they circulated throughout the eastern highlands, driven by their quest to uncover the region's riches and collect booty. They even ventured far outside the Muisca realm to investigate rumors of gold-filled palaces and mysterious tribes of Amazon women. They formed alliances with some Muisca leaders, fought against others, and participated in joint military campaigns against the Muisca's fiercest enemies, the Panches. Remarkably, only six Spaniards died during the expedition's first 13 months in Muisca territory, and none as a result of military conflict.

Of course, the fact that the Spaniards did not lose a man in combat does not mean that the conquest lacked violent encounters. Jiménez and his men regularly looted Muisca shrines or captured and tortured local leaders, from whom they demanded large ransoms. At times, such as when Jiménez and some of his followers seized the cacique (chief) of Tunja in August 1538, and with him, a booty of more than 140,000 gold pesos and 280 emeralds, these strategies proved highly profitable. At other times, the Spaniards met fierce resistance; the region's most powerful ruler, often referred to simply as "the Bogotá," refused to submit to the authority of the newcomers or surrender any of his rumored treasure of gold and emeralds. His resistance cost him his life; and while Bogotá's successor, named Sagipa, established a brief alliance with Jiménez, his refusal, even under torture, to reveal the

secret location of his predecessor's treasure, ultimately cost Sagipa his life as well.

But even without Bogotá's fabulous riches, if indeed such a treasure ever existed, the conquistadores of New Granada all gained handsome rewards. By June 1538, when Jiménez decided it was time to divide the spoils and distribute the shares, the "official" booty exceeded 200,000 gold pesos and more than 1,800 emeralds. For the 173 foot soldiers and horsemen still alive when the shares were distributed, the expedition proved to be among the most profitable campaigns of the 16th century, perhaps second only to the conquest of Peru.

Soon after Sagipa's death, Jiménez's small force received unexpected visitors. In February 1539, Nikolaus Federmann's expedition arrived from Venezuela; less than two months later, another expeditionary force, this one led by Sebastián de Belalcázar, arrived from Quito. It was with Belalcázar's arrival in Muisca territory that Jiménez finally learned of Fernández de Lugo's death. At Belalcázar's urging, Jiménez decided to establish three new cities in the region, an act that he believed would help secure his claims to the new territory. Thus, on April 27, 1539, Jiménez founded the city of Santafé de Bogotá, future capital of the New Kingdom of Granada; months later the cities of Vélez and Tunja were also founded.

MEXICO

The Spanish conquest of the Mexica (Aztec) capital of Tenochtitlán brought an expanding European empire into dramatic conflict with the most politically advanced civilization of 16th-century Mesoamerica, the Aztecs. The conquest of the Aztec Empire, however, was not a cultural or spiritual conquest but rather a political event, and the Spanish victory was in large part due to the nature of Central Mexico politics at the time.

The Spaniards' first American colonial experience was not in Mexico, but in the Caribbean. Columbus's famed 1492 voyage landed there first, and in 1493 his second voyage brought the first Spanish colonists to the Caribbean island of Hispaniola (modern-day Haiti and the Dominican Republic). From there, small groups of explorers set off to conquer other islands, such as Puerto Rico, Jamaica, and Cuba. The conquerors were not "soldiers" in the modern sense but partners in the colonial enterprise who earned a share of the spoils of any conquered lands.

Following this pattern of outward expansion, the first expedition to what is now Mexico set sail from Cuba in 1517. The Spaniards reached the Yucatán Peninsula first, where they encountered the Maya. Maya resistance to the Spaniards was fierce, and expedition leader Francisco Hernández de Córdoba returned to Cuba just two and a half months after he had departed; Hernández had lost nearly half of his men and one of his ships in that time.

Despite Hernández's failed effort, Spanish interest in mainland Mexico persisted. Cuban governor Diego Velázquez de Cuéllar organized a second and third expedition. The second trip, led by Juan de Grijalva, sailed in

1518 and again headed for the Yucatán coast. Grijalva's crew, however, continued sailing west around the peninsula beyond the Maya region and became the first Spaniards to reach the area of Mesoamerica dominated by the TRIPLE ALLIANCE of Central Mexico before heading back to Cuba.

The Triple Alliance was an alliance of three indigenous groups: the Mexica, had their capital at Tenochtitlán and were governed by the famed ruler MONTEZUMA; the Acolhua, who ruled from Texcoco; and the Tepanecs, who were based in Tlacopán. All of these groups were Nahuas (speakers of the NAHUATL language) and had been forcibly expanding their political control in the region for about a hundred years before the Spaniards arrived. Under Mexica leadership, the Triple Alliance exacted tribute from most of the indigenous groups from the Gulf coast to the Pacific Ocean. The growth of Triple Alliance control had led to resentment among many central Mexican indigenous groups, and into this political context of military expansion and growing discontent entered the third Spanish exploratory expedition from Cuba.

This third voyage was led by Hernando Cortés. However, Cortés's appointment by Governor Velázquez proved controversial, and Velázquez himself was ready to assign the expedition to someone else just before it departed. Cortés, however, gathered his men and supplies and left Cuba before he could be stopped. In defiance of the Cuban governor, he left for Yucatán and retraced the course followed by Grijalva, sailing east to west around the Yucatán Peninsula and then continuing along the coast into Triple Alliance territory.

On April 21, 1519, Cortés's ships arrived in a harbor in this region; there the Spaniards built a fortified city, which they named Veracruz. They were met by an official delegation sent by Montezuma and his allies, and the two groups exchanged gifts. The Spaniards did not understand Nahuatl but had two translators with them. One, a Spaniard named JERÓNIMO DE AGUILAR, spoke Maya (he had been shipwrecked off the coast of Yucatán years earlier). The second, a Nahua woman called La MALINCHE, spoke her native Nahuatl as well as Maya (she, too, had been held in Yucatán). Aguilar could move between Spanish and Maya, and Malinche could translate between Maya and Nahuatl. Thus, Cortés's group made themselves understood to the Triple Alliance representatives, and vice versa.

The Spaniards were intrigued by the Triple Alliance delegation; gifts of gold confirmed their suspicions that the Mexica possessed great riches. The Mexica, however, were less interested in the Spaniards and ordered them to come no closer to Tenochtitlán. The Spaniards had no intention of staying put but were ill prepared for a long trek from the coast into the central Mexican highlands to the capital.

It was another indigenous group who enabled Cortés to continue on his mission. Leaders of the local TOTONACS approached the Spaniards. The Totonac, tired of paying tribute and allegiance to the Triple Alliance, saw the Spanish arrival as an opportunity to cast off the Aztec imperial yoke and therefore offered their assistance. With Totonac guides, fighters, supplies, and valuable political knowledge, it was now possible for Cortés to plan a journey overland to Tenochtitlán. In June 1519, the expedition moved inland.

In the central Mexican highlands, the Spaniards encountered another group of Indians who harbored grudges against the Triple Alliance: the Tlaxcalans. The Tlaxcalans were also Nahuatl-speakers but were independent of and hostile to Triple Alliance control. They,

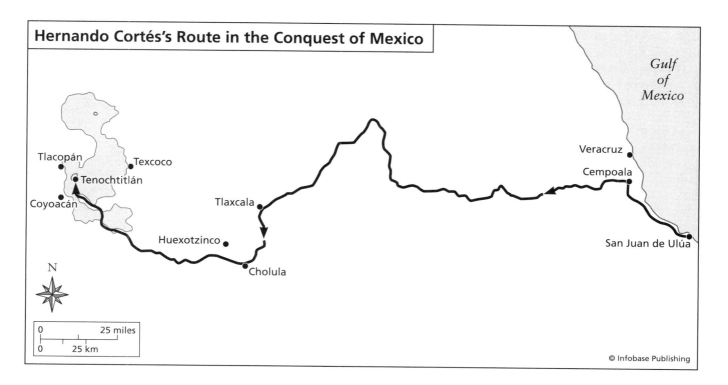

Hernando Cortés's Route in the Conquest of Mexico

© Infobase Publishing

like the Totonacs, saw in the Spaniards a valuable political ally. After a short period of hostility, they, too, joined the Spaniards against Montezuma and his allies.

In October 1519, Cortés left Tlaxcala with nearly 300 Spaniards and 5,000 or 6,000 Tlaxcalan fighters. Together, they marched toward Tenochtitlán and just outside the city, were met by Cacama, the ruler of Texcoco and Montezuma's nephew, who accompanied the Spaniards into Tenochtitlán to meet Montezuma himself.

The city of Tenochtitlán was built on a swampy island in the middle of the shallow lake Texcoco; it supported a population of at least 200,000. (Paris, Europe's largest city at this time, had only 150,000 inhabitants.) The small island was unable to contain such a large number of people, and the city's inhabitants began to expand the livable area of the city by mounding up mud from the lake bottom until small plots of land formed above the waterline. These fertile pieces of recovered land, called CHINAMPAS, provided additional space for homes and garden plots. Between these *chinampas* was an intricate web of shallow canals of lake water much like those in the European city of Venice. To reach the surrounding lake shore, three causeways extended out from Tenochtitlán to the north, south, and west. To the east, one could travel by boat across the lake to Texcoco.

Cortés and his men entered this booming metropolis from the south, and Montezuma invited the Spaniards to stay inside the royal palace complex. Most of the Tlaxcalans and other indigenous allies were obliged to remain outside the city on the lake shore. This arrangement left the relatively small group of Spaniards inside the city vulnerable and anxious, and when Cortés learned that the Aztecs had attacked their Totonac allies near Veracruz, he seized Montezuma and held him captive.

Montezuma's imprisonment restored Totonac and Tlaxcalan faith in Spanish power, but Cortés misunderstood the nature of government among the Nahuas. Montezuma did not rule Tenochtitlán in the same way that European monarchs governed, and allegiance to any Aztec ruler depended, at least partially, on that ruler's ability to govern. If other leaders perceived Montezuma to be weak or ineffective, then it was expected that he would be replaced. Cacama, the ruler of allied Texcoco, did indeed notice that Montezuma was losing control of Tenochtitlán, and he rallied the rulers of surrounding towns to join him in an attack on the Spaniards. Cortés learned of the impending strike, however, and arrested Cacama and his conspirators before they could carry out the plan.

At the same time that Cortés was working to frustrate the attempts of indigenous leaders, Spaniards elsewhere were working to thwart Cortés's mission. From Cuba, Governor Velázquez dispatched a group of 800 men led by PÁNFILO DE NARVÁEZ to capture Cortés, who had disobeyed the governor's orders by sailing to Mexico, and take him back to Cuba as prisoner. Cortés, however, learned of their arrival on the coast and set off from Tenochtitlán for Veracruz. Cortés attacked Narváez's

men at night, capturing Narváez and persuading most of his men to accompany him back to Tenochtitlán to assist in the conquest.

He returned to the capital to find that things were not going well for the Spaniards who had remained during his two-month absence. Cortés had left Pedro de Alvarado in charge, and Alvarado had massacred a large number of indigenous nobles attending a religious festival. The killings had provoked Tenochtitlán's residents to attack the Spaniards, and fighting forced the Spaniards to retreat into the fortified palace compound.

Cortés brought a large group of Spaniards (about 1,300) with him from the coast and 2,000 additional Tlaxcalans, but the city's residents far exceeded the number of men in Cortés's party. The now hostile residents allowed Cortés to reenter the city unopposed, only to trap him there. They laid siege to the palace compound for 23 days; the Spaniards were effectively imprisoned within the fortified walls, completely cut off from FOOD, ammunition, and the support of their indigenous allies.

In desperation, Cortés brought Montezuma out onto the rooftop of the palace to ask his people to end their attack. In the process, however, Montezuma was killed. The Spaniards, unable to withstand the siege, attempted to escape from the city during a strong rainstorm, late at night on June 30, 1520. The Mexica discovered them and attacked them as they fled on the causeway. Only a portion of the group, which included Cortés, reached the western shore of the lake alive.

These survivors marched north around the lakes towards the safety of allied Tlaxcala. They were attacked almost constantly; 860 Spaniards and 1,000 Tlaxcalans were killed before they finally reached Tlaxcala five days later. As the Spaniards rested and recovered from their injuries, the indigenous population of Central Mexico was overcome by the first wave of European diseases. With no natural resistance to these foreign illnesses, particularly smallpox, some 40 percent of the indigenous population of Central Mexico died.

Montezuma's successor, Cuitláhuac, contracted smallpox and died after only 80 days of rule. Cuitláhuac was followed in office by CUAUHTÉMOC. Nevertheless, the unexpected death of two Mexica rulers and the appearance of epidemic disease threw the capital into chaos. The Mexica were in no position to organize an offensive strike against the Spaniards as they recuperated in Tlaxcala. Cortés, on the other hand, had already renewed his quest to dominate Tenochtitlán.

First, Cortés began to secure the eastern road out of Tenochtitlán, which linked the city with critical supplies and support from the coastal city of Veracruz. Then he began construction of 13 ships in Tlaxcala, with which he could launch a lake-based attack on the island city. But, Cortés still needed access to the lake, and for this, he went to Texcoco on the lake's eastern shore. The ruler of Texcoco, Coanacoch, supported the Mexica, and frightened by Cortés's approach, he fled to safety in Tenochtitlán. His brothers Tecocol and Ixtlilxóchitl, however, were on unfriendly terms with the Mexica. They stepped in to fill the leadership void and readily agreed to assist the Spaniards.

From Texcoco, Cortés organized his attack on the capital. For four months, the reconstituted Aztec army sparred with the Spaniards and their allies in a series of battles for control of the area around the lake. On April 28, 1521, Cortés launched his ships into the lake from Texcoco. Aztec canoes were no match for the larger European vessels fitted with canon. The ships began a blockade of the island city, cutting off access to food and water (the lake's water was salty).

Ships were but one element of Cortés's conquest strategy. The conquistador also possessed ground forces composed of Spaniards and large numbers of indigenous fighters. For three months, these groups, under the protection of the Spanish ships, fought to enter the city from the causeways; still, these efforts met with failure. In June, Aztec fighters surrounded a group led by Cortés, and Cortés narrowly escaped capture. Sixty-eight other Spaniards were captured alive and sacrificed to the Aztec gods.

In July, Spanish fortunes changed: Spanish ships landed at Veracruz, bringing much needed supplies and fresh fighters. At the same time, the city of Tenochtitlán was succumbing to the lack of food and water. The Aztecs withdrew to the northern area of Tenochtitlán, Tlatelolco, as the Spaniards made their way up from the south. By August 1, the Spaniards had entered the large marketplace in Tlatelolco; on August 13, 1521, Cuauhtémoc was captured and the Aztecs surrendered. Spanish military and political conquest of Central Mexico was accomplished.

NORTHERN BORDERLANDS

From the Caribbean, Spaniards began to explore waters farther north at the turn of the 16th century. The first maps detailing portions of the Florida coast date from 1500 and 1502. Interest in the land bordering the Gulf of Mexico attracted Juan Ponce de León, who had participated in Columbus's second voyage and later conquered Puerto Rico in 1508. In 1513, Ponce de León sailed north into the Gulf of Mexico and encountered indigenous peoples off the coast of eastern Florida. Eight years later, in 1521, he returned to the coast of Florida after receiving permission from the Crown to conquer it. Calusa Indians along the coast attacked his expedition force, and Ponce de León died shortly thereafter from his wounds after having returned to Cuba.

Antonio de Alamiros and Alonso Álvarez de Piñeda explored the Gulf of Mexico in the first half of the 16th century. Álvarez demonstrated that Florida was a peninsula and explored the coastal areas of current-day western Florida, Alabama, Louisiana, and Texas, including the Mississippi River. Further explorations of the Atlantic coastline resulted in more encounters with Amerindians, some of whom were captured and enslaved to work in the Caribbean. In 1523, after presenting the Spanish Court with a captured indigenous person from islands off the coast of South Carolina, Lucas Vázquez de Ayllón obtained a license to colonize and convert native populations along the Atlantic coast. He recruited 600 colonists, including slaves and priests, and sailed to the coast, eventually erecting a small settlement called San Miguel de Gualdape on the coast of present-day Georgia. The colony failed, and fewer than one-third of the colonists made it back to Hispaniola. In the 1520s and 1530s, other Spanish explorations of the Atlantic and Pacific coasts resulted in increased knowledge of the North American coastline but failed to result in lasting settlements.

In 1528, Pánfilo de Narváez tried to explore and colonize Florida. The Timucua Indians, who lived north of Tampa Bay, sent the Spaniards away with promises of gold and resources farther inland. The Apalachees were at first friendly but attacked the expedition once it took one of their leaders hostage. The expedition split, and a detachment sailed along the Gulf coast, facing storms, attacks, and food shortages. They were shipwrecked on the coast of Texas, where Karankawas enslaved some of the survivors. Álvar Núñez Cabeza de Vaca and three others fled overland, acting as healers to ensure their safety until they met up with a Spanish slaving expedition in 1536.

Eleven years after the Narváez expedition, Hernando de Soto led another expedition to conquer Florida. De Soto's troops moved into territory inhabited by agriculturalist Mississippian peoples. There, de Soto captured slaves, robbed food stores, and killed those who resisted. Reports of gold drew his forces farther west, but after de Soto was killed in 1542, remnants of the group sailed down the Mississippi River and returned to Mexico.

Meanwhile, the northwestern frontier of the Spanish Empire had been the scene of a brutal expedition beginning in 1530 by Nuño de Guzmán, whose soldiers and indigenous allies stole, kidnapped, raped, and burned their way north. The province of Nueva Galicia was established in 1531 as a result, with its capital at Compostela. The crown awarded ENCOMIENDA grants to expedition members, and soldiers settled in the area. After several years, the Spanish settlements at Compostela and Chiametla greatly declined, while the indigenous population perished due to disease and harsh treatment. Nuño de Guzmán was arrested and imprisoned for his treatment of the Amerindians.

The return of Cabeza de Vaca's party in 1536 sparked renewed conflict in the north. In 1538, Fray Marcos de Niza accompanied Esteban, a member of Cabeza de Vaca's party, on an exploratory journey far north into Zuni country. While Esteban was killed, Fray Marcos's fantastic tales led to a large entrada force headed by Francisco Vásquez de Coronado in 1540. This force failed to find riches in modern-day Arizona and New Mexico but engaged in hostilities with the Pueblo peoples along the Rio Grande. A detachment traveled east over the great plains, but injuries and harsh winters led to the expedition's retreat to Mexico in 1542. Along the way, Coronado's force joined with troops under Viceroy Antonio de Mendoza to put down the fierce two-year rebellion of Cazcanes and Juchipilas. These indigenous peoples had laid siege to Guadalajara in a conflict known as the Mixtón War.

After the rebellion ended in 1542, the capital of Nueva Galicia was moved to Guadalajara, and more Spaniards moved to the frontier. In 1546, silver was discovered north of the Sierra Madre Occidental, and miners flocked to Zacatecas, Durango, Hidalgo, Guanajuato, Aguascalientes, San Luis Potosí, and Chihuahua in the 1550s. Presidios and missions were erected in these areas to attempt to control indigenous groups, but conflicts with peoples whom the Aztecs had called "Chichimecas" occurred frequently over the next century.

Coastal exploration of the northern frontier continued. In 1542, Juan Cabrillo sailed up the Pacific coast and landed at the harbor of present-day San Diego, California. After exploring the coast and exchanging arrows with the Ipai, the force traveled north to the site of present-day Los Angeles and then farther north until they reached the Rogue River in Oregon. The indigenous peoples they encountered communicated that other Spaniards had passed through the area. Cabrillo died during the winter, but Bartolomé Ferrer returned to Mexico in 1543. This expedition traveled more than 1,200 miles of coastline and bolstered Spanish claims to the territory. By the 1540s, it was clear that Baja California was a peninsula, but no permanent settlements were planted.

On the far northern frontier, conquest did not occur through military means. The Spaniards' chief gains were the knowledge of a good deal of coastal and some interior geography. By far, the largest effect of these early expeditions was the spread of disease. In Nueva Galicia, however, Spanish settlements were permanent by 1560. The discovery of silver created a strong motive for military presence and campaigns, such as the Mixtón War and against the Chichimecas.

PERU

In 1532, a Spanish force led by Francisco Pizarro captured the Inca ruler Atahualpa, obtained a vast treasure in gold and silver, and extended Spanish sovereignty into the Andes (see Incas). In some ways, the conquest of Peru seemed to replicate Cortés's conquest of Mexico (1519–21). Indeed, many of the factors that contributed to the Spaniards' success in Mexico also played a role in their conquest of Peru, including bitter rivalries and divisions among the indigenous groups, the Spaniards' technological superiority and horses, and the spread of Old World disease. There were also important differences, however. These included the fact that in the Andes, an apparently easy conquest, symbolized by Pizarro's capture of Atahualpa at Cajamarca in 1532, turned into a bitter struggle against Indian rebellions for a decade and the threat posed by a small neo-Inca state that endured until 1572.

The conquest of Peru was launched from Spanish strongholds in Central America. In 1522, Pascual de Andagoya sailed south from Panama to investigate reports of a rich, powerful indigenous culture called "Birú" (Peru). Those rumors, coupled with accounts of the vast riches won by Cortés and his men in the conquest of Mexico, captured the imagination and fueled the greed of men like Pizarro, one of governor Pedro Arias de Ávila's chief lieutenants. Eager to win gold and glory for himself, Pizarro formed a partnership with Diego de Almagro, a business associate, and with a priest named Hernando de Luque. The new partners bought Andagoya's three small ships and after gathering men and supplies, sailed south from Panama in November 1524. With great hardship, they reached the San Juan River, then returned to Panama.

Despite the failure of this first voyage, Pizarro, Almagro, and Luque entered into a formal contract on March 10, 1526; they agreed to share equally in the costs and profits of the endeavor to seize the wealth of Peru. Their second expedition sailed soon thereafter. Pushing much farther south, again with great difficulty, they reached Isla del Gallo along the central coast of Ecuador. There, many disgruntled participants abandoned Pizarro; however, "the famous thirteen" agreed to continue southward with Pizarro, encouraged by the discovery of several Amerindians on a raft laden with gold, silver, and fine cloth. The Spaniards struggled farther south and finally reached Tumbes, an Inca coastal city near the modern Peru-Ecuador border. Its wealth and splendor convinced Pizarro that the rumors and reports of Peru were indeed true.

Pizarro determined to return to Panama to organize an expedition of conquest. First, however, he returned to Spain and on July 26, 1529, secured from the queen a charter, the Capitulación de Toledo, authorizing the partners to undertake the conquest; the *capitulación* also granted Pizarro most of the rewards if the venture proved successful. While in Spain, Pizarro also met Cortés, with whom he discussed the conquest of the Aztecs. Finally, accompanied by half brothers Hernando Pizarro, Juan Pizarro, and Gonzalo Pizarro, as well as other recruits, Francisco Pizarro returned to Panama. On learning of the *capitulación*'s contents, Almagro became furious and was convinced that Pizarro had cheated him; nevertheless, he had few options other than to cooperate.

In late 1530, Francisco Pizarro set out for Peru with 180 men and 30 horses. They plundered the coast of Ecuador before reaching Tumbes in February 1532. The Spaniards discovered that the city had been partially destroyed in a civil war among the Incas. Huayna Cápac, the last great Inca ruler, had died around 1530, probably from smallpox, which had spread from the Caribbean and devastated the Andean peoples. Two of Huayna Cápac's sons, half brothers Huáscar and Atahualpa, fought to succeed their father. They represented rival PANAQAS, or royal lineages; Huáscar's power was centered in Cuzco, the Inca capital, while Atahualpa's power base lay in Quito, recently added to Tawantinsuyu, as the Incas called their empire. Furthermore, the Incas had created the Tawantinsuyu through conquest, and many of the recently subjugated people were unhappy with the new demands imposed on them. Pizarro was eager to exploit the indigenous dissension, just as Cortés had reported doing in Mexico.

With reinforcements from Panama, Pizarro departed from Tumbes in May 1532, moving into the mountains toward Atahualpa's army, which had recently defeated and captured Huáscar. Indigenous spies and emissaries visited the Spaniards, bringing ominous gifts such as plucked fowls and ceramic castles. Atahualpa knew the strangers' movements and might have destroyed Pizarro's men in a mountainous ambush. Overconfident, he instead allowed Pizarro and his men to reach Cajamarca, where Atahualpa and his forces were encamped. Atahualpa reportedly intended to kill all the Spaniards, except for the blacksmith and the barber, the latter because he seemed to have a magical ability to help the Spaniards regain a healthy appearance. They would be castrated and kept to serve at court.

After reaching Cajamarca and encamping in the city, Pizarro sent two squads, headed by Hernando de Soto and Hernando Pizarro, to the Indian camp. Using Indians seized during Pizarro's second expedition as translators, the emissaries conversed with Atahualpa, who agreed to visit the Spaniards in Cajamarca.

The following afternoon, November 16, Atahualpa was carried into the town on a litter accompanied by several thousand bodyguards armed with ceremonial weapons. Pizarro sent out Dominican friar Vicente de Valverde, who explained to Atahualpa (through a translator) the REQUERIMIENTO, a legalism that asserted Spain's sovereignty over the New World by way of papal donation and that encouraged the indigenous peoples to become Christian. Never having seen a book, Atahualpa asked to see the Bible carried by the priest but haughtily threw it on the ground when he could make nothing of it. At that point, the priest ran toward the Spaniards, who were hidden in buildings around the square. They fired on Atahualpa's men and then stormed out, the horses trampling the Inca's escort. The terrified Amerindians tried desperately to escape from the walled square but were cut down. Spaniards killed the men holding Atahualpa's litter, but such was the bearers' discipline that others quickly stepped forward to keep the Inca from falling. Francisco Pizarro himself captured Atahualpa.

With Atahualpa as their hostage, the Spaniards enjoyed great influence in Tawantinsuyu. Atahualpa's own faction grudgingly obeyed the captive's orders, fearful for his safety. To them, he was not only the supreme ruler of a highly centralized regime but also divine. Worried that the Spaniards might ally with his defeated half brother, Atahualpa secretly ordered Huáscar's execution. Eager to take revenge on Atahualpa, Huáscar's supporters assisted the Spaniards. Away from Cajamarca, Atahualpa's lieutenants struggled to maintain control over Tawantinsuyu. Hoping to buy his

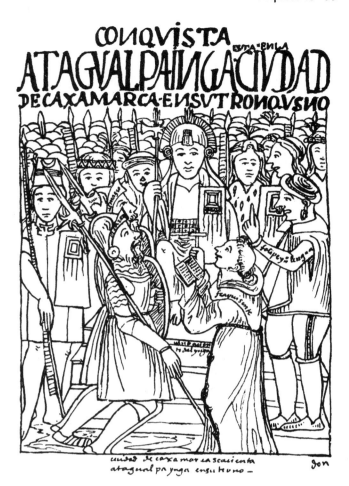

Felipe Guamán Poma de Ayala's illustration of Atahualpa seated before three kneeling Spaniards, Diego de Almagro, Francisco Pizarro, and Friar Vicente de Valverde. To the right of Valverde stands the indigenous translator Felipillo. (The Royal Library, Copenhagen, Denmark)

freedom, Atahualpa offered to fill a room once with gold and again with silver. While llama trains brought treasure to Cajamarca, the Spaniards reconnoitered.

In early 1533, Hernando Pizarro looted the great religious shrine at Pachacamac, near modern-day LIMA. Another contingent went to Cuzco, the Inca capital, where they stripped the walls of the Coricancha (Temple of the Sun) of 700 gold tablets, each weighing around 4.5 pounds (2 kg). By June, Atahualpa had amassed the promised ransom, making rich men out of all the Spaniards present at his capture; nevertheless, Francisco Pizarro refused to free him. Accusing Atahualpa of murdering Huáscar and organizing a rebellion, Pizarro executed his prisoner on July 26, 1533. Sentenced to be burned alive, the Inca converted to Christianity and was instead strangled, hoping thereby to save his remains for mummification and worship by his people, as was the case with his predecessors. Continuing his deceitful behavior, Pizarro ordered Atahualpa's remains burned and the ashes scattered. Hernando Pizarro left for Spain to pay the king's share (the royal fifth, or *quinto*) of the treasure and to inform Charles I of their exploits.

In an effort to maintain order in the Tawantinsuyu, Francisco Pizarro installed Túpac Huallpa, a member of Huáscar's *panaqa*, as a puppet Inca; then, reinforced by 150 men under Almagro, the Spaniards set out for Cuzco. At Jauja, Atahualpa's supporters, under the command of the great general Quisquis, attacked but were overwhelmed by Spanish horsemen. In open terrain, Andean soldiers, armed primarily with clubs and slingshots, were no match for horses and Spanish steel swords and body armor. On November 8, at Vilcaconga, the advance guard commanded by de Soto was ambushed and was saved only by the arrival of Almagro. They fought another battle outside Cuzco before Pizarro's forces entered the city on November 15, 1533. Túpac Huallpa, meanwhile, had died in October, forcing Pizarro to turn to another of Huayna Cápac's sons, MANCO INCA. Manco received the royal tassel in December 1533; however, he proved to be less willing to play the role of compliant puppet than the Spaniards hoped.

The Spanish may have held Cuzco, but they had not pacified Tawantinsuyu. Drawn from Panama by reports of the gold and silver to be had in Peru, more Spanish reinforcements arrived, including those led by Pedro de Alvarado, a captain under Cortés during the conquest of Mexico. During the first half of 1534, Sebastián de Belalcázar led the conquest of Quito. Convinced of the need for more secure contact with Panama than Cuzco could afford, Pizarro founded the "City of the Kings," or Lima, on January 6, 1535, thereby improving the Spaniards' maritime communications. Pizarro also attempted to resolve his differences with his partner, Almagro. To this end, Pizarro encouraged his partner to explore the lands south of Cuzco, and in July 1535, Almagro and a large contingent of Spaniards and Amerindians headed into CHILE.

Meanwhile, Manco Inca grew tired of Spanish abuse and exploitation. In 1536, he secretly organized a massive army and then slipped out of Cuzco. Soon Cuzco, defended by 200 Spaniards and their indigenous allies, was under siege. Using slingshots to hurl flaming missiles onto Cuzco's thatched roofs, Manco's warriors forced most of the Spaniards into the shelter of the Incan armory, Suntur Huasi. The battle for Cuzco grew ever more desperate for the Spaniards, but Manco's army could not deal the death blow. Juan Pizarro was killed trying to drive the attackers from the great fortress and temple complex of Sacsayhuamán, perched on a hill overlooking the city. From Lima, Francisco Pizarro sent several relief expeditions, but they were ambushed before they reached Cuzco. The Incas attacked Lima itself but could not take it. Neither did they capture Cuzco, despite their overwhelming numbers. As the fighting grew more bitter, so, too, did the atrocities committed by each side. After a siege of several months, Manco's army withdrew. Ethnic rivalries among the indigenous people weakened Manco's Great Rebellion; indeed, some remained firm Spanish allies.

The failure of the Great Rebellion sealed the Spanish conquest of Peru, although it did not bring general peace to the Andes. Manco Inca launched another rebellion in 1539 and then retreated into the mountains north of Cuzco, setting up an independent kingdom at Vilcabamba, which survived until 1572, when the Spaniards destroyed it. Almagro seized Cuzco from the Pizarros in 1537 but was defeated at the BATTLE OF LAS SALINAS and executed on July 8, 1538. In retaliation, Almagro's men murdered Francisco Pizarro in 1541. To assert royal control over the Andes, Charles I sent Blasco Núñez de Vela to Peru as VICEROY, with orders to limit the conquistadores' exploitation of the indigenous population. His arrival in 1544 touched off a rebellion against the Crown (see CIVIL WARS IN PERU). The viceroy died in the rebellion. Only in the mid-1550s, more than two decades after Pizarro had initiated the conquest, did royal authority over Peru become more secure.

SOUTHERN CONE

The conquest of the Southern Cone began early in the 16th century and refers to Spanish colonial incursions into what are now the nations of ARGENTINA, Chile, URUGUAY, and PARAGUAY. (The south of Brazil is often regarded as part of the Southern Cone, but Brazil's conquest is discussed in an earlier section of this entry.) The conquest of the Southern Cone began largely as an extension of Spain's conquest of the Inca Empire in Peru. By pushing south into Chile and from the Atlantic side, seeking the source of the Río de la Plata, or River Plate, the Spanish hoped to find more precious metals and ways to more efficiently ship the silver and gold they continued to seize from the Inca.

Juan Díaz de Solís discovered the mouth of the River Plate in 1516, but he and his men were all killed by local Querandí Indians soon after they arrived. FERDINAND MAGELLAN briefly explored the estuary as well in 1520, before continuing along his southerly route to the Pacific. Sebastian Cabot explored the Southern Cone's Atlantic coast in 1527 before founding the soon-to-be-abandoned town of Sancti Spiritus along the Paraná River. Cabot returned safely to Spain, where Charles I decided to fund an impressive force of 1,600 to accompany PEDRO DE MENDOZA in his attempt to settle the Southern Cone's east coast. Mendoza founded BUENOS AIRES in 1536, but such a large contingent proved difficult to provision. Spanish desperation stemming from lack of food and supplies provoked new hostilities with the Querandí, and Mendoza soon abandoned his men and died on his way back to Spain. In the meantime, Mendoza's subordinates had followed the Paraná upriver and founded Asunción in 1537. The remaining residents of Buenos Aires decided to abandon the town in 1541.

From Asunción, the Spanish planned to find mythical indigenous kingdoms with incredible wealth (see EL DORADO). Mendoza had named Juan de Ayolas to lead an expedition to find such kingdoms, but Ayolas disappeared while crossing the rugged Chaco wilderness.

With Mendoza dead and wealthy kingdoms nowhere to be found, Spanish colonists in Asunción shifted their focus from exploration to permanent settlement. The GUARANÍ were a sedentary people who occupied the southern Paraná Delta, where Asunción sits. Guaraní permanence in the area meant that if the Spanish were to occupy the region, the only two options were peaceful coexistence or a long and bloody war. With limited troops and resources, the Spanish favored the former. The indigenous political situation also favored a Spanish-Guaraní alliance. The Guaraní suffered frequent raids from nomadic tribes of the Chaco, such as the Guaycurú, Toba, Payaguá, Pilagá and Lengua, and therefore sought Spanish military assistance to repel them.

The architect of this alliance was Domingo de Irala, who became the default governor of Paraguay after Mendoza's departure. Charles I preferred a known entity, however, and in 1542, the king replaced Irala with Álvar Núñez Cabeza de Vaca. Initially, the new governor was well received; however, he soon wore out his welcome. Cabeza de Vaca appropriated 3,000 palm tree trunks that had been designated to finish the "old" conquerors' settlement, using them in part to build his own residence, the houses of the "new" conquerors, and horse stables. Cabeza de Vaca made some strides in solidifying the Spanish-Guaraní alliance but later permanently damaged the colonists' relationship with the Agace peoples who controlled the strategically important confluence of the Paraguay and Paraná Rivers. The governor lost additional allies when a catastrophic fire charred more than half of Asunción, including great quantities of stored food. After an unsuccessful 1544 expedition to the Chaco, in which many Spanish were killed or became ill, Cabeza de Vaca and a few of his aides were arrested, and the governor was sent back to Spain in irons.

Upon Cabeza de Vaca's arrest, Irala returned as governor of Paraguay. During the instability that followed the change of command, the Agace and Guaraní joined forces and launched an attack on Asunción in 1545. This was successfully repelled, and in 1547, Irala led an expedition to Peru. When he arrived, he discovered that the Spanish conquest had already reached the region. Stopping in the province of Chiquitos, Irala sent word to the governor of Peru, PEDRO DE LA GASCA, that he wished to meet with him. Fearing a power struggle, Gasca prohibited Irala from staying in Peru, and Irala returned to Asunción.

In Irala's absence, Francisco de Mendoza attempted to have himself elected governor. A revolt ensued, and Mendoza was tried and beheaded. When he returned, Irala set out to create a successful economy based on Guaraní labor.

On the other side of the Andes, Diego de Almagro played a leading role in the conquest of the Southern Cone. Almagro led the first Spanish expedition into Chile from Peru in 1535. With the help of Prince Paullu, the Inca Manco Cápac's brother, Almagro conquered the Andean provinces known to the Inca as Purumauca,

Antalli, Pincu, Cauqui, and Araucu. At the eastern entrance to the Aconcagua Valley, Almagro paused and sent his lieutenants forward. Almagro's subordinates reached the Maule River and fought the "skirmish" of Reinoguelén, at the junction of the Ñuble and Itata Rivers. This battle represented the first Spanish contact with the Mapuches and resulted in the death of two Spaniards and the capture of scores of Mapuches. Almagro and his subordinates eventually turned back, but their discovery soon prompted other explorers to try their luck in Chile. In 1541, PEDRO DE VALDIVIA led an expedition from Peru into Chile's Aconcagua Valley. Valdivia founded Santiago de la Nueva Extremadura, was declared Chile's first governor, and sent his lieutenants south and east into what would eventually become the Argentine province of Cuyo.

After founding the city of Santiago, Valdivia led a drive southward in 1546, which met with strong Mapuche resistance near the Bío-Bío River. Conflict only increased when the Spanish presence was stepped up in 1549, in response to the discovery of gold in the region. Valdivia's expedition established Spain's grip on much of Chile, but the conquest stopped short in 1553, when Valdivia was killed by Mapuches. Valdivia's former groom, Lautaro, had set an ambush for the governor as he rode to the aid of the Spanish fort of Tucapel.

See also BANDEIRAS (Vol. II).

—Bradley Thomas Benton
Eugene C. Berger
Kendall Brown
John F. Chuchiak IV
J. Michael Francis
Kristin Dutcher Mann
Erik Myrup
Stephen L. Whittington

Further reading:

José Ignacio Avellaneda. *The Conquerors of the New Kingdom of Granada* (Albuquerque: University of New Mexico Press, 1995).

Leslie Bethel, ed. *Colonial Brazil* (New York: Cambridge University Press, 1987).

Robert S. Chamberlain. *The Conquest and Colonization of Honduras: 1502–1550* (Washington, D.C.: Carnegie Institution of Washington, 1966).

Kathleen A. Deagan. "Sixteenth-Century Spanish-American Colonization in the Southeast and Caribbean." In *Archaeological and Historical Perspectives on the Spanish Borderlands*, edited by D. H. Thomas, 225–250 (Washington, D.C.: Smithsonian Institution Press, 1990).

J. Michael Francis. *Invading Colombia: Spanish Accounts of the Gonzalo Jiménez de Quesada Expedition of Conquest* (University Park: Pennsylvania State University Press, 1997).

Ross Hassig. *Mexico and the Spanish Conquest* (New York: Longman Publishing, 1994).

John Hemming. *The Conquest of the Incas* (New York: Harcourt Brace Jovanovich, 1970).

James Lockhart. *The Men of Cajamarca: A Social and Biographical Study of the First Conquerors of Peru* (Austin: University of Texas Press, 1972).

Jerald T. Milanich and Susan Milbrath, eds. *First Encounters: Spanish Explorations in the Caribbean and the United States, 1492–1570* (Gainesville: University of Florida Press, 1989).

Pedro Pizarro. *Relation of the Discovery and Conquest of the Kingdoms of Peru* (New York: Kraus Reprint, 1969).

Matthew Restall. *Seven Myths of the Spanish Conquest* (New York: Oxford University Press, 2003).

Matthew Restall and Florine Asselbergs. *Invading Guatemala: Spanish, Nahua, and Maya Accounts of the Conquest Wars* (University Park: Pennsylvania State University Press, 2008).

David Weber. *The Spanish Frontier in North America* (New Haven, Conn.: Yale University Press, 1992).

Copán Copán is a major MAYA archaeological site located in the hills of western HONDURAS. It is significant for its remarkable ART, ARCHITECTURE, inscriptions, and history.

Copán lies in a broad pocket of the Copán river valley, which contains the largest expanse of productive alluvial soils in the area. The site consists of a massive artificial acropolis, surrounded by extensive residential zones. The acropolis is composed of successive layers of civic-ceremonial construction spanning the Classic period (250–900 C.E.). Archaeologists have excavated tunnels throughout the acropolis to document the early architectural sequence of the site. The excavations indicate that the volume of construction increased most rapidly during the Early Classic period (250–550), suggesting the development of a centralized government.

The acropolis is organized around a series of courtyards. Major constructions include temples (Temples 11 and 16), palaces (the 10L-32 quadrangle), a ball court, and a council house (10L-22A). Numerous stelae (commemorative carved standing stones) and carved altars embellish the ceremonial center. The ceremonial buildings, especially the later major constructions, were built of fine masonry, each stone uniformly cut and coursed. The buildings are distinguished by elaborate mosaic architectural sculptures that were carved in place out of multiple blocks of stone.

The residential neighborhoods that surround the acropolis contained both elaborate elite residences and many middle- or lower-class dwellings. The total population of the site grew from a few thousand in the Early

Built during the reign of Copán's 13th ruler, Waxaklajun Ub'aah K'awiil (r. 695–738), this structure (Structure 10L-22) celebrates the first *k'atun* (20 years) of his rule. The structure is a symbolic representation of the Maya cosmos, with the building itself representing the mountain out of which maize was born. *(Courtesy of J. Michael Francis)*

This Maya glyph records the name of Copán's 13th ruler, Waxaklajun Ub'aah K'awiil. His lengthy reign (695–738) ended when he was captured and executed by the ruler of the vassal city of Quiriguá. *(Courtesy of J. Michael Francis)*

Classic period to 20,000–28,000 by its Late Classic apogee. The population collapsed during the mid-ninth century during the famous "Maya collapse."

Copán artwork is of outstanding quantity and quality. The style is distinctive, one major element being its three-dimensionality. Most monumental Maya art is low-relief carving, but the artwork of Copán is often carved in the round or in high relief. Examples include the major stelae dotting the site and the architectural sculptures that graced the facades and roofs of major buildings. The sculptural style is elaborate and baroque: The subjects of sculptures are often buried in a riot of stone tendrils and volutes laden with iconographic meaning.

The glyphic inscriptions of Copán are significant not only for their extent—they make up one of the largest inventories of texts—but also for their excellence. They are beautifully executed, and the creativity with which the complex script was used has led to advances in its decipherment.

Although archaeological remains in the Copán Valley date back to the second millennium B.C.E., the Maya city seems to have been founded by a foreign ruler named K'inich Yax K'uk' Mo' in 436–437 C.E. He may have been a minion of the Central Mexico city of TEOTIHUACÁN: He is portrayed in Mexican garb and is associated with Teotihuacán-style artifacts and architecture. Other major kings of Copán include the powerful Ruler 12, who reigned for most of the seventh century. His star-crossed successor, Waxaklajun Ub'aah K'awiil, was captured and sacrificed at the neighboring site of Quiriguá. Copán's last major king was Yax Pasaj, who erected a number of monuments shortly before the city drifted into its thousand-year sleep.

—Clifford T. Brown

Further reading:

E. Wyllys Andrews and William L. Fash, eds. *Copán: The History of an Ancient Maya Kingdom* (Santa Fe, N.Mex.: School of American Research Press, 2005).

Coronado, Francisco Vásquez de (b. ca. 1510– d. 1554) *Spanish conquistador and governor of New Galicia* A Spanish explorer, Francisco Vásquez de Coronado led an expedition into the U.S. Southwest in response to reports of seven rich indigenous CITIES in the land of Cíbola. The expedition made contact with the Hopi, Zuñi, and Pueblo peoples and provided important information about the geography of the Southwest, though it failed to find the riches it sought.

Born in 1510, Coronado was a friend and protégé of ANTONIO DE MENDOZA, the first VICEROY of New Spain (MEXICO). In Mexico, Coronado married Beatriz de Estrada, the daughter of New Spain's royal treasurer. He also headed forces sent by Mendoza to put down an indigenous rebellion in northwestern Mexico (New Galicia); he then became governor of the region.

When survivors of PÁNFILO DE NARVÁEZ's disastrous expedition to FLORIDA wandered into Mexico with stories of fabulously rich cities to the north, Mendoza named Coronado to head an expedition to investigate. This expedition made contact with the Zuñis at Hawikuh (the supposed Cíbola) on the Arizona–New Mexico border in July 1540. Coronado sent a party under Pedro de Tovar to the northwest to explore the lands of the Hopis, and another group under García López de Cárdenas found the Grand Canyon.

In late 1540, the expedition traveled into north-central New Mexico, having been invited to winter with the Pueblos. Again, no riches were to be found. Ill prepared for the weather, the Spaniards took FOOD and CLOTHING from their hosts and raped Pueblo WOMEN. In the ensuing Tiguex War, Coronado and his men committed further atrocities against the Pueblos.

In April 1541, Coronado led a small party eastward through Texas and Kansas, searching for the land of Quivira. The survivors of the expedition returned to Mexico in 1542. Accused of mistreating the NATIVE AMERICANS, Coronado was subject to legal investigations. He died on September 22, 1554. Despite his expedition's failure to find the anticipated riches, the undertaking revealed the breadth of the continent and discovered the Continental Divide. The expedition also provided other important geographical and ethnographic information for later Spanish colonization of the lands that Coronado had claimed for Spain.

—Kendall Brown

Further reading:

Herbert Eugene Bolton. *Coronado on the Turquoise Trail: Knight of the Pueblos and Plains* (Albuquerque: University of New Mexico Press, 1949).

Richard Flint. *No Settlement, No Conquest: A History of the Coronado Entrada* (Albuquerque: University of New Mexico Press, 2008).

Richard Flint and Shirley Cushing Flint, eds. and trans. *Documents of the Coronado Expedition, 1539–1542: "They were not familiar with His Majesty, nor did they wish to be his subjects"* (Dallas, Tex.: Southern Methodist University Press, 2005).

corregidor/corregimiento Within the Spanish system of government in the New World, the *corregidor* served as a local magistrate. The territory governed by a *corregidor* was known as a *corregimiento*. For all intents and purposes, in the colonial period prior to 1570, the office of *corregidor* was indistinguishable from that of the *gobernador* or *alcalde mayor*. In general, all were local magistrates who received their authority ultimately from the Spanish Crown. The *gobernador* frequently governed a larger or more important territory. Similarly, the *alcalde mayor* might govern a province and be nominally superior to the *corregidores* in his region.

The Crown held the power to appoint local magistrates. This power was delegated, in most instances, either to the VICEROY or to the local high court, the AUDIENCIA. Frequently, the viceroy and/or high court would appoint individuals from among their own following, retainers and friends, to local magistracies. By 1570, a significant number of local magistrates came from the ranks of the conquistadores. Initially, some conquerors who held ENCOMIENDA grants were also allowed to serve as magistrates; however, the NEW LAWS OF 1542 abolished this practice and offered, instead, appointment to magistracies as a reward to those who had lost their grants of *encomienda*. As a result, many of the mature children of the first conquerors were appointed as magistrates in recognition of their parents' service.

The local magistrate was responsible for the collection of royal taxes within his district. He also supervised local justice in areas outside legally established towns. Furthermore, he had a general mandate to protect the indigenous population. He supervised the allocation of land by the royal government, conducting surveys and investigations. He was paid a regular salary out of the Royal Treasury, although if the treasury lacked funds, it might be difficult to collect the salary. He sometimes appointed assistants, or *tenientes*, to aid him in the execution of his duties.

See also *CORREGIDOR/CORREGIMIENTO* (Vol. II).

—John F. Schwaller

Further reading:

Mario Góngora. *Studies in the Colonial History of Spanish America* (Cambridge: Cambridge University Press, 1975).

Cortés, Hernando (b. 1484–d. 1547) *Spanish conquistador of Mexico's Aztec Empire and its capital city of Tenochtitlán* Born in 1484 to minor nobility in Medellín, Spain, Hernando Cortés was a restless youth during the age of CHRISTOPHER COLUMBUS's transatlantic voyages. In his early 20s, Cortés defied his parents' wish that he become a lawyer; instead, he crossed the Atlantic where he found fortune and preferment in the Caribbean, as Spanish companies explored, conquered, and settled the islands. In 1506, Cortés settled on the island of HISPANIOLA; five years later, in 1511, he served as a captain in the CONQUEST of CUBA. It was not long before Cortés discovered his ambition and gift for leadership. In 1519, Cuba's governor, DIEGO VELÁZQUEZ DE CUÉLLAR, appointed Cortés to lead an exploratory expedition to the Mexican coastline. Cortés, however, had other plans, turning the exploration into a two-year war of conquest against the Aztec Empire (see AZTECS).

After fighting minor skirmishes on the Yucatán Peninsula and acquiring his invaluable interpreter, La MALINCHE, Cortés and his men founded the city of Veracruz. Soon after, its CABILDO ordered Cortés to disregard Velázquez's orders and authorized him to engage in independent conquests. On the coast, Cortés first received emissaries from MONTEZUMA. While these emissaries brought gifts for the new arrivals, their main mission was intelligence gathering. Advancing inland, the Spaniards encountered several indigenous communities, including the territories of Cempoala and TLAXCALA, an Aztec enemy. On the verge of defeat, Cortés sued for peace and convinced the Tlaxcalans to join him in marching on the Aztec capital, TENOCHTITLÁN.

Upon arrival, Cortés was welcomed into the city by the emperor in an apparent surrender. After several months living in the imperial residence, Cortés left the city to deal with a rival company of Spaniards sent by Velázquez. While Cortés was fighting his fellow Spaniards, a fellow captain, PEDRO DE ALVARADO, incited a massacre of Mexica warriors during a festival in Tenochtitlán. Although allowed to reenter the city, Cortés found himself trapped in a hostile city. The Spanish leader hoped to use Montezuma to broker a peace accord; however, in the process, Montezuma was killed, apparently by his own subjects. Surrounded and lacking political leverage, Cortés was forced to flee to Tlaxcala in July 1520. Over the next several months, he combined localized military assaults with diplomatic initiatives to build a regional alliance that isolated the Aztecs in their island capital. This strategy led to a protracted siege and culminated in a bloody assault by combined Spanish-indigenous forces. In the wake of the Aztecs' defeat in 1521, Cortés consolidated Spanish control over the former empire and adjacent regions.

Between 1521 and 1528, Cortés was the effective ruler of New Spain, the new colony formed from the Aztec Empire. King Charles I named him governor and captain general of New Spain. Later, in 1528, Cortés was made marqués of the Valley of Oaxaca, with vast entailed estates in southern MEXICO. Seeking to repeat his earlier success, he led various unremarkable expeditions, from California to HONDURAS, between 1522 and 1538. In his final years, he accompanied the king (but did not fight) in the 1541 North African campaign. Cortés died in Castelleja de la Cuesta, Spain, on December 2, 1547.

Even before his death, Cortés had become the archetypal conquistador, and he has remained legendary ever since. His success is undeniable: He acquired wealth, royal favor, and noble titles. Contemporary CHRONICLERS and his own writings emphasize that the conquest of the Aztec Empire was due to his military genius. He used superior European technology and manipulated credulous "Indians" and a superstitious Montezuma to lead a few hundred Spaniards to defeat of an empire of millions.

More realistically, however, European technology in the form of the steel sword always gave the Spaniards an advantage, and the "Indians" across the Americas were no more credulous than Spaniards, with indigenous leaders manipulating Cortés as much as he did them. Likewise, the Spanish could not have triumphed without the aid of tens of thousands of native allies. But, perhaps the greatest ally of all was the onslaught of epidemic DISEASES from the Old World that killed far more enemies than either the Spaniards or their allies.

Cortés's true gift lay in understanding the limitations of Spanish advantages and the vulnerability of invasion companies. His strength lay in caution, and his tempered use of diplomacy was often countered by unexpected and shocking displays of violence. While Cortés arguably achieved greater success and fame than any of his contemporaries, in the end, he was but one of many armed entrepreneurs, following similar procedures as other conquistadores—seeking royal patronage, gaining indigenous allies, and capturing Amerindian rulers.

—Matthew Restall

Further reading:
Anthony Pagden, ed. *Hernando Cortés, Letters from Mexico* (New Haven, Conn.: Yale University Press, 1986).
Hugh Thomas. *Conquest: Montezuma, Cortés, and the Fall of Old Mexico* (London: Hutchinson, 1993; New York: Touchstone, 1995).

Costa Rica

Costa Rica was an important geographical region, a place where many interactions between the inhabitants of South America and North America occurred. Archaeologists have divided Costa Rica into three major cultural regions: Greater Nicoya, the Atlantic Watershed/East-Central region, and the Gran Chiriquí-Diquís region.

The Paleoindian period (10,000–7000 B.C.E.) is represented by a Clovis quarry workshop at Turrialba, and Clovis stone points have been recovered at Guardiria, Lake Arenal, and Bolívar sites (see CLOVIS CULTURE). These spear points suggest that Costa Rica's early inhabitants lived in mobile bands and hunted large mammals, such as mastodons and giant sloths. Although mastodon bones have been found in the Atlantic Watershed/East-Central region, they are not associated with Paleoindian stone tools.

The archaeological record is somewhat sparse between 8000 and 2000 B.C.E.; however, it was during this period that climatic events led to the extinction of the megafauna and changed the lives of Costa Rica's pre-Columbian inhabitants. Evidence from Turrialba, Lake Arenal, Río Antiguo, Guardiria, and Florencia indicate a shift to hunting small game and gathering plant foods. The few stone tools and cooking stones that have been found show similarities to contemporary technology from central Pacific PANAMA.

The Early Formative period (2000–1000 B.C.E.) marks the beginning of settled, or nonmobile, life in Costa Rica, evidenced by the small and highly dispersed villages at Ni Kira, La Pochota, La Montaña, and around Lake Arenal. People constructed round houses and made elaborate vessels and CERAMICS; they also used quartz and oval siliceous flakes, possibly for MANIOC graters. Burial sites consisted of rectangular pits located between the houses.

Based on the tools excavated, these peoples' diet consisted primarily of root crops and tree fruits. Evidence dating back to 2000 B.C.E. in northern Costa Rica indicates that people there cultivated MAIZE, which they ground using stone *metates*; they also consumed palm nuts and fruits.

By the Late Formative period (300 B.C.E.–500 C.E.) other Mesoamerican influences were present in Costa Rica. Archaeologists have found items such as mace heads, carved jade pendants, and anthropomorphic stone pendants called ax gods with MAYA and Olmec designs (see OLMEC). During this time, evidence from the sites of Severo Ledesma, Barrial de Heredia, Tibas, Arenal-Tempisque, Nacascolo, Las Huacas, Mojica, and La Regla indicate a significant population increase. People lived in large houses in semidispersed agricultural villages; they practiced intensive maize agricultural activities on alluvial plains. Monumental stone sculpture, greenstone pendants, ritual *metates*, GOLD pendants from COLOMBIA, and gigantic granite balls are indicative of social stratification.

In Greater Nicoya, burial offerings such as jade pendants made of raw materials from the Motagua Valley (GUATEMALA) and trichrome pottery with Mesoamerican design elements suggest the existence of long-distance TRADE, especially in luxury items. However, archaeological evidence at East-Central sites such as La Montaña, Barrial de Heredia, and La Fábrica reflect greater influence from South America than from other parts of Mesoamerica.

During the Middle Polychrome period, between 500 and 1000 C.E., regional cultural differences become more evident. Population growth continued, as did the number of nuclear settlements. Sites such as Las Mercedes, La Zoila, and Costa Rica Farm contain mounds, stairways, cobble-paved causeways, and anthropomorphic stone sculptures. Archaeologists have found stone cist tombs containing offerings such as polychrome pottery from Great Nicoya and Greater Chiriquí pottery, which suggest a vibrant regional trade. At sites such as Vidor and Nacascolo in Greater Nicoya, people intensified their exploitation of marine resources. Despite this intensification, the general subsistence ECONOMY remained similar to previous periods, and people continued to hunt, gather wild fruits and nuts, and practice AGRICULTURE. Polychrome pottery incorporates Mesoamerican decorative elements, reflecting the migration of Oto-Mangue speakers into this area.

During the Late Polychrome period, around 1000 to 1550 at Nacascolo, La Guinea, and La Ceiba sites in Greater Nicoya, people settled in circular houses along the Pacific coast. Pottery designs show similarities with Mixtec-Puebla style (see MIXTECS). South American influences were observed at the East-Central and Gran Chiriquí-Diquís regions, where monumental architecture such as artificial mounds, stone causeways, and stone balls were found. Some of these balls were recorded at funerary sites such as Palmar and Piedras Blancas. People lived in villages such as San Isidro, Guayabo de Turrialba, La Cabaña, Rivas, and Murciélago, where they constructed circular houses. Flying-panel *metates* and human statues with trophy heads and metalwork also suggest South American influences. Subsistence was based on maize, beans, and the consumption of local tree fruits, in addition to the cultivation of tubers such as manioc. The local diet also included other goods such as molluscs, deer, peccary, tapir, agouti, and fish. People used lithic tools such as knives, scrapers, and *metates* to prepare plant and animal foods.

The first Spaniards who arrived in the 16th century at Greater Nicoya encountered highly stratified societies, such as Garabito, Pococí, Chira, Corobici, Orotina, Guetar, Tomi, and Chorotega. The Chorotega, who were of Mesoamerican origin, built villages arranged around a central plaza. They cultivated maize and beans and practiced rituals such as the *volador* (flying men) dance and *patolli* (a game with corn seeds). In other regions of Costa Rica, the Spanish encountered Chibcha groups such as the Bribri, Cabecares, Borucas, Cotos, Guaymí, and Quepos. Villages were divided into elite and nonelite groups and based their subsistence economy on agriculture, hunting, and gathering.

See also COSTA RICA (Vols. II, III, IV).

—Diana Rocío Carvajal Contreras

Further reading:

John Hoopes. "The Emergence of Social Complexity in the Chibchan World of Southern Central America and Northern Colombia, A.D. 300–600." *Journal of Archaeological Research* 13, no. 1 (2004): 1–47.

M. J. Snarkis. "La Costa Rica Precolombina." In *Artes de los pueblos precolombinos de America Central*, edited by M. J. Snarkis, 67–113 (Barcelona: Institut de Cultura, Museu Barbier-Muller, 2000).

cotton Cotton played a large role in the Americas both before and after the CONQUEST. Although cotton grows only in warm climates with generous rainfall, extensive TRADE networks and the collection of the fiber as tribute enabled cotton to be used by nearly all of the Americas' indigenous societies. Cotton cloth was produced for various purposes including decorative hangings or awnings for temples and marketplaces, marriage payments, battle armor, tortilla covers, or to adorn deities. It was most commonly used, however, to make CLOTHING.

The indigenous societies and economies of Mesoamerica relied heavily on cotton production and even used units of cotton as a form of currency. Cotton tied the MAYA into a broader Mesoamerican ECONOMY, connecting the Yucatán Peninsula with Central MEXICO and HONDURAS. Maya villages in the eastern interior paid their rulers raw cotton and cotton TEXTILES, which were then exchanged and sold to the central and western parts of the peninsula and, subsequently, to other distant regions of Mesoamerica.

Because cotton could not be grown in the climate of the Valley of Mexico, the AZTECS acquired cotton through the tribute they collected from those they conquered. Cotton paid in tribute came in a variety of forms but most commonly in lengths called *quachtli* and cloaks (*mantas*). A pictorial document listing the tribute owed to the Aztecs—the *matrícula de tributos*—indicates that 241,600 cotton cloaks were to be paid annually. When these are factored among the additional cotton items and *quachtli* most tribute provinces paid every year, the role of cotton in the Aztec Empire is quite remarkable. In addition, Aztec traders (*POCHTECA*) and market vendors collected a wide variety of cotton throughout the valley, each variety having a particular value.

The Inca Empire rivaled that of the Aztecs with regards to cloth tribute payments (see INCAS). Various provinces under Inca rule were assigned to provide either cotton or their labor to weave cloth from cotton already acquired by the state. Indeed, cotton textiles were one of the highest forms of tribute to the Incas. Moreover, Andeans used cotton to create tunics decorated with squares and other abstract patterns set in specific repetitive designs to identify the ethnicity of specific indigenous groups.

The importance of cotton did not diminish with the arrival of the Spanish. In 1496, CHRISTOPHER COLUMBUS required the native population of HISPANIOLA to pay a tribute of "a Femish hawk's bell . . . full of gold . . . or an *arroba* of cotton" every three months. Although cotton textiles did not play a role in the mercantilist colonial economy focused on the export of precious metals and other exotica, it helped to fuel the local economy. Spanish settlers depended on native cotton for local consumption. The demand for cotton textiles increased throughout the colonial period, especially in the cities and mining camps and was satisfied by tribute payments (this time to the Spanish) and the *obrajes* of Spanish settlers not endowed with ENCOMIENDA grants.

See also COTTON (Vol. III).

—Mark Christensen

Further reading:
Frances F. Berdan. "Cotton in Aztec Mexico: Production, Distribution and Uses." *Mexican Studies/Estudos Mexicanos* 3, no. 2 (Summer 1987): 235–262.

Council of the Indies (1524–1834)

The Council of the Indies served as the supreme governing body of the Spanish administration of the New World colonies. As an advisory council to the Spanish monarch, it had executive, judicial, and legislative control over the Indies.

With the Spanish exploration and CONQUEST of the New World, an empire began to form, and new governing institutions and administrative bodies for the administration of this empire evolved slowly from 1492 onward. At first, the Catholic monarchs Ferdinand and Isabella entrusted the governance of CHRISTOPHER COLUMBUS's newly established Caribbean colonies to Isabella's confessor, the bishop of Burgos, Juan Rodríguez de Fonseca (see MONARCHS OF SPAIN). The bishop of Burgos controlled the governance of the expanding colonies on behalf of both of the Spanish kingdoms from 1493 until the death of King Ferdinand of Aragon in 1516, when the crown of Castile formally received sole control over the New World. Under the new Castilian regent, Cardinal Francisco Jiménez de Cisneros, the governance of the Indies was handed to the newly formed Junta de Indias, headed by two members of the Council of Castile. From 1516 to 1524, the government of Spain's New World colonies was entrusted to this small subcommittee of the larger Council of Castile.

After the discovery and conquest of New Spain (see MEXICO) and parts of the Central American mainland, the new monarch, Charles I, decided that a separate, more permanent governing body should be in charge of the administration of the expanding New World empire. Thus, on August 1, 1524, the Real y Supremo Consejo de Indias (Royal and Supreme Council of the Indies) was formed. It had executive, judicial, and legislative functions, which increased over time. The Council of the Indies was given control over all aspects of imperial and local government in the Indies, and also over the CASA DE CONTRATACIÓN, or Board of Trade.

From its outset, the Council of the Indies was composed of a president, who each week during *consultas* informed the monarch of the affairs discussed in council and requested his action on petitions and legislation. A variable number of councilors also sat on the council, most of whom were lawyers or jurists with previous government experience in the Indies. A prosecutor (*fiscal*), and several secretaries, notaries, and other lesser officials (including an official historian, or chief chronicler, of the Indies), a royal cosmographer, and a host of other attorneys and jurists, also sat on the council (see CHRONICLERS).

In terms of its duties and jurisdictions, the Council of the Indies was entrusted with the planning and proposal to the Crown of all administrative policies relating to the New World colonies, including issues such as the conquest, population, immigration, and indigenous relations. It was the Council of the Indies, in consultation with local government agencies in the New World (such as the viceroyalties and AUDIENCIA courts), that proposed to the Crown the names of candidates for positions to be filled in the government of the Indies (see VICEROY/VICE-ROYALTY). The council also closely watched the activities of the officials it sent to the New World, formally administering and controlling the judicial reviews (*juicios de residencia*), or trials of exiting officials, that were held to ensure that no corruption or abuses were prevalent in their administrations. In addition, the council reviewed all ecclesiastical appointments and suggested candidates for church offices; its members also examined and either approved or rejected all papal bulls or ecclesiastical regulation. Each day, the council read, reviewed, and reported on the correspondence and petitions that thousands of New World residents sent back to Spain.

The Council of the Indies came to control all aspects of military planning, militias, authorizations of new conquest expeditions, and other martial affairs. Similarly, in its exercise of judicial functions, the council served as a supreme court of final appeal on all judicial questions, either civil or criminal, arising in the Indies. In its judicial function, the council was later limited in civil cases to hearing only those involving disputes of more than 1,000 pesos in value so as not to overburden the councilors with less important cases.

See also COUNCIL OF THE INDIES (Vol. II); MINISTRY OF THE INDIES (Vol. II).

—John F. Chuchiak IV

Further reading:
Clarence Henry Haring. *Trade and Navigation between Spain and the Indies in the Time of the Hapsburg* (Cambridge, Mass.: Harvard University Press, 1918).

Council of Trent (1545–1563)

The Council of Trent was convened by Pope Paul III as a response to the Protestant Reformation. As an ecumenical council, it had the authority to change the doctrines and practices of the CATHOLIC CHURCH. The council lasted until 1563, with deliberations falling into to three major periods, 1545–47, 1550–52, and 1562–63. While the council issued decrees on a wide range of issues, a few in particular had a major impact on the church in the New World. In general, the council established that bishops should truly serve as pastors of their dioceses. Thus, the practice of multiple appointments was curtailed, and bishops were expected to reside in their dioceses. The council regulated financial issues, such as the endowment and support of benefices and the creation and regulation of pious works. Lists of prohibited books were authorized, and restrictions were confirmed over the translation of the Bible into common languages. The council also passed various decrees seeking to reform the clergy and outlining the bishop's authority over clergy in his diocese. The council ordered the creation of catechisms for use in each diocese. While the canons and decrees of the council had the immediate effect of law within the church, each diocese and ecclesiastical province had to hold its own council or synod to implement them. These were held in MEXICO and PERU in 1565. Because of the long delay caused by distance, the full texts of the decrees of Trent did not arrive in either viceroyalty (see VICEROY/VICEROYALTY) until long after they were issued, so the provincial councils of Mexico and Lima gave blanket approval to Trent but later were unable to make any significant changes. The next provincial councils—Mexico (1585) and Peru (1582–83)—issued detailed rules on how the decrees of Trent were to be applied in the New World.

—John F. Schwaller

Further reading:
The Canons and Decrees of the Sacred and Oecumenical Council of Trent, edited and translated by J. Waterworth (London: Dolman, 1848).

coya

Coya is a QUECHUA term for the Moon, the INCAS' foremost female deity. The term was also used to refer to the principal wife of the Sapa Inca (chief ruler of the Inca Empire), as she embodied the Moon's most important daughter. Thus, the Sapa Inca was the son of Inti (the Sun), and the *coya* descended from the Moon.

The *coya's* link to the Moon gave her great power and authority in Tawantinsuyu, the Inca realm. She presided politically and religiously over Tawantinsuyu's WOMEN, leading their worship of female deities and heading female religious organizations. As leader of the lunar cult, she presided at the shrine of the Moon (Pumap Chupan) located next to the Temple of the Sun (Coricancha). Adorned with SILVER, the interior of Pumap Chupan stored the mummies of earlier *coyas,* which were brought out into the plaza for worship and to participate in important festivals.

The *coya* also filled important political duties. As mentioned above, she ruled over women, following the lead of Mama Huaco, *coya* of the legendary first Sapa Inca, Manco Inca (not to be confused with the 16th-century Inca). Mama Huaco was a fierce, warlike woman of great power, and later *coyas* were chosen for their abilities to lead and fulfill political and religious duties. At least some *coyas* seem to have been sisters of the Sapa Inca. The *coya* ruled CUZCO when her husband was absent on military campaigns.

Inca imperialism and the subsequent Spanish CONQUEST undermined the importance of the *coya.* The Sapa Inca and other important males practiced polygyny with women taken from the provinces, signaling not only the subjugation of those peoples but also the establishment of political bonds with them. Polyandry was not, however, permitted for the *coya,* and thus she could not extend her political influence in the same manner. The Spanish conquerors imposed a patriarchal political system that eliminated the *coya's* political role and introduced a religion that erased her ritual importance.

See also WOMEN (Vols. II, III, IV).

—Kendall Brown

Further reading:
Irene Silverblatt. *Moon, Sun, and Witches: Gender Ideologies and Class in Inca and Colonial Peru* (Princeton, N.J.: Princeton University Press, 1987).

One of the finest structures in the entire Inca Empire, Cuzco's Coricancha, or so-called Temple of the Sun, was perhaps the most important religious shrine in Tawantinsuyu. Within its remarkable stone walls, the Inca worshipped all the major celestial deities. The temple also housed the most important royal mummies. Moreover, the complex Inca *zeque* system of radial lines all emanated from the Coricancha. The base of the temple still remains, on top of which the Spaniards erected the monastery of Santo Domingo. *(Courtesy of J. Michael Francis)*

crime and punishment

MESOAMERICA BEFORE 1492

Native Americans in Mesoamerica before 1492 tended to regard the world as unstable and prone to chaos. For the AZTECS, MAYA, ZAPOTECS, MIXTECS, and others, crime, like capricious supernatural forces, could threaten the fragile social order. The need to guard against chaos acted as a kind of organizing principle for Mesoamerican societies. Much as people sought to placate the gods by routinely performing religious rituals such as fasting, so secular authorities tried to limit crime by inculcating normative values and by swiftly and severely punishing transgressors. Native Americans devised police and judicial institutions, including courts, to deal with criminal acts. These institutions operated on the basis of established laws that defined acceptable behavior. Authorities were especially concerned about interpersonal crimes, which threatened the social order by disrupting FAMILY and community relations. Prominent among these crimes were assault, drunkenness, and adultery. The courts also distinguished between crimes of an economic and political nature, as well as between civil and criminal litigation. Furthermore, the legal system recognized different juris-

dictions for the religious and military spheres, as well as in the conduct of war (see RELIGION, WARFARE).

In Mesoamerica, codified laws applied to everyone, and societies dealt with criminals through formal governmental and legal channels. In the Aztec Empire, the TLATOANI (ruler) of Texcoco, Nezahualcóyotl (1418–74), reformed legal codes and devised a legalist system that standardized existing laws and upheld their strict, uniform application. Nezahualcóyotl's reforms consolidated previous precedents, creating a legal system that helped integrate the Aztec Empire. In Texcoco, as elsewhere, the administration of justice began at the CALPULLI level of each ALTEPETL, and their equivalents in Mixtec, Zapotec, and Maya regions. Local communities typically had a jail as well as a retinue of staff for policing and judicial duties. For many crimes, the law distinguished between PIPILTIN (lords) and *macehualtin* (commoners; see MACEHUAL.) In NAHUATL-speaking areas, a lower court, known as the *teccalco*, arbitrated cases involving commoners, while another, called the *tlacxitlan*, judged nobles. Dynastic rulers usually presided over routine or minor cases and consulted with councils and judges in serious or complex cases. An appeals process complemented the local courts.

If a case required further consideration, it could be tried before authorities beyond the *altepetl*. Appeals could reach the *cihuacóatl*, the emperor's second-in-command, whose deliberations were assisted by a council of judges. Imperial councils dealt with especially contentious or serious cases, including those involving matters of state.

Beyond formal laws and judicial institutions, Native Americans devised customs and social practices to maintain order. These included the performance of religious obligations, which inculcated ideas about self-discipline, morality, and proper conduct. Failure to adhere to religious strictures could inspire divine retribution. Mayas and Aztecs associated physical illnesses with punishments meted out by the gods. Beyond the religious realm, people were warned of the perils of disorder and were exhorted to follow proscriptions against criminal behavior. EDUCATION instilled in children a sense of acceptable behavior. Parents expected their children to act with humility and to be obedient and courteous. Respect for one's elders also figured prominently in social conventions. When people deviated from the norms of acceptable behavior, courts determined whether their actions constituted crimes, and when they did, judges imposed exacting punishments.

Aztec and Maya legal codes meted out severe punishments for crimes they deemed contrary to social harmony. Drunkenness was seen as an especially unacceptable form of behavior not only because it was inherently disruptive but also because it could engender further problems by impoverishing families and creating conflict. Most groups viewed adultery, among other sex crimes, as particularly heinous because it struck at the heart of family relations, thereby jeopardizing one of the foundations of society. Authorities also prosecuted other sorts of social crime. These included unruly and disrespectful behavior, particularly toward one's superiors.

Seniority, status, and office defined a person's duties and rights. Special laws governed the conduct of soldiers and priests. People were expected to behave in accordance to their place and function in the social hierarchy, and position did not guarantee exceptional or lenient treatment under the law. The courts imposed severe penalties on nobles, particularly when they served in official capacities. Nobles were held to high standards of conduct in office because they were expected to set a good example. In one instance, Nezahualpilli, the son of Nezahualcóyotl, sentenced his wife (a daughter of the ruler of Tenochtitlán) to death for adultery, along with her lovers. For commoners, sumptuary laws regulated personal appearance, restricting the types of CLOTH-ING and jewelry people could wear. Such laws even extended to the kinds of property people could own. Contraventions of sumptuary laws could prompt harsh reprisals, even capital punishment.

Punishments may have been severe both to preserve the social hierarchy and to serve as a deterrent. They also reflected the perceived gravity of offenses. The courts commonly imposed physical punishments. Corporal pun-ishment sometimes included piercing, tattooing, and shaving the head to mark people as criminals. Other common punishments called for the removal of offenders from society, either through incarceration, banishment, or death. Death penalties applied in cases of recidivism and where land had been taken. Crimes such as adultery also warranted the death penalty, which was carried out either by stoning or hanging, regardless of a person's social position. Where appropriate, punishments could involve some form of reparation, particularly with property crimes and homicide. Courts required restitution for damaged goods or stolen property. In severe cases, Aztecs and Mayas imposed compensation by enslaving thieves and requiring them to serve their victims' families. Similarly, in cases of homicide, if the courts did not sentence perpetrators to death, they enslaved them to the family of the deceased. Because notions of justice were bound up with a concern for maintaining harmonious social relations, punishments had a restorative function and aimed to reestablish order.

SOUTH AMERICA BEFORE 1492

Chronicling societal responses to criminality in pre-Columbian South America is enormously difficult. The paucity of primary source material makes it difficult to provide accurate depictions of crime and punishment. Furthermore, as opposed to Mesoamerica, which harbored the prodigious Aztec and Maya civilizations, the only civilization of similar size in South America was that of the INCAS. Overall, it can be said that most legal systems in South America were not codified, hence common law practices were prevalent as societal response to crimes was observed, adopted, and handed down from one generation to the next. Nevertheless, from the evidence that is available, it appears that harsh punishments were common, even for relatively minor infractions.

Of course, the dearth of resources makes generalizations largely speculative. For instance, the MOCHE, who flourished in PERU between 200 and 700 C.E., depicted images of crime and punishment on their ornately painted CERAMICS. However, these depictions remain subject to interpretation and scholarly debate regarding the nature of Moche laws, crimes, and the treatment of criminals. By contrast, for the Incas, the evidence is much more complete.

For the most part, the Inca state did little to intervene in the legal affairs of conquered communities. They did not create a state legal code, nor did they have a judicial system that regulated their territory. Nevertheless, in some cases, the state did intervene in judicial affairs. For example, capital offenses included crimes committed against the Sapa Inca; likewise, acts of treason and the destruction of state bridges were punishable by death. The chief method of execution was bashing the criminal's skull with a club, throwing the criminal off a cliff, or binding and leaving the same to starve. Evidence of criminal incarceration is almost nonexistent, with a lone (but oft-cited) record of an "egregious traitor" who was locked in a dungeon with venomous snakes and other dangerous animals.

Lesser crimes precipitated a variety of other punishments, ranging from public condemnation and humiliation to chopping off appendages, banishment, and torture. A separate justice system was in place for royals; many crimes, such as incest (outside of sanctioned marriage), which were punishable by death for commoners invited only mild physical punishment if committed by a noble. Any crime perpetrated by a commoner against a noble promised a harsher punishment, usually death. Instead of torture or death, royals were expected to be deterred from crime by a public rebuke that served to lower their prestige in the community, ostracize them from other nobles, and ruin their relations with the emperor.

Some trials were convened by state officials; however, most infractions were dealt with by local officials or community elders. Ad hoc hearings of more serious charges were presided over by higher-level officials. In the case of treason or serious crimes committed by nobles, the emperor decided personally, often with guidance from a privy council. Verdicts were swift; judgment was administered in less than five days after an allegation was made and the criminal detained. In cases of notorious criminals, punishments extended not only to the criminal and that person's family; some sources indicate that entire villages were razed.

What little evidence exists regarding other Andean societies suggests that Inca responses to crime were not unique. For example, anthropological studies indicate that the Chimú civilization responded similarly, if not even more harshly, to crime. Murder, desecration of holy sites, and disrespect toward the deities was met with execution, with perpetrators thrown off a cliff or buried alive. Theft was another capital offense, predicated on the logic that all property was divinely bestowed; hence robbery was a religious sacrilege. Not only were the criminals quickly dispatched; anyone considered to have aided them was also summarily executed. Punishment, while sanctioned by state officials, was supported by the community at large to the extent that most of its members considered themselves to have been collective victims of the crime perpetrated.

Prior to 1492, justice in South America was uniformly decisive. Typically, criminals were physically punished, with death reserved for the most serious offenses. Societal hierarchies, both in terms of class and gender, were also reflected in the penal systems. Members of the nobility were often subject to milder punishments than were commoners. Still, the notion of redemptive justice was nonexistent, and the stunning effect of most punishments was directed toward deterring crime rather than exacting revenge. For the most part, responses to crime were considered to be a local matter, with the state intervening only when crimes affected imperial designs. In all, response to crime was quick, grave, and usually meted out by members of the community in which the crime occurred.

See also CRIME AND PUNISHMENT (Vols. II, III, IV).

—Richard Conway
Sean H. Goforth

Further reading:
Frances F. Berdan. *The Aztecs of Central Mexico: An Imperial Society* (New York: Holt, Rinehart & Winston, 1982).
Terence D'Altroy. *The Incas* (Malden, Mass.: Blackwell Publishing, 2002).
Diego de Landa. *The Maya: Diego de Landa's Account of the Affairs of Yucatán*, edited and translated by Anthony R. Pagden (Chicago: J. Philip O'Hara, 1975).
Jerome A. Offner. *Law and Politics in Aztec Texcoco* (New York: Cambridge University Press, 1983).
Irene Silverblatt. *Moon, Sun, and Witches: Gender Ideologies and Class in Inca and Colonial Peru* (Princeton, N.J.: Princeton University Press, 1987).

Cuauhtémoc (b. ca. 1497–d. 1525) *last supreme ruler of the Aztec Empire* Cuauhtémoc ("Descending Eagle," in NAHUATL) was the 11th and last *huetlatoani* (supreme ruler) of the Aztec Empire, ruling from 1520 to 1525 (see AZTECS). Despite his short and hectic rule, the life of Cuauhtémoc is one of the best recorded from this dynasty by both Aztec and Spanish CHRONICLERS. Cuauhtémoc was born ca. 1497 to the eighth Aztec emperor Ahuitzotl and Tiyacapantzin, a princess from Tlatelolco. He attended the main priestly school (*calmecac*) in TENOCHTITLÁN, the Aztec capital, and fought in several military campaigns against Quetzaltepec and Iztactlocan (see EDUCATION). In 1515 he was appointed as the "eagle ruler" of Tlatelolco.

In November 1519, Spanish conquistadores, led by HERNANDO CORTÉS, arrived at Tenochtitlán, only to be fiercely chased out in 1520 during the Noche Triste ("night of sorrows"). That same year, Cuitláhuac, who had replaced MONTEZUMA as the emperor, died of smallpox introduced by the Europeans (see DISEASE). Their cousin Cuauhtémoc was promptly chosen as the successor to the throne. He took Xuchimatzatzin, a daughter of Montezuma, as his wife and apparently killed one or more of Montezuma's sons, whom he considered potential rivals to the throne.

Unlike his cousin Montezuma, Cuauhtémoc was strongly opposed to the Spaniards' presence in his land. When the Spaniards and their allies returned in the summer of 1521 to lay siege to Tenochtitlán, Cuauhtémoc sought his own war allies among the Acolhuas and Tarascans, although with little success. Together with his smaller Aztec army, Cuauhtémoc confronted the Spanish attack but later attempted to flee the city and was captured. According to several sources, it was Cuauhtémoc himself who surrendered to Cortés and then begged him to take his life.

Cortés did not oblige; instead, Cuauhtémoc was taken prisoner in Coyoacán, where he was tortured to reveal the location of a hoard of gold that allegedly had been hidden from the conquistadores. Still, he was able to keep his *huetlatoani* title while in captivity. In October 1524, Cortés left for HONDURAS to subdue a rebellion;

fearing that Cuauhtémoc might revolt in his absence, he took Cuauhtémoc and other indigenous rulers of the TRIPLE ALLIANCE with him. On the way, Cuauhtémoc was accused of plotting a conspiracy against Cortés and was hanged in February 1525. With this act, the long line of Aztec sovereignty in MEXICO came to an end.

—Danny Zborover

Further reading:
Hugh Thomas. *Conquest: Montezuma, Cortés, and the Fall of Old Mexico* (New York: Simon & Schuster, 1995).

Cuba   Cuba, the largest island located in the Caribbean Sea, is surrounded by the Atlantic Ocean, the Gulf of MEXICO, the Straits of FLORIDA, and the Yucatán Channel. The island is defined by various terrains, ranging from rugged hills in the southeast, rigid mountains of the Sierra Maestra, and flat plains throughout.

The first peoples to inhabit the island were the Ciboney Indians, who arrived on the island around 1000 B.C.E.; and by 1000 C.E., the Ciboney had settled all across the island. However, they were soon joined by other waves of migrants. By 1050 C.E., Arawaks and their descendants, the TAINO, had also settled on Cuba. It was the Taino who first encountered the Spaniards upon their arrival in 1492.

The majority of what is known of Taino culture is derived from the chronicles of Spanish colonizers and the analysis of artifacts found in the region. The social structure of the Taino was matriarchal, with FAMILY names, material possessions, and social power passed down through the mother (as opposed to the father in many other societies). Organizationally, the Taino were divided into numerous chiefdoms throughout the Greater Antilles (Cuba, Jamaica, PUERTO RICO, and HISPANIOLA) with a CACIQUE, or chief, ruling over each. Recent research on the political structure of Taino society reveals highly organized chiefdoms. There is also some speculation that villages were socially divided between a ruling class, the *nitaínos*, and a subservient class, referred to as *naborías*. The *naborías* did the majority of the agricultural work and hunting, while the *nitaínos* supervised work, made ART and relics, and oversaw WARFARE.

Proof of the advanced state of the Taino ECONOMY stems from the technology used in AGRICULTURE, such as irrigation systems, and the extensive TRADE networks that extended across the islands of the Greater Antilles. Artifacts found in this region point to a deeply spiritual society, with a polytheistic RELIGION. Taino religious beliefs played important roles in society and daily life. Another central aspect of Taino life and culture was a ball game similar to soccer, found in many pre-Columbian societies in the region. The Taino version of the game was played with a hard ball on a paved court.

Taino culture flourished on the island until October 28, 1492, when CHRISTOPHER COLUMBUS landed in Cuba. Mistakenly believing it to be an Indian peninsula, Columbus claimed the land for Spain and called it "Juana." It was not until 1508 that Sebastián de Ocampo circumvented Cuba, proving that it was an island and not connected to the mainland. Columbus later wrote that upon arrival he encountered the Taino who were "very friendly" and explained that they "would be good servants and I am of opinion that they would very readily become Christians, as they appear to have no religion."

Though the Spanish overtook the indigenous population with relative ease, the Taino did put up a resistance. Shortly after Columbus landed in Cuba, Hatuey, a Taino cacique from Hispaniola, arrived to warn the local population of the Spaniards' intentions. Hatuey led the first indigenous revolt against colonial rule in Cuba, which lasted until 1512, when Hatuey was captured and burned at the stake. By that time, a large portion of the indigenous population in Cuba had been devastated through DISEASE and abuse; as the indigenous population declined, Spanish settlers sought new sources of LABOR. In 1513, the first recorded slaves were brought Cuba, with a larger group arriving in 1520 to work the newly established SUGAR plantations (see SLAVERY).

Columbus returned to Spain and in his place DIEGO VELÁZQUEZ DE CUÉLLAR took charge of the conquest of Cuba and established the settlements of Baracoa (1512), Santiago de Cuba (1514), and La Habana (1515). As governor, from 1511 until his death in 1524, Velázquez ruled with few restraints, instituting an *ENCOMIENDA* system, which fueled the exploitation of Cuba's indigenous population.

Havana quickly became the focal point of the island, and in 1537, the city became the seat of Cuba's colonial government. As a stopping point for merchant ships traveling to and from Spain, the city attracted both commerce and pirates (see PIRATES AND PIRACY). While the colonial city grew, so, too, did tensions between the indigenous, the slaves, and the colonizers. In 1533, the first major slave uprising occurred on the island, and with the assistance of disgruntled slaves, pirates succeeded in attacking and burning Havana.

Though the city was quickly rebuilt, deep social tensions continued. Another Taino cacique named Guamá led his wife and 50 other men in a guerrilla-style revolt against the Spanish; this uprising lasted until Guamá's betrayal and murder in the mid-1530s. By 1542, when the Spanish Crown promulgated the NEW LAWS OF 1542, which, among other things, sought to ban the *encomienda* system, the damage to the indigenous population proved devastating. By 1557, the Taino population in Cuba had dropped from 300,000 in 1492 to less than 500. The Spanish conquistadores had been able to overtake Cuba's indigenous population for two reasons: First, the Spanish weapons of war were more advanced than those of the native people, and second, the Taino concept of warfare varied greatly from that of the Spanish. Taino battles were won by capturing the enemy's WOMEN; heroes in warfare were those who captured material possessions and survived unscathed. The far more destructive strategy of capturing and killing indigenous leaders gave the Spanish an important military advantage.

By 1560, Havana had emerged as a leading center of commerce for the Caribbean and Central America, with a bright economic future in TOBACCO and sugar production. Tobacco, which Columbus encountered on his first visit to Cuba, was gaining popularity in Europe for its medicinal qualities (see MEDICINE). European demand for sugar was also on the rise. Columbus had brought sugarcane to the island during his second voyage in 1493, and with the steady arrival of 2,000 slaves a year from 1522 forward, Cuba's sugar industry grew quickly.

See also CUBA (Vols. II, III, IV); HAVANA (Vols. II, III, IV).

—Jennifer Schuett

Further reading:

Ramon Dacal Moure and Manuel Rivero De La Calle. *Art and Archaeology of Pre-Columbian Cuba* (Pittsburgh, Pa.: University of Pittsburgh Press, 1996).

William F. Keegan. *Taino Indian Myth and Practice: The Arrival of the Stranger King* (Gainesville: University Press of Florida, 2007).

Cuzco (Cusco)   In the middle of the 15th century, the Inca ruler PACHACUTI INCA YUPANQUI redesigned the city of Cuzco and had it rebuilt over preexisting settlements as the capital of the Inca Empire (see INCAS). A century later, the Spanish chronicler PEDRO CIEZA DE LEÓN, who was among the first Spaniards to enter the Inca capital, was stunned by the richness and wealth of one of its principal buildings, the Temple of the Sun (Coricancha). He described a garden in which the "earth" was lumps of fine GOLD, planted with golden stalks of corn. They were so well planted, he said, that no matter how hard the wind blew, it could not uproot them. Cieza de León saw more than 20 golden sheep, with golden lambs, and the shepherds who guarded them, their slings and staffs, were also all made of gold. Aside from this, he reported many tubs of gold, SILVER, and EMERALDS, as well as golden goblets, pots, and other kinds of vessels. He described rich carvings and paintings on some of the temple walls and concluded that it was one of the richest temples in the entire world.

The Coricancha and, by implication, Cuzco itself came to embody Spanish fantasies about the treasures to be found in the New World, and they quickly took possession of many precious objects. The temple was stripped bare and integrated into the church and monastery of Santo Domingo, whose monks continue to administer this Inca monument.

Coricancha was a large complex composed of courtyards framed by buildings and enclosed by a perimeter wall. Most of the buildings were constructed of finely cut and precisely fitted ashlars, in what is known as the Cuzco masonry style; they functioned as temples dedicated to forces of nature, such as thunder, lightning, the Moon, and the Sun (see RELIGION). The latter was the most prestigious temple, and its walls were covered with gold plating. Some Spanish writers mention a large gold disk personifying the face of the Sun, which is said to have stood on the curved wall that remains today. The Temple of the Moon was clad in silver plating.

Other focal points of Cuzco were the main plaza and the hilltop structures of Sacsayhuamán. The main plaza was situated in the city center and was divided into a larger section named Aukaypata and a smaller one known as Kusipata. Aukaypata was covered with a thick layer of sand from the coast and filled with many gold and silver vases, as well as human and animal figurines. These were all given as offerings to the god Viracocha. Somewhere near the middle of this plaza stood an important, politically and ritually charged stone, designated as an *usnu*. The *usnu* was connected to a basin and drainage canals for liquid offerings. It served further as an observation point of the Sun from which, most likely, the ruler followed sunrises and sunsets along the horizon line of Cuzco, which was marked by a series of large pillars.

Aukaypata was bordered by palaces attributed to specific Inca rulers. For example, the Casana compound at the northwest corner was the palace of the Inca ruler HUAYNA CÁPAC, and the Hatuncancha compound at the southeastern corner of the plaza may have contained the palace of Pachacuti. Aukaypata was also bordered by *kallanka* buildings, which were large halls with numerous doorways used as temporary accommodations for traveling troops or in which ceremonies could be staged in inclement weather.

Sacsayhuamán is the impressive building complex that overlooks the city from a nearby hill to the north. Its construction was most likely initiated by Pachacuti. It consists of the well-known three staggered rows of zigzag walls composed of huge, perfectly fitted stone blocks. The site also boasts many other buildings; a long, flat, open performance space; numerous sculpted rocks; and a water system. Sacsayhuamán served multiple purposes: It housed a sun temple, a number of storerooms, and perhaps a palace. Later, the Spanish used it as a military fortress.

Sacsayhuamán served as the center point of the *hanan*, or upper section of Cuzco. Overlaid on the *hanan-hurin* division was the partition into four quarters, or *suyus*, defined by four principal roads that departed from the main plaza and continued to the frontiers of the empire. Inca rulers referred to their empire as Tawantinsuyu, or "Land of the Four Quarters," whose point of origin lay at the convergence of the four roads in the heart of Cuzco. Chinchaysuyu was the north-

According to one Spanish chronicler, the Inca ruler Pachacuti Inca Yupanqui brought in 20,000 laborers on a rotating basis to construct this monumental architectural complex, located in the hills above the Inca capital of Cuzco. Sacsayhuáman served as a ceremonial, religious, and military complex. *(Courtesy of J. Michael Francis)*

western quadrant; Antisuyu, the northeastern one; and Collasuyu and Cuntisuyu were situated in the southeast and southwest, respectively.

The third important spatial division was the ZEQUE SYSTEM. The *zeques* were 42 imagined lines, all of which radiated out from the Coricancha in the center of Cuzco. These lines were marked by approximately 328 shrines, which could be buildings or natural features. The lines were subdivided into groups belonging to each *suyu;* each line was further assigned to one Cuzco lineage, whose task it was to service and maintain all shrines on its *zeque.* Researchers have argued that the *zeque* system extended conceptually throughout the Inca Empire and integrated metaphorically what the Incas constructed as sacred political landscape.

See also Cuzco (Vol. II).

—Jessica Christie

Further reading:

Brian Bauer. *Ancient Cuzco: Heartland of the Inca* (Austin: University of Texas Press, 2004).

———. *The Sacred Landscape of the Inca: The Cusco Ceque System* (Austin: University of Texas Press, 1988).

D

Dávila, Pedrarias   See ARIAS DE ÁVILA, PEDRO.

defensor de los indios (protector y defensor de los indios)   In general, the defense of the indigenous people of the New World was entrusted to all royal officials or functionaries until 1516, when the position of *defensor y protector de los indios* (defender and protector of the Indians) was created. Initially, it was only periodically exercised, by clergymen and even civilians; it did not become an established office, with a salary and specific duties and jurisdictions, until the creation of the general Indian court system (Juzgado General de Indios) in 1591.

The origins of the office of "protector and defender of the Indians" can be found in early Spanish civil and ecclesiastical laws, which entrusted local bishops in Spain with the protection of those considered minors or weaker members of society (widows, orphans, the sick, and the infirm) under the law. During the early administration of the Spanish colonies of the Indies, it became apparent that the indigenous peoples of the New World needed a similar protector to help mitigate the many abuses that colonists perpetrated against them. Although no official bishoprics were in place at the time, in 1516, the royal regent, Cardinal Francisco Jiménez de Cisneros, horrified at reports of abuses from the New World, saw the need to appoint a *protector y defensor de los indios* there. He selected BARTOLOMÉ DE LAS CASAS, then a local parish priest in CUBA, to serve as the first such protector. He sent a similar commission to the island of HISPANIOLA the same year, naming two Spanish Jeronymite friars as protectors there.

From 1516, the MONARCHS OF SPAIN began to designate and appoint at various times and in different places certain people, including bishops, friars, and civilians, as official defenders and protectors of the Amerindians. Since the position was only sporadically commissioned, defining the exact duties and powers of those who fulfilled it is difficult. In many instances, the officials were given jurisdictions that overlapped with those of local VICEROYS or AUDIENCIA judges (*oidores*), who also had a duty to protect the NATIVE AMERICANS. Many conflicts related to jurisdiction arose, as did complaints against the actions of the early protectors, and several wrote to the Crown requesting more specific information about their powers and responsibilities. After 1530, the Crown attempted to define more formally the duties and expectations of this official, yet between 1530 and the 1590s, commissions to the position were only sporadically awarded.

The formal, institutionalized, and salaried post of *defensor de los indios* was not created until the end of the 16th century, in regions with large indigenous populations, such as MEXICO and PERU. Individuals who held the position served as head of one of the newly created general Indian courts. These courts served as the courts of first instance for cases involving indigenous people, and the *defensor de los indios* had as his chief responsibility the protection of their rights and property. Eventually, a special annual half-*real* tax leveled on all indigenous tributaries raised the finances to fund the courts, which offered the New World's native people free or low-cost legal aid.

Regardless of their ultimate powers and duties, the early *defensores de los indios* became important officials, serving as an official voice and helping to reduce the abuses and violations of indigenous peoples by colonists and even royal officials.

115

See also Juzgado General de Indios (Vol. II); *letrado* (Vol. II).

—John F. Chuchiak IV

Further reading:
Woodrow Borah. *Justice by Insurance: The General Indian Court of Colonial Mexico and the Legal Aids of the Half-Real* (Berkeley: University of California Press, 1983).

de Soto, Hernando (b. ca. 1500–d. 1542) *conquistador in Central America and Peru, governor of Cuba, and leader of extensive expedition to Florida*   A native of Extremadura, Spain, Hernando de Soto first reached the New World as an adolescent in 1514. He arrived in Castillo del Oro (the isthmus of Panama) as a member of a large expedition led by Pedro Arias de Ávila, better known as Pedrarias. In Panama, de Soto participated in a number of small expeditions, one led by the famous conquistador Francisco Pizarro. Later, in 1532, de Soto accompanied Pizarro on an expedition to Peru that led to the conquest of the Inca Empire (see Incas) and made Pizarro, de Soto, and other participants some of the richest men in the New World. After the conquest of Peru, de Soto returned to Spain and used his newly acquired wealth and prestige to marry Isabel Bobadilla, the daughter of Pedrarias, thus forming an alliance with an important Castilian family. While in Spain, de Soto also petitioned the Spanish monarchy for the governorship of either Ecuador or Guatemala; however, he received neither. Instead, the Crown granted him the governorship of Cuba. De Soto was also granted the right to explore and conquer Florida and other regions of North America.

The expedition disembarked in present-day Charlotte Harbor, Florida, on May 30, 1539. Searching for large waterways, rich Indian settlements, and gold, de Soto and his men traversed parts of present-day Florida, Georgia, South Carolina, North Carolina, Tennessee, Alabama, Mississippi, Arkansas, Louisiana, and Texas. Several of de Soto's companions kept detailed accounts of their experiences, including their encounters with various Native American groups (see Native Americans). These writings provide some of the earliest demographic and ethnographic recordings of indigenous peoples in North America. The difficult and dangerous expedition significantly taxed the health of de Soto and his companions. Of the estimated 600 men who set out, only 311 survived. De Soto himself fell ill near the Mississippi River and died in June 1542. After his death, the remaining men abandoned the expedition, retreating overland to Mexico.

—Justin Blanton
Kathleen M. Kole

Further reading:
Lawrence A. Clayton, Vernon James Knight Jr., and Edward C. Moore, eds. *The De Soto Chronicles: The Expedition of Hernando de Soto to North America in 1539–1543*, 2 vols. (Tuscaloosa: University of Alabama Press, 1993).

diabolism in the New World   Although all classes of early modern Christian society believed in the devil, the perception of his power and influence underwent significant transformations in the early modern period. As the Decalogue, or Ten Commandments, came to influence a moral system that defined idolatry and witchcraft, even devil worship, as offenses against God, demonology rose to new heights in Christian theology. Both this focus on the devil and the discovery of "heathen" cultures inspired many ecclesiastics to reexamine the role and power of the devil within Christianity, the results of which laid the groundwork for a variety of opinions concerning diabolism in the New World.

In a way, the Spanish brought the devil to the New World. Prior to the arrival of Europeans, the indigenous peoples of the Americas had never heard of such a being, nor had they a comparable figure in their religions to this enemy of all Christendom. Indeed, the role of the devil in the New World before and after Spanish contact was an issue that evolved over time and inspired much debate among ecclesiastics. Upon their arrival, many friars came with hopes of a millennial age during which Amerindians would embrace Christianity and the devil would be defeated. At best, most friars viewed native people who had participated in idolatry, sacrifice, and other pagan rituals as naive and vulnerable to the deceitful devil or, at the worst, as malicious sorcerers who used demonic power against others, but not as devil worshippers. Bartolomé de Las Casas saw Native American paganism as compliant with natural law and their desire for God, and not diabolical in nature.

As idolatry and other practices persisted into the mid-16th century, however, ecclesiastics began to see the devil's hand interfering with their goals. Native people who continued to practice precontact rituals and believe in their own deities in the presence of Christianity were no longer seen as simply "misguided" but as devil worshippers. With millennial aspirations gone, the devil became a stronger foe. Indeed, ecclesiastics perceived the devil as actively attempting to thwart Christianity in the New World by taking advantage of the native neophytes and tempting them in myriad ways to maintain or return to their precontact practices, especially idolatry.

In response, in 1553, Fray Andrés de Olmos wrote a treatise in Nahuatl that defined idolatry not as mere malfeasance but as diabolism. José de Acosta, while defending many of the virtues of indigenous culture, simultaneously equated those indigenous practices that resembled Christian sacraments with idolatry, arguing that it was nothing more than the devil's envy of and attempt to imitate God's true church. Finally, in 1562, Fray Diego de Landa used idolatry's perceived link to devil worship to justify his violent campaign against the MAYA in Maní.

Moreover, in their efforts to instruct Native Americans on the diabolical roots of their continued idolatry and rituals, many 16th-century friars attempted to align the devil with indigenous deities thought to exhibit similar characteristics. In various publications, the Franciscan BERNARDINO DE SAHAGÚN identified the devil with Tezcatlipoca. In Nahua (Aztec) mythology, Tezcatlipoca, among other things, was a cunning deity who, through deceit and trickery, succeeded in overthrowing the more peaceful Quetzalcóatl. Seeing opportunity in aligning the two deceiving figures of the devil and Tezcatlipoca, Sahagún implanted the devil in precontact traditions. Furthermore, the illustrations in his *Historia general de las cosas de Nueva España* (*General History of the Things of New Spain*) portrayed two other major Nahua deities as the devil. With Tlaloc as a bearded goat and Huitzilopochtli as a demon, Sahagún made his view clear that these deities were not merely false idols but representations of the devil himself.

In Maya territory, Yucatec friars and their scribes followed similar patterns of aligning the devil with indigenous deities. Commonly, the deity Hun Ahau (One Lord) was used to represent the devil as the source of false wisdom. Maya myths of the underworld, creation, and death made Hun Ahau the most suitable choice. Associated with the day 1 Ahau, the Maya identified Hun Ahau with putrescence and the underworld; indeed, his POPOL VUH alias, Hunahpu, literally means "one lord of putrescence." Hun Ahau was one of the Hero Twins who descended into the underworld to play a ball game and undergo a variety of deadly ordeals against the lords of the underworld, or XIBALBÁ. Through trickery, cunning, and deceit, Hun Ahau overcame the challenges to earn an elevated position among the underworld deities. Indeed, Landa stated that Hun Ahau was the "prince of all the devils whom all obeyed," and the deity is listed in colonial Maya dictionaries as "Lucifer." Moreover, the *Ritual of the Bacabs* places Hun Ahau at the entrance to the underworld.

The friars not only tried to convince indigenous groups that those they esteemed as gods were actually devils, but they also faced the challenge of conveying who the devil was when not appearing as precontact deities. In addition, because the native population vastly outnumbered the friars, the devil needed to be portrayed in indigenous languages. In other words, ecclesiastics needed to create a place for a colonial devil by using preexisting native languages that had no real equivalent. For the Nahuas, ecclesiastics used *tlacatecolotl*, or "human owl," as the most common synonym for both the devil and his minions. In Nahua culture (see AZTECS), *tlacatecolotl* was a shape-changing shaman who took the form of an owl during his or her trances and who, while in this form, inflicted sickness and death on people at night. Ecclesiastics in the Mixtec region used a similar owl-per-

son, *tiñumi ñaha*, to represent the devil (see MIXTECS). For the Maya, ecclesiastical authors used the skeletal death god Kisin, or "flatulent one," as the synonym for the colonial devil. Kisin presided over the afterlife of the deceased and is often associated with the decay, filth, and the stench of decomposition.

Overall, the devil in the 16th-century New World took on many precontact and colonial forms. Throughout the colonial period, the CATHOLIC CHURCH continued to reevaluate the devil's role, power, and position in the New World. Indeed, diabolism seemed to wax and wane according to the native peoples' adherence to Christianity.

See also CATHOLIC CHURCH (Vols. II, III, IV).

—Mark Christensen

Further reading:
Fernando Cervantes. *The Devil in the New World: The Impact of Diabolism in New Spain* (New Haven, Conn., and London: Yale University Press, 1994).

Díaz del Castillo, Bernal (b. ca. 1495–d. 1584)
Spanish conquistador in Mexico and chronicler of the conquest
Bernal Díaz del Castillo was an eyewitness to one of the most defining moments in history, the Spanish CONQUEST of MEXICO, after which he wrote his detailed chronicle *Historia verdadera de la conquista de la Nueva España* (*The True History of the Conquest of New Spain*) (see CHRONICLERS). Díaz del Castillo was born in the Spanish town of Medina del Campo in ca. 1495 and arrived to the New World as a young man in 1514. Before participating in HERNANDO CORTÉS's fateful voyage in 1519, Díaz del Castillo took part in other expeditions as a foot soldier in Cuba and Yucatán. While his *Historia* covers the general period from 1517 to 1568, it focuses primarily on events from 1519 to 1521 and the downfall of TENOCHTITLÁN and the Aztec Empire (see AZTECS).

Although Díaz del Castillo seemed to have had sincere admiration for Aztec ingenuity and social complexity, he repeatedly highlights the cruelty of their rituals, such as HUMAN SACRIFICE; he also writes of Aztec hatred of indigenous groups opposed to the TRIPLE ALLIANCE. As a soldier, Díaz del Castillo paid particular attention to the military aspects of the conquest and claimed to have fought in about 119 battles. At the same time, he was a keen observer of the politics of Mexico, HISPANIOLA, and Spain and provided important insights into indigenous culture, RELIGION, and internal factionalism, not just those of the Aztecs, but also less-known groups such as the Tlaxcalans and Cholulans (see TLAXCALA).

Between 1524 and 1526, Díaz del Castillo accompanied Cortés to HONDURAS, where he witnessed the execution of CUAUHTÉMOC. He was granted ENCOMIENDAS in Tabasco and Chiapas as a reward for his services but lost them in 1530; finally, in 1540, he settled in GUATEMALA. During those years, Díaz del Castillo returned twice to Spain to defend his *encomendero* position, as well as Spanish actions in the conquest, which were challenged by Fray Bᴀʀᴛᴏʟᴏᴍᴇ́ ᴅᴇ Lᴀs Cᴀsᴀs. He began writing his retrospective *Historia* in 1551 and used Cortés's own letters to the Spanish king and Francisco López de Gómara's biographic chronicle, often taking a strong position against the latter. Many of the inaccuracies in Díaz del Castillo's chronicle are probably due to the fact he was writing three decades after the events he described. Furthermore, he was attempting to justify the Spaniards' actions during the conquest, depicting the conquistadores as the Christian liberators of New Spain both from the devil's influence and the brutal Aztecs. He emphasized his own poverty and the small return the conquistadores had received and thus hoped that his chronicle would guarantee prosperity for his heirs. Although a copy he sent to Spain in 1575 was published posthumously in 1632, he kept working on another version until his death in Guatemala in 1584. This manuscript was published as late as 1904 and is considered today one of the most detailed chronicles of the conquest of Mexico.

—Danny Zborover

Further reading:
Bernal Díaz del Castillo. *The Conquest of New Spain*, translated and edited by J. M. Cohen (New York: Penguin Books, 1963).

disease

THE AMERICAS BEFORE 1492

The pre-Hispanic Americas are sometimes described as a tropical, disease-free Eden. The 18th-century Mᴀʏᴀ of Yucatán remembered the pre-Hispanic world in idealized terms: "There was then no sickness," they wrote. "[T]hey had then no aching bones; they had then no high fever; they had then no smallpox; they had then no burning chest; they had then no abdominal pains; they had then no consumption; they had then no headache. At that time the course of humanity was orderly. The foreigners made it otherwise when they arrived here. They brought shameful things when they came." Disease and sickness were, of course, present long before the arrival of Europeans, though it is certainly true that they were limited in comparison with the massive series of epidemics that occurred during the 16th century.

Two main factors impeded the development and evolution of infectious diseases in the New World. First, interaction between humans and animals was relatively infrequent, which hindered the interspecies transfer of pathogens. Epidemiological scholarship has shown that many of the most lethal and contagious diseases, such as bubonic plague, smallpox, and the common cold, originated among animals. The domestication of cattle, swine, and fowl in the Old World brought humans in close, regular contact with ancestral forms of these diseases (see Cᴏʟᴜᴍʙɪᴀɴ

Exᴄʜᴀɴɢᴇ). Centuries of contact allowed mutations to cross between species and to humans. Given that relatively few animals were domesticated in the New World, the species barrier remained largely intact there, with relatively few diseases jumping from animals to humans.

Second, geographic variation limited the diffusion and migration of indigenous diseases, since pathogens, like all living organisms, evolve under specific climatic conditions. Broadly organized on the north-south axis of the Americas, where the altitude and climate vary widely, pre-Hispanic societies were often spread over different zones. The Aztec Empire, for example, included both the tropical lowlands of Central America and the high-altitude deserts of the U.S. Southwest (see Aᴢᴛᴇᴄs). To spread throughout the empire, the pathogens responsible for any disease would have had to withstand the heat of deserts, the cold of mountains, and the humidity of jungles. Furthermore, some pathogens depend on biological hosts that exist only in specific environs. For example, malaria can only be transferred to humans from mosquitoes, which live only in tropical conditions.

Our understanding of disease in the Americas before the arrival of Europeans is informed mainly by archaeological, iconographic, and epigraphic data. This reveals that American populations suffered from a host of ailments that can be broadly divided into three groups: congenital diseases, localized infections, and acute diseases. Burial sites in Pᴇʀᴜ, for example, detail the presence of tuberculosis in the Americas. Carved reliefs from Mᴇxɪᴄᴏ depict people with degenerative bone disorders.

A host of congenital diseases—broadly defined as degenerative ailments stemming from inherited traits—afflicted indigenous populations. Evidence of such diseases is easily identified in Classic-period (250–900 ᴄ.ᴇ.) Mesoamerican sculpture. Depictions of royalty from the city of Palenque during the seventh century show cases of acromegaly (enlarged facial bones) and polydactyly (extra digits) among several ruling families. These conditions did not hinder normal activity, nor did they pass between nonfictive relations. Palenque's lord Pakal, who led a massive period of expansion and reigned for more than 40 years, had an enlarged forehead and nasal bones.

Localized infections often stemmed from environmental conditions and often resulted in developmental disorders. Malnutrition or an imbalanced diet was the cause in many cases. Respiratory and gastrointestinal infections appear frequently in the archaeological record. For instance, Peruvian mummies from the 10th century show clear evidence of fatal cases of tuberculosis. While often deadly, such infections tended to affect individuals and generally were not contagious. Acute pathogens, on the other hand, could infect large populations, and variations of typhus, malaria, and syphilis were all found among pre-Hispanic populations. While many New World societies were concentrated in densely populated areas, these diseases do not appear to have spread beyond specific regions because of their geographic limitations. And while particularly the origins of typhus, malaria, and syphilis have been the subject of debate among scholars, most agree that variations of these diseases may have developed in both the Old and New Worlds. Syphilis, for example, seems to have evolved as a disease spread by topical contact in the New World, while in the Old World it was spread through sexual interaction.

The Nahuas of Central Mexico believed that illness was caused by a lack of equilibrium in the individual or society. Sickness was thought to be caused by many factors, including religious impropriety, sexual transgressions, extreme emotions, and physical stress (see RELIGION). The heart and soul, called *teyolia* in NAHUATL, were believed to be intertwined and were the keys to controlling disease and curing it. Sexual conduct with a person outside of one's social class could thrust one into a phlegm-ridden illness. Transgressions of this sort threatened the broader social order, and not surprising, recovery involved restoring harmony through sacrifice and penance. Another important concept in the Nahua ideology of disease involved disembodied life forces called *tonalli*, which were represented as spirit or animal companions that people had to appease. The spiritual essence of the *tonalli* was believed to reside in supernatural and natural spaces; disturbance of these spaces resulted in illnesses that correlated to specific sites on the human body. Finally, human life was thought to emanate from luminous gases called *ihiyotl*, which were powerful enough to both cause illness and heal sickness. Individuals who maintained social and personal balance were thought to give off beneficial emanations, while the ill gave off mal airs. Curing the infirm itself often involved pungent remedies.

EARLY COLONIAL LATIN AMERICA

The arrival of Europeans in the Americas initiated the most devastating series of endemic outbreaks of disease and demographic decline in human history. Diseases that evolved alongside humans in the Old World ravaged susceptible populations in the New World, transforming the social, political, and economic landscape. With basic social and political institutions weakened, the way was open for CONQUEST and exploitation. The Spanish apologist and chronicler BARTOLOMÉ DE LAS CASAS wrote that with the conquest came "illness, death and misery" (see CHRONICLERS).

In the century that followed the arrival of Europeans, native peoples fell victim to a host of highly communicable Old World diseases, including bubonic plague, hemorrhagic fever, influenza, measles, smallpox, and typhus. The outbreak and spread of disease among susceptible groups—referred to as "virgin-soil epidemics"—reduced indigenous populations by anywhere from 50 to 90 percent over the course of the 16th century. While before the arrival of Europeans the Amerindian population had numbered between 60 and 100 million, by the close of the 16th century, fewer than 10 million indigenous inhabitants remained.

A new disease affected everyone in indigenous society; old and young alike fell ill. Genetic weakness or biological inferiority had nothing to do with this, as concluded by some 19th-century imperials. The simple truth was that the native population lacked exposure to Eurasian diseases and so was not resistant to them. Moreover, many were already weakened by malnutrition, poverty, and overwork. Europeans, on the other hand, had built up their resistance to disease through exposure from a young age. They therefore might be passive carriers of a disease. And when they fell ill, the results tended to be less severe.

Although poorly understood by both native people and colonialists at the time, the introduction and spread of disease followed clearly identifiable patterns. First, diseases traveled along both human and animal corridors. With Old World settlers and their livestock came new diseases with variant strains. Some pathogens, such as smallpox and measles, were spread through person-to-person contact, while others, such as bubonic plague, spread through animal vectors. The earliest epidemic, which followed the arrival of the first European settlers in 1493, passed from animals to humans and then between humans. Old World livestock, particularly hogs, sparked the first outbreak of influenza among the native inhabitants of the island of HISPANIOLA (present-day Haiti and Dominican Republic). The sickness spread rapidly through both the island and region.

Second, disease often outpaced European contact. For example, in 1518, a Spanish ship touched ground along the coast of Yucatán; the vessel carried a slave who was infected with smallpox. The disease passed from village to village as indigenous communities communicated and traded (see TRADE). As a result, smallpox epidemics erupted in GUATEMALA in 1519 and in the Andes in 1524, years before the arrival of Spanish explorers. According to a MAYA chronicle of Guatemala, 1519 was a year when "First there was a cough, then the blood was corrupted." The next two years became known as the time that "the plague spread." When the Spaniards arrived, they encountered native communities already at war with Old World pathogens.

Third, virgin-soil epidemics touched entire native communities, regardless of sex, age, or social class. On the mainland, smallpox struck first. In 1520, the disease known as *huey zahuatl*, or "great spots," in NAHUATL reached TENOCHTITLÁN (present-day MEXICO CITY) and quickly spread throughout the city. "There came to be prevalent a great sickness, a plague," remembered an indigenous witness. "All were covered with pustules that were spread everywhere—on the face, on the head, on the breasts. . . . No longer could they walk, no longer could they move. They could not even turn their heads. They could not lie on their sides, belly, or on the back. And when they moved, they screamed."

Fourth, sociogeography influenced the rates of decline and recovery. In tropical, densely populated areas, including the Caribbean and mainland coasts, indigenous communities declined at rates that in some instances approached 100 percent. The speed and scale of decline left affected communities permanently debilitated, and the great majority never recovered. On the island of Hispaniola, for example, the native TAINO were virtually extinguished by 1590. In tropical, moderate to highly populated areas, such as the Yucatán and Central America, indigenous communities experienced slow but sustained population loss. Epidemic diseases occurred less frequently but consistently took their toll. Although the Yucatán was first New World site of smallpox, the native population continued to suffer from epidemic eruptions well into the 19th century. In temperate, densely populated regions, such as the Valley of Mexico and the Andes, indigenous societies suffered dramatic and widespread population loss during the initial outbreak of a disease; however, as the colonial period advanced, they slowly recovered. Large populations living in close proximity both sped the decline and promoted resistance. Epidemics may have spread through CITIES at staggering rates, but often they did not tear down the social institutions that supported the sick and infirm. Elite indigenous families, for example, continued to hold positions of authority in spite of suffering losses. Local populations in these areas proved to be the most resilient and eventually recovered from the series of epidemics.

Finally, diseases became regular and devastating occurrences. In the Valley of Mexico, indigenous and Spanish sources recorded the regularity of outbreaks, beginning with *huey zahuatl* (smallpox) in 1520. Successive epidemics included *sarampión* (measles) in 1531, *zahuatl* (a type of pox) in 1532, and a ravenous and highly destructive disease called *cocoliztli* (hemorrhagic fever) from 1545 to 1548. *Paperas* (mumps) erupted in 1550, followed by a general plague of nosebleeds, coughing, and skin abscesses in 1559 and 1550, *matlaltotonqui* (green fever) in 1563, and the return of *cocoliztli* from 1576 to 1580. While smallpox and measles claimed the most victims, the two outbreaks of hemorrhagic fever illustrate the pervasive, all-encompassing nature of epidemic disease. Weakened by the depopulation during the previous decades, hemorrhagic fever consumed the Valley of Mexico in both the late 1540s and 1570s. Spates of disease were sparked by a combination of factors: intense demands for native LABOR and several years of drought and pestilence had limited agricultural production, which led to widespread hunger (see AGRICULTURE). Normal relationships of reciprocity, such as caring for the ill, fell by the wayside as individuals struggled to meet even their most basic needs. A witness to the epidemic opined: "It is the nature of this illness that it causes great pain at the mouth of the stomach and comes with fever all over

the body. Death arrives after six or seven days." The psychological effects of these epidemics bore a heavy burden on indigenous people. Birthrates plummeted to nearly half of their preconquest rates, and colonial officials battled against infanticide.

The combination of epidemic diseases, WARFARE, economic exploitation, and environmental crises left many indigenous societies in a state of near or total collapse (see ECONOMY). Three hundred years after the arrival of Europeans, the Maya of Yucatán mourned: ". . . the mighty men arrived from the East [and] they were the ones who brought disease. . . . they wrote the charge of misery. . . . the introduction of Christianity occurs; blood-vomit, pestilence, drought, locusts, smallpox, and the importunity of the devil."

See also EPIDEMICS (Vol. II); MEDICINE (Vol. III).

—R. A. Kashanipour

Further reading:
Noble David Cook. *Born to Die: Disease and the Conquest of the New World, 1492–1650* (New York: Cambridge University Press, 1998).
Alfred Crosby. *The Columbian Exchange: Biological and Cultural Consequences of 1492* (Westport, Conn.: Greenwood Press, 1972).
Jared Diamond. *Guns, Germs and Steel: The Fates of Human Societies* (New York: W.W. Norton, 1998).
Alfredo López Austin. *The Human Body and Ideology: Concepts of the Ancient Nahuas*, translated by Thelma Ortiz de Montellano and Bernard Ortiz de Montellano (Salt Lake City: University of Utah Press, 1984).
Sandra Orellana. *Indian Medicine in Highland Guatemala: The Pre-Hispanic to Colonial Periods* (Albuquerque: University of New Mexico Press, 1988).

Dominican Republic See HISPANIOLA.

donatary captaincies During the first 30 years after the discovery of BRAZIL in 1500, the Portuguese Crown largely neglected the development and colonization of the new land (see CONQUEST). Preoccupied with its imperial aims in Asia, the Crown used Brazil primarily as a stopping place during the lengthy and dangerous journey to India. Accordingly, the first Portuguese to settle in Brazil were for the most part petty merchants, shipwrecked castaways, and penal convicts. The French, however, began to make inroads along Brazil's coasts in the 1520s in an effort to control the TRADE in Brazilian dyewood, which was becoming increasingly important in European markets (see DYES AND DYEWOOD). In response, the Portuguese Crown determined that the new land would have to be settled in a more systematic way if it were going to remain Portuguese. Accordingly, in 1534 King John III introduced donatary captaincies to Brazil.

Under the new system, Brazil's coastline was divided into 14 jurisdictions, or captaincies, with northern and southern borders that were separated by a fixed distance (generally between 90 and 300 miles) and extending indefinitely into Brazil's western interior. Each captaincy was assigned to a donatary (*donatário*), or lord proprietor, who was awarded certain privileges pertaining to colonization and settlement, including the right to establish towns, enforce laws, levy taxes, and receive tithes. The new system was based on earlier Iberian traditions—especially grants of feudal lordship in medieval Portugal—but was modified to meet Portugal's imperial aims in the Atlantic. The same system had been used in the settlement of Madeira, the Azores, and the Cape Verde Islands and reflected the limited resources of the Portuguese state at this time; in essence, it shifted the burden of colonization from royal to private interests.

If the Crown had high hopes for the captaincy system in Brazil, it was soon disappointed. Many colonists felt they were unjustly ruled by their *donatários* and soon denounced them. Rocky relations between Portuguese settlers and indigenous groups further contributed to the system's decline. Some captaincies, moreover, were never settled by their *donatários*, while others were left in various states of abandon. Of the original 14 captaincies, only two—Pernambuco and São Vicente—ever met with a measure of success, due largely to favorable indigenous relations and the introduction of sugarcane in the 1530s and 1540s (see SUGAR). Within a generation, it was apparent that the Crown would have to play a more active role in the colony's affairs if Portugal were not to lose control of Brazil to other European powers. Consequently, in 1549, the Crown sent Tomé de Sousa to serve as Brazil's first governor general; Sousa established the seat of royal government in the city of Salvador da Bahia. Although vestiges of the original 14 donatary captaincies remained for the next 200 years, the system itself effectively came to an end in the mid-16th century, as the Crown reasserted its control over the colony.

See also CAPTAINCIES GENERAL (Vol. II).

—Erik Myrup

Further reading:

Leslie Bethel, ed. *Colonial Brazil* (New York: Cambridge University Press, 1987).

dyes and dyewoods

Evidence of the use of dyes and dyewoods (varieties of wood used to dye TEXTILES, CERAMICS, and other items) prior to the arrival of Europeans has been found all over the Americas. The indigenous mastered the art of dying, and, in fact, dyes and dyewoods were often used as a form of tribute during the colonial period. The immense influence that dyes and dyewoods have had on global trade has been somewhat overlooked, though many of them are still in production. Indigo was perhaps the most important colonial export, behind SILVER; and cochineal was one of the most expensive. Indigo, *palo de Campeche*, cochineal, and brazilwood were all highly important to the European textile industry.

The extensive indigenous knowledge of natural dyes is often attributed to their ceremonial and medicinal value (see MEDICINE). While cultures outside of America often incorporated colors into certain hierarchies, the peoples of the New World saw them more often as universal. Colors were commonly associated with the cardinal points; red and white signifying the east or west, depending on the culture, blue signifying the south, and black the north. In some cultures, the color red represented fire, sun, or blood.

In his 16th-century chronicle, the Florentine Codex, the Franciscan friar BERNARDINO DE SAHAGÚN detailed the depth and complexity of indigenous knowledge of dyes (see CHRONICLERS). Written and compiled between 1547 and 1558, the codex described many of the processes and materials used in MEXICO and Central America. It discussed many unique dyes, as well as tempering agents. The dyes were used primarily for coloring textiles but also in other applications, such as to color pottery. Indigo, for example, could be used as a dye or as paint. Some of the more familiar dyes, dyewoods, and blends were the following:

Dyes, Dyewoods, and Blends

COLOR	COMMON/ENGLISH NAME(S)	INDIGENOUS NAME(S)	SPANISH NAME(S)	SCIENTIFIC NAME
Red	Cochineal/carmine	Nocheztli	Cochinilla, grana cochinilla	*Coccus cacti*
Red	Logwood	Hitzcuahuitl, huiscahuite	Palo de Campeche	*Haematoxylum campechia*
Yellow	Ochre	Tecozahuitl	Ocre	iron oxide
Blue	Indigo	Tlacehuilli, xiuhquilitl, jiquilite	Añil	*Indigofera suffructicosa*
Green	Cochineal and alum	Quiltic		

Pre-Columbian textiles, particularly early examples, are rare and often poorly preserved; nonetheless, the evidence suggests that indigenous groups from Mesoamerica to the Andes possessed remarkably varied palettes and created some of the finest textiles of anywhere in the world. Ancient specimens revealing resist-dyeing techniques, such as batik and tie-dye, have been unearthed at several sites in Peru, demonstrating not only the prolonged existence and use of dyes but also the mastery of advanced techniques.

Many dyeing techniques might have been lost had it not been for their economic value (see economy). The collection of cochineal, for example, is a difficult and time-consuming process. It is one of very few dyes made from an animal rather than a mineral or plant. The cochineal insect nests in the nopal cactus; in order to use it as a dye, it must be collected, boiled, dried, and otherwise processed. Indigo, because it is not water soluble, is likewise difficult to work with, yet it also was used for many purposes by the indigenous Americans. The use of pre-Columbian dyes, especially indigo and cochineal, has continued not only because of their unique properties and inimitable hues but also because of their global economic success and sustained value.

See also brazilwood (Vol. II); cochineal (Vol. II); indigo (Vol. II).

—Tyler Morell

Further reading:

Shawn William Miller. "Dyes and Dyewood." In *Iberia and the Americas: Culture, Politics, and History*, vol. 2, edited by J. Michael Francis, 420–421 (Santa Barbara, Calif.: ABC-CLIO, 2006).

Steven Topik, Carlos Marichal, and Zephyr Frank, eds. *From Silver to Cocaine: Latin American Commodity Chains and the Building of the World Economy, 1500–2000* (Durham, N.C.: Duke University Press, 2006).

E

economy

THE CARIBBEAN BEFORE 1492

The first inhabitants of the Caribbean islands, a cultural group known as the Archaic or Guanahatabey, were hunters and gatherers who likely arrived from FLORIDA or the southeastern United States. They did not produce CERAMICS or practice AGRICULTURE but did possess the skills to navigate the sea passages between the islands in search of raw materials and FOOD (such as mollusks and fish). The Caribbean ecosystem lacked large land animals, so hunting was limited to birds, reptiles, and different species of *jutía*, an indigenous rodent. Sea mammals such as manatees, the now-extinct Caribbean monk seal, and dolphins were also hunted for their meat, bones, and teeth.

Current archaeological evidence indicates that agriculture came to the Caribbean with immigrants from the Orinoco delta area in northern South America. These new arrivals, who belonged to the Arawakan linguistic family and were known as the Igneri or Saladoid, cultivated tuber crops such as MANIOC (also known as cassava or yucca), the batata, or sweet POTATO, and MAIZE. Manioc was grated to make a starchy flour, which was used to make *casabe* bread. The Saladoid peoples also grew *ají*, or hot peppers, COTTON and TOBACCO, as well as other plants for fibers, medicinal purposes, and dyes (see DYES AND DYEWOOD; MEDICINE).

TRADE appears to have been an important component of Saladoid economic activity. Raw materials as well as finished products made from stone, seashells, and presumably other perishable plant and animal goods were traded between villages and islands. Saladodid ceramics were decorated in hallmark white and red paint pain motifs and were also traded.

Recent archaeological records indicate that the Saladoid trade networks were extensive, stretching from Central America to the northern coast of South America. Ax heads and celts made of jadeite from the Motagua Valley in GUATEMALA have been found on the island of Antigua. Non-native peccary and jaguar teeth, together with condor-shaped carved figurines made from South American turquoise and jadeite, have been discovered at the La Hueca site on Vieques Island.

The Classic TAINO or Arawak culture, which arose from the Saladoid culture and later South American influences, saw the development of new agricultural practices, stone carving, and ceramic traditions. Economic activities were allocated according to gender and age. WOMEN undertook most of the productive work, including food preparation, making of pottery and textiles, and most domestic activities. Activities such as farming, hunting, fishing, trading, and the manufacture of weapons, tools, and ritual objects were male occupations.

Taino agricultural practices were adapted to the terrain and climate of the Caribbean. For example, in the Xaraguá region of the Dominican Republic, the Taino built terraces to farm hillside plots and developed irrigation techniques for their *conucos*, or fields. Spanish accounts describe extensive *conucos*, with hundreds of thousands of cassava plants.

Fishing continued to be an important activity, with intensive exploitation of tidal and mangrove areas. The production of cotton textiles, with dyed design and featherwork, was widespread. The Taino also introduced metalwork to the Caribbean. Naturally produced GOLD-SILVER or gold-copper nuggets, known as *caona* or *tumbaga*, respectively, were cold hammered to produce ornaments such as the *guanin*, or gold disk, that was worn by the CACIQUE or village chieftain as a symbol of authority.

Society revolved around the village, or *yukayeke*. The typical Taino village consisted of the cacique, supported by *nitaínos*, or nobility, with the *naborías*, or commoners, forming the bulk of the population. The *behique*, or spiritual leader, and skilled artisans who produced goods for trade and for the elite also enjoyed special positions within the village. There were regional polities in which a cacique was recognized as the overlord of a number of autonomous *yukayekes*. While the Taino did not develop CITIES, they did build large ceremonial centers, or *bateyes*, that consisted of plazas and ball courts lined with large stone monoliths, many of which were carved with petroglyphs. The inhabitants of neighboring villages gathered at these *bateyes* for religious celebrations and to conduct trade (see RELIGION).

Interisland sea trade and communication links were maintained by the Taino, whose canoes were made from trees trunks and could carry up to 80 passengers, or a sizable cargo. Trade was conducted by *nitaínos* with access to surplus foodstuffs, raw materials, and other valuable goods, although there is no evidence for a specialized trader class. Nevertheless, some regions and even islands were renowned for certain products. For example, the inhabitants of the small island of Mona produced an especially fine type of *casabe* bread, reportedly only for the caciques in neighboring HISPANIOLA and PUERTO RICO.

Despite adverse sea currents, there is some evidence of direct sea contact and perhaps trade between the Taino and inhabitants of Mesoamerica. BARTOLOMÉ DE LAS CASAS reported seeing beeswax, presumably from Yucatán, in CUBA. BERNAL DÍAZ DEL CASTILLO encountered a Taino woman from Jamaica, held captive by the MAYA of Cozumel. One Taino artifact, a manatee bone spatula, was found at the Classic Maya site of Altun Ha in BELIZE.

The Taino shared the eastern Caribbean with the Caribs, a distantly related group that also migrated from northern South America. Early European explorers remarked on the Caribs' aggressiveness and practice of CANNIBALISM. The Caribs inhabited both islands of the eastern Caribbean, as well as the mainland in what is now GUYANA. They maintained an extensive sea trade network, connecting their island outposts with South America. Carib society was in many ways similar to that of the Taino: They shared an economy based on the production of manioc and other agricultural products, supplemented with fishing, hunting, and gathering. The Caribs also produced excellent textiles and were skilled ceramists; however Carib society was uniquely organized around raiding neighboring nations and enslaving the inhabitants (see SLAVERY).

Among the Carib males, power and status were rewards for courage and success in WARFARE. While women (both native Carib and enslaved Taino) took care of the crops, produced utensils and textiles, and cared for the children, the men dedicated their time to hunting, fishing, and building and mending their canoes. Carib villages did not have a structured hierarchy. Rather, individual males with enough prestige and influence could mobilize the village for a particular purpose, such as launching a seagoing canoe or planning a trading voyage or raid.

Enslaving expeditions provided the Caribs with captives, who formed a large portion of their workforce. Generally, male prisoners were killed and ritually consumed, while females became the concubines of successful warriors. There is evidence, however, that the Caribs also traded with their neighbors. The large tree trunks used by the Caribs to make their canoes were available only on the larger islands inhabited by the Taino. The Caribs also traded for metals, foodstuffs, and textiles with the Taino and with groups on mainland South America.

MESOAMERICA BEFORE 1492

Cities and trade played prominent roles in Mesoamerica's pre-Columbian economy. Trade can be traced back to Mesoamerica's distant past, preceding even the establishment of settled societies with permanent agriculture. Variations in the availability of raw materials and the type of agriculture practiced gave rise to distinct local economies; thus, trade was crucial to supplying resources that were not available locally.

The rise of Mesoamerican city-states led to an expansion in the volume of trade. As urban centers with large populations consumed more goods, regional exchanges grew into long-distance trade networks that extended throughout Mesoamerica and beyond. Trade helped to integrate Mesoamerica's dispersed economic areas, and as a result, a change in the economic conditions in one area could have far-reaching consequences in another. Trade also helped promote a more stable supply of essential goods and generated wealth, which, in turn, further stimulated artisan production and the market. Prosperous cities embarked on monumental public ARCHITECTURE projects such as the pyramids of TEOTIHUACÁN, which further contributed to the economy by requiring LABOR and materials collected through trade or tribute. Prior to the Spanish CONQUEST, Mesoamerican societies such as the Aztec Empire (see AZTECS) had complex and highly regulated economies characterized by vibrant markets, specialist artisan production, slavery, compulsory labor drafts, and the receipt of tribute from conquered communities.

Agriculture formed the basis of Mesoamerica's economy. NATIVE AMERICANS practiced different kinds of agriculture, depending on factors such as topography and climate. In arid or tropical areas that were poorly suited to permanent agriculture, people relied on hunting, gathering, and fishing to supplement the FOOD they cultivated. To further bolster food supplies, people domesticated and raised animals such as turkeys, small dogs, and bees. Some communities relocated to follow the seasonal availability of food. Others moved in a regular cyclical fashion, as, for example, those who practiced slash-and-burn agriculture. While cultivation techniques could vary considerably, most people ate a staple diet of MAIZE, beans, and squash, supplemented by other local foods.

In areas of intensive, permanent agriculture, Mesoamericans employed generally similar forms of land tenure. Households owned plots of land, or MIL-PAS, which typically passed to subsequent generations through inheritance. Beyond household plots, there were community-owned lands set aside for the group's subsistence and to provide tribute in the form of food to religious and political elites. Dynastic rulers, nobles, and religious officials also had their own lands, particularly in larger and more socially stratified communities. These plots were tended by commoners, often in exchange for their own rights of access to land. In city-states, slaves captured in war also provided agricultural labor.

Permanent agriculture provided a basis for the rise of complex societies in Mesoamerica. Beginning with the Olmec civilization, which developed along the Gulf coast after 1500 B.C.E., city-states contributed to economic expansion and diversification. Large urban centers such as Teotihuacán (250 B.C.E.–750 C.E.), which arose after the decline of the OLMECS, were established in areas with fertile, rich soils and supplies of freshwater. Teotihuacán's irrigation network helped support the city's vast population, estimated to have been about 200,000 people at its height. Food surpluses in city-states contributed to greater social stratification. Slaves occupied the lowest level in society and lived apart from commoners and elites. Typically, commoners worked as farmers, artisans, and/or merchants, while the elite obtained their social position by fulfilling political and religious functions.

As cities grew in size and wealth, they embarked on the construction of monumental architecture. This included the famous basalt heads of the Olmecs and the pyramids of Teotihuacán and TIKAL, among others. City-states depended on complex labor arrangements to support these public works projects. At the household level, men worked as farmers or in trades, while women reared children, maintained the home, and raised crops and wove fabrics both for their families and for sale in local markets. Women also managed household income and often were responsible for meeting the FAMILY's tribute obligations. Beyond these daily tasks, households periodically came together to perform joint labor duties, as in times of harvest or in gathering essential materials such as wood. Residents also participated in public works projects, both at the village level and for larger polities. Although slaves supplied unskilled labor in cities, artisans and farmers also contributed to construction projects through rotational labor drafts. Highly skilled stone masons and sculptors were particularly important in the building of rulers' palaces, temples, and pyramids.

With the rise of city-states and the expansion of their spheres of influence, trade came to occupy an increasingly important place in Mesoamerican political and economic life. The Olmecs influenced both the societies that succeeded them and neighboring Mesoamerican areas. This cultural influence can be seen in the monumental architecture of ceremonial centers, as well as graphic writing systems and the adoption of long-distance trade. The Olmecs established formal trade mechanisms and developed markets for their goods; for instance, they exported rubber balls to groups that had adopted their ceremonial ball games. The Olmec legacy of regional and long-distance trading continued through the Classic period (ca. 250–900 C.E.) in city-states such as Teotihuacán and MONTE ALBÁN.

Because Mesoamerican communities relied on long-distance trade for much of their prosperity, economic dislocation in one place could have profound consequences elsewhere. The demise of Teotihuacán destabilized the economy of Maya areas, for example, fragmenting trade networks and thus interrupting the supply of OBSIDIAN and other valuable commodities from Central MEXICO. Such upheaval heightened rivalries between Maya city-states, precipitating warfare and enabling other urban centers to rise to dominance. Scholars argue about the causes of decline in Classic-era Maya kingdoms, proposing variously famine, DISEASE, or internal conflict, but diminishing trade may also have been either a cause or a symptom of the decline. The vacuum in long-distance trade was filled by the rise of the TOLTECS in Central Mexico (900–1150) and with them came a degree of economic revitalization in the Maya areas. For example, CHICHÉN ITZÁ rose to prominence as a commercial center at this time.

In Mesoamerica, goods were transported by human carriers because of the absence of draft animals. Rugged topography hindered long-distance transportation, as did problems of food supply. Because they had to employ people to carry goods, merchants preferred to trade lightweight and luxury goods that could command high prices. Obsidian remained a valuable commodity both because of the strength it lent to tools and its limited supply. The trade in obsidian thus underpinned regional and long-distance exchanges. Merchants turned to canoes as an efficient and affordable form of transportation on lakes and the few rivers that could be navigated. Canoes varied in size, from small craft to seafaring vessels more than 40 feet long. Larger canoes could transport considerable loads of goods and many passengers. The Maya switched to overseas transportation in the face of interruptions to overland trade after the demise of Teotihuacán. Cozumel became an important trading center for coastal transportation. The Maya dominated trade with markets as far away as the Valley of Mexico and the Gulf of HONDURAS. Some scholars argue that Mesoamerican trade extended as far north as modern-day New Mexico and perhaps as far south as COLOMBIA, or even PERU.

Trade occupied a crucial place in Mesoamerica's economy because people could generally obtain only a portion of the goods they needed locally. There were considerable variations in the availability of resources across different parts of Mesoamerica. Salt extraction, for example, was a mainstay of the economy in coastal regions in northern Yucatán. Obsidian deposits were confined mainly to the Pachuca area of Central Mexico and the highlands of Guatemala. Among metals, copper, gold, and iron ore (used to make mirrors) were found in western Mexico and Oaxaca. Tropical areas supplied other luxury items such as quetzal feathers and jaguar pelts. Coastal, lowland areas specialized in the cultivation of cotton, vanilla, CACAO, rubber, lime, and honey. By contrast, highland areas typically relied for their income on cochineal (see DYES AND DYEWOOD), textiles, and stones such as jade and turquoise fashioned into tools or jewelry.

The diversity in the location of raw materials also promoted specialization. Some communities were known for their trade specialties, for instance, the Mixtec metalworkers and Zapotec potters (see MIXTECS; ZAPOTECS). Indeed, elites from distant cities sometimes recruited esteemed artisans; thus, Zapotec craftsmen formed their own neighborhood in Teotihuacán. Throughout Mesoamerica, artisans usually lived in separate communities. They formed their own wards in larger polities. In Central Mexico, Xochimilco was renowned for its CHINAMPA agriculture, canoe making, and carpentry, while stonecutters, lapidaries, and tailors contributed to nearby Texcoco's prosperity. Artisans constituted a distinct social group in these polities. Skills tended to remain within the same families, with offspring commonly inheriting their parents' trades. Mesoamerica's artisans included carpenters, stoneworkers and sculptors, potters, basketmakers, weavers and tailors, and sandal and reed makers. In larger communities or those catering to lucrative urban markets, some artisans specialized as lapidaries, metalworkers, featherworkers, and papermakers. Painters and scribes provided their services to communities too, as did musicians, healers, scholars, priests, and warriors.

Artisans obtained raw materials and sold their finished goods in various types of markets. Marketplaces in village plazas catered to most people's daily needs, while regional markets offered a wider range of products. Transactions took place through commonly recognized means of exchange, such as cacao beans. Cacao beans functioned as a currency throughout Mesoamerica, although other acceptable currencies included copper axes and textiles, particularly cloaks. Native Americans coveted textiles as valuable items because their manufacture involved a considerable investment in highly skilled labor. Obsidian, jade, salt, and shells were also exchanged in commerce, particularly in Maya areas.

At the summit of regional commerce lay the city-state in whose marketplaces were sold commodities imported from throughout Mesoamerica. Government officials supervised the operations of these markets, ensuring that exchanges conformed to strict rules regarding prices and weights and measures. The preeminent market of Mesoamerica in the immediate precontact period was Tlatelolco, located in the island heart of the Aztec Empire. At the time of conquest, Spanish observers commented on Tlatelolco's orderliness, the immense number and range of goods, and its remarkable size, with thousands of customers visiting each day. Such was Tlatelolco's grandeur that the conquistador Bernal Díaz del Castillo wrote that several soldiers in his company, who had visited Constantinople and Rome, claimed they had never seen such an impressive marketplace.

Long-distance merchants delivered goods to markets such as Tlatelolco. Like artisans, merchants constituted a distinct, hereditary group with their own corporate organization. They occupied an intermediary place in society, neither commoner nor elite, although some Maya merchants approached the upper social ranks. Merchants maintained communities in distant lands and became agents for commercial exchanges and political relations. The POCHTECA, or long-distance merchants in the Aztec Empire, acted as ambassadors, establishing ties with trading partners. Indeed, the *pochteca* functioned as a kind of vanguard for Aztec imperial expansion, providing intelligence about economic, political, and military conditions that could assist in conquests and the formulation of state policies.

The size and complexity of urban economies called for careful planning and regulation. This proved especially important in supervising markets, labor recruitment, and securing essential resources through tribute. To this end, the Olmecs established regular land and river transportation routes while also building strategic settlements at the perimeter of their territory to promote defense and trade. Similarly, Teotihuacán's rulers pursued expansionist policies designed to monopolize the supply of obsidian. City-states frequently sought to extend control of their hinterlands. For the Aztecs, strategic marriages, military alliances, FLOWER WARS, and conquests formed part of a complex political economy that was bound up with imperial expansion and dominance.

SOUTH AMERICA BEFORE 1492

Due to its extreme variations in climate and physical geography, South America has many different economic systems. Braced between the Andes mountain range and the AMAZON River and its tributaries, South America features some of the world's most fecund, as well as most difficult, terrain. Vast arid plains consume huge swaths of land, most notably in modern-day ARGENTINA, BOLIVIA, CHILE, Peru, and URUGUAY. While common latitudes give rise to similar climates throughout much of the world, in South America, latitudinal variations have produced a rich diversity of ecosystems. The enormous altitudinous and latitudinal differences made travel and the introduction of technology exceptionally difficult, which was key in shaping of South America's economies. Sophisticated economic systems, most notably in the Andes, developed to overcome these impediments; they incorporated many of the traits that economists now praise, including division of labor, specialization, and long-distance trade networks. Finally, refinements to and expansion on the accomplishments of previous civilizations often enabled later civilizations to enjoy increasing levels of economic wealth prior to the arrival of Europeans.

The mixed blessing of geography produced disparate economies. Where larger and more sophisticated political systems emerged, economies were able to thrive by taking advantage of what economists now term *specialization*. Rather than everyone trying to produce everything, producers focused on a narrow range of products, according to their skills and abilities. In other areas, the inability of political regimes to coopt isolated producers stymied efficiency, leaving economies small and static. Therefore, by 1492, while some economic systems in South America were as sophisticated as those in contemporary Europe, others were more rudimentary, with nomadic foragers in the southernmost parts of the continent and more basic agricultural and farming economies elsewhere.

Still, even advanced South American economies differed in two salient ways from those in Europe. First, while many South American ethnic groups used metals to craft jewelry, metals were not widely used to make tools. Second, the European "beasts of burden" were never used in agricultural production in South America. Instead, due to the steep terrain of the Andes and the inability to adapt the wheel (which was used in several societies in building toys and the like) for transportation, animals such as the llama and alpaca were used mainly for transportation purposes. Given these limitations, it is no surprise that road systems were more complete and complex in high-altitude areas where the chief animal of transportation, the llama, thrived.

Although animals were for the most part not used in farming in South America, water-borne transportation systems and terracing for irrigation enabled long-distance trade and economic development. The majority of South American economies were characterized by a domestic mode of production; hence, self-sufficiency, developing plots of land for food, and manufacturing cloth and utensils were the cornerstones of economic activity. Gender-determined roles were prevalent in many daily activities, but given the number of tasks that required more than a single family to complete, such as construction and harvesting, communities tended to be made up of kin-based networks (see *AYLLU*). As a result, land and resources were viewed largely as communal.

Semipermanent agriculture-based economies built around the cultivation of tubers, beans, and cotton (crucial for the construction of fishing nets) began to emerge in South America at least 4,000 years ago. In economic terms, the most significant of the incipient settlements in the Americas was the Norte Chico civilization, which consisted of more than two dozen population centers in north-central Peru. Centralized control of the Norte Chico economy almost certainly emanated from an inland site, although two coastal sites indicate that trade networks were in place. The production of cotton and edible plants dominated economic activity, while bartering guaranteed the flow of goods. Norte Chico was less remarkable for

its economic dynamism than for the expansive reach of its economy (it included many of the high plateaus of the altiplano) and for laying the foundation for Andean trade that flourished in subsequent civilizations.

The establishment of communities along the Pacific coast of South America was aided by the incorporation of fish into the food supply; it provided much-needed protein into settlers' diets and facilitated permanent settlement. Communities in many lowland areas, which succeeded in domesticating only ducks, needed to hunt for game, which increased not only the rigors of daily life but stymied more permanent settlement and, hence, delayed the construction of infrastructure such as irrigation channels or roads.

The CHAVÍN civilization, which flourished along the Peruvian coast between 900 and 200 B.C.E., marked a high point of economic activity during the Early Horizon period and was instrumental in laying the foundations for later economic systems. The Chavín produced pottery and textiles in significant quantities, and their metallurgical skills were notably advanced. Cloth production was revolutionized during this time owing to their dedication to textiles, which they used both for individual and ceremonial purposes. The Chavín also developed a long-distance trade network, made possible by their domestication of the llama; this vast trade network extended north into Ecuador and south possibly as far as the northern coast of Chile.

The largest and most advanced pre-Columbian economic system in South America was that of the INCAS. Of course, the socioeconomic achievements of the Norte Chico, Chavín, WARI, TIWANAKU, and CHIMÚ, among other civilizations, laid the foundations for the Inca economy. Divided into four administrative sectors, the Inca Empire controlled more than a million square miles (2.59 million km²) of territory, with some 80 provinces composed of disparate indigenous groups. The Inca economy was controlled mainly by the state, which held large quantities of land and exercised significant control over the various modes of production and the redistribution of food, products, and even people (see *MITA; MITMAQKUNA; YANA*). The production of wool, cotton, and maize, for example, was mainly controlled by the state. The state could thus support a vast bureaucracy and maintain a large standing army; state-controlled resources were also used for ceremonial and martial purposes.

Cloth was the most prized product of Inca industry, and women were specially selected for weaving (see *ACLLA*). The main exception to state control was the cultivation of potatoes; households grew and harvested this vegetable in accordance with their needs. Though the Inca economy was advanced in many respects, a centralized monetary system was never introduced. Despite being perhaps the world's only civilization to cultivate crops at altitudes higher than 9,000 feet (2,743 m), the Inca economy thrived because of its long-distance exchange networks, including more than 15 miles (24 km) of roadways, integration of various pockets of skilled producers in different parts of the empire, and efficiency in addressing the basic needs of the citizenry.

Elsewhere, in the commodity-rich Colombian hinterland, the MUISCA flourished in the century prior to the arrival of Europeans. The mining of commodities such as coal, copper, gold, EMERALDS, and salt drove the economy. Coal, emeralds, and salt were in such abundance that they were used as de facto currencies. Other exchanges, for products from basic staples to luxury goods, relied on bartering. The Muiscas' destruction, however, was sown into their commodity-driven wealth: Their inordinate amount of gold, as well as its prominent use in ceremony, inspired the myth of EL DORADO, which captivated Spanish audiences and incited numerous expeditions just over a century after their rise.

The asymmetric development of economic systems in South America before 1492 was largely a by-product of geography and the availability of natural resources. In seeking to explain certain pockets of economic advancement, scholars have termed the more sophisticated South American economies *archipelagoes*. Economic specialization in the archipelagoes of South America can be traced back to at least 2400 B.C.E. The predominance of ceramics and embroidered textiles in burial sites on the Peruvian coast that date as far back as 1600 B.C.E. indicates the development of a state system of politics and remarkably sophisticated specialization and connotes unusual wealth. Still, in most parts of South America, economic activity remained in a basic agricultural phase until well after the arrival of Europeans. Access to protein-rich fish and long-distance trade networks ensured that the most sophisticated economies emerged along the Pacific coast of South America and to a lesser extent in pockets along the Amazon and Orinoco Rivers. Expansive road systems, which were often built upon those of preceding civilizations, increased the likelihood of economic vitality. At the time of Spanish contact, the Inca Empire dominated much of South America, and its economy rivaled those of Europe in its breadth and efficiency. The extraordinary wealth of advanced economies in South America, however, served only to attract the interest of European conquistadores.

EARLY COLONIAL LATIN AMERICA

The early decades of Latin America's colonial economy were dominated by the quest for precious metals, the accumulation and exchange of local products, and the control of indigenous labor. Of course, in much of the New World, pre-Columbian modes of production and exchange continued well into the colonial period; however, this does not imply that there were not fundamental changes for Native Americans. Initially, the first waves of Spanish conquistadores resorted to looting as a primary strategy for acquiring precious stones and metals. HERNANDO CORTÉS, for example, stole large quantities of Aztec gold during the early stages of the conquest of Mexico, only to lose it all when he and his men were forced to flee TENOCHTITLÁN during the Noche Triste.

In the conquest of Muisca territory, GONZALO JIMÉNEZ DE QUESADA and his band of 173 conquistadores pillaged more than 200,000 pesos of Muisca gold and more than 1,800 emeralds. And, most famously, following the capture of the Inca ruler ATAHUALPA, FRANCISCO PIZARRO and his men secured a ransom equal to more than 1 million pesos. Despite royal attempts to curb the practice, the early decades of the conquest witnessed extensive pillaging and looting of native gold, silver, food, and other products.

The prevailing economic doctrine of all the European powers was mercantilism, or the measuring of a country or empire's prosperity by the accumulation of wealth or capital. The most obvious wealth to come from the New World were the specie (coined money) of gold and silver. Official reports estimate that between 1500 and 1650, roughly 180 tons of gold and 16,000 tons of silver were sent from the New World to Spain; however, most of this wealth was generated after 1560, when silver production rose dramatically. Nevertheless, the search for precious metals helped to fuel the processes of exploration and colonization of the Americas.

Silver MINING in Mexico began less than a decade after the fall of the Aztec Empire, with the discovery of silver mines in Zumpango and Sultepec; these first strikes were followed by additional finds in 1534 at Taxco and Tlalpujahua, also in Central Mexico. However, none of these mines matched the tremendous silver deposits discovered at Zacatecas in 1546; in fact, only the silver mines of POTOSÍ in Peru, discovered in 1545, yielded more silver than those of Zacatecas during the 16th century.

In addition to silver, South America offered large quantities of gold, particularly in New Granada, where gold mining began in the early 1540s in places such as Popayán and Antioquia. Still, the early colonial mining techniques used by Spaniards relied heavily on preexisting indigenous methods of extraction and refining. For example, the Amerindians of the Andes had longstanding traditions of mining, smelting, and refining metals. Moreover, early settlers depended almost exclusively on native labor, which became increasingly problematic as populations declined as a result of disease, exploitation, and MIGRATION.

For both the Spanish and Portuguese, another major source of revenue was obtained from the production of SUGAR. By 1503, the first sugar mill was built on the island of Hispaniola, and as the demand for sugar rose, along with its price, early colonists in the Caribbean responded. By the 1530s, there were 34 sugar mills on Hispaniola. As Spain expanded its colonial possessions into Central and South America, so sugar followed. The Portuguese also sought to profit from Europe's growing demand for sugar, and by the early 16th century, sugar mills had begun to appear in BRAZIL.

Also crucial to both the Spanish and Portuguese Empires was the exchange of dyes and dyewoods, which included indigo, cochineal, and brazilwood. The export of cochineal was second to silver in New Spain, reaching a yearly value of 600,000 pesos in value by the late 1500s.

Other important industries were shipbuilding, which began in PANAMA and other parts of Central America.

While there is no denying the importance of mineral wealth, sugar, dyes, and other commodities, the most important source of wealth in the early colonial period was human labor. In the early decades of conquest in the Caribbean, much of this labor was forced Indian labor. As indigenous populations dwindled, Spaniards increasingly looked to other islands and the mainland as potential sources of slave labor. This pattern began to shift with the major conquest campaigns of Central Mexico and South America.

With the discovery of large population centers in Mexico, Peru, and Colombia, Spanish conquistadores (with royal authority) issued ENCOMIENDA grants to their most loyal followers. An *encomienda* grant included Indians, who were required to pay the holder, or *encomendero*, an annual tribute (typically paid in two annual installments). The size of these grants varied from one region to another, but many included hundreds, if not thousands, of tribute-paying Amerindians. In Peru, for example, some *encomenderos* regularly yielded annual incomes of 5,000 to 10,000 pesos. Again, the source of this wealth varied between regions; some *encomenderos* received payments in gold or silver, while others were supplied with cloth, agricultural products, salt, or other goods, which they then exchanged for specie. *Encomenderos* regularly used their subjects for personal services as well, forcing them to build houses, work private lands, or watch over herds. In many cases, these labor services were uncompensated.

The *encomienda* system dominated the early decades of the colonial economy; in 1542, the Crown attempted to curb the abuses of the *encomienda* system by prohibiting the granting of new *encomiendas* and mandating the transfer of existing *encomiendas* to the Crown upon the death of the current holder. However, these efforts were met with violent resistance (see CIVIL WARS IN PERU), and the Crown was forced to delay its efforts to abolish the *encomienda* system. By the middle of the 16th century, the steep demographic decline, largely due to the introduction of Old World diseases, began to threaten the economic viability of the *encomienda* system. Increasingly, as the indigenous population declined, Spanish and Portuguese settlers turned their focus across the Atlantic in search of a vast and inexpensive source of labor. In 1518, the Spanish Crown issued the first ASIENTO, or slave-trading contract, to transport African slaves to the New World.

See also ALCABALA (Vol. II); ALMOJARIFAZGO (Vol. II); ECONOMY (Vols. II, III, IV); MINTS (Vol. II); MONOPOLIES, ROYAL (Vol. II); QUINTO (Vol. II); SMUGGLING (Vol. II); WEIGHTS AND MEASURES (Vol. II).

—Richard Conway
J. Michael Francis
Sean H. Goforth
Francisco J. González
Christina Hawkins

Further reading:

Paul Bahn. *Archaeology: Theories, Methods and Practice*, 4th ed. (London: Thames & Hudson, 2004).

Peter Bakewell. *A History of Latin America* (Malden, Mass.: Blackwell, 2004).

Frances F. Berdan, et al. *Aztec Imperial Strategies* (Washington, D.C.: Dumbarton Oaks Research Library & Collection, 1996).

Richard E. Blanton, et al. *Ancient Mesoamerica: A Comparison of Change in Three Regions* (New York: Cambridge University Press, 1993).

Alfred W. Crosby Jr. *The Columbian Exchange: Biological and Cultural Consequences of 1492* (Westport, Conn.: Praeger Publishers, 2003).

Terence D'Altroy. *The Incas* (Malden, Mass.: Blackwell, 2002).

Bernal Díaz del Castillo. *The Discovery and Conquest of Mexico, 1517–1521*, translated by A. P. Maudslay (New York: Da Capo Press, 2004).

Eugenio Fernández Méndez. *Art and Mythology of the Taino Indians of the Greater West Indies* (San Juan, Puerto Rico: Ediciones El Cemi, 1972).

Kenneth G. Hirth, ed. *Trade and Exchange in Early Mesoamerica* (Albuquerque: University of New Mexico Press, 1984).

Thomas A. Lee Jr. and Carlos Navarrete, eds. *Mesoamerican Communication Routes and Cultural Contacts: Papers of the New World Archaeological Foundation* (Provo, Utah: Brigham Young University, 1978).

Marilyn A. Masson and David A. Freidel, eds. *Ancient Maya Political Economies* (Walnut Creek, Calif.: AltaMira Press, 2002).

Irving Rouse. *The Tainos: Rise and Decline of the People Who Greeted Columbus* (New Haven, Conn.: Yale University Press, 1992).

Vernon L. Scarborough and John E. Clark, eds. *The Political Economy of Ancient Mesoamerica: Transformations during the Formative and Classic Periods* (Albuquerque: University of New Mexico Press, 2007).

Ecuador Ecuador has a rich pre-Columbian history that extends from Paleoindian times to the Spanish CONQUEST. Geographically, the country has been divided in three distinct regions: the coast, the sierra, or highlands, and the AMAZON. Its resources and strategic position on the Pacific coast between Mesoamerica and PERU have played an important role in exchange networks and the origin and transmission of different pottery, metalwork, TEXTILES, and stonework styles and traditions.

Early Paleoindian occupation dates to around 11,000 B.C.E. at sites located mainly in the highlands, such as El Inga. There, scholars have identified two lithic traditions: fishtail points and Clovis fluted points, as well other spear points such as Ayampitin-like (teardrop and laurel leaf–shaped) and Paiján-like points, and various stemmed points (see CLOVIS CULTURE). El Inga was a campsite and workshop occupied by a mobile population who hunted megafauna. OBSIDIAN fishtail points have also been found at Tabacundo, Cayambe, Imbabura, and Quitoloma and basalt fishtail points at Tuquer, Chitán, and Tulcán. Barbed, lanceolate, and stemmed points and bone tools have been found at Chobsi cave and Cubilán. Obsidian points found at these highlands sites indicate an early regional trade with the coastal lowlands that extended from Mullumica-Yanaurco-Quicatola. Evidence of megafauna and associated human remains were found at Riobamba, and mastodon bones and stone tools have been found on the Santa Helena Peninsula.

Between 10,000 and 6000 B.C.E., the Las Vegas peoples inhabited various sites along the coast in Santa Elena Peninsula. After the extinction of the megafauna, these communities developed a diverse ECONOMY, exploiting marine, estuarine, and terrestrial resources. Between 8000 and 4000 B.C.E., they began to cultivate squash and root crops, and by 6000 B.C.E., they were cultivating MAIZE (see AGRICULTURE). Stone and shell tools were used for woodworking and in cultivation. These coastal communities lived in round houses. Their funerary practices, subsistence patterns, and stone tools have many similarities to those found in Cerro Mangote in PANAMA, suggesting early ties with Mesoamerican peoples.

Ecuadorean pre-Columbian inhabitants were among the first in the Americas to discover the mixture of clay, water, and fire that led to the invention of pottery, which started the Formative period around 5500 B.C.E. (see CERAMICS). Permanent communities that used Valdivia pottery at Loma Alta, Real Alto, La Emerenciana, San Pablo, Perinao, Punta Concepción, and Punta Tintina cultivated fields in the floodplains, using slash-and-burn agriculture. Along the coast, human populations fished, cultivated, and gathered plants and shellfish. At inland sites, they resided in U-shaped villages and dispersed hamlets, with oval houses built around a central plaza; these people also cultivated maize, squash, beans, and roots, which they stored in pits. To complement their diet, they later hunted terrestrial mammals, especially deer and other small game. Grounding stone tools such as *manos* and *metates* were used to process plant products. Sites that date back to this period also contained raised platforms, stone-faced terraces, and stone tools used to process COCA.

The Machalilla phase, or Middle Formative period, dates from around 2000 to 1000 B.C.E. Sites associated with this period have been identified in the sierra and on the coast and include La Plata, La Ponga, Cotollao, Chimborazo, Cañar, Loja, El Oro, Chanduy, Salango, and Cerro Narrio and in the Amazon region at Cueva de los Tayos. This period saw the intensification of maize cultivation, hunting, and fishing. Centers of ritual and exchange appeared in all three geographical zones, which helped to stimulate long-distance economic activity. The exchange provided exotic materials such as thorn oyster shells, pottery, turquoise, and lapis lazuli. These luxury items were used by the elite as symbols of their religious authority and social prestige.

The Late Formative, or Engoroy-Chorrera, period (1000–500 B.C.E.) manifested at sites such as Chanduy, Palmar, Salango, Putushio, La Chimba, Chorrera, Engoroy, Cerro Narrio, Peñón del Río, Isla Plata, and the Guayas. It saw a further intensification of agricultural activity, particularly the cultivation of maize and beans, as well as fishing, shellfish gathering, and the hunting of small game, including rabbits and deer. It also saw the introduction of animals from the south, such as llamas and GUINEA PIGS. Similarities between anthropomorphic Chorrera figurines and Ixtlán figurines suggest long-distance sea trade extending south to Peru and north as far as MEXICO.

The next period is called Regional Development and dates from 500 B.C.E. to 750 C.E. Social complexity and stratified societies emerged as a result of interaction and competition over long-distance exchange networks. Changes occurred in pottery styles and stone tools, both of which became highly diversified. This period was also characterized by widespread textile production, the introduction of metalwork, and the long-distance exchange of thorn oyster shells and obsidian. By this time, sociopolitical units, or *señoríos*, began to emerge in Ecuador at sites such as Tejar-Daule, La Tolita, Tuncahuán, Cerro Narrio, Jama-Coaque, Bahia, Guangala, Jambelí, Guadula/Selva Negra, and Consanga-Pillaro.

Along the coast, in the Amazon, and in the highland regions, inhabitants all cultivated and consumed maize, beans, POTATO, and MANIOC. They also exploited marine resources and domestic Muscovy duck, in addition to guinea pig, agouti, and deer. Tools consisted of net sinkers, root graters, spindle whorls, T-shaped polished stones axes, shell objects, and obsidian blades. Monumental ARCHITECTURE, such as elaborate tombs, platform mounds, and *tolas*, or earth mounds, have been found in ceremonial centers. These centers were important in both religious and economic activities (see RELIGION). Evidence of GOLD production at Chorrera burial sites dates to as early as 500 B.C.E. During this period, part-time specialists crafted elaborate gold ornaments and copper tools that were used by chiefs and placed in their graves.

The period of integration, between 500 C.E. to 1534, is characterized by the regional stratification of sociopolitical units, or confederacies (*confederaciones*). It also saw tremendous population growth, evidenced by clear signs of agricultural intensification. Specialized merchants and exchange trade networks, as well as the Inca conquest, also characterized this period (see INCAS). Evidence of these changes have been found at sites such as Manteño/Huancavilca, Atacames, Milagro/Quevedo, Capuli, Cuasmal-Tuza, Cosanga-Pillaro, Puruha, Cara, Paltas-Catamayo, and Napo.

Specialized merchants, or *mindaláes*, such as the Manteño, traded regional and luxury goods across great distances. Trade items included salt, dried fish, coca,

COTTON, thorn oyster shells, gold and copper ornaments, and fine TEXTILES. Some of these items were transported by sea, on large rafts made of logs; in this way, merchants took goods as far north as Mexico and down to Peru. Goods were also exchanged in local marketplaces, or *tiangueces*, located strategically between the highlands and lowlands. Local residents used hatchet-shaped copper as currency, which also has been found by archaeologists working in west Mexico and northern Peru.

These patterns were disrupted in the middle of the 15th century with the arrival of Inca forces from the south. Inca armies arrived in Ecuador around 1460, under the command of Prince Túpac Yupanqui, during the rule of the emperor PACHACUTI INCA YUPANQUI. Ecuadorean communities put up fierce resistance to the Inca's imperial campaigns; however, in the end, the Incas managed to subdue most of Ecuador. They accomplished this largely through alliances with local rulers, although they did have to militarily conquer Riobamba, Latacunga, Quito, Otavalo, and Caranqui, all important regions for the control of commercial activities and route trades between the highlands, the coast, and the Amazon. Following their arrival, the Incas built cities and administrative centers at places such as Tomebamba, Quito in the highlands, and Ingapirca in Hatun Cañar Province. It was in this sociopolitical environment that the Spanish conquistadores arrived in 1526 and founded the city of Quito in 1534.

See also ECUADOR (Vols. III, IV); GUAYAQUIL (Vols. II, III); NEW GRANADA, VICEROYALTY OF (Vol. II); QUITO (Vols. II, III).

—Diana Rocío Carvajal Contreras

Further reading:
J. S. and R. L. Burger. "Archaeology of Formative Ecuador: A Symposium at Dumbarton Oaks, 7 and 8 October 1995" (Washington, D.C.: Dumbarton Oaks Research Library & Collection, 2003).
Frank Salomon. *Native Lords of Quito in the Age of the Inca* (Cambridge: Cambridge University Press, 1986).

education

MESOAMERICA BEFORE 1492

What is known about educational practices in Mesoamerica during the Formative (1600 B.C.E.–200 C.E.) and Classic (200–850 C.E.) periods comes from the study of the social contexts in which writing systems and calendrical and astronomical calculations were employed and passed from one generation to another. More detailed ethnohistorical evidence regarding educational practices exists for the Postclassic period (850–1519), particularly in Mexica society (see AZTECS).

Perhaps the most specialized area of knowledge in Mesoamerica pertained to the calculation of calendrical cycles and their depiction in sculpture, pottery, and screenfold books, or CODICES. The divinatory calendar contained 260 days and was composed of two cycles: a progression of numbers (1–13) and a rotation of 20 day signs referring to animals, plants, and natural phenomena, with the names and depictions of these signs varying from region to region. Various Mesoamerican societies developed a highly formalized iconographic system to depict day signs, which continued to be used in sculptures and codices in the Postclassic period. Another time count was the 365-day year; the combined use of the 260-day and the 365-day cycles allowed for the unique designation of a specific day in a 52-year cycle. The MAYA also used a "Long Count," which placed dates within a cycle of 5,125.25 solar years. Given the expert knowledge involved in maintaining these cycles, relating them to social and astronomical phenomena, and divining potential outcomes on the basis of these data, only a small number of specialists and priests mastered the system. Although priests associated with major Classic-period ceremonial centers were in charge of orchestrating public ceremonies according to their calculations, there were also independent calendar specialists who tended to the needs of individual commoners.

Among the Maya, typically only members of the elite were trained as scribes, and the names and ranks of such individuals are known from some epigraphic texts that bear their creator's signature. It is also likely that Zapotec epigraphic texts were composed by elite scribes rather than by commoners (see ZAPOTECS). In the Postclassic period, there appears to have been a division of labor between a specialist who composed and painted pictographic texts on screenfold books—called a *tlacuilo* by the Nahuas—and the *amapohuani*, or specialist who recited these books' contents to an audience. Literacy seems to have been the province of members of noble lineages, who were selected by specialists to receive instruction in reading and writing. Nevertheless, the fact that the Aztec ruler Itzcóatl (r. 1427–40) ordered a public destruction of painted books suggests that literacy trickled down to some specialists regardless of their social status.

Most commoners were destined by birth to an informal education based primarily on the acquisition of knowledge necessary to practice subsistence AGRICULTURE, hunting, and animal husbandry on the one hand, and weaving, midwifery and cooking on the other; such a division of LABOR provided each gender with expertise in areas seen as complementary (see FAMILY; TEXTILES). Those who practiced a particular craft, such as stonecutters, masons, artisans, or fishermen, were expected to pass their knowledge on to their children, although some large urban centers, such as TEOTIHUACÁN in Central MEXICO, had workshops with master workers and large numbers of apprentices.

Due to the existence of detailed accounts compiled in the 16th century by the Franciscan BERNARDINO DE SAHAGÚN, more is known about Aztec education than any other such system in Mesoamerican society. Two verbs in

NAHUATL were used to convey the notion of "education": *huapahua*, meaning to "teach," "educate," and "render strong" or "firm," and *izcaltia*, meaning to "animate," "elevate," and "develop." Both terms signal that among the Aztecs, educational practices were seen as the long-term inculcation of pragmatic and moral precepts that reproduced collective values across all different sectors of society.

It is important to note that there was a major distinction between two Aztec educational institutions. The *calmecac* trained individuals to become *tlamacazqueh* (priests) or other religious specialists, while the *telpochcalli* prepared any able-bodied *telpochtli* (young man) for WARFARE (see RELIGION). Most of the youths who attended the *calmecac* were PIPILTIN, or nobles. The men and WOMEN who undertook this educational regime were required to do penance by bleeding themselves with thorns, to fast and to bathe only at precise intervals, and to commit to a life of celibacy.

If a young boy was offered by his parents to the *telpochcalli*, he would serve the community and become a warrior. Trainees began their career by sweeping and performing menial tasks; at age 15, they would be given heavy kindling loads to carry back to the community. Those who proved to have a "good heart" were called *tiachcauh*; those who were deemed judicious were called *telpochtlahto*, and they spoke for all of their peers. When a *telpochcalli* graduate became a warrior, he was awarded the title of *tlacateccatl*, *tlacochcalcatl*, or *cuauhtlahto* after he had captured four enemies in combat.

Aztec nobility was held to high moral standards; drunkenness, for example, was punishable by execution (see ALCOHOL; CRIME AND PUNISHMENT). Training in singing and lofty rhetoric was an integral part of an Aztec noble's education; some studied ceremonial singing at the Mixcoacalli (literally, "House of the Cloud Serpent") or at one of the various sites devoted to religious education in the Templo Mayor complex in the ceremonial center of the Mexica capital, TENOCHTITLÁN. An example of the broad range of oral performances that Aztec nobles and well-educated people were expected to master is found in the Huehuehtlahtolli, or "Words of the Elders." This collection of speeches to be given in specific contexts (for example, when greeting another noble or addressing a commoner audience) also includes oral performances for various life events, such as birth and marriage, regardless of social status. The transmission of knowledge in Mesoamerican societies sought to replicate an unchanging social order and tended to limit specialized knowledge—such as literacy and calendrical calculations—to a small group of individuals who were elite members or had strong ties to local elites.

SOUTH AMERICA BEFORE 1492

Because of a lack of written records, reliable evidence of educational opportunities in ancient South American civilizations is scarce. Pre-Columbian education systems in South America were largely informal. For those outside the royal classes, formal educational opportunities were largely nonexistent. What few educational opportunities existed were oriented toward specialized trades, such as weaving (see ACLLA), with women playing central roles. Despite the enormous gains made by South American civilizations over the millennia before the era of European contact and colonization, educational opportunities were typically limited to the verbal recounting of life experiences and wisdom passed from generation to generation; only the innermost cabal of a civilization's governing class may have enjoyed formal schooling. What formal educational opportunities that existed were restricted to Andean societies in the Inca Empire (see INCAS).

Given that formal education was inaccessible to commoners, knowledge was passed down to children from parents, community elders, and older siblings. For the children of the Inca nobility and provincial leaders, education took place in CUZCO over a four-year span. In their first year, students learned QUECHUA, the official language of Inca. In the second year, they were taught Inca religion. The third year focused on the use of the QUIPU, a specialized accounting system that involved representing values by tying knots into rope. The final year of study was dedicated to Inca history. Instruction was provided by the AMAUTA, or wise men, who ensured retention through a routine of practice, repetition, and application. Discipline was maintained by threats and beatings, limited to a single beating per day, administered by hitting the soles of the feet. Young women of the nobility were sometimes afforded specialized training, although this took place in the houses of elder noblewomen in Cuzco rather than in a formal school setting.

Outside of the nobility, the only group that had access to formal education was the adolescent women of conquered groups. The Incas selected girls around the age of 10 to train as "chosen women," or *aqllakuna*. These women were taken to provincial capitals where they studied several aspects of clothmaking, such as spinning and weaving, as well as brewing CHICHA and studying religion. The education module of *aqllakuna* was typically four years, after which they were taken to Cuzco and presented to the Inca king, who decided how they would be utilized.

See also BOOKS (Vol. II); EDUCATION (Vols. II, III, IV); UNIVERSITIES (Vol. II); UNIVERSITY OF MEXICO (Vol. II); UNIVERSITY OF SAN MARCOS (Vol. II).

—Sean H. Goforth
David Tavárez

Further reading:
Alfredo López Austin. *Educación mexica: Antología de documentos sahaguntinos* (México: UNAM, 1994).
Michael A. Malpass. *Daily Life in the Inca Empire* (Indianapolis, Ind.: Hackett, 2008).
Irene M. Silverblatt. *Moon, Sun, and Witches: Gender Ideologies and Class in Inca and Colonial Peru* (Princeton, N.J.: Princeton University Press, 1987).

El Dorado   The myth of El Dorado (a Spanish term meaning "the gilded one") has its origins in a Muisca tribal chief who, it was claimed, covered himself in GOLD dust and then bathed in a mountain lake, possibly Lake Guatavita, near modern BOGOTÁ. This practice was plausibly a part of a pre-Columbian Muisca ceremony; however, the original mythology quickly morphed into the rumor of the existence of a city of gold. Thus, the quest for El Dorado spurred numerous 16th-century Spanish expeditions throughout South America.

The story of El Dorado first caught the ear of the conquistador GONZALO JIMÉNEZ DE QUESADA, who led the first Spanish expedition into Muisca territory in COLOMBIA's eastern highlands. The story quickly traveled among Spanish conquistadores and, combined with other early contact rumors, produced a widely held belief that an El Dorado reigned over a kingdom of incalculable wealth. Unsatisfied with the riches found in Muisca territory, the Spanish misinterpretation of El Dorado was readapted literally, instigating searches for a city made of gold or replete with gold mines. In 1541, this myth spurred FRANCISCO DE ORELLANA and GONZALO PIZARRO to depart Quito and undertake an expedition of the AMAZON Basin in search of the mythic land. Instead, Orellena became the first European to navigate the length of the Amazon River. The 16th century featured a slew of other expeditions in search of El Dorado, most notably those by Philipp von Hutten (1541–45) and Sir Walter Raleigh (1595).

—Sean H. Goforth

Further reading:
John Hemming. *The Search for El Dorado* (London: Joseph, 1978).

El Mirador   The Late Preclassic MAYA site of El Mirador is located at 17.75° N latitude and 89.92° W longitude in GUATEMALA, four miles south of its northern border with MEXICO. El Mirador is one of the largest CITIES ever constructed by the Maya and contains enormous monumental ARCHITECTURE. Its rulers and 80,000 people dominated the region during its Late Preclassic prime (400 B.C.E.–100 C.E.). El Mirador succeeded its neighbor Nakbé, which had dominated the region in the Middle Preclassic. At the end of El Mirador's history, Maya power had shifted to the city of TIKAL.

El Mirador's urban plan included two major civic zones joined by a paved road (*sacbé*), which formed an east-west orientation 1.25 miles (2 km) long. El Tigre, a massive 215-foot (65.5-m) temple pyramid, protruded through the tall rain forest canopy in the Western Group. El Tigre faced eastward and consisted of multiple temples at various levels formed by basal platforms of stone rubble fill. El Tigre represents a Maya innovation—the triadic group—a layout with a large temple pyramid fronting a plaza and small flanking temple pyramids facing the plaza, with the whole arrangement organized in a C shape.

La Danta, the largest temple pyramid at El Mirador, is 230 feet (70 m) high. La Danta was supported by a 22-foot- (6.7-m-) high basal platform around a low hill,

View of La Danta pyramid at El Mirador, completely covered in vegetation *(Courtesy of J. Michael Francis)*

covering more than 950,000 square feet (88,258 m²) of terrain. Several small temple pyramids sit on the basal platform, including a small triadic group. Second- and third-level platforms rise another 90 feet (27.5 m), and the main triadic group of the Danta temple towers above all.

—Walter R. T. Witschey

El Salvador El Salvador is the smallest nation in Central America and the only one not to border the Atlantic Ocean. The development of present-day El Salvador was forged by indigenous groups that lived on the margins of Mesoamerica's most powerful civilizations, those of the AZTECS and the MAYA. Around 3000 B.C.E., the area of El Salvador was first occupied by Nahua Indians from MEXICO. These early peoples became known as the Nahua Pipil. The pre-Columbian history of El Salvador was dominated by the Pipil, though MIGRATION and outside influences, especially from the Maya, account for a few distinct native cultures and language systems that are often considered under the rubric of "Pipil." Pipil oral tradition emphasizes kinship with the Nahuas in Central Mexico, though scholars typically associate the history and culture of the Pipil also with the Maya, whose influence resulted from migration and CONQUEST. The Pipil enjoyed an AGRICULTURE-based ECONOMY and a social hierarchy similar to that of the Aztecs and Maya. Notably, the Pipil abolished HUMAN SACRIFICE early on in their society, a remarkable distinction from other groups in pre-Columbian Mesoamerica.

The character of Pipil culture was subsumed under the imposing control of the Maya in El Salvador for most of the first millennium C.E. Remains of limestone pyramids built by the Maya still adorn the countryside of western El Salvador. As Maya influence declined in the ninth century, the Pipil are believed to have organized their polity, known as Cuzcatlán, into two federal states, each divided into smaller principalities. The Pipil also constructed urban centers that remained populated into modernity, and some of which have become modern cities, such as Ahuachapán and Sonsonate. Sometime after 1000, another wave of migration brought a people known as the Izalco Pipil to the region from lands west of the Lampa River. Archaeological research and folklore suggest that these peoples were refugees from the Toltec Empire and had Toltec and Nahua ethnic roots (see TOLTECS). They also experienced significant Central Mexico influences and spoke NAHUATL.

The Pipil, with their various influences, accounted for most human settlement in El Salvador prior to the arrival of the Spanish. In 1524, PEDRO DE ALVARADO was dispatched from MEXICO CITY by HERNANDO CORTÉS to extirpate indigenous resistance south of Mexico. Alvarado was initially stymied by fierce Pipil resistance, led by a leader called Atlacatl. Alvarado was forced to retreat to GUATEMALA from El Salvador. After successive attempts

in 1525 and 1528, Alvarado finally subjugated the Pipil. The Spanish were disappointed to find that El Salvador harbored few precious metals.

See also EL SALVADOR (Vols. II, III, IV).

—Sean H. Goforth

Further reading:
John Bierhorst. *The Mythology of Mexico and Central America* (New York: William Morrow, 1990).

emeralds The term *emerald* is derived from a Persian word that appeared in Greek as *smaragdos*, meaning "green stone." Emeralds are found at only a few localities around the world and have long been valued by royalty and the wealthy because of their rarity and beauty. The only known source of the stones in the Americas before the arrival of Europeans was COLOMBIA. After the CONQUEST, however, other sources were discovered in BRAZIL and North Carolina. Sources were also reported to have existed in eastern ECUADOR, GUATEMALA, and PERU but are as yet unconfirmed.

Beryls, a compound of aluminum beryllium silicate, or $Al_2Be_3(Si_6O_{18})$, come in various colors, but emerald green ones are considered the most valuable. In emeralds, replacement of beryllium by alkali oxides and aluminum by chromic or ferric oxides is common. The emeralds' distinctive green color is caused by trace amounts of chromium or vanadium. Emeralds are often clouded by inclusions (known as *jardin*) and show an irregular color distribution. Characteristics of emeralds, including color, transparency, inclusions, trace elements, specific gravity, refractive index, appearance through filters, and fluorescence under ultraviolet light, vary depending on source. These traits allow identification of the source through microscopic, physical, chemical, or nuclear analysis.

Most emeralds occur in metamorphic rocks as a by-product of the environment that created the rocks, but Colombian deposits based on hydrothermal processes are unique in the world. Colombian shales at Muzo and Chivor were being mined by the MUISCA Indians earlier than 1000 C.E. Secondary deposits resulting from weathering or other decomposition of emerald-bearing matrix occasionally produce emeralds, but such deposits are rare. One is located at Ganchalá, Colombia.

During the pre-Columbian period, Colombian emeralds were traded as far south as BOLIVIA and as far north as MEXICO. Traders could have carried small emeralds from Colombia on foot or by boat along the Pacific coast with relative ease; alternatively, stones could have been passed from hand to hand through elite exchange. Polished emeralds used in jewelry have been found in graves at Sitio Conte, PANAMA, and date back to 700–900 C.E.

Emeralds and other beryls are the hardest naturally occurring substances in the Americas; therefore, evidence of worked emeralds is very rare for the period before the arrival of Europeans, who introduced hard metal tools. Polishing and carving could only have been accomplished through friction from beryl grit adhering to cords, reeds, or hides and laboriously rubbed against the stone's surface. One emerald of uncertain origin carved into the shape of a man (part of the Hudson Museum collection at the University of Maine) resembles stone figures produced in Guerrero, Mexico, between 900 and 600 B.C.E. Besides its overall shape, the stone is marked by straight cuts and conical drill holes.

Only one other description exists of what seems to have been a pre-Columbian carved emerald. During the period of CONQUEST, both FRANCISCO PIZARRO and HERNANDO CORTÉS sent emeralds to the Spanish Court. Cortés obtained most of his emeralds from the Aztec capital of TENOCHTITLÁN, but at least one came from the Hall of Justice in Texcoco. This emerald was reported to have the shape of a pyramid and to be as broad as the palm of the hand. The accuracy of the description cannot be verified because the object disappeared while en route to Spain.

—Stephen L. Whittington

Further reading:

J. Michael Francis. *Invading Colombia: Spanish Accounts of the Gonzalo Jiménez de Quesada Expedition of Conquest* (University Park: Pennsylvania State University Press, 2007).

encomienda   This term for an important institution of colonial Spanish America comes from the Spanish verb *encomendar*, meaning "to entrust." What was entrusted by governmental or royal officials to a recipient (usually a Spanish male) were the LABOR and tribute of an indigenous group. In exchange, each *encomendero* (holder of an *encomienda* grant) was supposed to provide protection and religious instruction to the Indians of his *encomienda* (see RELIGION). Fundamentally, an *encomienda* grant was the reward Spaniards expected for risking their lives and investing their own resources (weapons, horses, capital) in the various campaigns of CONQUEST and colonization. These expectations were not new; rather, they were based on previous experiences during the lengthy reconquest of Spain from the Moors (Reconquista). CHRISTOPHER COLUMBUS learned too late that the deep-seated anticipation of such prizes was a powerful force. Spaniards nominally under his command in HISPANIOLA soon turned away from the TRADE-oriented enterprises he favored, flouting his authority in order to operate within their own Reconquista traditions.

American realities both fulfilled and confounded Spanish ambitions. The most profitable *encomiendas* tended to be those in the two main conquest areas of MEXICO and PERU. Generally speaking, the grants in these areas were established faster, were larger, and included the delivery of both workers and goods. One of the main reasons they got such a quick start is that they were based on portioning out already-existing communities of peoples who lived much like Europeans. The numerous so-called imperial peoples of these two regions were already accustomed to the consequences of victory and defeat in ways that meshed with the *encomienda* system, so obligations to *encomenderos* were not entirely unexpected burdens. Thus, the TLATOANI of an ALTEPETL in the former Aztec Empire was prepared to channel labor and tribute to the new overlords just as he had previously to indigenous ones.

Both the *encomiendas* of Mexico and Peru benefited from a native rotary labor draft: the MITA (from the term for "turn") in the QUECHUA-speaking Andean region, and the *coatequitl* ("turn-work") in NAHUATL-speaking Mesoamerica. Nonetheless, Peruvian *encomenderos* enjoyed an initial advantage over their Mexican counterparts. Andean peoples had already developed highly effective techniques for MINING and refining SILVER (sometimes superior to imported European technologies), so *encomienda* labor could be more readily put into procuring this vital lubricant of international commerce.

Encomiendas tended to be less viable and valuable in regions where the peoples and natural resources were less like those of Mexico and Peru. Least amenable to Spanish demands were small groups of nomadic peoples who were unaccustomed to providing tribute and labor.

The *encomienda*'s fate varied within the vast reaches of Spanish America. A key variable was the sheer number of those demanding a share of indigenous labor. Where such claimants were fewer, *encomiendas* sometimes lasted until the end of the colonial period, but in regions where they were many and increasing, the colonial *encomienda* eventually gave way to other forms of labor procurement.

See also ENCOMIENDA (Vol. II); REPARTO (Vol. II).

—Barry D. Sell

Further reading:

Robert Himmerich y Valencia. *The Encomenderos of New Spain, 1521–1555* (Austin: University of Texas Press, 1991).

James Lockhart. "Encomienda and Hacienda: The Evolution of the Great Estate in the Spanish Indies." In *Of Things of the Indies: Essays Old and New in Early Latin American History*, 1–26 (Stanford, Calif.: Stanford University Press, 1999).

family Distinct patterns and values from both sides of the Atlantic informed family life in Latin America. Prior to European contact, the relative hierarchy of a given civilization in Mesoamerica or South America correlated to family structure. The definition of family therefore varied according to location. In Iberia, family laws and customs arose from centuries of overlapping Christian and Muslim influence, and family models and norms in Latin America changed dramatically after 1492 when Iberian and Amerindian traditions merged.

MESOAMERICA BEFORE 1492

In Mesoamerica and imperial Aztec society, families lived in organizational units known as *calpullis* (see AZTECS). Originally, these were based solely on kinship ties, though by the 15th century, the *calpulli* was more diverse in its makeup; it was a multigenerational grouping that shared communal land, worshipped together, and paid tribute collectively. Marriage was a crucial step in Aztec society, as it formally marked the transition to adulthood. Young men and WOMEN married between their late teens and early 20s. The ceremony began with a four-day period when both man and woman fasted and restrained from bathing. The fourth night saw physical consummation of the union followed the next day by a private ritual bathing and public wedding banquet. The new couple brought its productive and reproductive LABOR to the *calpulli*. In Aztec society, when a man and woman married, their union was primarily between two families (not between the couple and the church, as it would be in the colonial era).

The Aztec *calpulli* had an overarching family structure with both matrilineal and patrilineal descent. Aztec inheritance practices, for instance, were bilateral and could pass from mother to daughter as well as from father to son. Power in society could follow either female or male bloodlines, though it tended to follow the male. At marriage, a woman might join the *calpulli* of her husband or he might join that of her family. Scholars have suggested that this flexibility allowed men to take advantage of the family lines (blood or marriage) that best furthered their political goals.

This was particularly true for the elite in Aztec society, whose marriages stood apart from those of commoners (see *MACEHUAL; PIPILTIN*). For elite individuals, marriage often promoted political alliances between different regions, similar to marriage among European royalty to promote dynasties. Elite Aztec males and high-ranking imperial officers could take more than one wife. This helped to increase the size of a household and added labor power that could ultimately increase the family's wealth. While polygamy was common through much of the pre-Columbian Americas, it usually occurred only among the ruling class.

The relationship of sexuality and virginity to marriage differed in pre-Columbian societies from the Iberian world. In Aztec culture, sex was viewed as pleasurable activity rather than a sinful one, and those who engaged in sexual relations before marriage did not carry a stigma. Chastity as a value was emphasized mainly for the daughters of the elite. For married couples, however, sexual monogamy was the cultural norm, and adultery was severely punished (see CRIME AND PUNISHMENT). Overall, the institution of marriage was more flexible for the Aztecs than it was for Spaniards. For instance, if a couple reached an impasse in their relationship, they were permitted to

(continues on page 142)

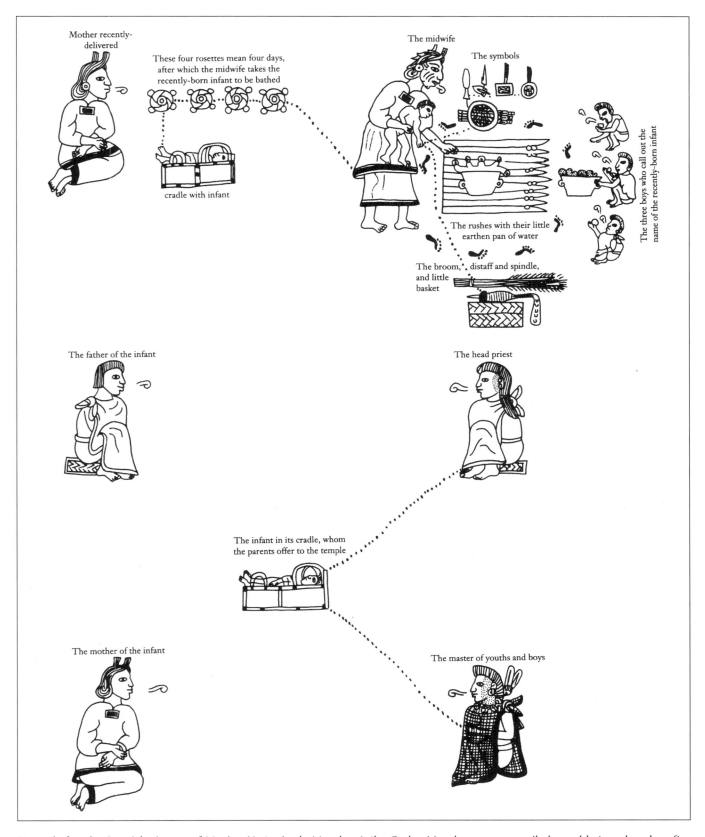

Named after the Spanish viceroy of Mexico (Antonio de Mendoza), the Codex Mendoza was compiled roughly two decades after the conquest of the Aztec Empire. The information contained in this remarkable work was gathered from Indian scribes and interpreters who had firsthand knowledge of the Aztec Empire before the arrival of Europeans. The image above and the four that follow illustrate some manners and customs in Aztec family life, from birth through childhood and marriage. The illustration above relates the customs associated with birth. *(Codex Mendoza, Courtesy of Frances F. Berdan and Patricia Reiff Anawalt)*

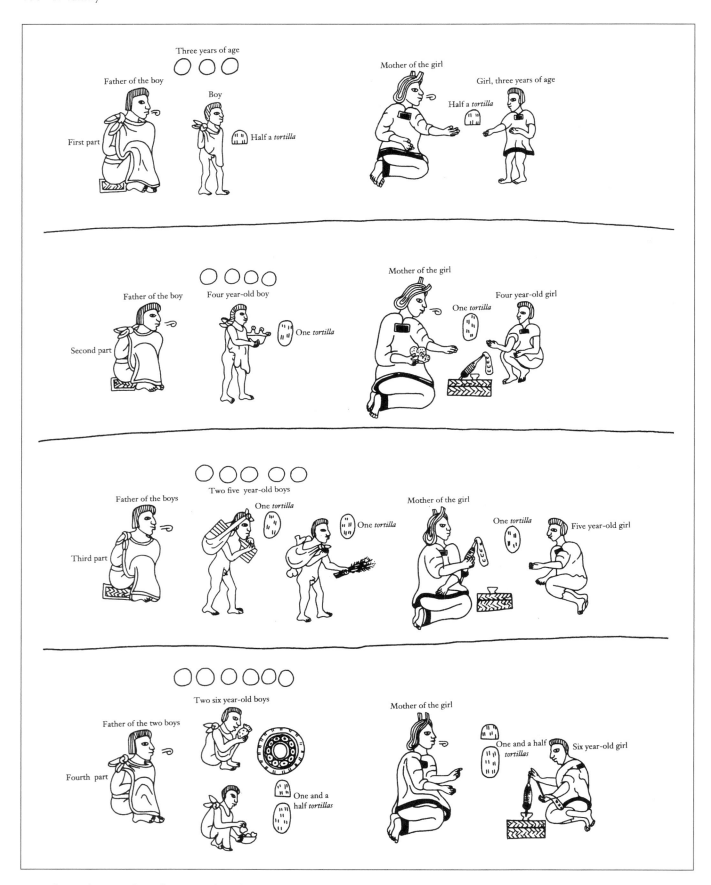

Here, the Codex Mendoza illustrates the education of young Aztec boys and girls between the ages of three and six, as well as their tasks and food rations. *(Codex Mendoza, Courtesy of Frances F. Berdan and Patricia Reiff Anawalt)*

These seven blue dots signify seven years.

Father of the children shown in this row

1st part

One and a half *tortillas*

A 7-year old boy is being taught by his father how to fish with the net he holds in his hands.

Mother of the children shown in this row

One and a half *tortillas*

A 7-year old girl is being taught how to spin by her mother

These eight dots signify eight years.

Father of the children shown in this row

2nd part

One and a half *tortillas*

Maguey spikes

An 8-year old boy is being warned by his father not to be deceitful, or he will be punished by being pierced in the body with maguey spikes.

Mother of the children shown in this row

One and a half *tortillas*

Maguey spikes

An 8-year old girl is threatened by her mother with maguey spikes, not to be deceitful.

These nine dots signify nine years.

Father of the children shown in this row

One and a half *tortillas*

3rd part

A 9-year old boy is pierced in his body with maguey spikes by his father, for being incorrigible.

One and a half *tortillas*

Mother of the children shown in this row

A 9-year old girl is punished for negligence and idleness by her mother, by piercing her hand with a maguey spike.

These ten dots signify ten years.

Father of the children shown in this row

A 10-year old boy is being punished by his father with a stick.

4th part[1]

Mother of the children shown in this row

A 10-year old girl is being punished with a beating, by her mother.

The drawings above include additional tasks for young boys and girls as well as the punishments they received for being negligent or disobedient. (*Codex Mendoza, Courtesy of Frances F. Berdan and Patricia Reiff Anawalt*)

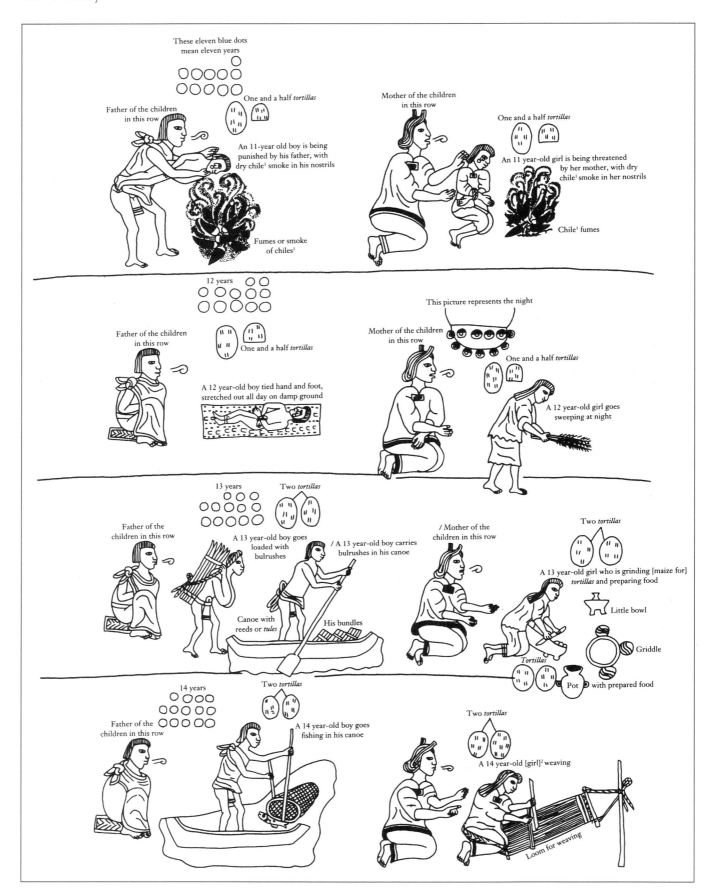

More punishments and tasks for boys and girls aged 11 to 14 (*Codex Mendoza, Courtesy of Frances F. Berdan and Patricia Reiff Anawalt*)

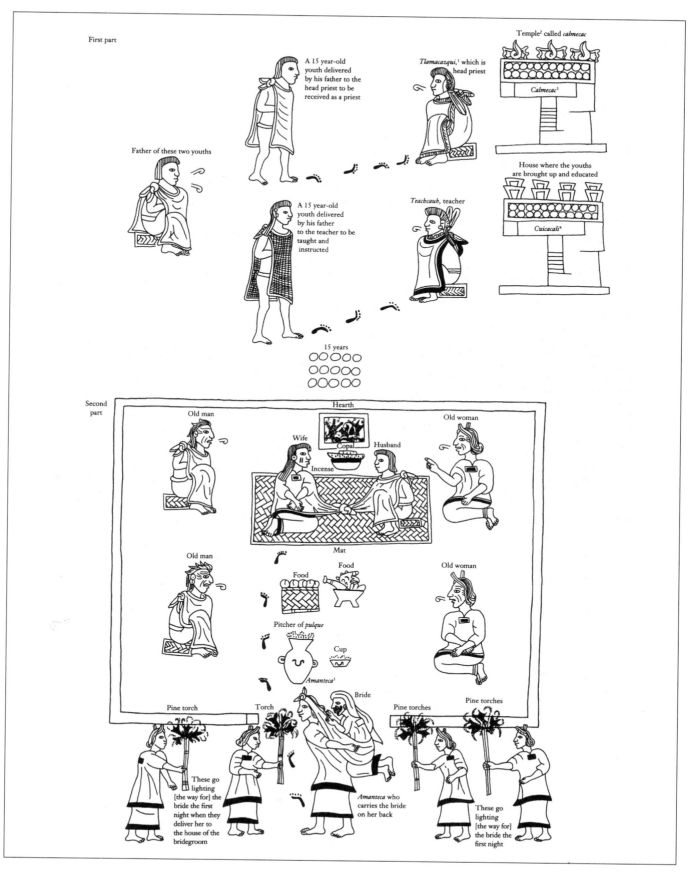

At the top, young adolescent boys enter one of two houses (the *calmecac* or the *cuicacali*) for formal education. Below is an illustration of a wedding ceremony. *(Codex Mendoza, Courtesy of Frances F. Berdan and Patricia Reiff Anawalt)*

(continued from page 136)

separate and could remarry if they so chose. Moreover, in some rural areas of the Aztec Empire, men and women lived together as man and wife after a betrothal but before a formal marriage ceremony. This practice, known as *montequitl*, was a kind of trial marriage.

To understand how families lived and related to one another, they must be examined in the context of labor and political structures in their respective societies. In many pre-Columbian societies, men's and women's work roles were complementary. Households depended on men and women, as well as members of several generations, in order to undertake the tasks necessary for survival, accumulate surplus materials, and reproduce. The Aztecs lived in a world of gender complementarity. Women's roles were respected, and women functioned in positions of power within the marketplace and the *calpulli*. While not fully egalitarian, the celebration of both female and male roles was very different from European culture of the same era. Some scholars have argued that gender hierarchy increased in Aztec society as the empire expanded during the late 15th century. Thus, at the height of Aztec power, women lost some of their status to men.

Other societies in Mesoamerica showed distinct patterns with regard to family. The MAYA civilization, which reached its height long before the Aztecs rose to prominence, had a more hierarchical society and emphasized male power over gender complementarity. Kin groupings among the Maya were based solely on patrilineal descent. The Nudzahui (MIXTECS) of Oaxaca, on the other hand, exhibited far more gender egalitarianism than the Aztecs did. They accorded power to women among the ruling group and female succession, and while this was not the norm, it did occur frequently.

SOUTH AMERICA BEFORE 1492

In pre-Columbian South America, scholars know most about family life in the Andes, and particularly in the Inca Empire, which was at its height when Spanish conquistadores arrived on the continent (see INCAS). Andean society was based on the kinship unit called the AYLLU. All members of an *ayllu* could trace their ancestry back to the same couple. Members of the same *ayllu* tended to marry each other, a practice known as endogamy. Like the Mesoamerican *calpulli*, the *ayllu* functioned as a way to structure labor, foster community, and reproduce. Men had access to *ayllu* resources such as land or herds through descent from their fathers. Women, likewise, had access to *ayllu* resources through their mothers.

In Andean cosmology, the relationship of male to female was complementary, and Andean society, be it in rulership, labor roles, or community structure, reflected that complementarity. Andean deities had clear gender identities and distinct domains. The female deity Pachamama, the earth goddess, needed male deities such as Illapa, the god of thunder and lightning, so that the earth and rain could together produce crops. Men's and women's daily roles in Andean life were held in similar balance; only by working together could men and women survive and flourish.

Children learned these gender-specific and complementary roles from birth. Spanish CHRONICLERS report that Andean boys and girls began to help their parents with light work at the age of five. Until the age of nine, though, play was the dominant aspect of children's lives. Through 12 years of age, girls practiced weaving, and boys hunted small game or watched over herds. When boys turned 18, they had to pay half-tribute to the Inca. Young women had increased duties. At 20, men owed full tribute. It was assumed that one would marry and become an adult in the community about this age, and so complementary were male and female roles that without the support of a woman, a man was unlikely to be able to meet his daily needs and pay full tribute.

Marriage was common in Andean society. In the marriage ceremony, the man and woman came together as different but equal beings; through speeches and ritual gift exchange, the couple acknowledged that both must play a role to ensure the proper functioning of their household. Within the *ayllu*, men plowed fields, herded animals, and fought. Women wove and made CLOTHING for their families, cooked, brewed, farmed, and raised children. The labor of each was a contribution not to the family per se but to the *ayllu*.

The Andean path to marriage could involve a form of trial marriage known as *sirvanacuy*, whereby a young man and woman lived together prior to a formal marriage ceremony. Typically, the couple would live in the household of the young man. This trial marriage allowed the couple, as well as their respective in-laws, to determine if the union was suitable. Should the couple decide to separate rather than marry, no formal mark of shame followed either. If the couple had children, those children were accepted into society without the mark of illegitimacy. Once a couple did marry through a formal ritual, it was expected that they would remain monogamous. Adultery was not tolerated within the *ayllu*. If a married couple chose to separate, the woman could move home to her family, but there was no formal divorce.

In regions outside of the Inca Empire, family life was marked by patrilineal kinship and prescribed gender roles. For the TUPINAMBÁ peoples, a seminomadic, forest-dwelling group in BRAZIL, leadership was a male preserve. The Tupinambá lived in settlements of 400 to 800 people, which were further divided into multifamily units. Gender and age determined daily activities. Women dominated agricultural life, growing mainly MANIOC and COTTON (see AGRICULTURE). Men cleared fields by taking down large trees and hunted and engaged in WARFARE. Marriage was a fundamental part of Tupí society; it could be polygamous and often tied kin further together.

EARLY COLONIAL LATIN AMERICA

After the conquest, family makeup and practices in the Americas changed. First and foremost, the DISEASES that came with the Europeans devastated indigenous populations, dramatically altering their way of life. Second, while relationships between indigenous (primarily women) and Spaniards (primarily men) cemented political alliances, they further challenged indigenous family structures as the power balance shifted to Spanish control. Third, Spanish society, through the laws of the Crown, the evangelization campaign of the CATHOLIC CHURCH, and Spanish cultural practices emphasized different values for family life and sexuality.

The demographic decline in the Americas after 1492 profoundly affected indigenous family life. As families shrank in number, there were fewer hands to respond to the demands of the Spanish rulers. In addition to death by disease, the forces fighting the Spanish were primarily male, so the death rate among young men increased also through war. When groups became too small to support themselves, they had to expand by adopting kin from outside. The movement of native men in this era—primarily to escape forced LABOR—also influenced family patterns by creating a gender imbalance at home. Many of these "outsiders," known in the Andes as *FORASTEROS*, had married into communities by the second and third generation of the colonial era. Ultimately, the increased death rate meant that families had difficulty transferring political power smoothly from one generation to the next, and their kinship ties were stretched thin. Families adapted creatively to these challenges; nonetheless, change in indigenous family structures was inevitable.

Over time, the Spanish influenced centuries-old Amerindian concepts of family, as well as norms and morals. In particular, scholars note that concepts of honor and shame associated with the Iberian Catholic tradition were transferred to indigenous groups. Long-held Aztec ideas about sex as both necessary and pleasurable were challenged by the Europeans' equation of sexual activity with sin. Likewise, Andean ideas about trial marriage were incompatible with the European emphasis on maintaining sexual purity until marriage in the case of young women. While this emphasis had something in common with the Aztec nobility's emphasis on chastity for its daughters, for indigenous society at large, the value associated with the loss of virginity marked a dramatic change for young women.

The power associated with mothers and grandmothers changed under Spanish rule. Whereas Inca and Aztec mothers had political and legal power alongside that of men, Spanish women had less recourse. Through the concept of *patria potestad*, the legal control of all members of a household rested with the father. Women did not have legal control over themselves or their children, making all members of a household, except the father, legal minors. Indigenous parents may have attempted to work within Spanish legal structures to continue traditional inheritance practices for several generations.

The conquest of Latin America also promoted new kinds of "family" structures hewn from pre-Columbian and Iberian traditions. Spaniards joined in sexual union with native women, and the idea that such unions could foster political relationships in HISPANIOLA, and later in MEXICO and PERU, was shared by indigenous as well as European men. Furthermore, as marriage had been fundamental in promoting political alliances in pre-Columbian society, the Spanish Crown passed a decree in 1514 that allowed the marriage of Spanish men and indigenous women. The Crown hoped that such marriages would help cement military alliances with native chieftains and quiet church critics who abhorred cohabitation. The law legitimated what was already occurring in practice. In Mexico, for instance, the king of the TLAXCALA gave numerous princesses to Spanish conquistadores, including HERNANDO CORTÉS. The Tlaxcalans, allies to Cortés and his small band of soldiers in 1519 through 1521, were eager to strengthen their political ties through a new generation born of these women. The Spanish men, however, for the most part took the princesses as concubines while waiting to take Spanish wives. This also occurred in the Andes.

While the norm was out-of-wedlock Spanish-indigenous unions, marriages did occur. Most commonly it was Spanish men who married indigenous women; there are very few documented cases of Spanish women marrying indigenous men. Catholic marriage was more common between elite native women and Spaniards because only marriage could ensure legal access to property. When a Spaniard contracted marriage with a native woman, the main motivation was not love but the acquisition of the lands and laborers tied to her family. In the Andes, Alonso de Mesa married the Inca noblewoman Catalina Huaco Ocllo in 1552. The daughters of Aztec king MONTEZUMA, Isabel and Leonor, also married Spanish men.

Whether in marriage or cohabitation, Spanish and indigenous unions produced a new generation of Latin American children. Known as mestizos, the first generation was accepted into Spanish society (see *MESTIZAJE/ MESTIZO*). Many mestizo children were taken from indigenous mothers to the households of their fathers in the Americas or sent to Spain to be raised by Spanish aunts and uncles. By the late 16th century, mixed-race children formed an increasing sector of the population and became less socially accepted. For those born out of wedlock, the status of illegitimacy carried significant legal implications: They could not receive inheritances, obtain an EDUCATION, or enjoy honorable social standing.

The importation of African slaves, a practice that picked up tempo in the late 16th century, had important implications for family (see SLAVERY). The Atlantic slave trade destroyed many traditional African family norms, especially the role of parents in choosing a marriage partner and the practice of bride wealth, the custom of the transfer of valuable property from the family of the groom to the family of the bride, most common among agricultural societies in Africa. African men and women struggled to create new kin networks in the Americas. They did so in the face of generally high child mortality and the inhumane practice of separating children from their mothers. Still, slaves used legal devices to gain the right to marry as well as the chance to remain in proximity to their spouses, rather than being sold away to new owners. They accumulated cash to buy freedom for their children. Thus, even within the institution of slavery, family ties emerged as a critical nexus of resistance.

Even for those who held the most political, social, and economic power in colonial Latin America, the conquest challenged family relationships. The disruption of marriage and domestic life by transatlantic travel had an important influence on the lives of women and children back in Spain. "Abandoned" wives often filed petitions with the king of Spain seeking to know the whereabouts of their husbands and to make them responsible for their financial obligations to the family. To this end, the Crown issued a decree in 1528 declaring that married men who resided in the Indies without their wives must either return to Spain or make arrangements to have their wives travel from Spain to the Americas. This decree did result in the reunification of some families, but many more remained separated by the events of conquest. Thus, women and children were left to forge ahead alone in a society where men's power and honor were paramount in the family structure.

The family unit was critical in restructuring society in the Americas after the arrival of Europeans. The larger and more hierarchical the society in terms of class or race, the more differentiation existed in terms of family groupings and the values attached to marriage and sexuality. Throughout the long period of transition, gender was a major indicator of family roles and responsibilities.

See also BIENES DE DIFUNTOS (Vol. II); FAMILY (Vols. II, III, IV); GODPARENTAGE (Vol. II); GRACIAS AL SACAR, CÉDULAS DE (Vol. II); LIMPIEZA DE SANGRE (Vol. II); SEXUALITY (Vol. III).

—Jane Mangan

Further reading:
Ondina E. González and Bianca Premo, eds. *Raising an Empire: Children in Early Modern Iberia and Colonial Latin America* (Albuquerque: University of New Mexico Press, 2007).
Susan Kellogg. *Weaving the Past: A History of Latin America's Indigenous Women from the Prehispanic Period to the Present* (New York: Oxford University Press, 2005).
Karen Viera Powers. *Women in the Crucible of Conquest: The Gendered Genesis of Spanish American Society, 1500–1600* (Albuquerque: University of New Mexico Press, 2005).
María Rostworowski de Diez Canseco. *History of the Inca Realm*, translated by Harry B. Iceland (New York: Cambridge University Press, 1999).

Federmann, Nikolaus (b. ca. 1505–d. 1542) *German conquistador, governor of Venezuela, and cofounder of Bogotá* Born in Ulm, Germany, Nikolaus Federmann was an official of Welser, a German banking firm that had been granted the governance of VENEZUELA in 1529. Serving under Ambrosius Alfinguer in the city of Coro on the northern coast of Venezuela, Federmann took command of the province of Venezuela while Alfinguer recovered from wounds received during an expedition to the interior. Acting against Alfinguer's orders, Federmann led 116 men south in search of a body of water that would lead to the Pacific Ocean, which Europeans at the time called the South Sea. Federmann and his men traveled more than 100 miles (160 km) south to the Llanos region of Venezuela before turning back, having failed to find access to the Pacific. Federmann returned to Coro. On his arrival, Alfinguer had him removed from Venezuela.

Federmann returned to Ulm, where he wrote a monograph about the different indigenous groups he had encountered. In 1533, Federmann learned that Alfinguer had died in Venezuela. He immediately approached the Welser company to return to Venezuela. Although initially named as governor of Venezuela, legal issues surrounding Federmann's earlier expulsion forced the Crown to name Georg von Speyer to that position instead. Federmann, serving as lieutenant governor, returned to Venezuela in 1535.

Federmann spent much of his first year arguing with local officials. With new restraints on Welser's power and with new demands made of him, Federmann found little political support in Coro. In 1536, against the instructions of Governor von Speyer, Federmann and a collection of men traveled southwest from Coro in search of the rich kingdom of EL DORADO. Losing men to hostile native groups, wild animals, and DISEASES, Federmann eventually made his way to COLOMBIA's eastern highlands, where he encountered another expeditionary force, led by GONZALO JIMÉNEZ DE QUESADA. With 160 men, Federmann began to settle the area around BOGOTÁ, where Jiménez de Quesada's men had arrived two years earlier. In an effort to secure his rights to the new region, Federmann returned to Spain in 1539 to present his claims. Federmann defended himself against the Welser firm, who charged him with withholding taxes and acting disloyally toward the Crown. Federmann solved the legal problems by relinquishing his territorial claims in the New World. He never returned to either Ulm or Venezuela and died in Valladolid, Spain, in 1542.

—Spencer Tyce

Further reading:
José Ignacio Avellaneda. *The Conquerors of the New Kingdom of Granada* (Albuquerque: University of New Mexico Press, 1995).

fleets/fleet system To protect and regulate their trade with their American colonies, first Spain and then Portugal organized their commercial shipping into fleets (*flotas*). These armed convoys guarded the traffic from foreign enemies but also hindered the development of intra-imperial trade.

Once Queen Isabella and her adviser Jorge Rodríguez de Fonseca forsook their plan to make commerce with the colonies a Crown monopoly, Rodríguez began to create the policies and institutions to oversee commercial activities. In 1503, Isabella established the Casa de Contratación (Board of Trade). Headquartered in Seville until 1717, it oversaw Spain's transatlantic shipping, registered goods and people going to and from the New World, trained pilots and navigators, and acted as a law court for crimes committed at sea and for maritime suits.

The Casa de Contratación regulated TRADE but increasingly had to deal with attacks on the ships by French pirates and privateers and to a lesser extent by Muslims. French corsairs plundered the Aztec treasure sent by Hernando Cortés to Charles I. By 1526, the king had ordered the Casa de Contratación and the Council of the Indies to require that ships no longer sail singly, but in twos or threes to better protect themselves (see PIRATES AND PIRACY). This failed to provide sufficient security, however, and in the 1540s, the Crown ordered that all merchant vessels sail to and from the Americas in large fleets. Heavily armed naval vessels accompanied each fleet.

By the 1560s, the fleet system had reached its maturity. Each year, two fleets sailed to the Spanish New World loaded with merchandise to sell to the colonists and returned with American treasure. The government collected the *avería*, or fleet tax, to pay for the armed escort. After its cargo and passengers had been registered by the Casa de Contratación, the *flota* departed in the spring from Seville, although as the years passed and larger ships made transitting the Guadalquivir between Seville and the ocean more difficult, many fleets left from Cádiz or Sanlúcar on the coast.

The *capitana*, a naval vessel commanded by the head of the flotilla, sailed at the head of the convoy, while the *almiranta*, another naval ship, sailed at the rear. Many of the merchants on board the ships were also well armed. The *flota* proceeded first to the Canary Islands and then navigated westward to the Caribbean. Some merchant vessels stopped in PUERTO RICO, HISPANIOLA, and HONDURAS, but most continued to Veracruz on the Mexican coast. The transatlantic transit generally took about two months. On arrival at Veracruz, the *flota* held a great fair at the nearby inland town of Jalapa, with merchants from MEXICO CITY arriving to buy goods.

The other convoy, destined for northern South America and PANAMA, was called the *galeones*. It set sail from Seville in August or September, putting in at Cartagena to trade and to send word to the Peruvian VICEROY in LIMA of its arrival. PERU's viceroy then sent a Pacific fleet (often called the *armada del sur*, or "southern armada") to Panama, carrying the Crown's revenues and merchants' SILVER. Lima's merchants bought goods in Panama from the *galeones* to sell throughout the viceroyalty. They then loaded them on

Modern view of the Guadalquivir River in Seville, Spain, with the Torre de Oro in the foreground *(Courtesy of J. Michael Francis)*

pack trains and hauled them over the isthmus, where they were embarked on the Pacific fleet (see TRANSPORTATION). The *armada del sur* had a difficult task in coordinating its arrival in Panama with that of the *galeones*. If the armada arrived long after the *galeones*, the European merchandise might decay in the tropical climate or be plundered by marauding buccaneers. On the other hand, if the armada reached Panama too early, the treasure they carried was exposed to pirates and was idle capital that might have been invested more profitably in another enterprise.

The *flota* and *galeones* usually gathered at Havana on the north coast of CUBA and sailed back to Spain together, starting out late in the year, once the hurricane season was over. The return trip was the most dangerous part of the voyage because enemies knew the vessels were laden with GOLD and silver. They preyed on vessels that became separated from the main fleet. Nevertheless, while some ships were lost to storms and others to corsairs, the fleet system generally succeeded in protecting the transatlantic trade in the 16th century. Only in 1628 did a Dutch squadron commanded by Piet Heyn capture the entire treasure fleet.

The Spanish fleet system also included a transpacific component, the Manila galleons. It began in the 1560s as a means of carrying mail, silver, and officials to Spain's outpost in the Philippines and made the return trip carrying a cargo of East Asian silks, spices, and other luxury goods. The Manila galleons sailed westward from Acapulco on the coast of MEXICO to Guam and then to the Philippines. From Manila, they had access to Chinese merchants. The return voyage followed favorable currents across the north Pacific to California and then southward to Acapulco. Spain tried to limit such shipping to one or two vessels per year to prevent American silver from leaking out of the empire, and the government prohibited Peruvian merchants from trading directly with China; nevertheless, there was probably a good deal of contraband trade.

The Portuguese did not develop a similar system to regulate and protect shipping to BRAZIL until the mid-1600s. Portuguese caravels plying the transatlantic waters tended to be small and set sail from a number of Lusitanian and Brazilian ports. The Portuguese Crown showed little inclination to centralize the commerce in the 16th century, and consequently merchantmen had to protect themselves against corsairs and privateers. Only in 1649 did Portugal create the Companhia Geral de Comércio (General Company of Commerce) to oversee and protect two annual fleets to Brazil.

Although the fleet system protected Spanish shipping, it hindered commercial development. It impeded the free flow of goods, favoring instead the interests of merchant guilds (*consulados*) in Seville, LIMA, and MEXICO CITY. With the decline of its maritime power in the 17th century, Spain could no longer send annual convoys, and often two or three years passed between the arrival of the *flota* or *galeones*. In the colonies, this created severe shortages of merchandise and huge fluctuations in the price of goods. These conditions, in turn, enticed the colonists to trade with Spain's rivals, such as French, Dutch, and English merchants who were drawn to Spanish waters with the aim of securing American gold and silver.

See also FLEETS/FLEET SYSTEM (Vol. II); MANILA GALLEONS (Vol. II); SHIPBUILDING (Vol. II).

—Kendall Brown

Further reading:
Clarence Haring. *Trade and Navigation between Spain and the Indies in the Time of the Hapsburgs* (Cambridge, Mass.: Harvard University Press, 1918).
Lyle N. McAlister. *Spain and Portugal in the New World, 1492–1700* (Minneapolis: University of Minnesota Press, 1984).

Florentine Codex This monumental work in NAHUATL and Spanish was completed under the direction of the famed Franciscan friar BERNARDINO DE SAHAGÚN. It is bound in three volumes, which are divided into 12 parts called "books." The Florentine Codex (see CODICES) currently rests in the Laurentian Library in Florence, Italy, having arrived there no later than 1588. Almost certainly, this remarkable codex was a present from the king of Spain to a leading member of the Medici family, Cardinal Ferdinando, who had a keen interest in rare and exotic manuscripts. Don Luis de Velasco delivered this gem of Nahuatl scholarship. Velasco was the son and namesake of an earlier VICEROY of New Spain and later followed in his father's footsteps and served in the same capacity.

The aura of prestige and importance implied by its donor, recipient, and bearer are justified by its contents. Sahagún conceived of it as something akin to an encyclopedic history of traditional Nahua (Aztec) life and culture (the first 11 books), culminating in an account of the CONQUEST OF MEXICO (book 12). As a description of a particular late precontact indigenous culture, it is unique in size, coverage, sophistication, and depth in the entire colonial Western Hemisphere. Its hundreds of folios are written in parallel Nahuatl and Spanish columns and copiously (if not fully) illustrated. Sahagún began work on the manuscript in the late 1540s. The copy that ended up in Florence was finished several decades later, although Sahagún's study of Nahuatl and the Nahuas continued until his death in 1590.

One of the primary purposes of the work was to demonstrate in context the many registers of the Nahuatl language: formal and colloquial, straightforward and allusive. This was to assist priests in learning the subtleties of Nahuatl in order to root out practices and beliefs contrary to Christianity (see DIABOLISM IN THE NEW WORLD). Thus, in addition to descriptions of such practical matters as occupations and the various names and uses of Mesoamerican flora and fauna, the Florentine Codex includes accounts of pre-Hispanic deities and their attributes and accouterments.

Enhancing readers' skill in preaching and hearing confession was another aim of the codex. One of the most notable sections is book 6, dedicated to "Rhetoric and Moral Philosophy." It includes examples of orations on the accession of rulers, parental advice to children, and prayers to some of the principal non-Christian gods and goddesses. Such features of traditional Nahuatl rhetoric as indirection, inversion, verbal ornamentation, and metaphor are demonstrated. Studying these and similar texts greatly helped conscientious clerics who attempted to master a language that in some respects differed greatly from European languages.

The authenticity of this massive text is due principally to the team that Sahagún assembled to gather, write down, and verify the information. Over several decades, accomplished Nahua Latinists (ex-pupils of the Franciscan) consulted with high-ranking Nahua elders from various ALTEPETL (city-states); Nahua scribes recorded the results. Hence, the Florentine Codex is a rich source for scholars working in fields as diverse as anthropology, linguistics, art history, ethnography, and history.

—Barry D. Sell

Further reading:

J. Jorge Klor de Alva, H. B. Nicholson, and Eloise Quiñones Keber, eds. *The Work of Bernardino de Sahagún, Pioneer Ethnographer of Sixteenth-Century Mexico* (Austin: University of Texas Press, 1988).

James Lockhart. "A Double Tradition: Editing Book Twelve of the Florentine Codex." In *Of Things of the Indies: Essays Old and New in Early Latin American History*, 183–203 (Stanford, Calif.: Stanford University Press, 1999).

John Frederick Schwaller, ed. *Sahagún at 500: Essays on the Quincentenary of the Birth of Fr. Bernardino de Sahagún* (Berkeley, Calif.: Academy of American Franciscan History, 2003).

Florida (La Florida)

During spring 1513, JUAN PONCE DE LEÓN set sail from the Caribbean in search of new islands to claim for the Spanish Crown. On Easter Sunday (Pascua Florida) he sighted land and named the newly discovered territory *La Florida*. Florida is a large peninsula located in southeastern continental United States. Made up almost entirely of karst terrain, the region's limestone beds are among its defining features. Additionally, the landscape takes its shape from two coastal plains and the Appalachian foothills in the eastern panhandle. In the early 16th century, the subtropical region of Florida rested on a low tidewater plain.

However, Florida's earliest human inhabitants, the Paleoindians, encountered a much drier climate when they entered the region 10,000 years ago. Consequently, they lived near limestone rain reservoirs, sinkholes, and springs. These freshwater resources also attracted large populations of game, including bison, camelids, raccoon, horse, sloth, muskrat, and deer. Florida's early inhabitants used unifacial and bifacial tools carved from wood, stone, and ivory to hunt and prepare FOOD. As a people dependent on hunting and gathering, the Paleoindians led a nomadic existence, moving according to the availability of food.

Several changes in the climate and ecosystem transformed Florida's Paleoindian societies. During the Archaic period, which began around 7500 B.C.E., warmer global temperatures melted the glaciers, and ocean waters covered nearly half of present-day Florida's surface area. On the other hand, the process also made freshwater more accessible. During the Late Archaic period, around 3000 B.C.E., population growth led to the founding of numerous towns along the coast and along the tributaries of St. John's River. A thousand years later, the Archaic peoples developed fired clay pottery (see CERAMICS). As this technology spread, new regional pottery styles came into being. For example, the Deptford culture developed a unique pottery style using quartz and clay particles in the post-Archaic period, around 500 B.C.E. Located along the Gulf coast, the Deptford subsisted primarily from marine resources. Furthermore, they used a variety of tools, wooden knives, clay fired pots, woven nets, baskets, canoes, and grinding stones (see METATE).

While Late Archaic villagers cultivated fields of squash and gourds, it was not until after 750 C.E. that the inhabitants of northeastern Florida began to harvest MAIZE. This practice eventually spread to other Indian communities. Maize production led to more stratified societies and to agriculturally based villages (see AGRICULTURE). Between 1100 and 1550, the Fort Walton culture emerged as one of the largest and most complex cultures in pre-Columbian Florida. The nearby Suwannee Valley culture also developed into an important agricultural society. This community preceded the TIMUCUA, which refers to a village in the Suwannee Valley and the language spoken by multiple indigenous communities in north and central Florida.

Other important indigenous groups present during the early colonial period included the Glades near Biscayne Bay (known to the Spanish as the Tequesta, Boca Ratones, and Santaluces), the Calusa located around Lake Okeechobee, the Ais near the southern extreme of the St. John's River, and the Guale of southeastern coastal Georgia.

Early Spanish explorations of Florida, inspired by Ponce de León's 1513 voyage, led to a series of failed expeditions during the early 16th century, including Lucas Vásquez de Ayllón in 1526, PÁNFILO DE NARVÁEZ in 1528, HERNANDO DE SOTO from 1539 to 1541, and Tristán de Luna in 1559 (see CONQUEST). It was not until 1565 that Spain established its first permanent colony: St. Augustine. The Spanish Crown enlisted PEDRO MENÉNDEZ DE AVILÉS to explore Florida, build and fortify two cities, and introduce the Catholic faith to the indigenous populations. After founding St. Augustine, Menéndez secured Spain's place on the Florida coast through alliances with local indigenous chiefs and the eradication of France's Fort Caroline.

Under Menéndez's governorship, secular priests established the first mission site at the Amerindian village of Nombre de Dios just outside St. Augustine. Menéndez traveled northward among the Guale-speaking villages and in 1566 founded the town of Santa Elena (near present-day Parris Island, South Carolina). The Spanish introduced domesticated livestock, such as chickens, cows, and pigs, as well as metal farming tools (see COLUMBIAN EXCHANGE). New agricultural crops were also brought to Florida, including peaches, peas, WHEAT, and oranges. Colonial contact led to cultural exchanges that dramatically transformed the diet and daily lives of Florida's indigenous communities.

—Kathleen M. Kole

Further reading:
Jerald T. Milanich. *Archaeology of Precolumbian Florida* (Gainesville: University Press of Florida, 1994).
Jerald T. Milanich and Susan Milbrath, eds. *First Encounters: Spanish Explorations in the Caribbean and the United States, 1492–1570* (Gainesville: University of Florida Press, 1989).

flower wars (flowery wars)   The flower, or flowery, wars (*xochiyaoyotl*, in NAHUATL) were unlike ordinary Aztec conflicts conducted for the purpose of CONQUEST or subduing revolts (sometimes called "angry wars"). Rather, these staged and highly formalized battles took place between the armies of the TRIPLE ALLIANCE and their opponents, on a prearranged date and within a consecrated space designated for the purpose. The fighting, often been preceded by visits and gift exchange between the antagonistic rulers, began with the ritual burning of paper and incense. Once the fighting had begun, the prime goal was apparently not to kill the enemy soldiers but rather to stun and capture as many of them as possible alive. Those who did not directly participate in the battles were not taken captive. Nevertheless, according to historical sources, many soldiers were indeed killed in these conflicts, and such a death was considered honorable and "blissful."

The context and purpose of this unusual practice was multifaceted and changed over time. The earliest recorded flower war was instigated in 1375 between the kingdom of Chalco and Acamapichtli, the first Aztec ruler, and may have lasted for 12 years (see AZTECS). This allowed both sides to demonstrate their military power and thus determined potential political dominance at a relatively low cost. Other historical sources claim that it was Montezuma Ilhuicamina's (Montezuma I) adviser, Tlacaélel, who first proposed the practice as a way of providing a ready supply of sacrificial victims for Aztec ceremonies (see HUMAN SACRIFICE). These public events at TENOCHTITLÁN and other regional CITIES surely served to intimidate potential adversaries of the Triple Alliance, and the name for these wars might have derived from the wall of flowers behind which the enemy rulers secretly observed the sacrifices. At the same time, sacrificial victims were also captured during the ordinary conquest wars, while in some flower wars more soldiers were killed than taken for sacrifice.

Another motive stated by the Aztecs for these wars was to provide battlefield experience for their soldiers and exercise military strategies. Potential opponents for a flower war were those armies considered equal in strength to the Aztec themselves, and emphasis was placed on hand-to-hand combat and individual fighting skills rather than indirect attack with spears and arrows. Thus, the flower wars required fewer men than for regular battles, and soldiers were occasionally chosen from among the nobility (although captured nobles were mostly released).

One prolonged flower war was fought between the Triple Alliance and their bitter enemies the Tlaxcalans (see TLAXCALA). According to the Aztecs, these recurring flower wars allowed the Tlaxcalans to "remain" unconquered, while providing their own armies with the necessary battlefield practice. However, the Aztecs experienced considerable losses in these wars, and it is likely that they were indeed trying to conquer and incorporate the Tlaxcalans into their empire by slowly wearing down their forces. These efforts failed, however, and the Tlaxcalans eventually joined the Spaniards in their conquest of Tenochtitlán.

—Danny Zborover

Further reading:
Ross Hassig. *Aztec Warfare: Imperial Expansion and Political Control* (Norman: University of Oklahoma Press, 1988).

food

MESOAMERICA BEFORE 1492
The Mesoamerican diet consisted of a rich array of wild and cultivated foods. The cultivation of New World plants and animals began around 10,000 B.C.E. and continued well into the Postclassic period. Mesoamericans ate mainly a vegetarian, carbohydrate-rich diet; nothing was more important to life than what is often described as the Mesoamerican trinity: MAIZE, beans, and squash.

According to the creation tale of the K'iche' (Quiché) MAYA of GUATEMALA, the POPOL VUH, human life was born from maize. As the principal staple crop throughout Mesoamerica, maize played a central role in the physical and spiritual lives of indigenous peoples. Maize was consumed daily in the form of tortillas, tamales, stews, and beverages. The crop's life cycle served as a metaphor for the intersection between the human and metaphysical worlds (see RELIGION). The farming of maize required careful and continuous attention, just as the deities required regular offerings (see AGRICULTURE). Unlike other crops, seeds can only be successfully germinated with human attention. Changes in weather patterns could turn future bounty into immediate scarcity, similar to the fickle nature of many Mesoamerican deities.

For both the Classic-period Maya and the Postclassic AZTECS, the god of maize controlled fertility and abundance. Growing maize, however, was not a single crop affair. Since the Preclassic period, beans and squashes were grown along with maize. Mirroring the stratification of the forest—with canopy, understory, and shrub layers—maize, beans, and squash were grown in a three-tiered fashion, with maize at the top, beans supported along the stalks, and squashes growing in the shade. Beans and squash also replenish nitrogen in the soil, which maize rapidly takes from it.

Although approximately 80 percent of the Mesoamerican diet consisted of maize, beans, and squash, a host of other foodstuffs were available. In the Classic period, the Maya, for example, raised MANIOC as a staple crop. Since the Preclassic period, farmers raised chilies, tomatoes, avocados, papayas, and CACAO, while deer, ducks, rabbits, and fish provided protein and other nutrients. Fields and forests existed as fluid areas of propagation and experimentation. Using mainly swidden, or slash-and-burn, agriculture, Postclassic Maya farmers from the Petén region allowed fertile fields to return to jungle but continued to collect from mature trees. Likewise, farmers in eastern GUATEMALA allowed domesticated and wild cacao stands to intermingle and harvested from both. In the Valley of MEXICO, domestic turkeys, dogs, and insects provided protein, while in Yucatán, wild deer and iguana supplemented the diet.

The production and consumption of food was subject to strict social and gender divisions. Highly valued foods, such as cacao and PULQUE, were reserved for the elite. Under the Aztecs' rigid hierarchy, the illicit sale and consumption of ALCOHOL brought severe penalties (see CRIME AND PUNISHMENT). Those caught selling alcohol to commoners were punished by death, as were drunken non-noblewomen under the age of 70. While restraint and moderation were typical in many Mesoamerican societies, during religious festivals, elites enjoyed massive feasts. Spaniards reported that in 1520, MONTEZUMA held a feast that consisted of more than 300 dishes.

Throughout Mesoamerica, the kitchen was the preserve of WOMEN, and the three-stone hearth was the center of the domestic ritual space. The preparation of food fell largely into the hands of women, and the clay griddle, or *comal*—a ritualized object—was exclusively the domain of women. Cooking was the focus of all girls' training and prestige. In addition to assisting in the fields, women of all ages learned the arduous and time-consuming task of maize preparation, which involved grinding dried maize into flour for tortillas and tamales. The continuous LABOR, according to one Spanish source, left women's hands "blistered, raw, and festering." Food preparation, however, was not just menial labor but a praiseworthy craft. At the time of the CONQUEST, the elite praised cooks for their commitment and skill. According to the 16th-century FLORENTINE CODEX, "the cook is the one who makes *mole*, [she] makes tortillas [and] is wiry and energetic. The good cook is honest, discrete, one who likes good food, an epicurious taster."

Mesoamerican subsistence and dietary patterns consisted of a rich but fragile balance of labor and ecology. With the production of food dependent on human labor, periodic shortages threatened even the most dominant societies. The so-called Great Maya Collapse in the ninth century seems, in part, to have been linked to a massive food shortage caused by ecological changes. Even during the expansionist period of the Aztecs, the capital city of TENOCHTITLÁN suffered widespread famine during the 1450s. While the arrival of Europeans in the 16th century strained Mesoamerican production, many of the basic forms of consumption and subsistence proved resilient to the pressures of colonialism.

SOUTH AMERICA BEFORE 1492

The history of the domestication and adoption of the first food crops in the Old World is better known than the trajectory of domestication and farming of food crops in the New World. The process began in both hemispheres at the end of the Pleistocene period but involved different kinds of crops. In the Old World, the emphasis was on the domestication of cereals, including barley, oats, and WHEAT, and large animals such as sheep, cattle, and horses for food, fiber, and transport (see TRANSPORTATION). In South America, the important plant domesticates were root crops, including sweet potato, manioc, and POTATO; seed crops were less important. The only large domesticated animals were the llama and alpaca; the llama was used for transport, meat, and fiber and the alpaca for fiber (see TEXTILES).

As the Ice Age waned, the early populations of hunter-foragers who had entered South America at least 11,000 years ago began to shift toward hunting smaller game, such as deer and peccary, and intensified their foraging for plant foods. Many of the earliest sites of human occupation in South America are found within a broad swath of territory that circled the core of the AMAZON rain forest, beginning in the northwest and extending across present-day COLOMBIA, VENEZUELA, and the Guianas, southwestward across eastern BRAZIL, and then to the west across southern Brazil and eastern BOLIVIA. These areas had more seasonal climates with a dry season of several months' duration and ranged from savannas to dry deciduous forests. In such environments, vegetation is controlled by rainfall and the length of the dry season. Some plants that adapted by storing starch in underground tubers or rhizomes against the dry months became important foods for foragers because their rhizomes and tubers were available when other foods were scarce. As the climate warmed at the beginning of the Holocene period, people began to foster and then cultivate some of these previously gathered foods.

This explains one of the central characteristics of South American foods: Many of them are roots rather than seeds. Another characteristic of these crops is that they can be propagated by sowing a piece of the tuber or rhizome rather than by seed. Arrowroot (*Maranta arundinacea*) was one root crop considered indigenous to northern South America and the Caribbean. The South American species of yam is *Dioscorea trifida*, which may have been domesticated between eastern Brazil and Guiana. Yams can survive for months without rainfall and can be stored dry for up to six months. Another crop, grown in the lowlands, along the Pacific coast and at lower elevations in the Andes was *achira* (*Canna edulis*). No longer cultivated as a field crop, *achira* is still found in house gardens today. The sweet rhizomes can be eaten raw or cooked. Mature rhizomes can be left in the ground for up to two years.

Two other lowland crops were even more important: sweet potato (*Ipomoea batata*) and manioc, or cassava (*Manihot esculenta*). Sweet potato is still a major food source, today second only to manioc, which was more important in the past. The sweet potato sets seed but can be grown from stem cuttings. It may have been domesticated in northern South America. In contrast, it has now been established that South American manioc was first domesticated in southern Brazil. Nicknamed the "bread of the lowlands," manioc is extremely productive. The crop can be stored in the ground for up to two years. There are two cultivated forms: bitter and sweet manioc. Bitter manioc contains chemical compounds called cyanogenic glucosides, which may have protected the plant from insect pests. These must be removed before it can be eaten. Sweet manioc does not contain these compounds. Both varieties of manioc can be processed into a dry meal (farina). Manioc sets seed but is commonly propagated from stem cuttings. It was one of the earliest domesticates and had spread to the west coast of South America by 9,000 years ago.

Potatoes were grown from the lowlands to the very highest altitudes of the Andes. Wild potatoes were eaten by early foragers in CHILE more than 13,000 years ago. There are many wild varieties, and by 10,000 years ago, some of these were being domesticated. There are eight domesticated species and literally thousands of varieties of this important crop. Special varieties can be grown at very high altitudes where no other crop will thrive. With special processing, these can be freeze-dried and made into a flour, called *chuño*, which keeps indefinitely; it is eaten in soups. Like the flour made from manioc, this was a lightweight transportable foodstuff that made long-range mobility possible. Many of the other potato varieties were developed to survive in particular microenvironments in the mountains. Farmers planted different varieties as insurance against loss from frost, drought, or excessive rain.

Other important plants contributed carbohydrates to the Andean diet. One was the peanut, another early domesticate from southern Brazil, which had made its way to the Pacific coast by 8,500 years ago. The peanut is a seed in a hard shell; it grows underground as an adaptation to the dry season. It is high in fats and proteins, which make it an important complement to crops that have high carbohydrate content but are low in fats and oils. Another important early domesticate was squash, which was prob-

ably first cultivated for its oil-rich seeds. Later, the flesh, which is stringy and bitter in primitive squashes, was improved through selection, and squash began to be cultivated as a vegetable. The principal domesticated squashes were *Cucurbita moschata*, the variety grown today in the lower and mid-elevations of the Andes, and *Curcubita ficifolia*, grown at still higher altitudes with cooler temperatures. The wild ancestor of *Curcubita moschata* may well have been domesticated again as a form adapted to the semiarid coast of ECUADOR and northern PERU; it is called *Curcubita ecuadorensis* and has not survived in its original form. It was reported from the Las Vegas site of coastal Ecuador with dates of 12,000 to 8,000 years ago. Seeds from a form slightly more like modern domesticates were found at sites in the Nanchoc Valley in northern Peru, with dates of 11,000 to 10,000 years ago.

Three different beans were domesticated in South America: the jack bean (*Canavalia plagiosperma*), which was probably eaten green; the lima bean (*Phaseolus lunatus*); and the common bean (*Phaseolus vulgaris*). The beans were also very early domesticates and provided important amounts of protein in the diet. Native South American seed crops were minor but highly nutritious. Best known are quinoa, a chenopod related to North America goosefoot, and lupine, an amaranth-like Old World millet. Maize was originally domesticated in southwestern Mexico. The earliest date for maize in South America, which comes from the western Amazon region, is nearly 7,000 years ago. Different varieties of popcorn and seed corn were developed in South America, some returning to Mesoamerica; however, corn, beans, and squash never became the staple triad in South America as they did in Mesoamerica and North America.

Other foods enhanced the indigenous diet and provided essential nutrients. There were four domesticated species of chili peppers (*Capsicum*) in South America: one in northern South America, two in the Amazon region, and one in the Andes and the Pacific coast. Peppers not only perked up an otherwise bland diet but were highly nutritious, providing vitamins and other nutrients. Most fruits were tree fruits and included *pacae* (*Inga pacae*), *lúcuma* (*Lucuma bifera*), avocado (*Persea americana*), and the tart fruits of *Bunchosia*. Cacao (*Theobroma cacao*) was apparently domesticated for its fruit in the Amazon. Amazonian peoples fostered but did not domesticate important nuts such as the Brazil nut and the peach palm, which were important sources of protein and oil.

While a lot is said about the importance of hunting as a source of meat, once people began farming, fishing may well have provided much of the protein people required. This is true for the farmers of the Amazon, who also hunted, and for those of the coastal valleys west of the Andes. In addition, the tradition of fishing and shellfish collecting along the littoral and the estuaries of the rivers on the Pacific coast dated back at least 10,000 years. Local wild animals, including some rodents and lizards and occasionally deer and peccary, were hunted. As farming became more important, fishers began to dry and salt large quantities of fish and shellfish, which were traded inland in exchange for agricultural products (see TRADE). Herding peoples in the high Andean grasslands also dried meat (*charqui*, or "jerky"), which they traded for crops grown at lower altitudes, particularly maize. Because llamas were so important as sources of fiber, small rodents were trapped and one, the *cuy*, or GUINEA PIG, was domesticated and raised in large numbers.

EARLY COLONIAL LATIN AMERICA

The arrival of European settlers to the Americas marked the beginning of a long process of culinary fusion. While Europeans settlers may have marveled at the bounty of New World foods, their palates were driven by their taste for Old World cuisines. Native peoples, cast to the bottom of the colonial hierarchy, were charged with feeding the colonizers but were generally prohibited from consuming Old World luxuries.

The first settlers unsuccessfully attempted to introduce European crops and animals to the Caribbean (see COLUMBIAN EXCHANGE). These ventures foreshadowed the trajectory of agriculture and food during the early colonial period. Staples struggled to survive, while livestock proved invasive. Shortages of food were frequent for colonizer and colonized alike. In 1493, for example, the first European settlers unsuccessfully attempted to grow wheat and barley in the Caribbean. These crops, adapted to high altitudes and cool weather, were unviable in the tropics. In 1494 and 1495, therefore, there was a dramatic shortage of grains. Old World livestock, on the other hand, thrived. Hogs quickly invaded every ecosystem and, incidentally, spread the first epidemic outbreak of influenza (see DISEASE).

The Amerindian pantry contained a rich diversity of foodstuffs. When Spanish soldiers marched in to the Valley of Mexico in 1520, they marveled at the quantity and variety of foods available in Aztec marketplaces. HERNANDO CORTÉS, writing to the Spanish king, described the markets as the largest and richest in the world. Maize was available in multiple forms—fresh, dried, and processed. The list of New World fruits seemed boundless and included avocadoes, chilies, squash, tomatoes, and melons.

The pre-Hispanic diet, which was based mainly on carbohydrate-rich vegetables, found little favor among Europeans. In Mexico, ubiquitous maize-based foods such as breads (tortillas and tamales), stews (*atoles*), and fermented beverages (pulque) offended European sentiments. The conquistador BERNAL DÍAZ DEL CASTILLO equated a diet based on maize with a life of misery. In the Andes, potatoes also found little favor among early European settlers. The potato was seen as a food of paupers.

A massive, weeklong series of banquets held in MEXICO CITY in 1538 were emblematic of the European palate in early colonial Latin America. The festivities took place on a grand scale in the central plaza of the city. Included on the menu were an assortment of meats, sweets, and liquors. Largely excluded, however, were Amerindian foods. The city plaza of the city had been staged as a hunting ground stocked with wild and domestic animals, including sheep, cattle, swine, deer, and chickens; turkeys were noticeably absent. Old World fruits, such as apples and pears, and delectables such as honey-coated marzipan were available in abundance. New World fruits, which every indigenous person consumed, did not appear on the banquet tables. Chocolate, in the form of a beverage, was the only New World item worthy of mention by the events' chroniclers.

For the early colonial indigenous, who were legally prohibited from consuming luxuries such as WINE and could not afford European commodities such as meat and wheat, the pre-Hispanic diet remained largely intact. Native Mesoamericans subsisted on maize, while native Andeans continued to farm potatoes. Colonial officials, however, placed great pressure on the ideological systems that reinforced those agricultural patterns. Priests and friars attempted to eliminate indigenous loyalties to agricultural deities by teaching new forms of subsistence (see RELIGION). In Mexico, they forwarded wheat, olives, and grapes—the principal components of the Eucharist—as alternatives to maize, beans, and squash. Nevertheless, these plants grew in only limited regions and were susceptible to disease. In the early colonial period, therefore, wheat tortillas, wine, and olive oil became markers of colonial status and Catholic piety.

While the kitchen existed as an important female-centered ritualized space in many pre-Hispanic societies, Catholic authorities attempted to move cooking to a secular realm during the early colonial period. For indigenous women, the home moved from being a source of power and prestige to a place that limited their authority and agency. Nahua (Aztec) midwives from the period warned newborn girls: "You will become fatigued, you will become tired; you are to provide water, to grind maize, to drudge."

The introduction of colonial subsistence and economic systems came with great costs (see ECONOMY). Periodic food shortages struck even the most fertile areas. In the 1540s and 1570s, the inhabitants of MEXICO CITY suffered widespread famine, which sparked massive outbreaks of *cocoliztli* (hemorrhagic fever) and killed nearly half the population. In the Mezquitil Valley north of Mexico, the introduction of sheep farming turned fertile plains into a barren desert in less than two decades. Subsequently, indigenous people and Europeans living in the area were forced to resettle.

See also FOOD (Vol. III).

—R. A. Kashanipour
Patricia J. Netherly

Further reading:

Sophia D. Coe. *America's First Cuisine* (Austin: University of Texas Press, 1994).

John C. Super. *Food, Conquest, and Colonization in Sixteenth-Century Spanish America* (Albuquerque: University of New Mexico Press, 1988).

forastero   In Spanish, the term *forastero* means "from the outside." It can also be used to refer to a person who "comes from a place outside of his or her native community." In colonial Spanish America, *forasteros*—also referred to as "vagabond Indians," or *indios vagabundos*—were, specifically, Indians who had left their natal communities to migrate to and integrate with other Indian communities. *Forasteros'* legal obligations and social status were defined in colonial society. As a distinct category of persons, they were seen in opposition to *originarios*, or Indians who lived in their native communities. The Crown perpetuated the *originario-forastero* dichotomy throughout the early colonial period.

In colonial Latin American society, *forasteros* were considered a social problem for several reasons. Their migrations confounded the Crown's tax- and tribute-collecting efforts. Moreover, Spanish *encomenderos*, who held grants to the right of indigenous LABOR on their lands, complained to the king about the NATIVE AMERICANS who became *forasteros* (see ENCOMIENDA). In particular, they noted that because vagabond Indians avoided taking their turns in the MITA, or forced labor obligation in the mines, they did not pay tribute to the Crown (see MINING). Ultimately, the movements of *forasteros* created shortages of labor in the mines and hindered the Spaniards' ability to extract natural resources using indigenous labor. To stanch the uncontrolled MIGRATION of *forasteros* throughout the New World Spanish colonies, numerous legislative attempts were made by colonial VICEROYS to restrict nonmandated Indian movements to places outside their native communities and, further, to move them back to their original communities.

See also FORASTERO (Vol. II).

—Tien-Ann Shih

Further reading:
Ann Wightman. *Indigenous Migration and Social Change: The Forasteros of Cuzco, 1570–1720* (Durham, N.C.: Duke University Press, 1990).

Franciscan millennial kingdom   This term refers to the belief shared by many Franciscan friars that the end of the world—the thousand-year reign of Christ on earth (the millennium)—was close at hand. The Franciscan order (Order of Friars Minor) was founded in the 13th century in Italy by St. Francis of Assisi (see RELIGIOUS ORDERS). It grew rapidly and gained great popularity in late medieval Europe. There were several internal disputes regarding the best way to follow the rule of the order, and as a result, the order split into several branches. The Observant branch was deeply influenced by the writings of a 13th-century Cistercian monk, Joachim of Fiore. Observant monks rigorously applied the Rule of St. Francis, embracing personal poverty and the notion that they could bring people closer to Christ by exemplifying a Christ-like life.

Fiore described the history of the world as falling into three eras, each identified with a part of the Trinity. The first age was that of God the Father and lasted until the coming of Christ. The current age is that of God the Son. Fiore believed that this current age would quickly end and usher in the era of the Holy Spirit, which corresponds to the Kingdom of Heaven on earth as described in the book of Revelation. This last age, the Franciscans theorized, would occur once the gospel had been preached to the last person on earth. As a result they took to the missionary effort in the New World with great fervor, confident that within their own lifetimes the Kingdom of Heaven would be at hand.

The millennial fervor of the Franciscans in the New World was seen most clearly in their evangelization in MEXICO. The friars who first arrived there were from an Observant province in Spain, the Holy Gospel Province, which had set about reforming the order from within. The friars were highly dedicated to regaining the early purity of the Franciscan rule, living in complete poverty, depending on the alms of the faithful, and living a life as close to that of Jesus as possible. They believed that in this way they could demonstrate the true nature of Christianity to the indigenous peoples of the New World, in spite of the language and culture barriers. Their efforts were chronicled by a member of the order, Fray Gerónimo de Mendieta, in his book *Historia eclesiástica indiana* (Ecclesiastic Indian history). In this history, Mendieta applied the tripartite division of history developed by Joachim of Fiore to the ages of the evangelization of the Indies. He felt that the "golden age" of evangelization had already occurred in the early 16th century with the efforts of the first missionaries, and that by the 1560s and 1570s, they had already entered the end times and witnessed a visible decline. The feeling that the end of the world was near continued to be an important theme for Franciscan missionaries.

See also CATHOLIC CHURCH (Vols. II, III, IV); FRANCISCANS (Vol. II).

—John F. Schwaller

Further reading:
John L. Phelan. *The Millennial Kingdom of the Franciscans in the New World*, rev. ed. (Berkeley: University of California Press, 1970).

Gasca, Pedro de la (b. 1493–d. 1567) *royal official, diplomat, bishop* Born into a modest hidalgo family in Navarregadilla, Spain, Pedro de la Gasca began his studies in canon law at the University of Salamanca (see SALAMANCA, SCHOOL OF) and continued at the University of Alcalá de Henares, receiving his law degree in 1521. He returned to Salamanca in order to continue his education and soon distinguished himself for his intelligence. Gasca became vicar of the archbishop of Alcalá de Henares in 1537 but soon began a political career as *visitador*, or inspector, of the Kingdom of Valencia and as a member of the Council of the Inquisition. Gasca established a reputation as a loyal and uncompromising royal servant, particularly for his hard-line stance toward the *converso* and MORISCO populations of Valencia.

In 1545, when news of GONZALO PIZARRO's rebellion in PERU reached Charles I, the king chose Gasca to reestablish royal authority in the new colony. A faction of *encomenderos* in Peru had risen against the VICEROY, Blasco Núñez Vela, after he had attempted to enforce the NEW LAWS OF 1542, which threatened *encomendero* authority and privileges (see CIVIL WARS IN PERU; ENCOMIENDA). Gasca sailed for Peru in 1546, with the authority to achieve order by any means necessary. He landed in PANAMA where he enacted his plan: He offered amnesty to Pizarro's supporters in exchange for their cooperation. For six months, Gasca built a coalition with whom he sailed for LIMA in 1547. There, he continued to undermine the rebel cause by political means. In 1548, Gasca's now-formidable army confronted Pizarro's dwindling forces outside CUZCO. Pizarro and his few remaining allies were annihilated.

Gasca left Peru in 1550 after initiating a series of administrative reforms. Charles I rewarded him on his return to Spain with the bishopric of Palencia, over which he presided until 1561, when he became bishop of Sigüenza.

—Jonathan Scholl

Further reading:

Teodoro Hampe Martínez. *Don Pedro de la Gasca, 1493–1567: Su obra política en España y América* (Lima: Fondo Editorial de la Pontífica Universidad Católica del Perú, 1989).

gold Gold was the object of desire for all conquistadores; CHRISTOPHER COLUMBUS required it of the native people in 1492, HERNANDO CORTÉS searched for it among the AZTECS of TENOCHTITLÁN in 1519, and FRANCISCO PIZARRO exacted it from the Andeans after his capture of ATAHUALPA in 1532. After the dust of CONQUEST had settled, Spaniards demanded gold as tribute from the indigenous population and even organized expeditions to find the mythical city of gold EL DORADO. Although the Spaniards' demand and search for gold met with varying degrees of success, gold played an important role in the initial conquest and colonization of the Americas.

Prior to the Spanish arrival, all of the Americas' settled indigenous cultures possessed and/or worked gold, though to varying degrees. The AZTECS called it *teocuitlatl*, "excrement of the gods"; the MAYA called it *takin*, "excrement of the sun"; and the INCAS referred to gold as the "sweat of the sun." The connection between gold and the divine was purely aesthetic. The luster of gold gave the metal a unique beauty, and its malleability made it a desirable metal for the ornamentation of shrines, temples, ritual objects, and various other artifacts. Indeed, gold items ranged from large masks to small, delicate bells. For indigenous cultures, the value of gold was in its beauty, not in its economic worth or buying power.

Understandably, the Amerindians found it strange that the Spaniards always appeared to be on the hunt for gold. More than one native person commented on how the Spaniards "thirsted mightily for gold; they stuffed themselves with it; they starved for it; they lusted for it like pigs." While such comments encourage the idea that the Spanish conquest was driven by the conquistadores' thirst for gold, this assumption fails to appreciate the role of precious metals in mercantilist Europe and the Spanish Empire (see ECONOMY). In an empire whose wealth was based on bullion, it was not enough for conquistadores simply to discover and claim new territories. New colonies required immediate economic viability, namely gold, to repay the debts conquistadores acquired to finance their expeditions. Unlike the native peoples, Spaniards saw little value in gold artifacts themselves, just the worth of the metal itself. Thus, once seized, items made of gold were melted down to facilitate the settling of debts, payment of the conquistadores' shares, and procurement of supplies. Because of its central financial role in conquest and settlement, the availability of gold in Central MEXICO and the Andes helped draw Spanish conquistadores and settlers, while the Yucatán Peninsula's dearth of gold helped discourage the foreigners' presence.

Moreover, in order to justify a new colony and be awarded positions of authority, conquistadores needed to discover gold to convince the Crown of the expedition's success. Men such as Columbus, Cortés, and Pizarro saw gold as a means to an end—the governorship of a new colony. In more practical terms, gold was also the most transportable, divisible, compact, nonperishable item of value that existed at the time. Thus, the significance of gold in the Americas shifted drastically after the Spaniards' arrival. Gold had a vital, unchallenged economic and political role in the conquest and early colonization of the Americas, and its eventual MINING and exportation throughout the colonial period created a demand for local products that helped shape regional economies.

See also GOLD (Vols. II, III).

—Mark Christensen

Further reading:
Peter Bakewell, ed. *Mines of Silver and Gold in the Americas* (Brookfield, Vt.: Variorum, 1997).

González Dávila, Gil (d. 1543) *explorer and conqueror of Nicaragua* Gil González Dávila explored and named NICARAGUA. González heralded from a noble family from Ávila, Spain, and benefited greatly from his family's ties to Bishop Rodríguez de Fonseca. In 1519, after serving

as royal treasurer on the island of HISPANIOLA, González received a commission from the Crown to explore the regions west of PANAMA, with Andrés Niño serving as his pilot. Despite the fact that the governor, PEDRO ARIAS DE ÁVILA (Pedrarias), had been ordered to provide the expedition with assistance, ships were not supplied. González was forced to transfer supplies over land to a Pacific base in order to build the ships for the expedition, which finally departed on January 21, 1522.

While Niño sailed on, González traveled by land up the Pacific coast, across what is now Panama and COSTA RICA, before turning inland. He claimed to have baptized more than 32,000 indigenous people en route and to have collected tribute from their chiefs. When he arrived at Lake Nicaragua (which he named after the local chief, Nicarao), his scouts reported that it drained into the Atlantic, sparking hope that it could be the much-sought sea passage across the isthmus. While González's first encounters with the indigenous population were peaceful, this came to an end when he was ambushed by the CACIQUE Diriangen.

With that, González retreated back to Panama and then to Santo Domingo to escape arrest by Pedrarias. By the time he returned in March 1524 to look for Lake Nicaragua's Atlantic drain via the eastern shore, several other explorers had taken an interest in Nicaragua. Pedrarias had sent his own expedition, and HERNANDO CORTÉS did likewise, from MEXICO. González established San Gil de Buenavista as his base, and a number of confrontations ensued. Ultimately, Francisco de las Casas, who had been sent by Cortés to deal with the treasonous explorer, took González to Mexico, from which he was sent to Spain for trial. He died in 1543.

—Angela Granum

Grijalva de Cuéllar, Juan de (b. ca. 1490–d. 1527) *explorer, conquistador, captain of expedition to Yucatán and Mexico's Gulf coast* Born in the Spanish town of Cuéllar near Segovia ca. 1490, Juan de Grijalva came to the New World before he was 20 years old. Together with his uncle, DIEGO VELÁZQUEZ DE CUÉLLAR, Grijalva took part in the CONQUEST and subjugation of the island of CUBA from 1510 to 1511. Velázquez had been given permission by the VICEROY of the Indies, Diego Columbus (CHRISTOPHER COLUMBUS's eldest son), to conquer the island and serve as its new governor. After the final conquest of the island and the establishment of a colony, Grijalva served under his uncle in minor governmental offices.

As soon as the governor of Cuba received the reports of the 1517 expedition to Yucatán, led by Captain FRANCISCO HERNÁNDEZ DE CÓRDOBA, Velázquez prepared to send a second, larger and stronger fleet to explore the new lands. Velázquez chose his nephew to serve as captain general of the new expedition. The expedition also counted on the navigator and pilot of the Córdoba expedition, Antón de Alaminos. To captain the four ships, in consultation with Grijalva, the governor selected PEDRO DE ALVARADO, FRANCISCO DE MONTEJO, and Alonso de Ávila.

On April 8, 1518, what came to be known as the Grijalva expedition set sail from Havana. With four ships and more than 300 men, the expedition was one of the largest expeditions formed in the Indies. The expeditions' chaplain, Juan Díaz, also served as the company scribe; Díaz recorded the entire voyage and its exploits in his publication, *Itinerario de la Armada* (The armada's itinerary).

Grijalva's ships arrived first at the island of Cozumel and then crossed to the mainland of the Yucatán Peninsula. There they saw three large towns with stone houses and large towers, which were later described by a member of the expedition, BERNAL DÍAZ DEL CASTILLO. The fleet continued along the coast of the Yucatán Peninsula and headed southwest toward the region of Campeche. While on shore, Captain Grijalva and his men had a violent encounter with a group of armed MAYA warriors. The Spaniards named the battle site Puerto de la Mala Pelea (harbor of the terrible battle).

Grijalva's expedition set sail once again, continuing southwest. Almost 100 nautical leagues (approximately 345 miles [555 km]) west of Laguna de Teminos the fleet came to the mouth of a large river, which the captain general named after himself. Soon, the fleet was met by more Maya, who expressed a desire to TRADE with the Spaniards. Urged by reports of GOLD, the fleet continued west along the coast, lands of the Totonac peoples (see TOTONACS). Just north of present-day San Juan de Ulúa, the Spaniards explored a large gulf with three islands; they named them the *Isla de Sacrificios* after finding evidence of HUMAN SACRIFICE. From there, Grijalva's fleet reached as far northwest as the mouth of the Río Pánuco (near today's Tampico, MEXICO) before turning back toward Cuba.

The significance of Grijalva's expedition lies in the fact that most of his captains and crew would take part in the subsequent conquests of Mexico and Central America. These included Alvarado (conqueror of GUATEMALA, 1522–24), Montejo (conqueror of Yucatán, 1527–37), and Alonso de Ávila (conqueror of Yucatán/HONDURAS, 1527–37). Although Grijalva himself would not take part in any of the major conquests, he did go on to command several smaller expeditions that explored and traded along the Central American coast. It was during one of these expeditions, in 1527, that Grijalva died from wounds inflicted during a battle with Central American indigenous people.

—John F. Chuchiak IV

Further reading:
Henry R. Wagner, ed. and trans. *The Discovery of New Spain in 1518 by Juan de Grijalva* (New York: Kraus Reprint, 1969).

Guadalupe, Virgin of   See VIRGIN OF GUADALUPE.

Guaraní

The Guaraní people occupied the regions of modern PARAGUAY, southern BRAZIL, southern BOLIVIA, and northern ARGENTINA. They are believed to be distant relatives of the Tupí peoples of the Brazilian AMAZON (see TUPINAMBÁ). The Guaraní language is considered part of the subfamily of Tupí languages and is the source of several English-language terms, such as *jaguar* and *piranha*. Much of what is known of Guaraní history has been passed down through oral transmissions, and these vary significantly by tribe. According to Guaraní mythology, the sun god Tupã, along with the moon goddess, Arasy, emerged from the earth in the hills of Areguá, Paraguay. From there, they created the rivers, seas, stars, animals; and from clay, they created the Guaraní people. Guaraní RELIGION centered on beliefs in nature. Because of the importance of religion, the leadership of tribes often fell to a religious leader known as the CACIQUE. The cacique also served as a practitioner of traditional MEDICINE.

Guaraní society was organized on a communal basis. Villages were composed of communal shelters that might house 10 or more families. As a seminomadic people, the Guaraní practiced subsistence farming and slash-and-burn AGRICULTURE. They grew MANIOC, MAIZE, beans, peanuts, and yerba maté, a tea. When the soil was depleted, within three to five years, villages moved to new locations. When the Spanish conquistadores arrived, beginning with the 1516 expedition of Juan Díaz de Solís, many Spanish towns were built on earlier Guaraní settlements (see CONQUEST). At the time of contact with the Spanish, estimates place the number of Guaraní at nearly 1.5 million. Over time, the Guaraní blended with the Spanish to form a nation of mestizos, and the region later became incorporated into the Viceroyalty of Río de la Plata (see *MESTIZAJE/MESTIZO*; VICEROY/VICEROYALTY).

See also GUARANÍ (Vol. II).

—Michael S. Coe

Further reading:
Barbara Ganson. *The Guaraní under Spanish Rule in the Río de la Plata* (Stanford, Calif.: Stanford University Press, 2003).

Guatemala

The first human settlers in Guatemala arrived from present-day MEXICO more than 12,000 years ago. Pre-Columbian Guatemala boasts one of the richest historical traditions in Mesoamerica; myriad well-preserved archaeological sites have provided great insight into the peoples that inhabited the country. High-quality CERAMICS and stone carvings, elaborate burial and religious temples, and a written language are among the achievements that have aided study of the nation's distant past. Throughout the era of ancient history, the OLMECS and MAYA dominated the region for some two millennia, until the arrival of the Spanish in the 16th century.

The earliest evidence of human settlement dates back as far as 18,000 B.C.E.; OBSIDIAN arrowheads from this time have been found in various parts of the country. More concrete evidence of contiguous human occupation dates to 10,000 B.C.E. The early peoples were hunter-gatherers, eventually adopting MAIZE from Mexico sometime around 3500 B.C.E. By 2500 B.C.E., several small-scale settlements had emerged around the lowland Pacific portion of Guatemala, including settlements around Tilapa, La Blanca, Ocós, El Mesak, and Ujuxte. Evidence of pottery in Guatemalan settlements emerged 500 years later.

The Monte Alto culture became the first large-scale civilization in Guatemala, as well as Mesoamerica, and a primary influence of the Olmec and Maya. The Pacific site of Monte Alto was first settled around 1800 B.C.E., and the area grew into a regional center between 400 B.C.E. and 200 C.E. Forty-five extant structures mark the remains of the Monte Alto culture, which feature carved stone heads and "potbellies," or male figures carved from boulders. These relics were often magnetized, making them the world's oldest magnetic artifacts. The sites and carving techniques used at Monte Alto were either contemporary to or heavily influenced by the earliest Olmec peoples.

The Olmecs, centered in southeastern Mexico, appear to have developed long-distance TRADE networks that widely affected Guatemala. Obsidian and jade were both highly prized commodities in Olmec culture and widely believed to have been of Guatemalan origin. As the Olmec culture declined between 400 and 350 B.C.E., offshoot cultures emerged that bridged the technological feats of the Olmec and the rise of Maya. Perhaps the most important archaeological site in Guatemala from this era is Tak'alik A'baj', located 120 miles from Guatemala City. Eighty-two structures, a dozen plazas, two recreational ball courts, and a hydraulic system that supported saunas ensured this locale was a thriving hub. Beyond being an important commercial center between the eighth century B.C.E. and ninth century C.E., Tak'alik A'baj' served as a nexus between pre-Olmec cultures, Olmec influences, and the rise of the Maya in Guatemala.

The seminal Maya settlements emerged about 1800 B.C.E. in the Soconusco region along the Pacific coast of southern Mexico and Guatemala. Over the succeeding centuries, the Maya expanded throughout much of southern Mexico and large swaths of Central America. By 800 B.C.E., the Guatemalan site of Kaminaljuyú had emerged as the chief source of jade and obsidian in the rapidly expanding Maya territory. ARCHITECTURE soon became a hallmark of the civilization, as crude burial mounds gave way to stone-tiered pyramids and large urban centers in such places as EL MIRADOR and, later, TIKAL.

The Maya also made significant achievements in astronomy and mathematics, having independently developed a series of remarkable innovations: the concept of zero by 36 B.C.E.; a complex calendrical system, with a 365-day solar calendar and a 260-day sacred calendar; and a host of impressive celestial observations. In fact, the Maya are believed to be the only pretelescopic civilization to accurately record the unique characteristics of the Orion Nebula. Aside from the sciences, the Maya developed the only complete written language in the pre-Columbian Americas.

Despite the immense achievements of the Maya over a wide range of fields, the Classic Maya civilization (250–900 C.E.) began to decline in the late eighth and early ninth centuries. Recent scholarship has focused on ecological factors such as overpopulation, endemic WARFARE, severe drought, and soil exhaustion as being central to the decline. Maya development from the first millennium on shifted north, as separate polities emerged in the Yucatán in the epoch prior to Spanish discovery. By the 16th century, the Maya had devolved into competing city-states, with rival cities constantly fomenting war against one another. Amidst this turmoil, the Spanish encountered the Maya in 1502.

The Spanish CONQUEST of Guatemala began in 1523 when HERNANDO CORTÉS dispatched PEDRO DE ALVARADO to Guatemala from MEXICO CITY. Initially, Alvarado allied with the Kaqchikel Maya to fight against their traditional rivals, the K'iche' (Quiché). Alvarado and his Kaqchikel allies began the conquest by confronting the K'iche', who mustered a force more than 8,000-strong. The combined forces easily defeated the K'iche', who were led by Tecún Umán, now regarded as Guatemala's national hero, on February 20, 1524. Destroying much smaller forces on his way, Alvarado burned the K'iche' capital on March 7, 1524. He then proceeded to IXIMCHÉ, where he established a base camp, and by 1525, Alvarado's forces had systematically sacked and destroyed nearby cities, including three regional capitals. For his service, Alvarado was named captain general in 1527.

Having solidified his power base in Guatemala, Alvarado turned against his Kaqchikel allies; after a long and bloody conflict, he eventually subdued them in 1530. Battles with other groups continued until 1548, when the last Maya, in Nueva Sevilla, was defeated, leaving the Spanish in control of the region. The Spanish quickly moved to institutionalize their power. The installation of the ENCOMIENDA system was met with fierce resistance by Guatemala's indigenous populations, and the colony's opposition was instrumental in the revision of the practice under the NEW LAWS OF 1542. In 1543, an AUDIENCIA was established in Guatemala, exercising jurisdiction over much of Central America.

See also GUATEMALA (Vols. II, III, IV); GUATEMALA CITY (Vol. IV).

—Sean H. Goforth

Further reading:

Arthur Demarest. *Ancient Maya* (Cambridge: Cambridge University Press, 2004).
Jared Diamond. *Collapse: How Societies Choose to Fail or Succeed* (New York: Penguin, 2005).
Wendy Kramer. *Encomienda Politics in Early Colonial Guatemala, 1524–1544: Dividing the Spoils* (Boulder, Colo.: Westview Press, 1994).

Matthew Restall and Florine Asselbergs. *Invading Guatemala: Spanish, Nahua, and Maya Accounts of the Conquest Wars* (University Park: Pennsylvania State University Press, 2007).

guinea pigs *(cuy)*　Over at least the last five millennia, domestic guinea pigs have played a multitude of roles in western South America. Known as *cuy* in the Andes, guinea pigs have an important role in folk medical diagnosis, are considered a great delicacy, and are regularly sacrificed to the gods. These medium-sized rodents appear regularly in archaeological deposits, colonial documents, shamanic rites, Andean households, and stewpots and for a time were even featured in a Peruvian comic strip (see FOOD).

Domestic guinea pigs are classified as *Cavia porcellus* and are probably related to the wild guinea pig (*Cavia aperea*), which is native to South America. Guinea pigs were domesticated by 2500 B.C.E., if not earlier. Domestication led to an increase in their average body weight and litter size and to the appearance of white or multicolored hair.

Documents from the centuries following the Spanish CONQUEST in 1532 show that guinea pigs played similar roles then as they do today, and based on archaeological data from sites such as Lo Demás, an Inca-era (ca. 1480–1532) site south of LIMA, PERU, these practices were pre-Hispanic (see INCAS). At Lo Demás, four naturally mummified guinea pigs with slit stomachs exactly replicate the use of these animals as diagnostic devices in modern healing ceremonies, in which the shaman rubs the patient with a live guinea pig and then slits its stomach open to see which organs are affected. Another Lo Demás specimen found as a burial offering had its throat slit. Similar finds have since been reported from other earlier sites.

—Dan Sandweiss

Further reading:
Edmundo Morales. *The Guinea Pig: Healing, Food and Ritual in the Andes* (Tucson: University of Arizona Press, 1995).
Daniel H. Sandweiss and Elizabeth S. Wing. "Ritual Rodents: The Guinea Pigs of Chincha, Peru." *Journal of Field Archaeology* 24 (1997): 47–58.

Guyana　The land now comprising modern-day Guyana in northeastern South America is characterized by diverse ecological zones. The territory includes an alluvial coastal plain, tropical forest hills and highlands, and interior savannas, crossed by large rivers such as the Branco and Essequibo, which are part of the Amazonia watershed. The earliest indications of human occupation of the area date back to between 10,000 and 8000 B.C.E., when small nomadic bands of Paleoindians using finely made flint and jasper spear points hunted now-extinct species of megafauna.

With climate change and the disappearance of large herbivores from the ecosystem, the local populations began to exploit other FOOD sources, foraging for

A 500-year-old guinea pig excavated at the Inca fishing site of Lo Demás in the Chincha Valley, Peru. The slit stomach indicates that this specimen was part of a curing ritual like those still carried out in the Andes today. *(Courtesy of Dan Sandweiss)*

shellfish, seeds, nuts, and fruits, in addition to hunting smaller animals and fishing. These new cultural adaptations to the environment, which included the Alaka culture near the Essequibo, produced less refined stone tools but left the first examples of rock ART, in both caves and shelters, including multicolored paintings of plants and animals and geometric designs.

AGRICULTURE and the production of pottery appeared around 4000 B.C.E., by which time the region's indigenous population had developed economic and cultural traits similar to those practiced when Europeans arrived (see CERAMICS). Seminomadic groups of farmers lived in large villages, where they cultivated MANIOC (cassava) and other tuber crops using slash-and-burn agriculture. They supplemented their diet through fishing and hunting. There is also evidence of extensive contact with neighboring cultural groups, such as influences from the Barrancoid culture of the Orinoco Delta to the northwest, which flourished between 800 B.C.E. and 1000 C.E.

By the 16th century, Guyana was inhabited principally by CARIB, Arawak, and Warrau-speaking groups. They continued to farm manioc, their principal crop, in addition to sweet POTATO and MAIZE. They also cultivated pineapples, avocados, papayas, and other tropic fruits and fished the many rivers of the interior, using traps, nets, and even poisons. Hunting deer, monkeys, tapir, and capybara was also an important activity. Both coastal and interior peoples participated in the wider TRADE networks that connected the Orinoco and AMAZON watersheds with the Guyana coast and even the Caribbean islands to the northwest.

The Carib, also known as the Karinya or Kalinago, were by far the most numerous group; they controlled the waterways of the Orinoco River, the upper Essequibo River basin, and into the southern part of the country. Like their relatives in the Leeward Islands of the Caribbean, the Carib of Guyana were feared warriors. The Akawois/Agawai, who were related to the Carib, were a seminomadic people whose territory extended across the region of the lower Essequibo. They eventually displaced the Carib from parts of the interior.

The Arawak or Lokono people inhabited mainly the coastal area, from the Orinoco Delta almost to the mouth of the Amazon River to the south. The Arawak shared many cultural traits with their relatives, the TAINO of the Caribbean islands, including well-developed and complex social structures. The Arawaks controlled much of the trade along the coast and the interior, especially that in luxury items such as metals and jewelry.

The Warrau/Warao inhabited the swamplands of the Orinoco Delta to the north and into northwestern Guyana. The Warrau were renowned as canoe makers and basket weavers and for their expertise at fishing.

During the mid- to late 16th century, European explorers (German, Spanish, and English) launched expeditions along the coast and into the interior of Guyana in search of EL DORADO, the legendary ruler of a gold-rich kingdom supposedly located in the region. While some indigenous peoples traded and established friendly relations with the Europeans, others resisted their encroachment by force. In either case, the lives of Guyana's native inhabitants were dramatically altered during the period of CONQUEST.

See also GUYANA (Vols. II, III, IV).

—Francisco J. González

Further reading:
Lal Balkaran. *Encyclopaedia of the Guyanese Amerindians* (Toronto, Canada: LBA Publications, 2007).
Anna Roosevelt, ed. *Amazonian Indians: From Prehistory to the Present* (Tucson: University of Arizona Press, 1994).

Guzmán, Nuño de (Nuño Beltrán de Guzmán)

(b. ca. 1490–d. 1558) *president of Audiencia of New Spain and conqueror of New Galicia* Nuño de Guzmán's career in MEXICO lasted barely a decade, during which he briefly became the most powerful authority there. Born around 1490 to a noble family of Guadalajara, Spain, with strong ties to the Crown, Guzmán's service to Charles I led to his appointment as governor of Pánuco Province, in northeastern Mexico, in 1525. Arriving in Mexico in 1527 he sponsored further bloody campaigns in Pánuco and exported thousands of indigenous slaves to the Caribbean islands in exchange for livestock (see SLAVERY). In 1528, he became president of the first high court, or *AUDIENCIA*, while still holding the governorship of Pánuco. Generally thought to have dominated the *audiencia*, Guzmán persuaded the *oidores* (judges) to sponsor an expedition to the west.

Beginning his campaign with the execution of the indigenous ruler of Michoacán, whom he accused of treason, Guzmán led thousands of conscripts from Central Mexico and Michoacán, as well as several hundred Spaniards, on a campaign that brought extensive violence and disruption to New Galicia (see CONQUEST). He established four enduring Spanish towns there; Compostela became the first capital. Guzmán's ambition was to join Pánuco and New Galicia into one vast jurisdiction and outflank HERNANDO CORTÉS; however, the arrival of ANTONIO DE MENDOZA as VICEROY in 1535 put an end to the ambitions of both men. Dismissed from the presidency of the *audiencia* even before he completed the conquest of New Galicia in 1531, Guzmán also lost the governorship of New Galicia in 1536. Arrested on charges relating to his various offices, he was jailed in MEXICO CITY and sent to Spain in 1538, where he lived until 1558 in a kind of legal limbo at court.

—Ida Altman

Further reading:
Donald E. Chipman. *Nuño de Guzman and the Province of Pánuco in New Spain, 1518–1533* (Glendale, Calif.: Arthur H. Clark Co., 1967).

Habsburgs (Hapsburgs)

Habsburgs (Hapsburgs) The Habsburgs were a central European royal family that ruled Spain from 1517 to 1700. Maximilian I, a Habsburg and Holy Roman emperor from 1508 to 1519, married his son Philip the Fair to Juana, the daughter of Ferdinand II of Aragon and Isabella of Castile in 1496 (see MONARCHS OF SPAIN). Juana inherited the throne of Castile when her mother died in 1504, but Juana's insanity prevented her from ruling (she is known to history as Juana the Mad). Her father acted as regent until his death in 1516, when Juana and Philip's son Charles became ruler of both Castile and Aragon.

Born in Ghent in 1500 and raised in the Low Countries, Charles I arrived in Spain in 1517 to become its first Habsburg monarch. Two years later, he was elected Holy Roman Emperor Charles V. He faced a serious threat to his power in 1520 with the outbreak of the Comunero and Germanías revolts, which reflected the Spanish nobles' dissatisfaction with Charles's reliance on non-Hispanic ministers and advisers. Nonetheless, with the Habsburgs' territories in central Europe plus Spain's overseas colonies, Charles ruled over the greatest European empire of the period. In 1524, he established the COUNCIL OF THE INDIES to govern the American colonies and sent high courts (see *AUDIENCIA*) and VICEROYS to MEXICO and PERU to wrest control of those lands from the conquistadores (see CIVIL WARS IN PERU; LAS SALINAS, BATTLE OF). American GOLD and SILVER flowed into Spain, although not in the great quantities reached at the end of the 16th century.

Foreign threats to the empire and Habsburg dynastic ambitions consumed much of Charles's energy and many Spanish resources. The Protestant Reformation began in 1517, the same year that Charles ascended to the Spanish throne, and Charles thrust Spain into the futile struggle to maintain Catholic hegemony in Europe. Meanwhile, he tried to block French expansion south into Italy. The Turks threatened Spanish and Habsburg interests in the Balkans and the Mediterranean. All of this led to a series of costly wars. His struggle against the Franco-Turkish alliance proved indecisive. Charles was forced to recognize his defeat in the Peace of Augsburg (1555) by the Schmalkaldic League of German Protestant princes. Exhausted, he abdicated in 1556 in favor of his son Philip II but divided the empire, leaving the Germanic and Austrian territories and the imperial title to his brother Ferdinand. King Charles spent only 16 years of his nearly 40-year reign in Spain.

Besides Spain, Charles left Philip the Spanish Netherlands, Italy, and the Americas. He had arranged Philip's marriage in 1554 to Mary Tudor, queen of England, in an attempt to protect Spain's hold over the Low Countries against France. The English alliance failed, however, with Mary's death in 1558 and the ascension of the Protestant Elizabeth to the throne. Philip dutifully pursued his father's foreign policies to protect Habsburg territorial interests and defend Catholicism. He found, however, that Charles's wars had left the monarchy bankrupt. Philip moved to consolidate Spanish hold over the American colonies and benefited from a great upsurge in treasure from the Mexican and Peruvian mines (see MINING). Nevertheless, even the American gold and silver was insufficient to offset the costs of Habsburg dynastic ambitions and WARFARE.

See also CHARLES I (Vol. II); PHILIP II (Vol. II).

—Kendall Brown

Further reading:
J. H. Elliott. *Imperial Spain, 1469–1716* (New York: Viking Penguin, 1990).
John Lynch. *Spain under the Habsburgs*, 2d ed., 2 vols. (New York: New York University Press, 1981).

Haiti   See HISPANIOLA.

Hernández de Córdoba, Francisco (d. 1517)

Spanish conquistador who led an ill-fated voyage from Cuba to Mexico   Little is known of Francisco Hernández de Córdoba's life prior to 1517, except that he was born in Spain and was evidently wealthy. At some point having migrated to CUBA, where he was unsatisfied with life, Hernández proposed westward exploration to the island's governor, DIEGO VELÁZQUEZ DE CUÉLLAR. The governor eventually gave his consent, enabling a convoy of 110 men on three ships to depart from the port of Santiago de Cuba on February 8, 1517. Among the men who accompanied Hernández were Antón de Aliminos, CHRISTOPHER COLUMBUS's chief navigator, and BERNAL DÍAZ DEL CASTILLO, who later chronicled the journey as part of his remarkable account of the CONQUEST OF MEXICO (see CHRONICLERS).

On March 4, 1517, Hernández's fleet was approached by 10 Indian canoes off the coast of the Yucatán. The following day, scores of canoes arrived to transport the Spanish ashore. Widespread apprehension about the native people's intentions proved well founded; as the conquistadores approached the nearby town of Catoche, they were ambushed. The technological superiority of the Spaniards' weapons permitted them to startle the Indians, and they beat a hasty retreat. The brief encounter produced two lasting results. First, the Spanish were able to capture two indigenous men, who later became the first interpreters of the Mayan language (see MAYA). Second, while the conquistadores were fighting for their lives, their chaplain entered the town and set about stealing some trinkets, made partly of GOLD, which proved instrumental in fomenting successive Spanish expeditions.

From Catoche, the Spaniards cautiously navigated the Mexican coast, landing some two weeks later, where they were again approached by Amerindians. Fearing conflict, the Spanish quickly refilled their water casks and departed. Ten days later, they went ashore at Champotón, to be surrounded once more. This time, fighting the Maya proved much more costly. Indigenous forces attacked the Spanish in waves. Díaz del Castillo recounts that the Indians cried "*calachumi*," meaning "leader" or "chief," which ignited focused attacks on Hernández, who was struck by at least 10 arrows. The Spanish broke camp and hurried to their ships, with only one man, named Berrio, left uninjured. Fifty Spanish sailors died that day, and another five died of their wounds days later. Aliminos encouraged a

circuitous return to Cuba, skirting FLORIDA in search of much-needed freshwater. The lack of freshwater exacerbated conditions aboard the ships. Francisco Hernández de Córdoba died of his wounds days after returning to Cuba, a fate also shared by three other men.

—Sean H. Goforth

Further reading:
Bernal Díaz del Castillo. *The Discovery and Conquest of Mexico: 1517–1521* (New York: Da Capo Press, 2004).

Hispaniola (La Española)

The island of Hispaniola is one of the Greater Antilles group in the Caribbean Sea; it is nestled between CUBA to the west, PUERTO RICO to the east, Jamaica to the south, and the Bahamas to the north. In 1697, the Treaty of Ryswick between Spain and France officially divided the island into two colonies. More than a century later, in 1844, the island acquired its present division into two nations, Haiti in the western one-third and the Dominican Republic in the east. The entire island was known to its indigenous inhabitants as Haiti; *Quisqueya* (*Kiskeia*) is the indigenous term used today to designate the island.

The entire island was once covered with dense tropical and pine forests, with a great diversity of flora and fauna. Human habitation, colonization, overgrazing, and recent development have caused the extinction of some species, as well as considerable deforestation; nevertheless, the island still supports unique ecosystems with endemic orchid species, birds, lizards, and native palms. An average daily temperature of 82 degrees is moderated by constant ocean breezes. Summer rains and hurricanes can be devastating. Earthquakes have destroyed entire cities, as happened to Santiago and La Vega in 1562.

The earliest evidence of human occupation on Hispaniola dates back to 4000 B.C.E., with the arrival of immigrants from Central America; this was followed by an Archaic, or preceramic, MIGRATION around 2000–1000 B.C.E. from northeast South America. A later migration from the Orinoco river system occurred at some point around 500 B.C.E.

Each of these human populations left evidence of their material culture and settlement patterns. From the preceramic migrations, hunters and gatherers left worked chert. There are signs of CERAMICS and cultivated root crops from 500 to 250 B.C.E.; by 1000 C.E., there is clear evidence of complex social, political, and religious organization, manifested in the construction of ball courts and ceremonial plazas, petroglyphs, ritual objects such as *zemies* (tripointed carved stones), and tools for grinding plants.

Between 1000 and 1492, preceramic settlers interacted with the latest migrants; through such interactions and adaptation to new environments, the TAINO Indians emerged as a distinct regional population. The Taino spoke an Arawakan language. These people adapted well to their environment and developed agricultural systems based mostly on root crops introduced from the mainland, such as yucca, or MANIOC (*Manihot esculenta*), MAIZE (*Zea mays*), beans, squash, and peppers (see AGRICULTURE). The Taino also were seafarers who constructed huge dugout canoes that could transport as many as 150 people (see TRANSPORTATION). Their economic prehistory up to the contact period shows successful adaptations to island environments, which combined farming practices with hunting and fishing (see ECONOMY). With the island's relatively low people-to-land ratio, the indigenous inhabitants were able to produce virtually everything they needed locally; however, they also supplemented local goods with products acquired through raids and TRADE with other islands and the mainland, creating a unique way of life that was at its height at the time of the Spanish invasion.

When CHRISTOPHER COLUMBUS arrived in December 1492, he and his men encountered the Taino. At the time, the Taino were a large population, with complex economic, political, and cultural organization. Taino settlements consisted of five principal *cacicazgos*, or chiefdoms, headed by CACIQUES named Guarionex, Caonabo, Behechio, Goacanagarix, and Cayacoa. Columbus also met the Ciguayos (who spoke a different language) in the region of Macorix. The Tainos had subsistence plots (*conucos*) and home gardens, where they planted manioc, maize, yautia (*Xanthosoma*), and fruit trees. COTTON and other plants were used to produce elaborately woven cloth, baskets, and hammocks (*hamacas*) (see TEXTILES). Settlements (*yucayeches*) were located around ceremonial plazas (*bateyes*), which were used for ball games and ritual musical performances (*areitos*) (see MUSIC). These plazas were surrounded with large rectangular houses for the caciques and round houses, or *bohios*, for extended families. Taino social organization exhibited hierarchies between *nitaínos* (elites) and *naborías* and included division of LABOR by gender and age, along with craft, medical, and religious specialization (see WOMEN).

The relationships between Tainos and Columbus, initially peaceful, soon turned violent as the Spaniards plundered villages, demanded GOLD, and raped, mutilated, and murdered. Before he returned to Spain, Columbus built the first fort, LA NAVIDAD, where 39 of his men remained. The following year, Columbus embarked on his second voyage to the Americas and returned to Hispaniola; he brought Old World plants such as sugarcane, and European livestock such as pigs, goats, and cattle (see COLUMBIAN EXCHANGE; SUGAR). However, when he arrived at La Navidad, he discovered the fort destroyed and the men killed.

Despite the setback, Columbus continued his plans to colonize the island. The first colonial settlement, La Isabela, was located in the north. The site, however, was eventually moved to the south-central region where Bartolomeo Columbus founded the city of Santo Domingo, which became the *sede virreinal* (seat) of the Spanish colonial enterprise (at least until 1600). Santo Domingo is today the oldest colonial city in the Americas.

Between 1493 and 1498, internal strife arose between Columbus and many of the Spanish settlers who had joined him; in part, the conflict was rooted in the settlers' refusal to engage in manual labor and their demands for land and riches. Consecutive governors sent by Spain organized a provisional power structure between 1500 and 1509, including *repartimiento* and later ENCOMIENDA grants (granting of lands and indigenous laborers to colonists); they also established a high court, or AUDIENCIA, to settle legal disputes.

Through the *encomienda* system, the Tainos were forced to pay tribute, work in gold mines and sugar mills, and to cultivate FOOD for the local Spanish population (see MINING). Mistreatment became so severe that many Taino committed suicide, and women aborted or committed infanticide. Others simply ran away to the mountains. Those who remained were devastated by WARFARE, forced labor, and DISEASES such as smallpox, influenza, and measles.

Census figures reveal a staggering rate of extinction for Tainos; from an estimated 200,000 at initial contact, to 40,000 by 1510, and 3,000 by 1519, around 500 of whom had escaped into the mountains with a leader named Enriquillo. In response to the dramatic population decline, Spanish settlers quickly introduced African slaves (see SLAVERY). As early as 1503, slaves were brought to the island to help replenish the dwindling Taino labor force. Less than 50 years after Columbus first set foot on Hispaniola, approximately 12,000 slaves had been introduced. By 1560, few Tainos remained on Hispaniola; however, food production techniques, land-people relations, place-names, as well as many Taino terms had been adopted by Spaniards, Africans, and the growing mixed population. These influences continue to survive.

The 30,000 square miles (77,700 km²) of Hispaniola, from prehistory to 1560, offer a remarkable example of biological, social, and cultural transformation. As the first territory in the Americas to be explored, conquered, and colonized by the Spanish, it witnessed momentous and devastating events that transformed the Americas and the rest of the world. From Hispaniola came the first European taste for important foods from the New World, such as manioc, maize, chili peppers, and tomatoes. Hispaniola also experienced the first hemispheric biological exchanges of animals, humans, and plants; likewise, it served as the location of the earliest New World experiments in plantation economies, based on monocrop production of sugar and TOBACCO.

See also DOMINICAN REPUBLIC (Vols. III, IV); HAITI (Vols. III, IV); HISPANIOLA (Vol. II); SANTO DOMINGO (Vols. II, III, IV).

—Lidia Marte

Further reading:

Samuel M. Wilson, ed. *Hispaniola: Caribbean Chiefdoms in the Age of Columbus* (Tuscaloosa: University of Alabama Press, 1990).

Honduras Honduras is a small country that straddles the Central American isthmus. GUATEMALA borders it on the west and NICARAGUA on the east, with EL SALVADOR on the southwest. It is mostly a mountainous country, which supported early agricultural communities in the Ulúa, Chamelecón, and COPÁN river valleys and around the shores of Lake Yojoa in the west (see AGRICULTURE). These early communities were mostly Lenca, whose language and culture differed from that of the MAYA, who established themselves in the Copán Valley. Evidence suggests that Lenca nobility interacted freely with the Maya and even established residences in the Maya capital of Copán, though there may have been racial tension between the two groups during the Classic period (250–900 C.E.).

The pre-Columbian history of Honduras was dominated by the rise and fall of Copán. The later centuries are told in historical inscriptions from that site, while archaeologists have relied on CERAMICS, soil samples, and excavations for information about the prehistory of Honduras. Scholars have concluded that the Preclassic period was marked by three main influences: the introduction of the Maya into Honduras, TRADE and cultural contacts with KAMINALJUYÚ, and the eruption of Ilopango Volcano.

It is not known precisely when the Maya arrived in the Copán Valley. Evidence from there and from Lake Yojoa indicate charcoal burning and MAIZE cultivation in Honduras as early as 4500 B.C.E. This is well before the rise of Izapa culture in the Late Preclassic period along the Pacific Guatemala coast. Kaminaljuyú in the Guatemala highlands, and Chalchuapa in the shadow of Ilopango Volcano in El Salvador, served as conduits of the Izapa and, later, their culture to western Honduras.

The spread of writing, belief systems, sculpture, ceramics, and ARCHITECTURE does not in itself infer the movement of people. Indeed, local chiefs in north and central Honduras, where Lenca dialects dominated, were able to command LABOR resources to build raised platforms for elite residences and places of worship at Yarumela, Los Naranjos, and Baida in the Comayagua Valley and at Santo Domingo, Río Pelo, and La Guacamaya to the north. These places bore spatial similarities to the much larger centers of Kaminaljuyú, Chalchuapa, and Usulután; and ceramics manufactured in the latter were traded throughout Honduras. Even Los Achiotes and Cerro Chino in the Copán Valley were organized on the pattern of the Lenca sites to the north and east.

The Copán pocket itself was different, however. While it shared in the Usulután trade, Copán did not develop monumental architecture during the Preclassic period. Then, sometime between 200 and 250 C.E., Ilopango Volcano erupted. The massive ashfall buried Chalchuapa and cut off Honduras from the Pacific coast. Trade connections with Kaminaljuyú were broken, and within a 60-mile (96.5-km) radius of the eruption much of the land was rendered unfit to support dense populations for up to 200 years. As a result of this disaster, many Lenca centers disintegrated; the Preclassic period was over.

The effects of the eruption spread far beyond Honduras. Trade from Central Mexico and the city of TEOTIHUACÁN shifted north to river routes through the Petén. EL MIRADOR and, later, TIKAL, CALAKMUL, Palenque, and other Maya sites rose to prominence. In Honduras, CACAO, which formerly was grown mainly on Pacific coast plantations, now began to be cultivated on the Caribbean coast.

It was at this time that the population of the Copán Valley, although still relatively small, began to grow and coalesce. A system of drainage canals was started, and the first ceremonial center, called Yune by archaeologists, was built. There is speculation that some of the refugees of the eruption brought their talents and families to Honduras and particularly to Copán. Curiously, structure 10L-7 at Copán bears a doorjamb inscribed with the Long Count date 8.10.10.10.16, which corresponds to April 4, 249 C.E. This is the end of the range of time for

The remarkable Stela 13 was commissioned by Tikal's ruler Siyaj Chan K'awiil II (r. 411–456). The front of the stela (pictured here) shows the ruler in ornate and archaic Maya regalia, with additional symbols that represent his Central Mexico ancestry. *(Courtesy of J. Michael Francis)*

The side of Altar Q at Copán shows Yax K'uk' Mo', the founder of the dynasty there, literally passing the torch to his 16th successor, Yax Pasaj Chan Yoaat. The latter, who commissioned this piece, is thereby claiming an unbroken chain of legitimacy from the founder. *(Courtesy of Janice Van Cleve)*

the Ilopango eruption and could be an important reference to it at Copán.

Two other early dates are recorded at Copán. Stela I, erected in 676 records that on December 18, 159 C.E., 120 years had been completed since some unknown event. The event occurred at or by "bent kawak" in the land of a person called "Foliated Ahau." Interestingly, the "bent kawak" also appears on Tikal's Stela 31 and at Yaxchilán, both in association with the foundations of dynasties. Stela 4 at Copán, raised in 726, also refers to the events of 159 and to Foliated Ahau.

Foliated Ahau is also identified on a carved peccary skull found in a tomb at Copán. The cartouche in the center shows two people sitting on either side of a stela and altar. The inscription reads *"hun ahau waxak chen kaltuun foliated ahau,"* which translates as, "On October 21, 376, the stone was bound by Foliated Ahau." This date is just two years before the invasion of Tikal by Siyaj K'ak and his Central Mexico army. The subordinate person on the left, who points to the text, is none other than Yax K'uk' Mo', who invaded Honduras in 427, killed the ruler, and

established a Maya dynasty at Copán that lasted almost 400 years. The person on the top right appears to be Yax Nuun Ayiin, the son of a ruler whom scholars have named Spearthrower Owl; it was Yax Nuun Ayiin who was placed on the throne of Tikal by Siyaj Kak in 378.

For years, archaeologists speculated on the identity of this Foliated Ahau person, but more recent analysis concludes that it is a title of royalty. The peccary skull translation is, therefore, more precisely, "On October 21, 376, the stone was bound by His Majesty." If "his majesty" is indeed Yax Nuun Ayiin of Tikal and Yax K'uk' Mo' is his subordinate, then the peccary skull is witness to a vassal relationship of Copán to Tikal. In fact, the Mayan name for Copán is *Xukpi*, which means "corner bundle." The "bundle" is Tikal, which is represented in the glyph for a hair bundle. The "corner bundle" would be a contemporary recognition that Copán was a frontier outpost of Tikal's authority.

As ruler, Yax K'uk' Mo' radically transformed both Copán and the entire river valley. In his new capital, he set in motion a massive building program, which included the construction of new temples, reorganizing the Yune platform, and laying out the great plaza. He drew villagers into urban centers and set up noble fiefdoms. He established a new RELIGION of blood sacrifice and direct intercession by the ruler between the deities and the populace. His son, Popol Hol, solidified his achievements and set in motion the Copán dynasty, which would eventually overshadow, if not subjugate, the Lenca centers in western and central Honduras. Copán's dominance persisted at least until 738.

In 738, the 13th ruler of the Copán dynasty, Waxaklajuun Ub'aah K'awiil, was defeated and killed by his rival in Guatemala; from that point on, the dominance of the capital over the rest of Honduras began to fade. In 822, the Copán dynasty failed, and local chieftains once again asserted their independence. By 1200, the cities were abandoned to the jungle. The Maya still existed in the countryside, and in 1530, a local chief named Copán Calel led a rebellion against the Spanish, and thus it was his name that became associated with the ruins of Xukpi. The first recorded visit to the site of Copán was by Spanish conquistador Diego García de Palacio in 1576.

See also HONDURAS (Vols. II, III, IV).

—Janice Van Cleve

Further reading:
Ellen Bell, Marcello Canuto, and Robert Sharer. *Understanding Early Classic Copán* (Philadelphia: University of Pennsylvania Museum of Archeology & Anthropology, 2004).

huaca (wak'a)   The term *huaca* (*wak'a*) is a QUECHUA word for an Andean sacred place or object. A *huaca* could be a temple, mountain peak, cave, spring, or any unusual natural object. Some *huacas* were idols. Adoration of *huacas* predated the rise of the Inca Empire (Tawantinsuyu) (see INCAS). Each AYLLU (clan or ethnic group) had its own *huacas*. Worship of *huacas* included prayer, rituals, offerings of FOOD and drink, and sacrifice of animals and occasionally humans (see HUMAN SACRIFICE). Andeans also considered mummies of important persons to be *huacas* and worshipped them. The mummies of deceased rulers were preserved in the Inca capital of CUZCO and were brought out to participate as *huacas* in important festivities. In their attempts to control conquered *ayllus*, the Incas sometimes carried off *huacas* to Cuzco, where they held the sacred objects hostage. By so doing, they hoped to ensure the cooperation of the subject peoples.

Spanish conquistadores looted many *huacas* as they searched for treasures, particularly GOLD and SILVER buried in elite tombs or used to adorn temples. They plundered the great pilgrimage shrine of Pachacamac on the coast near present-day LIMA. When FRANCISCO PIZARRO and his men arrived in Cuzco, they destroyed the mummies of the deceased Inca rulers as part of the campaign to stamp out indigenous RELIGION. Andean grave robbers were, and still are, called *huaqueros*.

The term continued in use after the CONQUEST to differentiate between Andean religion and Christianity. In the mid-1560s, Spanish priests discovered a revival of Andean religion, which became known as the TAKI ONQOY (dancing sickness). Its adherents chastised Andeans for abandoning the *huacas* and revealed that the *huacas* would rise up to kill or expel the Spaniards through DISEASE, earthquakes, and other disasters if Andeans would begin worshipping the *huacas* again. *Taquiongos* were messengers of the *huacas* or deities.

—Kendall Brown

Further reading:
Bernabé Cobo. *Inca Religion and Customs*, translated and edited by Roland Hamilton (Austin: University of Texas Press, 1990).

Huáscar (Washkar) (b. ca. 1495–d. 1532) *Inca emperor* Born sometime around 1495 in CUZCO, Huáscar was one of the Inca emperor HUAYNA CÁPAC's oldest sons and reputedly his designated heir: Huayna Cápac was said to have more than 50 sons, and after the untimely death of his chosen heir, Ninan Cuyochi, he named Huáscar as his preferred successor (see INCAS). Huáscar was groomed as an administrator from an early age.

Leaving Huáscar behind as an administrator in Cuzco, in 1524, Huayna Cápac journeyed to the northern provinces near present-day Quito, ECUADOR, to continue his conquests; there, he joined the company of his favorite son and trusted general, ATAHUALPA, and his designated heir, Ninan Cuyochi. Atahualpa was both Huáscar and Ninan Cuyochi's younger half brother. During the campaigns near Quito, Ninan Cuyochi died of a strange DISEASE, which may have been smallpox.

After the death of Ninan Cuyochi, Huayna Cápac continued to expand the empire; however, now having more affection for his surviving son Atahualpa, and reportedly at Atahualpa's urging, he realized that the empire was too large to be ruled by a single Inca from the capital of Cuzco. Before his death by disease in 1527, Huayna Cápac made the fateful error of dividing the empire into two halves. One half was to be ruled from Cuzco, with Huáscar as its emperor; the other was to be ruled jointly by Huáscar and his younger half brother, Atahualpa.

Huáscar was envious of Atahualpa's status as Huayna Cápac's favorite son. Even before the death of their father in 1527, the empire and its armies and administrators had divided into factions that supported either Huáscar or Atahualpa. A majority of the administrators, nobility, and bureaucrats in Cuzco supported Huáscar. Atahualpa, on the other hand, enjoyed the support of the bulk of his father's army, which was stationed in the north. When Huayna Cápac died, the empire was thrown into a long, bitter, and violent civil war that did not end until 1532, with the arrival of the Spanish conquerors under the command of FRANCISCO PIZARRO.

Late in 1532, Atahualpa's armies, led by his general Quizquiz, managed to take Cuzco and capture Huáscar. Despite being imprisoned by the Spaniards, Atahualpa sent the order to have Huáscar murdered. But after Huáscar's brutal death in late 1532, his supporters and allies continued to fight against Atahualpa and his followers; moreover, they offered aid to the Spaniards in the ultimate CONQUEST of PERU.

—John F. Chuchiak IV

Further reading:
Juan de Betanzos. *Narrative of the Incas*, translated and edited by Roland Hamilton and Dana Buchanan (Austin: University of Texas Press, 1996).

Huayna Cápac (Wayna Qhapaq, Tito Cusi Gualpa)

(d. ca. 1527) *Inca emperor* Huayna Cápac was the last great Sapa Inca (r. ca. 1493–1527) before the Spanish CONQUEST of PERU in the 1530s. His death touched off a civil war between factions headed by two of his sons (HUÁSCAR and ATAHUALPA), and the Spaniards exploited the conflict to defeat the INCAS.

Before his unexpected death in the mid-1490s, Huayna Cápac's father, Topa Inca Yupanqui, had named two of his sons to succeed him. He first designated as his heir Tito Cusi Gualpa, the youngest son of his principal wife (COYA), Mama Ocllo. Shortly thereafter, however, the Inca changed his mind and settled on Cápac Guari, the son of one of his secondary wives. Supporters of Tito Cusi Gualpa killed the rival in the ensuing struggle, and he became Sapa Inca, assuming the name Huayna Cápac. He was a young boy, however, and for several years his uncle, Huaman Achachi, acted as regent. When he began to rule, Huayna Cápac ordered the execution of two of his brothers, whom he perceived as dangerous rivals, and married his sister Cusi Rimay. When she died, he married another sister, Chimbo Ocllo. As was customary, he also had secondary wives and concubines taken from provinces throughout Tawantinsuyu (the Inca Empire).

Huayna Cápac ruled for a quarter-century and founded the Tumipampa PANAQA (royal AYLLU, or lineage group). He repelled a minor invasion of GUARANÍ-speaking Chiriguanos from PARAGUAY. Huayna Cápac's predecessors had already extended Tawantinsuyu throughout the central and northern Andes, and he added to it Quito (whose conquest had begun under his father) and the territory of the Chachapoyas.

A smallpox or measles epidemic spreading southward from the Caribbean killed Huayna Cápac around 1527 (some scholars have placed his death as early as 1525 and as late as 1530) (see DISEASE). He had designated a son named Ninan Cuyochi as his heir, but he, too, died during the epidemic. Two other sons, Atahualpa and

Huáscar, each supported by rival *panaqas*, fought a bitter civil war to succeed Huayna Cápac. This conflict greatly facilitated the Spanish conquest of Peru, as FRANCISCO PIZARRO and his men arrived just as Atahualpa's faction had triumphed.

—Kendall Brown

Further reading:
Maria Rostworowski de Diez Canseco. *History of the Inca Realm*, translated by Harry B. Iceland (New York: Cambridge University Press, 1999).

human sacrifice

Human sacrifice appears to have been an important facet of cultures in the Americas before European contact, particularly in Mesoamerica. South of Mesoamerica, the Chibchas of PANAMA, Caucas of COLOMBIA, Jíbaros of ECUADOR, the TUPINAMBÁ of BRAZIL, and various cultures in PERU offered human sacrifices in religious rituals and to commemorate important events (see RELIGION). Eyewitness accounts, depictions in pre-Hispanic ART and documents, and skeletal remains recovered from caves, cenotes (sinkholes), and other deposits provide convincing evidence of the practice. However, scholarly debates continue about the extent, scale, and disparate purposes of these sacrificial rites.

Sacrificial victims could be men, WOMEN, or children, depending on the context. For example, in some regions, a principal motivation for WARFARE was to take captives for sacrifice; not surprisingly, most of these captives were male. In other contexts, women were sacrificed by being buried alive or poisoned in order to accompany a deceased leader into the afterlife as wives or servants. Children became sacrificial victims because of their innocence or because their tears resembled rainfall, which the priest hoped to stimulate. Some cultures treated future victims with respect, granting them special privileges and even adopting captive members of enemy groups for a period of time. This partly explains why some went willingly to their deaths, but ALCOHOL and drugs also reduced resistance.

The lives of sacrificial victims were terminated through diverse means. Possibly the most widespread practice was decapitation with a knife or ax. Decapitation was associated with the Mesoamerican ball game; friezes show that losing the game often meant losing one's head. The head might be displayed on a skull rack (called a *tzompantli* by the AZTECS) or deposited in a pit beneath a building or in a plaza.

Heart extraction was another common method of human sacrifice. In Mesoamerica, priests stretched the victim over a sacrificial stone, opened the chest with a knife, and tore out the still-beating heart. In areas under influence from Central Mexico, the heart was thrown into a receptacle held by a reclining stone figure (Chac-Mool) and burned. In some Mesoamerican rituals, sacrificial

A section of the stone skull rack, or *tzompantli,* at the Aztec ruins of the Templo Mayor complex in Mexico City *(Courtesy of J. Michael Francis)*

victims were bound to scaffolds and shot with arrows or *atlatl* darts or disemboweled with spears. A series of carved stone relief panels at MONTE ALBÁN, Oaxaca, depicts disemboweled and sexually mutilated men.

On other occasions, victims were thrown from cliffs or down stone stairways. Some ball game reliefs show victims rolling down stairways with their arms and legs tied behind them. In Yucatán, individuals were pushed off the edge of the sacred cenote at CHICHÉN ITZÁ to drown in the deep water (see MAYA).

War captives in the Aztec and Tupinambá cultures fought gladiatorial battles using inferior weapons against fully armed warriors. Children were taken to mountaintops in the Andes and given intoxicating beverages before being left to die of exposure. Victims' eyes were stabbed with sharp instruments and their skulls were smashed with clubs. Some victims were roasted over fires. The scalp was torn from the skull, skin was cut from the face of living victims, and ceremonial suits were tailored from flayed skin.

Europeans in the early colonial period responded to these practices with disgust. Despite their concerted efforts to abolish human sacrifice, it continued in remote areas.

—Stephen L. Whittington

Further reading:

Nigel Davies. *Human Sacrifice in History and Today* (New York: Dorset Press, 1981).

Incas The Incas were a group who settled in the Cuzco Valley in the south-central Andes of South America between 1000 and 1400 C.E.; there, they founded the city of Cuzco (in modern-day PERU) on the site of earlier settlements. The new city quickly emerged as the capital of the largest empire ever forged in South America.

The Andes Mountains are situated between a narrow and arid coastal desert strip in the west and jungle and rain forest regions to the east; many peaks in the ranges reach elevations above 19,685 feet (6,000 m) and are covered in snow. Although initially a highland culture, the Incas' territorial expansion acquainted them with contrasting topographic and climatic zones; they learned to adapt to and exploit the many micro-environments concentrated in relatively small areas. The Incas traded surplus goods with their neighbors for those that they lacked (see TRADE). This system founded the important Andean principle of complementarity. The Incas indigenous language was QUECHUA, which continues to be spoken by their descendants, primarily in the central Andean region. What we know about the Incas comes from Spanish chronicles and historical documents and from archaeological excavations.

Before 1400 C.E., the Incas formed but one of a multitude of localized ethnic polities, or *señoríos*, rivaling for power in the Cuzco Basin. Scholars characterize preimperial Inca society as a chiefdom. Sometime around 1400, the Incas began to emerge as the dominant regional polity, conquering, subjugating, and forging alliances with their neighbors. The archaeological record of these neighbors is dominated by Killke CERAMICS, which have been found in the center of Cuzco, in the Cuzco Valley, as well as in outlying areas. Some of the larger and more powerful ethnic groups were the Anta and Ayarmaca to the west and northwest of the Cuzco Valley, the Cuyo to the north, and the Pinahua to the southeast. Over the course of several generations, Inca society transformed from a small, localized state to a vast empire, encompassing contiguous territories from southern COLOMBIA to CHILE and northwestern ARGENTINA. This empire, known as Tawantinsuyu (Land of the Four Quarters), was ruled from the capital city of Cuzco, which became its physical and ideological center.

One of the strategies the Incas used to justify and legitimize their growing power was to veil their origins in mythology. The archaeological record has identified and confirmed certain sites mentioned in Inca oral traditions, and the chronology of the ethnographic accounts squarely matches the archaeological data. The two dominant origin tales say that the Incas were not locals but foreigners sent by deities from supernatural places. The first narrative puts their point of origin on the Island of the Sun in Lake Titicaca, in modern BOLIVIA. It was there that the creator god Viracocha called forth the Sun, the Moon, and the stars from holes in a sacred rock outcrop. This outcrop became one of the most important pilgrimage sites in the Andes and was appropriated by the Incas into their state ideology. The outcrop has been identified and investigated as the principal sanctuary on the Island of the Sun and is situated in its northern sector. After setting the celestial bodies in motion, Viracocha fashioned humans. The Sun named Manco Cápac and Mama Ocllo as the principal couple, brought them forth from the rock outcrop, and sent them on an underground journey in a northwestern direction to find a "chosen" valley for their people to settle. They reemerged at a location known as Tampu T'oqo.

Scholars believe that the official Inca myth centered on this site and on another called Pacariqtambo. Tampu T'oqo was a place with three caves, located near Pacariqtambo. Today, a town named Pacariqtambo is situated in the province of Paruro, south of Cuzco. The ancient Pacariqtambo has been identified as the Inca site Maukallaqta and is located less than six miles (9.6 km) north of contemporary Pacariqtambo. The nearby carved rock outcrop, called Pumaurqu, is thought to have been the origin place Tampu T'oqo. The creator called forth Manco Cápac and Mama Ocllo and their three brothers and three sisters; from them came the Inca ancestors from the central cave, and the Maras and Tampu peoples from the adjoining caves. The brothers and sisters were paired as couples, with Manco Cápac and his sister-wife Mama Ocllo assuming leadership. The four couples began to search for fertile lands, followed by many local groups. From the mountain of Huanacauri (outside present-day Cuzco), they saw a fertile valley. A golden rod was cast into the earth, and when it stuck firmly in the ground, the Inca knew they had found their home. Manco Cápac led his party into the pre-Inca settlement that was to become Cuzco. Manco was the only brother left because the other three had been transformed into stone or locked in a cave during the journey.

RULERS

Manco Cápac was the first in a line of 13 Inca sovereigns (Sapa Incas) who governed before the Spanish invasion of 1532; these 13 rulers (also referred to simply as Inca) included three who governed in the postcontact 16th century. The term *Cápac*, meaning "noble" or "of high status" in Quechua, was adopted by some later rulers and lineages to signal that they were close to the royal descent line that, beginning with Manco Cápac, identified rulers as sons of the Sun and emphasized their close linkage with rock shrines. The history of Inca rulers is known through partial biographies by a number of Spanish CHRONICLERS. Manco Cápac and his followers were the first to live in what was to become the imperial capital of Cuzco. At the time of their arrival, the future site of Cuzco was a village called Acamama, whose inhabitants produced Killke ceramics. This settlement consisted of four sections: Quinti Cancha, or the District of the Hummingbird; Chumbi Cancha, or the District of the Weavers; Sairi Cancha, or the District of Tobacco; and Yarambuy Cancha, likely a mixed district inhabited by Aymara (Aymara is the indigenous language spoken by people in the southern Andes and particularly in Bolivia) and Quechua speakers. Acamama was also divided into upper (*hanan*) and lower (*hurin*) halves. The quadripartite and dual spatial divisions (which the Inca appropriated and integrated into their capital and state organization), therefore, were present in the pre-Inca settlement. Concepts of a four-part order as well as binary oppositions and complementarity were part of a pan-Andean thought system, which the Inca shared and manipulated to their political advantage.

There is no consensus as to whether the first seven Inca rulers were actual historical figures or mythological individuals. The chronology implied by the Spanish chroniclers is not confirmed by the archaeological record. The rulers' names are reported as Sinchi Roca, the son of Manco Cápac and the second ruler, followed by Lloque Yupanqui, Mayta Cápac, Cápac Yupanqui, Inca Roca, and Yahuar Huacac. Beginning with the eighth ruler, Viracocha Inca, the records become more extensive. Much of the information relating to Viracocha Inca focuses on military conquests; in fact, it may have been this ruler who changed Inca military strategies from raiding and alliances to territorial expansion.

The notorious CHANCA WARS are widely discussed in the literature. The Chancas were another local *señorío*, with ambitions to enlarge their own territory; their expansionist strategies eventually led to a violent clash with the Incas. The Chanca army vastly outnumbered that of the Inca, which caused Viracocha Inca to abandon Cuzco and flee to his estate at Caquia Xaquixaguana (Juchuy Qosqo). There, he was joined by Inca Urcon, his son and heir, and most of Cuzco's elite. However, his other son, Inca Yupanqui (see PACHACUTI INCA YUPANQUI), decided to remain in Cuzco with a few equally committed men who vowed to defend the city or die trying.

The night before the decisive battle, Inca Yupanqui prayed for assistance and the Creator God appeared to him in a dream and vision, promising additional warriors and final victory. And, so it happened: During the battle, the number of Inca fighters magically increased, as stones transformed into warriors, and they repelled the Chanca assault. Based upon detailed narratives provided in several chronicles, archaeologists engaged in survey work on the plains west of Cuzco believe they may have identified the site of this battle, which took place in 1438.

This remarkable victory was followed by a period of tension between Inca Yupanqui and his father, who remained at Caquia Xaquixaguana. But, eventually, Viracocha Inca traveled to Cuzco, placed the fringe of rulership on Inca Yupanqui's head, and gave his son the title "Pachacuti Ynga Yupangui Capac Yndichuri," which means "change of time, King Yupanqui, son of the Sun." In the end, Pachacuti Inca Yupanqui accepted his father's apologies for past offenses, including a failed assassination attempt, and the two participated in the festivities of Cuzco together until Viracocha Inca's death.

While stories such as the tale of the Chanca wars are popular, and the result of the historical mindset of colonial Spanish chroniclers, systematic archaeological survey work in areas surrounding Cuzco has demonstrated that Inca state formation did not result from the victorious outcome of the Chanca wars. Rather, the Inca state and imperial expansion were based on long-term regional social, political, and economic processes, which included multiple wars with different ethnic groups as well as more peaceful strategies, such as marriage alliances (see WARFARE).

The Inca site of Ollantaytambo, Peru. The image shows the terraces and ceremonial sector with the so-called Sun Temple. *(Courtesy of Jessica Christie)*

Pachacuti Inca Yupanqui's reign is dated to the middle of the 15th century. True to his title, he is credited with transforming the emerging Inca state into an empire; he is also credited with redesigning Cuzco as a capital that would materialize his imperial ambitions.

Of course, Inca settlements soon extended well beyond the city itself. Other significant architectural constructions dotted the closer environs of Cuzco (see ARCHITECTURE). These were the royal estates of individual rulers, many of which lined the Urubamba Valley, a fertile agricultural zone that provided most of the crops for Cuzco's residents. Well-known Inca sites along the Urubamba River, such as Pisac, Ollantaytambo, and MACHU PICCHU, have now been identified as royal estates of Pachacuti. Royal estates were multipurpose architectural complexes maintained by retainers (see YANA) of the sovereign: They showcased agricultural terraces, storage buildings, temples, and country palaces where the ruler and his courtiers enjoyed leisure time in settings tightly linked to the natural surroundings. There was no architectural canon for royal estates; each represented a personalized discourse between the ambitions of the royal patron and the natural landscape.

Inca rulers built numerous country estates, in part because of the split-inheritance system. When a sovereign died, his eldest son inherited the highest office; all his material possessions, however, passed on to members of his lineage (PANAQA), who administered his properties and maintained the cult of his mummy. The new ruler had to acquire, and that meant conquer, new lands and build new palaces. Thus, the most desirable areas, such as the Urubamba Valley, were quickly taken. HUÁSCAR, the 12th Inca ruler, is said to have become angry with the dead because they owned all the best properties which, he argued, should be given to the living.

In terms of military conquests, Pachacuti and his son, Topa Inca Yupanqui, together accumulated a territory that extended from Cuzco in the center to much of modern Ecuador in the north, and into southern Bolivia to the south. Nevertheless, strips of the central and southern coasts were not yet part of the Inca Empire. Pachacuti's successors continued to focus on territorial expansion. Topa Inca Yupanqui acceded in 1471, and he is widely seen as the conqueror par excellence. He added vast territories to the east into the lowland jungle areas, southeast, and south beyond today's Santiago de Chile and northwestern Argentina. In the north, Topa Inca conquered Quito, and on the central coast, he annexed the area that now includes LIMA. His best-known estate is Chinchero, which was located in the highland zone between Cuzco and the Urubamba Valley.

HUAYNA CÁPAC succeeded Topa Inca in 1493. He was said to have made military expansion and administrative organization equally important priorities. While part of his military campaigns involved securing borders, he also advanced to the north beyond Quito and to the southeast beyond Samaipata, a site known for the largest rock outcrop sculpted by the Inca. Thus, the Inca Empire reached its widest territorial expansion under Huayna Cápac. He turned Tumipampa in Ecuador into a second imperial capital, where political and military might were focused during his reign. While he was fighting in the north, an epidemic broke out and Huayna Cápac died from it ca. 1527. His heir designate, Ninan Cuyochi, experienced the same fate, which precipitated a conflict over succession.

Following Huayna Cápac's death and that of his heir, HUÁSCAR and ATAHUALPA, two royal sons by different mothers, fought a bitter civil war over the title of rulership; the costly conflict lasted until just before the arrival of the Spaniards in 1532. Initially, it was Huáscar who became emperor in Cuzco, with the consent of the nobility. His half brother Atahualpa may have accepted his rule at first. However, after he had several of Atahualpa's messengers murdered, the latter challenged the emperor's authority from his base of power in the north, now Ecuador, where part of the Inca army was stationed. Huáscar responded with military action. Bloody battles were waged for several years, claiming the lives of thousands and severely weakening Inca power on the eve of the Spaniards' arrival. In the end, Huáscar was captured, and Atahualpa came out of the war victorious. Atahualpa's officials took Huáscar to Cuzco, where he was forced to watch the execution of most of his immediate family and relatives.

Atahualpa himself was still in Cajamarca, waiting for the defeated Huáscar, when he received word that a contingent of strangers had arrived at Tumbes on the north coast. The small Spanish force, under the leadership of FRANCISCO PIZARRO, quickly made its way up into the Andes and arrived at Cajamarca on November 15, 1532 (see CONQUEST). There, in a surprise attack, Atahualpa was taken prisoner; the captured Inca responded by offering an immense ransom of GOLD objects in exchange for his freedom. Eight months later, after the ransom had been paid, Atahualpa was convicted of treason and executed.

The Spaniards then marched on to Cuzco, which they entered unopposed on November 15, 1533. Pizarro gave most of Cuzco's palaces and other buildings to members of his own party, and they set about plundering the Inca capital of its wealth. The most valuable treasures were found in the Coricancha (Temple of the Sun), which was looted despite the loud protests of its priests. In December 1533, following traditional ceremonial protocol, MANCO INCA was installed as the new Inca ruler. Manco Inca, another of Huayna Cápac's sons, had escaped the massacre inflicted by Atahualpa's men. Pizarro believed that Manco would be a compliant puppet through whom he himself could govern.

Manco Inca, however, had higher ambitions. He escaped from Cuzco, assembled an army, and became the leader of a resistance movement. In 1536, his forces laid siege on Cuzco and attacked the newly founded Ciudad de los Reyes (Lima) on the coast. Manco's goal was to expel the Spaniards from the entire Andean region.

During the siege, the Spanish were far outnumbered; they barricaded themselves at Sacsayhuamán, the fortified citadel above Cuzco. In the end, the Spaniards and their allies held the capital, and the attack on Ciudad de los Reyes failed as well. Still, the resistance movement did not give up; instead, it went underground into the eastern lowland jungles. After his initial escape from Cuzco, Manco Inca founded Vilcabamba as his new capital. For the next 36 years, the Inca maintained an independent state at Vilcabamba, where they enjoyed their liberty, fomented plans to regain their lands, and organized campaigns against the invaders. Over that period, Vilcabamba was governed by three rulers: Manco Inca was succeeded by Titu Cusi, who in turn was followed by Túpac Amaru. Vilcabamba has been identified as a large archaeological site near the present village of Espíritu Pampa, in Peru. Ongoing archaeological investigations are revealing that Manco Inca used many of the same architectural and sculptural design features as found in Cuzco.

The Spaniards were thoroughly annoyed by this resistance and sent several expeditions into the forests to subjugate the rebels. These efforts proved of no avail until Viceroy Francisco de Toledo himself led an expedition and conquered Vilcabamba in 1572. The last Inca ruler, Túpac Amaru, was taken to Cuzco and sentenced to death. The imposition of stable Spanish rule was a slow process. The first decades were plagued by civil wars among the conquistadores (see CIVIL WARS IN PERU) and by epidemics of European DISEASES, which wrought devastation on the Andean people. Estimates suggest that within four decades of the invasion, the population had been reduced by half. Beginning in the 1550s, the Spanish Crown dispatched a series of VICEROYS to Peru to establish order and civil administration.

ADMINISTRATION

The stunning rise and expansion of the Inca Empire began in the early 1400s; in less than a century, the empire covered most of the Andes, from modern Ecuador to southern Chile and northwestern Argentina. This expansion was made possible by a well-organized administrative system, anchored in religious practices that transformed newly conquered territories into ideological landscapes. The primary administrative units were the provinces into which newly acquired territories were shaped and which were ruled by governors. Archaeologists have identified major settlements as the seats of provincial governments, such as Vilcashuamán, Huánuco Pampa, Cajamarca, and Tumipampa in the north and Hatunqolla, Chucuito, and Tambo Colorado south of Cuzco. These provincial centers were state installations and often copied architectural designs and political protocol of the capital. They were physically and administratively very different from the private royal estates of Inca rulers, such as Pisac, Ollantaytambo, and Machu Picchu in the Urubamba Valley, or Topa Inca's estate at Chinchero. The Sapa Inca and his court frequently traveled and

resided at both types of settlements. Throughout the empire, the Incas grouped households into units of 10 to 10,000 who were responsible for civil duties, such as farming, herding, and arts and craft production, as well as military service (see ART). Each unit of 100 or more households was led by a hereditary local chief, called a KURAKA. All units were required to send tribute based on their local resources to the state, centered in Cuzco; they were also required to provide rotational LABOR service to the Inca state (see MITA). Another strategy was forced resettlement: Inca officials selected thousands of families and entire communities from each new province to be moved to different locations, often thousands of miles away, to establish enclaves of settlers referred to as *mitimas*. The main goal of this policy was to break up societies that posed security threats to the Inca state; another motive was to create communities of economic specialists whose products were vital to the state. Most significant in arts and craft production controlled by the state were metallurgy, TEXTILES, and ceramics. The most valuable and symbolically charged metals were gold and SILVER, which were associated with the Sun and the Moon and reserved for the ruling family. High-quality *cumbi* textiles were woven from COTTON and wools, and ceramic styles were dominated by flared-rim jars with constricted necks and pointed bottoms, often called *aribalos*, drinking cups or tumblers (*queros*), and large storage jars, all of which generally exhibited geometric black linear designs on a reddish brown ground. Many of these objects were displayed, used, or given away at public events, such as feasts, which helped forge loyalties between the administration and its subjects.

To maintain communication links between Cuzco, the provinces, and the periphery, the Incas developed two highly effective administrative tools: They kept records with knotted-string devices called QUIPUs, and they constructed the most far-flung road system in precontact America. A *quipu* consisted of a main cord and a series of attached pendant cords. The pendant strings displayed sets of different knot types at equal intervals, which stood for decimal units. The lower units, ones and tens, were situated farthest away from the main cord, and the higher units were closer to the top. Different string colors may have indicated that different objects were counted. *Quipus* were knotted, read, and stored by *quipu* specialists called *quipucamayocs* and registered statistical information related to census data, tribute collection, and religious service, all of which were vital to the state.

The road system (Cápac Ñan) consisted of two main north-south transportation routes. One route was located in the highlands and the other along the coast, and both were connected by numerous smaller roads. Together, the road system linked roughly 25,000 miles (40,225 km) of roadway. Inca roads were traveled by the CHASQUI (runners who disseminated messages), traders, and armies. Further, Inca roads held an important place in state-imposed religious ideology. They connected Cuzco with powerful pilgrimage sites, such as the Island of the Sun in Lake Titicaca and Pachacamac on the central coast, and they were often marked by rock shrines (see HUACA). Roads were also traveled by parties of provincial officials, who brought sacrificial items, including children, to the capital to be sanctified. They then returned to their villages, walking in straight-line paths, and presented the sacrifices to all local *huacas* (see ZEQUE SYSTEM). The practice of *capac ucha* was important in building and maintaining links between the state center and its periphery. It cast the road system in the religious context of linking various *huacas*, which may be seen as a large-scale duplicate of local *zeque* systems, thus integrating all Inca territories.

RELIGION

The Inca worldview did not include the Western subject-object separation; rather, the world was a lived bodily experience in which all objects and features were endowed with a life force. Mountains were personified, caves and water sources provided access to the animated world below, and living humans interacted with dead ancestors. The source of all waters was the Pacific Ocean, from which water rose in the form of clouds to fertilize the earth as rain; to complete the hydraulic cycle, it collected in rivers and lakes to return to the ocean. Stone was the essence of mountains, and selected boulders and outcrops were sculpted for a number of purposes; they served as seats, offering tables for the earth, counting devices, and trail markers from which visual links with certain mountains could be constructed. Rock outcrops were further integrated into architecture, and the scale and variety of stone modification played out the discourse between the Incas and their natural surroundings; ultimately, stone formulated a specifically Inca political landscape.

Many natural features were perceived as origin places of the Inca dynasty and of individual AYLLUs (extended lineages defined not only by blood relations but also by land and water rights). The ancestor of an *ayllu* was said to have emerged from a specific cave or water body, and it became the duty of all descendants to maintain this feature as a *huaca*. In case an *ayllu* was relocated by the state, its members carried a piece of the rock or a vessel of the water taken from their origin place (*pacarisca*) and added it to a similar feature at their new settlement to create a new *pacarisca*.

Machu Picchu's Intiwatana stone sculpture served in the observation of the movements of the Sun. *(Courtesy of Jessica Christie)*

Specific deities manipulated by the state to legitimize the authority of the emperor were Inti, the Sun, and Viracocha, the Creator God. Both played a vital role in Inca origin narratives and were understood by the Incas as the protagonists of creation in the Lake Titicaca region. All large settlements had a temple dedicated to the Sun, where the ruler performed his pivotal role as son of the Sun on earth. The central and richest of these temples was the Coricancha in Cuzco, which housed a golden image of Inti, known as Punchao. Secondary deities populated the landscape; they included the *apus*, or spirits of high mountain peaks; Inti-Illapa, the god of thunder; Mama-Quilla, mother moon; and Pachamama, the earth mother. Inca rulers, assisted by a class of priests, honored these deities through ceremony and sacrifice organized by a ritual calendar that culminated in the Cápac Raymi and Inti Raymi festivals held on the December and June solstices. The main purpose of both events was to honor the Sun, which was done through dancing, feasting, and drinking CHICHA, an alcoholic drink made from fermented MAIZE (see ALCOHOL). By doing so, the Incas reinforced social order and cemented loyalties.

Based on Spanish accounts and archaeological data, the Incas were a highly organized society in which the political, religious, social, and economic realms came together to shape a cultural system led by a single sovereign whose ambitions were challenged only by the natural setting of the Andes, which could become his ally or enemy. Inca society functioned until the last ruler, Túpac Amaru, was executed by the Spaniards.

—Jessica Christie

Further reading:

Terence D'Altroy. *The Incas* (Malden, Mass.: Blackwell Publishing, 2002).

Iximché   Founded in the 1470s or 1480s, Iximché was the capital of the expanding highland Kaqchikel MAYA state. Following the Spanish CONQUEST, the site briefly became the first Spanish colonial capital of GUATEMALA. Between the late 1950s and early 1970s, archaeologist George Guillemin excavated and reconstructed architecture in the elite area of the site. Today, Iximché is an important national monument and remains a focus of Kaqchikel religious pilgrimages.

The Kaqchikels were vassals and mercenaries who lived in K'iche' Maya territory until factionalism within the ruling K'iche' lineage forced them to flee. They first settled at present-day Chichicastenango but soon founded a new city in a defensible location, surrounded on three sides by steep ravines. They made their new location even safer from attack by cutting a ditch through the narrow neck of land that connected the area of elite palaces, temples, and ball courts to rich agricultural fields and commoner households (see AGRICULTURE).

Their efforts to create defensive works were justified, as the Kaqchikels faced military assaults from their old overlords. In addition, an internal revolt by the Tukuché faction convulsed Iximché. The faction's defeat on May 18, 1493, was so significant that all subsequent Kaqchikel history was recorded in relation to that date. During the late 15th and early 16th centuries, rapid Kaqchikel territorial expansion involved aggressive military action against the surrounding K'iche's and other peoples. Deposits of decapitated skulls found during the site's excavation provide physical evidence of both aggressive and defensive WARFARE.

News of the arrival of Europeans to the Caribbean may have reached Iximché as early as 1510, when the Aztec emperor sent reports of their presence in the Antilles. After learning of the Spanish successes in the conquest of MEXICO, and seizing an opportunity to defeat their opponents and expand their own territorial holdings, in 1520, Kaqchikel rulers invited the Spanish into Guatemala.

When the Spaniards arrived in 1524, Kaqchikel warriors initially supported PEDRO DE ALVARADO, his Spanish troops, and indigenous allies from Central Mexico; the combined forces joined to attack the Kaqchikels' enemies. Early in the conquest period, the Kaqchikels and Spaniards enjoyed cordial relations. Alvarado and his troops moved into Iximché and rechristened the settlement Santiago de los Caballeros de Guatemala.

Relations soon deteriorated, however, as the Spanish increased their demands for GOLD and LABOR from their Kaqchikel allies. In response, the Kaqchikels abandoned the city and fled into the surrounding mountains, where they engaged in protracted guerrilla warfare against their former allies. In 1526, while Alvarado was in HONDURAS with HERNANDO CORTÉS, disgruntled Spanish conquistadores rebelled and burned much of Iximché; after the fire, only a small Spanish contingent remained in the city, and Iximché never recovered its former glory. Eventually, the site was abandoned entirely.

—Stephen L. Whittington

Further reading:

C. Roger Nance, Stephen L. Whittington, and Barbara E. Borg. *Archaeology and Ethnohistory of Iximché* (Gainesville: University Press of Florida, 2003).

J

Jiménez de Quesada, Gonzalo (b. 1509–d. 1579)
Spanish conquistador in Colombia's eastern highlands and founder of Bogotá   Little is known about the early decades of Gonzalo Jiménez de Quesada's life. Even his place of birth is disputed, although the best evidence suggests that he was born in Granada in 1509. In his early 20s, Jiménez served as a soldier in the Italian campaigns before returning to Granada, Spain, in 1530 to study law. However, after completing his studies he did not remain in Spain for long. In November 1535, Gonzalo Jiménez de Quesada was one of 1,200 passengers who departed from the Canary Islands with Pedro de Fernández de Lugo's fleet. The fleet arrived in Santa Marta, COLOMBIA, in January 1536, where Fernández de Lugo began his appointment as governor. After just a few months in Santa Marta, Lugo appointed Jiménez as his lieutenant governor; he then chose Jiménez to lead an ambitious expedition up the Magdalena River to search for an overland route to PERU, as well as access to the Pacific Ocean. A lawyer by training, Jiménez led a force of 800 Spaniards and scores of indigenous carriers and African slaves up the Magdalena River (see SLAVERY). The expedition proved costly, with nearly three-quarters of his men perishing in the first 12 months; however, the 179 survivors, Jiménez included, successfully crossed into Colombia's eastern highlands, where they initiated the CONQUEST OF MUISCA territory. This three-year expedition proved to be one of the most profitable conquests in the New World. Nevertheless, much to his own dismay, Jiménez never achieved the fame or fortune of HERNANDO CORTÉS or FRANCISCO PIZARRO.

Jiménez and his men remained in Muisca territory for almost two years, during which time they looted enormous sums of GOLD and EMERALDS. Over that same period, his small force had no contact with other Europeans. In fact, most of Santa Marta's residents believed that Jiménez and his men had all perished. However, in an odd coincidence, two separate Spanish forces, one from VENEZUELA and another from ECUADOR, arrived in Muisca territory in early 1539. The unexpected arrival of competing expeditions forced Jiménez to take actions to legitimize his claim to the region. Before he returned to Spain to petition the Crown, he founded three cities, one of which was Santafé de BOGOTÁ.

When he returned to Spain in 1539, Jiménez faced a series of charges, including fraud, torture, and murder (he had been accused of torturing and killing a Muisca CACIQUE named Sagipa). Moreover, several veterans of the expedition filed suits against him, claiming that they had been promised shares in the spoils. Jiménez successfully defended himself against most charges; however, he did have to pay a series of fines and was forbidden from returning to the lands he had conquered. In fact, it was not until 1548 that Jiménez was granted license to return to the New Kingdom of Granada.

He returned the following year and spent the next few decades in New Granada. Nevertheless, he remained bitter that he had not achieved the same fame or wealth as Cortés or Pizarro. In his *PROBANZA DE MÉRITO* (proof of merit petition) from 1562, Jiménez boasted that neither Cortés nor Pizarro had discovered or settled better or richer provinces than he. His quest for fame and fortune continued to inspire him to even greater conquests. In 1569, Jiménez de Quesada led a disastrous expedition into the Llanos of eastern Colombia; after three years in search of a rich new kingdom to conquer, Jiménez limped back to Bogotá. Most of the men who had joined him were either killed or had fled. Jiménez himself had lost a great deal of his fortune; he never found his kingdom of gold and died in relative obscurity in Mariquita in 1579.

—J. Michael Francis

Further reading:

J. Michael Francis. *Invading Colombia: Spanish Accounts of the Gonzalo Jiménez de Quesada Expedition of Conquest* (University Park: Pennsylvania State University Press, 2007).

K

Kaminaljuyú   Located at 14.63° N latitude, 90.55° W longitude, Kaminaljuyú is the largest early MAYA site in highland GUATEMALA. Most of the visible ruins today are found in the Kaminaljuyú National Archaeological Park, within Guatemala's modern capital, in a mountain valley some 5,000 feet (1,524 m) above sea level. Kaminaljuyú was well situated for regional TRADE, near river headwaters that fed both the Caribbean and the Gulf of Mexico. Significantly, Kaminaljuyú also controlled the nearby OBSIDIAN source at El Chayal.

Human settlement at Kaminaljuyú dates back to between 1200 and 1000 B.C.E., which corresponds to the end of the Early Preclassic period. In the Middle Preclassic (1000–400 B.C.E.), Kaminaljuyú grew considerably in area, as evidenced by earthen monumental ARCHITECTURE and irrigation infrastructure, including a large canal from Lake Miraflores (now dry) southward to farmlands. At this time, the inhabitants of Kaminaljuyú produced carved stone monuments, as found at many Classic-period Maya sites.

Kaminaljuyú continued to grow, and in the Late Preclassic period (400 B.C.E.–200 C.E.) two more high-capacity irrigation canals were constructed. Toward the end of this period, Lake Miraflores dried up, and the irrigation system fell into disuse.

During the Early Classic period (200–400 C.E.), Maya migrants from the highlands to the west established a new order at Kaminaljuyú, thus ending the eight-century-long practice of carving stone monuments to portray rulers, their captives, and royal trappings.

In the next two centuries, Kaminaljuyú was greatly influenced by the city of TEOTIHUACÁN in Central MEXICO, exchanging goods and cultural features. Notable is the use in Kaminaljuyú of the *talud-tablero* architectural style, which is ubiquitous at Teotihuacán. Though populated for another few hundred years, Kaminaljuyú was abandoned prior to the Spanish CONQUEST in the early 16th century.

—Walter R. T. Witschey

Further reading:
Robert J. Sharer and Loa P. Traxler. *The Ancient Maya*, 6th ed. (Stanford, Calif.: Stanford University Press, 2006).

kuraka (curaca, quraqa)   A *kuraka* was an ethnic lord or chieftain of an Andean lineage (*AYLLU*). Spaniards often used the Caribbean term *CACIQUE* instead of *kuraka*. The *kurakas* predated Inca imperial expansion (see INCAS). Reciprocal obligations conditioned a *kuraka's* relationship with the *ayllu*. He (nearly all *kurakas* were men) received LABOR tribute from the people. In return, he was expected to defend the *ayllu* against external threats; fairly distribute the land according to families' needs; oversee the storage of FOOD, cloth, and other goods; and ensure the timely and proper performance of religious rituals to garner divine protection and blessing for *ayllu* members (see RELIGION). Much of the *ayllu's* surplus economic production ended up in the *kuraka's* hands through tributary obligations (see ECONOMY). Nonetheless, he reciprocated by feeding members of the *ayllu* and providing raw materials for those involved in the production of TEXTILES.

One of the *kuraka's* most important responsibilities was to supply the food, CHICHA (MAIZE beer), and other goods needed for festivals and rituals. A *kuraka* who failed to reciprocate for the labor he demanded might be deposed, and some were killed. The *kuraka*'s status depended on the number of people he ruled (and thus the amount of labor he controlled) rather than the amount of territory he governed. The typical *ayllu* was divided into an upper (*hanan*) and lower (*hurin*) half, with a different *kuraka* ruling over each. Although it did not necessarily pass to the eldest son, the *kurakazgo* (chieftainship) was usually hereditary.

As the Inca Empire expanded, local *kurakas* were subordinated to the empire. Those who cooperated with the Incas retained their positions; however, they then also served as intermediaries between the local population and the empire. The Inca ruler became a type of supreme *kuraka*, appropriating part of the *ayllu*'s surplus through labor tribute but also assuming the reciprocal obligations. The Incas also began to introduce a new form of *kurakazgo* based on a base-ten system (with a *kuraka* ruling over 10, 100, or 1,000, etc.), an innovation that challenged traditional practices. The Incas' forced resettlement of peoples to other regions of the empire to break down ethnic solidarity also undercut the *kurakas*' position (see MITMAQKUNA).

The Spanish CONQUEST of PERU brought additional changes. Many chieftains initially welcomed the Incas' defeat because it seemed to liberate them. The Spaniards used the *kurakas* to govern the *ayllus* and to mobilize ENCOMIENDA labor. In the years immediately after the conquest, in fact, the *kuraka*'s role was very similar to what it had been under the Incas: He was an intermediate official who provided labor for the Spaniards and who also retained part of the *ayllu*'s output for himself. But, there were some important differences: The Spaniards assumed no reciprocal obligations for the labor they extracted; moreover, they provided no food for the workers, and in many cases, their demands were so onerous that the *kuraka* had to decide whether to try to protect his people or to cooperate fully with the Europeans. Conditions for *kurakas* worsened when the Spaniards began demanding monetary rather than labor tribute, forcing *kurakas* to provide MITA workers for mercury and SILVER mines, and resettling Andeans in *reducciones* that often ignored *ayllu* divisions (see CONGREGACIÓN; MINING).

See also KURAKA (Vol. II).

—Kendall Brown

Further reading:

Susan Ramirez. *The World Upside Down: Cross-Cultural Contact and Conflict in Sixteenth-Century Peru* (Stanford, Calif.: Stanford University Press, 1996).

Steve J. Stern. *Peru's Indian Peoples and the Challenge of Spanish Conquest* (Madison: University of Wisconsin Press, 1982).

L

labor

THE AMERICAS BEFORE 1492

Labor systems in the Americas prior to 1492 largely reflected the hierarchical societies of many different ethnic groups. Peasants or commoners were taxed in the form of labor paid to the nobility. Conquered peoples were expected to labor as a form of tribute. Another pool of labor was met by slaves (see SLAVERY). Slaves occupied the lowest stratum of society and were used as a massive, and oftentimes expendable, labor force. This approach to labor probably has great depth in the annals of the pre-Columbian Americas, but it is only in relation to the capstone civilizations—the AZTECS, INCAS, and MAYA—that scholars have detailed information. Among these civilizations, the salient and lasting achievements—immense road networks, large stone temples, terraced fielding, the construction of CITIES that were among the largest in the world—have provenance in the use of forced labor.

Labor was often viewed as a tax, owed to the state, or its nobility. As a tax, commoners were expected to contribute labor to nobles in the form of military service, agricultural labor, so-called "kitchen" labor that entailed grinding MAIZE and the like, and spinning and weaving to create cloth (see AGRICULTURE; TEXTILES; WARFARE). This form of labor contribution was regarded as reciprocal—it was provided in exchange for public services and the security offered by the state.

Tribute also played a crucial role in many labor systems. As the Aztec and Inca Empires expanded, the conquered peoples were ordered to pay annual tributes to the state, which came in the form of a certain amount of designated goods, or as a labor tax (see MITA). These tributes were a critical element of state finances. By 1519, the Aztecs were collecting significant amounts of tribute from all the regions they had conquered. Tribute obligations were often a significant burden to those paying them, and throughout the century of Aztec imperial expansion, numerous city-states defied the empire's demands for the same. The Incas kept strict account of the tribute and labor taxes they exacted from conquered regions, information that they carefully recorded on their QUIPUS; the state stored these goods in a vast network of storage systems. State goods were then distributed to local leaders (see KURAKA), the vast Inca armies, artisans, bureaucrats, and urban dwellers. Some stores were kept in case of emergencies, such as drought or frost.

Slavery accounted for much of the labor surplus required by the Aztecs, Incas, and Maya. Slaves were often drawn from longstanding enemy groups that were ultimately conquered. Criminals were also made slaves in some instances, and in some cases, citizens could sell themselves into slavery in order to avoid abject poverty. Slave labor was integral to the construction of large public works projects, temples, and cities.

Many American civilizations, especially the Aztecs, Incas, and Maya, controlled large amounts of surplus labor, believing a large labor pool was crucial to the territorial expansion of their civilization. Labor was extracted from citizens, conquered peoples, and slaves, and hence labor systems often featured gradations. The context of the Americas should also be considered. The stringent requirements on human labor was partly the result of prohibitive and undulating terrain and partly a product of an inability to domesticate large animals to serve as beasts of burden, increasing the demands on human labor. This tradition of massive pools of human labor being harnessed by the state and parsed to reflect the gradations of social hierarchy provided opportunities for Spanish conquistadores to take advantage of internal divisions and disputes (see CONQUEST).

EARLY COLONIAL LATIN AMERICA

Labor practices in early colonial Latin America drew from Iberian traditions, including African slavery, and were closely linked to developing maritime and mercantile contacts beyond Europe. They also followed patterns of demographic change. During the reconquest of the Iberian Peninsula (Reconquista), Iberian monarchs distributed ENCOMIENDA grants of labor or tribute as rewards to military leaders. These *encomiendas* were transplanted first to the Canary Islands and then to the Caribbean. In the Caribbean, Spanish settlers were allocated shares of Native American labor, known as *repartimientos*. Indigenous people labored in the agrarian ECONOMY and in MINING scarce precious metals. Settlers supplemented *encomienda* labor with that of *naborías* (personal servants or dependents of CACIQUES) and slaves captured in warfare.

With epidemic DISEASE and the catastrophic population decline among TAINO and CARIB Indians, who all but disappeared in the 16th century, Spaniards increasingly used enslaved Africans for labor. A similar situation developed in BRAZIL, where the Portuguese initially recruited and enslaved indigenous people to obtain dyewood and then work on SUGAR estates (see DYES AND DYEWOOD). Demographic collapse in the Caribbean inspired opposition to exploitative labor practices by ecclesiastical figures such as the friar BARTOLOMÉ DE LAS CASAS. Moral debates surrounding the treatment of NATIVE AMERICANS lay behind the LAWS OF BURGOS (1512), which sought to regulate the *encomienda* system.

As Spaniards ventured beyond the Caribbean, they extended slavery and *encomienda* systems to mainland areas. Africans participated in the conquests of Mesoamerica and the Andes, as did thousands of Native American allies (see CONQUEST). Following earlier precedents, many conquistadores in Mesoamerica and the Andes received *encomienda* grants. They used thousands of laborers as auxiliaries for exploration and military campaigns. *Encomienda* laborers also generated wealth for Spaniards, especially after the discovery of SILVER. Concerned over the potential of *encomenderos* (recipients of *encomienda* grants) to rival royal authority and seeking to regulate the treatment of Native Americans, the Crown promulgated the NEW LAWS OF 1542, which abolished indigenous slavery and sought to return *encomiendas* to the Crown by restricting inheritance. The New Laws were met with fierce opposition in the Americas, provoking conflict in PERU (see CIVIL WARS IN PERU). Implementation of the New Laws was not always stringently enforced, and some privately held *encomiendas* survived the entire colonial period. Indian slavery also continued in peripheral areas such as CHILE, where hostile populations resisted conquest.

After the conquest, Spaniards preserved the rotational draft labor systems of the Aztec and Inca Empires, known as *coatequitl* and *mita* in NAHUATL and QUECHUA, respectively. Formalized under the rubric of *repartimiento*, Native American corporate communities such as the ALTEPETL and AYLLU supplied a share of their unskilled laborers to work for limited periods in agriculture and pubic works projects. *Repartimiento* drafts also recruited skilled workers, often carpenters and masons, who worked in church construction, among other tasks. Before the arrival of Spaniards, Native American artisans had worked in lapidary arts, feather working, textile manufacture, and CERAMICS, among other specialized trades (see ART). Some of these traditions lingered in the postconquest period, supplemented by Spanish craftsmen who brought with them such European trades as blacksmithing. Over time, Spaniards and people of African and mixed ancestries came to dominate the artisan production.

Spaniards sought to consolidate Native American communities that had been depopulated by disease through resettlement programs, known as *congregaciones* (see CONGREGACIÓN). Likewise, in peripheral areas, semi-nomadic groups were encouraged or forced to reside in mission complexes and forts. The geographical mismatch between *encomiendas* and silver mines in MEXICO meant that Spaniards drafted a significant proportion of labor outside institutional parameters, with Africans and *macehualli* (commoners in Nahua society) playing a significant role in labor allocation (see MACEHUALLI). In the Andes, by contrast, large population centers corresponded with the location of silver deposits, particularly in POTOSÍ, where the *mita* system endured longer. Elsewhere, *repartimiento* became increasingly redundant as employers competed for decreasing supplies of labor to work in mines, textile workshops (*obrajes*), and large landed estates (haciendas). Employers increasingly obtained labor by offering wages or through coercive practices such penal labor, debt service, and slavery.

Atlantic slavery developed from Iberian trade contacts with Africa. The vast majority of slaves came from West and Central Africa. They were supplemented by Native American slaves captured in peripheral areas and a few slaves imported from Asia. Slaves went to work as domestic servants in urban households, artisan shops, and *obrajes*, as well as in sugar and TOBACCO cultivation. The relatively high cost of slaves tended to limit their dispersal through the colonial economy, with the overwhelming majority going to sugar-producing areas, particularly Brazil. Over time, the influx of African slaves contributed to processes of *mestizaje*, or racial mixture, initiated with the conquest, gradually transforming the demographic composition of the America (see MESTIZAJE/MESTIZO).

See also LABOR (Vols. III, IV).

—Richard Conway
Sean H. Goforth

Further reading:

James Lockhart and Stuart B. Schwartz. *Early Latin America: A History of Colonial Spanish America and Brazil* (New York: Cambridge University Press, 1983).

Charles C. Mann. *1491: New Revelations of the Americas before Columbus* (New York: Knopf, 2005).

ladino   The Spanish term *ladino* originated in Roman times, when it referred to a native of the Iberian Peninsula who could speak the language of the conquering Romans. By early medieval times, ladino had come to mean the vernacular Romance language commonly spoken in what would become Spain (excluding Catalonia). The term's meaning shifted again between the 11th and the 13th centuries, after Latin rites adopted by the Christian Council of Burgos in 1080 replaced the Visigothic liturgy, and as Romance-based spellings became more common. Eventually, Christian writers ceased to use the term *ladino* to describe their own Romance vernacular languages. In particular, Castilian Romance developed its own nomenclature as *castellano*. Iberian Jews, however, continued to call their vernacular language, a hybrid of Hebrew and Romance, "ladino."

In the 16th century, *ladino* could refer not only to the aforementioned language of the Sephardim but also to anyone who spoke Castilian as a second language ("to a Moor or a foreigner," according to the early linguist Sebastián de Covarrubias in 1611) and/or to a person's wisdom or cleverness. Transferring the notion to the early colonial Americas, it came to refer most basically to bilingualism. Although *ladino* sometimes referred to Spaniards who had learned native Amerindian languages, such as NAHUATL in Mesoamerica or QUECHUA in the Andes, most often *ladino* described a Native American or African who was bilingual in his or her native language and Spanish. Additionally, *ladino* suggested the adoption by non-Spaniards of not only the Spanish language but also Spanish dress, religion, customs, and values.

Despite its many positive connotations, the meanings of *ladino* in the early colonial Americas could be ambivalent or even negative. Spaniards often favored *indios ladinos*, who frequently acted as trusted cultural brokers between Spanish invaders and indigenous communities. Precisely because of their mediating role, some *indios ladinos* were suspected by Spaniards of betrayal or even fomenting rebellion. (The same can be said of Africans, who in some parts of Spanish America would eventually become part of a racialized ladino population, along with

deculturated indigenous people and mixed-race peoples.) Likewise, *indios ladinos* often played a powerful role in the defense of native communities but were sometimes resented by their neighbors as coercive agents and enforcers of colonial rule. *Ladino* in early colonial Latin America could therefore be a compliment, an insult, or a mixture of both, used to describe acculturated non-Europeans who occupied an ambiguous place in colonial society.

—Laura Matthew

Further reading:

Rolena Adorno. "The Indigenous Ethnographer: The 'indio ladino' as Historian and Cultural Mediation." In *Implicit Understandings: Observing, Reporting, and Reflecting on the Encounters between Europeans and Other Peoples in the Early Modern Era*, edited by Stuart Schwartz, 378–402 (Cambridge: Cambridge University Press, 1994).

La Navidad   La Navidad was a doomed settlement constructed from the wreckage of the *Santa María*, CHRISTOPHER COLUMBUS's flagship. In the early morning hours of Christmas 1492, just weeks after first reaching the Americas, the *Santa María* ran aground on a sandbar as it skirted the Haitian coast (see HISPANIOLA). Columbus ordered the ship's supplies to be hauled to the mainland once he realized the *Santa María* was lost, despite the crew's frantic efforts to save it. With the assistance of the island's chieftain, Guacanagari, the ship's contents were moved ashore, where they were secured. On the basis of Guacanagari's accounts of GOLD, Columbus opted to leave 39 members of the crew on the island while he returned to Spain.

Columbus ordered that the wood from the *Santa María* be used to build a crude fort just along the shore to protect any recovered gold, though his diary reflects his low regard for the native people's ability to muster a threat. He also appointed his mistress's cousin, Diego de Arana, as governor of the settlement. Columbus left the settlers on January 4, 1493, anxious to track down the *Pinta*, which he had not seen for some weeks.

Columbus's second voyage returned him to the island in November 1494, where he expected to find his marooned settlers operating a viable outpost. Instead, the corpses of 11 of his men were strewn along the beachfront, and the fort was destroyed. The TAINO Indians reported that the Spanish settlers had harassed and abused the local indigenous people, who eventually killed them in retaliation. The area of La Navidad was lost to history for the next 500 years, until a local farmer introduced an archaeologist to the site in 1977.

—Sean H. Goforth

Further reading:

Samuel Eliot Morison. *Admiral of the Ocean Sea: A Life of Christopher Columbus* (Boston: Little, Brown & Co., 1942).

The *Santa María*, a *nao*, was the largest of the three vessels in Christopher Columbus's 1492 voyage. While the precise dimensions of the *Santa María* are unknown, the ship's measurements likely did not exceed 19.2 feet (5.85 m) in width, 38.5 feet (11.73 m) in length along the keel, and 57.7 feet (15.79 m) on the lower of the two decks. The *Santa María* ran aground on the island of Hispaniola on Christmas Day, 1492. *(Courtesy of J. Michael Francis)*

Landa, Diego de (b. 1524–d. 1579) *Franciscan friar and bishop of Yucatán*   Born in 1524 in the Spanish town of Cifuentes, Diego de Landa entered the Franciscan monastery (see RELIGIOUS ORDERS) in Toledo when he was 16. Nine years later, at the age of 25, Landa committed himself to the missionary challenge of Spain's new Mexican colonies, arriving in Yucatán just seven years after the 1542 founding of the provincial capital of Mérida (see MEXICO). Assigned to pastoral duties at the new monastery at Izamal, Landa soon revealed his ambitions; he quickly learned Yucatec Mayan and wrote religious guides and other works. He also traveled extensively throughout the peninsula, preaching to MAYA communities and destroying their "idols."

In 1558, Landa was elected custodian of the Franciscan order in the colony, and three years later became provincial head of the order. As custodian, he became involved in a legal dispute between the church and one of the colony's founding conquistadores, Francisco Hernández; Landa harried Hernández mercilessly for years, until at last, lying mortally ill, Hernández confessed his "crimes" against the ecclesiastical authorities. Other conquistador

families would not forget Landa's role in this affair, which symbolizes well the difficult relationship between colonists and clerics that persisted throughout the colonial period in Yucatán. Ironically, Landa's fall from power and exile to Spain in the 1560s was not a result of his confrontation with local colonists. Rather, it stemmed from a dispute with another Franciscan (Francisco de Toral) and Landa's brutal persecution of the Maya.

In 1560, Fray Francisco de Toral became the province's first resident bishop; however, he did not arrive until August 1562, by which time Landa had already begun investigating the alleged "return to their ancient and evil customs" (including HUMAN SACRIFICE—by crucifixion) by dozens of Maya communities. Their leaders and others, mostly nobles, were arrested under accusation of practicing idolatry (see DIABOLISM IN THE NEW WORLD). Some 4,500 Maya, including WOMEN, were tortured (nearly 200 to death). Landa held *autos de fe* (acts of faith) in Maní, Sotuta, and Hocaba-Homun, at which Maya "heretics" who had survived torture were whipped and publicly chastised; moreover, Landa oversaw the destruction of more than 5,000 "idols" and 27 hieroglyphic books.

This act caused the Maya much grief, as Landa himself acknowledged. In response, Bishop Toral immediately began to dispute the legality of Landa's use of violence and the veracity of the confessions thereby extracted. Many of the colonists agreed with him.

In 1563, Landa returned to Spain to defend himself in court. There, he wrote his great *Recopilación*, a pioneering ethnographic study of Yucatán, its people, and its history before and after the CONQUEST. The only surviving portion of this work is an excerpt copied in the 18th century and entitled *Account of the Things of Yucatán* (*Relación de las cosas de Yucatán*). Drawn from the friar's own observations and from his conversations with two Maya informants, Nachi Cocom and Gaspar Antonio Chi, the *Relación* is unique to Yucatán and one of the most important such manuscripts to have survived colonial Mexico. Perhaps, if viewed as conducted in the spirit of care and concern for the Maya, Landa's inquisition and their suffering at his hands can be reconciled with the book's veritable celebration of the Yucatec people.

In exile, Landa also worked for his political rehabilitation with typical fervor and tenacity; when Toral died in 1571, Landa himself was appointed Yucatán's bishop. He returned in 1573, older but vindicated and no less determined to uproot Maya "idolatry." Despite the opposition of both colonists and Maya leaders, Landa promoted the authority of the CATHOLIC CHURCH with an iron hand until his death in 1579; he was buried in the Franciscan monastery at Mérida. As a defender of the Franciscan order and ecclesiastical authority, Landa was no doubt "a great friar," as his colleagues wrote in 1570. But, as a man who compiled knowledge about the Maya yet burned books that were sources for the same subjects and who strove to protect indigenous people from Spanish settlers yet campaigned for the brutal torture of their leaders, he offers a fascinating and tantalizing window on Mexico's colonial experience.

See also *AUTO DE FÉ* (Vol. II); FRANCISCANS (Vol. II).

—Matthew Restall

Further reading:

Inga Clendinnen. *Ambivalent Conquests: Maya and Spaniard in Yucatán, 1517–1570* (Cambridge: Cambridge University Press, 1987).
William Gates. *Yucatán before and after the Conquest, by Friar Diego de Landa* 1937. (Reprint, New York: Dover, 1978).

Las Casas, Bartolomé de (b. 1484–d. 1566) *Dominican friar and "protector and defender of the Indians"* The Dominican friar Bartolomé de Las Casas, named "protector and defender of the Indians," was an early reformer of Spanish colonial enterprises (see *DEFENSOR DE LOS INDIOS*; RELIGIOUS ORDERS). A critic of the actions of Spanish settlers in the New World, Las Casas argued that the indigenous people were rational and civilized and, therefore, deserving of Christian conversion. His most notable work, *Brevísima relación de la destrucción de las Indias* (*A Very Brief Account of the Destruction of the Indies*), became a principal source on the brutality of colonialism and moved Las Casas into mythical status.

Born to a merchant family in Seville, Spain, in 1484, Las Casas embodied the contradictions of early colonial enterprises. After postponing his training in letters under the grammarian Antonio de Nebrija, Las Casas immigrated to HISPANIOLA in 1502 invested with a modest ENCOMIENDA, which proved to be a financial failure. During the next decade, Las Casas witnessed the dramatic collapse of the island's native population. By his own account, his life's trajectory turned in 1511 after hearing Fray ANTONIO DE MONTESINOS describe the mortal sin of exploiting the indigenous. In 1514, Las Casas renounced his own *encomienda* and began his campaign for an imperial agenda that did not exploit the native populations. In 1516, he was appointed *protector y defensor de los indios*. However, in 1522, following the failure of his settlement at Cumaná, VENEZUELA, Las Casas abandoned his political post and entered the Dominican order.

Over the next two decades, Las Casas navigated the religious-political bureaucracy of the Spanish colonies, working with important figures such as Bishop Juan de Zumárraga and Viceroy ANTONIO DE MENDOZA to create protective colonial legislative policies (see CATHOLIC CHURCH; VICEROY/VICEROYALTY). No stranger to the royal court, in 1531, Las Casas argued before the king that all Amerindians should be subject to the same rights and burdens as Spanish citizens. Following that logic, Las Casas drafted a confessional manual in which he characterized indigenous people as humble neophytes and Spaniards as vain sinners; he would continue this argument in *A Very Brief Account of the Destruction of the Indies*. As the vicar of GUATEMALA and later the bishop of Chiapa (Chiapas), Las Casas circulated his notorious manual, which was a clear act of defiance against colonial authorities. In 1547, Las Casas returned to Spain to answer charges of treason levied by the famous humanist JUAN GINÉS DE SEPÚLVEDA. In Valladolid, from 1550 to 1551, the two figures debated the nature of Indian humanity before high royal officials and learned scholars. Building on Thomist-humanist philosophy, which emphasized the divine rationality of people, Las Casas condemned the brutality of the conquistadores and the cruelty of settlers, an argument that he articulated in *Apologética historia* (ca. 1552).

Cleared of the charges, Las Casas wrote two major works following the debate in Valladolid. *A Very Brief Account of the Destruction of the Indies* was (published in 1552). In it, Las Casas described natives as Christian neophytes who were savagely attacked by Spanish settlers. This description quickly circulated throughout Europe, and this work became the source of the "Black Legend" of the brutality of Spanish colonialism. In his *Historia de las Indias* (*History of the Indies*; completed in 1559 and published in 1875), Las Casas provided an ethnology of native civilizations. In 1566, at the age of 82, Las Casas died in Madrid, Spain.

See also DOMINICANS (Vol. II).

—R. A. Kashanipour

Further reading:
Daniel Castro. *Another Face of Empire: Bartolomé de Las Casas, Indigenous Rights and Ecclesiastical Imperialism* (Durham, N.C.: Duke University Press, 2007).
Lewis Hanke. *All Mankind Is One: A Study of the Disputation between Bartolomé de Las Casas and Juan Ginés de Sepúlveda in 1550 on the Intellectual and Religious Capacity of the American Indians* (DeKalb: Northern Illinois University, 1974).

Las Salinas, Battle of (April 6, 1538)

Fought near the city of CUZCO in 1538, the Battle of Las Salinas pitted Spaniard against Spaniard, as the forces of DIEGO DE ALMAGRO and those of the Pizarro brothers fought to dominate PERU. FRANCISCO PIZARRO and Almagro had formed a partnership to undertake the CONQUEST of Peru. Following the capture and execution of the Inca ruler ATAHUALPA and the Spanish occupation of the Inca capital at Cuzco, however, Pizarro claimed much of the territory for himself (see INCAS). A disgruntled Almagro led a fruitless expedition into the deserts of northern CHILE, returning in 1537 to find Cuzco under siege in MANCO INCA's Great Rebellion. Almagro relieved the siege but arrested GONZALO PIZARRO and HERNANDO PIZARRO, who opposed his occupation of Cuzco. Meanwhile, Francisco Pizarro was in LIMA on the coast.

As a result of his negotiations with the Pizarro faction, Almagro freed the Pizarro brothers. The two sides, however, were unable to resolve their contention. Seeking revenge, Hernando Pizarro led an army of 700 Spaniards from Lima to Cuzco. Almagro rejected his Inca ally Paullu's suggestion that they ambush Pizarro's force in a narrow mountain valley. Reluctant to make war on his fellow Spaniards, Almagro decided instead to defend Cuzco.

With Almagro incapacitated by syphilis, Rodrigo Orgóñez led the Almagro army. He chose a site a few miles south of Cuzco near some salt leaches (*salinas*) to fight the Pizarrists. On the morning of April 6, 1538 (not April 26, as some historians have written), the two forces engaged. Almagro's smaller army, weakened by desertion and abandoned by the Inca supporter Paullu, succumbed after two hours of fighting. Only 50 or so Spaniards died during the battle, but reprisals afterward claimed many more. Orgóñez was wounded and executed on the field. The Pizarrists captured Almagro, tried him for treason, and executed him.

Although minor in terms of its military importance and the number of casualties, the Battle of Las Salinas was a chief factor in Charles I's decision to send a VICE-ROY to Peru to take power from the conquistadores and establish order in the colony.

—Kendall Brown

Further reading:
Paul Stewart. "The Battle of Las Salinas, Peru, and Its Historians." *Sixteenth Century Journal* 19, no. 3 (1988): 407–433.

Laws of Burgos (1512)

The Laws of Burgos, promulgated in 1512, were the first Spanish laws created to govern the Indies and regulate relations between Spaniards and the indigenous peoples of the New World. From the beginning of Spanish colonization in the New World, the basic laws and ordinances of the Kingdom of Castile were assumed to serve also in the governance of the Indies. Castilian law, as opposed to the legal codes of Aragon or other Spanish kingdoms, constituted the basic form of civil and criminal law in the new colonies. Nevertheless, the administrative distance, as well as the new peoples and lands discovered, were so different that events in the Indies quickly mitigated the creation of new laws to meet the special conditions there.

As early as 1499, when initial instructions concerning the proper treatment of the indigenous peoples were issued to Governor FRANCISCO DE BOBADILLA (CHRISTOPHER COLUMBUS's replacement as governor of the colony of HISPANIOLA), the Crown realized that new regulations were needed, especially in terms of regulating the relations between Spaniards and the indigenous peoples of the Caribbean. One of the most important proponents of new legislation was the Dominican friar ANTONIO DE MONTESINOS, who in 1511 not only complained and sermonized about Spanish abuses of the Indians but also wrote a lengthy report about these to the Crown.

In response to Montesinos's complaints and other reports, in 1512, King Ferdinand convened a theological and academic council at the city of Burgos to look into the legal questions concerning Spain's rights over the dominion of the Indies. The Ordinances for the Treatment of the Indians (Ordenanzas para el tratamiento de los indios), more commonly called the Laws of Burgos (1512), were the legislative fruit of the council's findings. These ordinances reflected the council's formal conclusions, which established a series of legislative principals that would inform and shape all subsequent royal laws related to the Indies.

The Junta de Burgos concluded that first, the Indians were, indeed, free vassals of the Crown. Second, the Catholic monarchs were the natural lords of the Indians, due to their subdelegated duty from the pope in Rome to evangelize and convert the native people to Christianity (see RELIGION). In order to accomplish the goals of conversion and colonization, the council also stated that the Indians could be obliged to work for the Spaniards but only if the LABOR was tolerable and was compensated with a just salary or payment. In a more negative tone, the Junta de Burgos also stated that war against the native people and their enslavement was justified if they refused to accept Christianity (see CONQUEST; SLAVERY; WARFARE). In order to alert the Indians of their rights and obligations to the Crown, the Laws of Burgos authored an official *REQUERIMIENTO*, or legal "requirement," which had to be read to the indigenous people before any "just war" could be waged against them.

These Laws of Burgos were issued officially by King Ferdinand on December 27, 1512, and they officially regulated the relations between Spaniards and the conquered peoples of the New World. The ultimate goals were to ensure the spiritual and material welfare of the Amerindians, who were often mistreated by their Spanish conquerors.

Among the many legacies of the Laws of Burgos of 1512 was the first official use of the Castilian legal term *ENCOMIENDA*, with its medieval reciprocal duties for both conqueror and conquered. The transplantation of the medieval concept of the *encomienda* system, both a duty and a privilege, was meant to replace the more arbitrary and abusive division of the NATIVE AMERICANS in the early *repartamientos*, or forced labor divisions granted to Spanish conquerors.

Although many of the various aspects of the Laws of Burgos had good intentions, the laws were largely unenforceable. Regardless of their enforceability, however, the laws represent Spain's first attempt to limit the abuse of the indigenous peoples of the New World by the Spanish.

—John F. Chuchiak IV

Further reading:

Lesley Byrd Simpson. *The Encomienda in New Spain: The Beginnings of Spanish Mexico* (Berkeley: University of California Press, 1966).

———. *Studies in the Administration of the Indians in New Spain: The Laws of Burgos of 1512* (Berkeley: University of California Press, 1935).

Lima Located at 12° S latitude and 77° W longitude, the city of Lima emerged after the CONQUEST as the capital of Spanish PERU. The Spanish conquistador FRANCISCO PIZARRO founded the city in 1535.

Lima is situated in the Rimac river valley, one of many such valleys on the desertlike Pacific coast of Peru. The Humboldt Current and Andean rain shadow control the climate and weather in the region. Lima has moderate summers, with the temperature averaging 80° Fahrenheit (26.6°C) from December to March, and humid overcast winters, with temperatures averaging between 55° Fahrenheit (12.7°C) and 60°F (15.5°C).

The region has considerable preconquest time depth, known archaeologically from Inca and pre-Inca sites in the urban area, the Rimac Valley, and the surrounding region (see INCAS). The first settlers were descendants of the Asian population that had crossed the Bering land bridge or sailed along the Pacific Rim. The evidence of the first settlers in Peru is from secondary archaeological sites that date to 5,000–10,000 years ago; the primary Pacific shore sites of these early inhabitants were destroyed by rising sea levels.

Early hunter-gatherers began to settle near Lima in about 4500 B.C.E., taking advantage of the rich seafood harvest. Settlements at Paloma and Chilca grew in size and cultivated COTTON, from which they made fishing nets and lines, as well as TEXTILES.

By 2000 B.C.E., construction had began at El Paraíso, about 70 miles north of Lima; El Paraíso is considered the largest preceramic monument in the Western Hemisphere (see CERAMICS). Nine masonry multiroom palaces contain 100,000 tons of quarried stone. El Paraíso initiated an architectural tradition of large courtyards within U-shaped structures; the style lasted for some 3,500 years (see ARCHITECTURE).

In 200 C.E., in the Rimac Valley, a distinctive cultural pattern of buildings and residential patterns began and endured for several centuries. The remains of this "Lima culture" are buried under modern Lima.

The huge oracle site of Pachacamac was constructed early in the first millennium at a prominent coastal site 20 miles (32 km) south of Lima. Pachacamac was an active pilgrimage site for centuries, ultimately being taken over by the Incas shortly before the Spanish conquest.

By the 1400s, the Inca Empire, with complex taxation and statecraft and a road system that extended some 15,000 miles (24,140 km), dominated both the Andes and the coast, including the Lima region. This domination came under threat even before the arrival of Pizarro and his men, however; six years before the Spanish conquest, European-borne smallpox swept into South America, killing the Inca ruler HUAYNA CAPÁC (see DISEASE).

Huayna Cápac's death sparked a violent dynastic dispute, leading to civil war. Pizarro arrived on the north coast of Peru during the civil disruption that followed, then marched inland to Cajamarca, and in a remarkably short time captured, ransomed, and killed the Inca emperor ATAHUALPA. He then marched to and seized the Inca capital, CUZCO.

Following the conquest, the Spaniards found the 11,500-foot (3,505-m) altitude of Cuzco, though rich in GOLD, to be intolerable. Europeans were ill adapted to cope with hypoxia, edema, and the high rate of spontaneous abortions and, instead, chose to settle on the Pacific coast in 1535. Their port of Callao, founded by Pizarro for shipping Inca gold to Spain, is now part of the modern metropolis of Lima and the largest port in Peru.

The founding of Lima was centered at the Plaza Mayor (Plaza de Armas), which is dominated by the cathedral (begun by Pizarro on January 18, 1535, and dedicated in 1540) and the adjacent archbishop's palace on the east side, the presidential palace on the north, and the city hall on the west. Thus, with the conquest of the Inca Empire, the center of power in South America shifted from the high Andes to the coast at Lima.

See also Callao (Vol. II); Lima (Vols. II, III, IV).

—Walter R. T. Witschey

Further reading:

James Higgins. *Lima: A Cultural History* (New York: Oxford University Press, 2005).

literature

MESOAMERICA

Mesoamerican literature probably originated in the oral traditions that predate the New World migrations. The earliest Mesoamerican literature appeared in the second half of the first millennium b.c.e., when pictographic, ideographic, and phonetic glyphic writings were developed by the Zapotecs and other groups. Although such short inscriptions cannot be fully considered "literature," these ruler names, toponyms, dates, and complex symbolic images were often accompanied by oral interpretations and performances, which would breathe life into the symbols; this practice continued throughout the pre-Hispanic and early colonial period.

The Mesoamericans' literary subject matter was diverse. It included the origins of the physical and spiritual worlds and the place of humans within them, the mythical deeds of deities, politics and the economy, local and imperial histories and genealogies, and astronomy and mathematics. For the most part, these subjects were not mutually exclusive, with several commonly being found in the same document. Literacy was limited to the nobility, thus most literature was produced by the ruling elite and government officials, as well as priests and priestesses. At the same time, the schematized pictographic style would have been comprehensible to the majority of the population and even to those who spoke different languages. Except for a few cases among the Maya, we do not know the names of any early authors, although they were most likely from the elite.

One of the earliest and most enduring Mesoamerican literary genres is the "territorial narrative" through which rulers legitimized their territorial charters by means of historical and mythical stories; an early example can be found in the first-century c.e. conquest slabs at Monte Albán. Shortly thereafter, several cultures began to record their historical and political literature in more detail. Much early Mesoamerican literature was written on screenfold codices. Fragmentary evidence suggests that these books appeared as early as 600 c.e., although Classic-period narratives have survived until today only on nonperishable stone stelae, murals, lintels, and portable items such as ceramic vases and figurines (see ceramics).

The Maya, who created the most complex writing and calendrical systems in Mesoamerica, left extensive inscriptions that delineated the accomplishments and genealogies of their kings and queens. Like all political and dynastic histories, these contained their share of implicit and explicit propaganda aimed at elites and commoners alike; a fine example is the Hieroglyphic Stairway at the Maya site of Copán, in Honduras, which is the longest carved inscription found anywhere in the Americas.

Codices appeared during the Postclassic period; the few preserved examples come from the Mixtec and Maya peoples (see Mixtecs). The still unprovenanced Borgia group are the only surviving codices of a vast religious literature that might have been in possession of high priests and priestesses in the Mixteca-Puebla area (see religion). Since these documents were often edited and expanded over various generations, different themes are found in the same document; for example, one side of the Mixtec Codex Vindobonensis is dedicated to the mythological creation of the Mixtec cosmos, while the other, added much later, provides genealogical information. Other Mixtec codices tell the "epic saga" of the 11th-century lord Eight Deer; this tale uses historical events as well mythical beings and locations. The Maya Codex Dresden contains complex astronomical calculations, which, although certainly motivated by the Maya's own curiosity about the heavenly bodies, were nevertheless devised as an attempt to predict the actions of divine entities.

By the time the Spanish landed in Mesoamerica in the early 16th century, there were numerous literary genres within indigenous society, each with its own document type. The Aztecs, for example, distinguished between *teomoxtli* and *teotlahtolli* books, dedicated to religious and mythological prose, respectively; *tonalamatl*, for determining individual destinies by the sacred calendar; *huehuehtlahtolli*, which were speeches from parents to their children and rulers to their subjects, as well as philosophical, ethical, and religious teachings; *tequiuhamatl*, in which tribute records and census lists were recorded; and *cuicamatl*, or books of songs (many that survived are attributed to Nezahualcoyotl, the 15th-century Texcocan king). Mesoamerican authors employed various literary devices in their compositions, such as parallel sentences and couplets for symbolic expressions and complex metaphors of the kind also employed in the earliest Mesoamerican inscriptions.

Although the Spanish often commented on the abundance of indigenous literature in their own chronicles, much of it was destroyed during the early years of the conquest, when codices and complete libraries were put to the torch as works of the devil (see chroniclers). Nevertheless, numerous codices were hidden, and literary works continued to be transmitted orally. The codex tradition itself was altered to suit the new colonial reality by focusing on such "secular" themes as history, tribute, and territory, and overall, more than 500 Aztec and other codices survive from the early colonial period. Among the most common genres produced in the Valley of

MEXICO were the sequential year-count "annals," such as the Codex Aubin, which narrates a selected Mexica history from 1168 to 1608.

The encounter of the Mesoamerican and European traditions created new literary forms, such as the "ethnographic codices" produced mostly by the indigenous for European eyes. One of the most famous examples is the Codex Mendoza, which narrates in pictorials and glosses the history of the Mexica rulers. It also provides a catalog of conquered places and the tribute they paid to the empire and deals with the daily life of Aztec commoners (see MACEHUAL). Even more impressive in its amount of pictorial and written detail is the FLORENTINE CODEX, an encyclopedic manuscript composed between 1540 and 1580 by Friar BERNARDINO DE SAHAGÚN together with Aztec scribes. Its 12 volumes include both pictorials and alphabetic texts in Spanish and NAHUATL and contain the most complete description of indigenous society before the Spanish conquest. This work also relates the fateful clash of cultures from the native perspective.

At the same time, indigenous nobles began to learn how to write in the Roman alphabet in order to reaffirm their elite status under the new Spanish administration. This resulting corpus of alphabetic documents in indigenous languages is only starting to be explored but has already revolutionized our understanding of indigenous literature before and after the Spanish conquest. One such scholar was Fernando de Alva Ixtlilxóchitl, a descendant of Nezahualcoyotl and the Aztec emperor Cuitláhuac, who wrote a history of his people based on earlier documents and oral traditions still available to him. At least in part, some of these manuscripts are postconquest transcriptions of pre-Columbian codices, such as the Mayan POPOL VUH (Council Book), in which the K'iche' (Quiché) people recorded their mythology, history, genealogies, and religion. This last is also our main source of information for understanding the pre-Columbian epic of the "Hero Twins," which appeared in Maya iconography as early as 100 B.C.E. Other important early colonial Maya literature includes the books of Chilam Balam, which was written by Yucatec Maya priests and includes prophecies and historical narratives starting from the seventh century C.E., and the Ritual of the Bacabs, which contains esoteric knowledge and medical incantations. Documents known as "community histories," a subgenre of the pre-Columbian territorial narratives, flourished during the early colonial period. These often focus on the original migration to the land, the conquest wars and settlement of the indigenous polity, and the ruling dynasty, such as that depicted in the Historia Tolteca-Chichimeca from the Valley of Puebla. These pictorial and/or alphabetic documents were created either to solidify communal identity or for the purpose of land litigations in Spanish courts, mostly against other indigenous communities. Several were composed for the purpose of requesting privileges from the Spanish king on the basis of actual or alleged loyal service during the conquest. Other documents in indigenous languages and Spanish were created within the community and included wills and testaments, personal letters, and land transactions.

The Spanish produced their own literature in their "new world." "Conquest narratives," such as those written by both HERNANDO CORTÉS and his men, recorded the events that brought about the downfall of empires, in this case the Aztec Empire. Other conquistadores recorded their adventures in other parts of Mesoamerica. Many of these chronicles, such as that by BERNAL DÍAZ DEL CASTILLO, were written in response to a growing body of literature that criticized the Spaniards' cruelty toward the Indians, criticisms perhaps best exemplified in the works of the 16th-century Dominican friar BARTOLOMÉ DE LAS CASAS.

Other early writings were produced by ecclesiastical authorities, commonly in the form of catechisms and dictionaries. Several Spanish priests even began adapting the pictorial system to their own ends in order to convert with greater success the indigenous population to Christianity. In the 1560s, DIEGO DE LANDA, a Franciscan friar and later bishop of Yucatán, wrote a detailed account on the Maya way of life; nevertheless, he burned dozens of their religious codices. The establishment of the Spanish Crown in New Spain also resulted in a wealth of bureaucratic literature, which often provides important details about the lives of both the Spanish and indigenous in early colonial society. The *Relaciones geográficas* were compiled around 1580 as a survey for the Spanish king Phillip II; ironically, this geographical questionnaire produced the largest-known collection of indigenous MAPS, many of which followed the traditional pictorial traditions of territorial narratives.

THE ANDES

It is likely that pre-Columbian oral literature was as rich in the Andean region as it was in Mesoamerica, as seen in the pictorial narratives on MOCHE ceramics or the *tocapu* designs on TEXTILES and cups. Still, South American cultures apparently did not develop phonetic writing systems. In the Andes, the most intricate apparatus to record complex information before the Spanish conquest was the QUIPU, used extensively by the INCAS and other cultures in the region before them. According to the 16th-century chroniclers, *quipucamayoc* specialists were able to record and then recount information concerning tribute, censuses, ritual, laws, political organization, calendars, genealogies, and the official history of the empire. However, scholars are still debating whether the *quipu* is indeed a decipherable writing system or merely a mute mnemonic device; this issue cannot be resolved from the examples found thus far.

Therefore, unlike Mesoamerica, for the Andean region, we currently lack direct literary continuity from the pre-Columbian to the early colonial period, when much of the surviving historical information was narrated from *quipus* and then recorded alphabetically by the early chroniclers. Not by chance, much of this early indigenous literature came from the Inca Empire, and more specifically, was narrated by the ruling families of Cuzco.

Among the earliest literature produced in the Andes were the Spaniards' conquest narratives, which for the most part attempted to undermine the Incas' autochthonous achievements and questioned the legitimacy of their rule. Among the writers were Francisco de Xerez, Francisco Pizarro's personal secretary, who in 1534 published an official version of the conquest of Peru; Miguel de Estete, who wrote his firsthand experiences on his travels and conquests with Pizarro; and Dominican friar Gaspar de Carvajal, who chronicled the first Spanish expedition to the Amazon River in 1542. A more observant and "ethnographic" account of the Andean people is contained in the soldier Pedro de Cieza de León's four volumes about the Spanish conquest and first decades of European hegemony in the central Andes.

Other important early Spanish chroniclers were Cristóbal de Molina, who recorded numerous Incaic traditions; and Sarmiento de Gamboa, who attempted to produce a unified historical narrative for the Inca Empire but became frustrated by the multiple "partisan histories" of the competing factions. Juan de Betanzos, a Spaniard who married an Inca princess and mastered the Quechua language, recorded in much detail one of the provincial histories from his wife's indigenous family and compiled a short Spanish-Quechua dictionary. In addition to ecclesiastical and legal documents, Spanish officials produced a large corpus of records about land ownership and resources, most notably the *visitas*, formal inspections undertaken in the first decades after the conquest, which provide detailed historical and political information on groups outside the Inca imperial core.

As in Mesoamerica, the Andean indigenous elite similarly adopted the Roman alphabet for their purposes and composed documents, mostly in Spanish, Quechua, and Aymara, in an attempt to validate their royal status and property rights through noble pedigrees. A few indigenous chroniclers from royal bloodlines wrote more lengthy descriptions of their people. Among the most exceptional was Guamán Poma de Ayala, whose detailed narrative is accompanied by 400 drawings of Andean mythological and historical subjects before and after the Spanish conquest, as well as a critique on the harsh colonial rule in Peru directed to the Spanish king. Other comprehensive accounts include those of Titu Cusi Yupanqui and Santa Cruz Pachacuti, and that of the mestizo Garcilaso de la Vega, who idealizes life under the Incas. Although these texts were written a few decades after the conquest and show strong Christian worldviews mixed with the indigenous, these "insider" perspectives strongly challenge the official histories of the Spanish conquistadores.

Much 16th-century Andean literature written by both indigenous and Spaniards consists of sequential histories of individual Inca kings from accession to death, along with the story of the patrilineal descent group founded by each one. According to Garcilaso de la Vega, *amautas* were responsible for structuring these historical events into short stories, while the *harauicus* wrote them down as poems. The chroniclers occasionally refer to these epic praise-poems telling of war, victories, and other memorable events in the Inca Empire, which were sung and accompanied by music and dance in elaborate ceremonies and funerals. Oral recitations used literary devices and poetic conventions such as metaphors, rhythm, and patterned repetition as memory aids and might have first been recorded on *quipus*. The cosmogonic literature consisted of two distinct mythic cycles, one emphasizing Lake Titicaca, where the god Viracocha created the Sun, Moon, and humans; and the other, the emergence of the Inca ancestors from a cave in Pacariqtambo. An important early document is the *Huarochiri Manuscript*, which consists of tales and legends in Quechua collected from indigenous informants and edited by the priest Francisco de Ávila; it opens a window on 16th-century Andean indigenous religious practices.

See also Garcilaso de la Vega (Vol. II); literature (Vols. II, III, IV); printing press (Vol. II).

—Danny Zborover

Further reading:
Miguel León-Portilla and Earl Shorris. *In the Language of Kings: An Anthology of Mesoamerican Literature—Pre-Columbian to the Present* (New York: W. W. Norton & Co., 2001).

Joanne Pillsbury, ed. *Guide to Documentary Sources for Andean Studies, 1530–1900* (Norman: University of Oklahoma Press, 2008).

M

macehual One of the most important features of Nahua society was the hereditary division between nobles and commoners (see AZTECS). This social reality quickly became familiar to colonizing Spaniards. As a consequence, the NAHUATL term *macehualli* (plural, *macehualtin*), or "commoner," soon passed into Mexican Spanish as *macehual* (plural, *macehuales*). At times, the hispanized term was extended beyond the Nahuatl-speaking areas to describe the majority of the settled working population in other regions of Mesoamerica, which was made up of MIXTECS, MAYA, and other groups.

Broadly speaking, the *macehualtin* were those who raised crops and animals, rendered tribute goods to the ALTEPETL and its TLATOANI, performed the hard physical LABOR required for community projects under the traditional *coatequitl* (rotary labor draft), occupied themselves in various crafts, and engaged in local and long-distance TRADE. Before the enforced peace brought by colonization, the *macehualtin* also made up the bulk of the fighting forces that an *altepetl* dispatched against another. Being a commoner did not always imply straitened circumstances; indeed, some specialized craftsmen and long-distance merchants (POCHTECAS) acquired as much wealth as many nobles.

A special aspect of *macehualli* was its meaning in the possessive form as someone's "subject" or "vassal." Since the nobles were formally subjects of the *altepetl*'s leader, the *tlatoani*, they, too, were sometimes described as *macehualtin*. In yet another sense, since the typical inhabitant of an *altepetl* was a *macehualli*, the term (perhaps its primary original meaning) could mean "human being" or "person." This might explain why by 1600 it started to become the Nahuatl equivalent of *indio*, or "Indian," in Spanish.

Nahua society before and after the CONQUEST occasionally allowed for social mobility. A prime example from the early colonial period is Antonio Valeriano. Born a *macehualli*, he became the most renowned Nahua Latinist of his time: Valeriano married into MONTEZUMA'S FAMILY and was governor of MEXICO CITY for 26 years.

—Barry D. Sell

Further reading:

James Lockhart. *The Nahuas after the Conquest: A Social and Cultural History of the Indians of Central Mexico, Sixteenth through Eighteenth Centuries* (Stanford, Calif.: Stanford University Press, 1992).

Kevin Terraciano. *The Mixtecs of Colonial Oaxaca: Ñudzahui History, Sixteenth through Eighteenth Centuries* (Stanford, Calif.: Stanford University Press, 2001).

Machu Picchu Machu Picchu was established as a royal estate by the Inca emperor PACHACUTI INCA YUPANQUI in the mid-15th century (see INCAS). Situated on a mountain ridge above the Urubamba River, it is lower in elevation and milder in climate than the Inca capital of CUZCO. Like many royal estates, it contained housing for the Inca emperor, his retinue, and a multitude of servants who maintained the estate in his absence, as well as numerous shrines for religious activities. The terraced fields that existed just below the site, as well as the rich agricultural fields in the valley farther down, were also in royal possession. Royal estates would pass to the AYLLU of the Inca ruler when he died. These royal *ayllus* were called PANAQAS. The *panaqa* would then manage

One of the world's most magnificent archaeological sites, Machu Picchu was likely built as a royal estate for the Inca ruler Pachacuti Inca Yupanqui (r. 1438–63). *(Courtesy of J. Michael Francis)*

the estate, providing income from its surrounding lands to sustain the dead king's FAMILY and funding ceremonies and rituals in his memory. A dead ruler was considered a powerful ancestor with influence in the spirit world; thus, honoring him and maintaining ties with his family was of practical importance.

Machu Picchu is made from shaped stones, fitted tightly against each other without mortar, and was roofed with thatch. High-status buildings featured stones that were highly smoothed and of a more regular shape (see ARCHITECTURE). Stones were spiritually important to the Incas, who believed that they had the power to turn into humans. Structures at the site emphasize important aspects of royal Inca life and symbolic power. These include a building that marks the June solstice, a large rock whose shape resembles a nearby mountain, and ritual fountains and baths throughout the site, symbolically demonstrating Inca power over earth and water and the elite's relationship with the heavens.

—Sarahh E. M. Scher

Further reading:

Richard L. Burger and Lucy C. Salazar. *Machu Picchu: Unveiling the Mystery of the Incas* (New Haven, Conn.: Yale University Press, 2004).

Magellan, Ferdinand (Fernão de Magalhães) (b. ca. 1480–d. 1521) *Portuguese navigator and explorer*

Born in Villa de Sabroza in northern Portugal to a family of minor nobility, Ferdinand Magellan gained experience as a navigator and military man while participating in expeditions to India, the East Indies, and North Africa. In 1513, Magellan approached King Manuel of Portugal to request leadership of a voyage that would sail west to the Spice Islands. After being denied twice, Magellan took his request to King Charles I of Spain. The Spanish Crown granted Magellan's request and agreed to provide him with five ships and the majority of the funds required to outfit the expedition. On September 20, 1519, Magellan left Sanlúcar de Barrameda with a crew of 250 men.

The expedition sailed first to the Canary Islands, then to Cape Verde and south down the African coast to Sierra Leone before eventually sailing west across the Atlantic to BRAZIL. The expedition remained in Brazil for roughly two weeks before heading south to what is now ARGENTINA. Magellan decided to remain there for five months in order to repair damage to the ships. During this time, many of his crew members grew restless, and a dispute arose between Magellan and the Spanish captains. This developed into a mutiny, which was thwarted by Magellan and his supporters. During the mutiny, one of Magellan's ships deserted and returned to Spain; another vessel was sunk.

The three remaining ships continued the expedition and eventually passed through the strait that now bears Magellan's name and into the South Sea, which Magellan renamed the Pacific. The expedition headed north along the coast of CHILE, before sailing west across the Pacific. In March of 1521, Magellan reached Guam in the Marianas. The expedition continued on until it arrived at Cebu, in what is now the Philippines. In an attempt to forge an alliance with the indigenous people of Cebu, Magellan agreed to attack their enemies who resided nearby at Matan. This decision proved to be disastrous, and Magellan was killed in battle. The surviving members of the expedition could man only two ships and decided to burn the third. The ships sailed on to the Moluccas Islands, where they took various spices on board. One of the ships, the *Trinidad*, then headed east in an attempt to sail back across the Pacific; the other, the *Victoria*, commanded by Sebastián del Cano, continued west and eventually rounded the Cape of Good Hope and arrived back in Sanlúcar de Barrameda on September 1, 1522, thus completing the first circumnavigation of the globe.

See also MAGELLAN, STRAIT OF (Vol. II); SANLÚCAR DE BARRAMEDA (Vol. II).

—Justin Blanton

Further reading:
Hugh Thomas. *Rivers of Gold: The Rise of the Spanish Empire from Columbus to Magellan* (New York: Random House, 2003).

maize   Before the arrival of Europeans in the Americas, domesticated maize (*Zea mays*) was a staple crop of cultures from the St. Lawrence Valley (Canada) to CHILE (see AGRICULTURE). Through the process of selective breeding, the caloric yield of the maize plant increased immensely, and its physical characteristics underwent radical transformations. The rows of large kernels of domesticated maize are tightly packed on a cob that is surrounded by a tough husk; because the kernels cannot scatter, the plant is no longer capable of reproducing without human intervention. Maize was such an important staple that it became integrated into religious beliefs and myths wherever it was grown (see RELIGION). Characteristics of gods and goddesses were based on maize's physical characteristics and life cycle. Because of its centrality to ancient cultures in the Americas and, after the CONQUEST, to cultures throughout the world, archaeologists and geneticists have searched diligently for its wild ancestor and place of origin.

Several varieties of maize on display in the Peruvian Andes near Cuzco *(Courtesy of J. Michael Francis)*

Three primary hypotheses have been offered for the ancestry of maize. According to the tripartite hypothesis, domesticated maize arose from a now-extinct wild pod-popcorn ancestor. The second theory, known as the teosinte hypothesis, postulates that maize is descended from teosinte, a tassel-bearing wild grass. Lastly, the tripsacum-diploperennis hypothesis suggests that maize resulted from a cross between teosinte (*Zea diploperennis*) and *Tripsacum*, genus of tassel-bearing wild grass.

Archaeologist Richard S. MacNeish focused his search for the origin of maize on dry caves in the highlands of MEXICO; plant materials are generally better preserved at such sites. According to MacNeish, genetic evidence indicated that the ancestor of maize was a highland grass; pollen evidence showed it originated somewhere between MEXICO CITY and Chiapas. Excavations between 1961 and 1964 in the Tehuacán Valley also revealed many remains of maize. MacNeish argued that some recovered cobs were 7,000 years old, came from the wild ancestor of maize, and supported the tripartite hypothesis. Domesticated maize appeared around 5000 B.C.E. in Mesoamerica, a conclusion based on uncalibrated conventional radiocarbon dating of charcoal associated with maize remains. MacNeish believed the Tehuacán Valley was not necessarily the earliest place where maize cultivation occurred.

MacNeish's work, however, did not settle all matters concerning the ancestry and origins of maize. A "lowland model" proposed that maize arose from mutations to teosinte growing in the Río Balsas drainage of Guerrero, Mexico. Accelerator mass spectometry (AMS) radiocarbon dates obtained directly from cobs excavated by MacNeish in the Tehuacán Valley are almost all considerably younger than the conventional dates originally reported. A group of biologists and geneticists has declared that biological evidence of the teosinte hypothesis is overwhelming; reports of a successful *Tripsacum*-teosinte hybrid are not credible, and evidence is lacking that the maize genome is a mixture of the *Zea diploperennis* and *Tripsacum* genomes. Currently, the earliest widely accepted evidence of domesticated maize is two calibrated AMS dates (4355–4065 B.C.E.) on cobs of primitive maize that show strong influence from teosinte in its ancestry; this evidence was obtained from excavations at Guilá Naquitz Cave in Oaxaca, Mexico.

Although maize provides essential dietary calories, it lacks important nutrients. Mesoamericans discovered that maize prepared by soaking the kernels in a water-lime mixture (known as *nixtamal*) and then grinding the blend on stones (called *manos* or *metates*) resulted in better human health than maize prepared in other ways. Despite this innovation, a diet that included beans and squash provided better nutrition than one based exclusively in maize.

See also MAIZE (Vols. II, III).

—Stephen L. Whittington

Further reading:

John E. Staller, Robert H. Tykot, and Bruce F. Benz, eds. *Histories of Maize: Multidisciplinary Approaches to the Prehistory, Linguistics, Biogeography, Domestication, and Evolution of Maize* (Boston: Elsevier Academic, 2006).

Malinche, La (Malintzin, Malinalli, Marina) (b. ca. 1500–d. 1541?)

Nahua woman who served as Hernando Cortés's translator in the conquest of Mexico   La Malinche, or simply Malinche, also referred to as doña Marina, Malintzin, Malinalli, La Chingada, or La Llorona, is one of the most intriguing protagonists of the Spanish CONQUEST OF MEXICO. *Malinche* is a Spanish corruption of her indigenous name, *Malintzin*, or *Malinalli*, which probably derived from her sacred calendar birthday sign. Born into a noble Nahua family in the Coatzacoalcos region, she was sold into SLAVERY by her stepfather and ended up as a servant in a MAYA noble family in Potonchán, Tabasco. On March 15, 1519, she was offered as a gift to HERNANDO CORTÉS, who after baptizing and renaming her *doña Marina*, gave her to his lieutenant Alonso Hernández Puertocarrero. To communicate with these Maya nobles, Cortés had used GERÓNIMO DE AGUILAR, a Spaniard who had been shipwrecked on the Yucatán shore and had learned the language in captivity. But, Cortés soon realized that Malinche was bilingual not only in Maya and NAHUATL but also in both the colloquial and noble vernaculars, so she was promptly employed to complement Aguilar in communicating with the emissaries of the TRIPLE ALLIANCE (see AZTECS). By virtue of her position as Cortés's personal interpreter, Malinche soon learned to speak Spanish; she also developed an intimate relationship with Cortés. She was instrumental in Cortés's first meeting with MONTEZUMA on November 9, 1519, in TENOCHTITLÁN, during the events of the Noche Triste (night of sorrows) through to the subsequent defeat of CUAUHTÉMOC.

Beyond her linguistic skills, Malinche possessed an extensive knowledge of indigenous culture and society and thus became a key adviser to Cortés. In fact, the two were so inseparable that the Mexica referred to Cortés also as "Malinche." Malintzin may not have objected to the notion of the foreign conquest and, in fact, might have deliberately manipulated the interaction between indigenous and conquistadores for her own political and personal ends, as might have been the case in the notorious Cholula massacre. Perhaps as a result, Malintzin was further known by her Nahuatl nickname, *Tenepal*, or "vigorous speaker," although this might have been given to her after the conquest.

In 1522, Malinche bore a son to Cortés, named Martín, who is often considered New Spain's first mestizo (a person of mixed indigenous and European blood). Between 1524 and 1526, she accompanied Cortés on his military expedition to HONDURAS, and she interpreted Cuauhtémoc's last confessions. This is also where she was formally married to Juan Jaramillo, one of Cortés's lieutenants, and was awarded an ENCOMIENDA near Coatzacoalcos as a dowry from Cortés. Malinche later gave birth to Jaramillo's daughter, named María. In 1537, she still served as Cortés's interpreter in MEXICO CITY, where she might have died from smallpox as late as 1541.

Although the Spanish chronicles mostly underemphasize her role in the conquest of Mexico (Cortés rarely mentions her in his letters to the king), in indigenous documents such as the *Lienzo de Tlaxcala* and the FLORENTINE CODEX she is depicted as nearly an equal to Cortés. At the same time, much of her background story is told by the Spanish conquistador BERNAL DÍAZ DEL CASTILLO and also by Cortés's secretary, Francisco López de Gómara, who portrayed Malinche as a model of those indigenous who had willingly accepted the political and social transformation of Mesoamerica. Today, the concept of "La Malinche" has been used in different and often contradictory contexts, such as the image of the deceived Indian, the traitor, or as the "mother" of modern Mexican identity (see MESTIZAJE/MESTIZO).

—Danny Zborover

Further reading:
Sandra Messinger Cypess. *La Malinche in Mexican Literature: Myth and History* (Austin, University of Texas Press, 1991).
Camilla Townsend. *Malintzin's Choices: An Indian Woman in the Conquest of Mexico* (Albuquerque: University of New Mexico Press, 2006).

Manco Inca (b. ca. 1513–d. 1544) *Inca emperor installed by the Spanish and founder of neo-Inca rebel state*   Manco Inca was a son of the Inca ruler HUAYNA CÁPAC, whose death touched off a civil war within the Inca Empire between two of Manco's half brothers, ATAHUALPA and HUÁSCAR. The Spaniards exploited the turmoil to conquer PERU (see CONQUEST). Seeking a puppet ruler to oversee the empire, the conquistadores installed Manco as the new emperor in December 1533. At the time, he was about 20 years old.

Given his youth and his Spanish backing, Manco struggled to win the support of his people. They knew the Spaniards controlled him, and some wondered if another of Huayna Cápac's sons might better defend the people. A few conspired against him, and Manco persuaded DIEGO DE ALMAGRO, one of the Spanish leaders, to have these murdered. Manco resented the Spaniards' abuse of the Indians and particularly their mistreatment of his royal person. As a consequence, he conspired to overthrow and expel the Spaniards; on April 18, 1536, he escaped from CUZCO and raised a huge army. The army besieged Cuzco and ambushed Spanish relief expeditions sent from LIMA.

Although Manco nearly captured Cuzco, the siege ultimately failed, and his army disintegrated. He withdrew with several thousand followers northwest of Cuzco

to Vilcabamba, where he established a new Inca state. A civil war among the Spaniards temporarily relieved pressure on Manco, but he lacked the power to control the Inca nobles who had joined him at Vilcabamba (see CIVIL WARS IN PERU). He executed those whom he distrusted or whom he perceived as rivals to his authority, but this only handicapped further resistance against the Spaniards. On occasion, Manco negotiated with the Spaniards; he even allowed several Spaniards to take refuge at Vilcabamba after they murdered FRANCISCO PIZARRO in revenge for the execution of Almagro. In 1544, hoping to please the new Spanish VICEROY, Blasco Núñez de Vela, the Almagrists murdered Manco while he was playing quoits. Vilcabamba survived another quarter century until it was destroyed by the Spaniards in 1572.

—Kendall Brown

Further reading:
John Hemming. *The Conquest of the Incas* (San Diego, Calif.: Harcourt, 1970).

manioc (cassava, yucca)   Manioc (*Manihot esculenta*) was the most important cultivated crop of the AMAZON lowlands (see AGRICULTURE). It was also important on the Pacific and Caribbean coasts. Most manioc varieties are adapted to seasonally dry regions; however, others are grown in the Amazon rain forest, where manioc is the principal and most reliable source of calories of any FOOD, though it is low in protein and other nutrients. Manioc is highly productive and can flourish in poor soils. It was first domesticated in south-central BRAZIL at the beginning of the Holocene period (roughly 8000 B.C.E.) in areas of dry open forest, to which it had adapted by storing starch in enlarged roots. Manioc is grown under cultivation from stem cuttings. It is eaten boiled or taken as a fermented beer (*masato*) (see ALCOHOL). Later in the history of manioc cultivation, farmers in central and eastern Brazil began to cultivate bitter varieties, which were high in toxins that had to be removed before eating. After processing it into a coarse meal, manioc is usually baked in cakes on a griddle or dried and ground into flour (farinha). Farinha is light and easily transported and can be stored for a year. This innovation created a surplus, which could support larger populations.

—Patricia J. Netherly

Further reading:
Dolores R. Piperno and Deborah M. Pearsall. *The Origins of Agriculture in the Lowland Neotropics* (San Diego: Academic Press, 1998).

maps   It is likely that before the Spanish CONQUEST the indigenous people of the Americas used diverse cartographic expressions to orient themselves in the terrestrial, celestial, or mythological landscapes; in fact, the surviving evidence suggests that for them space and time were closely interrelated. The earliest known maps date to the Formative period, when the OLMECS, the MAYA, and the Izapán represented their cosmos on public monuments so that their rulers could symbolically position themselves at the center of the universe. These cosmic maps continued in use up to the Late Postclassic period; horizontal depictions of the cosmos are shown in the Central Mexico Codex Fejérváry-Mayer and the Mayan Codex Madrid. In addition, maps of the heavens and constellations are sometimes found on carved stones or painted in CODICES. Since these cosmological representations were intimately linked to indigenous RELIGION, they soon disappeared as a result of the Spanish spiritual conquest.

At the same time, terrestrial maps are one of the most enduring graphic expressions in Mesoamerica. Indigenous rulers were clearly concerned with recording their territorial extent from early on in their history. Many Mesoamerican groups recorded place-names in logographic and phonetic fashion; the earliest known example is found at MONTE ALBÁN, where a series of stone slabs symbolize the towns conquered by this Zapotec state during the first century C.E. (see ZAPOTECS). Similar territorial charters appeared later in the Mixtec codices from the Late Postclassic period, where complex iconic representations of the Mixtec landscape serve as backdrops in depictions of elite marriages and rituals (see MIXTECS).

This ancient tradition of graphic territorial narratives is probably best exemplified by the "community maps," usually painted on a single sheet of paper (mapas) or canvas (lienzo). Although early eyewitness accounts ascertain that this is a pre-Columbian tradition, all the surviving examples postdate the Spanish conquest. It seems that this cartographic genre was restricted mainly to the area between Hidalgo, Michoacán, and Oaxaca, with only a few examples from the Maya region. For the most part, they are highly idealized depictions of indigenous kingdoms' boundaries and territorial extent and include prominent geographical features such as rivers and roads, as well as the centrally located head town and subject and/or antagonistic towns.

In the Mesoamerican fashion of melding space and time, the accompanying pictorial narrative is often concerned with the original MIGRATION to the land, the conquest wars, the settlement of the kingdom, and the genealogy of the ruling family. These pictorial narratives often served to legitimate the territorial claims of a ruler in the face of competing demands or land disputes and to fortify communal identity. Indeed, after the Spanish conquest, they served as valuable evidence in Spanish courts of law. A fine early 16th-century example of this tradition is the Lienzo de Tecciztlan y Tequatepec, which depicts an alliance between the Chontal people of Oaxaca and a powerful indigenous headtown on the Pacific coast. Other examples include maps of long-distance migrations, such as the Aztec peregrinations from Aztlán in the Mapa Sigüenza and the Tolteca-Chichimeca "itinerary histories" in the Cuauhtinchan maps. These early maps do not seem to demonstrate any conventionalized scale or orientation, although east is commonly at the top. Furthermore, scale often decreases as the observer moves away from the central community. Due to the "circular" distribution of pictorial elements and narratives in many of the maps, it appears that they were occasionally meant to be appreciated horizontally, so that viewers could walk around the document.

More localized maps are known from the Valley of MEXICO, where Aztec bureaucracy demanded the creation of cadastral land plots. These maps include the exact area of the property, the owner's name, and even the property's soil type (see AZTECS). Other maps are known from CHRONICLERS' descriptions, but no examples of these have survived. The Aztecs apparently used detailed maps for way-finding (similar to road maps), and MONTEZUMA even gave such a map to HERNANDO CORTÉS on his expedition to the Coatzacoalcos River. The POCHTECA traders were said to have used their capacity as spies to draw maps of distant towns, which the Aztec armies would later use to conquer them. The closest surviving example of a city map is that of the Aztec capital, TENOCHTITLÁN, in the Codex Mendoza, though it is very emblematic and metaphorical.

After the Spanish conquest, indigenous and European cartographic traditions often merged. The largest corpus of these hybrid maps is found in the Relaciones geográficas of 1580, painted by indigenous people as a response to a detailed Spanish questionnaire designed to gather information about Spain's colonial possessions. One such map from the town of Teozacoalco helped scholars to place the pre-Columbian Mixtec codices in the geographical and historical context of the Mixtec people. It seems that both scale and orientation were standardized in these later maps, probably through the influence of European cartographers, who aimed to record their newly conquered land as accurately as possible. These maps usually do not contain indigenous mythical narratives or indigenous historical content.

Pre-Columbian mapping in the Andes is harder to identify than in Mesoamerica; likely there are landscapes represented on TEXTILES and rock ART, and models of houses were commonly expressed in CERAMICS and stones. However, all surviving examples are highly iconic and might not have functioned as maps per se. The INCAS also carved complex landscapes on large boulders, such as the Sayhuite and the Quinku stones near CUZCO; nevertheless, these carvings do not seem to be associated with the actual geography. Perhaps better examples of maps are the large ground drawings of Nazca, which might have been used to guide pilgrims across the featureless desert (see NAZCA LINES). The later ZEQUE system of the Incas served a similar purpose in addition to dividing the physical landscape into territories pertaining to certain social groups. It has been suggested that geographical information linked to the organization of the zeque system, such as the relative location of the HUACAS and the distance between them, could have been recorded on QUIPUS, which thus functioned as maps.

After the Spanish conquest, several indigenous chroniclers drew maps to accompany their manuscripts. Santa Cruz Pachacuti sketched a celestial map that was once represented on the wall of the Coricancha (sun temple) in Cuzco, and Guamán Poma de Ayala drew several maps that integrated Andean worldviews with European cartographic conventions, including one of the Inca Empire and the "pontifical world." The evidence for pre-Columbian mapping in lowlands South America is even more scant but might have included numerous petroglyphs that represented both geographical and celestial landscapes. Their configuration, however, is for the most part highly abstract, and interpretations are often drawn from ethnographic analogies with the Amazonian tribes (see AMAZON).

—Danny Zborover

Further reading:
David Woodward and G. Malcolm Lewis, eds. *The History of Cartography*, vol. 2, book 3: *Cartography in the Traditional African, American, Arctic, Australian, and Pacific Societies* (Chicago: University of Chicago Press, 1998).

marriage   See FAMILY.

Maya   The Maya are a group of peoples speaking related languages who occupy a large contiguous area of eastern Mesoamerica. The Maya region consists of the eastern parts of the Mexican states of Tabasco and Chiapas and all of the states of Yucatán, Campeche, and Quintana Roo (see MEXICO). It also includes all of GUATEMALA and BELIZE and the western portions of EL SALVADOR and HONDURAS. Although Maya culture varied throughout this large region, the native peoples shared basic cultural patterns including languages, elements of social structure and RELIGION, and basic subsistence practices. The archaeological evidence suggests that the Maya have lived in the same area for several thousand years.

A small outpost of Maya people also stands at the opposite end of Mesoamerica, in northern Veracruz and adjacent parts of the neighboring states. These people, known as the Huastecs, speak a language distantly related to the main branch of the language family.

GEOGRAPHY

The main Maya region is physiographically and environmentally diverse. Elevation slowly increases from north to south, until the mountains in the south descend abruptly to the Pacific. Rainfall increases from the northwest to the southeast. The northwest corner of the Yucatán Peninsula is a virtual desert, while parts of the southern and southeastern lowlands receive 100 inches (2,540 mm) or more of rain each year.

Thus, the northern lowlands, which include most of the Yucatán Peninsula, are relatively hot, flat, and dry. The peninsula is composed of limestone strata, which encouraged underground drainage and mitigated against the development of rivers. Except for a small number of lakes, the only sources of water are sinkholes, or cenotes. Soils in the north tend to be shallow and stony, limiting their agricultural potential (see AGRICULTURE). The highest vegetation consists of low thorn forest, although the trees become taller as one travels south.

The southern lowlands, also known as the Central Maya area, grow hillier as one travels south. Extensive seasonal swamps, known as *bajos*, meander among the hills and ridges. There are more rivers in the south than in the north. Several slow, winding rivers drain the eastern part of the southern lowlands through Belize into the Caribbean. Much of the western part of the area drains into the Usumacinta River, a major artery for transportation and commerce. The highest vegetation in the southern lowlands is tropical forest.

The Maya highlands, also known as the Southern area or southern highlands, consist of tall, folded, and dissected mountain ranges that run roughly parallel with the Pacific. The mountains extend from Chiapas across the base of the Maya region into Honduras. They reach their highest elevations in Guatemala. The highlands are marked by deeply incised rivers, extensive valleys, and picturesque lakes. Soils are deep in many parts of the highlands and include fertile volcanic and alluvial sediments.

LANGUAGES

The 30 or so Mayan languages make up a language family, meaning that they descended from a common ancestral language, known as Proto-Mayan. While Mayan languages are still spoken by millions of people today, some are on the verge of passing entirely out of use.

The most divergent of the Maya languages are Huastec and Chicomuceltec. The linguistic evidence suggests that the Huastec languages split off from the main branch several thousand years ago. In the broad northern lowlands, the four closely related Yucatecan languages are Yucatec, Lacandón, Itzá, and Mopán. Yucatec, the most widely spoken, is actually called "Maya" in the native tongue. It seems almost certain that the glyphic script of the Maya CODICES was recorded in the Yucatec language. It is also likely that many, perhaps all, of the stone inscriptions of the northern lowlands were written in Yucatec.

The southern lowlands were largely depopulated at the end of the Classic period, but it is generally believed that the inhabitants spoke Cholan Maya languages, which consist of Choltí (now extinct), Chortí, Chol, and Maya Chontal. Many scholars believe that the extensive glyphic inscriptions carved on stone monuments in the southern lowlands were written in an ancestral form of the Cholan languages, and while this assumption seems logical and credible, it has been difficult to prove, and other hypotheses remain in contention. The Cholan languages are

Major Maya Sites in Mesoamerica

Komchén

Dzibilchaltún

Mayapán

Uxmal

Chichén
Itzá

Cobá

Gulf of Mexico

Cozumel

Sayil

Edzná

Becán

Calakmul

Nohmul

Cuello

*Caribbean
Sea*

Palenque

El
Perú

Uaxactún

Lamanai

Altun Ha

Piedras Negras

Tikal

Holmul

Yaxchilán

Caracol

Altar de Sacrificios

Seibal

Lubaantun

Cancuen

Quiriguá

Copán

Kaminaljuyú

PACIFIC OCEAN

0   100 miles

0   100 km

N

© Infobase Publishing

closely related to the Tzeltalan languages of highland Chiapas, which borders the southern lowlands.

The Maya highlands possess the greatest linguistic diversity of the region. The large numbers of distinct languages there may be partly attributable to the difficulty of communication across this rugged terrain and also to the complex political history of the area. The highland languages are commonly divided, based on their degree of historical relationship, into Eastern and Western groups, and then into smaller categories.

Because of their speakers' long tradition of interaction and communication, Mayan languages also form a language area distinguished by loans and shared elements that have diffused across the area.

CHRONOLOGY

The origins of the Maya people remain shrouded in mystery. Some Archaic sites of hunter-gatherers have been found in the Maya area, but their connection to the later Maya agriculturalists is unclear (see AGRICULTURE). In the southern lowlands, there is paleoecological evidence of extensive forest clearance around 2000 B.C.E., presumably related to the initial expansion of agriculture settlement; nevertheless, evidence of corresponding settlements has not been found. The earliest archaeological remains of agriculturalists in the region are found on the coast of Guatemala and Chiapas. This Ocós culture dates from 1800 to 1400 B.C.E., but the people are not thought to have been Maya.

The earliest archaeological remains in the lowlands that are clearly related to the later Maya are found at sites such as Cuello, Belize, and EL MIRADOR, Guatemala, and date from around 1000 B.C.E. In the Middle and Late Preclassic periods, populations increased dramatically, large sites emerged, and, during the Late Preclassic (ca. 400 B.C.E.–250 C.E.), all the characteristics of complex, state-level societies emerged, with social stratification, political centralization, economic specialization, elaborate ART and ARCHITECTURE, long-distance TRADE, and glyphic writing (see ECONOMY; LITERATURE).

The Classic period (250–900) saw the development of many large sites with substantial populations that engaged in complex political and economic interactions, including WARFARE. At this time, the population of the Maya lowlands was in the millions, which is much larger than it is today. The subsistence system needed to support these populations combined arboriculture, pisciculture, horticulture, and intensive agriculture. The economy included diverse specialization and mass production, as well as extensive trade. The social structure evidently was founded on extended families forming lineages (see FAMILY). It is generally believed that the lineages were defined on patrilineal principles, but it is also possible that some Maya peoples were bilineal (having both matrilineages and patrilineages). Populations, social complexity, art, and architecture all achieved a peak in the Late Classic (600–900).

At the end of the Classic period, the population collapsed in the southern lowlands and in parts of the northern lowlands. The causes for this are a matter of debate. There is evidence for drought, environmental degradation, overpopulation, and chronic internecine warfare in different places and times. No one theory adequately explains all the evidence. The collapse seems to have come about through a complex series of events spread over at least two centuries, rather than a single event.

Around the end of the Classic period, the Puuc Hills region of Yucatán experienced a final, remarkable flourish. Many large sites were built or expanded at this time, such as Uxmal, Sayil, Kabah, and Nohpat. It is possible that this region, which enjoys unusual agricultural potential but lacks sources of drinking water, received immigrants from elsewhere in the lowlands.

At about the same time, at the end of the Classic and the beginning of the Postclassic period (ca. 1000), CHICHÉN ITZÁ grew into the most important political capital of the northern lowlands. The influences apparent at Chichén are cosmopolitan and eclectic. Central Mexico contacts are obvious, but whether these came from the TOLTECS proper is a matter of debate. Many think that Chichén had a novel form of government called a "joint government," or *mul tepal* in Maya, which was apparently a kind of confederacy of lineages. This differed from the Classic-period governments, which were based on a cult of divine kingship.

In the Late Postclassic period (ca. 1200–1542), the largest city in the Maya area was MAYAPÁN, in Yucatán. Mayapán was, according to colonial-period records, the seat of a *mul tepal*, which eventually fell in a bloody internecine conflict. The art and architecture exhibit some Mexican influences, mixed with the revitalization of some Maya traditions, such as the erection of stelae. At the same time, the southern Maya lowlands were largely unoccupied except for smaller settlements along the Caribbean coast and in the lake region of the central area. The Maya highlands increased in population in the Postclassic period, and groups such as the K'iche' (Quiché), Mam, and Kaqchiquel all developed small but powerful states that fought bitter battles against the Spanish (see CONQUEST).

GLYPHIC WRITING

The Mayan glyphic writing system, or script, was used throughout the Maya-occupied lowlands of the Yucatán Peninsula, Tabasco, Chiapas, Guatemala, and northern Honduras from as early as the Late Preclassic period (400 B.C.E.–250 C.E.) and, at least in some areas, continued through Spanish contact and well into the colonial period. Currently, the earliest known instances of lowland Mayan writing consist of painted wall fragments at the site of San Bartolo, Guatemala, that probably date to the third through first centuries B.C.E. What was probably a very similar writing system was used in the southern highlands of Guatemala and El Salvador during the Late Preclassic period, at sites such as Kaminaljuyú and Takalik Abaj. The nature of the relationship between the Mayan writing system and the contemporary Isthmian script used in places just to the west of the Maya area, such as Veracruz, remains unclear. Although many of the early Mayan texts remain poorly understood, their content appears to be somewhat similar to that of later periods.

Examples of Mayan writing from the Classic and Late Classic periods (250–1000 C.E.) are more numerous and widespread, and better understood. Although changes in the script did occur, the classic writing system itself remained remarkably standard in form, despite being used over such a wide area for more than eight centuries. Even though several different Mayan languages were probably spoken across this area, the writing system seems to record a rather uniform language, probably most closely related to the Eastern Cholan subgroup of Mayan languages. It is thought that this language may have been a high "courtly" language used for important official communications by Maya rulers, the nobility, and palace officials, much as French was a prestigious language throughout much of Europe during particularly the 12th and 13th centuries. The Maya

scribes and sculptors who produced written texts appear to have been predominantly elite courtesans (including sons of rulers) trained in sophisticated scribal and artistic traditions. Certainly, the content of the vast majority of existing Mayan texts is related to predominantly elite activities and concerns. This elite-oriented subject matter and the lack of examples of writing from low-status households may imply that literacy was a privilege of the upper echelon of Maya society, although commoners may have been able to recognize calendrical information and the names of rulers.

Mayan writing has been found on a wide variety of objects made from a number of different materials. Whether carved in stone or wood, sculpted in plaster or stucco, or painted on fig bark paper or clay vessels or plastered walls, the glyphs themselves are often executed in a style firmly rooted in the flowing lines of calligraphy. In fact, the Maya term *tz'ihb* designates both "painting" and "writing," which accords well with the painterly calligraphic writing style and the frequent association of text and image. Many texts were carved or incised on free-standing stone monuments, such as stela (large, upright monoliths), tablets, thrones, and circular "altars." Texts are also found

Copán's Stela A, with entrance to cache below. Copán's stelae were unique in the Maya world for their elaborate subterranean vaults for offerings. (*Courtesy of Janice Van Cleve*)

The back of Copán's Stela A documents a ritual performed on the bones of Waxaklajuun Ub'aah K'awiil's grandfather. The side of this remarkable stela records that the rulers of Tikal, Calakmul, and Palenque were present to witness the event. (*Courtesy of Janice Van Cleve*)

carved on architectural features such as stone or wood lintels over doorways, as well as stone door jambs, wall panels, building cornices, stairways, and stuccoed facades. Some architectural texts are very long, such as the 1,300-glyph block inscription on the Hieroglyphic Stairway of Temple 10L-26 at COPÁN, Honduras, or the three large interior wall panels of the Temple of the Inscriptions at Palenque, Chiapas. Most glyphic texts are intricately linked with pictorial or iconographic images, such as in the famous painted murals of Bonampak, Chiapas.

Texts such as these commonly start with a standardized formula, noting the date as well as astronomical and other cyclical information, such as the lunar position and other nine- and seven-day cycles. Much of the content focuses on historical events pertaining to rulers and, to a lesser extent, to other nobility and high-status officeholders. These events included births, childhood rituals, taking-of-office ceremonies, wars, captive taking, and deaths. Particularly important were records of the erection of stelae and rituals performed by the reigning ruler at the end of certain calendrical periods. Other important content included records of founding events, conjuring of deities and ancestors, and the ruler's royal genealogy and venerated names and titles. These records, which included dates according to the 260-day ritual calendar, apparently served a legitimizing function for rulers, whose activities or ancestry were sometimes linked to events and deities in the mythic past (such as the creation of the world) or the distant future. WOMEN were often the subjects of monumental texts, whether they were the daughters of rulers sent to other locales in marriage alliances, the mothers or wives of rulers, and/or acting monarchs in their own right.

The Maya also carved, painted, or inscribed texts on small, portable ceremonial objects or elite personal items, including wooden or stone boxes, wooden mirror backs, and small sculptures, often identifying their owners. Such "name tagging" has been found on bone awls and weaving pins, greenstone celts and earflares, and shell implements such as inkpots and trumpets (see MUSIC). Several scribes and sculptors "signed" their ceramic or monumental works by using a similar format to identify themselves as the artists responsible. Stone features such as stela, lintels, and stairways could also be "tagged." A large number of ceramic vessels were inscribed around the rim with a standardized formula identifying the type and function of vessel (plate, cup, "drinking vessel"), its contents (varieties of chocolate, corn gruel, tamales), and the owner's name and titles. The main body of ceramic vessels often included writing as well, often identifying painted figures and sometimes even representing their speech. Painted texts have also been found on the walls of caves; they often record the ceremonies undertaken in these sacred ritual locales and perceived entrances to the underworld (see XIBALBÁ).

Other than a limited number of texts mentioning tribute items and bundles of chocolate beans, few examples of economic record-keeping are known, although these may have been recorded on perishable materials such as palm leaves, wooden tablets, or in paper books. It is possible that such perishable media may also have been used to record such things as legends and myths, poetry, and songs. Only four examples of Maya painted fig-bark-paper books, or CODICES, are known to exist (the authenticity of one is still debated). Although these were painted in the Postclassic period (1000–1517), some content may have been copied from Classic-period texts. The codices include records of astronomical tables (including tracking of, and perhaps corrections to, the cyclic stations of Venus and lunar and solar eclipses), mythic events associated with the creation of time periods and the cosmos, and divinatory almanacs (probably used to record days considered auspicious for particular ceremonies and activities).

Clearly dated inscriptions in stone from the southern lowlands date to as late as the beginning of the 10th century; however, glyphs continued to be inscribed on stone monuments and other objects at sites in the northern Yucatán Peninsula for at least another century. The practice of carving glyphic texts in stone diminished drastically during the Postclassic period, with only a handful of stelae known from sites such as Mayapán, Yucatán, and possibly Flores, Guatemala. Although few examples remain today, the painting of texts in murals and in books did continue throughout the lowlands. Mayan writing was still in use after the conquest, and some friars were said to have learned how to read and write in the glyphic system. The 16th-century Franciscan friar DIEGO DE LANDA's writings contain a brief description of a set of glyphic syllables and their sound values (mistakenly thought to be an "alphabet"). Subtle clues found in colonial indigenous works written in Mayan languages, yet using the Latin alphabet, suggest that literacy in the glyphic writing system persisted in both the lowlands and highlands at least into the early part of the colonial period, despite Spanish missionaries' efforts to repress it.

Given that it was Friar Landa who orchestrated public burnings of Maya books in 16th-century Yucatán, it is ironic that it was his recorded "alphabet" that set the stage in the mid-20th century for a major breakthrough in the long process of deciphering the Mayan glyphic writing system. Previously, generally only the number system, chronological framework, and astronomical cycles were well understood due to the efforts in the 19th and early 20th centuries by researchers from Germany, Britain, France, the Yucatán, and the United States. In fact, some scholars had felt that the inscriptions dealt only with calendrical matters, with individual glyphs representing ideas rather than designating sounds. However, in the 1950s, Russian scholar Yuri Knorosov showed, using the sound values provided by Landa and by relating images to their corresponding hieroglyphs in the Maya codices, that phonetic syllables were used to spell words. In the 1960s, the Russian-born researcher Tatiana Proskouriakoff demonstrated the historical nature of some texts, correctly identifying births and deaths of depicted individuals. Work in the 1970s and 1980s allowed scholars to recognize verbs, translate entire phrases, decipher additional syllables, and read lists of Classic-period kings.

It is now clear that the Mayan writing system could adequately express anything that the language would require, including grammatical elements such as verb endings. This was accomplished by using a mix of phonetic syllables (consisting of consonant and vowel) along with logograms (glyphs that represent the stem of a word, usually in the form of consonant-vowel-consonant). Research in recent decades has greatly expanded the number of syllables and logograms able to be read, although many continue to elude decipherment, and a certain number occur too rarely to ever be read. The general gist of the large majority of extant Mayan texts is understood, while many are now able to be read in full. Over the last two decades, indigenous Maya researchers have begun to investigate and reuse their ancient script, even adapting it for use with modern highland Guatemalan languages.

THE BALL GAME

The ritual ball game is one of the defining traits of Mesoamerican civilizations. Ball courts are prominent architectural features at most large archaeological sites throughout Mesoamerica, including the Maya area. Specific features of the game, including the manner of scoring, number of players on each team, size of the court, equipment used, and outcome for the winners and losers, varied between cultures and CITIES, as did the purpose of playing. Extant records indicate that games could be played between two individuals as a means of predicting the future, based on the outcome, or between multiplayer teams for entertainment and gambling. Some records suggest that losers might have been killed, while others state that winners lost their lives. Certain types of goals were rare enough that the team that scored one had the right to chase spectators and take whatever they were carrying or wearing.

The Maya ball court usually had a playing surface in the shape of an I. Sloping benches or vertical walls designed to keep the ball within bounds ran along the long sides of the court. Single or multiple markers along the sides or in the center of the court functioned as goals. At Copán, the main ball court has three markers on each side, one in the center and one on each end of sloping side benches, and each is shaped like the head of a macaw. Three carved markers are also inset into the playing surface. At Chichén Itzá, one stone ring decorated with intertwined serpents is set high on each side wall. At Copán, players had to hit the markers to score, while at Chichén Itzá they attempted to hit the ball through the rings.

The game involved a solid rubber ball about the size of a softball or soccer ball. Players were allowed to hit it with their hips or torso and were supposed to keep it in the air. A solid ball that would bounce energetically off

A rubber ball used to play the ball game that was ubiquitous throughout Mesoamerica. This ball is on display at Mexico City's National Museum of Anthropology and History. *(Courtesy of J. Michael Francis)*

stone or plaster playing surfaces would be dangerously heavy and hard against the body. Healed broken bones of an elite male buried in the acropolis area of Copán may represent injuries from the ball game.

Ball players wore heavy padding around their hips and chests to absorb the shock of the ball's impact. Hip protectors, known as yokes, were probably made of wood, hide, and fiber stuffing. Other ball game equipment included *hachas*, *palmas*, and *yugitos*, probably also made of perishable materials. Ceramic figurines and wall friezes show flat carved *hachas* and phallic *palmas* mounted on the front of yokes; players wore *yugitos* to protect their elbows and knees during diving saves. Players sometimes carried hand stones (*manoplas*) to support themselves when leaning close to the playing surface or possibly to hit the ball in some variations of the game. Archaeologists have excavated stone yokes and *hachas* at numerous Maya sites. These heavy objects might have been used as trophies, handicaps for good players, or markers for temporary ball courts.

The ball game had many religious connotations and associations with warfare and HUMAN SACRIFICE. The ball's flight through the air above the playing surface represented the Sun's passage across the sky during the day. In the K'iche' POPOL VUH, a creation story written down in the 16th century, much action revolves around ball courts and games involving supernatural beings on earth and in the underworld (Xibalbá). Losers are often decapitated or otherwise put to death. This was also true of games played on actual courts. *Hachas* frequently were carved to represent skulls or skeletons. Ball court friezes at Chichén Itzá show the fate of a defeated player: His head is in the hand of the victor and his kneeling body spouts serpents from the neck. A carved ball on one frieze

La Esperanza ball court marker from the Maya site of Chinkultic, in Chiapas, Mexico. The stone is slightly more than 21.5 inches (54.6 cm) in diameter and 5.5 inches (14 cm) thick. The center features a ball player in action, dressed in full regalia. The marker indicates that the ball court had a dedication Long Count date of 9.7.17.12.14 (591 C.E.) and is on display at Mexico City's National Museum of Anthropology and History. *(Courtesy of J. Michael Francis)*

This carved limestone panel shows two Maya ball players. The figure on the left is the Maya ruler of Toniná, K'inich B'aaknal Chaak. In the center, the glyphs above the ball record the date, which corresponds either to November 12, 675, or October 30, 727. The identity of the figure on the right is less clear, but it might be the ruler of Calakmul, Yuknoom Took' K'awiil. *(Courtesy of J. Michael Francis)*

contains a skull. Scenes of ball games at Yaxchilán and Tikal show that losers were rolled down steep flights of stairs with their arms and legs tied tightly behind them. To make the connection between losing and death absolutely clear, the trussed bodies appear within balls.

In portraits, Maya rulers are often depicted wearing ball game paraphernalia. Playing the game was a requirement for royal males, and game imagery was integral to the ideology that supported the ruling elite. Leading warriors into battle against other cities was a dangerous activity for elite males, as they particularly were targeted for death or capture. The blood of nobles and members of the royalty was highly potent as an offering to the gods. Elite captives stripped of their finery were forced to play the game against opponents from the victorious city before being sacrificed.

Despite strong associations with death, the Maya ball game also was symbolically connected with rebirth. In the Popul Vuh, One Hunahpu lost his life while playing ball against underworld gods, was buried beneath a ball court, and eventually was resurrected. The story of One Hunahpu, whom scholars equate with the Maize God, parallels the life cycle of MAIZE, where buried seeds give rise to plants whose heads are removed to permit the continuation of existence.

CALENDARS

Maya calendars were the most complex calendars developed in Mesoamerica. Some elements probably originated as a farmer's almanac and divinatory tool in the Zapotec area and reached the Maya via the OLMECS and other peoples on the western and southwestern margins of Maya territory (see ZAPOTECS). Observations of astro-

nomical events such as equinoxes and solstices formed the basis of Mesoamerican calendars. Some buildings, such as the Caracol at Chichén Itzá and Group E at Uaxactún, were carefully oriented and positioned to permit the observation of the rising and setting of celestial bodies at the horizon. The Maya conceptualized time primarily as cyclical, with past and present events linked by similar locations within long and short time cycles, but also as linear for counting the eternally repeating cycles of days.

The Sacred Round, or Tzolk'in, was a cycle of 260 days, composed of the numbers 1 to 13 and 20 day signs. A bar represented 5 and a dot was 1 in writing numbers. An example of a sequence of days is 1 Imix, 2 Ik', 3 Ak'bal through 13 Ben, then continuing from 1 Ix through the remaining day symbols. The day 1 Imix recurs only after completion of a 260-day cycle. Date of birth became part of one's name, though Classic rulers did not follow this practice. A supernatural being associated with each day symbol determined the personality and fate of people born on that day, and prediction tables in codices listed positive or negative features of each day symbol. The number in front of the day symbol modified its effect, so there were 260 different possible forecasts. The Sacred Round also influenced communal activities, such as religious festivals.

The Haab' (Vague, or Common, Year) lasted 365 days, a complete agricultural cycle. It consisted of 18 months of 20 days each and a period of five unlucky unnamed days at the end of the cycle, the Wayeb'. Each month had a supernatural patron or protector. A "zero" day, described during the Classic as the "seating" of the new month, introduced the patron who would influence the next 19 days. An example of a sequence of Haab' days is Seating (0) Pop, 1 Pop, 2 Pop through 19 Pop.

Since the Haab' was about six hours shorter than the tropical solar year, the two quickly got out of alignment. It is not known whether the Maya periodically inserted extra days to make corrections, so it is unclear if the Haab' always began in mid-July, as it did in the 16th century. According to Friar Landa, the new year festival was the most important: People swept out their houses, replaced old utensils with new ones, and put new covers on bundles of relics and images of gods and goddesses.

The Calendar Round was a period of 18,980 days (52 years) that resulted from the combination of the Sacred Round and Haab' cycles. A particular date, such as 3 Ak'bal 2 Pop, would not recur until an entire Calendar Round had passed. Dates in inscriptions were most commonly recorded using this form. The Haab' new year could only begin on one of four Tzolk'in day symbols, each of which was associated with a particular color, direction, and prophecies that influenced the entire year. A Bakab, a supernatural being who held up a corner of the sky, was "year-bearer" for each of these day symbols.

The Long Count was a place notational system for recording longer progressions of days. It appeared in the last century B.C.E. in chiefdoms on the Pacific coastal plain of GUATEMALA and Chiapas. The earliest use anywhere in the world of a symbol to represent the number 0, usually a shell, occurs in a Long Count.

Scholars define the beginning of the Classic period as 292 C.E., the first date on a Maya monument that is contemporary and not retrospective. Long Count dates on monuments generally begin with an introductory glyph that has a central variable element representing the patron of the appropriate Haab' month, followed by periods of time in decreasing order. A *bak'tun* was a period of 144,000 days, or 20 *k'atun*; a *k'atun* was 7,200 days, or 20 *tun*; a *tun* or *haab'* consisted of 360 days or 18 *winal*; a *winal* was equivalent to 20 days, or *k'in*; a *k'in* was one day. Long Count dates are transcribed so that larger units are on the left and smaller ones are on the right, separated by decimal points: 9.8.10.12.1. The Maya had a vigesimal (base-20) numbering system, based on the number of human fingers and toes, and the Long Count corresponds to this system, except for the *tun*, which was modified to correspond more closely to the length of a solar year. *Tun* also means "stone," probably related to the custom of erecting stone monuments at the end of certain calendrical cycles.

Long Count units higher than the *bak'tun* are known. The base date for the Long Count, the date of the creation of the world, is 4 Ajaw 8 K'umk'u, or September 8, 3114 B.C.E. in the Julian calendar, which was used in Europe until 1582. The world's creation was not the beginning of time, however, and Long Count dates much earlier than the base date help to place the creation within a larger context.

The initial series is a Long Count date that often appears first in inscriptions and reaches a day and month in the Calendar Round. Distance numbers, or secondary series, ordered lists of *k'in, winal,* and other units, appear after the initial series and count forward or backward from it. The initial series is itself a distance number from the base date. Some distance numbers mark *tun* anniversaries or the end of Long Count periods.

The supplementary, or lunar, series is a group of glyphs often appearing between the day and month glyphs of the initial series that provides information about the Moon for that particular day. The lunar series involves Moon cycles, including one based on a sequence of nine glyphs for the Lords of the Night, or deities ruling over the night.

The Maya also observed and recorded other cycles. They made tables of an 819-day cycle based on the product of the magic numbers 7 (Earth), 9 (the heavens), and 13 (the underworld). This cycle was important for Classic ceremonies concerning world directions and colors and the god K'awiil; it often appears in association with the birthday or accession of a ruler. The date of creation occurred on the third day of one of these cycles, which was associated with east and red and was propitious for the creation of the world and life. Finally, the Maya developed tables of solar and lunar eclipses, the 584-day cycle of Venus, bringer of misfortune and war, and 13 constellations of the zodiac.

The Sacred Round was still being used at the time of the conquest and is used in highland Guatemala today. Determining the relationship between Long Count dates and the European calendar is challenging because the Maya did not record the Long Count during the last few centuries before contact. Most scholars favor a correlation of 9.15.10.0.0 with June 30, 741. The current Long Count will end in December of 2012.

RELIGION

The Maya cosmos was composed of three realms, the upper world (heavens), the middle world (world of humans), and the underworld (Xibalbá). Nine levels, stacked in a sort of pyramid, made up the upper world. A two-headed reptile represented the path of the Sun, Moon, and other celestial bodies. The middle world was the back of a crocodile or turtle floating in a pool with water lilies. The underworld was a watery place of nine levels resembling an inverted pyramid. Different supernatural or mortal beings inhabited each realm.

The middle world was divided into quadrants that resemble the cardinal directions. Each quadrant was related to the Sun's daily journey and associated with a particular color, tree, animal, bird, and other characteristics. The east was the "emerging Sun," and its color was red. The west, whose color was black, was the "entering Sun." "Left hand of the Sun" was the direction that corresponded with the white north and was associated with the Sun's zenith. Opposite was the "right hand of the Sun," the yellow south associated with Xibalbá.

In the center of the middle world was the World Tree (Wakah-Chan), represented by a giant ceiba, whose roots descended into the underworld and branches reached into the heavens. The World Tree was a path by which inhabitants of the various worlds could travel and communicate.

The color of the center was blue-green (the Maya did not distinguish between those colors). Maya codices and modern religious practices among living Maya demonstrate that the pathway used in the ritual cycle started in the east and then passed to the north, west, south, and, finally, center.

Numerous deities with characteristics of males, females, or animals inhabited the three worlds. Some belonged to pairs or triads of gods or goddesses, while others were avatars of other deities. Itsamnaaj was the supreme creator deity, inventor of writing, and patron of learning and sciences, who inhabited the starry sky with his wife, Chak Chel, goddess of weaving, childbirth, MEDICINE, and the waning Moon. Together, they were the progenitors of the other gods and goddesses. A nubile version of Chak Chel (Ix Chel or Ix Ch'up) was the young Moon Goddess, who dallied with other gods. Associated with the east, the Sun God (K'inich Ajaw) may have been an aspect of Itsamnaaj. Venus was associated with the west and brought misfortune and WARFARE.

The underworld was inhabited by ugly, smelly, and terrifying supernatural beings. These included the Lord of Death (Yum Kimil) and the old God L, god of destruction. Gods associated with the center were the Maize God (Hun-Nal-Ye) and K'awiil, deity of divine lineages and regent of the quadrants of the cosmos. In the middle world, Pawahtuun was the patron of scribes and painters; he also presided over the Wayeb', the five unlucky days that follow the end of the 360-day solar calendar. Pawahtuun also held up the four corners of the cosmos as four beings, each equivalent to a Bakab who held up a corner of the sky. Chaak, the god of rain, was another deity associated with the center when he was singular, and with each quadrant of the cosmos when he was quadripartite.

After the Sun God disappeared beneath the western horizon each evening, he became the Jaguar God of the underworld, passing through Xibalbá before rising triumphantly in the east the next morning. Humans provided the Sun God with sacrificial offerings so that he could complete his dangerous nighttime journey. The most appropriate offering was human blood, whose potency increased with the social rank of the source. Royal personages were expected to draw blood through autosacrificial rites. Men pierced the foreskin of the penis, and women drew a thorn-studded cord through the tongue to produce blood that they dripped onto paper and then burned.

Kings and nobles participated in warfare by leading troops into battle. One of the purposes of warfare was to take enemy captives, particularly kings and nobles. Captives were marched back to the victors' city, where they were made to play the ritual ball game, tortured to produce quantities of blood, and ultimately killed. The passage of the rubber ball through the air during the game symbolized the passage of the Sun through the sky.

The Popol Vuh, or Council Book, based on oral tradition written down in the 16th century by a former K'iche' nobleman, is the source of much information about ancient Maya religion. The book summarizes various creations and destructions of the world but focuses on the current (fourth) creation and the rise of the K'iche'. According to the Popul Vuh, the gods tried to fashion humans out of various substances, including mud and wood; however, these efforts failed and the gods were not satisfied with the result until they used maize. In the story, One Hunahpu and his brother Seven Hunahpu offended the gods of the underworld with their noisy ball playing. The gods invited the brothers to play in Xibalbá, where they were defeated and killed. Hanged in a calabash tree, the decapitated One Hunahpu's head spat into the hand of a daughter of one of the underworld gods, impregnating her; this act led to the birth of the Hero Twins, Hunahpu and Xbalanque. The Hero Twins followed in the footsteps of their father and uncle but used their wiles to defeat the underworld gods and resurrect their father. Thus the world was made safe for humans. Scholars equate One Hunahpu with the Maize God, Hunahpu with Venus, and Xbalanque with the Sun.

The Maya believed that each person had multiple souls, one of which could continue its existence in an afterlife. A king hoped his soul's journey after it was swallowed by the Maw (cave) of the underworld would emulate the Maize God's, passing through the travails of Xibalbá to rise to the heavens, where it would join the souls of venerated ancestors. Mourners brought food and drinks for the soul's journey through the afterlife; these offerings were placed in ceramic vessels decorated with painted or inscribed images that often paralleled scenes in the Popul Vuh. These probably functioned as road maps for the soul, showing it how the Hero Twins defeated the underworld gods. Nevertheless, not all treatment of the dead was meant to help the soul's journey. Mass graves and defleshing the face of decapitated persons may have been designed to destroy or suspend the journey of an enemy's soul.

The Maya used various means to enter altered states for religious purposes. Blood loss during autosacrificial rituals allowed participants to conjure the Vision Serpent and communicate with ancestors. Strong native TOBACCO induced visions when smoked or used as an enema. Glands in the skin of a large toad (Bufo marinus) produced poisonous and hallucinogenic substances that were mixed with tobacco or used in enemas. Fermented alcoholic beverages taken orally or anally also provided access to alternate realities (see ALCOHOL). Sleeping and dreaming permitted interaction with or transformation into one's way, an animal spirit companion of each person, ancestor, or god or goddess.

Aspects of Maya religion, such as belief in resurrection and the use of crosses (the foliated cross represented maize), paralleled aspects of Christianity. Religious SYNCRETISM developed during the colonial period and continues in present practices such as veneration of Maximón in highland Guatemala.

—Jeff Buechler
Clifford T. Brown
Stephen L. Whittington

Further reading:
Michael D. Coe. *Breaking the Maya Code*, rev. ed. (New York: Thames & Hudson, 1999).
———. *The Maya*, 7th ed. (New York: Thames & Hudson, 2005).
Michael D. Coe and Justin Kerr. *The Art of the Maya Scribe* (New York: Harry N. Abrams, 1998).
Arthur Demarest. *Ancient Maya: The Rise and Fall of a Rainforest Civilization* (New York: Cambridge University Press, 2004).
David Freidel, Linda Schele, and Joy Parker. *Maya Cosmos: Three Thousand Years on the Shaman's Path* (New York: HarperCollins, 1993).
Simon Martin and Nikolai Grube. *Chronicle of the Maya Kings and Queens: Deciphering the Dynasties of the Ancient Maya*, 2d ed. (New York: Thames & Hudson, 2007).
E. Michael Whittington. *The Sport of Life and Death: The Mesoamerican Ballgame* (London: Thames & Hudson, 2001).

Mayapán   Mayapán is a large MAYA archaeological site located in the state of Yucatán, MEXICO, in a hot, dry, flat thorn forest. It is known to have been the political capital of a large state that controlled most of the northern peninsula. It is a late site, dating to 1200–1450, in the Late Postclassic period. A few earlier artifacts from the Preclassic (before 250 C.E.) and Classic periods (250–900) have also been found at the site, but all the structures investigated by archaeologists date from the Late Postclassic. The site measures more than 1.5 square miles (3.9 km²) and is surrounded by a substantial defensive wall, more than five miles (8 km) long. Within the wall, more than 4,000 pre-Hispanic structures have been mapped. Outside the wall, a narrow belt of additional residential settlement occupies a fringe of land. Mayapán was by far the largest Maya site of the Late Postclassic period and has been the subject of several significant archaeological investigations.

Several Spanish colonial-period texts chronicle Mayapán's history, both in Spanish and in the native Yucatec Mayan language. In the 16th century, the Spanish bishop DIEGO DE LANDA recounted that Kukulkán, the Maya version of the hero-god QUETZALCÓATL (Plumed Serpent), founded Mayapán after the fall of CHICHÉN ITZÁ. He unified the Yucatecan nobility, and under his leadership, they built Mayapán and divided the towns and provinces among themselves. After Kukulkán left, the nobles chose the head of the Cocom lineage as ruler. The Cocom rulers eventually became repressive, sustaining their regime by introducing Aztec mercenaries (see AZTECS). Finally, the Xiu lineage, which had settled earlier in the hill country south of Mayapán, joined the other nobles to overthrow the Cocom tyranny. As a result, Mayapán burned and was abandoned in the mid-1400s.

The story told in the Yucatec language chronicles is different in emphasis. It focuses on an ethnic group called the Itzá, apparently a group of "Mexicanized" Maya. The Cocom were probably an Itzá lineage. The Maya texts mention a "joint government" (*mul tepal*) at Mayapán but also discuss a ruler named Hunac Ceel. He was implicated in treachery and witchcraft: A love potion and an abducted bride caused the city's overthrow by Chichén Itzá and Izamal.

The ART and ARCHITECTURE of Mayapán have a Mexican flavor. For example, flat beam-and-mortar roofs, a Mexican trait, are the norm, while Maya corbel vaults are rare. Round temples, a Mexican form, are also common at Mayapán. Balustrades, serpent columns, and colonnades are other significant Mexican traits. Murals and stuccos uncovered in excavations reflect the Mixtec-Puebla style of Central Mexico. The only well-preserved stela at the site exhibits carving suggestive of the Mixtec-Puebla style. Nevertheless, the presence of stelae suggests the persistence of an earlier Maya tradition, as does the use of glyphs.

Overall, Mayapán exhibits an eclectic mix of Maya and Mexican traditions. It was probably a multiethnic city that played an important role in long-distance TRADE. The fruitful and complicated blend of cultures was undoubtedly the result of the complex political and economic dynamics of the region and period.

—Clifford T. Brown

Further reading:
Susan Milbrath and Carlos Peraza Lope. "Revisiting Mayapán: Mexico's Last Maya Capital." *Ancient Mesoamerica* 14, no. 1 (2003): 1–46.

medicine   Early colonial medicine in Latin America developed as an amalgamation of indigenous and European ideas and practices. Building on the mass of indigenous knowledge of the natural environment, colonial healing systems incorporated indigenous medicines into European ideas about DISEASE and the body.

Pre-Columbian concepts of health and sickness varied as widely as native societies themselves. Among the small-scale cultures of the Sonoran Desert, for example, disease was believed to be tied to the natural environment. For many of the urban societies of Mesoamerica, individual health correlated to the overall order of society. In this context, ailments could indicate violations of individuals as well as ruptures in the norms and organization of the community. Native societies maintained a variety of healing specialists. For the MAYA of the Yucatán, professional healers, including midwives, surgeons, herbalists, and bone setters, treated specific ailments and conditions.

Since Spanish and indigenous interaction took place mainly in the Valley of MEXICO, Nahua concepts and practices were critical to early colonial medicine (see AZTECS). The Nahuas believed that illness was the product of individual and social disequilibrium. In this context, sickness was caused by many factors, including religious impropriety, sexual transgressions, extreme emotions, and physical stress (see RELIGION). The heart and soul, called *teyolia* in NAHUATL, were believed to be intertwined and the keys to controlling individual disease and healing. Sexual activity with someone of a different social class, for example, could thrust a person into a phlegm-ridden illness. Transgressions of this sort threatened the broader social order, and not surprisingly, recovery involved restoring harmony through sacrifice and penance.

Another important concept in the Nahua ideology of disease involved the disembodied life forces called *tonalli*, which were represented as spirit or animal companions that individuals had to appease. The spiritual essences of the *tonalli* were believed to reside in supernatural and natural spaces; disturbances to these spaces resulted in illnesses that correlated to specific sites on the human body. Finally, human life was thought to emanate from luminous gases called *ihiyotl*; these gases could cause illness, as well as heal. Individuals who maintained social and individual balance were thought to give off beneficial emanations, while the ill gave mal airs. Curing the infirmed, therefore, often involved pungent remedies.

After the CONQUEST, Nahua medical practices and ideas found favor among Spaniards. While the colonizers often disparaged indigenous religious practices, they praised the Nahuas' emphasis on social order and individual responsibility. Indigenous concepts of penance and sacrifice were equated with Christian notions of sin and redemption. Spaniards also saw disease as a reflection of metaphysical disorder and disharmony and drew parallels between the indigenous emphasis on blood with European ideas of the humors, which identified blood, phlegm, black bile, and yellow bile as the sources of sickness. In this context, Spaniards believed that sickness was caused by imbalances in the body's fluids, and healing therefore involved returning the body to a state of balance. Furthermore, Spaniards were anxious to learn about the natural world from knowledgeable sources. Indigenous elites and medical practitioners served as repositories of information on the region's flora and fauna. Early colonial medicines, then, evolved through the cross-pollination of diverse medical traditions.

Remedies involved treating both the specific ailment and the moral condition of the infirmed. BERNARDINO DE SAHAGÚN, a Franciscan friar with a keen interest in indigenous culture, described the conjuncture of religion and medicine, writing "preachers and confessors are physicians of the soul . . . [and] it is appropriate that they have practical knowledge of medicine and of spiritual illnesses." Indigenous midwives commonly treated infirm newborns with a blessing of water believed to cleanse the heart/soul (see WOMEN). Noncertified local healers, or *curanderos*, specialized in herbal remedies and prayers for ailments that involved physical and psychological distress.

European interest in indigenous medicine began early in the colonial period. The priest Ramón Pane recorded TAINO remedies and practices in the Caribbean during CHRISTOPHER COLUMBUS's second voyage of 1493. In the 1550s, Sahagún interviewed Nahuatl-speaking nobles and began compiling a massive 12-volume description of indigenous religion and culture, which contained 225 descriptions of healing herbs. During the same period, a native healer and professor of medicine from MEXICO CITY, Martín de la Cruz, prepared a description of local medicinal herbs. Given as a gift to King Charles I, the manuscript was not held in public view until the 20th century. In 1565, the Spanish physician Nicolás Monardes published an account that incorporated useful American remedies into European Galenic medicine.

In 1570, King Philip II named the well-known Spanish physician Francisco Hernández as the chief medical officer of the Indies, or *protomédico general*. Although charged with regulating medical knowledge and investigating all things related to natural history throughout the Spanish colonies, Hernández spent the entirety of his six-year tenure surveying healing plants in the Valley of Mexico. While in Mexico, Hernández witnessed the massive 1576 outbreak of *cocolitzli*, which killed scores of the region's indigenous inhabitants; he also witnessed the devastation caused by European diseases at the Hospital Real de los Naturales (Royal Hospital for Indians). He summed up his own feeling of helplessness, both personally and professionally, in poetic hexameters:

What do I say? Why did it fall to me to test the medicinal plants on myself?
And at the same time put my life at great risk?
Or those diseases, which caused me such excess fatigue, with which I am still afflicted, and which will affect me for the rest of my life. . . .

The Spanish Crown attempted to regulate and control medical information and practices through Hernández's appointment and the subsequent creation of a governing board of physicians, the Protomedicato. Government and religious officials regularly complained of illicit practices in curing. Clerics, for example, frequently charged indigenous female healers with invoking WITCHCRAFT in their remedies. The Protomedicato established certifying examinations for physicians, surgeons, apothecaries, and midwives. Despite these attempts to regulate and control medical practices, healing largely remained a local and unregulated affair. Both apothecaries and indigenous healers thrived through their use and knowledge of healing herbs.

See also MEDICINE (Vol. III).

—R. A. Kashanipour

Further reading:

Francisco Guerra. *Searching for the Secrets of Nature: The Life and Works of Dr. Francisco Hernández,* edited by Simon Varey, Rafael Chabrán, and Dora B. Weiner (Stanford, Calif.: Stanford University Press, 2000).

Alfredo López Austin. *The Human Body and Ideology: Concepts of the Ancient Nahuas,* translated by Thelma Ortiz de Montellano and Bernard Ortiz de Montellano (Salt Lake City: University of Utah Press, 1984).

Sandra Orellana. *Indian Medicine in Highland Guatemala: The Pre-Hispanic to Colonial Periods* (Albuquerque: University of New Mexico Press, 1988).

Mendoza, Antonio de (b. 1495–d. 1552) *first viceroy of New Spain and viceroy of Peru*

Antonio de Mendoza was the first VICEROY of New Spain (MEXICO), appointed by Charles I in 1535. He governed until 1550, when he was appointed viceroy of PERU. Mendoza came from one of the most powerful clans within the Spanish nobility. His father, the count of Tendilla, had been an important figure in the conquest of Granada. Mendoza was a younger son in the family and, thus, did not fall in line of succession for the title. His appointment initiated a pattern whereby viceroys would be chosen from among the titled nobles or bishops and archbishops. It also established a pattern whereby many viceroys would serve first in New Spain, then later in Peru. The viceroy's major obligation was to provide the colony with a physical embodiment of the king, a "vice-king," to act as a counter to the high court, or *AUDIENCIA*, which had already been established.

During his term of office in Mexico, Mendoza oversaw the expedition of FRANCISCO VÁSQUEZ DE CORONADO to the U.S. Southwest and expeditions up the Pacific coast to modern-day San Francisco and witnessed an indigenous uprising in the west known as the MIXTÓN WAR. He also supervised the creation of the first MINING codes, issued the first important land grants, developed regulations for the cattle industry, and supervised the major construction projects that would characterize MEXICO CITY (see ARCHITECTURE). He is also known for his handling of the promulgation of the NEW LAWS OF 1542. These laws mandated the eventual abolition of the *ENCOMIENDA* system under which indigenous people paid tribute to and labored for Spanish settlers and conquistadores. Mendoza invoked the traditional right of a governor to refuse to enforce parts of the laws, saying *"Obedezco pero no cumplo"* ("I obey, but do not comply"). This recognized both the monarch's right to issue the law and a governor's right to enforce it as necessary.

—John F. Schwaller

Further reading:

Arthur Scott Aiton. *Antonio de Mendoza, First Viceroy of Mexico* (1927. Reprint, Durham, N.C.: Duke University Press, 1967).

Mendoza, Pedro de (b. ca. 1487–d. 1537) *Spanish conquistador and founder of Buenos Aires*

Born to a noble family in the Grenadine town of Gaudix, Mendoza grew up in the inner circle of Spanish politics. In 1529, he offered to explore the southern half of South America at his own expense. A few years later, this offer was accepted by King Charles I of Spain (Holy Roman Emperor Charles V)

largely through the influence of Pedro's mother, María de Mendoza. Mendoza set sail in 1534 with considerable forces at his side and an even more generous grant from Charles: He was appointed *adelantado* of New Andalusia, granted a license to conquer as much land as he wanted (up to 600 miles north of New Toledo), provided 2,000 ducats for undertaking the expedition, with another 2,000 contingent on developing the region within two years, and promised half the treasure of the local tribal leaders he killed and 90 percent of the ransom paid for kidnapping them.

Mendoza departed Spain with an impressive fleet, but his aspirations quickly foundered. Storms struck the fleet along the Brazilian coast, spreading his forces. His second-in-command was assassinated soon thereafter, possibly on the orders of Mendoza, who suspected him of disloyalty. By 1535, Mendoza was making his way up the mouth of the Río de la Plata (see ARGENTINA). He founded the city of BUENOS AIRES on February 2, 1536. Conditions worsened as the local Querandí people became hostile and DISEASE broke out among Mendoza's men. Diego de Mendoza, Pedro's brother, led an attack against allied tribes at the Battle of Luján River; as a result, Diego and more than three-quarters of his men were killed. Later that year, another brother, Gonzalo de Mendoza, arrived with fresh forces and successfully founded the city of Asunción, capital of PARAGUAY. Pedro embarked for Spain in 1537, dejected and in ill health. He died on the voyage.

—Sean H. Goforth

mestizaje/mestizo

The CONQUEST and settlement of the Americas brought together human groups that had previously had little or no contact. As Europeans entered the Americas, they found themselves face to face with a whole new hemisphere of humanity. From the Spanish point of view, the new social order that developed from their conquests contained three types of people: Spaniards, initially referred to as "Christians" or "Castilians"; *indios* (Indians), subdivided into different ethnic groups; and *negros*, or "blacks" (both free Africans and slaves), who were sometimes differentiated by ethnic group.

Mestizaje describes the process by which these three founding groups formed formal and informal unions, which in turn engendered offspring of mixed ancestry. While inseparable from Spanish colonialism, the term *mestizaje* was not used by early colonial Spaniards. In the 16th century, Spaniards did not have a racial conception of human groups. Although they did not envision race in the modern sense, they did construct differences between themselves and others. These differences were often grounded in the complex intersection of RELIGION, culture, and physical difference.

Among the three founding groups, Spaniards perceived themselves to be superior. Much of this superiority was based in the belief that their success in conquering the Americas derived from divine provenance as a reward for having completed the reconquest of the Iberian Peninsula, the Reconquista. Their success in conquest and the subsequent decline in the indigenous population also reinforced a belief in the physical inferiority of native peoples, who came to be seen as frail and sickly. Resistance to conversion and continued idolatry after conversion convinced many Spaniards that the indigenous were stubborn and dim witted. While Spaniards viewed African slaves as physically superior to both *indios* and themselves, Africans were disparaged as the most savage and intellectually inferior group. This view derived from both environmental and cultural conceptions. Spaniards, and other Europeans, believed that the heat and climate of sub-Saharan Africa led to Africans' dark skin, physical robustness, and simple-mindedness. At the same time, frequent internecine WARFARE and the associated practice of interethnic SLAVERY led Spaniards to view Africans as violent and savage.

The Spanish sought to differentiate those of mixed ancestry in the New World. This desire stemmed from the belief that individuals would inherit the traits of both parents; moreover, it was thought that the creation of new categories would help maintain order and control. The term *mestizaje* shares its root with the most privileged category of mixed ancestry, namely *mestizo*. Meaning "mixed," this word was used to describe an individual born to a Spaniard and an Indian, or someone of equal parts Spanish and indigenous ancestry. During the 16th century, mestizos were often the illegitimate or unrecognized children of Spanish men and indigenous WOMEN, although the reverse did occur more frequently over time. In general, mestizos were considered stronger than *indios*, both physically and mentally; however, they were often accused of being undependable and prone to vice. If not attached to a Spanish patron, they could be accused of being vagabonds and wastrels. The application of this category could depend on the status of the Spanish parent. Very often, biologically mestizo children born to and recognized by elite Spaniards were not labeled *mestizo*. In the immediate postconquest period, publicly recognized offspring, legitimate or not, between indigenous nobility and Spanish conquistadores were never labeled *mestizos* and were considered *españoles*, or Spaniards.

Originating in 15th-century Iberia, the term MULATO was used to describe the child of an African and a Spaniard. This term derived from the word *mula*, or "mule," the cross between a horse and a donkey. In Spanish America, *mulatos* were more highly regarded than Africans, slave or free, but were seen as more dangerous and less governable than mestizos. Their African ancestry led to a presumption of inherent aggressiveness; however, Spanish ancestry implied a greater intellectual capacity. Together, the perceptions that *mulatos* were both stronger and more violent than Spaniards but more intelligent than Africans led to fears that *mulatos* were more capable and more apt to revolt than African slaves or *indios*. Despite these prejudices, free *mulatos* did generally aspire to higher-status occupations than free Africans or indigenous people.

Technically, the term *zambaigo* described an individual of African-indigenous ancestry. Most frequently, this term appeared in laws and ordinances issued by colonial authorities; however, quotidian documentation, such as baptismal records, criminal cases, and petitions, rarely used *zambaigo* to describe Afro-indigenous individuals. Common usage labeled anyone of mixed African ancestry as a *mulato*. Many Afro-indigenous *mulatos* were raised in close proximity to indigenous culture and could move fluidly in both indigenous and Hispanic society. This helped these individuals form mixed unions with other groups and further the process of *mestizaje*.

Mestizaje began as soon as Europeans and Africans entered the Americas and accelerated over time. In general, European-indigenous unions were more common during the period of initial conquest and settlement. As the number of African slaves in the Americas increased, so too did mixed unions with Africans. Although demographic data is scarce, the evidence suggests that where indigenous populations survived in large numbers, Afro-indigenous *mulatos* came to outnumber Afro-European *mulatos*. In areas where indigenous populations disappeared or declined dramatically, such as in the Caribbean, BRAZIL, and parts of northern South America, Afro-European *mulatos* predominated. These demographic differences across the Americas have led to vastly different legacies of *mestizaje* in modern Latin American nations.

See also CASTAS (Vol. II); MAMELUCO (Vol. II); MESTIZAJE/MESTIZO (Vol. II); PARDO (Vol. II); *zambo* (Vol. II).

—Robert Schwaller

metate   A *metate* was a carved grinding stone used in FOOD preparation to crush seeds, grain, chilies, and CACAO. The term *metate* is derived from the NAHUATL word *metlatl*, which means "grinding stone." *Metates* varied in size, but typically they were carved from porous volcanic rock. The *mano*, a smooth handheld stone used to grind the food, was cut from the same stone.

Metates have been discovered in archaeological sites throughout the Americas, but especially in the southwest United States and in Mesoamerica. In the pre-Columbian period, *metates* were used by WOMEN to grind MAIZE (corn) into a powder form. Mesoamerican cultures used processed maize in various ways, such as to make corn tortillas, tamales, and *atole* (a hot corn beverage). *Metates* were also used to grind other grains and seeds such as acorns, cacao, chili peppers, coarse rock salt, spices, and vegetable foods.

—Stephanie Lozano

Further reading:

Scott Cook. "Price and Output Variability in a Peasant-Artisan Stoneworking Industry in Oaxaca, Mexico: An Analytical Essay in Economic Anthropology." *American Anthropologist* 72, no. 4 (1970): 776–801.

A *metate* and *mano* from Guatemala *(Courtesy of J. Michael Francis)*

Mexicas   See Aztecs.

Mexico

When HERNANDO CORTÉS and his fellow conquistadores arrived in what is now Mexico in 1519, they encountered a large number of distinct indigenous groups who spoke hundreds of different languages and represented a broad spectrum of sociopolitical complexity. Some indigenous groups were nomadic, some lived in small villages, and still others had organized themselves into complex states and empires that represented some of the world's most advanced civilizations at the time.

The first inhabitants of Mexico arrived during the last ice age, some 11,500 years ago, and lived as nomadic hunters and gatherers. By 1800 B.C.E., however, Mesoamericans had become more adept farmers and small villages had begun to form (see AGRICULTURE). By 1200 B.C.E., some of these villages had grown substantially both in size and political complexity. The OLMECS of Mexico's southern Gulf coast flourished between 1200 and 500 B.C.E. during the Preclassic period (1800 B.C.E.–200 C.E.). Their stone monuments, which include large carved heads and altars, make them unique among Mesoamerican civilizations of the period. While little is known about the Olmecs, the archaeological evidence suggests that their society was highly stratified and ruled by a powerful elite and that they practiced a widespread state RELIGION.

As the Olmecs declined around 500 B.C.E., another civilization in Mexico rose in power. In the Valley of Oaxaca, about 250 miles (400 km) south of MEXICO CITY, the Zapotec-speaking peoples founded their capital at MONTE ALBÁN (see ZAPOTECS). Monte Albán is believed to have been the first urban state polity in Mesoamerica (see CITIES). It began as a union of several smaller political "chiefdoms" in the Oaxaca valley that grew over time to govern nearly all of the Zapotec speakers and even some non-Zapotec groups in the area. Because of this political expansion, Monte Albán might also have been the first imperial state in Mesoamerica. The civilization at Monte Albán is credited with the creation of the region's first glyphic writing system and sacred calendar. Evidence of this early writing endures in carved stone monuments; the glyphs are composed both of elements that visually depict meaning and of elements that represent phonetic sounds.

By 200 C.E., or the beginning of what scholars call the Classic period (200–900) of Mesoamerican history, the Zapotec "empire" had grown to its largest size. Between 600 and 900, Monte Albán's political dominance was increasingly weakened by challenges from smaller urban centers in the region. Cities such as Lambityeco and Suchilquitongo asserted themselves as independent polities, free from Monte Albán's control; moreover, these sites began to rule over parts of the region that Monte Albán once governed. Additionally, non-Zapotec groups began to encroach into Zapotec territory. By the time the Spaniards arrived in the 16th century, virtually all the Zapotec sites were dominated by outsiders.

Just as Monte Albán reached its peak in the Valley of Oaxaca around 200 C.E., a second large Classic-period civilization rose to prominence to the north. This civilization was located at TEOTIHUACÁN in Mexico's central high plateau; by around 200, Teotihuacán had come to dominate all of Central Mexico; over the next 300 years, the city grew to become perhaps the largest urban center in Mesoamerica. The city's population likely exceeded 150,000 inhabitants. The city covered eight square miles (20.7 km^2) and was dominated by sacred monuments. The most famous of these monuments today are the large pyramids at the site, the so-called Pyramids of the Sun and the Moon. These names are misleading, however; the Pyramid of the Sun was probably built to honor, not the Sun, but the rain god, to whom Teotihuacán's residents were particularly devoted.

Teotihuacán's power was not limited to its ability to build large and impressive monuments (see ARCHITECTURE). In fact, Teotihuacán maintained extensive long-distance TRADE and built frontier defenses to protect its traders and political boundaries. Among Teotihuacán's most important commodities were fine OBSIDIAN (volcanic glass) products. Teotihuacán was located close to major obsidian mines, and the city's skilled obsidian craftsmen turned the rock into knives, blades, arrowheads, and other sharp instruments (see MINING). The obsidian trade helped fuel the local ECONOMY and attracted people from other ethnic groups, such as the Zapotecs and those from Gulf coast cultures, who settled in Teotihuacán. Around 650, a portion of Teotihuacán society revolted, and the center of the city was set on fire. As a result, many of Teotihuacán's residents abandoned the city, and by 900, nearly all of the city's residents had found new homes away from the urban center.

A third important Classic-period civilization in Mexico was that of the MAYA. The Maya are perhaps the most studied of Mesoamerica's pre-Hispanic peoples; they were remarkably advanced in ART, architecture, astronomy, writing, and agriculture. The Maya lived (and continue to live) in an area that now includes eastern Mexico (the Yucatán Peninsula and Chiapas), GUATEMALA, BELIZE, and parts of HONDURAS and EL SALVADOR. The landscape varies widely across this region, which led to significant cultural and linguistic diversity among the Maya. Indeed, there are more than 30 distinct Mayan languages.

The most emblematic of the various Maya groups are perhaps those who occupied the lowlands of the Yucatán Peninsula, Chiapas, Guatemala, and Belize. In fact, the term *Classic period* originally referred to the period in which the lowland Maya reached the height of their cultural complexity and production.

The Maya were never as politically or demographically centralized as, for example, the civilizations based at the cities of Monte Albán and Teotihuacán. Rather, the Maya had several centers of power that, over time, engaged in both alliances and conflict. In the Classic period, these centers included southern lowland sites at CALAKMUL, TIKAL, CARACOL, COPÁN, and Palenque, which have long impressed scholars with the richness of their culture. The most visually impressive aspect of this culture is the large stone stelae (tall inscribed slabs) and altars that the Maya erected to commemorate important events in their history. These stelae and altars are covered with Maya glyphic writing, which was more developed than its Zapotec counterpart.

The end of the Classic period is characterized by the decline of these important southern lowland Maya sites. Scholars have not been able to agree on why these centers—and the Classic-period culture that they propagated—ceased to thrive. Most believe that problems arose as a result of population growth and social instability. Whatever the reason, many of the southern sites were abandoned, and the center of Maya civilization during the Postclassic period (900–1520) shifted to the northern Maya lowlands.

Postclassic-period Maya culture was characterized by increasing urbanization and the concentration of power. In the Early Postclassic period, the site of CHICHÉN ITZÁ in the Yucatán Peninsula dominated the Maya world. By the 13th century, Chichén Itzá had fallen, and the city of MAYAPÁN had replaced it as the most important Maya center. Both of these Postclassic cities differed from their Classic-period predecessors; their art and architecture reflected greater contact with civilizations from the Central Mexico highlands, particularly that of TULA in modern-day Hidalgo State.

The civilization at Tula, also called Tollan, is poorly understood and heavily debated among scholars. Tula's past is clouded, in part, because it figures prominently in legendary accounts written by Central Mexico peoples soon after the Spanish CONQUEST. In fact, the term *Toltec* (someone from Tula) also had the more general meaning of a "wise" or "cultured person" (see TOLTECS). Nevertheless, there is evidence of a complex civilization at Tula from around 900 to 1200.

The city of Tula itself seems to have represented a combination of several Mesoamerican cultural traditions. The most important of these related to the MIGRATION of peoples from the north. These migrants are often called the "Chichimeca" or "Tolteca-Chichimeca" in colonial-period sources and were probably the first NAHUATL speakers of Central Mexico (Nahuatl was the language spoken by the AZTECS when the Spaniards arrived). The Tolteca-Chichimeca were a powerful political force. At the height of Tula's power, Toltec influence and control could be felt throughout Central Mexico, the Gulf Coast, Yucatán, and Chiapas. The most visually recognizable feature of this influence is the spread of religious devotion to the feathered, or plumed, serpent deity, QUETZALCÓATL. The rep-

Basin of Mexico on the Eve of the Spanish Conquest, ca. 1519

Lake Zumpango

Lake Xaltocan

Lake Texcoco

• Texcoco

Azcapotzalco •

• Tepeyac

Tlacopán •

Tlatelolco

• Tenochtitlán

Chapultepec •

Coyoacán •

• Culhuacán

Lake Xochimilco

Xochimilco •

Lake Chalco

• Chalco

N

AJUSCO MOUNTAINS

Elevated area

0   7 miles

0   7 km

resentation of this Toltec god is particularly strong in the Maya city of Chichén Itzá in the Yucatán Peninsula.

Though the city of Tula declined and was abandoned in the 13th century, its cultural traditions persisted in Central Mexico. Many of the leaders of Central Mexico polities at the time of conquest legitimized their rule by emphasizing their Toltec ancestry. In the 14th century, however, still more migrants arrived in Central Mexico from the north; their arrival transformed regional politics and the balance of power. These late arrivals were the Mexicas, or Aztecs.

The Mexicas were but one of the ethnic groups that constituted the Nahuas, or speakers of the Nahuatl language, in Central Mexico. Their arrival brought an end to the rule of another Nahua group, the Tepanecs. In the early 15th century, the Mexica overthrew the Tepanecs with the help of neighboring Nahua groups; the victors then formed what scholars have called the "TRIPLE ALLIANCE," a military and economic accord between the Mexica and the Nahuas from Texcoco and Tlacopan. This alliance brought much of the surrounding area under its control. Neighboring polities were compelled to either submit to the Triple Alliance and pay tribute to it or be subjugated by force.

The Triple Alliance was still expanding when the Spaniards appeared off the Gulf coast in 1519. In the Mexica capital city of TENOCHTITLÁN, the famed MONTEZUMA held the position of TLATOANI, or ruler. Cacama ruled in Texcoco. These two, together with the regent in Tlacopan, exacted money and loyalty from the Gulf of Mexico to the Pacific Ocean.

Nonetheless, the Spaniards, led by Cortés, were able to exploit the prevailing political situation in Central Mexico to their advantage. Many of the indigenous groups that had been forced to pay tribute to the Triple Alliance were easily persuaded to join the Spanish. By the time he arrived at the Mexica capital from the coast, Cortés had amassed a large number of indigenous allies. Initially, the Triple Alliance mounted a successful defense of their capital, despite the number of Cortés's supporters. As a result, the Spaniards were forced to flee the city, in what they later called the "Noche Triste," or "night of sorrows." Cortés was undeterred, however, and made preparations for another attack. As he did so, the first waves of European DISEASES swept through the indigenous population. The Indians had no natural resistance to diseases such as smallpox, and as a result many thousands died. Cortés used this to his military advantage and successfully defeated the Triple Alliance in 1521.

The Spaniards continued their campaign in the rest of Mexico and were eventually able to bring other groups under their political control in areas such as the Valley of Oaxaca, the Gulf Coast, and the Yucatán Peninsula (though only after protracted conflict in this last region). Political defeat, however, did not signal the end of indigenous society and civilization. Although the Spanish replaced indigenous leaders at the highest levels of government, native patterns of social and political organization often remained intact (see *ALTEPETL*; *CAH*).

In fact, the Spanish Crown was often obliged to rely on pre-Hispanic systems of taxation and LABOR draft in order to govern effectively. Additionally, indigenous languages continued to be used, even within the Spanish court system and bureaucracy. Many of these languages and cultures continue to flourish in Mexico today.

See also MEXICO (Vols. III, IV); MEXICO, INDEPENDENCE IN (Vol. II); MEXICO CITY (Vols. II, III, IV); NEW SPAIN, VICEROYALTY OF (Vol. II).

—Bradley Thomas Benton

Further reading:
Michael D. Coe and Rex Koontz. *Mexico: From the Olmecs to the Aztecs*, 5th ed. (New York: Thames & Hudson, 2002).
Matthew Restall, Lisa Sousa, and Kevin Terraciano, eds. *Mesoamerican Voices: Native-Language Writings from Colonial Mexico, Oaxaca, Yucatán, and Guatemala* (Cambridge: Cambridge University Press, 2005).
Michael E. Smith and Marilyn A. Masson, eds. *The Ancient Civilizations of Mesoamerica: A Reader* (Malden, Mass.: Blackwell Publishers, 2000).

Mexico City At first glance, in November 1519, HERNANDO CORTÉS and his men were astonished by the grandeur of Aztec capital city of TENOCHTITLÁN (see AZTECS). They claimed it as their own, nonetheless, in the name of the king of Spain. On July 1, 1520, less than nine months after their historical encounter with the Aztec ruler MONTEZUMA, the Spaniards were ferociously chased out of the city during the tragic events of the Noche Triste (Night of Sorrows). The Spanish left behind a ruined city, its nobility nearly all massacred, and hundreds of soldiers dead on both sides. In the year that followed, the Spaniards made several failed attempts to conquer the island, first facing the Aztec king Cuitláhuac and later the persistent CUAUHTÉMOC. After a siege of 75 days during which Tenochtitlán's water and FOOD supplies were cut off, Cuauhtémoc finally surrendered himself and the city on August 13, 1521 (see CONQUEST). The swift downfall of the strongest Mesoamerican city by a relatively small force of Spanish conquistadores was only possible thanks to the tens of thousands of indigenous allies (primarily the Tlaxcalans), Spanish firearms and metal swords, and, perhaps most important, European DISEASES, which already had devastated the besieged population (see TLAXCALA).

The restructuring of the city began in 1522, and according to one chronicler, more than 400,000 indigenous workers were employed for the task. The Catholic cathedral was built in front on the main temple complex, the Templo Mayor (in fact, the church was built with stones dismantled from the ruins of the latter), while Aztec deities were replaced by Christian saints. Although built by native hands, houses for the Spaniards took on a European appearance, and the city was slowly adapted to

This photo shows the ruins of the Templo Mayor, with Mexico City's cathedral in the background. *(Courtesy of J. Michael Francis)*

a grid pattern. Cortés claimed the palace of the defeated Montezuma; however, in 1560, the building passed to New Spain's colonial government and today is the site of the National Palace.

Similarly, the Aztec "pleasure palace" in Chapultepec, a garden complex the indigenous nobility used for retreat and feasting, became the property of the New Spain's VICEROYS. The four *calpultin* neighborhoods were largely maintained in their original form and size, although their function as military units was abolished (see *CALPULLI*). Tribute was still collected as before, and LABOR, required. Specialized crafts were allowed to continue, though in a modified fashion; for example, featherwork previously used for Aztec shields and war costumes was now employed to depict Christian motifs. The Aztec *calmecac* and *telpochcalli* schools were replaced by Catholic religious schools, and the Colegio de Santa Cruz (College of the Holy Cross), the first college for noble Aztec boys, was established in Tlatelolco in 1536. While many classes were still given in NAHUATL, students were also taught to speak Spanish; the glyphic writing of the preconquest period was largely replaced by the Latin alphabet.

Spanish officials and institutions took over from their Aztec counterparts, with the establishment of the royal *AUDIENCIA* (high court) in 1527 and the appointment of the first viceroy, ANTONIO DE MENDOZA, in 1535.

Despite the introduction of Spanish institutions, the native political organization below that level was kept relatively intact. Even if the fall of Tenochtitlán marked the end of Aztec hegemony in Mesoamerica, in political and economic terms, much survived well into Spanish rule; native leaders continued to exercise control over the indigenous population of New Spain from the newly established capital of Mexico City.

See also MEXICO (Vols. III, IV); MEXICO CITY (Vols. II, III, IV).

—Danny Zborover

Further reading:
Hugh Thomas. *Conquest: Montezuma, Cortés, and the Fall of Old Mexico* (New York: Simon & Schuster, 1995).

migration   The land bridge theory, also known as the Bering Strait theory, is the most commonly accepted explanation of the first human migrations to the Americas. It contends that hunters and gathers from Siberia traveled over the Bering land bridge and into Alaska in pursuit of big-game animals between 50,000 B.C.E. and ca. 9000 B.C.E. After crossing the land bridge, they migrated south and eventually reached South America through the Panamanian isthmus. Another theory suggests that humans migrated along the Asian coast by boat or canoe and traveled across ice blocks to reach the Americas. A further possibility is put forward in the Pacific coast theory, which says that at some point during the southward migration from Alaska, some migrants traveled by boat or canoe along the Pacific coast. However, both of the coastal theories have substantially less evidence than the land bridge theory to support their claims.

It is unclear exactly how the earliest migrants spread out once they reached South America. Early settlement sites have been discovered along the lowlands of both sides of the landmass, suggesting that some groups traveled down the Pacific side, while others crossed to the Caribbean and Atlantic coasts. Although the specific routes and dates of migration are unclear, the evidence of movement is not. Scholars have uncovered evidence of human life in MONTE VERDE, CHILE, and Taima Taima, VENEZUELA, dating back to at least 12,500 B.C.E.; from the southernmost tip of Tierra del Fuego dating to 11,000 B.C.E.; and in ECUADOR and PERU dating to 10,800–10,000 B.C.E.

These sites are highly diverse in terms of environment and FOOD sources, both of which would have determined the migrants' length of stay in any given location. In some regions, available resources were limited, so multiple migrations took place; this occurred, for example, in the arid deserts and grasslands of Chile, Peru, BRAZIL, and ARGENTINA. By contrast, in places such as the Andean lowlands, food sources were more abundant and diversified throughout the seasons; this allowed groups of people to remain in one place for longer, which provided opportunities for exploration and, eventually, settlement in the areas most conducive to their skills. Temperate and tropical forests as well as wetlands also provided subsistence options and did not require specialization in a particular resource.

South American Arawaks first began migrating to the Caribbean along the Orinoco River as far back as 1500 B.C.E. This migration continued for hundreds of years. The three major indigenous groups of the Caribbean—the Ciboney, TAINO Arawak, and CARIB—all descended from the successive migration waves of South American Arawaks. The Ciboney were the earliest to arrive in the Caribbean and settled primarily in CUBA and other islands of the Greater Antilles. The Taino inhabited the Bahamas, Greater Antilles, and the northern islands of the Lesser Antilles. They were seafarers who traveled extensively throughout the islands on trading expeditions (see TRADE). The expansion of the Taino kingdoms displaced the Ciboney to the western side of the island of HISPANIOLA; by the early 16th century, the Taino had largely absorbed the Ciboney. The Caribs were the last migrant group to settle in the Caribbean, and they dominated the Lesser Antilles. Throughout most of the 15th century, the Taino were driven northeast as a result of raids by the Caribs to the south.

The largest pre-Columbian civilization was that of the INCAS, which emerged in the early 13th century in the highlands of Peru. Inca imperial expansion was rampant in the 14th and 15th centuries; by the end of the latter, the empire extended from the capital in CUZCO as far north as

southern COLOMBIA, and well into Chile to the south. At its height, the population of the empire was 6–13 million. The Incas displaced many groups in areas where land was ripe for the cultivation of MAIZE; they also moved large numbers of peoples from regions that were susceptible to rebellion. The state then resettled the areas with people loyal to the empire, moving troublesome subjects closer to Cuzco.

Despite the remarkable reach of the empire, most of South America never fell under Inca rule. Hundreds of other ethnic groups inhabited the region. For example, the Guaycurus lived in the mountains of the Gran Chaco; their territories extended on both sides of the Paraguay River into the north and northwestern PARAGUAY frontiers and into the province of Matto Grosso, Brazil. The nomadic fishing and foraging Charrúa inhabited parts of modern URUGUAY, northeastern Argentina, and Brazil. The seminomadic communities of Tupí and GUARANÍ moved mainly within Brazil (see TUPINAMBÁ). The Mapuche inhabited southern Chile and southern Argentina and were able to resist both Inca and Spanish attempts to subjugate them. The Ona lived in Patagonia and are believed to have migrated from the mainland across the Strait of Magellan by canoe. Farther south, the nomadic Yahgans traveled the southernmost islands, where they sustained themselves by collecting shellfish and hunting sea lions.

In Mesoamerica, the Classic-period MAYA emerged beginning ca. 250 C.E. Classic Maya sites covered a broad territory, including the Yucatán Peninsula, Tabasco, Chiapas, GUATEMALA, BELIZE, and parts of HONDURAS. Between the eighth and ninth centuries, the southern Maya lowlands experienced sharp population decline; soon after, many of the large urban centers there were abandoned. The causes for this remain unclear; the many theories include resource depletion, long-term drought, endemic WARFARE, overpopulation, and environmental degradation. Whatever the causes, it appears that large numbers of Maya fled north to the northern lowlands of the Yucatán Peninsula. That region flourished well past the ninth century and maintained a large population until the arrival of Europeans in the 16th century.

One of the most fascinating migration stories concerns the Mexicas, or AZTECS. They are said to have originated in 1168 on an island called Chicomoztoc, meaning "seven caves," in the middle of a lake in northern MEXICO. They were commanded by their patron god Huitzilopochtli to undergo a long migration to Central Mexico in search of the site to build their great city; according to Huitzilopochtli, the Mexicas would know where to settle by the appearance of an eagle perched atop a cactus, with a snake in its beak. The Aztecs arrived in the Valley of Mexico in 1248 and by the early 14th century had begun to build the city of TENOCHTITLÁN on an island on Lake Texcoco. Between the 14th and 16th centuries, the Aztecs dominated much of Mesoamerica. They accomplished this through warfare and CONQUEST, expanding the empire far beyond its origins in the Valley of Mexico. At its height, the Aztec Empire stretched from the northern part of Guatemala to Central Mexico and from the Pacific Ocean to the Gulf of Mexico.

The population of the New World prior to 1492 is still debated, with estimates ranging from 8 million to 112 million people. Most scholars accept that there were approximately 54 million people living in the entire Western Hemisphere before 1492. The New World inhabitants were concentrated mainly in Mexico, where the population reached 17.2 million; the Andes in South America likely supported a population that exceeded 12 million. Some have suggested that the other regions of South America (that is, outside the Inca Empire) supported a population of some 8.6 million; however, recent archaeological findings in the AMAZON regions of Brazil and Peru are beginning to challenge such claims. Central America was inhabited by 5.6 million people, a population two-thirds smaller than in Mexico and Andes. The Caribbean had the smallest number of inhabitants in the New World, with slightly more than 3 million spread across the islands.

The arrival of CHRISTOPHER COLUMBUS launched a period of unprecedented migration, both within the New World and from outside. Waves of migrants arrived from Europe, and it was not long before the new settlers began to import large numbers of African slaves. During the conquest and early colonial period, large numbers of Amerindians moved as well.

In the following two decades, Spaniards from southern Spain (Andalusia) represented the largest single group of migrants, accounting for 60 percent of the migration flow to the New World between 1493 and 1508. These Andalusian migrants, both men and women, were predominately from the large urban center of Seville. This migration pattern occurred for several reasons. Andalusia was home to the most populated cities in Spain, with the greatest population density in Seville. Seville's proximity to ports exposed the population to influential travelers and accessible opportunities to emigrate on the ships departing for the New World. Thus, from 1493 to 1520, one out of every six migrants was from the city of Seville, one out of five was from the province of Seville, and one out of three colonists was from the Andalusia.

Following HERNANDO CORTÉS's expedition to Mexico in 1519 and the conquest of the Aztec Empire in 1521, news of untold wealth in the Americas reached the Old World and the origins of emigrants began to diversify. While Seville remained a predominate source of outward migration from 1520 to 1540, half of the total number of immigrants to the New World came from six Spanish provinces: Seville, Badajoz, Caceres, Toledo, Salamanca, and Valladolid. Additionally, the New World now witnessed the arrival of migrants from Portugal, Italy, and France, among 35 other countries. Their destinies varied widely. Spanish migrants from the Castile region settled in higher numbers than Andalusians in PUERTO RICO and on the mainland. Castilians were predominant in Colombia and Venezuela and had a significant popula-

tion in NICARAGUA. The Río de la Plata region had the highest number of non-Spaniard migrants, at 12 percent. The migrants were primarily Portuguese and had been members of expeditions rather than individual travelers.

With the colonization of Mexico and Peru, the Caribbean islands' foreign populations declined dramatically. From 1520 to 1530, only 11 percent of migrants settled in Santo Domingo on the island of Hispaniola; by contrast, Peru became home to 10.8 percent of the migrant population. Mexico received an estimated 32.4 percent of the total migration flow from the Old World and 50 percent of Old World migrants who went to mainland America. In this same period, Europeans migrated to various other destinations throughout the Americas: 8.8 percent of migrants settled in the Río de la Plata region; 7.7 percent in PANAMA; 7.3 percent in New Granada; 3.7 percent in Guatemala; 2.8 percent in Venezuela; 1.6 percent in Cuba; 1.1 percent in Nicaragua; 0.9 percent in Puerto Rico; and 0.6 percent in Honduras. Of course, these figures are problematic, as they are based on the destinations listed in the official passenger manifests. Once they reached the New World, migrants often moved from one place to another, making it virtually impossible to quantify specific population figures in any one region.

European migration also spurred large-scale migrations of both the Amerindian and African populations. Indigenous populations throughout the New World experienced migration, often by means of enslavement, conscripted LABOR, and/or displacement (see SLAVERY). In addition to forced movement, their populations declined dramatically through disease, labor exploitation, warfare, and starvation. On the island of Hispaniola, for example, the indigenous population dropped from an estimated 1 million to 600,000 between 1492 and 1510; in the following 30 years, it fell to a mere 5,000, which represents a 98 percent rate of decline in a matter of decades. Devastating population loss occurred virtually everywhere in the New World, as Old World diseases spread through populations that had no immunity.

As the indigenous populations declined, Europeans turned to Africa to replenish their falling labor pool. A 1511 report to the Spanish king Ferdinand II suggested that one black slave's labor was equal to that of four Indians. From 1510 to 1530, nearly 35,000 African slaves, most of whom were already enslaved in Europe, were sent to the New World; their numbers were soon augmented by slaves brought directly from Africa. In 1530, the Spanish Crown began to issue licenses for the direct importation of African slaves to the New World (see *ASIENTO*). This was done to compete with Portugal's burgeoning slave trade to Brazil. Between 1521 and 1550, an estimated 15,000 slaves arrived in the Americas.

See also IMMIGRATION (Vol. II); MIGRATION (Vols. II, III, IV); POPULATION (Vol. II).

—Kathryn Plummer

Further reading:
Peter Boyd-Bowman. *Patterns of Spanish Emigration to the New World (1493–1580)* (Buffalo: State University of New York Press, 1973).
Philip Curtain. "Distribution in Space: The Hispanic Trade." In *The Atlantic Slave Trade: A Census*, 15–50 (Madison: University of Wisconsin Press, 1969).
William Denevan. *The Native Population of the Americas in 1492* (Madison: University of Wisconsin Press, 1992).
Thomas D. Dillehay. "Migration, Adaptation, and Diversity." In *The Settlement of the Americas: A New Prehistory*, 249–262 (New York: Basic Books, 2000).

milpa *Milpa*, also known as "swidden," "slash and burn," or "shifting," is an agricultural method that necessitates the slashing, cutting, felling, and burning of forested areas for the planting of garden plots or agricultural fields, also called *milpas*. It is often associated with patterns of shifting cultivation, in which soil exhaustion or weed intrusion requires plot rotation and fallow cycles. Tropical soils are fragile, thus AGRICULTURE in the tropics tends to deplete soil-based nutrients rapidly, resulting in decreasing yields after just a few seasons. In order to stimulate the regeneration of soil nutrients through the growth and decay of tropical vegetation, *milpa* agriculturalists typically abandon plots for as many as 25 years. These cycles of field preparation, cultivation, and fallow, and the need to shift cultivation to new fields on a cyclical basis, play an important role in the social, economic, and political configurations of peoples who practice *milpa* agriculture.

It is common practice for a FAMILY to have several small plots (*milpas*) under cultivation. At any one time, the fields are scattered among various landforms, soil types, or hydrological settings in order to maximize production and minimize the risk brought on by unpredictable climate changes. Though requiring extensive land, *milpa* cultivation is highly LABOR efficient and has been widely practiced in areas of high vegetation and seasonal rainfall patterns. In Mesoamerica, the typical plot was planted with MAIZE, supplemented by beans and squash.

Swidden cultivation systems can be intensified by a number of strategies beyond shortening the fallow cycle. Increasing the diversity of crops planted in individual plots can extend the growing season, make maximum use of horizontal space, and increase their resistance to insects. Tree crops can be planted and succession species managed to maintain the productivity of the plot while it is fallow. Agricultural production under rainfed cultivation systems was intensified in ancient times through a number of field-surface management strategies that modified soil conditions, moisture availability, and microclimate in order to promote crop growth. Ridging and mounding of soils is a common cultivation technique. *Milpa* is a relatively efficient and ecologically sound system of agricultural production, especially compared to the labor- and resource-intensive permanent and irrigation-based system that dominates the modern nation states.

—John M. Weeks

Further reading:
Scott L. Fedick, ed. *The Managed Mosaic: Ancient Maya Agriculture and Resource Use* (Salt Lake City: University of Utah Press, 1996).
Peter D. Harrison and B. L. Turner, eds. *Pre-Hispanic Maya Agriculture* (Albuquerque: University of New Mexico Press, 1978).

mining The conquistador HERNANDO CORTÉS was said to have told the Aztec emperor MONTEZUMA that he suffered from an ailment of the heart for which GOLD was the only specific (see AZTECS). The first Inca subjects to greet FRANCISCO PIZARRO along the coast of PERU were said to have wondered if Spanish horses ate gold, so desperate were their masters to lay their hands on it (see INCAS). True or false, these legends from the era of contact betray the *aurum sacra fames*, or "sacred hunger for gold," that engulfed Europe, and particularly Spain, following the voyages of CHRISTOPHER COLUMBUS. What economic historians term the early modern *bullion famine* in fact encompassed most of Eurasia (see ECONOMY).

As depicted in early MAPS and writings, America was from the start both a figurative and a literal gold mine. With the discovery of the "Rich Hill" of POTOSÍ in present-day BOLIVIA and similarly rich sites in MEXICO in the mid-1540s, the Americas became the richest source of SILVER the world had yet known. In the first decades after discovery, European, African, and indigenous mining and refining techniques were combined so that by 1560, Spanish merchants and officials shipped tons of raw gold and silver, mined and processed mainly by forced indigenous workers and enslaved Africans, across the Atlantic each year (see SLAVERY). By the 1570s, tons of Spanish American silver went annually across the Pacific to the Philippines and China. Nevertheless, mining in the Americas was not new.

Prior to the arrival of Europeans in the Americas in 1492, Amerindian societies, including the great empires of the Aztecs and Incas, were lithic in that they relied mostly on stone rather than metal tools and weapons. The archaeological record is replete with stone axes, hammers, scrapers, projectiles, and points. Metals, where found, were used primarily for ritual and display, being universally regarded as divine residues that naturally attached to and enhanced chiefly or kingly power. Iron was known only in its meteoric form, although its oxides hematite and magnetite were used as pigments. Cinnabar, or mercury sulfide, was similarly used and collected from surface deposits, if not mined. Decorative stones such as nephrite, turquoise, EMERALDS, and quartz were also associated with divinity and often appeared in shamanic divination and healing kits, even among nonsedentary forest dwellers (see RELIGION). Prospecting, mining, and quarrying were marginal activities in most of the Western Hemisphere prior to 1492, and metallurgy even more so.

There were, however, some spectacular exceptions. Copper mining and metallurgy date to remote times in both North and South America, and gold mining and refining are probably at least as old, if not older. Sheet-metalworking in copper and gold dates to at least 1500 B.C.E. in the southern Andes, the oldest of the Americas' several ancient metal-smithing centers. The development of silverworking, along with the smelting of complex copper-based alloys, was in evidence in Andean South America at least 2,000 years ago, as was the world's only known premodern use of platinum. The Andes was also known for its deposits of tin and arsenic, both of which enabled experimentation with utilitarian alloys, and bronze and arsenical bronze tools and weapons were common by 1000 C.E. The Incas claimed the invention and spread of bronze as imperial legacies, but both clearly predated them. More localized and small-scale bronze production appears to have developed independently in Michoacán, Mexico, a few hundred years before the arrival of the Spanish in 1519 (see CONQUEST).

All these advances in metallurgy spurred mining activity to a greater or lesser degree, depending on the demands of chiefs and other rulers, merchants, and ordinary consumers. Copper axes from Peru and CHILE were traded to coast, mountain, and AMAZON rain forest peoples, sometimes in exchange for gold dust panned from streams (see TRADE). Copper "axe money" soon followed, although its ritual-versus-monetary functions remain uncertain. Turquoise mined near Santa Fe, New Mexico, was traded as far south as GUATEMALA, and copper mined in Mexico was sent north in return, usually in the form of bells and tweezers. Such items abound in ancestral Pueblo graves. Emeralds from COLOMBIA were combined with local gold in PANAMA and ECUADOR, and nephrite from Guatemala was sent to COSTA RICA in exchange for copper-gold alloys. The long-distance trade in mined or quarried flint and OBSIDIAN is older still, stretching back to the era of the great mammoth hunters. Quarrying for building stone was also ancient but was more commonly restricted to sedentary urbanites. Far more ancient and widespread, and frequently undertaken by WOMEN, quarrying for clay suitable for pottery making can also be considered a type of mining (see CERAMICS).

COPPER

Relatively abundant and malleable, though not easy to melt (at 1,981° Fahrenheit, or 1,083°C), copper has long drawn the attention of humans. In the Americas, deposits of native copper in the Great Lakes region of eastern North America, southern Arizona, Mexico's Sierra Madre ranges, and various sites in the central and southern Andes enabled early prospectors to gather workable metal without much digging. Copper was also found and worked in Colombia and Costa Rica, but deposits were much more scarce. Short of finding pure native copper, even the richest ores required development of high-temperature furnaces. Bellows appear never to have been used, but copper, like gold and silver, can be melted with blowpipes on charcoal. It was then poured into clay molds or hammered into various shapes with stone hammers.

While copper mining and surface collecting were clearly ancient practices in the Americas, it is an extraordinary find in Chile that stands out as a landmark in global mining history. In 1899, prospectors in Chuquicamata, in the Atacama Desert, found a naturally mummified sixth-century C.E. miner apparently killed in a cave-in. His tools included a shovel, stone hammer, and ore basket. Archaeologists have since identified ancient copper mines and associated tools in northwest ARGENTINA and at Batán Grande, in north coastal Peru. All these known ancient mines were excavated with hafted stone tools. Much later copper-silver mines in southwestern Mexico show signs of fire splitting, or the use of fires to help make ores more friable, a practice common in the Old World. Substantial copper deposits were also found in northwestern HISPANIOLA and southeastern CUBA, although it is difficult to know how extensively they were worked prior to the arrival of the Spanish.

GOLD

Though far less abundant than copper, gold does not readily oxidize and therefore can be found in its native state in many places, particularly where ancient mountain ranges were eroded by rivers and streams. Most pre-Columbian gold mining, or "placering," was undertaken with wooden gold pans and digging sticks in and along the stream banks from Mexico to Chile. Not all gold deposits were worked, however. The extensive placers of the Brazilian highlands and Amazon Basin appear to have been entirely unexploited in pre-Columbian times (see BRAZIL). The same was true of nearly all North American placers outside Mexico.

Few pre-Columbian gold mines went underground, as far as is known, although there were exceptions in northwestern Colombia, in the department of Antioquia, where miners dug pits and shafts with staves. These underground tunnels were made possible thanks to highly oxidized and therefore friable quartz veins. Extracted ores were easily milled with harder stones, and the resulting sands were washed in the wooden pans for free gold. No mercury amalgamation was practiced. If early Spanish CHRONICLERS can be trusted, the Colombian diggings were dozens of feet deep, a considerable achievement given the lack of iron or bronze excavation tools.

SILVER

Unlike gold and even copper, silver rarely occurs in its native state. It is highly susceptible to oxidation and other forms of chemical bonding and thus has to be separated from its host material through crushing, smelting, and other refining processes. Despite the existence of massive silver deposits in the mountains of Mexico and HONDURAS, it was only in the Andes that silver mining and metallurgy were substantially developed in pre-Columbian times. There, in places such as Porco, Bolivia, and Huantajaya, Chile, indigenous miners using hafted stone hammers followed rich veins of ore. Stone furnaces known as *huayras* (from Quechua *wayra*, or "wind") were built on ridges where breezes could stoke their llama-dung fires. Silver was smelted in this way in the hills around Potosí even after the Spanish conquest. Copper-silver alloys appear to have been mined and worked in western Mexico, but silver was not apparently separated and treated in isolation.

PLATINUM AND ALLOYS

Platinum, a hard, brittle metal with a high melting point (3,225° Fahrenheit, or 1,773.8°C), is also rarely found in its native state. Indeed, it is rarely found at all. The first significant discovery of platinum in the world was in the Pacific lowlands of Colombia, where it appears alongside gold dust in many river basins. While its density and resistance to oxidation make it similar to gold, it is far harder to manipulate. The name platinum comes from the Spanish *platina*, or "silver-like," and only with the advent of modern chemistry in the 18th century was it identified as an element, hailed in the scientific world around 1750 as the "eighth metal." Attempts to smelt and work Colombian platinum, which was freely supplied to scientists by the Spanish Crown, were mostly unsuccessful until just before 1800.

Amazingly, pre-Columbian metalworkers living along the Pacific shore of northwest South America developed techniques for working with platinum using only charcoal pits and blowpipes some 2,000 years ago or earlier. Workshop evidence and artifacts from the La Tolita-Tumaco culture of the Ecuador-Colombia border region have shown that locally mined platinum was combined with small amounts of gold and welded into workable ingots. These were beaten and burnished with hard stones into plates, nose rings, and earplugs, among other items. Platinum artifacts appear not to have been widely traded, and the techniques for making them were lost with the decline of the La Tolita–Tumaco chiefdoms by ca. 350 C.E.

PRECIOUS STONES

While jadelike nephrite was quarried from shallow outcrops in Guatemala in ancient times, what would today be regarded as mining of precious stones was limited to Colombian emeralds. Emeralds, a species of beryl, were found on the eastern and western slopes of the Eastern Cordillera, just north of BOGOTÁ. The stones were closely associated with chiefly power among the ruling MUISCA of the region, and at the time of Spanish invasion in the late 1530s, large-scale emerald mines were worked in the region now known as Chivor. Under the control of a chief named Somondoco at the time, the emerald mines were said to have been worked by hundreds of people using wooden digging sticks and substantial dams and canals. Hydraulic mining, or hushing, was particularly well suited to the recovery of emeralds, which are neither dense nor easily discovered amid the friable black shales in which they occur. In contrast, the celebrated emeralds, diamonds, topazes, and aquamarines of Brazil went undiscovered until late colonial and even modern times.

MINING TECHNIQUES

From the 1490s to 1510s, Spanish-run gold mines on the island of Hispaniola appear to have been placer operations of a fairly simple type, with no significant innovations other than iron tools for excavation and processing and bellows furnaces for smelting gold dust into ingots. The famous diggings of the Cibao Mountains in the island's northern interior were probably as dependent on indigenous and African techniques of canal and irrigation management as they were on Spanish or other European mining practices. By 1505, enslaved African miners, some of whom may have had experience with gold washing and perhaps smelting, were present in the diggings. According to the chronicler Gonzalo Fernández de Oviedo and other eyewitnesses, many of the earliest mineworkers, especially panners, were women. Men handled excavation, canal construction, and furnace operations. This gendered division of LABOR was continued on a lesser scale in Cuba and PUERTO RICO and was also seen in Panama and at locations on the mainland.

According to archaeologists, the Spanish-run copper mines at the western end of Hispaniola near modern-day Cap Haitien entailed the excavation of shallow underground mines and smelting of raw ore rather than medium-grade ore, but even this was not a particularly capital-intensive business. The early SUGAR industry, which incidentally consumed copper kettles and other hardware, probably had much higher entry costs. Copper mining on Hispaniola partly justified the minting of copper *maravedí* coins, the only ones produced in the Americas.

Only when gold miners in what is today Colombia and Ecuador went underground in pursuit of low-grade ores after about 1550 did gold mining become as capital intensive as it was labor intensive. The newly discovered silver mines of Bolivia and Mexico required even more capital and technological innovation to be profitable, conditions that were offset by their richness and the burgeoning world demand for the white metal. Creditors to Charles I included the Welser and Fugger families of Augsburg, both of whom had mining interests in the silver districts of central Europe. Through these and other connections, German milling and refining technologies flowed through Spain to its overseas colonies. German miners and millwrights were present in the Sultepec silver district of Mexico by the 1530s and throughout the Andes by at least 1550.

But it was a Spanish merchant from Seville, Bartolomé de Medina, who arguably had the greatest impact on the future of precious metals mining in the Americas. By 1554, Medina had developed a process to amalgamate silver ores that was workable on a large scale with minimal inputs of fuel and water. By 1556, he had patented his process, which made use of a variety of salts as reagents. Prior to discovery of mercury deposits in highland Peru at Huancavelica in 1564, the necessary quicksilver came from the mines of Almadén, near Ciudad Real in south-central Spain. The Fuggers of Augsburg were major investors in these, mostly convict-staffed mines. Although they had no need of Medina's formula, hard-rock gold miners in Colombia and Ecuador also used mercury amalgamation from the 1550s.

By 1560, mining in the Americas was the most significant producer of both public and private revenue, most of it in silver but still including significant quantities of gold. Precious metals far exceeded sugar, TOBACCO, hides, dyestuffs, and other products in export ledgers (see DYES AND DYEWOOD). Mining towns were the motors of the colonial ECONOMY, giving rise to long-distance commerce and many secondary supply sectors, some of them proto-industrial in character. The search for new deposits, meanwhile, remained the primary factor behind territorial expansion. Expanding mining frontiers in turn spurred the demand for labor, most of it forced. By the 1550s, the dangerous and onerous work of underground mining and mercury-based refining were performed by armies of forced indigenous draft workers and enslaved Africans, although a trend toward specialization and even wage work was evident before 1600. For reasons unknown, locally produced gunpowder was not used in Spanish-American mining until the later 17th century.

Gunpowder production required sulfur and saltpeter, the former mined from volcanic deposits or recovered after burning pyrite, or iron sulfide, and the latter either mined from natural deposits or distilled from uric acid. Ordinary salt, or sodium chloride, was mined extensively from seaside saltpans and inland springs and deposits. Some was used in silver refining. Most colonial sources of salt, such as the massive Colombian deposits of Zipaquirá, near Bogotá, had been exploited since remote pre-Columbian times. Tar pits, such as those at Lake Maracaibo, VENEZUELA, and Ecuador's Santa Elena Peninsula, were also valuable to the colonial economy. Once refined, petroleum tar was used for shipbuilding and to seal WINE jugs. Calcium carbonate in the form of lime was also widely manufactured from quarried stone for building purposes. A vast corpus of mining laws was quickly developed to regulate all aspects of this burgeoning industry.

Colonial miners exploited copper deposits in Cuba, Mexico, and Chile, along with some tin in Bolivia; however, the colonial failure to mine and forge iron from local deposits remains something of a conundrum. In short, it was the power of Seville's merchant guild, or Consulado, which needed as many European export products as possible to send to the colonies in exchange for ever greater amounts of silver and gold, that killed any hope of an indigenous iron industry. Iron and steel from the Basque Country of northern Spain, Habsburg Bohemia, Sweden, and other parts of Europe would thus continue to flow to the Americas until the end of colonial times. It arrived in the form of tools, weapons, bars, and rods. One variety was known as early as the 16th century as *hierro platino*, or "silvery iron." True platinum, when first discovered, was discarded as useless.

See also COPPER (Vol. III); GOLD (Vols. II, III); HUANCAVELICA (Vol. II); MERCURY (Vol. II); MINING (Vols. II, III, IV); SILVER (Vols. II, III); ZACATECAS (Vol. II).

—Kris E. Lane

Further reading:
Peter Bakewell. *Mines of Silver and Gold in the Americas* (Aldershot, U.K.: Variorum, 1997).
Alan Craig and Robert C. West, eds. *In Quest of Mineral Wealth: Aboriginal and Colonial Mining and Metallurgy in Spanish America* (Baton Rouge: Louisiana State University Press, 1991).
Colin McEwan, ed. *Pre-Columbian Gold* (London: British Museum, 2000).
David A. Scott and Warwick Bray. "Ancient Platinum Technology in South America: Its Use by the Indians in Pre-Hispanic Times." *Platinum Metals Review* 24, no. 4 (October 1980): 147–157.

mita (mit'a)   The *mita* was a pre-Columbian LABOR system in the Andes, adopted and expanded by the INCAS, in which all able-bodied citizens provided tribute in the form of work to their community. It began at the local, or AYLLU, level as a reciprocal form of exchange called *ayni*, in which members of the *ayllu* would lend their labor according to their abilities on a rotating basis. The work shifts were tied to the annual, seasonal cycles of AGRICULTURE and animal husbandry, and the workers were, as the word *mittaruna* signifies, "those that take their turn." The local *mita* helped Andeans achieve self-sufficiency and maintain kinship and ethnic bonds.

As the Inca state expanded, so, too, did the *mita*; eventually, this labor system formed the basis for the payment of most tribute in the empire, from military service to MINING, to transcontinental road building. The Incas became remarkably efficient at organizing work projects, keeping detailed records on their QUIPUS, and using the system in their political expansion and the incorporation of rival ethnic groups. Once an unincorporated ethnic group submitted to Inca dominion, that group would provide labor services and receive benefits in the reciprocal exchange of the *mita*. Inca leaders would also assign *mitas* to care for their agricultural lands and mines. Surpluses produced on state lands were stored and redistributed to the people in times of need, thus strengthening the imperial ideology of reciprocity between Inca and commoner and between the state and local *ayllus.*

Mita also provided the structure for forming religious ties between the Andean people and their deities (see RELIGION). Records show that HUACAs, local Andean religious shrines, were sustained through *mita* labor. Community members gave a certain amount of work to maintain the shrine and related ceremonial and symbolic elements, such as the ZEQUES, or sacred lines that marked the ceremonial landscape in the Andes. In return, Andeans hoped to receive benefits from their deities in the form of bountiful crops and fertile animals. The Inca state religion, appropriating this same model, dedicated agricultural lands to the Sun and the Moon, whose productivity depended on the *mittaruna.* As conquered peoples were incorporated into the Inca Empire, so were their deities, who were serviced through *mita* as part of the process the Incas used to extend broader reciprocal relationships and maintain their hegemony.

After the Spanish CONQUEST, the conquistadores and *encomenderos* took advantage of the elaborate pre-Columbian *mita* system by continuing the practice of mandatory work projects, often in cooperation with local KURAKAs and in conjunction with Spanish colonial officials (see ENCOMIENDA). Viceroy Francisco de Toledo is credited with reorganizing the colonial ECONOMY beginning in 1569, when he expanded *reducciones* of Indians into Spanish settlements and centralized the state organization of forced labor (see CONGREGACIÓN). The colonial *mita,* organized through the *repartimiento* system, became a major source of labor for mining, farming, *obrajes,* public works projects, and the construction of buildings and churches. It also contributed to the further degradation of indigenous society by forcing Indian laborers into virtual debt peonage, separating families for long periods of time, and exposing *mita* workers to widespread abuse and dangerous work environments.

See also MITA (Vol. II); REPARTO (Vol. II); TRIBUTE (Vol. II).

—Michael J. Horswell

Further reading:
Steve J. Stern. *Peru's Indian Peoples and the Challenge of Spanish Conquest: Huamanga to 1640* (Madison: University of Wisconsin Press, 1982).

mitmaqkuna The *mitmaqkuna* (singular, *mitmaq*), or "persons living away from their homeland," were male heads of household and their families who had been sent away from their native place and group either by their KURAKA (ethnic lord) or by the Sapa Inca (see INCAS). The institution was pre-Inca in nature, grounded in the needs of local and regional polities, but taken over and transformed to meet the needs of the Inca state. The *mitmaqkuna* did not provide personal service directly to their *kuraka* or the Inca, and they continued to be counted in

their group of origin. Before the Inca, *mitmaqkuna* were sent away from their core territory to carry out specialized tasks, such as growing COCA, chilies, or COTTON at lower, warmer altitudes; herding at high altitudes above the crop line; or MINING and smelting. They were assigned lands to cultivate for their own support. It appears that only a few families were involved from each group; however, different social divisions or even different ethnic groups might send families to the same special resource zone.

With imperial expansion, the Incas used this institution initially to gain access to LABOR for state fields and private holdings of the Inca and his close relatives. As the state expanded, the *mitmaqkuna* became part of a geopolitical strategy of control. *Mitmaqkuna* from the coast, who knew how to make rafts from gourd floats, were moved to strategic river crossings. New lands for MAIZE or coca production were created through terracing and irrigation by bringing in groups who knew these technologies. The Incas established many new hilltop fortresses, or *pukara,* and brought in *mitmaqkuna* from other areas to man them. In these cases, groups of 50 or 100 households from the same core group could be moved.

In order to secure newly conquered areas and control potentially resistant populations, massive numbers of people were moved as *mitmaqkuna* both out of and into these regions. In some cases, as much as half the original population was moved out of their home area. The *mitmaqkuna* were granted lands for cultivation in their new home, which may have been those held by groups that had been moved out. The *mitmaqkuna,* particularly those from the Cuzco region, were accorded high status, so in addition to giving up lands and population, the Incas adjusted the rank order of the AYLLUS in the *hanan/hurin* moieties so that the *mitmaqkuna* had higher rank than the autochthonous groups.

Under the last Incas, thousands of *mitmaqkuna* were used to cultivate maize and coca for state use; this produce went into the state storehouses to maintain the Inca armies and state institutions. These *mitmaqkuna* were drawn from different ethnic polities and cultivated fields or portions of fields assigned by their group of origin, all in a complex system that equalized the area and quality of land assigned to each. The lands given to the *mitmaqkuna* for their subsistence lay outside the Inca fields. The Inca need for TEXTILES, CERAMICS, fine masonry, and articles of stone, wood, and metal became so great that artisans were also moved away from their groups of origin as *mitmaqkuna* too (see ART). Some received lands for cultivation, while others may have been maintained from state storehouses. At this level, the *mitmaqkuna* had become industrial-scale producers in a preindustrial state.

—Patricia J. Netherly

Mixtecs The term *Mixtec,* literally meaning "people of the cloud place," is a NAHUATL appellation for one of the major ethnic groups in MEXICO. They called themselves the

Tay Ñudzahui. The Mixtecs inhabit the modern Mexican states of Oaxaca, Puebla, and Guerrero, which are geographically subdivided into the Alta, Baja, Coast, and Valley regions. Small groups of Mixtec agriculturists settled in this area as far back as 1500 B.C.E., when they diverged from other Otomanguean groups such as the ZAPOTECS. During the Classic period (250–1000 C.E.), the Mixtec population and settlements grew in size and complexity. Many sites were located on defensive hilltops, indicating local conflicts. In the Postclassic period (1000–1519), settlements were relocated to valley floors, while the old sites continued to be used for ceremonial purposes. Prior to the Spanish CONQUEST, several Mixtec towns had fallen under the influence of the TRIPLE ALLIANCE and were required to pay tribute to the Aztec Empire (see AZTECS).

The Mixtec subsistence economy was based largely on the unique *lama-bordo* agricultural terracing technique, which supported the growing population (see AGRICULTURE). By the time of the Spanish conquest, 500,000 people lived in the Mixteca region, making it one of the most densely occupied regions in Mesoamerica. The Mixtecs further developed a system of "vertical integration," in which agricultural produce and other specialized goods were exchanged between diverse ecological zones, and periodically congregated in large markets between major towns.

At the head of the Mixtec social structure were the ruling elite and hereditary nobility who resided in central towns, while the majority of commoners lived in the surrounding subject villages. The small kingdoms thus formed were interconnected through endogamous marital alliances among the royal lineages. The Mixtecs also created a network of political and economic ties that extended far beyond the Mixteca. In the late 11th century, the Mixtec lord Eight Deer forged a vast kingdom on the Pacific coast. He founded and named his new capital Tututepec, which grew to be one of the largest Mesoamerican cities during the Postclassic period.

Mixtec RELIGION was based on a pantheon of supernatural beings (*ñuhu*), the most important of whom was Dzahui, the Rain God. In fact, the Mixtecs' autodesignation of Tay Ñudzahui meant "people of the rain place." Although the Mixtecs did not construct monumental temples like the Zapotecs and the MAYA, they were known for their sacred ARTWORK, executed most notably in GOLD, bone, and stone, such as was found in a tomb of a Mixtec noble in MONTE ALBÁN. One of the most widely distributed polychrome ceramic traditions during the Postclassic, the Mixteca-Puebla style, was produced in part by the Mixtecs (see CERAMICS).

The ancient Mixtecs are probably best known today for their eight surviving pictorial CODICES, produced during and after the Postclassic period. Their writing system is among the most important and influential scripts in Mesoamerica and can be found on vessels, murals, and in early colonial documents such as *lienzos*. The codices are archaeologists' main source for understanding Mixtec mythology, religion, genealogies, chronology, and geography. They refer to a place called Apoala from which the primordial couple and kingdom are believed to have emerged. After the Spanish conquest, Mixtec society underwent major changes but retained some of its social structure and ancestral lands, which the Mixtec people continue to occupy.

—Danny Zborover

Further reading:
Ronald Spores. *The Mixtecs in Ancient and Colonial Times* (Norman: University of Oklahoma Press, 1984).

Mixtón War (1540–1542) The culmination of a decade of violence and disorder that followed NUÑO DE GUZMÁN's conquest of New Galicia (western MEXICO), the indigenous-Spanish conflict now known as the Mixtón War began in the fall of 1540 in the area north of Guadalajara. The indigenous communities of New Galicia were ethnically diverse, relatively small, autonomous entities on which the Spaniards had attempted to impose their demands for tribute, LABOR, and personal service. Fierce resentment of these demands coupled with the apparent opportunity offered by the departure of Governor FRANCISCO VÁSQUEZ DE CORONADO for the "New Land" (New Mexico) led local people to fortify and supply strongholds, known as *peñoles*. Following scattered attacks on Spanish *encomenderos* and their personnel and property, Spaniards discovered these centers of revolt, which eventually attracted large numbers of adherents (see ENCOMIENDA). The VICEROY, ANTONIO DE MENDOZA, sent aid, but during the first year of the conflict, the Spaniards experienced a series of defeats. PEDRO DE ALVARADO died after a disastrous retreat from Nochistlán. Soon after the Spaniards had fended off a concerted attack on Guadalajara, the viceroy arrived from MEXICO CITY with a large force of Spanish horsemen and infantry, as well as thousands of indigenous troops from Central Mexico. In the fall of 1541, they succeeded in turning the tide of the war. The viceroy's forces overwhelmed the *peñoles*, and hostilities ended in 1542. Thousands of people died or were taken captive and enslaved, while others fled to the mountains or were relocated, indelibly altering the ethnic map of New Galicia.

—Ida Altman

Further reading:
Arthur Scott Aiton. *Antonio de Mendoza: First Viceroy of New Spain* (New York: Russell & Russell, 1927).
Ida Altman. *The War for Mexico's West: Indians and Spaniards in New Galicia, 1524–1550* (forthcoming).

Moche The Moche people occupied the northern coast of modern-day PERU from approximately 50 to 800 C.E. Centered on the Moche river valley, their culture expanded north and south over the centuries in a loose affiliation of polities. The Moche elite oversaw

An in situ reconstruction of the lavish tomb of the lord of Sipán. He was buried with a large array of luxury items, such as jewelry and headdresses, which reflected his political and religious importance in Moche society. *(Courtesy of Sarahh E. M. Scher)*

the building of large adobe-brick structures, such as the Pyramids of the Moon and the Sun (see ARCHI-TECTURE). Some of these structures hosted elaborate ceremonies that included HUMAN SACRIFICE intended to ensure agricultural success in the difficult, mostly desert coastal environment (see AGRICULTURE). The Moche were prolific craftspeople and artists, excelling especially in CERAMICS and metalwork (see ART). Their ceramic vessels are highly naturalistic and depict many aspects of Moche life, including animals, plants, people, and supernatural beings in both two and three dimensions. Some vessels portray individual men from young adulthood to old age. Moche metalworkers created elaborate items from GOLD and SILVER alloys. Many of these metal pieces were part of the ritual costume worn by the elite during religious ceremonies (see RELIGION). Ear and nose ornaments, necklaces, and elaborate headdresses have been found in Moche graves, along with large caches of ceramic vessels. The most famous of these graves were excavated at Sipán, in the Lambayeque river valley.

The Moche political structure seems to have been in crisis by the 700s, and by 800, it appears that the culture had collapsed. The causes for this are subject to debate but include the possibility that the El Niño weather event caused such massive flooding that irrigation canals were destroyed. Without an irrigation system, and along with the other destruction caused by the flooding, the Moche people would have been unable to produce adequate FOOD. It is speculated that this led to the breakdown of Moche political power, and the people broke into smaller, more sustainable groups, in which they remained until the advent of the Lambayeque culture and CHIMÚ Empire several centuries later.

—Sarahh E. M. Scher

Further reading:
Steve Bourget and Kimberly L. Jones, eds. *The Art and Archaeology of the Moche: An Ancient Andean Society of the Peruvian North Coast* (Austin: University of Texas Press, 2008).
Margaret A. Jackson. *Moche Art and Visual Culture in Ancient Peru* (Albuquerque: University of New Mexico Press, 2009).
Joanne Pillsbury. *Moche Art and Archaeology in Ancient Peru* (Washington, D.C.: National Gallery of Art, 2001).

Moctezuma   See MONTEZUMA.

monarchs of Portugal   Portugal's second ruling dynasty, the House of Avis, governed the kingdom of Portugal from 1385 to 1580. During this period, the interests and ambitions of the Crown were intertwined with the early history of the Portuguese Empire. The history of the Avis dynasty and its role in Portuguese expansion is distinct from what was seen in Spain. Unlike the Kingdoms of Castile and Aragon, which were not effectively united under a single head until the early 16th century, Portugal—a single kingdom—had established its borders nearly 250 years earlier as part of its own Christian reconquest (to remove the Moors from Iberia). Together with other factors, including the increasingly commercial role of Lisbon and the concomitant growth of a Portuguese merchant class, the political stability of the House of Avis created an ideal environment for the pursuit of Portugal's overseas ambitions in the early 15th century. Accordingly, although the voyages of CHRISTOPHER COLUMBUS and Vasco da Gama were separated by only a few years, the origin of Portugal's Atlantic empire began nearly a century before, with the invasion of Ceuta (near modern-day Morocco) in 1415.

Today, scholars often cite religious, economic, and political motives to explain Portugal's conquest of Ceuta. But, the ultimate decision by Portugal's first Avis monarch was also personal in nature, being in no small part due to the influence of his third son Henrique, who looked to Africa for personal glory, riches, and knowledge. Known more commonly today in English as Prince Henry the Navigator (1394–1460), he went on to become a patron of subsequent Portuguese voyages and discoveries. He encouraged the development of the caravel, the first ship that was reliable on the high seas; he also fostered the creation of navigational technology and detailed MAPS of Africa and the Atlantic. Under Henry's patronage, the Portuguese went on to establish factories, or trading posts, along the coasts of western Africa (see TRADE). They also discovered and colonized various islands in the Atlantic, including Madeira, the Azores, and the Cape Verdes. These early discoveries, during the early to mid-15th century, established patterns of settlement that the Portuguese would later use in BRAZIL, including fortified trading posts, the establishment of SUGAR plantations, and the use of African SLAVERY.

Although the Portuguese Empire initially grew on account of the patronage of its monarchs, country and Crown also suffered important losses. Indeed, the end of the Avis dynasty is traced in large part to the decision of King Sebastian to invade northern Africa once again. Fighting at Alcácer-Quibir (in northwest Morocco) in 1578, Sebastian's forces were decisively defeated, and he himself was killed (along with nearly all of Portugal's nobility). A relatively young monarch without heirs, Sebastian's death set off a dynastic crisis that was not resolved until 1581, when Philip II, a Spanish Habsburg, took possession of the Portuguese throne (see HABSBURGS).

See also AVIS DYNASTY (Vol. II); JOHN VI (Vol. II); PEDRO I (Vol. III); PEDRO II (Vol. III).

—Erik Myrup

Further reading:
C. R. Boxer. *The Portuguese Seaborne Empire, 1415–1825* (New York: Alfred A. Knopf, 1969).

monarchs of Spain The marriage of Isabella of Castile (b. 1451–d. 1504) to Ferdinand of Aragon (b. 1452–d. 1516) in October 1469 laid the foundation for the union of Spain's Christian kingdoms. Their conquest of the kingdom of Granada in the southern part of the Iberian Peninsula in 1492 eliminated the final remnants of Muslim political power and marked the end of the Reconquista (see MORISCO). In the same year, Isabella's backing of CHRISTOPHER COLUMBUS resulted in the discovery of the New World. The two monarchs ruled their kingdoms separately, but when Ferdinand died in 1516 (Isabella had died in 1504), their grandson Charles I inherited the combined thrones of Aragon and Castile. He was also heir, through his father, to the Habsburg territories of central Europe, and ruled the Holy Roman Empire as Charles V (see HABSBURGS). All this made the Spanish monarchy 16th-century Europe's foremost power.

Mid-15th century Castile was a kingdom torn by struggles between the nobility and the reigning monarch, Henry IV, Isabella's half brother. The aristocratic faction accused Henry of, among other things, Muslim sympathies, homosexuality, and sexual impotence. They demanded that he name his younger half brother Alfonso his heir, and when the boy died, they forced Henry to accept Isabella as his successor. She had already married Ferdinand of Aragon against Henry's wishes, in part to protect her interests in Castile but also because of what seems to have been a genuine romantic attraction between the two. When Henry died in 1474, the Castilian nobles prevented his daughter Juana from taking the throne and gave it instead to Isabella. Ferdinand succeeded to Aragon's crown in 1479. Although the couple ruled Christian Spain, their individual kingdoms retained their legal and fiscal traditions, with no institutional or legal unification.

The "Catholic Kings," as they became known, laid the foundations for Spain's Golden Age. Through military might and social and economic concessions, they managed to win the nobility's political support. They established the Inquisition in 1480 to deal with the problem of *conversos* (Jewish converts to Christianity) who still practiced Judaism, although the tribunal became a tool of tremendous abuse and persecution. Convinced that the *conversos* would never become true Christians while living with Jews, Ferdinand and Isabella ordered the expulsion of all Jews in 1492. Ferdinand intervened diplomatically and militarily in Italy, a traditional Aragonese sphere of interest, but it was Isabella's funding of Columbus's first voyage that forced Castile, and thus Spain, to look westward. Pope Alexander VI awarded the discovered lands to Castile, along with the responsibility of converting their inhabitants to Christianity, a task that the devout Isabella took seriously (see RELIGION). Nevertheless, despite the long-term importance of the American discoveries, the Catholic Kings undoubtedly considered the conquest of Granada, the last Muslim stronghold in the peninsula, as their greatest achievement. It brought an end to the reconquest and almost eight centuries of Muslim political power in Iberia. As a sign of the importance they accorded Granada, they chose to be buried there in the royal chapel of the city's cathedral.

Despite their other achievements, Ferdinand and Isabella were less successful in providing an heir to their kingdoms. As it turned out, their daughter Juana, married to the Habsburg Philip I of Burgundy (Philip the Fair), inherited not only the throne but also a strain of insanity from Isabella's Portuguese mother. With Philip's death in 1506 and Juana's madness (she is known to history as Juana la Loca, or Joanna the Mad), Ferdinand governed Castile as regent until his death in 1516. A critical influence during that period and earlier was Francisco Ximénez de Cisneros, religious reformer, clerical leader, and Renaissance scholar. Cardinal Ximénez had been Isabella's confessor and adviser, and after her death, he continued to serve Ferdinand.

Following Ferdinand's death, Cardinal Ximénez governed until the teenager Charles (b. 1500–d. 1558) arrived in 1517 to rule his grandparents' kingdoms. In his person, Spain was united, although he did not sweep away the individual kingdoms' laws and fiscal privileges but agreed to rule each as a separate jurisdiction. Elected Holy Roman emperor in 1519, Charles was irresistibly drawn to protect Habsburg interests in central Europe. The Protestant Reformation began at almost the same time as Charles became emperor. He confronted Martin Luther at Worms but the German clerical refused to back down. In part from religious commitment and in part to assert their independence of Habsburg authority, many German princes rebelled and formed the Schmalkaldic League, which fought Charles to a standstill. Charles finally recognized that he was unable to defeat the German Protestants and agreed to the Peace of Augsburg (1555), which stipulated that each ruler could determine the religion of his people. Meanwhile, he continued the traditional Spanish and Habsburg rivalry with France, particularly over control of northern Italy. There, Charles was more successful. He defeated and captured Francis I at the Battle of Pavia (1525). He also married his son and heir, Philip, to Mary Tudor in an attempt to win English support for the anti-French struggle. France's own Wars of Religion, however, so convulsed that monarchy that it did not constitute a major threat to Spanish imperialism for the remainder of the century.

Still, the Habsburg territories that conferred such grandeur on Charles and Spain proved a tremendous burden. He squandered Spanish resources on futile attempts to roll back the tide of Protestantism, to shore up his territories in the Low Countries and Germany, and to thwart the expansion of the Turks. Nonetheless, his domains stretched around the globe, and with the CONQUEST of MEXICO and PERU, significant quantities of American GOLD and SILVER found their way into the royal treasury; unfortunately, Charles's European wars left him bankrupt by the time he abdicated and turned Spain over to his son, Philip II, who ruled from 1556 to 1598. Both father and son were energetic, intelligent rulers. They were the most powerful monarchs of their time, largely due to Spanish resources, but their pro-Habsburg and anti-Protestant policies proved in the long run detrimental to Spain.

See also CHARLES I (Vol. II); CHARLES II (Vol. II); CHARLES III (Vol. II); CHARLES IV (Vol. II); FERDINAND VI (Vol. II); FERDINAND VII (Vol. II); HABSBURGS (Vol. II); *PATRONATO REAL* (Vol. II); PHILIP II (Vol. II); PHILIP III (Vol. II); PHILIP IV (Vol. II); PHILIP V (Vol. II).

—Kendall Brown

Further reading:

John Edwards. *Ferdinand and Isabella* (New York: Pearson/ Longman, 2005).

J. H. Elliott. *Imperial Spain, 1469–1716* (New York: St. Martin's Press, 1964).

John Lynch. *Spain, 1516–1598: From Nation State to World Empire* (Cambridge: Blackwell, 1992).

Monte Albán

Among the most important archaeological sites in MEXICO, Monte Albán rises about 1,000 feet (305 m) above the Valley of Oaxaca. Founded in 500 B.C.E. by a confederacy of Zapotec chiefdoms on an uninhabited hilltop, the site slowly grew in size and population to become one of the first urban centers of Mesoamerica, covering an area of about eight square miles (21 km²) (see ZAPOTECS). Its strategic central location allowed Monte Albán's rulers to coordinate local TRADE and exchange and thus establish a new political order in the valley and beyond. Between 500 and 100 B.C.E., members of the Zapotec elite at Monte Albán oversaw the building of monumental temples, palaces, patios, and public buildings around a main plaza carved out of the artificially leveled hilltop. The lower classes lived on hundreds of residential terraces surrounding the site's core, mostly in single-family dwellings.

Apart from its remarkable location, Monte Albán is exceptional for the discovery of more than 300 carved stone slabs, each depicting a slain war captive (originally misidentified and labeled as Danzantes, or "dancers," due to their grotesque positions). Many of the slabs include glyphs in Zapotec dating to about the first century C.E., making them among the earliest examples of writing in the Americas. Later (100 B.C.E.–350 C.E.), other stone slabs were carved with the places and rulers conquered by the expanding state of Monte Albán. During the same period, an arrow-shaped structure was constructed in the main plaza; it was carefully oriented to important astronomical events. From about 200 to 350 C.E., Monte Albán's rulers started to interact with the powerful elite of TEOTIHUACÁN in the Valley of Mexico. By 600, Monte Albán had reached its peak population of about 25,000 inhabitants.

For reasons not entirely understood, major construction activity stopped around 800, and the population left for other cities in the valley. During the Postclassic

The hilltop Zapotec capital of Monte Albán, view from the South Platform toward the main plaza and the North Platform. The arrow-shaped Building J is seen in the foreground. *(Courtesy of Danny Zborover)*

period (800–1521), the now-deserted urban core continued to be used sporadically as a ceremonial center and a fortress and as burial grounds for numerous groups. In 1932, the Mexican archaeologist Alfonso Caso discovered a spectacular burial chamber, which contained GOLD and other precious artifacts left by the MIXTECS.

—Danny Zborover

Further reading:
Joyce Marcus and Kent Flannery. *Zapotec Civilization: How Urban Society Evolved in Mexico's Oaxaca Valley* (London: Thames & Hudson, 1996).

Montejo, Francisco de (b. ca. 1479–d. 1553) *Spanish conquistador and adelantado in Yucatán, Tabasco, and Honduras* A native of the town of Salamanca, Spain, Francisco de Montejo was born ca. 1479 to Juan de Montejo and Catalina Álvarez de Tejeda, apparently members of the local lesser nobility. Before he left for the Indies, Montejo had an illegitimate son, baptized Francisco, with a prominent woman from Seville named Ana de León.

Montejo made his way to the West Indies and quickly came to serve as a member of several major Spanish CONQUEST expeditions. Arriving in CUBA early in 1514, he participated in the organization of an expedition under PEDRO ARIAS DE ÁVILA to conquer the region known as Darién on the isthmus of PANAMA. Based on his experience in logistics and his organizational skills, the Spanish explorer JUAN DE GRIJALVA similarly selected him to serve as one of the captains in his 1518 expedition to explore the newly found coasts of mainland MEXICO. Montejo went on to serve again as one of the captains of the 1519 expedition led by HERNANDO CORTÉS.

In one of his most important missions, Cortés sent Montejo, along with Alonso Portocarrero, to escort the king's royal fifth (*quinto real*) of treasure from Mexico back to Spain. From his arrival in Spain until late in 1522, Montejo served Cortés's interests at the Spanish Court. In reward for his services, Cortés granted Montejo an ENCOMIENDA in the city-state of Azcapotzalco, to the north of the new capital of MEXICO CITY. Enjoying his prosperity for only a few years, Montejo was again selected by Cortés and the municipal council of the new colony of New Spain in 1524 to serve as their representative at Court.

By 1526, a wealthy man in his own right, Montejo sought to win royal favor to launch his own expedition of conquest. On November 19, 1526, he presented his initial plans to conquer and colonize the Yucatán Peninsula to King Charles I and his councilors. The king and the COUNCIL OF THE INDIES quickly accepted his plan, and on December 8, 1526, Montejo received the royal charter, or *capitulación*, giving him the right to begin the conquest and colonization of Yucatán. As a reward for his services, Montejo was awarded the title of *adelantado* of Yucatán, to be held by himself and his heirs in perpetuity; he was

also given the offices of governor and captain general of the province for the term of his natural life. During this same time, Montejo met and married the wealthy widow, Beatriz de Herrera from Salamanca, who gave Montejo much of the funding required to outfit his expedition.

Although his first expedition to Yucatán (1527–29) was a failure, Montejo did not give up on his plans. Instead, in order to create a supply line for his subsequent expeditions of conquest to the region, he conquered and pacified the regions of Tabasco, HONDURAS, and Chiapas. Although only moderately successful in these conquests, Montejo did come to have effective political control over most of these regions by 1539.

Although Montejo never again personally led military expeditions of conquest in Yucatán, he entrusted the leadership of new expeditions to his son, Francisco "el Mozo" (the Younger), and his nephew, also named Francisco de Montejo. Together, son and nephew triumphed in the final conquest of Yucatán with the creation of the first permanent Spanish capital at the MAYA site of Tihó, which the Spaniards named *Mérida* on January 6, 1542.

The elder Montejo returned to govern the province of Yucatán from 1546 to 1548, but his authoritarian rule was resented by many of the major conquistadores, who felt Montejo kept too many of the spoils for himself. Fearing that his vassal was growing too strong, the Spanish king listened to the criticisms of the conquistadores and colonists in Yucatán and removed Montejo from government. In 1550, an official *residencia* trial of his conduct in office was held, and the negative charges and subsequent removal of many of his powers and privileges forced Montejo to return to the Spanish Court to defend himself in a countersuit with the Council of the Indies. Montejo did not live to see the end of his case. Before the suit was concluded, the *adelantado* died of a fever in Salamanca on September 8, 1553.

—John F. Chuchiak IV

Further reading:
Robert S. Chamberlain. *The Conquest and Colonization of Yucatán, 1517–1550* (New York: Octagon Books, 1966).

Montesinos, Antonio de (d. ca. 1530) *Dominican friar and advocate for the indigenous* Antonio de Montesinos was a Dominican friar who won lasting fame as the first advocate of human rights for the indigenous peoples of the Caribbean. Almost nothing is known about his early life, but he was one of the first Dominicans to arrive in the New World after CHRISTOPHER COLUMBUS first discovered it (see RELIGIOUS ORDERS). Appalled by the Spaniards' abuse of the islanders, in 1511, Montesinos and some of his fellow Dominicans decided to chastise their countrymen. The Dominicans chose Montesinos, who was known for his stern and energetic sermons, to give the sermon on the Sunday before Christmas in 1511; in it, Montesinos publicly criticized the Spaniards' treatment

of the Amerindians. Another Dominican, BARTOLOMÉ DE LAS CASAS, preserved the content of the sermon, for which Montesinos took as his text, "I am a voice crying in the wilderness" of this island. He asserted the basic humanity of the NATIVE AMERICANS and denounced Spanish cruelties. He told his listeners, who included the islands' elite and Governor Diego Columbus, that they had no more hope of salvation than did the infidel Muslims.

His sermon outraged those in attendance, who insisted that he retract his accusations. Nevertheless, in a second sermon delivered the following Sunday, the Dominican laid out further arguments in support of his original position. Montesinos's opponents persuaded King Ferdinand in 1512 to order the friar to keep silent about their treatment of the Indians. Montesinos returned to Spain and advocated his cause at Court. He then returned to the New World, evangelizing for some time in PUERTO RICO and then in VENEZUELA, where he reportedly died around 1530.

Montesinos apparently had a hand in the conversion of Las Casas, arguably the greatest Spanish exponent of indigenous rights. Las Casas gave up his ENCOMIENDA in part because of Montesinos's urging.

See also DOMINICANS (Vol. II).

—Kendall Brown

Further reading:
Lewis Hanke. *The Spanish Struggle for Justice in the Conquest of America* (Boston: Little, Brown, 1965).

Monte Verde
Monte Verde is an archaeological site located along the low mountains of the sub-Antarctic region of CHILE, about 500 miles (805 km) south of Santiago. Discovered by a veterinary student in 1975, early research suggested the site was more than 14,000 years old. This claim stirred tremendous controversy in the 1970s and 1980s. If indeed the site was that old, it would predate—by a millennium—what was widely believed to be the earliest known site of human existence in the Americas, at Clovis, New Mexico (see CLOVIS CULTURE). Since the 1990s, scientists have moved toward consensus that Monte Verde is, in fact, the earliest human settlement in the Americas. As a consequence, a new model of human MIGRATION from Siberia along the western coasts of the Americas has been developed.

Researchers believe that Monte Verde was occupied by a small number of people, perhaps 20 to 30, between 12,800 and 11,800 B.C.E. The settlers erected a 20-foot-long (6 m) tentlike structure, with two hearths, that was probably for communal use. Remnants of stone tools were found, as well as series of mastodon bones, a human footprint, fossilized dung, and nearly four dozen different plant, seed, or berry remains were found at the site. Many of the items consumed at Monte Verde originated from well over 100 miles (161 km) away, suggesting that Monte Verde's residents had established a TRADE network. This challenges the widely held belief that the first settlers in the region were nomadic foragers. The preservation of the site's artifacts is credited to a turf blanket created by a swamp that enveloped the area after its occupancy. In 2008, new radiocarbon tests performed on algae and seaweed found on the upper layer of the site, known as Monte Verde II, reconfirmed the site's age.

—Sean H. Goforth

Montezuma (Moctezuma Xocoyotzin, Montezuma II) (b. ca. 1466–d. 1520) *ruler of Aztec Empire at the time of the arrival of the Cortés expedition*
This ill-fated figure was born ca. 1466 and died in 1520, apparently stoned to death by his own people. He is enshrined in the popular imagination as the cowardly loser to HERNANDO CORTÉS. His name carries such a heavy charge of defeat that the U.S. Marine Corps celebrates its martial triumphs by opening its hymn with the words "From the halls of Montezuma. . . ."

Montezuma's early years did not presage such an unfortunate destiny. Nahuatl-language accounts usually list him as either *Moteuçoma Xocoyotl*, or more formally with the reverential suffix *-tzin*, as in *Moteuçomatzin Xocoyotzin* (in MEXICO, his name is rendered *Moctezuma Xocoyotzin*). The second element of his name means "Younger," in reference to the earlier Montezuma (Moteuçoma Huehuetzin), who ruled 1440–69. Both headed the ALTE-PETL of TENOCHTITLÁN, capital of the Mexicas (AZTECS). Montezuma I allied with the nearby cities of Texcoco and Tlacopan to successfully extend the Aztec Empire's reach east and south (see TRIPLE ALLIANCE). Montezuma II ruled from 1502 to 1520. Before Cortés's arrival, Montezuma II was feared by friend and foe alike; indeed, the name he shared with his predecessor speaks to his initial fearsome reputation: "He frowns angrily in a lordly manner."

Montezuma II ruled over the Aztec Empire for almost two decades. During that time, he struggled to consolidate the empire. The number of military campaigns under his rule was unprecedented, even if the empire did not grow significantly. Montezuma also continued the long-standing efforts to conquer TLAXCALA, which, like his predecessors, he did not succeed in. Had the Spaniards not arrived in 1519, it is likely that Montezuma would have continued with his imperial ambitions. He had implemented a series of reforms designed to increase his own power and that of the Mexica nobility. Nevertheless, Cortés's arrival initiated the fall of the empire, as the Aztecs' enemies allied with the newcomers to topple it.

It is curious that Montezuma himself is often blamed for the empire's collapse. The most-cited evidence of his submissiveness is his supposedly fawning speech to Cortés as the Spanish conquistadores entered Tenochtitlán on November 8, 1519. In reality, he gave the Nahuatl equivalent of the Spanish *mi casa es su casa* ("my house is your house"), a polite phrase hardly to be taken literally. The notion that Montezuma was responsible for the Spanish conquest began early, with many on the losing side finding it convenient to make him a scapegoat.

The conquistadores' successes have more plausible explanations. The help of numerous indigenous allies, such as the Tlaxcalans, was critical. European military technology such as steel weapons, their horses, and unfamiliar military tactics were also important factors. In addition, diseases such as smallpox wiped out and demoralized many indigenous people both during and after the conquest.

—Barry D. Sell

Further reading:
Ross Hassig. *Mexico and the Spanish Conquest* (Norman: University of Oklahoma Press, 2006).
James Lockhart. *We People Here: Nahuatl Accounts of the Conquest of Mexico* (Berkeley: University of California Press, 1993).

Morisco   In early modern Spain, the term *Morisco* was applied to Christian converts from Islam. While some Iberian Muslims had converted voluntarily during the medieval period, many were forcibly baptized at the beginning of the 16th century. Following the 1492 conquest of the Kingdom of Granada by the Catholic monarchs Ferdinand and Isabella, the Muslim population was protected under surrender treaties. Nevertheless, by 1499, increasing persecution and pressure to convert under the cardinal Francisco Ximénez de Cisneros led to the first Alpujarras uprising, as the Granadan Muslims protested the breach of the treaties' terms. Once the uprising had been suppressed, the Granadan Muslims were forced to choose between baptism and exile from Spain. Upon accepting baptism, they fell under inquisitorial scrutiny.

Tensions mounted on the peninsula as Spanish authorities became increasingly concerned that the Moriscos were neither good Christians nor loyal subjects. In 1526, Charles I granted the Granadan Moriscos a three-year "period of grace" during which they were to receive instruction in Catholicism but not be subject to the Inquisition. Additionally, the Moriscos faced prohibitions on wearing traditional dress, speaking in the Arabic dialect, and giving their children Muslim names. By the mid-16th century, inquisitorial persecution of Moriscos increased, as ecclesiastical authorities feared that they continued to practice Islam clandestinely.

Geographic differences within Spain meant that the label *Morisco* could refer to peoples holding beliefs that ranged from Islam to Catholicism. In Aragon and Valencia, the Moriscos' proximity to Muslims in the Mediterranean and the presence of Muslim religious leaders (*alfaquíes*) suggests that they were able to maintain some of their practices. In Castile, many Moriscos had been Christians for several generations, and some even claimed "old Christian" status in the courts. The Granadan noble families of Morisco descent similarly claimed to have converted before the forced baptisms and to have partici-

pated in the Christian reconquest (Reconquista). Members of these elite families were not subject to the legislative restrictions on the majority of Granadan Moriscos and thus could bear arms, join military orders, and acquire prestigious offices. They were also exempt from restrictions on travel to Spanish America. Nevertheless, after the second Alpujarras uprising in 1568–72, the expulsion of the Granadan Moriscos, and their forced resettlement across Spain, Moriscos on the peninsula were labeled as rebels by jurists who favored their expulsion. In 1609–14, the Crown expelled the Moriscos from Spain.

Due to concerns that they would influence indigenous religiosity, royal decrees prohibited Moriscos from immigrating to Spanish America. Nonetheless, some obtained false licenses and traveled there. Morisco and North African Muslim slaves were also prohibited from traveling to Spanish America, yet royal decrees suggest that they were taken there as well, some of them serving on the Spanish galleys that skirted the Caribbean coast (see slavery). In the Americas, Moriscos faced accusations similar to those they had encountered in Spain. Inquisitors tried Moriscos suspected of praying in Arabic, invoking Muhammad, and behaving inappropriately during Mass. Free Morisco immigrants held a range of occupations, such as artisans, medical practitioners, and laborers. Some, who achieved high status following their exploits during the conquest, became *encomenderos* (see ENCOMIENDA). By the late 16th century, Morisco descent was invoked in disputes over offices and *encomiendas*. If proven to be a Morisco, an individual could lose his or her social standing and possessions and be deported to Spain.

See also *CONVERSOS* (Vol. II).

—Karoline P. Cook

Further reading:
James Tueller. *Good and Faithful Christians: Moriscos and Catholicism in Early Modern Spain* (New Orleans, La.: University Press of the South, 2002).

Motolinía   See BENAVENTE, TORIBIO DE.

Muisca   The Muisca (Chibcha) Indians inhabited the fertile mountain plains of COLOMBIA's eastern highlands. Muisca territory corresponded roughly to the modern Colombian departments of Cundinamarca and Boyacá and covered a territory of more than 1,000 square miles (2,590 km²). When the first Spanish conquistadores reached Muisca territory in 1537, the region supported a population that exceeded 500,000.

Despite the fact that the eastern highlands were settled as early as 12,500 B.C.E., the earliest signs of Muisca culture did not appear until thousands of years later. The Early Muisca period is quite recent, dating to 800–1200 C.E.; these early Muisca were perhaps Chibcha-speaking migrants from northern Colombia or VENEZUELA. The Early Muisca period saw the emergence of ceremonial centers, a dramatic growth in interregional TRADE, an intensification in WARFARE, and the introduction of GOLD work and mummification.

The Late Muisca period (1200–1537) witnessed further population growth, an increase in long distance trade, and a proliferation of different forms of pottery (see CERAMICS). It was also characterized by a dramatic growth in village size, as well as the emergence of centers of political power.

According to the 17th-century Spanish chronicler Fray Pedro Simón, the term *Muisca* derived from the Chibcha word *muexca*, meaning "man" or "person" (see CHRONICLERS). However, it should be noted that the term itself is a European imposition. The Indians never referred to themselves as "Muisca," but rather by the name of the various chiefdoms in which they resided. Some scholars have suggested that when the first Spanish expedition arrived in 1537, Muisca territory was divided into two separate kingdoms, one ruled by the Zipas of BOGOTÁ and the other governed by the Zaques of Tunja (see CONQUEST). However, more recent studies suggest that Muisca territory was far more decentralized.

In addition to staple crops such as MAIZE and POTATO, the Muisca cultivated a variety of tubers, beans, and chilies (see FOOD). They also grew several types of nuts and an impressive variety of fruits and vegetables. Highland lakes and rivers were stocked with an abundance of fish, and the Muisca exploited a series of rich salt beds. Moreover, they cultivated COTTON, COCA, and TOBACCO; collected honey, wax, and turpentine; and used *cabuya* to make rope and cords. All of these goods circulated through a well-developed system of regional markets, through which products from different ecological zones circulated within Muisca territory and throughout much of Colombia.

The Spanish conquest ushered in a series of important and often devastating changes for the Muisca population. While the conquest itself followed a much less violent path than that of the conquests of MEXICO or PERU, the long-term effects on the Muisca proved disastrous. Within a century, the combined effects of European DISEASE, miscegenation, exploitation, and outward MIGRATION saw the Muisca population fall by as much as 80 percent.

—J. Michael Francis

***mulato* (mulatto)** Beginning in the 15th century, Portuguese traders began to transport slaves from sub-Saharan Africa to Europe (see SLAVERY). In Iberia, the offspring of these African slaves and Europeans were called *mulatos*. This term derived from the word *mula*, or "mule," the cross between a horse and a donkey. In Iberia, the term *loro*, referencing the color of dried laurel leaves, was also used to denote an individual of mixed African-European ancestry. Once transported to the Americas, the term *mulato* came to include the children of Africans and NATIVE AMERICANS. Occasionally, royal

and other official documentation used the term *zambo* or *zambaigo* to describe an Afro-indigenous person; however, this term never entered popular usage.

Most 16th-century observers, including VICEROYS and CHRONICLERS, noted that the majority of *mulatos* born in the Americas were Afro-indigenous, not Afro-European. The growth of these *mulato* populations occurred despite consistent attempts to prevent African-native interaction. Generally, the children of *mulatos* inherited the label *mulato*, even if they had a non-*mulato* parent. This tendency broadened the label further, and by the mid-16th century, this term was used to describe anyone of mixed ancestry who was believed to have some African forebears.

See also *MULATO* (Vol. II); *Zambo* (Vol. II).

—Robert Schwaller

music

THE AMERICAS BEFORE 1492

The indigenous peoples of South America, the Caribbean, and Mesoamerica possessed rich musical cultures. Music was integrated into their daily lives and their understanding of the world. Singing or chanting in a raised voice was associated with the creation of the world in stories such as the Mayan POPOL VUH.

The archaeological record includes a large array of indigenous musical instruments and confirms that their use was widespread. Bone, cane, and clay flutes, some more than 3,000 years old, have been found over a large area: *Ocarinas* were most common in Central and South America; *antaras*, or panpipes, were a key feature of the music of the Paracas of PERU. Whistles were used to produce several different pitches and were often made of clay and shaped, then baked, into human or animal forms. The shape of the whistle—whether lizard, frog, turtle, bird, snake, coyote, or human—affected its volume and pitch. Clay flutes had between two and five holes, and reed flutes were also common. The *quena*, an end-blown flute of reed or bone, was widely used in the music of the MOCHE and then INCAS.

Some aerophones had interlocking parts and produced several pitches, demonstrating an advanced knowledge of acoustics. Trumpets were often associated with creation, rain, and the sea. Clay and conch shell trumpets were used to call groups together and in rituals directed to the gods and goddesses. Shell trumpets sometimes had mouthpieces made of clay or bone. Percussion instruments were abundant. These were made of items from the natural environment. Dried gourds containing seeds and/or pebbles served as rattles, and animal bones and sticks as rasps. Dancers often wore bracelets or ankle adornments made of nutshells, metal disks, or dried fruits, which jingled as they moved. Drums of different varieties were used for communication and ceremonial dances. The Aztec *teponaztli*, a horizontal, wooden slit drum played with sticks or animal bones, produced two tones and was elaborately carved (see AZTECS). The *huehuetl*, a vertical drum of varying sizes, was made of a hollowed-out log, over which animal skin was stretched. The Aztecs considered the *teponaztli* and *huehuetl* to be sacred and thus used them in important ceremonies. The Maya crafted a *timbal*, a small, U-shaped clay drum to accompany ceremonies. Stringed instruments were rare, although a few groups possessed a musical bow.

Music served many functions in pre-Columbian communities. It was intimately involved in communication with deities. Singers, dancers, and musicians made supplications to the gods for rain, plentiful harvests, and victory in warfare. In central Mesoamerica, drumming and singing were part of ceremonies for ritual sacrifices. These performances helped solidify Mexica (Aztec) control over the peoples that made up the Aztec Empire. Song and ceremony were also used to combat illness. Shamans intoned music as part of their rituals to heal the sick (see medicine). Music also served important civic functions in indigenous life. An excavated Maya mural at Bonampak shows a procession of musicians playing rattles, tortoise shells, and drums. Two men playing wooden trumpets also appear in this mural, which depicts a ceremony honoring the ascension of a youth to power. The accession of a new ruler, victory over rival groups, and success in hunting were all celebrated in song. Daily tasks, such as grinding maize, tending to children, and preparing meals were also accompanied by song. Bartolomé de Las Casas described large groups of Taino women singing as they shredded manioc for cassava bread.

It is difficult to overestimate the importance of song and dance in the ritual lives of indigenous groups. Codices from Mesoamerican societies contain lyrics, depictions of dances, and images of musicians. Epic songs recounted the history of military conquests and important leaders and events. Singing was involved in Incan ancestor worship, and songs, such as the *cantares históricos*, preserved the memory of a ruler's deeds and exploits. Early Spanish observers were often stunned by the number of musicians and the length of ritual performances. According to chroniclers, an elaborate Inca ceremony commemorating the maize harvest in 1535 involved a double choir intoning songs in harmony from sunrise until sunset for more than a week.

Dances were performed before and after military expeditions, at planting and harvesting times, and to honor individual gods and goddesses and political leaders. Much of this music was made in groups and involved rhythmic stamping accompanied by rattles, rasps, aerophones, and unison song. Another key feature of precontact indigenous music was the wide variations in regional and ethnic forms of song and dance.

Musicians performed important roles in precontact indigenous societies and were highly esteemed and carefully taught. Aztec musicians were trained in the *calmecac*, or school for noble youth. There, young men learned to play instruments and perform songs that told the history of Aztec military success or honored the gods. Maya musical leaders, or *holpops*, held a prestigious place in their communities. Among the diverse groups of the northern deserts and mountains, musicians were specialists in rituals; they could heal, converse with the deities, and prepare for war or the harvest through song and dance.

THE EARLY COLONIAL PERIOD TO 1560

As early as Christopher Columbus's first voyage to the Caribbean, members of Spanish expeditions gave thanks for safe journeys by chanting antiphons such as the "Salve Regina." Missionaries accompanied conquering forces and chanted mass. Drums, flutes, and handheld harps provided entertainment and military music. Chroniclers of the Spanish expeditions described dances and loud songs performed by indigenous peoples upon their first encounters.

Because of the important place it occupied in both Spanish and indigenous societies, music soon became one of the most important tools in the spiritual conquest of indigenous peoples (see religion). Fray Pedro de Gante, a Flemish Franciscan who arrived in New Spain (Mexico) shortly after the fall of Tenochtitlán, helped establish schools at Texcoco and the Convento de San Francisco, where Nahua boys were taught to read, write, and sing. Motolinía (Toribio de Benavente), among others, wrote enthusiastically about the success of music as an aid in teaching doctrine and attracting Native Americans to the church. Other than schools where music was taught, cathedrals became centers of musical production in early colonial Latin America. The cathedrals at Mexico City and Lima hired students of prominent composers of the Spanish cathedrals to direct musical programs. Soon, cathedrals in Puebla (Mexico), Guatemala City, and Bogotá (Colombia) were also known for their elaborate music.

Indigenous peoples responded positively to the introduction of European-style music. Working as a musician was far more attractive than other forms of labor, and in some areas, musicians were exempt from tribute payments. Orchestras and choirs were filled with recent converts; some were able to rise to prominent positions; for example, Atahualpa's son Diego Lobato became chapelmaster of the Quito cathedral.

Music served political as well as religious purposes. Elaborate ceremonies marked the installation of a new viceroy, the visits of important officials to rural areas, and events in the lives of the royal families (see family). After the death of Charles I in 1559, the chapel master at the cathedral in Mexico City orchestrated a massive procession, followed by a performance of newly composed music by a double choir.

Spaniards not only introduced liturgical and civic music but also brought stringed instruments such as the guitar and harp, as well as the bowed stringed instruments of the viol family. Indigenous peoples learned to play these instruments and also became expert craftsmen. Furthermore, musical notation, the heptatonic scale, and European harmonies were spread through convent schools and mission choirs. While the oldest music book printed in the Americas was a chant book printed in Mexico in 1556, much early music spread by ear. Juan de Torquemada wrote that indigenous teachers spread Spanish polyphonic

Both European and indigenous instruments, such as these preserved in the Iglesia de Santo Domingo de Guzmán in Oaxaca, were used in the evangelization of the Americas. *(Courtesy of Kristin Dutcher Mann)*

villancicos, or religious hymns, into even remote settlements. Secular songs introduced by settlers, including romance ballads and sung poetry such as the *décima*, reflected the rich and multiethnic culture of Renaissance Spain. Dances such as the *moros y cristianos*, which re-created the defeat of the Moors in southern Spain, were fused with indigenous dances and themes (see MORISCO).

From the first decade of the 16th century, Africans began arriving in the Americas (see SLAVERY). Thereafter, African instruments, such as the marimba, and rhythms, tunes, and call-and-response patterns combined with European and indigenous music. In the Caribbean, rhythmic songs accompanied repetitive work tasks such as planting, harvesting, or hauling heavy materials.

A recurring theme in the early musical encounters between Spanish officials, missionaries, and indigenous and African peoples was the attempt to control cultural practices deemed offensive, threatening, or pagan. The First Mexican Provincial Council of 1555 ruled that music could be used for evangelization purposes, but that indigenous songs in the vernacular must reflect Christian doctrine. Dancing was permitted only during daylight hours outside of church buildings, and no instruments other than the organ were suitable for use during litur-

gical services in the churches. Rules such as these, and the fear that new converts would return to indigenous practices, resulted in the destruction of some indigenous instruments and a prohibition on native dances. A second set of restrictions was issued in 1565, indicating that the Spanish church authorities were still concerned with controlling musical content, form, and performances.

In the period after 1560, the struggle to define appropriate music intensified as the church engaged in prolonged attempts to extirpate idolatrous practices. Indigenous groups adjusted their musical practices in order to maintain their cultural identity in the face of colonial pressures. In the larger towns, composers were heavily influenced by the baroque music of Spain, while missionaries continued to rely on music as an important tool of conversion.

See also MUSIC (Vols. II, III, IV); THEATER (Vol. II).

—Kristin Dutcher Mann

Further reading:

Dale A. Olsen. *Music of El Dorado: The Ethnomusicology of Ancient South American Cultures* (Gainesville: University Press of Florida, 2002).

Robert Stevenson. *Music in Aztec and Inca Territory* (Berkeley: University of California Press, 1976).

N

Nahuas See AZTECS.

Nahuatl Nahuatl is the language spoken by the Nahuas, including the Mexica (AZTECS). *Nahuatl* was the name designated by its pre-Columbian speakers. Many contemporary Nahuas now use the term *mexicano* for their language, the thrust in this case being "the language of the Mexicans." In early colonial documents, the word appears most often in such compounds as *nahuatlatolli* (the Nahuatl language) and *nahuatlato* (interpreter, or expert in Nahuatl). It literally means "clear, intelligible, agreeable sound." The notion that one's native tongue is pleasingly comprehensible is often accompanied by the feeling that other tongues are opaque gibberish. Hence, the Nahuatl accounts of the Spanish CONQUEST OF MEXICO contained in the FLORENTINE CODEX include the observation that Spaniards spoke in a "babbling tongue."

Nahuatl belongs to the Uto-Aztecan family of languages. It covers an area whose northernmost reaches include Ute speakers in Utah and continues through Mexico and as far south and east in Central America to speakers of Pipil in NICARAGUA. For much of this area, Nahuatl was the lingua franca.

By the late 1530s, Nahua scribes began switching from pictographs and ideographs in *ALTEPETL* recordkeeping (see CODICES) to the Roman alphabet. Thousands of pages of alphabetical records are still extant, providing a rich source of information about early Nahuatl and Nahuas.

Nahuatl continues to be a presence in Mesoamerica and beyond. The names of two colonial regions that are now countries are Nahuatl: Mexico ("Place of the Mexica") and GUATEMALA (from hispanized *Quauhtemallan*, "Place of the Woodpile"). It has also contributed words to Mexican Spanish that have made their way into English and other languages, such as coyote, tomato, and chocolate. Nahuatl is still spoken by as many as 2 million people.

—Barry D. Sell

Further reading:

R. Joe Campbell and Frances Kartunnen. *Foundation Course in Nahuatl Grammar* (Austin: Institute of Latin American Studies, University of Texas, 1989).

Jane H. Hill and Kenneth C. Hill. *Speaking Mexicano: Dynamics of Syncretic Language in Central Mexico* (Tucson: University of Arizona Press, 1986).

Narváez, Pánfilo de (b. 1470–d. 1528) *Spanish conquistador who led a failed expedition to Florida* Pánfilo de Narváez was born a Castilian duke in 1470. In 1509, he participated in the CONQUEST of Jamaica. In 1512, he went to CUBA to support DIEGO VELÁZQUEZ DE CUÉLLAR's conquest. While there, he led expeditions to the eastern end of the island, accompanied by BARTOLOMÉ DE LAS CASAS. Then, in 1520, under Velázquez's orders, Narváez left Cuba for MEXICO in order to arrest HERNANDO CORTÉS and bring him back to Cuba. Despite his sizable force, Narváez's efforts were frustrated by attacks from indigenous groups and then defections of his men to Cortés. On May 24, 1520, Narváez was defeated by Cortés at Veracruz. Narváez, having lost an eye in the battle, was taken prisoner, only to be released by Cortés to return to Spain in 1521.

In 1526, Narváez was issued a royal grant by King Charles I to colonize FLORIDA. He left Spain in June 1527, commanding five ships carrying 600 passengers (some of whom were wives, slaves, and servants). The expedition first landed in HISPANIOLA, where about 100 of Narváez's forces deserted. Narváez then sailed to Cuba, before diverting two of his ships to Trinidad, where they were destroyed by a hurricane. The remaining ships suffered continued setbacks in Cuba before finally reaching present-day Tampa Bay, Florida, in mid-April 1528.

On May 1, despite the protest of his second-in-command, ÁLVAR NÚÑEZ CABEZA DE VACA, Narváez decided to send 300 of his men north in search of riches, while the remainder would sail up the coast to meet them. First one ship, then the remaining three, sailed to Cuba to pick up the expedition's fifth ship. They would never see Narváez's land forces. Instead, Narváez's contingency was harassed and attacked by Apalachee Indians throughout much of the summer, devastating his forces. By September 1528, only 242 men remained alive. An attempt to build boats and sail back to sea resulted in a horrific voyage across the Gulf of Mexico. Narváez likely perished when his ship capsized in the Gulf. Approximately 80 survivors made it to the Texan coast; the others died of thirst or as a result of a second hurricane. From Texas, the group meandered through much of the present-day U.S. Southwest, their numbers constantly dwindling. In July 1536, the expedition's only survivors, Cabeza de Vaca, two other Spaniards, and a Moorish slave, encountered a Spanish slave-taking patrol, ending the journey eight years after the group had reached Florida.

—Sean H. Goforth

Native Americans

CARIBBEAN BEFORE 1492

Archaeologists have identified the oldest human settlement in the Caribbean islands at Banwari Trace, in Trinidad. The site is associated with the Preceramic or Mesoindian period, which dates from 7,900 to 2,000 years ago. A small animal-hunting and shellfish-gathering culture, this Archaic group is thought to have settled in Trinidad about 7,000 years ago and, over time, to have migrated up to the Greater Antilles until about 2,000 years ago. Surviving cultural items for this time period include a variety of shell implements and stone tools such as pestles, grooved axes, celts, chipped flint and bone projectile points, fishing spears, and bone needles.

Like most of the archaeological record for the region, the proposed migration up to the Greater Antilles is speculative and a source of heated debate. While scholars have identified Mesoindian sites in the Greater Antilles similar to that at Banwari, evidence suggests that smaller islands may have been bypassed and the larger islands settled first. However, because of changes in sea level, as well as modern regional development, many early sites could have been destroyed.

The islands of CUBA, HISPANIOLA, and PUERTO RICO are noted for the greatest concentration of Mesoindian

sites. The Mesoindian period in the Greater Antilles had two distinct subseries, the Ortoiroid and the Casimiroid (6,900 to 4,500 years ago). These Preceramic cultures are generally associated with hunter-gatherer groups.

The Ortoiroid culture originated in South America, with intermittent artifact discoveries up to the Virgin Islands through Puerto Rico to the Mona Passage. Said to be the product of multiple MIGRATIONS and cultural interactions, the diverse Casimiroid culture is associated with cultures from the Yucatán or Central America. Archaeologists assume that migrants to the mainland came by sea to western Cuba via a now-submerged chain of islands. A people called the Ciboney who were said to inhabit parts of Cuba and Hispaniola at the time of European contact are often associated with Casimiroid culture. These sites are noted for lithic artifacts, including core tools, blades, burins, awls, scrapers, anvils, and hammerstones. The Casimiroid are further subdivided into the Courian subseries of Cuba, Haiti, Puerto Rico, and the Virgin Islands and the Redondan subseries of Cuba.

Many of these "open camp" Mesoindian sites consist of small shell middens found on or near the coast, with faunal material consisting of the remains of fresh- and salt water shellfish, fish, and sea and land animals. There was seemingly a heavier reliance on land-based hunting resources in the earlier part of the Mesoindian period than in the latter part.

Ever the cultural melting pot, from about 2,000 years ago to the first European contact more than 500 years ago, the Caribbean region seems to have experienced several waves of migrations by distinct cultures. Significant changes in cultural manifestations such as CERAMICS, the increased importance of AGRICULTURE and TRADE, and sedentism can be traced through the archaeological record. This period is often referred to as the Ceramic, or Neoindian, period.

As a result of trace materials and stylistic continuities, archaeologists suggest that a significant migration into the Antilles took place approximately 2,000 to 1,400 years ago, dominated by a culture identified as the Saladoid. It is generally accepted that this culture originated in the lower Orinoco river valley; these migrants brought with them horticulture that featured MANIOC and MAIZE. Early settlers seemed to favor flat coastal plains and alluvial valleys, while the later Saladoid period saw expansion into the mountainous island interiors. Debate continues as to whether these groups pushed the Mesoindian populations out or transculturation occurred over time. A growing body of evidence supports the latter view.

One of the characteristics of Saladoid pottery is white paint used on a red background; this style can be found in modern-day VENEZUELA. The Saladoid also decorated jars, bowls, trays, platters, and bell-shaped vessels with polychrome designs in white on red, white on red with orange slip, black paint, and negative-painted designs.

On Puerto Rico and the Virgin Islands, the Saladoid fashioned pendants from exotic materials such as jasper-chalcedony, amethyst, crystal quartz, fossilized wood, greenstones, carnelian, lapis lazuli, turquoise, garnet, epidote, and possibly OBSIDIAN. Although production of these artifacts seems to have faded about 1,400 years ago, their wide Antillean–South American distribution is evidence of extensive trading in raw and manufactured goods.

Archaeologists further contend that from approximately 1,400 to 1,200 years ago, either another wave of emigrants came out of the Orinoco area and spread throughout the Antilles or the Saladoid evolved into a culture identified as Ostionoid. The ceramic style of this culture focused on incised decoration rather than painting. Another important cultural manifestation attributed to the Ostionoid phase is the development of large, complex communities and multifunctional ceremonial centers, which included ball courts or plazas, called *bateys*. During this phase, the indigenous population increased in the highlands of Puerto Rico, Hispaniola, and Cuba, while Jamaica and the Bahamas were beginning to be settled. Reports also indicate a marked loss of cultural continuity between the islands and South America during this time period, evidenced by a lack of exotic trade goods.

Scholars have identified later elaborations of the Ostionoid as Elenoid and Chicoid, which appeared from about 1,200 to 850 years ago and 850 to approximately 500 years, respectively. Another very different Ostionoid variant is identified as Melliacan or Mellacoide. Mellacoide ceramics appeared in Cuba around this time. Defined by the distribution of specific ceramic styles, it is these people that scholars suggest were called the Arawak or TAINO by the Spaniards during the early stages of colonization.

Scholars suggest that the Taino-Arawak culture in the Greater Antilles reached its peak shortly before the arrival of Europeans. The Taino established complex societies, with communities ranging from about 1,000 to 5,000 residents. While Taino settlements extended throughout the Greater Antilles, the Bahamas, and even southern Bimini, the most elaborate political systems and expressive culture were seen at Puerto Rico and Hispaniola. Organized into *iukaieke* (chiefdoms) where the *kasike* (CACIQUE) held hereditary political power based on "matrilines," these communities sustained themselves through agricultural production, supplemental hunting, trade, fishing, and shellfish gathering. Socioreligious manifestations included petroglyphs and the development of *cemíes* (spirit effigies), which were associated with ceremonial practices. *Cemíes* could be carved from stone, wood, bone, or shell or created from clay. Consistent with the Ostionoid subseries, petaloid stone celts were also made during this period. Although Taino craftspeople excelled in stone and hard wood working, their pottery varied and evolved throughout the region, from polychrome to an incised style, which often featured rim "lugs," or "*adornos*," in the form of human, animal, or spirit heads on the rims.

While major manifestations of Taino culture—both material and linguistic—can find their origin and parallels in South America and other circum-Caribbean cultures, many aspects of Taino culture are unique. Ball courts, for example, are found in Central and South America, the lower United States, and Mesoamerica; however, their central role in Taino sociopolitical life is as distinctive as the ball game's cultural associations.

That the Taino world was culturally and linguistically diverse is evidenced by the existence of various ethnic groups (such as the Ciboney and Macorix) and several recorded languages or dialects. The Taino from Cuba were said to be able to communicate well with peoples in the Campeche region of Yucatán. At least three languages were spoken on Hispaniola alone. Two of these were quite different, while one was known as the island's universal language. Ethnic differences also appear to have been greater on Hispaniola than on other islands, even though archaeologists generally consider all or most of these peoples Taino.

One of the most notable cases that supports a cultural synthesis of Saladoid and Archaic cultures is based on a careful examination of Mellacoide assemblages. Melliacan pottery currently has no precedents on Hispaniola or in the Antilles or South America. Thus, it has been proposed that Mellacoide ceramics resulted from a lithic migration that fused this style with the Ostionoid medium. The relationship between Ostionan and its variants Melliacan and Chican is not sequential; rather, they existed at the same time in various locations on Hispaniola and continued until the time of European colonization. Thus, from this multicultural past, a complex Taino society emerged, which at times displayed marked differences but also retained many similarities across a vast land area.

Just a few hundred years prior to contact, other indigenous peoples identified as CARIB are believed to have migrated to the Caribbean, again from the Orinoco river valley region. Historically, it has been suggested that this group "displaced" the Arawak populations and "controlled" the Lesser Antilles up to the Virgin Islands. It is also argued that the so-called Carib migration was brought to a halt when it reached the island of Puerto Rico.

Whether the group that apparently made its way up the Lesser Antilles was of true Carib, or Karina, stock has been long debated. As a result, these peoples are often referred to as Island Caribs in order to highlight their difference from mainland communities. While some cultural differences did exist between the Greater and Lesser Antillean groups, including population density, a separation of men's and women's houses, and arrow tip styles, other cultural aspects were not dissimilar. Manioc production, petroglyphs, *cemí* stones, and pelatoid celts are all found in the Lesser Antilles, although with less frequency. Like the Taino, the so-called Island Carib language is classified as Arawakan. It contains many words in common with the Taino language.

Despite more than 500 years of colonization, indigenous peoples of the region have important insights into Caribbean "prehistory." From contemporary Yucatán MAYA accounts relating that the Caribbean islands were a trade route and "bridge" to South America, to the oral tradition of the Unishido Lokono Arawak clan of Venezuela, which states that the Taino were one of five ancient clans that moved into the islands, these accounts complement academic assertions of pre-Hispanic Caribbean multiculturalism. The Kalinago of Dominica maintain an oral tradition that within their ancestral memory, groups of men came from South America and integrated with local communities. This integration and exchange resulted, not from WARFARE, but from trade and local alliances. Local oral tradition in Puerto Rico maintains that such alliances were made with groups coming from Vieques. These arrangements allowed visitors among the mainland communities for trade.

Perhaps the most poignant indigenous version of Caribbean prehistory is the Taino emergence story from Kasibahagua, which states that the Taino were born of the islands themselves. This same oral tradition recognizes the existence of other peoples, highlighting a culturally diverse awareness. Unlike the Kalinago, the Taino do not recount any migration memory, indicating a very long presence in the islands.

The Caribbean has always been an area where cultures interacted, adapted, and, in the case of the Great Antilles, synthesized to evolve into unique and complex cultures. Viewed through this lens, the Caribbean provides a rare instance where two versions of history, indigenous and nonindigenous, are complementary.

MESOAMERICA

The origins and subsequent development of Mesoamerica's indigenous peoples are best understood as part of broader cultural processes that took place on the continent. While most scholars agree that Mesoamerican indigenous peoples developed independently from the Old World civilizations up until Spanish contact in the early 16th century (the 11th-century Viking colony in Newfoundland apparently had no impact on Mesoamerica), others maintain that cultural similarities might be the result of incidental or intentional transoceanic contact. At the same time, countless regional variations have always existed in Mesoamerica, and apart from occasional phenomena that affected all of its inhabitants, such as drastic climatic change, each culture developed unique characteristics and changed at a different rate. Our current understanding of Mesoamerican native cultures is still limited to those areas that have been explored archaeologically, and while significant discoveries are constantly shaping the picture, many pieces of the puzzle are still missing.

Paleoindian Period (40,000?–8000 B.C.E.)

Humans did not evolve on the American continent but rather populated it as fully modern humans during the Late Pleistocene Ice Age and the Early Holocene period. Scholars mostly agree that there were one or more migrations from northeast Asia (Siberia) across the now submerged Bering Straits and south to the Americas through terrestrial corridors cleared of ice fields and by boat along the coastlines. The date of the initial migration, however, is still debated. There is clear evidence that humans were living in South and North America from at least 13,000 B.C.E., though some argue that the date could be as early as 40,000 B.C.E. At present, the most secure evidence for early human presence in Mesoamerica comes from the site of Iztapán, in the Basin of MEXICO, where hunter-gatherers hunted the now extinct mammoth some 10,000 years ago using projectiles with Clovis points (see CLOVIS CULTURE). Small groups of hunter-gatherers, who pursued big game and inhabited caves and rock shelters, spread from there throughout North and Central America. As the population increased, smaller groups started to break away and occupy the diverse ecological niches. Through time, this continuous process resulted in the linguistic and ethnic diversity that characterizes Mesoamerica to this day.

Archaic Period (8000–2500 B.C.E.)

Around 8000 B.C.E., the warmer climate of the Early Holocene allowed most of these early egalitarian groups to establish in a relatively defined territory, although they still moved each season. The remaining Pleistocene megafauna such as mammoths, mastodons, and wild horses were all hunted to extinction, and the hunters started to follow smaller game, such as deer, rabbits, birds, and iguanas. However, it was the plant gatherers (possibly WOMEN) who were responsible for one of the most important cultural revolutions in the Americas, that being the development of agriculture. This began with simple experiments in domesticating plants such as teosinte (wild maize), and it is possible that the cultigens thus produced were used initially for ritualistic purposes rather than as sources of FOOD.

The charred remains of plants and grinding stones found in Early Archaic caves in Tamaulipas, the Tehuacán Valley, and Oaxaca indicate that by 5000 B.C.E. the intentional cultivation of domesticates such as beans, squash, chilies, avocado, tomato, amaranth, and, most important, maize was well under way. The domestication of animals soon followed, and dogs and turkeys were bred as sources of food. Macrobands started to establish semisedentary camps next to these predictable and relatively secure sources of food, which in turn led to a gradual rise in population. By 3500 B.C.E. permanent settlements had appeared throughout the Gulf Coast and Central Mexico; pit houses dating to the end of the Archaic period have been discovered in this region. Other groups along the Pacific coast exploited the swampy coastal environment and built large shell mounds, which are among the earliest monumental constructions in Mesoamerica. The changes in settlement patterns and mobility also saw the beginnings of the Mesoamerican spiritual life, which included complex burial ceremonies and HUMAN SACRIFICE.

Formative (or Preclassic) Period
(2500 B.C.E.–300 C.E.)

Many of the archetypical "building blocks" that would distinguish Mesoamerica from the cultural areas of North, Central, and South America were developed during the Formative period. By 2500 B.C.E., the majority of the population of Central Mexico (and probably other regions) was gathered in horticultural villages but continued to practice hunting and gathering. Around this time the first pottery, a revolutionary technology that might have been adopted from non-Mesoamerican groups farther to the south, appeared along the western Pacific coast, then later in the Tehuacán Valley. Fired clay vessels largely replaced containers made from gourds and woven baskets; figurines for ritual purposes also began to be produced.

The transformation from dispersed villages to nucleated centers intensified, and settled life brought about faster community integration and the need to create communal spaces, such as a house dedicated for public gatherings and the ball court at the coastal site of Paso de la Amada. At the same time, people's different access to natural resources and the resulting accumulation of wealth heralded the onset of social stratification. There are clear signs that a ruling elite emerged in the Soconusco area and at San José Mogote in the Valley of Oaxaca around 1500 B.C.E.; these people's achieved or ascribed status and association with the divine realms allowed them to assume control over the majority of the population. Powerful elites lived in large houses built on raised platform mounds, controlled small chiefdoms of two or three-tiered settlement hierarchy, and exchanged luxury goods with rulers from other villages and regions. The Valley of Mexico also underwent major social transformation around 1200 B.C.E.; the pottery-laden burial sites at Tlatilco's cemetery attest to the spiritual and technological sophistication of this region's culture.

These Early Formative societies led to the development of the Olmec culture. The OLMECS inhabited the tropical Gulf coast of Veracruz and Tabasco from around 1200 to 500 B.C.E. Even if theirs was not the all-inventive Mesoamerican "mother culture" as previously thought, the Olmecs still stood above all others with their extensive settlements, such as San Lorenzo and La Venta, where they erected monumental pyramids and colossal sculptures dedicated to their rulers. The Olmecs also participated in an interregional trading network, and their religious symbols circulated on decorated ceramic vessels and carved greenstone celts. One chiefdom with which the Olmec interacted was located at Chalcatzingo in Morelos, where the Gulf Coast and Central Mexico cultures had blended.

As the Olmec culture began to decline around 500 B.C.E. (for reasons still unknown), the Maya culture emerged in the lowlands of GUATEMALA and northern BELIZE. Ruler-priests in cities such as Cuello and Nakbé took the lead, while massive pyramids adorned with stucco masks representing deities or rulers were erected in Late Formative cities such as Cerros and EL MIRADOR.

To support the growing population around these civic-ceremonial centers, the Maya developed a sophisticated agricultural intensification system of raised fields.

The ZAPOTECS, in the Valley of Oaxaca, invented the first known writing system and sacred calendar in the Americas around 600 B.C.E. and shortly thereafter established the first imperial state, which originated at MONTE ALBÁN. At the same time, the Valley of Mexico saw the emergence of warring city-states, but these were soon overshadowed by the rise of the powerful theocratic state of TEOTIHUACÁN after its rival city, Cuicuilco, was destroyed by a volcanic eruption around 100 B.C.E.

The Classic Period (300–900 C.E.)

The cultural elements developed during the Formative period were formalized during the Classic period. Between 300 and 600 C.E., Teotihuacán grew to be one of the most influential religious and political centers in ancient Mesoamerica and one of the largest CITIES in the world. Its inhabitants exported fine green obsidian along with their military-religious ideology as far as Oaxaca and Guatemala; evidence of their presence can be found in the ARCHITECTURE and inscriptions of Monte Albán, KAMINALJUYÚ, and TIKAL. At the same time, Zapotecs and Maya formed artisan neighborhoods in Teotihuacán. Early in the Classic period, Cholula similarly emerged as an important religious center; it combined elements of the Gulf Coast, Maya, and Central Mexico cultures.

The Classic period is perhaps best known for the florescence of the lowland Maya people, who created the most complex writing system and calendar known in the Americas, the recent decipherment of which has revolutionized our understanding of Maya culture. Although once considered as the apogee of Mesoamerican civilizations in terms of ART, architecture, mathematics, and astronomy, it is now also known that the Classic Maya practiced intense interpolity WARFARE and human sacrifice. In this period of shifting dominance and alliances between the numerous Maya city-states, the antagonistic cities of Tikal and CALAKMUL emerged as "super-states" in the Petén region. Powerful royal lineages emerged in other important Maya cities such as COPÁN and Palenque, both of which extended their political influence through conquest and marital alliances.

The cultural and natural landscape started to change notably around 500 C.E., when the overpopulation of Mesoamerican cities led to disease, malnutrition, and high mortality rates. At the same time, the overexploited environments called for a redistribution of food products from the hinterland to the nonproducing urban sectors. Additionally, a period of severe drought began at about this time and lasted until the 11th century. Teotihuacán was among the first great cities to be affected; the ceremonial center was attacked and burned by 600 and then left mostly abandoned. Monte Albán held up until 800, when construction stopped and its inhabitants left for other centers in the Valley of Oaxaca.

In the Maya lowlands, the fragile ecosystem rapidly reached its maximum carrying capacity; warfare between city-states in search of new resources became endemic and only added to the friction between the ruling elite and commoners. Around 800, the lowland Maya centers began to collapse; glyphic inscriptions stop at about 900. Although some Maya kingdoms in Belize and elsewhere seem to have remained fairly intact, the majority of the lowland Petén cities were completely abandoned, with many people migrating north to the Yucatán Peninsula. Still, in the two centuries following the fall of Teotihuacán, other cities grew. The numerous ball courts at El Tajín on the Gulf coast, for example, attest to that city's religious and political importance during this transitional period.

The Postclassic Period (900–1521 C.E.)

Following the Classic-period abandonment of major cities, the Postclassic period began with large migrations of people across the landscape and the reorganization of the political structure. Independent polities started to interact through a shared market ECONOMY and religious ideology, each with well-defined territory and specialized economic activities. Trade was commercialized and long-distance POCHTECA merchants moved obsidian, pottery, salt, CACAO, and cloth to the farthest reaches of Mesoamerica (see TEXTILES).

Maritime trade networks developed along the coastlines of Mesoamerica and lower Central America, probably as far as South America. Luxury goods previously procurable only by the elite gradually became available to most commoners in the open market economy. Although warfare between city-states was still endemic, a new "international" style of religious symbols developed, integrating the different ethnic groups in Mesoamerica into a single "world system." This might have involved the introduction of a unified Mesoamerican religion surrounding the cult of QUETZALCÓATL, the Feathered Serpent deity, whose major religious center was located at the Great Pyramid of Cholula.

At about 900, the TOLTECS stepped up to fill the political and economic vacuum left by the fall of Teotihuacán; they soon controlled Central Mexico from their capital in Tollan (see TULA). Similar to their predecessors, Toltec military conquests and religious ideology reached far and wide, mainly through a long-distance exchange network encompassing the U.S. Southwest to HONDURAS. The Maya royal lineages reemerged around Lake Petén-Itzá, the highland regions of Guatemala, and the Yucatán Peninsula, where the inhabitants of the dominant city of CHICHÉN ITZÁ interacted closely with the Toltecs; Chichén Itzá itself showed a close resemblance to Tollan. In the Mixtec area, a large unified kingdom was created during the 11th century by Lord Eight Deer "Jaguar Claw" from his vast city of Tututepec; he, too, might have legitimized his rule through the Toltecs. The expansion of the MIXTECS was also notable in the Valley of Oaxaca, where lavishly decorated cities such as Mitla demonstrate a mixture of Zapotec and Mixtec cultural traditions.

Yet another major shift occurred in Mesoamerica around 1200, when these and other centers declined for reasons that might be linked with climatic change. Around the same time, migrant groups from the northern deserts entered the Valley of Mexico; among these newcomers was the small Mexica tribe that would later form the mighty Aztec Empire (see AZTECS). The previous "international" style had transformed into the geometric and highly standardized Mixteca-Puebla iconographic style, which was expressed on polychrome ceramics, CODICES, and murals. This religious-ideological set of symbols was less dependent on phonetic components than the Formative- and Classic-period writing systems and thus was shared between numerous linguistic groups, from northern Mexico to NICARAGUA.

In Yucatán, the city of MAYAPÁN replaced Chichén Itzá as the regional capital, the massive defensive wall surrounding the former indicating a period of unrest and large-scale warfare. Soon after the violent collapse of Mayapán in 1441, Postclassic Maya society again fragmented into smaller city-states, while in the Guatemalan highlands the K'iche' (Quiché) Maya from the Gulf of Mexico established their capital at Utatlán; they, too, claimed Toltec ancestry. In the late 15th century, the Zapotecs of Oaxaca broadened their influence to the Isthmus of Tehuantepec, where they established a powerful kingdom. The Tarascans of Tzintzuntzán also succeeded in establishing a large conquest empire in western Mexico and developed techniques for working copper and bronze.

Overshadowing all these Late Postclassic developments was the emergence of the most powerful indigenous group in Mesoamerican history, the Aztecs. In less than 150 years, these late migrants to Central Mexico had formed an enormous empire that extended over much of present-day Mexico and ruled over hundreds of indigenous communities. The Aztec Empire was dominated by a TRIPLE ALLIANCE between the cities of Texcoco, Tlacopan, and TENOCHTITLÁN; nevertheless, it was the warlike Mexica people of Tenochtitlán who soon took the lead. In addition to a powerful conquering army, the Aztecs extended their control through a complex web of marital alliances throughout Mesoamerica and traded with groups that did not form part of their empire, such as the Tarascans and the Tlaxcalans (see TLAXCALA).

Agricultural intensification and urbanization in the Valley of Mexico triggered rapid population increase, and by the late 15th century there were about 1.6 million people living in the valley alone. The empire came to an abrupt end, however, when in 1521 a handful of Spaniards and tens of thousands of indigenous auxiliaries conquered Tenochtitlán and took over the empire (see CONQUEST). This year is often regarded as the end of the pre-Columbian era in Mesoamerica and the beginning of the colonial period. Still, despite the alarming mortality rate among the indigenous from exploitation and DISEASES during the first decades of the conquest, Mesoamerican people prevailed by adapting to drastic change and assimilating the Old World into their millenary cultures.

SOUTH AMERICA

Human occupation of the Americas resulted from the migration of nomadic groups across the Bering Strait by means of a temporary land bridge at least 14,000 years ago. It was once widely thought that North America was the site of the first human settlement; however, more recent archaeological deductions indicate that migration down the Andean spine of South America may have facilitated some of the earliest human settlements. For instance, evidence from around MONTE VERDE, CHILE, which hosted some two dozen settlers between 12,800–11,800 B.C.E., has swayed scholarly opinion in favor of a migratory pattern in a much more southward trajectory. Other than the Paleoindian tribes in Monte Verde and El Abra in COLOMBIA, scant evidence exists of the Americas' earliest peoples, hunter-gatherers at the end of the last ice age. Over the successive millennia several dozen Native American civilizations staked out a distinctive identity before European contact. From what is known, these societies' level of sophistication depended largely on the discoveries of previous civilizations. The comingling and success of various Native American groups over time eventually produced some impressive results. At the time of the Spaniards' arrival, the Inca Empire was highly accomplished, as indicated by their mathematics, agricultural and farming techniques, and overland trade networks (see INCAS).

The Norte Chico culture is widely believed to have been the first large-scale civilization to emerge in South America, around 3000 B.C.E. Some 30 well-populated hubs of the Norte Chico flourished in northern PERU, before the civilization collapsed around 1800 B.C.E. At roughly the same time, the Valdivia culture emerged near the modern-day town of Valdivia, ECUADOR. The Valdivian people grew maize, beans, and other vegetables. They also created ceramics, which became increasingly elaborate over the centuries. The CHAVÍN culture followed the Valdivia and the Norte Chico, populating coastal Peru and influencing a much larger swath of the littoral Andes from roughly 900 to 200 B.C.E. Existing at about the same time as the ancient Egyptians, the Chavín employed advanced metallurgical techniques, wove textiles to make cloth, practiced agriculture, and had an extensive trade network. These achievements, coupled with the domestication of the llama, helped lay the foundation for successive advances of Native American cultures in South America.

The MOCHE culture occupied the northern coast of Peru between 100 and 800 C.E. The civilization was in many respects fragmented, as it did not feature a centralized political authority and operated mainly as a loose affiliation of communities that were notable for their creation of mold technology, painted ceramics, gold crafts, and extensive irrigation systems. The Huaca del Sol, an enormous pyramid-shaped adobe, is believed by many to be the largest pre-Columbian structure in Peru, though it was heavily damaged by the first Spanish arrivals.

The WARI (Huari) people populated the highlands and coast of southern Peru, from 500 to 900 C.E. The Wari capital was just north of modern-day Ayacucho, though the society's most well-preserved ruins are near Quinua and the town of Pikillaqta, a short distance southeast of Cuzco en route to Lake Titicaca. Scholars believe the Wari developed an advanced sociopolitical hierarchy, with different administrative divisions between the main poles of the civilization. The Wari utilized terraced fielding techniques and an extensive road network that was a significant legacy for the Incas when they began to expand in the area several centuries later.

The MUISCA confederation dominated the eastern highlands of Colombia in the century before Spanish contact in 1537. The Muisca inhabited an area equivalent in size to modern-day Switzerland and spoke a language known as Chibcha, believed by linguists to be older than Aramaic. The confederation seems to have been efficiently administered, and the governance of the Muisca was notable because it neither featured a monarch nor sought territorial expansion or the subjugation of other tribes. The Muisca economy was vibrant, centering on local and long-distance trade, the MINING OF EMERALDS, coal, copper, salt, and GOLD; these commodities immediately spurred Spanish interest and provided the primary evidence for the mythological city of EL DORADO.

The Inca Empire was the largest civilization in the Americas at the time of European contact. It arose in the Peruvian Andes in the 13th century, with the Incas quickly coopting or conquering other ethnic groups and vast swaths of South America, especially along the Andes. From 1483 through about 1533, the Inca Empire swelled to include parts of modern-day ARGENTINA, BOLIVIA, Chile, Colombia, Ecuador, and Peru. The empire (called Tawantinsuyu) was governed under a federal system partitioned into four quadrants, with the capital located in Cuzco. The chief language of the Incas was QUECHUA, though literally dozens, if not hundreds, of local languages were spoken in the empire.

Under the governance of PACHACUTI INCA YUPANQUI, who reigned from 1438 to 1471, the size of the Inca kingdom grew extensively. Pachacuti shrewdly reconnoitered the lands of neighboring civilizations and often made overtures to the royal classes. In many cases, he offered to induct them into the royal hierarchy of the Incas and promised increased wealth for the entire society if they came under the cloak of the Sapa Inca. Recognizing the hegemony of the Incas, most acceded to their demands, swelling the ranks of the noble class and coopting other domains under the Inca umbrella.

The Incas created a large, smooth-running economy based on exchange and taxation of certain goods. Much scholarship on the Inca economy indicated that the civilization adopted a form of socialism to ensure that the basic needs of all were met; however, more recent research on the topic complicates the matter, and the degree to which socialism was practiced seems to have varied. Regardless, studies indicate that the Incas enjoyed an extensive trade network, which was impressive given both the vastness of the empire and the ruggedness of the terrain in the Andean highlands, that ensured a free flow of goods throughout Inca lands and the specialization of goods by producers.

Inca society featured many refinements and notable innovations in the fields of architecture, agriculture, engineering, and mathematics. Various terraced fielding techniques, developed by previous civilizations and used widely by the Incas, ensured that agricultural staples were grown in the mountainous terrain that was naturally ill suited to sustainable food production. They also adapted irrigation techniques to improve the production of maize, squash, tomatoes, peanuts, chilies, melons, COT-TON, and POTATOES.

Architecture was viewed as the highest form of art by the Incas, whose large-scale stone works resulted in the creation of MACHU PICCHU and other sites, which had enormous stone temples. Beyond temples and housing, the sophisticated understanding of construction led to the creation of two enormous road systems, one through the highlands running essentially the length of Peru for more than 3,200 miles (5,150 km) and a coastal road that ran some 2,500 miles (4,023 km). This made communication and TRANSPORTATION very rapid; messengers could be expected to travel some 150 miles (241 km) a day (see CHASQUI). When the Spanish first encountered the Incas in 1536, their appetite for conquest was peaked by the immense achievements of the Incas and the enormous reach of their empire, spanning more than 15,000 square miles (38,850 km²) and including 9–14 million inhabitants.

See also ARAUCANIANS (Vol. II); CHICHIMECAS (Vol. II); NATIVE AMERICANS (Vols. II, III, IV).

—Roberto Múrako Borrero
Sean H. Goforth
Danny Zborover

Further reading:

Susan Toby Evans. *Ancient Mexico and Central America: Archaeology and Culture History* (London: Thames & Hudson, 2004).

Kim MacQuarrie. *The Last Days of the Incas* (New York: Simon & Schuster, 2007).

Charles C. Mann. *1491: New Revelations of the Americas before Columbus* (New York: Knopf, 2005).

Jerald T. Milanich and Susan Milbrath. *First Encounters: Spanish Explorations in the Caribbean and the United States, 1492–1570* (Gainesville: University of Florida Press, 1989).

Irving Rouse. *The Tainos: Rise and Decline of the People Who Greeted Columbus* (New Haven, Conn.: Yale University Press, 1992).

Samuel M. Wilson, ed. *The Indigenous People of the Caribbean* (Gainesville: University Press of Florida, 1999).

Nazca lines The Nazca lines are immense ground drawings, also called "geoglyphs," which cover approximately 400 square miles (1,036 km²) of the Nazca desert on the southern coast of PERU. This archaeological mystery had been studied since the lines were first brought to scholarly attention during the 1920s. By far, the most common are the 762 extremely straight lines, often several kilometers long, which radiate from 62 central points called "ray centers." Others geoglyphs include 227 geometric and abstract designs, such as zigzags, spirals, triangles, and trapezoids, one of which is as long as 10 football fields. Additionally, there are several human figures positioned on hillsides, and over 50 zoomorphic and botanical geoglyphs, such as flowers, birds, fish, a monkey, and a spider; the largest is the figure of a cormorant, which is about 985 feet (300 m) long.

The majority of the geoglyphs were created between 200 B.C.E. and 600 C.E. by the local Nazca people. They used a simple method of creating the lines by clearing and rearranging stones and the sun-baked dark topsoil, thus exposing the lighter subsurface. Still, the Nazca lines are the result of hundreds of years of continuous practice, and many are superimposed by later ones. While the human figures might have been created first, the lines and geometric designs are clearly later than the animals, which might have been created between 600 and 1000 C.E., or as late as the 15th century.

Although archaeologists now better understand how, when, and who created the geoglyphs, the reason why still baffles those who study them. Their monumental size, along with the fact that they can be best seen from higher elevations, has attracted some wild theories, including spaceships, and suggestions that the Nazca used some kind of hot-air balloons. Recent experiments have shown that the process of creating the large figures was in fact quite straightforward and could have been accomplished by a small group of people using simple instruments.

Some scholars have attemped to understand the phenomenon in its cultural context and immediate natural surroundings. One of the earliest interpretations was that the lines served as a giant agricultural calendar, with the lines directed toward celestial events such as sunsets and rising stars; however, more recent studies have demonstrated that only some of the lines could have had astronomical significance, while others probably functioned as ceremonial pathways for pilgrims in a fashion similar to today's pilgrimages common among indigenous Andean people. In addition to the lines, several archaeological sites of the Nazca culture have been excavated (such as the pilgrimage center of Cahuachi), and their polychrome CERAMICS have been collected from along the lines. It has been further demonstrated that the ray centers were located adjacent to streambeds and foothills, while trapezoids were closely associated with water flow and might have served in rituals to summon water to the arid land. Similar theories link the animal geoglyphs to fertility cults and the worship of mountains as the creators of water and to the humid tropical forest iconography that appears on Nazcan ceramics and TEXTILES. Thus, the Nazca lines might have been a precursor to the Inca ZEQUE system, which combined all of these elements, though on a much smaller scale.

—Danny Zborover

Further reading:

Anthony Aveni. *Between the Lines: The Mystery of the Giant Ground Drawings of Ancient Nasca, Peru* (Austin: University of Texas Press, 2000).

New Granada   See COLOMBIA.

New Laws of 1542

The New Laws of 1542 were a series of laws designed at the request of Fray BARTOLOMÉ DE LAS CASAS, which aimed to prevent the brutal exploitation of the indigenous peoples under the repressive ENCOMIENDA system. Meant to replace the 1512 LAWS OF BURGOS and eventually eliminate the *encomienda* system, the 1542 laws were met with fierce resistance in the New World, forcing the Crown ultimately to rescind many of them, at least in part.

As the CONQUEST of the New World progressed, there were many complaints from clergymen about the conquistadores' and settlers' abuses of the indigenous peoples. Chief among the critics of the Spanish regime in the New World, the Dominican friar Las Casas incessantly petitioned the Crown to do something to correct the abuses of the *encomienda* system. These New Laws, as they came to be called, were issued as the result of a reform movement begun in Spain to correct the abuses and failures of the old laws of Burgos and thus ensure the protection and freedom of Amerindians, especially those living in the newly conquered mainland colonies. Las Casas's ultimate goal was the eradication of the *encomienda* system, which forced the indigenous peoples into almost slavelike tribute and LABOR relations with their Spanish conquerors.

The New Laws were passed in 1542 and amended in 1543. They contained regulations that addressed the reform and restriction of the *encomienda* system; among the most important of these was the strict prohibition against Indian SLAVERY. Other provisions limited *encomienda* grants to one's lifetime; however, this provision was later amended to permit the renewal for a second lifetime only. These provisions, if enforced, would have led to the gradual abolition of the *encomienda* system in the New World within a generation or two. The New Laws also prohibited the forced labor of indigenous peoples on plantations and in the mines (see MINING). They also required that all indigenous labor be paid a fair wage, and that Indian tribute payments and taxes be assessed fairly and moderately.

The reaction to the promulgation of the New Laws in the Spanish colonies was violent and swift. In PERU, GONZALO PIZARRO and other supporters rose up in revolt against the Spanish Crown, and this eventually led to the overthrow of the royal official (VICEROY) sent to govern the region of Peru, Blasco Núñez Vela, who attempted to enforce the laws. The viceroy in New Spain (MEXICO), ANTONIO DE MENDOZA, more wisely decided to mitigate against a possible revolt by suppressing the New Laws and their enforcement. Applying the informal right to "obey but not comply" (*obedezco pero no cumplo*), Viceroy Mendoza averted what could have been a disastrous rebellion in New Spain.

Alarmed by the negative reaction of the colonists in the New World, on October 20, 1545, King Charles I reluctantly decided to suppress more than 30 of the New Laws' most disputed regulations. With the repeal of these regulations, the *encomienda* system and the quasilegal exploitation of the indigenous people of the New World continued. Nevertheless, some of the more lasting reforms, such as the prohibition against Indian slavery, were strictly enforced, which limited some of the most notorious abuses of the Spanish colonial system. In the end, the New Laws had mixed results; though not strictly enforced, they did tend to mitigate the most flagrant abuses of indigenous rights during the remainder of the colonial period.

—John F. Chuchiak IV

Further reading:

Lesley Byrd Simpson. *The Encomienda in New Spain* (Berkeley: University of California Press, 1966).

Henry Stevens, ed. *The New Laws of the Indies* (London: Chiswick Press, 1893).

New Spain   See MEXICO.

Nicaragua

Nicaragua is aptly nicknamed the "land of lakes and volcanoes." Two great lakes partly fill the Nicaragua Depression: the vast Lake Nicaragua (known in ancient times as Cocibolca) and the smaller Lake Managua (once known as Xolotlán). The depression stretches diagonally across the entire country, from the Gulf of Fonseca, past the lakes, and down the Río San Juan to the Caribbean. Tectonic forces also created the extraordinary chain of volcanoes that stretches across the country along the depression.

Nicaragua divides naturally into several major physiographic zones. The Pacific coastal lowlands, including the area around the lakes, are hot and humid with deep fertile soil; this region carried the largest human populations in prehistory. The central highlands consist of rugged volcanic mountains interspersed with lush, fertile valleys. The wide Atlantic coastal lowlands are watered by broad meandering rivers that run down from the rain forest-clad hills to the sandy coastal lagoons covered by scrub pine.

Culturally and archaeologically, Nicaragua combines multiple varieties of Mesoamerican, South American, and other indigenous traditions. The Spanish left several chronicles describing the native peoples of Nicaragua (see CHRONICLERS). Colonial chronicles say that the peoples of the Pacific lowlands were emigrants from Mesoamerica. The Chorotegas apparently moved in from Central MEXICO after 700 c.e. Chorotega is an Otomanguean language, one of a diverse group of languages in Mesoamerica. The Subtiabas, who lived near modern León, spoke a language closely related to Tlapanec, another Otomanguean language that is still spoken in the Mexican state of Guerrero. The most recent immigrants were NAHUATL-speaking peoples related to the AZTECS. They immigrated during the Postclassic period (1000–1519), displacing some of the earlier migrants. All these peoples brought Mesoamerican cultural traits with them and interacted with other Mesoamerican peoples.

The peoples of the central highlands and Atlantic slope were culturally distinctive. Their languages belong to the Misumalpan and the Chibchan families. The former includes Matagalapan, Miskito, and Sumu. The Matagalpas occupied a large part of the north-central highlands. The Miskitos and Sumus still live in northeastern Nicaragua. The Chibchan speakers included the Ramas, who still live in small numbers on the east-central Atlantic coast. The indigenous cultures of central and eastern Nicaragua possess a complex mix of autochthonous traits and Costa Rican and Panamanian cultural patterns (see COSTA RICA; PANAMA).

The outline of Nicaraguan prehistory is incomplete. Virtually nothing is known of the Paleoindian and Archaic periods. The wide Caribbean lowlands have for the most part not been explored by archaeologists. Most research has been undertaken in the Pacific coastal lowlands, especially around Rivas, Masaya, and Granada and on the islands of Lake Nicaragua. For example, on Ometepe Island in Lake Nicaragua a ceramic sequence extending deep into the Formative period has been recovered (see CERAMICS). The earliest pieces appear to be related to the early ceramic complexes of the Pacific coast of GUATEMALA and Chiapas. Later Formative materials include TRADE goods typical of southern Mesoamerica. The ceramics corresponding to the Mesoamerican Classic period (250–1000) include a wide variety of well-made and iconographically complex polychrome types. The iconographic motifs and symbolism become progressively more Mesoamerican in character with time. The Postclassic materials share

decorative patterns with the widespread Mixteca-Puebla style of the Mesoamerican Late Postclassic period, although overall technique, forms, composition, and execution remain indigenous.

Mound complexes were common in the Pacific lowlands and the north-central highlands in later prehistory. The most famous sites in the country are ceremonial complexes that include elaborately carved monumental standing stones. The carvings from the great lakes region usually include a main anthropomorphic figure with an associated animal, often interpreted as a familiar spirit or alter-ego. The most famous of these sites are those on Zapatera Island in Lake Nicaragua.

See also NICARAGUA (Vols. II, III, IV).

—Clifford T. Brown

Further reading:
Frederick W. Lange, et al. *The Archaeology of Pacific Nicaragua* (Albuquerque: University of New Mexico Press, 1992).

Nicuesa, Diego de (b. ca. 1464–d. 1511) *Spanish conquistador and first governor of Castilla del Oro*

Diego de Nicuesa was a Spanish conquistador with close ties to the Spanish Crown. He was intent on colonizing the area known as the Tierra Firme on the northern tip of South America. This same area was nicknamed "Castilla del Oro," a name given to the region based on CHRISTOPHER COLUMBUS's claims of rich GOLD deposits.

The Spanish Crown decided that the Tierra Firme would be governed by two men: Diego de Nicuesa was granted the province of Castilla del Oro, and ALONSO DE OJEDA was awarded New Andalusia. However, the king failed to specify the precise demarcation line between the two territories.

On arrival in the New World, Nicuesa turned out to be a disastrous navigator whose arrogance prevented him from recognizing his mistakes, even in the face of his crews' pleas. Stranded on the Panamanian coast, Nicuesa and his crew were nearly destroyed by starvation and Amerindian attacks (see PANAMA). Eventually, a rescue fleet retrieved them, and from then on, Nicuesa governed his colony with an iron fist. Nevertheless, the settlement eventually failed. The Spanish Crown then ordered Nicuesa to govern Ojeda's former colony, Nueva Antigua. When the residents of the struggling society heard of Nicuesa's merciless and arrogant ways, they trapped him and sent him back to HISPANIOLA in 1511. However, the ship never reached the island, and Nicuesa was never heard from or seen again.

—Christina Hawkins

obsidian Obsidian, or fine black or gray volcanic glass, was among the most prized goods in pre-Columbian Mesoamerica. Obsidian is largely silicon dioxide, sometimes streaked with green or brown by the presence of iron or magnesium, and is used by modern eye surgeons for its ability to form a sharp edge.

In pre-Columbian Mesoamerica, pieces of obsidian of six to eight inches (15–20 cm) in size were typically reduced by hammering to a "core." From the core, pressure flaking with wood, bone, or antler produced long (eight-inch [20.3 km]) blades of a thin cross-section, which had two sharp edges, like a double-edge razor. These obsidian blades may have been sharper than steel, since pressure flaking produces edges to a thinness of a few molecules.

Obsidian blades were widely used for cutting and dressing meat. Likewise, they were embedded in the heads of wooden war clubs (see WARFARE). Members of the elite used larger pieces of obsidian as mirrors. MAYA elites also used obsidian blades during ritual bloodletting ceremonies.

Obsidian was prized among the pre-Columbian indigenous peoples of Mesoamerica and was traded throughout the area (see TRADE). Control of obsidian sources became a powerful source of economic wealth for CITIES such as KAMINALJUYÚ and TEOTIHUACÁN (see ECONOMY). The most important known ancient obsidian sources were the highland GUATEMALA volcanoes El Chayal, near Guatemala City; Ixtepeque, in eastern Guatemala; and San Martín Jilotepeque, in western Guatemala.

Obsidian sources show a unique chemistry that links the obsidian to the particular volcano in which it formed. Laboratory tests can determine the chemical makeup of obsidian by neutron activation analysis, allowing archaeologists not only to determine its source but also to highlight trade routes and trading partners.

—Walter R. T. Witschey

Further reading:

Arthur Demarest. *Ancient Maya: The Rise and Fall of a Rainforest Civilization* (Cambridge: Cambridge University Press, 2004).

Ojeda, Alonso de (b. ca. 1465–d. 1515) *Spanish conquistador and first governor of New Andalusia* Born ca. 1465 into a family of the minor nobility, Alonso de Ojeda made a name for himself by accompanying CHRISTOPHER COLUMBUS on his second journey to the New World in 1493. As a teenager, Ojeda had worked his way up the ranks in the home of the duke of Medinaceli. By establishing influential contacts, Ojeda earned his passage on the voyage with Columbus. He returned to Spain in 1496; however, three years later, in 1499, Ojeda journeyed back to the New World. This time, he had his own mission with Juan de la Cosa, an important ally to the Crown and Ojeda's close friend.

Once settled in the New Granada area (which corresponded roughly to what is now the Colombian city of Cartagena), Ojeda's men attempted to subjugate and convert the indigenous population to Christianity. Their efforts met with fierce resistance, with the Indians mounting a series of counterattacks. Almost all of Ojeda's men were killed, including de la Cosa. While in a sorry state of defeat, Ojeda was spotted by a Spanish force offshore, led by his competitor, DIEGO DE NICUESA; Nicuesa sent aid to the struggling settlement. Ojeda subsequently avenged the murder of de la Cosa by leading a massacre against the Amerindians.

Over time, the settlement of New Andalusia came under several indigenous attacks by warriors armed with poisonous arrows. The settlers also suffered from starvation and other hardships. Eventually, Ojeda lost control of the colony and was replaced by Martín Fernández de Enciso.

—Christina Hawkins

Further reading:
Martin Dugard. *The Last Voyage of Columbus* (New York: Little, Brown & Co., 2005).

Olmecs The Olmec culture thrived along the tropical southern Gulf coast and on the floodplains of Veracruz and Tabasco from about 1200 to 500 b.c.e. The term *Olmec* is also used broadly to refer to a widespread style of ART found at archaeological sites from the Basin of MEXICO and Guerrero on the Pacific to GUATEMALA and EL SALVADOR. Its early florescence and distinct style had previously established the Olmec culture as the Mesoamerican "Mother Culture," although more recent theories have linked these developments to large-scale processes that occurred during the Formative period (1500 b.c.e.–250 c.e.).

The archaeological record suggests that Olmec society was organized into chiefdoms and that the Olmecs' diet consisted of MAIZE, beans, squash, fish, dogs, deer, rabbits, and iguanas. The Olmecs might have been the first to erect stone monuments in Mesoamerica. Due to the humid lowland conditions and the accumulation of sediments, small Olmec villages with no monumental ARCHITECTURE are extremely hard to locate, and archaeologists' knowledge is limited to only a handful of sites, the largest being San Lorenzo and La Venta. San Lorenzo was built on an artificially modified hill and was occupied from 1150 to 900 b.c.e. Archaeologists have found large houses dedicated to public gatherings erected on low platforms there. La Venta flourished later (900–500 b.c.e.), and there, archaeologists have found pyramids and monumental structures, plazas, stone mosaic pavements, tombs with jadeite caches, and tabletop thrones. These sites also had subsurface stone conduits through which freshwater was distributed to the elite.

Recent discoveries of epi-Olmec glyphic texts from the region suggest that the Olmec language was related to the Mixe-Zoquean group of linguistic families. While *Olmec* is a late NAHUATL term meaning "people of the rubber land," it is still not known what Olmecs called themselves. Regardless, the area is true to its Nahuatl name; the Olmecs exploited the rich rubber sap, which they traded throughout the region (see TRADE). Rubber balls found at the Olmec site of El Manatí provide the earliest evidence for the practice of the Mesoamerican

ball game (see MAYA). The Olmecs also produced some of Mesoamerica's first and finest ART, including small jadeite statues, fine CERAMICS, and carved stone stelae, as well as the famous colossal stone heads. The last are larger-than-life portraits of Olmec rulers wearing their typical headgear. The basalt for these multiton sculptures was extracted from the distant Tuxtla Mountains, although how it was transported remains unknown.

Olmec religious iconography deals with zoomorphic and anthropomorphic representations, such as feline motifs, a crocodilian earth deity, and a water deity represented by a sharklike monster (see RELIGION). Among the most curious are the widespread "baby face" figurines, some carved out of wood, as those found at the El Manatí bog as ceremonial offerings. Olmec ritualistic and mythical imagery are often found in caves or on natural rock faces. The reasons for the eventual decline of Olmec culture around 500 b.c.e. are still uncertain, although it seems that the later Classic Maya elite were influenced by their Olmec predecessors.

—Danny Zborover

Further reading:
Christopher A. Pool. *Olmec Archaeology and Early Mesoamerica* (Cambridge: Cambridge University Press, 2007).

Orellana, Francisco de (b. 1511–d. 1546) *Spanish conquistador, first European to navigate the Amazon River, and founder of Guayaquil* Born in Trujillo, Spain, in 1511, Francisco de Orellana was a childhood friend and, by some accounts, a distant cousin of FRANCISCO PIZARRO. In 1527, at the age of 17, Orellana left Spain and sailed to the Indies. In 1533, he joined Pizarro's forces in PERU and quickly distinguished himself by helping quell the revolt of DIEGO DE ALMAGRO (see CIVIL WARS IN PERU). After Pizarro defeated Almagro's forces, Orellana was appointed governor of La Caluta and successfully reestablished the port city of Guayaquil, ECUADOR, which had twice been sacked by native peoples.

In 1541, Orellana was appointed one of GONZALO PIZARRO's lieutenants on a voyage east of Quito, into the South American hinterland in search of EL DORADO, the mythic City of Gold, as well as the Land of Cinnamon. Orellana's mandate was to scout the Coca River, but his men threatened to mutiny if he did not proceed farther. In response, Orellana ordered the construction of a larger sailing vessel, and the expedition soon followed the Coca River into the Napo River, then into the Negro River on June 3, 1542. From there the force continued, sailing into the Amazon River. Orellana bestowed the name *AMAZON* because of the repeated attacks on the expedition by female warriors reminiscent of the mythological Amazons (see AMAZON WOMEN). Despite improbable odds, Orellana managed to navigate the length of the Amazon, reaching the river's mouth on August 24, 1542.

A small tributary of the Amazon River in Peru *(Courtesy of J. Michael Francis)*

Soon thereafter, Orellana returned to Europe. He landed first in Portugal, where the Portuguese king tried to persuade him to return to the Americas as the leader of a Portuguese expedition. Balking at the idea, Orellana made his way to Spain. Orellana's discoveries highlighted one of the primary tensions of the era—territorial claims in the Americas by both Spain and Portugal, which the Treaty of Tordesillas had only partially resolved. The Spanish king, Charles I, appointed Orellana as governor of the Amazonian region, which was dubbed New Andalusia, and chartered another expedition to the area for settlement by 300 men and 100 horses, with the objective of founding two cities. Orellana's new fleet of four vessels set sail on May 11, 1545, only making it to Brazil in December after a harrowing journey. Once there, the following year was marked by intermittent attempts to explore the Amazon Delta, although the harsh conditions devastated the expedition. Of the 300 men who started out, only 44 survived to be rescued by a Spanish ship the following year; Orellana had died sometime in November 1546.

—Sean H. Goforth

Further reading:

Anthony Smith. *Explorers of the Amazon* (Chicago: University of Chicago Press, 1994).

P

Pachacuti Inca Yupanqui (d. 1471) *Inca emperor* Pachacuti Inca Yupanqui acceded to rulership after his victory over the Chanca in 1438 and remained in power until 1471. The most notable project Pachacuti undertook as Sapa Inca was the rebuilding of the city of Cuzco. The Spanish writer Juan de Betanzos offers a vivid account of this, depicting Pachacuti as a far-sighted urban planner and effective organizer of LABOR. Pachacuti first outlined the city and made a clay model to show how he wanted it built. He then mobilized a crew of 50,000 workers, who labored for 20 years, from the first improvements of channeling the Tullumayo and Saphy Rivers that flow through Cuzco until the completion of the building program. When the city was finished, Pachacuti held a town meeting and assigned houses and lots to members of Cuzco's nobility and to all other residents. He had people of lower social rank settle between the Temple of the Sun (Coricancha) and the point where the two rivers joined. Pachacuti named this section of his city Hurin Cuzco (lower Cuzco); the far end was called Pumachupa, which means "lion's tail." The area from the Temple of the Sun on up, between the two rivers to the hill of Sacsayhuamán, he distributed among the prominent lords of his lineage and his own direct descendants. This section became Hanan Cuzco (upper Cuzco). Based on this description, Cuzco's new layout is understood as visualizing the body of a puma, with its tail at Pumachupa and its head at Sacsayhuamán.

Pachacuti's other significant accomplishments were early territorial expansions to the southeast and northwest, as well as the formulation of a political landscape and sacred geography. Pachacuti commissioned the construction of various royal estates in the Urubamba Valley, the most famous of which is MACHU PICCHU.

—Jessica Christie

pajé The shamans of the indigenous peoples of Amazonia and neighboring regions were known as *pajés* (from the TUPÍ-GUARANÍ word for "spiritual leader"). *Pajés* were the repositories of special knowledge about the world and were intermediaries between the human and supernatural worlds. The peoples of the tropical forest, despite their different cultures, languages, and ethnicity, generally considered the natural environment to be inhabited by spirits that interacted not only with humans but also with plants, animals, rivers, and other elements of the landscape (see AMAZON). *Pajés* were highly regarded by their societies and respected for their ability to heal; as a result, they were often rewarded with political authority and material wealth. Since in many cultures it was believed that sickness was caused by enemy sorcerers or witches, *pajés* also led military expeditions against the groups they claimed were responsible (see WITCHCRAFT).

Pajés underwent years of apprenticeship with established shamans, often secluded from the rest of the community. This training likely included the mastery of a large volume of information, from memorizing creation myths to the elaboration of herbal remedies.

Renowned for their knowledge of medicinal plants, including hallucinogenic plants such as the ayahuasca vine that was used both for healing and to communicate with the spirit world, *pajés* are still an important element of folk MEDICINE among both indigenous and non-Indian communities in modern Latin America.

—Francisco J. González

Further reading:
Anna Roosevelt, ed. *Amazonian Indians: From Prehistory to the Present* (Tucson: University of Arizona Press, 1994).

Panama For centuries, Panama has served as a land bridge, allowing the exchange of plants, animals, people, goods, and technologies between North and South America (see MIGRATION). Archaeological, linguistic, and genetic data demonstrate that Panama has been occupied continuously since the initial colonization of the Americas. Although animal bones found at La Trinadita date to 45,000 B.C.E., no associated Paleoindian tools have been found. The earliest evidence for human occupation comes from pollen and Joboid tools collected at La Yeguada and Lake Alajuela and dates to around 9500 B.C.E. Two lithic bifacial stone tool traditions and pollen remains are the only evidence of later human occupation. These are associated with the North American Clovis and South American fishtail projectile heads used by hunter-gather populations who inhabited the region around 9000 B.C.E. (see CLOVIS CULTURE). The tools have been found in open sites and rock shelters on the central Pacific coast, at locations such as La Mula-West, Nieto, and Vampiros.

During the Preceramic period, around 7000 to 5000 B.C.E., humans inhabited coastal sites and rock shelters along the central Pacific coast. They used bifacial stone tools and milling stones called "edge-ground cobbles" to prepare a variety of foodstuffs, including rodents, shellfish, freshwater turtles, estuarine fish, and plants. There is evidence of early AGRICULTURE during this time. Slash-and-burn cultivation was practiced to grow crops such as arrowroot, MAIZE, and squash, all of which were originally domesticated outside Panama.

After 5000 B.C.E., the use of unifacial stone tools became more common. Early inhabitants continued to use animal and plant resources. MANIOC, sweet potatoes, and yams were added to the diet, and agriculture continued to expand (see POTATO). In western Panama, between 4000 and 2500 B.C.E., human groups living in small camps and rock shelters used stone tools that differed from those used in central Panama. Bifacial wedges and axlike tools of basalt and andesite were used for woodworking. These people collected palm nuts and tree fruits; cultivated maize, manioc, and arrowroot; and probably hunted peccary, deer, and small game.

Pottery was developed in central Panama around 3000 B.C.E. at coastal and inland sites such as Monagrillo (where it was first identified), Zapotal, Corona, Río Cobre, Calavera, and Ladrones (see CERAMICS). In central Pacific Panama, there was an intensification of agriculture, particularly in the drier foothills, but otherwise, most cultural patterns continued from the preceding Preceramic period. Throughout Panama, material culture became more diverse during this period, and three distinct cultural regions emerged in western, central, and eastern Panama.

By the first millennium B.C.E. until 300 C.E., Panama experienced relatively rapid cultural development and agricultural intensification. Regional pottery styles developed in western Panama (Concepción complex style), central Panama (La Mula style), and eastern Panama (zoned linear incised). The growing population began settling in nucleated agricultural villages. In central Panama, people settled along the alluvial plains of the main rivers in the lowlands, at sites such La Mula–Sarigua, Sitio Sierra, Natá, Cerro Juan Díaz, Búcaro, La India, Cañazas, El Indio, and El Cafetal; similar processes occurred at La Pitahaya and Cerro Brujo in western Panama. New technologies were introduced. In central Panama, sites from this period indicate the broad usage of legless slab *METATES* (grinding stones), *manos*, and polished axes, all typically associated with maize cultivation, a staple FOOD in the region. In addition to maize, people consumed white-tail deer, fish, crabs, and shellfish.

The period between 400 and 800 C.E. saw the establishment of stratified societies and settlement hierarchies. Elite individuals controlled and displayed luxury goods made of stone, shell, ivory, and GOLD and mobilized LABOR for the construction of cemeteries, mounds, stone sculptures, stone pavements, and buildings. Evidence of this can be found at sites such as Sitio Conte, Barriles, La Pitahaya, Sitio Pitti-Gonzalez, Miraflores, Rancho Sancho, Cerro Juan Díaz, and El Caño.

After 800, the production of maize, hunting of game, and exploitation of marine resources intensified. Polities consolidated in regional centers such as Cerro Cerrezuela and El Hatillo, and populations increased along the river valleys. Tools, pottery, and other commodities were produced mainly by craft specialists, and burials reflect increased social stratification.

When the Spanish arrived in 1501, Panama had a variety of settlement types of different sizes. Communities were stratified and spoke diverse Chibcha languages in central and western Panama and the Cueva language in eastern Panama. There is also evidence of long-distance TRADE between polities, as well as WARFARE. In eastern Panama, Cueva speakers were organized in dispersed villages ruled by a local chief. Their ECONOMY was based on hunting, gathering, and agricultural activities. Spanish CHRONICLERS described stratified communities ruled by paramount chiefs in central Panama. These nucleated villages were located in major river valleys, surrounded by a wide variety of habitats from which the inhabitants obtained abundant game and fish; they also cultivated maize, manioc, sweet potatoes, and squash. In western Panama at the time of the CONQUEST, groups such as the

Catebas, Guaymis, Dolegas, and Dorasques lived in dispersed hamlets surrounded by agricultural fields.

See also PANAMA (Vols. II, III, IV).

—Diana Rocío Carvajal Contreras

Further reading:
R. Cooke. "Prehistory of Native Americans on the Central American Land-Bridge: Colonization, Dispersal and Divergence." *Journal of Archaeological Research* 13 (2005): 139–188.

panaqa (panaka, panaca) The term *panaqa* is a QUECHUA word referring to a royal kin group (see AYLLU) of Inca elites based in the imperial capital of CUZCO, PERU (see INCAS). Each sovereign in the conventional list of Inca emperors was revered as the founder of a royal kin group; at the time of the Spanish CONQUEST, there were 10 royal kin groups based in Cuzco. Like an *ayllu*, a *panaqa* was organized around shared kinship, landholdings and ritual-ceremonial groupings. This royal kin grouping was further divided, according to the principle of dual corporate organization, into upper (*hanan*) and lower (*hurin*) divisions. Reflecting Inca social organization, which integrated *ayllus* into a single, hierarchical society, *panaqas* were bounded and ranked according to factors such as ritual status, mythohistorical tradition, and the founder mythologies of the kin groups.

The *panaqa* as a kin unit played important political, economic, and ritual roles in Inca society. *Panaqas* inherited the estates of their kin group founders and managed these lands with the resources developed by the deceased ruler during his lifetime. These estates were located across varied ecological zones so that a wide range of resources could be exploited as a source of wealth for the monarch and his descendants. The resources provided by the estates of royal kin groups allowed them to underwrite political and ceremonial activities that were crucial to the maintenance of royal power and, perhaps most important, to support the privileged obligation the *panaqa* held of maintaining ancestral mummies, a practice critical in Inca and, more broadly, Andean religious practice (see RELIGION).

—Tien-Ann Shih

Further reading:
Maria Rostoworski de Diez Canseco. *History of the Inca Realm*, translated by Harry B. Iceland (Cambridge: Cambridge University Press, 1999).

Paraguay Paraguay is a republic located in the middle of South America. It takes its name from the river that bisects it, the word *Paraguay* originating from the GUARANÍ terms for "river" and "place." Modern Paraguay is landlocked but is bordered in the southwest and south-east by major rivers—the Paraná and Pilcomayo—that separate it from URUGUAY and ARGENTINA. Paraguay shares borders with BOLIVIA and BRAZIL to the north.

Before the Spanish CONQUEST, Paraguayan territory was occupied mainly by the Guaraní, who occupied the southern Paraná Delta, where Asunción sits. They lived in patrilineal communal homes, with up to 60 families in the same building. Their diet consisted primarily of fish, MAIZE, and calabashes. The Guaraní suffered frequent raids from nomadic tribes of the Chaco such as the Guaycurú, Toba, Payaguá, Pilagá, and Lengua. These persistent assaults eventually convinced the Guaraní to establish an alliance with Spanish settlers. Guaraní communities were organized by lineage, each lineage governed by its own chief. There appeared to be no formal head of state, and little if any ceremony surrounded the death of a ruler. Nevertheless, there was some degree of hierarchy in Guaraní society; one's status was often based on inherited class membership. In the case of shamans or healers, status and power often had more to do with an individual's charisma.

The Spanish appeared in Paraguay after abandoning attempts to settle nearer to the Atlantic coast. Juan Díaz de Solís discovered the mouth of the Río de la Plata (River Plate) in 1516, but Querandí Indians killed him and all his men shortly after landfall. Sebastian Cabot explored the Atlantic coast in 1527 before founding Sancti Spiritus along the Paraná River. Sancti Spiritus was soon abandoned, but Cabot returned safely to Spain, where Charles I decided to fund an impressive force of 1,600 to accompany PEDRO DE MENDOZA's expedition to settle the Río de la Plata. Mendoza founded BUENOS AIRES in 1536, but such a large contingent proved difficult to feed. The Spaniards' lack of FOOD and supplies provoked new hostilities with the Querandí, and Mendoza soon abandoned his men; he later died on his way back to Spain. In the meantime, Mendoza's subordinates had followed the Paraná upriver and founded Asunción in 1537.

From Asunción, the Spanish initiated their quest to find indigenous kingdoms said to hold incredible wealth. Mendoza had named Juan de Ayolas to lead an expedition to find such a kingdom, but Ayolas disappeared while crossing the rugged Chaco wilderness. With Mendoza dead and the mythical kingdoms nowhere to be found, Spanish colonists in Asunción dramatically changed their strategy and sought an alliance with the Guaraní.

In 1542, ÁLVAR NÚÑEZ CABEZA DE VACA was appointed governor of Paraguay. However, instead of reestablishing royal authority, his arrival touched off a conflict between "old" and "new" conquerors. Cabeza de Vaca appropriated 3,000 palm tree trunks that had been designated to finish the "old" conquerors' settlement and had them used in part to build his residence, the houses of the "new" conquerors, and horse stables. This act angered many of the city's old residents. Nevertheless, Cabeza de Vaca made some strides in solidifying the Spanish-Guaraní alliance but later permanently damaged the colonists' relationship with the Agace peoples who controlled the strategically important confluence of the Paraguay and Paraná Rivers. As time passed, the governor rapidly lost allies; his popularity was further damaged when a catastrophic fire charred more than half of Asunción, including vast quantities of stored food. After an unsuccessful 1544 expedition to the Chaco, during which many Spanish were killed or became ill, Cabeza de Vaca was arrested and sent back to Spain in irons.

As a result of the instability following Cabeza de Vaca's arrest, the Agace and Guaraní joined forces and launched an attack on Asunción in 1545. The new governor, Domingo de Irala, was able to drive the attackers back; he then turned his attention to seeking reinforcements from Spain. After two years of waiting for imperial support, Irala decided to lead an expedition to PERU. On arrival, he discovered that the region had already been settled by the Spanish. Stopping short of LIMA, in the province of Chiquitos, Irala sent word to Peru's governor, PEDRO DE LA GASCA of his wishes to meet with him. Fearing a power struggle, Gasca prohibited Irala from staying in Peru. Irala's only option was to return to Asunción.

In Asunción, Francisco de Mendoza had in the meantime tried to have himself elected governor. Irala's allies had Mendoza arrested, and he was sentenced to death and executed. Once Irala had reestablished the peace for the second time in five years, he began an expansion of Paraguayan territory in an attempt to create easier access to the sea. This expansion was moving toward Brazil and the Río de la Plata in 1552 when Irala received a message from Charles I that confirmed his status as governor but also prohibited further expansion. This turn of events prompted Irala to ignore the royal ban on issuing ENCOMIENDA grants, which the governor began to institute as a source of labor for Paraguay's Spanish settlers. With no hope of trade with Spain nor a union with Peru, Irala set out to create a successful ECONOMY based on the exploitation of Guaraní labor.

The establishment of *encomiendas* marked the beginning of the "transition phase" in Paraguay's colonial history. In this phase, wealth would not be gained through the accumulation of GOLD and SILVER (which were scarce in Paraguay) but through the exploitation of indigenous labor primarily in AGRICULTURE.

See also ASUNCIÓN (Vol. II); PARAGUAY (Vols. II, III, IV).

—Eugene C. Berger

Further reading:

Efraím Cordozo. *Breve historia del Paraguay* (Buenos Aires: Editorial Universitaria de Buenos Aires, 1965).
Elman R. Service. "Spanish-Guaraní Relations in Early Colonial Paraguay." In *Anthropological Papers* (Ann Arbor: University of Michigan Press, 1954).

Pedrarias See ARIAS DE ÁVILA, PEDRO.

Peru Peru, a large nation in South America, is oriented north-south along the Pacific coast, with ECUADOR to the north, CHILE to the south, and BOLIVIA and BRAZIL to the east. In terms of its geography, Peru boasts three major environmental regions: The first is a narrow coastal desert that runs along the Pacific shore, interrupted by 40 rivers flowing generally westward from the Andes mountains. The central region is dominated by the Andes Mountains. To the east of the Andes, Peru is dominated by the rain forest of the AMAZON. In all, modern Peru covers an area of approximately 500,000 square miles (1.29 million km²).

This varied environmental complex is largely responsible for major aspects of Peru's rich pre-Columbian history, with people attracted to the bountiful seafood harvest of the Pacific, the lush river valleys that run from the Andes to the coast, and the high mountain valleys in the Andes. Moreover, at various points in its history, cultural groups extended beyond the borders of modern Peru. For example, the Inca Empire extended into regions of modern Chile, Bolivia, ARGENTINA, Ecuador, and COLOMBIA (see INCAS).

Peru's pre-Columbian past is both highly diverse and remarkably complex. In terms of historical time, Peruvian prehistory initially is divided into "periods"; however, beginning about 400 B.C.E., scholars separate periods by "horizons."

Periods in Peruvian Prehistory

PERIOD OR HORIZON	DATES
Lithic period	Settlement to 3000 B.C.E.
Preceramic period	3000–2000 B.C.E.
Initial period	2000–400 B.C.E.
Early Horizon	400 B.C.E.–1 C.E.
Early Intermediate period	1–600 C.E.
Middle Horizon	600–1000 C.E.
Late Intermediate	1000–1450 C.E.
Late Horizon	1450–1533 C.E.

Knowledge of Peru's first inhabitants is sparse; two lines of evidence, however, place the earliest arrivals by 11,500 years ago. Early human occupation sites elsewhere and blood typing of indigenous Peruvians confirm that the first arrivals were from Asia, crossing into the Americas via the broad Bering land bridge that linked Asia and North America during a time of low sea levels. MONTE VERDE, Chile, a 15,000-year-old campsite south of Santiago, documents a sophisticated level of cultural activity, including framed hide huts, sewing, harvesting numerous wild plants, obtaining seafood, and killing mammoths. These people mostly likely arrived via a multigenerational MIGRATION down the west coast of Peru. It is reasonable to assume the existence of similar sites along the Peruvian coast, now inundated by rising sea levels.

Blood typing and genetic studies suggest that the New World was populated by three or four waves of migrants, only one of which was significant in populating South America. The "founder effect" postulates that as the small original populations crossed into South America, they gave rise to peoples among whom blood type O predominates, type A is rare, and type B is altogether absent.

Peru's early inhabitants (after about 10,000 years ago) began to confront the varied challenges of the regions's diverse environment and left suites of stone tools. In the northwest, homes were small, consisting of huts roughly six feet (1.8 m) in diameter. Tools were primarily choppers, scrapers, and flakes, used to craft other tools and wooden projectiles.

Needlelike projectile points used for spearing fish date back 12,000–7,000 years ago; these points distinguish the Paiján tradition along the north coast. Again, rising sea levels likely inundated their primary seaside sites. In the Andean north, early settlers relied extensively on game hunting.

By the end of the Lithic period (ca. 3000 B.C.E.), the Chinchorro coastal culture, which straddled the Peru-Chile border, became the first group in the world to mummify human remains. Their complex mummification process consisted of removing flesh and organs, treating the skin, and reassembling the skeleton with wood supports. A final coat of mud plaster preserved the mummy until burial at some later date.

The first evidence of plant domestication in the New World, evidenced at the Guitarrero Cave and Tres Ventanas Cave, date back to the Lithic period 10,000 years ago. While there is evidence of cultivated crops such as beans and chili peppers, there is even greater evidence for the domestication of plants used to produce woven and knotted goods; these sites reflect the early beginnings of a long textile-production tradition in Peru (see TEXTILES).

The Preceramic period (3000 B.C.E.–2000 B.C.E.) in Peru initiated a precocious process of social complexity and organization. Significant monumental sites emerged during this period, including Caral, the "oldest city in the New World" (see CITIES). At Caral, the ARCHITECTURE reflects a tradition of building sunken circular courtyards, known as *plazas hundidas*, with diametrically opposed entry stairways. This practice began during this period and continued for centuries. Knotted and woven textiles are frequently found at Preceramic sites, bearing intricate portrayals of double-headed serpents, condors, and other figures. In addition to the Chinchorro region to the south, major cultural remains have been found along the Pacific coast from LIMA (the Rimac Valley) northward in nearly every river valley up to the MOCHE and Chicama Rivers.

Beginning during the Preceramic period, the Kotosh religious tradition demonstrates cultural vigor in the Andes and its Amazon tributaries. Excavations at Kotosh, the cultural type-site, in two large solid platform mounds, revealed 10 construction phases, the two earliest without CERAMICS. La Galgada, located 50 miles (80.5 km) from the coast,

reveals clear evidence that goods flowed from the coast to the highlands and into the Amazon: Tombs at La Galgada contained both Pacific shell and Amazon bird feathers.

In an interesting variation on the Neolithic revolution, numerous Preceramic groups of sites along the Río Supe, including Caral, seem to have chosen either fishing or farming as their primary ECONOMY, with active exchange of foodstuffs and other goods the norm. In this era, foodstuffs included arrowroot, sweet potatoes, squash, beans, pacaya, guava, jicama, MANIOC, MAIZE, oca, ulluco, white POTATOes, shellfish, kelp, and anchovies (see FOOD).

The Initial period is marked by three major changes: the spread of ceramics southward from their early appearance in Ecuador in the Valdivia culture, the widespread construction of U-shaped platforms along the coast north of Lima, and the extensive use of irrigation AGRICULTURE. At numerous coastal rivers, local populations constructed canals to support irrigated crops at higher river elevations; these canals then fan out from the river to their fields as the elevation drops. This technological innovation greatly increased the amount of available arable land along the coastal desert region. Moreover, increased rainfall during the Initial period fostered the growth of local traditions there.

The construction of U-shaped platforms followed the earlier tradition of placing baskets of earth fill, complete with the basket, in place to carefully account for LABOR. Later, this tradition included marking adobe bricks to account for the labor contribution of individual villages. U-shaped platforms may have had their origins at El Paraíso; however, the largest, most complex examples are found at Sechín Alto and Huaca Los Reyes.

As devastating drought brought the collapse of most coastal sites and U-shaped platform complexes, a new tradition, CHAVÍN, emerged at a major 10,000-foot (3,050-m) high Andean site, Chavín de Huántar. The dramatic spread of Chavín influence to coastal Ica by 400 B.C.E. marked the beginning of the Early Horizon.

Chavín de Huántar, unlike its earthen counterparts on the coast, was finely crafted with masonry and riddled with rooms and passages. The first "old temple" construction is C-shaped, with a central *plaza hundida*. Within the lower labyrinth where passageways cross, archaeologists found a 15-foot (4.5-m) stela, the Lanzón, configured as a point-down knife blade, with a carved "Smiling God" deity. A removable stone in the passage above the Lanzón permitted Chavín's priests to bring voice to the stela. Imagery at Chavín de Huántar also includes raptors, anthropomorphic figures with hallucinogenic cacti, and crocodiles from the Amazon.

Prosperity gave way to drought, and the Chavín influence gave way to more regional cultures in the Early Intermediate period. Of particular importance were the Moche on the north coast, the Lima culture of the central coast, and the Nazca culture on the south coast, famed for its large desert geoglyphs of gigantic geometric figures and outlines of birds, fish, and other animals, all etched on the desert landscape (see NAZCA LINES). At this time, isolated Andean groups formed small pockets in the highlands, while to the south, the TIWANAKU culture formed around Lake Titicaca.

Two large adobe constructions, the Huaca del Sol and the Huaca de la Luna dominated the Moche capital, Cerro Blanco; however, over time looters have ravaged the site. After the CONQUEST, Spanish looting of the extensive rich tombs within them was achieved by "hydraulic mining," or the manual diversion of the Moche River in order to wash away the adobe structures and expose the interred GOLD within. The remains of the Huaca del Sol, now less than half its original size, are still 1,100 feet (355 m) long, 520 feet (158.5 m) wide, and 130 feet (40 m) tall.

Nevertheless, the Moche left one of the richest artistic legacies in pre-Columbian Peru. Creative Moche ceramic and textile arts depict animals, mythical figures, real-life portraits, and religious themes, including the caste of the warrior priest, who sacrifices captives taken in battle. The iconography of the warrior priest matches with high accuracy the details of the tomb of the Lord of Sipán in the Lambayeque Valley, which rivals the tomb of the Egyptian pharaoh Tutankhamen in the richness of its grave goods (see ART).

Environmental disaster brought enormous changes to Peruvian cultures at the end of the Early Intermediate. Earthquakes damaged and dislocated irrigation canal segments. At least eight major El Niño events, beginning in 511 C.E., triggered drought conditions between 562 and 594; during the period, rainfall dropped by one-third. Flooding also destroyed a major section of the Moche capital.

During the Middle Horizon, a period characterized by widespread societal disruption, the Andean WARI culture began to spread through north and central Peru. The Wari relied on high-mountain terraced fields and tribute collections from distant groups that fell under Wari control. Both these elements were precursors of later Inca statecraft and agriculture.

To the south, the Tiwanaku culture of Lake Titicaca flourished, refining earlier lakeside irrigation farming techniques to substantially improve agricultural production. Canalized fields covering 250,000 acres relied on irrigation water in a process that warmed the water during the day to mitigate frost effects at night. Around 1100, an extraordinary drought dropped the water level of Lake Titicaca by 40 feet (12 m), rendering much of the irrigated land unusable and bringing an end to the Middle Horizon.

During the Late Intermediate, Peruvian peoples were once again isolated into smaller regional polities. Coastal river valleys supported a series of independent ethnic groups, which dominated relatively small territories. From north to south, these cultures included the CHIMÚ, Sicán, Chancay, Ica, and Chiribaya. Despite their size, some of their constructions were truly monumental, including the large Chimú capital at CHAN CHAN and the Sicán city of Batán Grande.

In the Andes, the Wanka occupied the region east of Lima, the Aymara kingdoms occupied the Lake Titicaca region, and the Incas first emerged in the Lucre Valley. Out of the drought conditions of the Late Intermediate, the Incas emerged as masters of the environment and of neighboring peoples. Knowledge of the Incas and Late Horizon times is both archaeological and historical, based on accounts of the Spanish CHRONICLERS.

Radiating outward from what would become their capital city of CUZCO, the Incas, led by their ruler PACHACUTI INCA YUPANQUI, pursued conquest of their neighbors; these campaigns continued through 1463, and under Pachacuti's leadership, the Incas refined their statecraft. They introduced a broad taxation system, applied to agricultural production, textiles, and community labor. Goods were stored in a vast network of state warehouses, reprising the earlier approach introduced by the Wari.

Pachacuti's successor, Topa Inca, extended the empire to the north and south, spanning 2,500 miles (4,023 km) from central Ecuador to central Chile. Topa Inca's heir, HUAYNA CÁPAC, assumed the throne in 1493, a time of marked unrest. The domination and assimilation of cultures conquered by Topa Inca were far from solidified. Efforts to relocate entire villages, as well as attempts to force the spread of the QUECHUA language, characterized this era of great unrest.

Huayna Cápac campaigned in Ecuador and established a second northern capital at Tumibamba; however, the empire soon erupted in civil unrest. Six years before FRANCISCO PIZARRO and his men set foot in Peru, the first agent of conquest, namely smallpox, struck Inca territory. Both Huayna Cápac and his chosen heir are believed to have succumbed to the DISEASE, and their deaths sparked a bitter internal war. This bloody conflict not only threatened the empire from within; it also facilitated the process of the Spanish conquest.

Five years of civil war raged as a tug-of-war developed between HUÁSCAR, who claimed the Inca throne from Cuzco, and ATAHUALPA, who advanced his claim from Tumibamba. In 1532, a military encounter in Ecuador led to Huáscar's defeat and capture. Following the capture of Huáscar, Atahualpa began to march his victorious forces toward Cuzco.

While on this fateful journey in 1533, the conquistador Francisco Pizarro, sailing along the coast, learned of these circumstances and marched inland toward Cajamarca; there, in a surprise attack, he captured Atahualpa and held him ransom; with the ransom paid, Pizarro accused Atahualpa of plotting an uprising against the Spaniards, and after a brief trial, he ordered Atahualpa's execution. Pizarro continued his march to Cuzco, defeated the capital, and ultimately retired to the coast where he founded Lima in 1535.

See also CALLAO (Vol. II); LIMA (Vols. II, III, IV); PERU (Vols. II, III, IV); PERU, VICEROYALTY OF (Vol. II).

—Walter R. T. Witschey

Further reading:
Michael E. Mosley. *The Incas and Their Ancestors* (London: Thames & Hudson, 1992).

pipiltin   This Nahuatl term for "nobles" (singular, *pilli*) referred to the hereditary elite of preconquest and early colonial Nahua society (see Aztecs). The majority of Nahuas were MACEHUALES, or commoners. Social convention dictated that the unmodified term referred either to men or both men and WOMEN. When referring specifically to women, it became *cihuapipiltin* (singular, *cihuapilli*), or "noblewomen." Nahuas shared the noble/commoner distinction with other Mesoamerican peoples, such as the Mixtecs, Zapotecs, and Maya.

Broadly speaking, Nahua nobles took the lead in administering the resources of the *ALTEPETL* (city-state). They also conducted important religious ceremonies and directed TRADE relations (see RELIGION). They stood out from commoners by such features as dress. Whereas before the Spanish CONQUEST they might wear rare feathers and earplugs as evidence of their noble status, after the conquest they increasingly took to wearing European-style clothes and carried swords and muskets.

There were also clear distinctions within the nobility itself. At the highest level was the ruler, or *TLATOANI*, of the *altepetl*, who was drawn from a select group known as *teteuctin* (plural of *teuctli*, or "lord"); both offices were then followed by ordinary *pipiltin*. Wealth did not automatically lead to higher status. Some commoners involved in crafts and trade were just as wealthy as many nobles but never achieved noble status.

Noble status could be earned, nevertheless. Before the conquest and colonization imposed peace on warring *altepetl*, an outstanding warrior who was a *macehual* might become a *quauhpilli*, literally "eagle noble" and less literally "nobleman through merit." Marriage provided another avenue for social advancement. The renowned Nahua Latinist Antonio Valeriano was born a *macehual* but married into the Montezuma family and became a member of the highest Nahua nobility.

—Barry D. Sell

Further reading:
James Lockhart. *The Nahuas after the Conquest: A Social and Cultural History of the Indians of Central Mexico, Sixteenth through Eighteenth Centuries* (Stanford, Calif.: Stanford University Press, 1992).

Kevin Terraciano. *The Mixtecs of Colonial Oaxaca: Ñudzahui History, Sixteenth through Eighteenth Centuries* (Stanford, Calif.: Stanford University Press, 2001).

pirates and piracy   A pirate is defined as someone who robs or plunders ships at sea or attacks settlements without a legitimate commission from a recognized king or queen. The actions, depredations, and plunder of these sea raiders are known as piracy. In the Caribbean region, the bulk of piracy was directed against the Spanish. Shortly after Christopher Columbus's last voyage to the New World in 1504, the Caribbean became a booming source of mineral wealth and TRADE for Spain. Eager to protect its new possessions from foreign interlopers and possible competition from Portugal, in 1493, Spain negotiated the Treaty of Tordesillas, which effectively divided the entire non-European world between Spain and Portugal. A north to south line, which began 270 leagues (approximately 932 miles [1,500 km]) west of the Cape Verde Islands, was drawn along the globe. The treaty granted all the territory to the east of this imaginary line to Portugal, while all lands to the west went to Spain.

Of course, the other European monarchs were not consulted on the issue, and many of them resented Spain's claim to dominance in the New World. Sending out semilegal sanctioned pirates, called "privateers," and sponsoring or condoning outright acts of piracy and plunder against Spain quickly resulted. The French king Francis I reportedly issued the following sarcastic comment on the Treaty of Tordesillas: "The sun shines for me as for the others, I would like to see the clause in Adam's will that writes me out of my share of this New World."

As early as the 1520s, Spanish shipments of GOLD and SILVER bullion from the New World began to attract pirates from rival European nations such as France, England, and the Netherlands. Acts of piracy occurred both in the Caribbean and throughout the greater Atlantic world, making the route from the Indies to Spain ever more dangerous and the likelihood of pirate attack an omnipresent danger.

As early as 1522, the French pirate Jean Fleury attacked and seized three Spanish ships loaded with Aztec treasure taken by Hernando Cortés on their way back to Spain (see Aztecs; conquest). Fleury was the first of a long series of French pirates who conducted raids and other acts of piracy against Spanish shipping and settlements throughout the 16th century. Bolder acts of piracy were to come. In 1544, French Huguenot pirates captured and burned the city of Cartagena. Ten years later, in 1554, the French pirate François Le Clerc captured Santiago, Cuba, and the next year his associate and fellow Protestant pirate Jacques de Sores captured and sacked the city of Havana. In 1564, while looking for a safe place to develop a new colony to serve as a base for future piracy against Spain, the French established the first non-Spanish colony in the New World at Fort Caroline in Florida. Although the Spanish destroyed this pirate colony in 1565, Spain's exclusive rights to colonization in the New World had ended.

Similarly, from the 1540s forward, England entered into the race for plunder and colonization. English pirates (technically privateers who either held letters of marquee or had informal permission from Queen Elizabeth) sacked Spanish shipping and port cities from the 1560s to the 1590s. In fact, England's best sailors and explorers almost always engaged in acts of piracy against Spain's possessions in the Indies; these infamous pirates included Sir John Hawkins, Sir Francis Drake, John Davis, and many others. Sir Francis Drake, England's most successful pirate (or privateer), echoed the general English disdain for Spanish claims to the territories outlined in the Treaty of Tordesillas when he swore to his queen, "We will give the Spanish no peace beyond the line!" Living up to his oath, Drake successfully raided and conducted piracy against Spanish settlements, sacking and plundering the cities of Nombre de Dios, PANAMA (1572); Valparaiso, CHILE (1579); Santo Domingo, HISPANIOLA (1586); Cartagena, COLOMBIA (1586); St. Augustine, Florida (1586); and, finally once again, Nombre de Dios (1595).

In order to protect its New World empire from these growing foreign incursions, the Spanish established key settlements on the largest of the Caribbean islands and throughout the Caribbean coasts of Central and South America; this region came to be known as the Spanish Main. After repeated pirate attacks against these key settlements, Spain was forced to build expensive walled cities and defensive works in towns in Cuba, Hispaniola, the isthmus of Panama, as well as Veracruz and Campeche along the coasts of MEXICO, and Cartagena and Maracaibo, VENEZUELA on the South American coast.

Moreover, to offset the danger to its treasure fleets, in the 1560s the Spanish CASA DE CONTRATACIÓN (Board of Trade) and the COUNCIL OF THE INDIES created the treasure fleet system. This system limited the number of FLEETS sent each year, concentrating them into two rotating fleets that sailed in convoys escorted by heavily armed warships. This new system created the need for another Pacific fleet and a silver train system, the latter designed to transport the vast quantities of silver from PERU and BOLIVIA overland across the Isthmus of Panama for transshipment to Spain on the *Tierra Firme* treasure fleet. Although meant to protect Spain's TRADE with the Indies, these new treasure fleets and the silver train system provided new targets for pirates and thus were victims of acts of piracy throughout the 17th century.

In terms of control over the Caribbean and mainland Central and South America, the Spanish could not afford a sufficient military presence to control such a vast territory and thus eliminate piracy. Weaker regions of Spanish control quickly fell to new attempts at Caribbean colonization by England, France, and the Netherlands. The result was that whenever a war was declared in Europe against Spain, acts of piracy occurred throughout the Caribbean. The ultimate success of these pirate expeditions eventually led to the establishment of new non-Spanish European colonies in the New World, especially on the islands of the Lesser Antilles.

See also HAWKINS, JOHN (Vol. II).

—John F. Chuchiak IV

Further reading:
Kris Lane. *Pillaging the Empire: Piracy in the Americas, 1500–1750* (Armonk, N.Y.: M. E. Sharpe, 1998).

Pizarro, Francisco (b. ca. 1478–d. 1541) *Spanish conquistador of Peru* Francisco Pizarro, the legendary conquistador of PERU, was born in the late 1470s in Trujillo, capital of Spain's Extremadura Province; his exact birth date is not known. Francisco was the illegitimate eldest son of Gonzalo Pizarro Rodríguez de Aguilar (1446–1522), a hidalgo with a limited estate in Trujillo and a royal infantry captain in the War of Granada and the War of Navarre, in which he died serving King Charles I. Francisco's mother was Francisca Gonzáles, from a family of peasants known as the Roperos for their probable relationship with the local convent of San Francisco as keepers of the wardrobe and where Francisca worked as a servant. Francisco, second cousin to HERNANDO CORTÉS on his father's side, most likely spent his childhood between the two households, though he seems not to have received the education that his younger brothers did.

Pizarro left for the Indies in 1502 as part of the fleet led by Nicolás de Ovando, governor of HISPANIOLA. There are few details of his early years in the Caribbean; however, through his military feats in expeditions against the indigenous peoples of the islands and eventually in PANAMA, Pizarro won the favor of Governor PEDRO ARIAS DE ÁVILA, known as Pedrarias. He participated in the Spanish "discovery" of the Pacific Ocean under the command of VASCO NÚÑEZ DE BALBOA, and in 1519, Pedrarias named him *REGIDOR* of the city of Our Lady of Assumption of Panama, where he became one of the most important *encomenderos* (see ENCOMIENDA). It was from this economic and political base that Pizarro, then one of the richest and most powerful men in Panama, launched his expeditions to South America (see CONQUEST).

After Pascual de Andagoya returned incapacitated from the first expedition of exploration along the Pacific coast in 1522, Pedrarias authorized Pizarro and his two partners, DIEGO DE ALMAGRO and Hernando de Luque, to continue the venture, which became known as the Compañía del Levante (Levant Company). The new partners were inspired by Andagoya's reports of a fabulously wealthy empire to the south, mistakenly understood to be named *Virú* or *Birú*; this region soon came to be called "Peru." Pizarro's first expedition, financed by an array of investors-adventurers in Panama, set sail in November 1524. It ended in failure, however. Pizarro and company (80 men and 40 horses) advanced no farther than Pueblo Quemado (on the Colombian coast) where a skirmish with Amerindians, in addition to FOOD shortages, forced them back to Panama (see COLOMBIA).

Pizarro and the Levant Company's second expedition sailed in November 1526; it consisted of two ships, 160 men, and a few horses. While Pizarro established a camp at the San Juan River, his pilot, Bartolomé Ruiz, sailed farther south, crossing the equator for the first time in the Pacific. Ruiz also glimpsed the rumored riches of Peru when his ships crossed paths with an ocean-going balsa raft off the coast of Manta, ECUADOR. The raft, believed to be on a trading mission with the INCAS farther south, was laden with SILVER, GOLD, precious stones, and elaborate TEXTILES, as well as other ornate objects indicative of an advanced civilization. Ruiz captured three Indians from the raft to train as interpreters for future expeditions. He then rejoined Pizarro, and together they continued south, reaching the Isla del Gallo, where their men began dying at alarming rates from hunger and DISEASE. Many wished to return to Panama, where the new governor, Pedro de los Ríos, had decided to recall the Levant Company.

This recall led Pizarro to deliver his famous speech, during which he drew a line in the sand and declared "There lies Peru with its riches; here, Panama and its poverty. Choose, each man, what best becomes a brave Castilian." Thirteen men, the renowned "Thirteen of Fame," chose to stay with Pizarro and continue the expedition. They were rewarded the following year when they reached, first, the Gulf of Guayaquil and then made it as far south as the Peruvian river Santa. These explorations and landings revealed the first Inca city encountered by Europeans, Tumbes, and other signs of the vast, unknown empire of riches that awaited the conquistadores. In Tumbes, Pizarro gathered various samples of the region's wealth and curiosities, such as llamas; significantly, before he returned to Panama, he also acquired his famed interpreter, Felipillo.

Once back in Panama, Pizarro was unable to secure permission from Governor de los Ríos for a third expedition; he therefore decided to go directly to Spain for royal assent. This astute move both reduced the risks from rival conquistadores in the Indies and secured wider financial backing. His visit to King Charles I's court coincided with his cousin Hernando Cortés's return to Spain with tales of his marvelous exploits of the conquest of MEXICO. Not only did this coincidence inspire the Court's confidence in Pizarro's proposals, but it aided in his recruitment of adventurers, many of whom were from his native Trujillo. On July 26, 1529, Queen Isabella, in Charles I's absence, signed the Capitulación of Toledo, which authorized Pizarro, Almagro, and Luque to discover and conquer the territory known as Peru. Pizarro was named governor, captain general, and *adelantado* of Peru, while Almagro was appointed commandant of Tumbes; Luque was named protector of the Indians and future bishop of Tumbes. This unequal distribution of power among the three led to Almagro's

This 20th-century sculpture of a mounted Francisco Pizarro sits in the Plaza Mayor of Trujillo, Spain, Pizarro's hometown. The sculpture is the work of the American artist Charles Rumsey. *(Courtesy of J. Michael Francis)*

eventual disagreements with Pizarro and the infamous civil wars following the conquest of Peru (see CIVIL WARS IN PERU).

After recruiting his half brothers JUAN PIZARRO, GONZALO PIZARRO, and HERNANDO PIZARRO from Trujillo, along with other soldiers, and procuring provisions and horses, Francisco returned to Panama. Then, on December 27, 1530, Pizarro launched his third expedition to Peru. Following several difficult months exploring the Ecuadorean coast, the company reached Tumbes to find the city in ruins, reportedly due to a civil war between rival Inca leaders and half brothers, HUÁSCAR and ATAHUALPA. The ensuing months were spent exploring the northwest arid region of Peru, until Pizarro founded the first Spanish city in Peru, San Miguel de Piura. From there, Pizarro marched southeast, into the sierra, toward the heart of the Inca Empire. He reached Cajamarca on November 15, 1532. There, he found Atahualpa resting and fasting after his victory over his half brother, Huáscar. Pizarro led a surprise attack against the Sapa Inca and his retinue of hundreds of high officials, capturing Atahualpa and effectively destroying the leadership structure of the Inca Empire. After collecting a remarkable ransom for Atahualpa's release, and in fear of an impending counterattack by Atahualpa's general Rumiñaui, Pizarro executed Atahualpa on July 26, 1533. Pizarro then turned his sights on the Inca capital, CUZCO. After winning four decisive battles on the road from Cajamarca, Pizarro and his men entered Cuzco unchallenged on November 15, 1533.

Pizarro dedicated the remainder of his life to the establishment of the colonial administration of Peru, his expansive business interests, fighting Inca resistance and rebellions, and managing the internal political intrigues that ultimately led to his demise. He first founded his capital at Jauja but later decided it more advantageous to locate the capital on the coast, where he established LIMA, the "City of Kings," on January 18, 1535. He became fabulously wealthy from the numerous *encomiendas,* silver mines, and estates he controlled. In recognition of his success, Charles I granted him a marquisate, along with a new coat of arms. Pizarro fathered four children: Francisca and Gonzalo by the Inca princess Inés Huaylas and Francisco and Juan by the Inca princess Añas, or Angelina Añas Yupanqui. The rivalry with his partner of more than 20 years, Almagro, led to ever-greater disputes over the spoils of the conquest, especially over jurisdictions of territory Almagro claimed were granted to him. After saving Cuzco from MANCO INCA's siege, Almagro claimed the city as part of his territory, a claim that was disputed by the Pizarro brothers; ultimately, the Pizarros defeated Almagro's army at the BATTLE OF LAS SALINAS in 1538 and executed Almagro. The bad blood between the Almagristas and the Pizarros continued until Almagro's son's followers murdered Pizarro on the night of June 26, 1541. Pizarro's remains, confirmed to be legitimate in 1977, rest in Lima's cathedral.

—Michael J. Horswell

Further reading:
James Lockhart. *The Men of Cajamarca: A Social and Biographical Study of the First Conquerors of Peru* (Austin: University of Texas Press, 1972).
Rafael Varón Gabai. *Francisco Pizarro and His Brothers: The Illusion of Power in Sixteenth Century Peru* (Norman: University of Oklahoma Press, 1997).

Pizarro, Gonzalo (b. ca. 1502–d. 1548)

Spanish conquistador, governor of Quito, and leader of rebellion against the Spanish Crown Born in Trujillo, Spain, Gonzalo Pizarro was the fourth son of a father of the same name. Pizarro had already dedicated himself to a military career when he accompanied his half brother FRANCISCO PIZARRO to the Americas in 1530 with the intention of conquering PERU. Gonzalo Pizarro served as a lieutenant in the first war against the INCAS and was rewarded handsomely for his service with a portion of ATAHUALPA's treasure, as well as a coveted *repartimiento.* Pizarro distinguished himself as a military leader throughout the 1530s by pacifying indigenous rebellions and helping put down a challenge from his brother Francisco's former partner, DIEGO DE ALMAGRO. After this war between the rival Spanish forces, Francisco rewarded Gonzalo with the governorship of Quito (see CIVIL WARS IN PERU).

Envisioning still greater conquests, Pizarro led a 1541 expedition east from Quito into the AMAZON Basin, hoping to discover the legendary Lands of Cinnamon. A lack of supplies, combined with a general ignorance of the harsh territory, led to the deaths of the vast majority of the 200 Europeans and almost 4,000 indigenous people who accompanied him. When Pizarro returned to Quito the following year with his few surviving companions, he learned of the assassination of Francisco by supporters loyal to Almagro (the Almagristas).

Francisco's death left Gonzalo as the only Pizarro brother in Peru (see HERNANDO PIZARRO; JUAN PIZARRO). He expected to inherit his brother's position as governor but was disappointed upon the appointment of a royal official who had not taken part in the conquest. He was further alienated upon the promulgation of the NEW LAWS OF 1542, which limited the authority of *encomenderos* in Spanish America (see ENCOMIENDA). By the time Viceroy Blasco Núñez Vela arrived in Peru in 1544 charged with the implementation of the New Laws, Pizarro had established himself as the leader of a strong resistance prepared to defend *encomendero* privileges, by arms if necessary (see VICEROY/VICEROYALTY).

Núñez Vela showed himself unwilling to compromise. His royalist forces met Pizarro's rebel army for the decisive battle outside Quito in 1546. The rebels routed the loyalists, killing the viceroy in battle. Unwilling to endure such insubordination in his kingdoms, Charles I appointed PEDRO DE LA GASCA president of Peru and empowered him to restore order by any means necessary.

Pizarro, meanwhile, moved to consolidate his authority in Peru in order to prevent royal reprisals.

Gasca sailed for Peru in 1546. He would demonstrate a conciliatory tendency that his predecessor lacked. Gasca promised pardons to Pizarro's supporters in exchange for their assistance in putting down the rebellion. He bided his time and continued to win allies until 1548, when he led his army from Lima to confront Pizarro outside Cuzco. Even as the sides lined up in battle formation, many of Pizarro's forces sensed defeat and deserted to join Gasca. Pizarro was taken prisoner in the battle and was beheaded the following day.

—Jonathan Scholl

Further reading:

Rafael Varón Gabai. *Francisco Pizarro and His Brothers: The Illusion of Power in Sixteenth Century Peru* (Norman: University of Oklahoma Press, 1997).

Pizarro, Hernando (b. ca. 1501–d. 1578) *Spanish conquistador* Hernando Pizarro, Francisco Pizarro's half brother, was born in the capital of Spain's Extremadura province, Trujillo, in approximately 1501. Hernando Pizarro was the legitimate son of Gonzalo Pizarro Rodríguez de Aguilar (1446–1522). His mother was Isabel de Vargas. He was Gonzalo's only legitimate son, was educated and highly literate, experienced as a captain of infantry in Spain's military campaigns in Navarre, and had contacts at the court of Charles I. Hernando traveled to the Indies with Francisco in 1530 to take part in the third expedition to Peru. He became one of Francisco's most influential collaborators and one of the most important protagonists in the conquest of the Inca Empire (see Incas), enriching himself and improving his family's stature in Trujillo (which seemed to be his priority, rather than governing Peru, like his half brothers Francisco and Gonzalo Pizarro).

After participating in the capture of the Inca ruler Atahualpa, Hernando was sent back to Spain to represent Francisco's interests at Court and to ensure the Pizarros' privileged position in the new colonial government of Peru, especially in light of Diego de Almagro's political moves to obtain greater benefits. Hernando wrote an informative, if not self-aggrandizing report, which he sent to the High Court of Santo Domingo; the account offered testimony to his participation in the first years of the conquest of Peru (see *AUDIENCIA*). Highlighted among his deeds were his interview with Atahualpa, as well as the exploration of Pachacamac, a coastal pre-Inca oracle that

The Palace of the Conquest dominates the main square in Trujillo, Spain, ancestral hometown of the Pizarro family. *(Courtesy of J. Michael Francis)*

the Incas had incorporated into their pantheon of deities (see RELIGION). In his letter, Pizarro described the temple complex and its idol, which he destroyed. He was also responsible for capturing the Inca general Chalcuchima, one of the most powerful of Atahualpa's military cohorts, who commanded a large army.

After returning from Spain, Pizarro joined his half brothers Gonzalo and JUAN PIZARRO in the governing of Cuzco and led the city's defense during MANCO INCA's rebellion and siege. In 1537, Almagro returned from CHILE to take Cuzco under his control, imprisoning both Hernando and Gonzalo. Hernando was eventually released; later, he returned to Cuzco, along with Gonzalo, to retake the city after defeating Almagro and his men in the BATTLE OF LAS SALINAS. Following Almagro's execution, in 1538, which he ordered, Hernando was again sent to Spain to intervene on behalf of his brother Francisco's administration and to increase his financial and political standing. This time, however, his entreaties were met with official reproach, and he was sentenced to prison for 20 years at La Mota in Medina del Campo, Spain.

Although in prison, he enjoyed the comforts afforded to him by the revenues of his Peruvian investments, especially the SILVER mines of Porco, second in production only to the nearby POTOSÍ (see MINING). In 1552,

Hernando married his niece, Francisca Pizarro, the daughter of Francisco Pizarro and the Inca princess Inés Huaylas. Francisca had inherited her father's fortune, making her a most attractive marriage partner for the aging patriarch of the Pizarro clan, whose objective was to keep the Pizarro estates, mines, and ENCOMIENDAS in the family. They had five children, three of whom lived to adulthood. Hernando was released from prison in 1561 and returned with Francisca to Trujillo, where they built the Palacio de la Conquista (Palace of the Conquest) on the main square. Hernando spent the rest of his life consolidating the family's wealth and contesting the Crown's and other adversaries' challenges to his family's legacy.

—Michael J. Horswell

Further reading:
James Lockhart. *The Men of Cajamarca: A Social and Biographical Study of the First Conquerors of Peru* (Austin: University of Texas Press, 1972).

Pizarro, Juan (b. ca. 1510–d. 1536) *Spanish conquistador* Juan Pizarro, FRANCISCO PIZARRO's half brother, was born in the capital of Spain's Extremadura Province,

A view of the monumental architectural complex of Sacsayhuamán, located in the hills above the Inca capital of Cuzco *(Courtesy of J. Michael Francis)*

Trujillo, in approximately 1510. Like Francisco, Juan was the illegitimate son of Gonzalo Pizarro Rodríguez de Aguilar (1446–1522). His mother was María Alonso, which made him a full brother of GONZALO PIZARRO. Unlike Francisco, Juan Pizarro seems to have been raised in the manner befitting a member of the lesser nobility. He grew up under the tutelage of his half brother HERNANDO PIZARRO and his aunt, the matriarch of the Pizarro family in Trujillo, Estefanía de Vargas.

In 1530, Pizarro sailed to the Indies with his brothers and quickly assumed positions of responsibility in the CONQUEST of PERU. Reported to be affable and well liked among the Spaniards, in contrast with his half brother Hernando, Juan rose to the rank of captain and was effectively put in charge of the family's interests in the city of CUZCO. He served on the founding CABILDO (town council) of the city and later was named its CORREGIDOR. Juan died from wounds sustained in a heroic charge he led to retake the fortress of Sacsayhuamán during MANCO INCA's 1536 siege of Cuzco. He left his entire inheritance to his brother Gonzalo and never recognized a mestiza daughter he had fathered with an Inca noblewoman in Cuzco (see MESTIZAJE/MESTIZO).

—Michael J. Horswell

Further reading:
James Lockhart. *The Men of Cajamarca: A Social and Biographical Study of the First Conquerors of Peru* (Austin: University of Texas Press, 1972).

pochteca Constituting a long-distance merchant class within Aztec society, the *pochtecas* were organized hierarchically into 12 guildlike groups (see AZTECS). Originally based in the city of Tlatelolco, the *pochtecas* resided in closed neighborhoods with internal laws, practiced intermarriage, and celebrated private feasts and performed rituals to their patron god Yahcateuctli. The *pochteca* title was hereditary, though outsiders were occasionally admitted to the group.

These specialized merchants operated in the open mercantile economy of the Late Postclassic Aztec Empire (1400–1520), which established long-distance exchange networks between the Valley of MEXICO and highly specialized production areas (see ECONOMY; TRADE). In the absence of draft animals, the *pochtecas* traveled lengthy intervals on foot, carrying raw materials and finished items on their backs or with the aid of porter caravans. Among the trade items that moved to and from the empire's center were TEXTILES, jaguar pelts, feathers, CERAMICS, shells, OBSIDIAN, precious stones, bronze, GOLD, salt, CACAO beans, and slaves (see SLAVERY). Some of the imported utilitarian goods were sold to commoners in the markets of Tlatelolco and TENOCHTITLÁN.

The *pochteca* trading expeditions were commonly sponsored by the Mexica (Aztec) nobility, who required exotic goods to enhance their prestige and status. Since they were not considered nobility, the *pochtecas* could not normally keep their luxury merchandise. Nevertheless, the Aztec rulers granted them special privileges and generous rewards, and many *pochtecas* became as wealthy as the nobles who hired them. Their unique position as merchants for the elite gave the *pochtecas* the right to travel freely throughout the Aztec Empire and beyond, and they often acted as ambassadors to foreign rulers. This made them the eyes and ears of the emperor; they gathered news, created MAPS, and frequently spied on politically unstable regions. Occasionally, when a *pochteca* trader was murdered by a hostile group, the Aztecs retaliated with brute military force.

After the Spanish CONQUEST, the *pochtecas* started to compete with European merchants and merchandise; however, they were severely restricted by the colonial bureaucracy, and soon after the conquest, the organized guild was dissolved.

—Danny Zborover

Further reading:
Ross Hassig. *Trade, Tribute, and Transportation: The Sixteenth Century Political Economy of the Valley of Mexico* (Norman: University of Oklahoma Press, 1985).

Ponce de León, Juan (b. ca. 1460–d. 1521) *Spanish explorer, conquistador, and governor of Puerto Rico* Juan Ponce de León was born in Santervás de Campos near Valladolid sometime around 1460. Prior to the discovery of the Americas, he served the MONARCHS OF SPAIN Ferdinand and Isabella in their campaign against the Muslim kingdom of Granada. After its CONQUEST, Ponce de León ventured to the Americas in 1493 on CHRISTOPHER COLUMBUS's second voyage. He participated in the conquest and early government of HISPANIOLA. In 1508, Ponce de León received royal permission to conquer the nearby island of Borikén. He renamed the island San Juan de PUERTO RICO and founded the first Spanish settlement there, Caparra. In 1509, Ponce de León was named governor of the island. His tenure as governor was brief; he was removed from his position when Diego Columbus was granted privileges that had been taken from his father.

In 1513, Ponce de León sought to improve his position by engaging in a new conquest. Outfitting several ships, he ventured north where he claimed the "island" of La FLORIDA. After traveling along most of Florida's Atlantic coast, his ships passed around the Florida Keys and entered into the Gulf of MEXICO. On this journey, he discovered the Gulf Stream Current, which would become invaluable to transatlantic navigation. Ponce de León also searched for the "Fountain of Youth." According to Spanish CHRONICLERS of the time, this myth had been recounted to him by the TAINO Indians in Puerto Rico.

In 1521, Ponce de León organized a second expedition of two ships and approximately 200 men to conquer

Florida. His men faced strong resistance by the Calusa Indians, and Ponce de León himself was seriously wounded. After retreating to Cuba, he died from his wounds.

—Robert Schwaller

Popol Vuh Literally meaning "Council Book," the Popol Vuh is a valuable source of information on the history, genealogy, religion, mythology, and social organization of the K'iche' (Quiché) Maya people of Guatemala. Its known history began as a K'iche' alphabetic transliteration of a pictorial document, most likely a pre-Columbian codex, composed by members of three noble lineages between 1554 and 1558 in the colonial town of Santa Cruz Quiché (see codices). At the beginning of the 18th century, the manuscript was discovered in the town of Chichicastenango by Fray Francisco Ximénez, who translated it into Spanish. The document was brought to scholarly attention soon after Guatemalan independence in 1821 and is currently held in the Newberry Library in Chicago. As one of the most complete and detailed indigenous texts of Mesoamerica, the Popol Vuh has provided scholars with a wealth of information regarding Maya religious iconography, which appears to record a Maya history that dates back to as early as 100 b.c.e., as seen for example on the San Bartolo murals (see religion).

The Popol Vuh begins by recounting the Maya gods' creation of the physical world and the humans who inhabit it, the latter succeeding only after four attempts, when humans were made out of maize. Their descendants eventually became the founders of the K'iche' lineages, who wandered the land to establish kingdoms and eventually settled in Guatemala's central highlands. They received their ruling legitimacy first from a powerful city in the east and later from a great ruler in the lowlands somewhere off the Yucatán shore. These K'iche' nobles returned to their kingdoms with items of rulership, among which was the original pictorial document that would later be translated and named the Popol Vuh.

At the heart of the narrative is another story concerning Hun Hunahpu and Vucub Hunahpu, the sons of the first calendar diviners. The firstborn twin sons of Hun Hunahpu were to become the patrons of writing and the arts. Although Hun Hunahpu and Vucub Hunahpu were later sacrificed by the lords of the underworld, Hun Hunahpu miraculously fathered a second pair of twin sons, Hunahpu and Xbalanque, with the daughter of an underworld lord. The narrative then focuses on the adventures of these later Hero Twins—both on earth and in Xibalbá, the underworld, where they overcome trials posed by the lords therein. Eventually, they allow themselves to be burned to ashes, only to be resurrected in the disguise of magicians who can raise the dead. They perform their miraculous act on the lords of death, but after sacrificing them, they do not revive them. After avenging their father's and uncle's

deaths and paying a visit to their burial place, the Hero Twins then rise to heaven as celestial bodies. These protagonists' movements between the surface and the underworld probably represent those of the Sun, Moon, planets, and stars through the sky, thus the Popol Vuh should be read as an allegorical tale similar to the Greek and other great mythologies of the world.

—Danny Zborover

Further reading:
Allen J. Christenson. *Popol Vuh: The Sacred Book of the Maya* (Norman: University of Oklahoma Press, 2007).

potato The potato (*Solanum*) is a food crop of the New World comparable in age to the wheat and barley of the Old World. There are more than 235 species of wild potato. These have successfully resisted frost, extreme altitudes, drought, insect pests, and microbial diseases. Early human populations in southern Chile were gathering and roasting wild potatoes 13,000 years ago. Potatoes have been cultivated in the Andes for at least 10,000 years, about the same length of time as beans and squash. During this long period, Andean farmers developed eight species and thousands of varieties of domesticated potatoes (see agriculture). One reason they were able to do this is the enormous number of microclimates in the Andes, where small changes in altitude led to changes in temperature and moisture. A second reason is in the genetic makeup of the *Solanum* genus. This remarkable diversity led to high productivity and a reduction of risk to farmers.

Of the eight species of cultivated potatoes, *pitiquiña* is closest to its wild forebears. The other seven species of domesticated potatoes were developed from *pitiquiña*, which is highly nutritious. Its tubers are extremely variable, both in form and in color. The yellow potato (*limeña* or *papa amarilla*) is deep yellow and especially tasty. It is adapted to the shorter days of the central Andes and is not found outside that region. The *phureja* potato is grown at low to mid-altitudes (7,200–8,500 feet [2,195–2,590 m] above sea level) on the warm moist eastern slopes of the Andes from Venezuela to Argentina. Its small, irregular-shaped tubers are nutritious with good flavor. *Phureja* lacks a dormant period and sprouts immediately. This is good for continuous cropping but a drawback for storage.

There are literally thousands of varieties of the *andigena* potato, which is found from Argentina to Venezuela. The tubers are large, and the modern *tuberosum* species is closely related. Two frost-resistant species of potatoes are grown at high altitudes in southern Peru and Bolivia; they are *ajanhuiri* and *rucki*. *Ajanhuiri* is grown between 12,000 and 1,300 feet (3,658–396 m) in the region around Lake Titicaca. The tubers are nutritious but are too bitter to eat without processing. *Rucki* potatoes (actually two species) are grown at even higher altitudes and are even more frost resistant; they also require processing to be edible.

Long ago, Andean farmers devised a process of leaching potatoes in running water, then drying them in the sun and freezing them at night; this process created a lightweight flour called *chuño* that is highly nutritious, portable, and can be stored indefinitely. *Rucki* potatoes are still planted today to reduce the risk of crop loss in extreme conditions. In the Andes, potatoes provided the calories and nutrition for survival and population growth in one of the most challenging environments in the world. Technical developments—the creation of new varieties and the invention of *chuño*—made the development of civilization possible.

—Patricia J. Netherly

Further reading:
James Lang. *Notes of a Potato Watcher* (College Station: Texas A & M University Press, 2001).

Potosí   Located high in the eastern Andes Mountains (14,764 feet [4,500 m] above sea level) on an alluvial plain in modern-day BOLIVIA, Potosí served as a center for SILVER MINING from its founding in 1545 through the end of the 17th century. The huge quantities of silver extracted from Potosí made it synonymous with wealth throughout Europe. The forced LABOR methods employed there contributed to the Black Legend, an understanding of Spanish colonial rule that emphasized its cruelty toward and exploitation of indigenous peoples.

Increased activity in the eastern Andean highlands during the GONZALO PIZARRO rebellion enabled the Spanish to discover the extensive silver ore deposits of the Cerro Rico (Rich Mountain) around which the city of Potosí developed (see CIVIL WARS IN PERU). This discovery is the subject of folklore, for despite evidence of pre-Hispanic silver mining by communities in the immediate vicinity of the Cerro Rico, even the rich surface ores remained virtually untouched. One story emphasizes the destined arrival of the Spaniards. At the height of Inca rule, agents approached the site to examine it (see INCAS). A voice from inside the mountain commanded them not to take the silver; it was meant for other masters.

Following the 1548–49 pacification of the Pizarro rebellion, settlement in Potosí began in earnest; Spaniards throughout Peru flocked to the city in order to stake their claims. They brought with them the *YANA* and *ENCOMIENDA* Indians who provided the labor force during the initial phase of silver mining. The terms of service differed depending on the demands of the Spanish master and the legal status of the indigenous laborer, but most miners owed their masters a fixed quantity of ore or refined silver, which was to be given at intervals. Upon fulfilling this duty, native individuals were usually free to extract ore for their own profit.

The early period of extraction (1545–60) was limited primarily to surface mining. Ore was crushed by means of human- or animal-powered mills and was then refined in traditional Andean furnaces, called *guayras*. When placed on the windswept hills around Potosí, air rushing through strategically cut vents over flaming llama dung produced temperatures capable of separating impurities from the silver ore. Ores of sufficient quality could be made into pure, coinable silver.

By 1550, as many as 25,000 native Andeans resided in Potosí. Fifteen years later, that number had more than tripled. Many came to fulfill the demands of the Spaniards to whom they were pledged, but some came in hopes of escaping the onerous tribute demands of their masters. The urban ECONOMY of Potosí offered indigenous people a means of subsistence apart from their traditional *AYLLUS*.

The exhaustion of surface ores led to a decline in silver production beginning in the late 1560s. This, in turn, instigated the mass departure of Amerindian laborers. The introduction of water-driven mills and a new amalgamation technique solved the problem of dwindling surface ores and made the refining process more efficient. Amalgamation, a process developed in New Spain (MEXICO) in the 1550s, involved adding mercury to pulverized ore inside a refining tank. The resulting chemical reactions enabled silver to be separated from less valuable components of the ore. Amalgamation made it possible to refine even low-quality ores into pure silver. The resulting increase in profitability made cutting mineshafts a worthwhile enterprise. Spanish settlers managed to ensure a sufficient indigenous workforce by reviving the pre-Hispanic *MITA* labor draft system. Silver production spiked in the late 1570s. Output leveled off in the 1590s, but production remained high through the first few decades of the 17th century.

See also POTOSÍ (Vol. II).

—Jonathan Scholl

Further reading:
Peter Bakewell. *Miners of the Red Mountain: Indian Labor in Potosí, 1545–1650* (Albuquerque: University of New Mexico Press, 1984).

pottery   See CERAMICS.

probanza de mérito   The Spanish Crown never possessed the resources necessary to fund the enormous costs of the exploration, CONQUEST, and settlement of the New World; instead, the MONARCHS OF SPAIN often negotiated private agreements with individuals or corporations, offering financial rewards, offices, and titles to those who organized, equipped, and funded these early ventures. Likewise, the thousands of conquistadores who participated in the conquest were not part of a formal Spanish army; rather, most joined the early conquest expeditions in the hope that their services would be rewarded with money, offices, and titles. Thus, the *probanza de mérito*, or "proof of merit" petition, served to highlight individual services to the Crown. Thousands of these petitions are housed in archives in Spain and throughout Latin America, offering rich details about the various conquest campaigns. Scholars have too often overlooked the value of these documents, claiming that the self-serving purpose of these records exaggerates individual accomplishments and thereby distorts the history of the conquest. Nevertheless, individual petitioners had to be careful not to exaggerate their achievements, as witnesses often contradicted such claims. Colonial *probanzas* provide some of the richest documents for reconstructing the history of the campaigns of conquest and their participants.

—J. Michael Francis

Further reading:

Murdo J. MacLeod. "Self-Promotion: The *Relaciones de Méritos y Servicios* and Their Historical and Political Interpretation." *Colonial Latin American Historical Review* 7, no. 1 (Winter 1998): 25–42.

Puerto Rico   Part of the much larger Caribbean culture area, Puerto Rico presents the longest continuous span of occupation in the Antilles. The archaeological record indicates that human settlement began on the island during the Mesoindian or the Preceramic period, from 7,900 to 2,000 years ago. It is presumed that early migrants made their way east from Yucatán or Central America to Mona Island and Puerto Rico from 6,600 to 4,500 years ago (see MIGRATION). These sites are identified with the Casimiroid culture, which is noted for the lithic artifacts associated with hunter-gatherer cultures.

From around 2,000 years ago to the first contact with Europeans, about 500 years ago, dramatic cultural changes occurred around the Caribbean. These was characterized by diverse ceramic styles and increased population density (see CERAMICS). The first group that migrated into the Antilles during this period were the Saladoid. Making their journeys between 2,000 to 1,400 years ago, the Saladoid brought with them horticulture that featured MANIOC and MAIZE, as well as polychrome pottery technology. Within the area of Puerto Rico and the Virgin Islands, subregional Saladoid cultures named the Huecan and the Cedrosan developed permanent settlements; they are associated with ceremonial centers and ball courts.

While some accounts identify Puerto Rico and its aboriginal population as Carib, the indigenous peoples that CHRISTOPHER COLUMBUS encountered at the end of the 15th century are generally known as TAINO (see CARIBS). Columbus symbolically took possession of the island of Borikén, as it was known among the Taino, in the name of Spanish Crown in 1493, yet Spanish settle-

ment of the island did not begin until 1508. When the island's first Spanish governor, JUAN PONCE DE LEÓN, arrived on the island and renamed it *Puerto Rico*, there were approximately 20 loosely confederated indigenous political territories. The CACIQUE (chieftain) Agueibana was the most politically influential and had the largest traditional territory. As with the prior colonization of HISPANIOLA, and under orders from the Spanish Crown, Ponce de León set out to control the island's resources and subdue its inhabitants. To accomplish his mission, he established a now legendary yet peaceful relationship with Agueibana. After Ponce de León entered into the "making relations ceremony" with Agueibana, it would seem that this early association between the Spaniards and Puerto Rico's Taino was at the least amicable.

While Ponce de León did set out to subjugate the Taino, his initial strategy was not militarily oriented. Rather, his first economic endeavors were agricultural initiatives (see AGRICULTURE). Puerto Rico's Taino were not subject to overt military extermination policies nor was the overall population forced to exploit GOLD (see MINING). Of the Taino who were pressed into such service, it was consistently reported that "those natives who could escape fled to the interior, away from the slave driving masters."

By 1515, only 5,500 indigenous people were officially distributed in the Spanish ENCOMIENDAS in Puerto Rico. The *encomienda* was a Spanish trusteeship LABOR system that institutionalized "rights and obligations" between the *encomendero* (grantee) and the people under his "care." An expansion of medieval feudal institutions, Indian lands were theoretically to remain in the Amerindians' possession; nevertheless, they were required to pay tax (tribute) and provide free labor at certain times of the year to the *encomendero*. In exchange, the *encomendero* was responsible for their welfare, their assimilation into Spanish culture, and their Christianization.

From 1515 to 1518, outbreaks of smallpox are said to have wiped out two-thirds of Puerto Rico's indigenous inhabitants, as well as a significant percentage of Spaniards (see DISEASE). These estimates relate solely to those Indians within the *encomienda* system, as no censuses were taken in the mountainous region at this time.

Just three years after the initial colonization of the island in 1511, and one year after the first gold smelter was ordered built, more than 11,000 aboriginal islanders began the first of a series of military offensives against the Spanish. Although Puerto Rico received the least number of enslaved Africans in the Indies, many of those who arrived joined the Taino in the mountainous interior (see SLAVERY). In what the Spanish named the "Cimarron Rebellions," these two distinct cultural groups combined forces in military campaigns against the Spanish Crown.

While Old World diseases, slavery, low birth rates after the CONQUEST, malnutrition, suicide, intermarriage, departure to other islands, and outright WARFARE all reduced the indigenous population, these factors did not lead to a complete extinction of Puerto Rico's Taino Indians, despite what has been promoted historically.

See also PUERTO RICO (Vols. II, III, IV).

—Roberto Múkaro Borrero

Further reading:
Loida Figueroa. *History of Puerto Rico from the Beginning to 1892* (New York: Anaya Book Co., 1972).
Olga Jiménez de Wagenheim. *Puerto Rico: An Interpretive History from Pre-Columbian Times to 1900* (Princeton, N.J.: Markus Wiener Publishers, 1998).
Peter E. Siegel, ed. *Ancient Borinquen: Archaeology and Ethnohistory of Native Puerto Rico* (Tuscaloosa: University of Alabama Press, 2005).

pulque   Pulque is the slightly sour, carbohydrate-rich fermented product of the sap of the xerophytic agave or maguey (*Agave americana* and others). Consumed in Central and western MEXICO, it is a prominent traditional beverage associated with ritual intoxication. Part of a constellation of products—FOOD, fiber, construction material, fuel, and fertilizer—derived from the agave, pulque (*octli*, in NAHUATL) is weakly alcoholic and appears white due to the suspension of a diverse community of yeast and eubacteria (see ALCOHOL). Viable as a beverage for a brief period of 24–36 hours, pulque undergoes putrescent decomposition, developing a mucilaginous body and a disagreeable odor. Its artisanal production begins with the collection of sucrose-rich *aguamiel* from specially prepared, mature plants of six to 12 years of age. Once collected, the *aguamiel* is transferred to fermentation containers; during the preconquest period,

these were large, flared-neck ceramic jars (see CERAMICS). Roots were traditionally added during fermentation to increase intoxicating effects. Among the AZTECS, special intoxicating pulques were prepared for use in ritual (see RELIGION). Pulques flavored by the addition of fruits may have precolonial roots; however, most are of later invention. Agave use is documented in the Early Preclassic period, although the production of pulque may have begun sometime later as the plant came under increasing cultivation. Representations of agave and pulque occur at the Classic-period metropolis of TEOTIHUACÁN (200–800 C.E.). Representations are also common in Postclassic-period CODICES. A highly significant food resource for the large Postclassic-period populations of Central Mexico at the eve of the Spanish CONQUEST, agave cultivation is strongly associated with xeric areas where *aguamiel* and pulque augmented the traditional MAIZE and legume-based diet and provided a potable source of water in areas with limited surface water supplies.

See also PULQUE (Vol. II).

—Christopher Von Nagy

Further reading:
Henry J. Bruman. *Alcohol in Ancient Mexico* (Salt Lake City: University of Utah Press, 2000).
Jeffrey Parsons and Mary Parsons. *Maguey Utilization in Highland Central Mexico: An Archaeological Ethnography* (Ann Arbor: Museum of Anthropology, University of Michigan, 1990).

punishment   See CRIME AND PUNISHMENT.

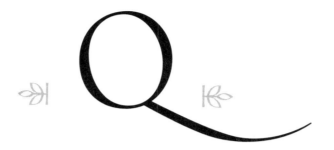

Quechua Quechua is best described as a group of seven related languages, which are not mutually intelligible as they are divided into many dialects. Today, there are at least 10 million Quechua speakers in the Andean republics, ranging from southern COLOMBIA, ECUADOR, PERU, and BOLIVIA to northwestern ARGENTINA. There is an extensive record of oral LITERATURE, poetry, and song; written Quechua is now taught in bilingual schools.

Most Quechua speakers are found in Peru and Bolivia. It was long thought that the great extent of Quechua was related to the expansion of the Inca state, which introduced Quechua as the language of administration and that the language was further spread by the Spanish colonial authorities (see INCAS). However, studies in historical linguistics have shown that in the centuries before 500 B.C.E., the original language, proto-Quechua, was spoken on the central Peruvian coast and adjacent highlands. From 0 to 500 C.E., divergent forms of Quechua expanded into the central highlands, including Junín and along the coast to the north and south of the original area.

In the centuries that followed, further expansion and diversification occurred into the north-central highlands and coast and along the southern coast into the southern highlands and the WARI heartland, displacing Aymara-related languages and extending to the south of CUZCO. By about 800 C.E., one divergent dialect, very different from the dialect spoken in Cuzco, had moved north from Chachapoyas into highland Ecuador, long before the arrival of the Incas. To the south, the expanding Inca state seems to have facilitated the spread of Quechua into eastern Bolivia and

northwestern Argentina, without penetrating a block of Aymara, Puquina, and Uruquilla dominance around Lake Titicaca and extending south to Lake Poopó. Thus, the early expansion was fostered by spontaneous contact between peoples, who were probably multilingual, through TRADE or pilgrimage. For many of these groups, the Quechua dialect of Cuzco was another language to be learned.

—Patricia J. Netherly

Further reading:

Alfredo Torero. *Idiomas de los Andes: Lingüística e historia,* 2d ed. (Lima, Peru: Editorial Horizonte, 2005).

Quetzalcóatl (Kukulkán) In NAHUATL, this deity's name means "feathered serpent." Called Kukulkán among the MAYA, the god Quetzalcóatl has great time depth and geographic spread throughout Mesoamerica, where he was revered as the patron of rulers, learning, and merchants.

Although serpent iconography dates to Olmec times (1000–400 B.C.E.), such as on Monument 19 from La Venta, most archaeologists place the serpent-plus-feathers motif later (see OLMECS). For example, within the citadel (Ciudadela) on the Street of the Dead in TEOTIHUACÁN in Central MEXICO, stands the Temple of Quetzalcóatl (150–250 C.E.). This terraced, truncated pyramid has multiple copies of a feathered serpent head, with ruffed neck feathers, on the terrace risers.

In the Yucatán Peninsula, feathered serpents are also common at Uxmal (800–1000 C.E.), where pairs

A feathered serpent head representing Quetzalcóatl adorns the Aztec Templo Mayor. *(Courtesy of J. Michael Francis)*

adorn building facades in long intertwining patterns. The Nunnery Quadrangle and Governor's Palace are noteworthy in this regard. Moreover, the Itzá held the feathered serpent as central to worship. Feathered serpent images at CHICHÉN ITZÁ (800–1100) adorn several ceremonial structures, including the largest ball court in Mesoamerica, where feathered-serpent columns are used in the upper and lower Temple of the Jaguars, and feathered serpent balustrades flank stairways. The Temple of the Warriors features large feathered serpent columns. Similar columns are found at the Toltec site TULA, in Hidalgo, north of MEXICO CITY (see TOLTECS). The AZTECS borrowed widely from Toltec traditions and beliefs, and Quetzalcóatl became one of their most venerated deities.

The Temple of Kukulkaán (also referred to as the Castillo), Chichén Itzá's largest structure, has large stone serpent heads at the foot of the north balustrades. At the equinoxes, the setting Sun shines light across the terraces, which casts a light-and-dark shadow to create the pattern of a diamond-back rattlesnake from the stone heads at the foot of the pyramid to the top. Feathered serpent motifs are evident at MAYAPÁN (1200–1450) as copies of the ARCHITECTURE at Chichén Itzá. Given that numerous Mesoamerican rulers adopted the name *Quetzalcóatl* as their own, religious ritual became mixed with history and myth into legends about real people (see RELIGION).

—Walter R. T. Witschey

quipu   The *quipu* (*quipo, khipu*) is an Andean device that predates the rise of the Inca Empire (see INCAS). In general, *quipus* consist of a series of variously placed knotted cords (called "pendant threads") connected to a central cord. The position, color, length, and design of these cords allowed Inca *quipucamayoc* (specialists who created and "read" the *quipus*) to record and "read" the information that each *quipu* contained. The precise nature of the information encoded on these *quipus* has been the source of much scholarly contention, however. Most scholars have argued that *quipus* served principally as mnemonic devices and that the information encoded on the different knots was used mainly to

Felipe Guamán Poma de Ayala's illustration of a *quipucamayoc* (Inca accountant and treasurer), holding a *quipu* in his hands *(The Royal Library, Copenhagen, Denmark)*

record numerical quantities, such as census data, troop numbers, and the contents of storehouses. Indeed, it appears that most *quipus* recorded information of that nature.

Nevertheless, over the past several decades, the debate over other possible uses of Inca *quipus* has intensified, and many modern Andeanists now believe that *quipus* were used to record much more than numerical information. Indeed, recent scholarship suggests that Inca *quipus* reflected a striking degree of uniformity and could be used to record sophisticated grammatical constructions; in other words, it has been argued that *quipus* could in fact record language and therefore could be "read." It should also be noted that many Spanish colonial accounts claimed that *quipus* were used to record non-numerical information, such as myths, legends, history, and poetry. For several decades after the Spanish CONQUEST, *quipucamayocs* continued to function in colonial PERU, often appearing in Spanish courts, where they were asked to read from their *quipus*. Transcriptions of these testimonies have begun to yield fascinating new clues about the information encoded on Inca *quipus*.

—J. Michael Francis

Further reading:
Catherine Julien. *Reading Inca History* (Iowa City: University of Iowa Press, 2000).

R

regidor Council members, or *regidores*, represented their CITIES and towns at the local level in the basic political unit of the Spanish Crown, the *CABILDO*. From the moment the first Spaniards settled in the New World, they introduced concepts of government based on medieval codes of law and customary practice. The *cabildo*, or municipal council, was the cornerstone of Castilian society. In America, the Spaniards used the founding of a town and the election of *cabildo* members as a means of colonization.

In MEXICO CITY, after the defeat of the TRIPLE ALLIANCE in 1521, Spaniards founded a *cabildo* and set about rebuilding the capital city from the ashes of TENOCHTITLÁN. The *cabildo* was composed of alcaldes, who typically functioned in a judicial capacity, and *regidores*. As political administrators, *regidores* collected tribute and enforced regulations related to local markets and commerce, building projects, and infrastructure. They also oversaw the organization of municipal celebrations, royal receptions, and religious festivities. Most *regidores* involved in the formation of Mexico City had been granted *ENCOMIENDAS*, which gave them access to indigenous tribute or LABOR; others held interest in MINING, SUGAR cultivation, cattle, and TRADE. Access to labor and resources fostered resentment and political factionalism among the early Spanish elite.

Royal administrators took the notion of the *cabildo* and superimposed it on indigenous communities organized around *repúblicas de indios*, a Spanish term often used to refer to semi-independent groups of Indians who controlled a given portion of land (see *REPÚBLICA DE INDIOS*). While royal provisions stipulated that membership of indigenous *cabildos* should include only native people, the expanding presence of *castas*, a term used to identify those of mixed-blood ancestry, compromised this practice (see *ALTEPETL; CAH; MESTIZAJE/MESTIZO*). During the colonial period, *cabildo* members from Indian towns stand out as some of the most active mediators between the Spanish and indigenous worlds.

See also *REGIDOR* (Vol. II).

—Alex Hidalgo

Further reading:

Charles Gibson. *The Aztecs under Spanish Rule: A History of the Indians of the Valley of Mexico, 1519–1810* (Stanford, Calif.: Stanford University Press, 1964).
Lyle McAllister. *Spain and Portugal in the New World, 1492–1700* (Minneapolis: University of Minnesota Press, 1984).

religion

CARIBBEAN BEFORE 1492

On October 12, 1492, CHRISTOPHER COLUMBUS landed on a small island in the Caribbean, which he named San Salvador. It was there that he made initial contact with the TAINO. His perceptions of the native people, as well as those of the other early colonial CHRONICLERS, were affected by a variety of factors, including a Christian and patriarchal value system, fear, a sense of isolation, and culture shock at being in an alien environment. Columbus's financial debt to Queen Isabella and his need to validate his geographical theories further impaired his judgment and affected his treatment of the indigenous population. All of these factors are important to keep in mind when attempting to understand pre-Columbian religious beliefs and practices in the Caribbean.

The archaeological evidence is scanty and inconclusive. Over the centuries since initial contact, most indigenous ceremonial and burial grounds have been looted or destroyed. Nevertheless, on his first voyage to the Caribbean, Columbus described the artifacts he saw. His original journal was lost, but the Dominican friar BARTOLOMÉ DE LAS CASAS recorded the following excerpt in his *Apologetica historia de las Indias*: "We have found many beautifully carved statues and masks in the shape and likeness of women. I do not yet know whether they are for the purpose of adornment or religious devotion."

It is clear from this entry that Columbus was curious about the beliefs of the Amerindians. In March 1495, Columbus commissioned a Catalan missionary from the Jeronymite order, Fray Ramon Pané, to live with and learn about the Taino people. Pané was a simple man who had come to the New World to serve as a chaplain to the newly arrived Spanish settlers. Over a three-year period, he wrote extensively about the Taino belief system. While his writing style reflects a lack of EDUCATION, he nonetheless mastered the native language. Pané went on to write the most complete and reliable account of Taino customs and beliefs ever recorded.

According to Pané, Taino religion and mythology included aspects of animism, shamanism, totemism, and polytheism. The two major deities in the Taino pantheon of gods and goddesses were Yucahu Bagua Maorocoti and Attabeira Yermao Guacar Apito Zuimaco, his mother, who was also mother of the celestial waters, human fertility, and the Moon. One of Attabeira's names identifies her as the creator and supreme deity. The *batey*, the sports field and ceremonial grounds of the native population, was named after Atabey (Attabeira), and representations of her abounded at these locations. Some scholars have suggested that the games played on these fields were imbued with religious significance and helped predict the future.

The name Yucahu Bagua Maorocoti translates as "lord of the yucca, the seas, and without male ancestor" (see MANIOC). This indicates that Attabeira, like Tiamat in the Enuma Elish, is the great mother and the one creator. It was she alone, like the Egyptian creator Nun, who without the aid of a male engendered Yucahu and all the other deities. It was also she who was represented in the elliptical stone objects (*cemíes*) depicting a snake eating its own tail—she with no beginning and no end. *Cemíes* were an important part of the Taino belief system, as the spirits of their deities and their ancestors resided within these sacred objects. Other *cemíes* were usually tripointed, mountain-shaped statues made of stone or wood.

The Taino belief system played an integral part in the people's daily existence. The Taino believed that DISEASE was the result of one of two things: disordered thinking (stress or anxiety) or a nutritional deficiency. Illness was therefore treated with spiritual counseling, directed by a *behique*, or shaman. Upon entering a hallucinogenic trance after inhaling a powdered herb (*cohoba*), the *behique* would speak to the spirits in order to ascertain the cause of an illness. At times, a ritual sacrifice involving abstention and/or fasting was prescribed. Other times, an exorcism was performed. Most often, the cure was as simple as creating a *cemí* of an ancestor or protective spirit for the patient. The Taino are recorded to have been very free with all their possessions, sharing everything they had except for their personal *cemíes*, which they guarded religiously.

Other deities who figured strongly in the Taino pantheon are Yaya, Spirit of Spirits and Father of the Sky, and Itiba Cahubaba, Ancient Bleeding One and Mother Earth. It is not clear whether these were other manifestations of Attabeira and Yucahu or separate deities. In addition, Pané described other *cemíes* the Tainos worshipped and their characteristics. These included Maquetaurie Guayaba, lord of the dead, and Guabancex, mistress of the hurricane, the Amazon woman (see AMAZON WOMEN).

The Taino religious pantheon was complex and seemed to be representative of the dual nature of all things. According to their creation myth, the Taino originated in a land called Caonao (land of GOLD) on a mountain called Cauta (sacred mountain). On this mountain, there were two caves. One was called Caciba Jagua (cave of the sacred tree), and the other, Amayauna (cave of no importance). The Taino people emerged from Caciba Jagua; all other people emerged from Amayauna.

Like many other indigenous cultures, Taino cosmology included a belief in the power of four sacred elements: earth, fire, water, and air. Everything coming from the earth, including herbs and other plants, roots, and fruits were considered medicinal as well as nutritional (see MEDICINE). Newborn babies were blessed and purified by being immersed in water and, in addition to abstaining from sexual relations and fasting, men washed themselves before undertaking any potentially dangerous journey for protection. Healing herb potions (*jarabes*) were heated over a fire to activate their healing powers, and great leaders were often burned on a pyre to purify their spirits. The *behique* often used the power of breath to suck or blow spiritual forces into or out of his patients, and upon burning on a ritual pyre, dead men were said to expel or confess truths.

The belief system of pre-Colombian Caribbean peoples had many similarities and a common origin with both North and South American native cultures. There is evidence that these groups traded on a regular basis; hence, cultural diffusion would have occurred, contributing to the multifaceted, rich, and complex nature of Taino spirituality (see TRADE).

MESOAMERICA BEFORE 1492

Although unique in their own ways, the religions of Mesoamerica's settled cultures shared some fundamental beliefs. Mesoamericans believed that the earth was a middle world, positioned between the various levels of the upper world and underworld, they believed in a similar pantheon of deities who served roles within these worlds, and they imbued their deities with attributes of the flora and fauna associated with these worlds. Mesoamerican deities were connected with the clouds, rain, the Sun, and the Moon. Some took the form of humans, MAIZE, snakes, jaguars, and lizards. Still others, especially those associated with death and the underworld, took the form of skeletons, spiders, bats, and owls. Moreover, many deities appear in both masculine and feminine guises, reflecting the Mesoamerican belief in the duality of all things.

Mesoamericans also shared similar creation myths, in which deities created the world and humankind through their labor and/or sacrifice. By way of gratitude and in order to receive continued favor, humans were expected to show respect for their deities through specific rituals. Indeed, the relationship between humans and deities was tightly bound to reciprocation.

Creation myths and the reciprocal obligations they formed were honored at ceremonial centers with special connections to the underworld and upper world, such as caves and mountains, respectively. In addition, individual polities typically constructed primary ceremonial centers that commonly took the form of pyramid temples. The great pyramids formed a ritual center that included government buildings, markets, shrines, upper-class dwellings, and sometimes ball courts. They also formed a religious center where rulers performed rituals that affected the entire community and its relationship with the cosmos. Just as the pyramid was the center of the world of the community, it was also the symbolic center of the community's link to the universe and its deities. Indeed, through these pyramids, the temporal and religious world of each culture was made and ordered.

Once created, Mesoamerican cultures needed to maintain the correct balance within the universe. This was a delicate matter—shortage or excess could result in disaster. For example, drought, hurricanes, and crop failure were seen as signs of the deities' disapproval. Mesoamericans maintained the balance by fulfilling their obligations to deities through rituals and sacrifice. Because in most creation stories the deities bled or even sacrificed themselves to create the earth and humans, they required human blood for their sustenance, although sometimes animal blood was acceptable. Indeed, bloodletting rituals and HUMAN SACRIFICE were common elements in Mesoamerican religious observance.

These rituals not only "fed" the deities and fulfilled humanity's obligations but maintained the world itself. In the Nahuas' (AZTECS) creation myth, after the Sun was created it failed to move across the sky until the deities had sacrificed themselves. Similarly, humans were required to offer their blood to sustain the world; however, Mesoamericans also believed that the world was created and destroyed on a cyclical basis. For example, at the time of the Spanish CONQUEST, the Nahuas thought that the universe had already passed through four cycles and that they were living in the fifth age. At the end of each era,

the deities would create a new world and the cycle would repeat itself. Failure to sustain the world in its present cycle could result in its destruction. Thus, droughts, hurricanes, and earthquakes were also seen as warning signs to center and balance the world through religious ritual.

The community's responsibility to the deities and the world they had created fell upon the shoulders of the elite. Indeed, elite corps of warriors, priests, and rulers were responsible to the people for maintaining both the temporal and supernatural reciprocal relationships of the community. These responsibilities reinforced the elites' social and religious status by creating an extraordinary focus on elite people themselves. As the highest-ranking members of the elite, Mesoamerican rulers were not only heads of government but religious heads. As spiritual leaders, they possessed sacred powers to intervene with deities and the cosmos on behalf of their communities.

Nevertheless, the elite did not carry all the responsibility for maintaining balance; people were responsible for the daily order of their homes and individual lives. Mesoamericans believed that the human body was a miniature replica of the cosmos. Like the cosmos, the body followed a cycle of creation and destruction. The body also possessed supernatural forces that required maintenance through personal rituals and observances. Overall, religion bound together the sociopolitical units of Mesoamerica, reinforcing the roles of rulers, elites, and commoners, while giving each group a part to play in the maintenance of their natural and supernatural worlds.

Complex calendars governed the religious rituals to ensure their observance. As all Mesoamericans were agriculturalists who needed the favor of the gods to ensure a good crop, calendric rituals usually coincided with key events in the agricultural cycle such as sowing, sprouting, growing, and harvesting, and the rainy and dry seasons (see AGRICULTURE). The calendars also represented the Mesoamerican concept of time. Time existed in three separate yet constantly intersecting planes: human time, the time of the gods, and the time before the deities created humans. Every day, these natural and supernatural times intersected, and humanity received an imprint from the deities.

The Calendar Round was created to predict such imprints. This calendar consisted of two interconnecting cycles. The first, called the *tzolkin* by the MAYA, or *tonalpohualli* in NAHUATL, was the 260-day count composed of 20 day names and 13 numbers that rotated to create 260 individual days. Each day had its own omen and destiny that came to define the day itself and the characteristics of those born on that day. For example, someone born on the day of Akbal would have the propensity to be wealthy, feminine, and a skilled orator. This calendar interlocked with a 365-day calendar that followed the solar year, consisting of 18 months of 20 days, plus an additional month of five days. As both calendars rotated, numbered days became aligned with numbered months to form a date that would not repeat for 18,980 days. Thus, the day

1 Kan 2 Pop would not recur for another 52 years. This 52-year cycle was a large part of Mesoamericans' belief in cyclical creation and destruction and, as such, was a focus of significant ritual in all cultures.

The Aztecs believed that although each era of existence lasted for several 52-year cycles, the world was always in danger of being destroyed on the last day of each cycle. Thus, they celebrated what is known as the New Fire Ceremony. During the five days preceding the end of the cycle, all fires were extinguished, possessions were broken, and the people practiced a state of mourning. On the last night, Nahua priests would await Pleiades' passing through the meridian at midnight. On the star's passing, a man was sacrificed, and a fire was started in his chest, which subsequently kindled all the fires throughout the Valley of MEXICO. The next day, the renewal of another cycle was celebrated with feasting, bloodletting, and sacrifice. All settled cultures practiced similar rituals at the end of each cycle.

Astronomical observations greatly influenced Mesoamerican calendars and religious beliefs. Buildings were carefully aligned with the cycles of celestial bodies including the Moon, Sun, and Venus. For example, the Aztecs constructed the Templo Mayor so that on the spring equinox, the Sun rose directly between the two shrines—one for the god Huitzilopochtli, the other for the god Tlaloc—at its summit. The Maya aligned the sun temple at Dzibilchaltún so that on the equinoxes, the Sun would seem to rise in the middle of its main doorway. Likewise, the pyramid "El Castillo" at CHICHÉN ITZÁ was constructed in such a way that during the equinoxes, the Sun would cast a shadow of the pyramid's platforms on the side of the staircase to make a body of light that connected to the illuminated head of a snake positioned at the bottom of the stairs. For the Maya, the scene appears as though Kukulkán, the feathered serpent, is moving down the pyramid (see QUETZALCÓATL).

Finally, Mesoamerican religions were inclusive in nature. Mesoamerican cultures allowed conquered peoples to continue venerating their own deities as long as they also now venerated those of the conquerors. Additionally, the conquerors could adopt the deities of their subjects, such as the Nahuas' appropriation of Xipe Totec, an Oaxacan god of agriculture, spring, and goldworkers. In the end, this inclusiveness contributed to the creation of common beliefs among Mesoamerican religions.

SOUTH AMERICA BEFORE 1492

At the time of the Spanish conquest, the vast continent of South America was home to tens of millions of people, divided into distinct ethnic groups, with diverse languages, cultures, and religious traditions. While very little is known about the religious beliefs and practices of the majority of pre-Columbian groups, recent advances in archaeological and ethnohistorical research are beginning to provide more detailed information. Religious beliefs and practices in pre-Columbian South America

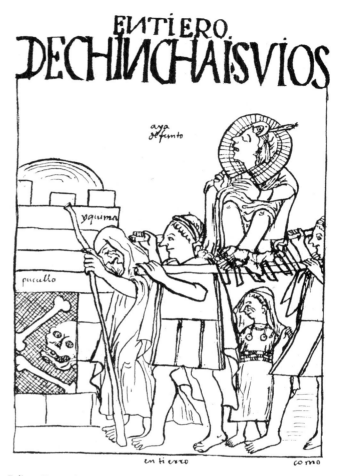

Felipe Guamán Poma de Ayala's illustration of the burial practices of the Chichaysuyus, who resided in one of the four quarters of the Inca Empire *(The Royal Library, Copenhagen, Denmark)*

were remarkably diverse, with localized networks of gods, sacred shrines, rituals, and spiritual leaders. Unlike much of Mesoamerica, where many ethnic groups shared common deities, South American religion was far more diverse. Nevertheless, despite the many different religious traditions, some commonalities do appear to have existed.

First, virtually all religious traditions in pre-Columbian South America were polytheistic, consisting of a diverse pantheon of terrestrial and celestial deities. Andean peoples, for example, believed that the sacred resided all around them, in streams, rivers, mountains, boulders, and even small stones. All of these elements of the physical world were capable of embodying the divine and thus of exerting influence on their daily lives. Local cults emerged throughout the Andes, from COLOMBIA to CHILE, linking populations with the divine powers and spirituality of the land that surrounded them.

Second, most religions or cultural practices included human and animal sacrifice. Religious traditions throughout the continent also reflected profound concern about the afterlife, and most groups venerated deceased ancestors.

The use of religious symbolism was ubiquitous in pre-Columbian societies. In fact, the most reliable primary resource from which to study these religions is the ARCHITECTURE and other material remains discovered by archaeologists. For example, several ceramic pieces found in the northern Andes of South America included two or more animals combined into one, such as half-feline and half-eagle, or even an animal body with a human face (see CERAMICS). Another common theme found in these pieces was the polarity of man and woman, usually featuring a pair of human beings side by side, some with feline legs and feet.

Of all the pre-Columbian cultures of South America, the ethnic group about whom the most is known is the INCAS. With polytheistic beliefs, the Incas worshiped many deities, all of whom had some connection to the natural elements of the Earth. An example was the Sun God, Inti. In addition to the Sun, the Incas venerated an ultimate creator, the weather/thunder god, the Moon Goddess, and a goddess of the sea. The Sun God was the figurehead of all religious and cultural aspects of life and dictated the authoritative structure of the society. The ruler of the empire was believed to be a direct descendant of Inti.

An important yet controversial aspect of Inca religious and cultural practices was the chewing of the COCA leaf. In its natural form, coca has both mental and medicinal effects; it was chewed throughout much of South America, well beyond the borders of the Inca Empire. Hallucinogenic drugs or plants also played a significant part in religious rituals; these mind-altering substances allowed a shaman to travel to the otherworld in order to communicate with the deities. The use of hallucinogenic substances was highly regulated, their consumption often restricted to all but shamans.

See also COFRADÍA (Vol. II); CURANDERA/CURANDERO (Vol. II); INQUISITION (Vol. II); MISSIONS (Vol. II); RELIGION (Vols. II, III, IV); SANTERIA (Vol. III).

—Mark Christensen
Rosalina Diaz
Christina Hawkins

Further reading:

Davíd Carrasco. *Religions of Mesoamerica: Cosmovision and Ceremonial Centers* (San Francisco: Harper & Row, 1990).

Ramon Pané. *An Account of the Antiquities of the Indians: Chronicles of the New World Encounter*, edited by José Juan Arrom, translated by Susan Griswold (Durham, N.C.: Duke University Press, 1999).

religious orders

religious orders   Within the CATHOLIC CHURCH, all nuns and some priests are members of religious orders. Generically, members of religious orders are known as "regulars," or "regular clergy," in that they follow the special rules (Latin, *regula*) of their order. There are three major types of religious orders. Orders for men are known as "first orders," with female orders being known as "second orders" since historically male orders preceded female orders, while the latter tended to adopt the rules of the first. A third order consists of laypeople who voluntarily follow the regulations of an order as best they can in their daily lives. Both male and female orders played a vital role in the development of the church in early colonial Latin America.

The Dominican and Franciscan orders were the most famous of the missionary orders in the New World. Both were founded by charismatic leaders in the 13th century, and both sought to revitalize the Catholic Church at the time. The Franciscans, founded by St. Francis of Assisi, were openly a missionary order. The Franciscans felt that by personally imitating Christ through poverty and humility, they could draw people to a deeper form of Christianity. The Dominican order, founded by St. Dominic de Guzmán, sought to attract converts to the faith through preaching and to deepen the faith of existing Christians. The members of these two orders took strict vows of poverty and sustained themselves through begging. As a result, the Franciscan and Dominican orders were known as "mendicant" orders. They practiced a strict egalitarianism, and individual members were known simply as "brothers," and in English also as "friars."

Other mendicant orders important in the evangelization of the New World were the Mercedarian and Augustinian orders. The Mercedarians (Order of Our Lady of Mercy) had as their goal the redemption of Christian captives held by Muslims. The Mercedarian order quickly became one of the most important orders in early Latin America, with several of the chaplains on important expeditions, such as those of HERNANDO CORTÉS, coming from this order. The Augustinian order played an important role in early educational efforts in Latin America and was one of the largest religious orders in MEXICO during the colonial period (see EDUCATION).

Religious orders took great pride in having been the first in any given missionary field. While some clergy accompanied the armies of CONQUEST, normally it was the arrival of an organized band of missionaries that gained precedence for a specific order. Although a Mercedarian accompanied Cortés in the conquest of Mexico, the Mercedarians are not usually considered the first order to have Christianized Mexico. The arrival of 12 Franciscans some three years after the conquest of the AZTECS initiated the evangelization of that country. The Dominicans are generally credited with being the first order in PERU.

In each major territory, different religious orders developed specific geographical regions, often on the basis of where other orders had failed to have a presence. In the case of Mexico, the Franciscans tended to first carry out their mission in the central region around modern MEXICO CITY, although Franciscan influence was also found elsewhere. The Dominicans concentrated their efforts on the southern region between Mexico City and

Oaxaca. The Augustinians were active in central regions not already claimed by the other orders, but especially in the west, in the region of Michoacán. In a similar manner, other orders came to dominate entire regions of the New World; for example, the Mercedarians were the dominant order in GUATEMALA, although other orders had a presence there.

The primary mission of the religious orders was the conversion of the indigenous people to Christianity. At the onset, the missionaries faced several major obstacles, the greatest of which was communication. The friars did not know the native languages; and the NATIVE AMERICANS did not know Spanish. Rather than train the indigenous people in Spanish or Latin, the missionaries learned the native languages, focusing on a few widely spoken languages, such as NAHUATL among the peoples of Central Mexico, Mayan in the Yucatán and Central America (see MAYA), and QUECHUA and Aymara in the Andean regions. The friars copied the languages in Latin characters, writing grammars, dictionaries, and handbooks for indoctrination. The first book published in the New World was a Christian catechism in Nahuatl, written for use in the conversion of the Aztecs.

While converting Amerindians to Christianity was the central goal, the missionary techniques of the religious orders differed. One of the major controversies of the early colonial period had to do with the administration of the sacrament of baptism. The Franciscans believed that after a relatively short period of indoctrination, native people could be baptized by a priest in a simple ceremony, using holy water and oils. The other orders, especially the Dominicans, held that native people needed a long and protracted period of study of Christian doctrine, followed by the full ritual involving new garments, salt, saliva, and other features, just as in any other baptism in Europe. Similarly, the Franciscans believed that indigenous people could be baptized at any time of the year, while the other orders restricted the sacrament to Easter and Pentecost Sundays.

Some sacraments could only be performed by the local bishop, particularly the sacrament of confirmation. In the early days of the missionary effort, there were no bishops, and when they did arrive, they served in the Spanish CITIES, often far from the remote indigenous villages. As a consequence, the friars secured permission from the pope to exercise the functions of bishops in regions located over two days' ride from the local bishop. The final permission from the pope, contained in a letter called Omnimoda, granted not just powers of bishop but all the powers of the pope himself to the missionaries operating in remote regions.

Religious orders had important vocations beyond conversion. In the towns and villages of the New World, it was the religious orders that started schools, both at the lower and university level. The Dominicans were especially active in the field of education. The Franciscans also set up schools, their most famous in Mexico being the College of the Holy Cross in Tlatelolco, a suburb of Mexico City. That school was founded to train the sons of the Aztec elite in both Christian doctrine and European culture. It was thought that if the sons of the nobility embraced Spanish culture, their subjects would be more willing to embrace Christianity. While several students at the college went on to important leadership roles in indigenous society, none were allowed to join the religious orders or the clergy. While it seems the first missionaries hoped that the young native boys who were under their tutelage could eventually become friars and priests, within a few years most came to believe that the indigenous lacked the necessary moral direction to become priests. Nonetheless, native individuals continued to serve in the monasteries and convents in an ancillary manner. Frequently called *donados*, some took the habit of the order but did not take its religious vows. Others served in the parishes, teaching Christian doctrine, leading prayer services, playing MUSIC and singing, or helping to maintain the churches and cloisters.

The majority of the religious orders sustained themselves through gifts and bequests, either of outright cash donations or property. The property could be sold for cash or maintained by the order and rented for ongoing income. The orders also established endowments to support special causes, such as saying memorial masses or providing dowries for poor young WOMEN, either to marry or to enter the convent. Funds received for endowments, and all funds in excess of what was needed for the daily expenses, were invested in property in the form of mortgages. The interest on a mortgage was used to pay for the purposes of the endowment, such as masses or dowries. Only the Franciscans refused to accept property or make investments.

See also AUGUSTINIANS (Vol. II); DOMINICANS (Vol. II); FRANCISCANS (Vol. II); JESUITS (Vol. II); MERCEDARIANS (Vol. II); MISSIONS (Vol. II).

—John F. Schwaller

Further reading:

Robert Ricard. *The Spiritual Conquest of Mexico*, translated by Leslie Byrd Simpson (Berkeley: University of California Press, 1966).

Antonine Tibesar. *Franciscan Beginnings in Colonial Peru* (Washington, D.C.: Academy of American Franciscan History, 1953).

república de indios   In many records of colonial MEXICO, the terms *república de indios* (republic of Indians) and *república de españoles* (republic of Spaniards) appear with great frequency, often in legal and social contexts that assume two fully segregated domains, one populated by indigenous people, the other by Spaniards, creoles, mestizos, and Africans. However, the various social, economic, and political practices recorded in colonial documents suggest that while initially these two terms referred to two highly differentiated groups of people, by late colonial times this differentiation was not so clear in some domains, such as large urban settlements, and increased in geographically isolated communities. The term *república de indios* should therefore be regarded as a bureaucratic concept for a set of legal dispositions, not always reflecting social realities, through which the Spanish Crown attempted to maintain politically expedient territorial, legal, and social divisions between indigenous and nonindigenous peoples.

After the CONQUEST, the Spanish Crown had to contend with local lineages and traditional notions of rulership. Thus, it allowed for the appointment of what were called "natural lords," lineage rulers who maintained their standing in early colonial governance systems. This duality was reflected in the designation of a local ruler as "CACIQUE and governor." For the most part, the Crown did not interfere directly with the election of indigenous rulers for the first two generations or so after the conquest; however, it did prepare the ground for their demise. The Crown seized the initiative during indigenous inheritance crises, inserting nonelites and even outsiders into the local sphere as governors at these times. The date of rupture with the lineage ruler varies across regions; it occurred in 1564 in Texcoco, around 1560 in Pátzcuaro and by 1560 in the Toluca valley, and from 1579 onward in central Yucatán. By the end of the 16th century, indigenous communities had been placed under the direct authority of the Crown and the centralized clergy. In this manner, the Crown succeeded in mapping a regional political chain of command onto Indian communities without overtly replacing elite groups or triggering major rebellions.

In 1516, a Spanish priest named BARTOLOMÉ DE LAS CASAS presciently argued for the major social and political features that came to characterize *pueblos de indios* (Indian towns): segregated indigenous villages directly controlled by Crown officials, with a church and a hospital governed by a qualified priest, and a population subject to rotating, periodic LABOR obligations related to labor-intensive colonial enterprises such as MINING and manufacture, and to community needs. To this general framework should be added land-tenure laws, which restricted the sale of indigenous communal or private land to non-Indians, and land-tenure patterns that emphasized communal landholdings but allowed elites and influential Indian townspeople to usufruct some portions of land. The indigenous community could be a *cabecera de doctrina*, or the head of the smallest colonial administrative unit (*sujeto*, or dependency). *Cabeceras* had a resident priest who managed the doctrinal education, mass, and public registers and periodically visited the *sujetos*.

Indians could elect lower-level local officers to serve in the town's CABILDO (city council), which consisted of two alcaldes (local magistrates), about four REGIDORES (city council members), and an *escribano* (notary). Although offi-

cials usually did not serve consecutive terms, in practice, these positions rotated among males with kinship ties to traditional elite groups or ambitious males who wished to increase their social standing; the amount of personal resources and responsibilities required for these offices acted as deterrents for overburdened commoners.

Amerindians had a variety of obligations to the Crown and to their local community. A fixed monetary yearly tax was collected from each adult indigenous person: WOMEN were assigned a lower tax, which did not automatically translate into a reduced obligation, since they had unequal access to monetary income; men contributed a fixed number of days of free labor per year—often one full day per week—to various community and Crown projects. Community funds were held in a communal box with three keys with symbolic assignations: one for the Indian head of government, another for the priest, and the third for high colonial officials. These labor and tax obligations were a heavy burden to most commoners. Labor service at regional mines and workshops contributed, along with epidemic DISEASE, to the catastrophic indigenous mortality rates during the late 16th and early 17th centuries (see MINING).

In contrast to the more complex social status of urban Indians, the relative independence and isolation of rural community residents allowed them to acquire a corporate identity that was based on local sociopolitical and religious institutions. This identity became increasingly localistic and parochial with the passage of time. The rise in rural populations that began with the demographic recovery of indigenous communities in the mid-17th century resulted in the creation of more rural communities, or pueblos, in the late 17th and the 18th centuries. The basic requirements for a *pueblo de indios* was a population of at least 80 families, a church building, and an adequate political rationale. The creation of new pueblos often called for the submission of 16th-century *títulos primordiales* (primordial titles) establishing land rights given to the community by a Spanish court; this resulted in a proliferation of new *títulos*, which imitated the style and content of earlier documents.

Paradoxically, even groups of people whose main ethnic background was not indigenous established settlements that shared traits with *pueblos de indios*. For example, the early northern Puebla community of Tenampulco, which had disintegrated due to depopulation in the late 16th century, lent its name to a new community that settled beside the former's abandoned church building in the mid-18th century. Although the new community functioned virtually as a *pueblo de indios*, most of its residents were MULATO ranchers rather than indigenous people. In this manner, the *pueblo de indios* contributed to the formation of a strong local identity in rural communities. This form of group identity has persisted in the face of numerous attempts at centralization and nation building in independent Mexico.

—David Tavárez

Further reading:

Margarita Menegus Bornemann. *Del señorío a la república de indios: El caso de Toluca, 1500–1600* (Madrid, Spain: Ministerio de Agricultura, Pesca y Alimentación, 1991).

Arij Ouweneel and Simon Miller, eds. *The Indian Community of Colonial Mexico* (Amsterdam, Netherlands: CEDLA, 1991).

requerimiento   The *requerimiento* (requirement) was a legal document that constituted, in the words of historian Patricia Seed, a "protocol for CONQUEST." It was used by the Spanish to legitimize their conquests in the Americas. In competition with the Portuguese for overseas territories, the Spanish sought to prove their legal title to the Americas. By the second decade of the 16th century, questions were being raised about the legitimacy of the conquests. For example, in 1511, the Dominican friar ANTONIO DE MONTESINOS preached a series of sermons on HISPANIOLA that denounced the exploitation of indigenous peoples. In response, the Crown convened a panel of theologians in 1513. One member of the panel, Juan López de Palacios Rubios of the Council of Castile, drafted the *requerimiento*.

Influenced by medieval Spanish legal traditions, the *requerimiento* outlined the hierarchy of Spanish colonial authority. It traced how God had granted the popes not only spiritual but also temporal authority over all peoples of the world, the descendants of Adam and Eve. When Pope Alexander VI donated the Americas to the Catholic Kings (Isabella and Ferdinand) in his bull Inter Caetera in 1493, he transferred jurisdiction of its lands and peoples to them. As a legal document, the *requerimiento* named indigenous peoples as vassals of the Crown and demanded that they submit to the pope and Spanish authority and allow Christian missionaries to preach freely. If they rejected these terms, the Spanish could justifiably wage war upon and enslave them.

The *requerimiento* was intended to be read aloud to indigenous peoples in the presence of a notary and an interpreter. Gonzalo Fernández de Oviedo, who later assumed the position of royal chronicler, accompanied the first expedition that reputedly used the *requerimiento*, namely that of PEDRO ARIAS DE ÁVILA to Tierra Firme in 1514. Other CHRONICLERS and historians described its use in the conquests of MEXICO, PERU, and other parts of Spanish America.

A vocal opponent of the enslavement and exploitation of the Amerindians, Dominican friar BARTOLOMÉ DE LAS CASAS, riled against the *requerimiento*. In his *History of the Indies*, Las Casas wrote that even if indigenous peoples understood Spanish, the terms of the *requerimiento* were still opaque. He argued that the concepts expressed in the document—a monotheistic god as creator, papal authority, and Christianity—would be incomprehensible without adequate religious instruction. Indigenous peoples did not have the information necessary to accept the terms of the document. The *requerimiento* effectively gave the Spanish a legal justification for waging war on indigenous peoples and conquering and enslaving them.

—Karoline P. Cook

Further reading:

Lewis Hanke. *The Spanish Struggle for Justice in the Conquest of America* (Dallas, Tex.: Southern Methodist University Press, 2002).

S

Sahagún, Bernardino de (b. ca. 1499–d. 1590) *Franciscan friar in Central Mexico* This member of the Order of Saint Francis was born ca. 1499; in 1529, he left Spain for MEXICO, where he remained until his death in 1590. While extremely active in the foundation of the Mexican church and its ministering to millions of NAHUATL-speaking parishioners, he is best known today for his work on the FLORENTINE CODEX, a monumental study of Nahua society, culture, and history (see AZTECS). Sahagún's work on the Florentine Codex has earned him such titles as the "first anthropologist," "pioneer ethnographer," and even "father of modern anthropology." However, while the codex was completed under Sahagún's careful supervision, it should be noted that the Florentine Codex was a collaborative endeavor, involving numerous Nahua (Aztec) aides. These assistants gathered information for the friar; they conducted extensive interviews with Nahua elders, many of whom were alive when the Spanish first arrived. Moreover, these assistants recorded the text in the Nahuatl language. Not surprisingly, the Florentine Codex is considered among the most important written works of the entire colonial period.

Among his many other accomplishments, Sahagún achieved fame as a teacher of Latin to select Nahua youth at the College of the Holy Cross in Tlatelolco. This was the first institution of higher learning in the mainland Western Hemisphere. Some of his students later became teachers there and collaborated with him on his Nahuatl writings.

Sahagún is associated with many seminal Nahuatl texts. His collection of Christian songs in Nahuatl, *Psalmodia Christiana*, appeared in 1583. Other pieces include catechistical works and examples of traditional high rhetoric. His earliest extant effort is a collection of sermons. Written in 1540, a copy made in 1548 on native *amate* (fig bark) paper and bearing Sahagún's own handwritten notations from 1563 currently rests in Chicago's Newberry Library. As an original composition, it is the oldest sermonary from the Americas.

Sahagún's linguistic expertise was well recognized. He was the lone expert censor, and for good reason. Perhaps no other European in 16th-century Mexico aside from the author of the first published Nahuatl dictionary (1555), the equally renowned Franciscan Alonso de Molina, could match Sahagún's understanding of the Nahuatl language.

See also Franciscans (Vol. II).

—Barry D. Sell

Further reading:

Miguel León-Portilla. *Bernardino de Sahagún: First Anthropologist* (Norman: University of Oklahoma Press, 2002).

John Frederick Schwaller, ed. *Sahagún at 500: Essays on the Quincentenary of the Birth of Fr. Bernardino de Sahagún* (Berkeley, Calif.: Academy of American Franciscan History, 2003).

saints Saints played an important role in 16th-century Spanish Catholicism (see CATHOLIC CHURCH). As people who had lived lives worthy of emulation and beatification, saints could intercede on behalf of those who prayed to them. As material objects, saints' images not only served to perpetuate the narrative of their lives and teach moral behavior but acted as objects to which people could make offerings and petition in times of need. In Spain, the communal aspects of local RELIGION allowed each city or town to select saints they believed would best serve the needs of its inhabitants. Saints protected Spanish communities and individuals against plagues, crop failure, and other natural disasters, and each saint had a particular niche in the cosmos as the patron of rains, harvest, childbirth, and so on. Moreover, saints had designated feast days that were arranged within the liturgical calendar year.

The Spanish conquistadores and friars brought the cult of saints to the Americas. After removing the AZTECS' idols from their main temple in TENOCHTITLÁN, HERNANDO CORTÉS erected shrines to the Virgin Mary and Saint Christopher in their place. Additionally, from the time they began establishing churches, friars insisted that each indigenous polity have a patron saint. From what is understood about the early friars and their methods, it is unlikely that they tried to replace indigenous deities with saints possessing similar characteristics. They also promoted the patron saints of their particular order and wrote hagiographies in indigenous languages to educate the native people about them. Yet given the relatively small number of ecclesiastics and the significant linguistic barriers, it would have been difficult for the friars to be the sole transmitters of information about Catholic saints. It is likely that the indigenous people also gradually learned about saints through their increasing contact with ordinary Spaniards and the ecclesiastics' linguist-aides.

Thus, when indigenous CITIES, towns, and provinces began to acquire their own patron saints, their inhabitants usually had only limited knowledge of those saints and their supernatural properties. Nevertheless, this did not impede indigenous acceptance of saints. Indeed, of all the aspects of Catholicism, saints had the most significant impact on the lives of the Indians throughout Latin America. Saints' names were given to people, churches, towns, and confraternities, and saints appear in the earliest examples of indigenous documentation, from testaments and municipal documents to primordial titles and annals. The Nahuatl term *santopan*, "where a saint is," was even occasionally employed as a general term for the subunits of *ALTEPETL*. Although documentary evidence suggests that the cult of the saints did not fully emerge in New Spain (MEXICO) until around the 1580s, saints became a part of the Indians' lives from the time they were introduced.

The close parallels between Spanish and precontact American religious traditions no doubt played an important role in native acceptance of saints. Catholicism's association between martyrdom and blood and the figures of Christ and many saints likely appealed to many indigenous people, as did the Catholic tradition of honoring saints with processions, decorative accoutrements, flowers, incense, dances, and MUSIC. Furthermore, the Nahuas (Aztecs), MAYA, MIXTECS, and INCAS already had patron deities for cities, towns, and households. The idea that towns and households could venerate supernatural beings who provided protection against myriad disasters was not new to the indigenous peoples of many areas of the New World, nor was the idea of adopting conquerors' deities into existing ideologies (although the Spaniards' demand for the exclusive worship of their god was a novelty). Indeed, the newly adopted patron saint of a city or town, like the precontact deities before them, served to unify the polity and its constituent parts. Thus, following tradition, Amerindians quickly embraced Catholic saints and combined whatever limited knowledge about them they had gleaned from friars and other Spaniards with their existing understandings of patron deities and their veneration (see SYNCRETISM).

It is understandable that the saints of New Spain took on indigenous qualities and characteristics. For example, because of Saint John the Baptist's association with water, Nahuas celebrated the saint's feast day with rituals once used to venerate Tlaloc, the precontact deity of water. Additionally, the native people viewed saints as dualistic deities who were capable of both blessing and punishing, as their older deities had been. Indeed, because the feast day of Saint Francis coincided with the end of the rainy season and the start of the cold season in Central Mexico, a change that frequently brought about a loss in crop, Nahuas referred to the saint as "the cruel." Moreover, because both indigenous people and Spaniards celebrated supernatural figures according to religious calendars based on agricultural cycles, saints and precontact deities were frequently celebrated on similar days. Such similarities allowed Saint Joseph to be associated with Xipe Totec, the Virgen de las Candelas with Chalchiuhtlicue, and Holy Week with the rites to Tezcatlipoca.

Similar to Christians in 16th-century Spain, communities in New Spain sought the intercession and appeasement of their saints, and a saint's feast day provided the opportunity to acquire both. It was not uncommon for communities to spend enormous amounts on the feast day of their patron saint. Similar to precontact rituals, communities honored their saints (whom they took to be the actual saints and not just images) with music, dancing, CACAO, PULQUE, and feathers (see ALCOHOL). Such devotion trickled down to individual homes and families. By 1560, images of saints had appeared in the homes of many Indians. Documentary evidence suggests that some indigenous people even had specific places of worship set aside in their homes for saints.

To be sure, the impact of the cult of saints varied from region to region. Yet by the end of the 17th century, Central Mexico saints were at the center of confraternities, an important part of the native religious experience and had even begun to "own" land. Although such manifestations were not quite apparent in 1560 throughout all of New Spain, the seeds for such devotions were being sown at that time.

—Mark Christensen

Further reading:

William A. Christian Jr. *Local Religion in Sixteenth-Century Spain* (Princeton, N.J.: Princeton University Press, 1981).
Martin Austin Nesvig, ed. *Local Religion in Colonial Mexico* (Albuquerque: University of New Mexico, 2006).

Salamanca, School of

Salamanca, School of   As a result of Spanish endeavors in the New World, intellectuals in the Iberian Peninsula debated over the legality of the CONQUEST and the nature of the NATIVE AMERICANS. During the 1520s and 1530s, a group of theologians led by Dominican friar FRANCISCO DE VITORIA expounded on these issues in a series of lectures held at the University of Salamanca in Spain. Collectively, this group of scholars is known as the School of Salamanca.

The early 16th century saw an influx of information to Spain from the New World that described incidents of violence and oppression against the indigenous population of the Americas. In 1512, King Ferdinand commissioned a *junta*, or meeting, of royal officers, theologians, and academicians to discuss the polemic surrounding the validity of the conquest. Partly to satisfy Ferdinand's desire to justify the Crown's actions, this group of intellectuals put together a legal code known as the LAWS OF BURGOS to regulate relations between Spaniards and native peoples.

A decade later, as information from the colonies continued to stir controversy, a group of scholars led by Vitoria attempted to rationalize the conquest along theological lines. For Vitoria and his followers, this meant a close examination of natural law, or the universal norms that direct people's behavior. Vitoria challenged the idea that the Indian was a natural slave who could not adequately govern himself. Proponents of this view pointed to anthropophagy and HUMAN SACRIFICE as evidence of the barbaric nature of the Amerindian. The fact that Christianity had not appeared in the New World until the arrival of the Spaniards also contributed to the image of the native person as a natural slave subject to the rule of the more powerful Spaniards (see SLAVERY).

In a series of lectures held in Salamanca between 1538 and 1539, Vitoria, unsolicited by the Crown, reexamined the issues surrounding the conquest known to contemporaries as the "affairs of the Indies." In *De Indis*, Vitoria systematically addressed questions of FAMILY, law, political structure, and urban development, items closely associated with European ideals of civilized life. While some Caribbean groups had led a primitive lifestyle, the Aztec and Inca Empires had been highly organized polities that were, in the minds of some early explorers, worthy of imitation (see AZTECS; INCAS). In addition, Vitoria examined the notion that the development of industry, TRADE, and RELIGION represented markers of civility. He found little to substantiate claims that these elements were absent among the Amerindians, pointing instead to the hierarchical organization of religion, the ascetic nature of New World priests, and the observation of feasts and holidays. He concluded that in terms of natural law, the Indians were neither barbarians or natural slaves but simply people subjected to negative influences.

Vitoria held the Prime Chair of Theology at Salamanca from 1529 to 1546. His work charted the course of theological inquiry at Salamanca and influenced the work of other members such as Domingo de Soto and Melchor Cano, as well as that of the Jesuits Luis de Molina and Francisco Suárez.

—Alex Hidalgo

Further reading:
Anthony Pagden. *The Fall of Natural Man: The American Indian and the Origins of Comparative Ethnology* (Cambridge: Cambridge University Press, 1982).

Santa Fe, Capitulations of

Santa Fe, Capitulations of   See CAPITULATIONS OF SANTA FE.

Santo Domingo

Santo Domingo   See HISPANIOLA.

secular clergy

secular clergy   See CLERGY, SECULAR.

Sepúlveda, Juan Ginés de

Sepúlveda, Juan Ginés de (b. ca. 1490–d. 1574)
Spanish humanist, renowned philosopher, and defender of military and Christian conquest of the Americas   Born to an elite family from Córdoba, Spain, sometime in the 1490s, Juan Ginés de Sepúlveda led an influential life, much of which he spent among Catholic royalty. In 1521, sponsored by the powerful de' Medici family, he attained his doctorate in philosophy from the College of Bologna. From 1523 to 1526, he resided at the papal court where he wrote his first tome, an Aristotelian tract called *Dialogus de appetenda Gloria*, which challenged the concept of pacifism. After nearly a decade as a canon of Salamanca and *visitador general* in the Spanish court, in 1536, Sepúlveda became the royal historian to Charles I (Holy Roman Emperor Charles V) and official tutor to the future king Philip II (see MONARCHS OF SPAIN). He compiled the 30-volume narrative about Charles I entitled *De rebus gestis Caroli Quinti*, which praised the Holy Roman emperor for his aggressive stance against heresy and paganism.

Influenced by juristic humanism, which emphasized the classical binaries of sacred and profane, Sepúlveda wrote *Democrates secundus* (published in 1547) in which he defended the CONQUEST and subjugation of the Americas as a just war aimed at wiping out indigenous barbarism and expanding the Christian realm, a position that brought Sepúlveda into direct conflict with the Dominican friar BARTOLOMÉ DE LAS CASAS. In 1550, the two influential figures debated the nature of native people before a distinguished group of royal scholars in Valladolid. Referring to the numerous European accounts of CANNIBALISM, idolatry, and HUMAN SACRIFICE, Sepúlveda charged that the Amerindians' barbarity left them in a state of natural SLAVERY. The colonial enterprise, he argued, merely reestablished the divine and natural hierarchy of the world. While official policy shifted away from the enslavement of native peoples, Sepúlveda's views found receptive audiences among Europeans wishing to justify the institutions of colonialism.

—R. A. Kashanipour

Further reading:
Lewis Hanke. *The Spanish Struggle for Justice in the Conquest of America* (Philadelphia: University of Pennsylvania Press, 1949).

silver Prior to the European CONQUEST of Latin America, silver, GOLD, and other precious metals served multiple purposes. The ancient Andeans of South America became experts at extracting silver from the earth and converting it into jewelry, decorations for religious rituals, tools, and various household items. The CHIMÚ people were among those who mastered the art of "silversmithing," constructing portraits and decorative pieces out of the precious metal.

By the time the Spanish arrived in PERU, the INCAS had formed one of the wealthiest and largest empires in the world. Inca ART was almost always made out of precious metals such as gold and silver, and some royal buildings were decorated with the same. Indeed, the preconquest silversmiths were found to possess equal or greater skill than their Spanish and other European counterparts. On their arrival in the New World, Europeans immediately began exploiting both silver and gold in massive quantities, thus establishing MINING as the primary colonial industry.

Until the Spanish and Portuguese settlers discovered MEXICO in the 1520s, the primary specie (coined money) exported from the New World was gold; however, with the fall of TENOCHTITLÁN and the discovery of silver in Mexico (and later Peru), silver soon replaced gold as the most important source of wealth in the New World. Nevertheless, in the first two decades after the conquest, productivity was slow and profits were minimal. Yet, with the discovery of rich silver deposits of POTOSÍ (modern BOLIVIA) in 1545 and Zacatecas (Mexico) the next year, productivity had dramatically increased by the 1540s and 1550s.

The indigenous peoples of South America had used silver primarily to display their prestige, and therefore, it was extracted from the earth with the intent of paying homage to the ruling religious and political authority. It was not used as currency. Not surprisingly, European demand for silver drastically conflicted with indigenous perceptions and usage of silver; for Europeans, silver and gold were viewed primarily as sources of power and wealth. Therefore, European merchants and monarchs alike fought to acquire as much of these metals as possible.

Given that the economic well-being of Spain was dependent on the incoming shipments of precious primary commodities from the New World, the increase in silver production only increased Spain's dependency on

the metal. Well known during this time period was the "king's share," or the *quinto* (royal fifth), which awarded the Spanish monarch with a one-fifth tax on total consignments. Nevertheless, it is important not to exaggerate the role that silver played during the early decades of the colonial era. For example, King Phillip II's income from American silver represented only 20 percent of the Crown's total revenue. Even so, as the colonial era advanced, silver did become increasingly important to Spain's economy.

See also MERCURY (Vol. II); MINING (Vols. II, III, IV); SILVER (Vols. II, III).

—Christina Hawkins

Further reading:
J. H. Elliott. "Spain and America in the Sixteenth and Seventeenth Centuries." *The Cambridge History of Latin America*, vol. 1 (New York: Cambridge University Press, 1985).

slavery

THE AMERICAS BEFORE 1492

Slavery was widespread in the Americas before 1492, just as it was in almost all regions of the world in ancient times. Nevertheless, this type of slavery had nothing in common with the African slave trade later established by Europeans in the Atlantic world. Slavery in the Americas was not chattel slavery: Enslaved people were not considered to be objects, and the condition was not inheritable.

The form of ancient American slavery archaelogists know the most about existed in Mesoamerica, where documents related to it were written by indigenous people as early as the 1540s, using the Roman alphabet to write phonetically in their own languages. From these sources, we know that people could sell themselves or their children into slavery in times of famine or other calamity or be pressed into servitude as punishment for a crime (see CRIME AND PUNISHMENT). In Texcoco (one of the Nahua states in Central MEXICO), for example, a highly refined code governed people's voluntary passage into an enslaved state and guaranteed them certain protections, such as that they could "buy themselves back."

WARFARE, however, produced the greatest numbers of slaves in Mesoamerica. When one ethnic state conquered another, a whole people could pass into a type of servitude. This did not mean that they all became personal slaves but that they lost ownership of their land and became tenants on the land of others. Warriors taken prisoner on the battlefield became slaves in the more modern sense: They were bound and taken to the homes of the victors to work or were later sacrificed in religious ceremonies (see HUMAN SACRIFICE). Indeed, a key element of Mesoamerican warfare was the collection of slaves who could be sacrificed to the deities. At times, individuals other than captured warriors were enslaved. WOMEN and children might become slaves, and some were sacrificed to the deities, but most lived on in the households of nobles or successful warriors as domestic workers, concubines, or even lesser wives. Though a woman's sense of identity was likely torn asunder, her children, at least, had equal footing in society.

Only the larger parameters around the transfer of prisoners into slavery are known. In the Aztec world, slaves not claimed by a particular warrior as his own booty could be sold in a market, such as the one at Azcapotzalco (see AZTECS). Sometimes, such slaves were bought by clans in need of sacrifice victims; others were sent east to work in the part of Mesoamerica most committed to the production of COTTON cloth (though they themselves probably did supportive tasks in order to free local women for weaving, which was considered a holy act). LA MALINCHE, famous for having been HERNANDO CORTÉS's translator during the CONQUEST, was born in the NAHUATL-speaking world but was later enslaved and sent east. Cortés came across many such enslaved people on the MAYA coast.

It is impossible to enter into the mental world of such slaves, though a lament of a female domestic does survive as it was written down in about the 1560s. In the song, the woman cries aloud that her master should not treat her arrogantly, as she was a prisoner of war, not someone sold voluntarily by her own family. This supports the idea that whatever sadness may have been experienced by women taken as slaves during times of conflict, they did not necessarily feel any sense of shame or inferiority (perhaps a motivating factor in Malinche's participation in the Spanish conquest).

Evidence of slavery has also been recovered from the Inca world of South America and includes several texts written by both indigenous scribes and Spanish priests (see INCAS). From these accounts we know that the Inca king collected *aqllakuna* from each ethnic state conquered by his armies and that these women became wives of leading figures and/or lived in walled seclusion, where they wove cloth and brewed CHICHA for the empire (see ACLLA). (A small number were sacrificed in religious ceremonies or became priestesses in Inca temples.) While in one sense the *aqllakuna* were enslaved, theirs was also a position of honor. It has even been argued that they played a central role in the expansion and consolidation of the Inca realm.

There is less information about slavery in other regions of the hemisphere; nevertheless, it is clear that slavery was generally associated with warfare. Among both nomadic and semipermanent cultures, people made war to secure hunting rights in certain areas, gather particular resources, and take captives. Enemy warriors might be tortured to death—and were accorded great honor if they managed to show no feeling—particularly if a group needed to avenge the loss of its own warriors. Individual men might be allowed to live on as slaves. ÁLVAR NÚÑEZ CABEZA DE VACA was a Spaniard who was enslaved on the Gulf coast shortly after PÁNFILO DE NARVÁEZ's failed 1527 expedition to conquer FLORIDA. He later wrote of his experiences, which likely reflected pre-Columbian local practices. Like other male slaves, Cabeza de Vaca worked hard at the least pleasant tasks necessary to the group's survival and was always somewhat hungry. Nevertheless, his status as a slave was not permanent.

Women and children taken in war, although known as slaves at first, were usually eventually adopted as citizens of their new communities and thus lost their slave status. The years after 1492 produced many "captivity narratives" in North America from which the experiences of enslaved women in general before 1492 can be inferred. For example, Mary Jemison, a colonist's daughter, was taken by the Shawnee in the mid-18th century when she was 15 years old and sold by them as a slave to the Seneca of the Six Nations Iroquois (or Haudenosaunee). Later, she married and became a full member of society. When she had a chance to return to her biological people, she chose not to go, although she did dictate her memoirs. Clearly, Jemison no longer considered herself to be enslaved. On the other hand, Gandeaktena, a 17th-century Algonkian woman in what is today Canada, who was captured by the Iroquois, never felt at peace with her situation even though she had married into the culture. She described herself to Jesuit priests as a slave and asked to be allowed to convert to Christianity and live with them instead of remaining where she was, and she was not the only woman who responded in this way.

Among the nomadic and seminomadic peoples of pre-Columbian America, a slave was the property of the warrior who had captured him or her until he chose to sell or give his prize to another. Occasionally, however, an ethnic state attempting to achieve dominance over a particular area would disband an entire settlement or group of settlements, selling dozens of people into slavery. There is archaeological and textual evidence that slaves followed the major TRADE routes used for other goods like copper, shells, or turquoise. People undergoing such passage never existed in great numbers, however.

Though slavery was found almost everywhere in the Americas, it did not dominate life anywhere in the hemisphere. Indigenous slavery differed profoundly from that practiced by Europeans.

EARLY COLONIAL

Immediately on encountering the Caribbean islands, Spanish colonizers sought to enslave their indigenous inhabitants. Following the Spanish Crown's direction in 1509, the Spanish governor of HISPANIOLA ordered colonizers to bring the inhabitants of the Bahamas, or Lucayas, to the main island to serve as slaves or servants for life (a status called *naboría*). Expanding their raids to other islands, colonizers enslaved TAINOS (indigenous people of the Caribbean) to work in the GOLD mines and on SUGAR estates and cattle ranches (see MINING). Gradually, colonizers carried out slave raids throughout the Caribbean and the mainland, including Florida, Central America, and the coastal regions of VENEZUELA and COLOMBIA.

The resistance of the Taino, combined with their susceptibility to European DISEASES such as smallpox, influenza, and typhus, quickly prompted Spanish colonizers to petition the Crown to allow the importation of Muslim and black Iberians as slaves (see MORISCO). And, by the 1520s, colonizers had petitioned the Crown for black Africans, whom they considered to be easier to control than the black Iberians. Imported slaves, along with their indigenous counterparts, worked in the households, mines, farms, and estates of the Spanish colonizers on Hispaniola.

By the 1520s, fugitive slaves had joined resistant Taino communities in the interior of Hispaniola, and they gradually populated the smaller islands of the Caribbean. Africans joined in the rebellion against the Spaniards led by Enriquillo, a Taino leader who was eventually defeated. A few years later, in 1521, enslaved Wolofs, herders, and horsemen from West Africa led a rebellion on a sugar estate on Christmas Day. Enslaved Muslims and Canary Islanders joined the revolt, which was put down by an armed cavalry. Nevertheless, the Spanish Crown then banned Wolofs from being imported to the Americas because of their "excitable and rebellious spirit."

Upon encountering the advanced civilizations of the Aztecs in Mexico (1519) and the Incas in PERU (1532), clerics and legal scholars debated the consequences and legality of enslaving indigenous people. The most famous was the Dominican BARTOLOMÉ DE LAS CASAS. After returning from the Caribbean, where he had witnessed firsthand the suffering of the Tainos in CUBA, Las Casas spent the next five decades arguing and petitioning against the exploitation of indigenous people. For years, he returned to the Americas, where he worked to convert the indigenous to Christianity; moreover, he argued for restitution to the Indians and refused to minister to Spaniards who kept indigenous slaves.

In 1550, Las Casas engaged in an influential public debate on the treatment of Amerindians. According to the Dominican cleric, the justification for Spanish rule in the Americas was the conversion and "good governance" of indigenous peoples. His opponent, JUAN GINÉS DE SEPÚLVEDA, argued that wars against the indigenous were just because the Indians were clearly slaves by nature who would benefit from serving a superior people, the Spanish. No formal mandate was established, but Las Casas's views heavily influenced Crown policy, and the enslavement of peoples who peacefully submitted to Spanish colonization and converted to Catholicism was eventually outlawed.

Following the award of the first ASIENTO, or slave-trading contract, in 1518, the Spanish expanded into the mainland of Mexico and Peru. The armies of Cortés included several hundred enslaved men, who Cortés led in the conquest of Mexico in the 1520s. Likewise,

FRANCISCO PIZARRO and DIEGO DE ALMAGRO held almost 2,000 slaves in their armies during their conquests in the 1530s and the subsequent CIVIL WARS IN PERU of the 1540s. Enslaved men and women also served as domestic servants in the new CITIES of the Americas. Slaveholders valued enslaved men and women also for their symbolic worth, since the ownership of slaves indicated wealth and honor. Some owners provided silk CLOTHING, shoes, and even weapons for slaves who accompanied them in public as both guards and for display. In Peru, where the Spanish established a coastal city and the climate was ideal for the cultivation of sugar and grapes, as well as WHEAT, enslaved Africans and their descendants labored on small farms and mid-size estates. By the mid-1550s there were about 3,000 slaves in the Peruvian viceroyalty, half of them in the viceregal capital of LIMA (see VICEROY/VICEROYALTY).

Indigenous laborers worked mainly in the highland SILVER mines, while other enslaved men labored in alluvial gold deposits in the tropical lowlands. By the 1540s, Africans and their descendants worked in gangs of 10 to 15 in the southern Andes and, eventually, coastal ECUADOR and lowland southern Colombia. In Mexico, enslaved men and women also worked in Spanish households as domestic servants, as well as on the lowland and coastal sugar estates. Initially, enslaved African and African-descent men also worked in the northern silver mines, including Zacatecas, Guanajuato, and Pachuco. In EL SALVADOR (which was part of GUATEMALA in the 16th century), enslaved men and women would eventually work on the cacao and indigo estates. In HONDURAS, by 1545, almost 1,500 slaves worked in the gold mines.

With the early, expanding silver economy, Peru was a critical destination for captives who entered the Spanish Empire through the Caribbean port of Cartagena before crossing Central America to the Pacific city of Panama. There, indigenous slaves figured prominently in the early conquest expeditions. By the 1530s and 1540s, native slaves taken from Honduras and NICARAGUA labored as cargo bearers and canoeists in the river and overland routes across the Panamanian isthmus. Though the Spanish Crown outlawed indigenous slavery in 1550, native people scarred with brands from across Central America and CHILE continued to serve as slaves along these Pacific routes.

Enslaved Africans and their descendants proved critical to the upkeep of roads, ports, and cities throughout the Spanish Americas. The municipal councils in PANAMA purchased teams of enslaved men to monitor the roadways; others quarried rocks in order to build fortresses to defend the empire's Pacific coast. Eventually, enslaved men served as muleteers and rowers along the isthmus roads and waterways.

Many enslaved men and women arrived in the Americas as Catholics; others converted in order to benefit from the protections afforded by the CATHOLIC

CHURCH. According to ecclesiastical mandates, slave-holders could not separate enslaved couples; rather, they had to allow them at least a nominal proximity, if not cohabitation. Church law also urged slaveholders to allow enslaved people to attend Mass on Sundays and holidays, and secular law prohibited extreme physical abuse of slaves. While these laws were repeatedly violated in Spanish America, many enslaved people did claim their rights as spouses and Catholics.

Initially, enslaved men and women were sold from Iberia to the Americas. As the Portuguese (with some Spanish merchants) gained control of the slave trade into the Americas, captives from Senegambia, Guinea-Bissau, and Sierra Leone in West Africa were among the largest numbers of Africans in the early colonial Americas. Enslaved, and eventually free, Africans and their descendants intermarried and developed kinship relationships with each other. In some cases, enslaved people formed bonds with men and women who served as the godparents to their children (see FAMILY). In other cases, slaves named each other as "shipmate" kin or fellow captives who had survived the transatlantic passage together. Using Catholic institutions for their own purposes, enslaved people also joined *cofradías*, or religious confraternities, that functioned as mutual aid societies, thus ensuring their members would be buried and particular SAINTS would be properly celebrated (see RELIGION).

Enslaved men and women resisted enslavement by, most notably, establishing fugitive communities. For example, in 1549, escaped pearl divers established one such settlement (called a *palenque*) on the island of Margarita, off the coast of Venezuela. From 1553 to 1558, a fugitive leader called King Bayano established a fugitive settlement on the Panamanian isthmus. In coastal Ecuador, the fugitive settlement of Esmeraldas was formed by the captive survivors of shipwrecks (1545 and 1553), who mixed with local indigenous populations. Seeking to secure a route from the highlands to the coast, coastal authorities launched numerous unsuccessful military expeditions to conquer the region. In other cases, fugitive communities were established in close proximity to colonial urban areas, such as those outside the Caribbean port of Cartagena. Members of fugitive settlements traded FOOD from their fields for needed goods or, in times of scarcity, raided Spanish and indigenous communities for the same.

In urban centers throughout Spanish America, enslaved men served as blacksmiths, tailors, shoemakers, and masons. Skilled laborers were often rented out by their owners and, in turn, they paid a daily, weekly, or monthly *jornal*, or "wage," but were allowed to retain additional earnings. Enslaved women also sold their labor as cooks or wet nurses but were best known for selling bread, sweets, prepared food, and other goods on urban streets and plazas. Enslaved men and women could use their earnings to purchase themselves or another

family member and secure an official record of manumission or freedom.

See also BRAZIL, ABOLITION (Vol. III); CHARTER OF SLAVERY (Vol. III); *COFRADÍA* (Vol. II); LAW OF THE FREE WOMB (Vol. III); SLAVERY (Vols. II, III).

—Rachel Sarah O'Toole
Camilla Townsend

Further reading:

Herbert Klein and Ben Vinson III. *African Slavery in Latin America and the Caribbean*, 2d ed. (New York: Oxford University Press, 2007).
Jerome Offner. *Law and Politics in Ancient Texcoco* (Cambridge: Cambridge University Press, 1983).
Fernando Santos-Granero. *Vital Enemies: Slavery, Predation, and the Amerindian Political Economy of Life* (Austin: University of Texas Press, 2009).
Irene Silverblatt. *Moon, Sun and Witches: Gender Ideologies and Class in Inca and Colonial Peru* (Princeton, N.J.: Princeton University Press, 1987).
Camilla Townsend. "'What Have You Done to Me, My Lover?': Sex, Servitude and Politics among the Pre-conquest Nahuas as Seen in the *Cantares Mexicanos*." *The Americas* 62, no. 3 (2006): 349–389.

Soto, Hernando de   See DE SOTO, HERNANDO.

sugar   The sugarcane plant is native to Asia and was first domesticated near the Indian subcontinent. As a crop, sugarcane was relatively unimportant until the discovery of methods to preserve its natural sugars in a solid, granulated form. Extracting sugar solids from the plant requires grinding or crushing the cane, reducing the resulting pulp over heat, and then allowing the mixture to dry into a crystalline solid. The basic process of refinement was developed in Asia in the fourth century and spread along with the plant.

In the first millennium C.E., sugar production expanded from India into the Middle East. Islam helped further the spread of sugarcane by introducing its cultivation in the conquered regions of North Africa and Iberia. Christian crusaders brought back an appreciation for sugar from their journeys in the Holy Land. Although Europeans desired this curious, sweet "spice," its rarity and cost excluded it from the diets of all but the wealthiest individuals.

The 15th century saw a major expansion of sugar production in western Europe. In the 1420s, sugarcane was being grown in parts of the Iberian Peninsula and on the Canary Islands. The Portuguese CONQUEST and colonization of Madeira in 1455 led to the development of sugar plantations, which would come to dominate sugar production for the next three centuries. Large-scale sugar production requires a great deal of manual

LABOR. While little labor is needed during the growing cycle, once sugarcane stalks are ready for harvest, they must be cut and crushed and the resulting pulp refined, all with little delay. If the cane is cut too late or the pulp not extracted quickly, the natural sugars in the plant will spoil, ruining the harvest. Consequently, sugarcane estates required many laborers, skilled and unskilled, to ensure timely cutting, quick transport, and efficient refining. On Madeira, the Portuguese began sugar production using a mixed labor force of free wage laborers and African slaves (see SLAVERY). Over time, as Portuguese merchants gained better access to the internal African slave TRADE, sugar growers on Madeira increasingly began to rely on slave labor.

Sugarcane was brought to the Americas with the earliest explorers and settlers in the 1490s. Despite its early arrival, sugarcane was not a primary crop in the initial decades of colonization. Most Spaniards sought to accumulate wealth through control of native goods and easily exploited natural resources; however, once these began to wane, they quickly looked to sugar as a valuable cash crop. The first sugar estates were founded in the Caribbean and in MEXICO. By the mid-16th century, the Portuguese had begun cultivating sugarcane in BRAZIL. For the next three centuries, growing European demand for sugar would lead to increased production and an ever-increasing demand for African slaves. The global impact of sugar production should not be overlooked; more than any other commodity, sugar helped create and define the complex colonial relationship between Europe, the Americas, and Africa (see COLUMBIAN EXCHANGE).

See also *ENGENHO* (Vol. II); SUGAR (Vols. II, III).

—Robert Schwaller

syncretism
Syncretism is the union or reconciliation of the beliefs and practices of two different cultures that results in a hybrid manifestation. Colonial cultures have frequently been described as syncretistic because they tend to combine elements of both the indigenous culture and that of the colonial power. In early colonial Latin America, the areas of greatest syncretism were language and RELIGION.

In language, the native cultures first adapted their own words to describe the new Spanish items. Later, they adopted Spanish nouns, using them according to their own rules of grammar. For example, the Nahuas (AZTECS) first described European horses as "*mazatl*," the native word for "deer." Later, they adopted the Spanish word (*caballo*) and used it according to NAHUATL rules, resulting in *cahuallo*. The most common area of borrowing into Spanish occurred when Europeans lacked words or names, especially for the new plants and animals they encountered in the New World. In MEXICO and PERU, the Spanish developed different vocabularies, especially for local products. In Mexico, fresh corn (MAIZE) became known as *elote* (from the Nahuatl *elotl*), while in the Andean region it came to be known as *chocllo*, a QUECHUA word.

In the area of religion, indigenous cultures variously embraced aspects of the Christian religion and grafted them onto their own. In the Andean highlands, for example, various aspects of the earth goddess Pachamama were identified with the Virgin Mary in Christianity. Likewise, although the Nahuatl term *Tonantzin* (our revered mother) frequently appeared in pre-Columbian contexts as a form of address for various female deities, it came to be applied to the Virgin Mary (see SAINTS).

The process of syncretism, though perhaps seemingly haphazard, was more often quite logical. Indigenous cultures attempted to understand the Spanish in terms of their cultural assumptions, just as the Spanish attempted to understand the NATIVE AMERICANS according to their own European cultural assumptions. Where each culture saw a similarity to its own, it assumed that the underlying tenets were the same. Consequently, the Spanish missionaries heard one of the Nahua gods described as "He through whom all things live." This resonated with them as an apt description of the Christian god, and they adopted this locution as an epithet for God, yet the native peoples heard it as an epithet for their own deity Tezcatlipoca. What ensued was what one scholar has described as the "double-mistaken identity." The missionaries assumed that the Nahuas understood that they were describing God, while the Nahuas understood that the missionaries must be describing Tezcatlipoca.

—John F. Schwaller

Further reading:
James Lockhart. *The Nahuas after the Conquest* (Stanford, Calif.: Stanford University Press, 1992).

Taino (Taíno)   The Taino were an ethnic and cultural Arawak-speaking group that inhabited most of the Caribbean islands of HISPANIOLA, CUBA, Jamaica, PUERTO RICO, the Bahamas, and the Virgin Islands. Originally from the region of the Orinoco river delta in northeastern South America, the ancestors of the Taino, known as the Saladoid, or Igneri, began to migrate to the Leeward Islands around the year 100 C.E., displacing or incorporating the earlier inhabitants (see MIGRATION). The Taino culture arose out of the Saladoid around the year 1200 with unique social and technological adaptations to their island environments.

Taino villages had a complex social structure. The CACIQUE, or chieftain, most often a male (although there were some female caciques), inherited rank and status from his (or her) maternal lineage. The *behique*, or shaman, ranked second after the cacique. Below them, the *nitaínos* constituted a type of nobility, with the *naborías*, or commoners, making up the bulk of the population. The Taino were skilled stone carvers, with many of their idols (*cemíes*) and ritual belts comparable in technical execution to the best Mesoamerican stone artifacts (see ART). Taino religious and social life centered on communal ceremonies known as *areitos*, which were held on broad stone-lined plazas; the largest of these plazas thus far discovered are at Caguana and Jácanas in Puerto Rico (see RELIGION). The Taino believed in supreme deities that controlled various aspects of nature: Examples are the storm god, named Huracán, and a supreme creator, known as Yocahu. The *cemíes* or spirits of the ancestors served as intermediaries with the deities and protected the living during their daily activities.

The years between 1200 and 1500 were characterized by a flowering of Classic Taino culture in Hispaniola and Puerto Rico, with independent villages falling under the rule of regional caciques, increased population growth, and a more intense exploitation of local resources. Taino AGRICULTURE, based on the cultivation of MANIOC, produced large surpluses and allowed for further diversification of the ECONOMY. COTTON, TEXTILES, TOBACCO, and GOLD, as well as carved stone and wood objects, were produced for the elite and for TRADE.

There is little evidence of conflict between Taino villages or regional chiefdoms. Indeed, many caciques and *nitaínos* married into elite families from neighboring islands. However, migrating bands of CARIBS, moving from the South American mainland, began to displace the Taino on the Leeward Islands; the Caribs also launched raids as far west as Cuba and Jamaica. Despite some military conflicts, relations between the Carib and Taino also included trade, intermarriage and, in some cases, military and political alliances.

The Taino were devastated by the Spanish CONQUEST; much of their language and culture was suppressed. Nevertheless, the Taino survived and their descendants in Cuba, the Dominican Republic, and Puerto Rico are beginning to rediscover their original language, religion, and culture and claim recognition for their legal rights.

—Francisco J. González

Further reading:
José J. Arrom, Ricardo E. Alegria, and Fatima Becht, eds. *Taino: Pre-Columbian Art and Culture from the Caribbean* (New York: Monacelli Press–Museo del Barrio, 1997).

Taki Onqoy (Taqui Ongoy, Ayra, Aira)   Taki Onqoy is a QUECHUA term meaning "dancing sickness" that was used to describe a resurgence of Andean RELIGION in the 1560s as a form of resistance to the Spanish CONQUEST of PERU and the imposition of Catholicism. Uncovered by Spanish priest Luis de Olivera in 1564, the movement flourished in the central Andes north and west of CUZCO.

Taki Onqoy reflected Andean despair about oppressive Spanish colonialism. A messianic movement, its adherents (*takiongos*) believed that the old indigenous deities would rise up to destroy the Spaniards through DISEASE, earthquakes, and other natural disasters and return Peru to indigenous rule (see *HUACA*). Taki Onqoy did not call on Andeans to take up arms against the Europeans, for the dieties would destroy them. *Takiongos* urged Andeans to stop practicing Christianity and to offer sacrifices to the *huacas* once again. Followers were expected to undertake five-day periods of abstinence from salt, MAIZE, chili peppers, and sexual relations. They were also to stop worshipping the Christian god, eating Spanish FOOD, and dressing in European CLOTHING. Those who had been baptized as Christians engaged in frenzied dances, shaking and trembling while cursing the Christian faith.

Although men and children joined the movement, WOMEN seem to have played a particularly prominent role in it. Spanish investigators found thousands of *takiongos* among the Lucanas and Soras indigenous groups. Cristóbal de Albornoz, whose reports constitute the most important historical source about the movement, was a leader in the campaign to root out the heresy. More than 8,000 Indians were punished, many with temporary or permanent exile, before Taki Onqoy subsided.

—Kendall Brown

Further reading:

Steve J. Stern. *Peru's Indian Peoples and the Challenge of Spanish Conquest: Huamanga to 1640* (Madison: University of Wisconsin Press, 1986).

Tawantinsuyu   See INCAS.

Tenochtitlán   Located on a small island in Lake Texcoco in the Valley of MEXICO, Tenochtitlán grew from a humble village to the capital of the Aztec Empire within a century (see AZTECS). Although there is some archaeological evidence for human occupation on this island as early as 1000 C.E., according to Aztec historical accounts, it was a small group of Mexica nomads who first settled there in 1325, under the territorial dominion of Azcapotzalco. The Mexicas overthrew Tepanec rule (from Azcapotzalco) in 1428 and formed a TRIPLE ALLIANCE in which Tenochtitlán took the dominant role. As tribute flowed into the city, it experienced rapid urban growth. By 1519, on the eve of the Spanish CONQUEST, Tenochtitlán had reached the size of 4.5–5.8 square miles (12–15 km²),

Located in Mexico City's National Museum of History and Anthropology, this model reconstruction shows the ceremonial precinct of the Aztec capital city of Tenochtitlán. The main temple, or Templo Mayor, is depicted in the back center. *(Courtesy of J. Michael Francis)*

This picture shows a Chac-Mool from the Aztec Templo Mayor complex, in the historic center of Mexico City. Various Chac-Mools have been located in Central Mexico and the Yucatán Peninsula. Their forms are similar, and the bowl or plate that rests on their stomachs was likely used to receive offerings or sacrifices. Excavated in the early 1980s, this Chac-Mool was found fully polychromed. *(Courtesy of J. Michael Francis)*

with a population of 125,000 to 250,000, making it larger than any city in Spain at the time (see CITIES).

The capital was physically and conceptually divided into quarters; at the center, where these quarters converged, was situated the most important structure in the entire empire: the Templo Mayor (Great Temple). This temple served as an *axis mundi* to the Aztec quadripartite universe and was oriented to the rising Sun during the equinoxes. Further echoing the dual nature of the Aztec cosmos, the temple's top platform accommodated two of the most important gods in Aztec mythology: The southern red shrine was dedicated to Huitzilopochtli, the Aztec tribal war god and sun deity; the northern red shrine was dedicated to Tlaloc, the god of rain and agricultural fertility. The temple itself represented Coatepetl (Serpent Mountain), where Huitzilopochtli was mythically born, and Tonacatepetl, Tlaloc's "Sustenance Mountain."

Recent excavations have revealed seven different construction phases to the Templo Mayor, each completely enveloping the former structure while expanding its size; while the first structure, dating to 1325, was merely a humble shrine, the last one of the early 1500s measured 262.5 feet (80 m) at the base, and the dual tem-

ples at the top had reached a maximum height of 147.6 feet (45 m), accessed by twin staircases of more than 100 steps each. Throughout these expansion phases, the Aztecs had buried more than 100 offerings, mostly exotic animal remains, HUMAN SACRIFICES, and luxury goods from distant parts of the empire, located so that they would reflect their relative geographical position. They even included artifacts of bygone civilizations such as the TOLTECS and the OLMECS, as well as smaller temples in the TEOTIHUACÁN architectural style (see ARCHITECTURE). Thus, the Templo Mayor in itself became a microcosm for the Aztec world, both in space and time.

Surrounding the Templo Mayor was the walled-off Sacred Precinct, which in its last construction phase included about 80 minor temples dedicated to the different gods and deities. Other buildings included schools for the nobility, a ball court, a temple for the Eagle Knights, and the *tzompantli* wooden racks where more than 100,000 skulls of the sacrificial victims were publicly displayed. Surrounding these were the palaces of the Aztec kings and queens and other nobles.

Transport of people and merchandise was made through water canals that transected the city, although paved streets also existed. Four large avenues and canals departed toward the cardinal directions from the Sacred Precinct, three of which connected the island to the mainland and to the pleasure palaces of the nobility (such as Chapultepec's zoological park and gardens). All of the city quarters were further divided into *calpultin*, neighborhoods where the commoners resided, each equipped with its own temples and schools (see CALPULLI). Around these were the CHINAMPAS, agricultural fields that fed both commoners and elite (see AGRICULTURE).

—Danny Zborover

Further reading:

Michael E. Smith. *The Aztecs* (Cornwall, U.K.: Blackwell Publishing, 2003).

Teotihuacán One of the most influential urban centers in the Basin of MEXICO and beyond, Teotihuacán came to power around 100 B.C.E., after its rival city, Cuicuilco, was destroyed by a volcanic eruption. By 300 C.E., more than half of the basin's population had migrated to Teotihuacán; population estimates range between 40,000 to 200,000, making it one of the largest CITIES in the world at the time. The city covered an area of some eight square miles (21 km²), of which less than 5 percent has been excavated. Its design, characterized by a carefully laid out grid pattern, was unparalleled in pre-Columbian times.

RELIGION played a central role in the city's location, and Teotihuacán soon became an important pilgrimage center. Religious processions took place along its main axis, the so-called Avenue of the Dead, which was oriented to important astronomical events. Flanking it are two of the largest temples ever constructed in the Americas, the Pyramid of the Moon and Pyramid of the Sun, the latter constructed above a semi-artificial cave with mythical significance. At the other end is the Ciudadela complex, the site of the pyramid dedicated to QUETZALCÓATL (the "feathered serpent" god). The remains of hundreds of people, probably warriors, were discovered in dedicatory caches under the pyramids. Other temples were dedicated to Tlaloc (the storm god) and to Cihuacoatl, the great goddess of fertility. In their midst were palaces for the rulers and priests and numerous peripheral apartment compounds for the lesser nobility and artisans, among which were wards for ZAPOTECS and MAYA groups. These temples and residences had a unique architectural style and were lavishly decorated; they contained stone sculptures, and

The ceremonial and administrative center of Teotihuacán: view of the Avenue of the Dead and the Pyramid of the Sun (to the left), seen from the top of the Pyramid of the Moon *(Courtesy of Danny Zborover)*

many walls were painted with colorful murals depicting religious themes (see ARCHITECTURE; ART). Except for a few graphic signs, there is no clear evidence for a local writing system, and the language or ethnicity of the Teotihuacános is still debated.

Teotihuacán drew its economic power from the control of nearby OBSIDIAN sources and its strategic location along major TRADE routes. Along with material goods, Teotihuacán exported its religious ideology, which emphasized military symbolism and the cult of war, throughout Mesoamerica (see WARFARE). At its height, Teotihuacán's religious, political, and economic influence reached as far as the Zapotecs of Oaxaca and the Maya of GUATEMALA.

Teotihuacán's decline began around 500 C.E., archaeologists have discovered evidence of deliberate temple burning at that time. DISEASE had further affected the population, and there are signs of environmental degradation. Although the ceremonial center was finally abandoned around 600, numerous people continued to live in the surrounding hinterland. Almost 800 years later, the AZTECS visited the site and worshipped there and gave it its current NAHUATL name, *Teotihuacán*, which translates as "City of the Gods." Even at that time, the ruined site was impressive enough that the Aztecs believed this was the place where the Sun and Moon were born.

—Danny Zborover

Further reading:
Annabeth Headrick. *The Teotihuacán Trinity: The Sociopolitical Structure of an Ancient Mesoamerican City* (Austin: University of Texas Press, 2007).

textiles The indigenous peoples of Mesoamerica used various techniques to make textiles, including weaving, embroidery, and twining. From early on, textiles served both functional and decorative purposes. They were used to make CLOTHING, which also signified the wearer's geographic origins, gender, occupation, social status, and religious associations. They were also used to make containers and wall hangings.

Indigenous cultures valued certain textiles above CERAMICS, ARCHITECTURE, and even metalwork. Textiles were regarded as valuable and sacred objects, revered for the sophistication of their design and embedded social meanings. This sensibility is referred to as "textile primacy" and runs counter to the Western tendency to value precious metals and jewels more highly than textiles. Sixteenth-century accounts of gift giving between indigenous populations and Spanish conquistadores underscore this difference. While the Spanish marvel at native jewelry and metalwork, they barely mention textiles. Native accounts, on the other hand, emphasize the quality and function of the ritual attire they gave to Europeans.

TECHNOLOGY
To make cloth, threads first needed to be produced. Threads were made by manually spinning raw plant or animal fibers around a spindle (a pointed stick) to produce long, thin strands. In Mesoamerica, only plant fibers were used. In the highlands, COTTON was reserved for the elite, while coarser fibers made from maguey, palm, and yucca (MANIOC) were for commoners. Because cotton is grown at lower altitudes close to the coast, the coastal people in South America wove mainly with cotton.

Once produced, threads were woven, embroidered, or twined together to create cloth. Twining was the simplest technology and the first to emerge in the Americas. It is a nonloom technique similar to macramé, in which threads are wrapped around each other by hand. Weaving, however, was the most common process by which threads were made into fabric. The backstrap loom was the traditional weaving equipment in the Americas. It consisted of a series of sticks, one tethered by a cord to a fixed object (commonly a tree) and another attached to a belt that went about the hips of a sitting or kneeling weaver. The weaver's own weight was used to hold the warp (vertical) threads taut as the weft (horizontal) threads were passed through the loom.

Embroidery produced the finest textiles, known as tapestries. Embroidery is a superstructural technique in which threads are sewn on to a thin layer of ground cloth to create a design. The weft threads are packed tightly together in order to obscure the warp threads and create a highly durable textile. Tapestry is LABOR intensive because the designs are individually stitched onto the fabric.

TEXTILES AND FEMALE IDENTITY
Throughout the Americas, weaving was most commonly undertaken by WOMEN (see FAMILY). In both Andean and Mesoamerican cultures, spinning and weaving were so intimately linked to womanhood that they were considered to symbolize the act of reproduction. While a full spindle is diamond shaped, like the female genitalia, the act of spinning itself was likened to conception and the growth of the fetus in the womb. Similarly, weaving, or the process by which threads become fabric, was associated with giving birth.

SOUTH AMERICA
Textile production in South America dates back as far as 10,000 B.C.E. The largest number of ancient South American textiles have been found in coastal PERU and BOLIVIA, where the arid desert climate helped to preserve them. Some relatively well-preserved textiles have been found in oxygen-deprived caves in the Andean highlands and at other high altitude sites with perpetual freezing conditions. The earliest known textile fragments were excavated from Guitarrero Cave in the north-central Andes of Peru. These early examples, as well as the more famous Huaca Prieta textiles (ca. 3000–1800 B.C.E.), were made by twining individual plant fibers.

The Paracas textiles, which were found in burial sites along Peru's southern coast, are among the most widely studied pre-Columbian fiber structures. They date to ca. 0–200 C.E. and were used in a complex funerary tradition in which the desert sands along the south coast served as an acropolis for Paracas rulers, nobility, and retainers. The textiles were wrapped around the bodies of the deceased, encasing mummified figures placed in a fetal position.

Paracas textiles were created in two decorative styles: linear and block color. The linear style was developed first. Abstract designs or geometric patterns were embroidered onto ground cloth (a simple, thin woven textile). The block-color style, on the other hand, was used to depict the natural and human worlds. The most common motifs were humans dressed in the region's ritual costume, shamans, and predatory animals. The figures depicted on the textiles used to encase mummies might have related to a deceased's social or political status.

The WARI (Peru) and TIWANAKU (Bolivia) (ca. 500–800 C.E.) both produced tapestry textiles that were worn mainly as tunics to communicate the wearers' political dominance over their vast domains. By donning images of specific deities, Wari and Tiwanaku elites declared their divine right to political authority. The two empires shared much of the same iconography, the most ubiquitous being the staff-bearing figure also found on the famous Gate of the Sun at the Tiwanaku archaeological site. The two styles did differ in some respects, however. While the patterns on Tiwanaku textiles were able to be "read" by most people, those of the Wari were more abstract and therefore were legible to only a select few.

The INCAS, perhaps best known for their monumental architecture, also created magnificent textiles (ca. 1450–1532). Royal weavers called *aqllakuna* (see *ACLLA*) were women chosen from childhood to weave for the Inca ruler. It is also known that fine textiles were burned as offerings to the deities and that textiles played other important roles, such as delineating between classes of people in the highly stratified Inca society. Extensive tribute systems were in place to create *cumbi* (tapestry) cloth for the elite.

Perhaps the most fascinating form of Inca textile work is the *QUIPU*, which consists of a series of small cords knotted to a single, larger cord. *Quipus* were used to record numbers (particularly tribute figures) but may also have documented verbal language. The *quipu* was "read" according to the number of strings, number of knots on each string, and the type and position of each knot. As a recording device constructed entirely from fiber, it was the ultimate manifestation of textile primacy.

MESOAMERICA

As in South America, dress was a major source of identity in Mesoamerica. The AZTECS, in particular, had laws concerning the type of dress a person could wear, according to his or her ethnicity and social status.

The dampness and humidity of the Mesoamerican climate left little in the way of textiles themselves for archaeologists to study. Nevertheless, important information has been discovered from other sources. While most pre-Columbian CODICES were destroyed, colonial codices contain detailed depictions of pre-Columbian garments.

The male loincloth is the garment shown most frequently in the codices, but other garments include the hip cloth, cape, kilt, quilted armor, warrior costume, and ceremonial attire. Female garments included skirts, capes, and ritual attire. These are general categories, as each garment differed widely according to the wearers of the garment.

Archaeologists have recovered some extant Mesoamerican textiles. Findings from Guila Naquitz in Oaxaca, MEXICO, include non-loom baskets, cordage, and knotted netting made from plant fiber (ca. 8000 B.C.E.). The largest discovery of textiles was made in CHICHÉN ITZÁ's sacred cenote, an oxygen-deprived limestone sinkhole on Mexico's Yucatán Peninsula. The textiles, having been submerged in water for hundreds of years, had blackened and their designs largely lost; nevertheless, they have provided valuable information about the variety and complexity of weaving practices among the MAYA. Three types of plain weaving were identified. The textiles also used bound openwork, or netlike twined spacing intermixed with traditional weaving.

A polychrome textile from the Postclassic period (ca. 900–1521) in Chiapas, Mexico, resembles clothing depicted in the Mayan Nuttall Codex. It is one of the only extant textiles that retains its original decorative scheme. Three figures are shown in procession on a yellow band, which represents the surface of the earth. The figures are wearing warrior regalia and symbolize the mythic struggle between life and death.

—Elena FitzPatrick

Further reading:

Margot Blum Schevill, Janet Catherine Berlo, and Edward B. Dwyer. *Textile Traditions of Mesoamerica and the Andes: An Anthology* (Austin: University of Texas Press, 1996).
Rebecca Stone-Miller. *To Weave for the Sun: Ancient Andean Textiles in the Museum of Fine Arts, Boston* (New York: Thames & Hudson, 1994).

Tikal The city of Tikal (in the kingdom of Mutal) was one of the two great supercenters of Classic MAYA culture; the other was its archrival, CALAKMUL. Tikal was located in the heart of GUATEMALA's Petén district, in an area between the San Pedro and Macal river systems; this location gave Tikal strategic control over TRADE between the Gulf of Mexico and the Caribbean. At its height, Tikal was home to 100,000 people, covered an area of some 25 square miles (65 km²), and produced a wide

Tikal's Temple 1 was built as the mortuary pyramid for the ruler Jasaw Chan K'awiil (r. 682–734), whose tomb was discovered inside in 1962. Though barely visible, the magnificent roofcomb is decorated with the image of a seated sculpture of Jasaw Chan K'awiil. *(Courtesy of J. Michael Francis)*

View of the Classic-period Maya city of Tikal, taken from the site's largest structure, Temple 4. Standing at 212 feet (64.5 m) in height, Temple 4 dates to the mid-eighth century and is the largest Maya structure of the Late Classic period. *(Courtesy of J. Michael Francis)*

array of CERAMICS, inscriptions, and ceremonial ART that continues to define Classic Maya culture.

Construction began in this area as early as 200 B.C.E. Tikal achieved enormous power and influence under the leadership of Siyaj K'ak (Fire Born), a conqueror who had been sent from the Central Mexico metropolis of TEOTIHUACÁN. Siyaj K'ak entered Tikal in January 378 C.E., Tikal's ruler died that same day, ushering in a new royal dynasty, perhaps from Teotihuacán itself. The new leadership launched what became a 150-year campaign of expansion and growth, one which made Tikal the dominant force in the Maya southern lowlands. Tikal's dominance experienced an unexpected challenge when northern rival Calakmul began its own power bid in the mid-500s; Tikal ultimately managed to defeat the upstart in the late 600s. The victory initiated a new phase of growth and ceremonial construction, but the rivalry and subsequent frenzy of growth depleted resources and manpower. These stresses, combined with overpopulation, long-term drought, and the fall of Teotihuacán and its accompanying economic power, initiated a long process of decline in the Maya lowlands. The last recorded date for Tikal is 869.

After the Classic Maya collapse, Tikal lay abandoned for nearly a millennium. In 1848, the chief of Guatemala's Petén district, Modesto Méndez, managed to locate the ruins following a tip by local *MILPA* farmers. For the next century, Tikal received an intermittent stream of gentleman-travelers and occasional academic surveys. Extensive scientific excavation and reconstruction only began in the mid-1950s, first under the University Museum of Pennsylvania and subsequently under Guatemala's Proyecto Nacional Tikal. While much work remains, these and subsequent projects have helped make Tikal one of the most visited archaeological sites in the world.

—Terry Rugeley

Further reading:
Jeremy A. Sabloff, ed. *Tikal: Dynasties, Foreigners, and Affairs of State* (Santa Fe, N.Mex.: School of American Research Press, 2003).

Timucua   Before the arrival of French and Spanish colonists in the 16th century, the Timucua indigenous peoples had occupied the interior of northern FLORIDA, the interior of southern Georgia, and the coastal regions of northeast Florida and southeastern Georgia for some 11,000 years. Originally living as small bands of hunters and gatherers, they later formed the hunter-gatherer, horticulturist, and large agriculturalist chiefdoms that were encountered by Europeans (see AGRICULTURE).

Subsistence strategies were based on environmental conditions, while the boundaries of chiefdoms were usually dictated by physical geography and tribal affiliations.

Consisting of at least 15 distinct political and cultural groups spread across a large area and a range of ecological environments, the Timucua were linked mainly as speakers of varieties of the same language. They were not a single cultural group, as has been widely assumed. Indeed, many groups were never united, either politically or ethnically, and some were at war with each other.

Long before the Timucua were given their name by French explorers and Spanish conquistadores, at least 15 tribes spoke at least 10 varieties (dialects) of what came to be called the "Timucuan" language. The tribes that are known to have spoken Timucua were the Acuera (Diminiyuti or Ibiniyuti), Agua Dulce, Casagne, Icafui, Mocama (Tacatacuru), Ocale, Ocone, Potano, Saturiwa, Tucururu (Tucuru), Utina, Yufera, Yui (Ibi), and Yustega. The names of many of the dialects indicate which tribes spoke them. Almost certainly, there was a greater population of Timucuan speakers in Florida, who were wiped out by DISEASE before Spanish CHRONICLERS could collect information about them.

—Rebecca D. Gorman

Further reading:

John H. Hann. *A History of the Timucua Indians and Missions* (Gainesville: University Press of Florida, 1996).

Jerald T. Milanich. *The Timucua* (Oxford: Blackwell Publishers, 1996).

John Worth. *Timucuan Chiefdoms of Spanish Florida*, vols. 1 & 2 (Gainesville: University Press of Florida, 1998).

Tiwanaku (Tiahuanaco)   The term *Tiwanaku* carries multiple meanings: It refers to a long-known ART style, a monumental site in BOLIVIA near the southern end of Lake Titicaca, a civilization, and an archaic Andean state. Tiwanaku culture flourished from 400 to 1100 C.E. in the altiplano, the high plateau between PERU and Bolivia. It arose through a process of intensification of economic strategies over time (see ECONOMY). Community-based inland farmers developed a number of technologies to increase production of potatoes and minimize risk, including hillside terracing, creating artificial ponds, and constructing raised field systems in the lake plain (see AGRICULTURE; POTATO).

In the high puna grasslands, herding peoples tended flocks of llamas and alpacas, which were important for their wool and meat and for TRANSPORTATION. Another group, the Uru, exploited the aquatic resources of Lake Titicaca and possibly practiced rainfall farming. Warm-climate crops such as MAIZE and COCA were obtained through exchange with groups in the valleys of the Pacific coast and the eastern mountain valleys; groups

from the altiplano later established colonists in these valleys (see FOOD; TRADE).

Throughout this period, llama caravans were used to transport goods between distant communities. Language and ideas were also transported by those who made these long journeys. By 500 C.E., CERAMICS decorated with distinctive religious iconography had spread throughout the area through Tiwanaku networks, from the altiplano around Lake Titicaca to the warm valleys of the western cordillera. At the same time, the Aymara and QUECHUA languages were spreading, at the expense of Puquina and Uruquilla.

At this time, the urban site of Tiwanaku itself was a larger ceremonial destination in a landscape dotted by urban settlements with relatively modest ceremonial structures (see CITIES). At Tiwanaku, there was a series of large and imposing ceremonial precincts built of fine stone masonry, which was brought from distant quarries. Additionally, there were palaces for the elite and special areas for artisans and the general population. While the permanent population of Tiwanaku was relatively modest, it was vastly increased by the arrival of pilgrims for religious feasts; they brought with them foodstuffs and other supplies.

Later, after 800, Tiwanaku became a highly centralized polity. Extensive areas of a neighboring valley became part of a centrally controlled raised field production system. This continued until 1100, when a prolonged drought caused the abandonment of the raised fields, as well as the abandonment and destruction of the urban center and its temples. Nevertheless, the underlying complementarity of altiplano society persisted, and llama caravans continued to link maize producers of the high coastal valleys with potato farmers near the lake and the herders of the puna; now, however, these exchanges were on a smaller, regional scale. Tiwanaku civilization coexisted with the WARI culture, centered in the southern Peruvian highlands, until about 850. While these two cultures shared some ideological elements, as seen in their art styles, they were distinct and seem not to have attempted CONQUEST or other forms of contact.

—Patricia J. Netherly

Further reading:

John Wayne Janusek. *Ancient Tiwanaku* (Cambridge: Cambridge University Press, 2008).

tlatoani   This NAHUATL term was the title used to define the ruler of an *ALTEPETL* (city-state). It literally means "one who says things," that is, "speaker," in the sense of someone who gives commands. While grammatically gender neutral, in its unmodified form, it referred to males. On the infrequent occasions when a woman occupied the position of *tlatoani*, the term was modified to *cihuatlatoani*, or "female ruler." Sometimes, the title was enhanced, as in *huey tlatoani* or "great ruler," as MONTEZUMA was sometimes called. In its plural form, *tlatoque* (occasionally *tlatoanime*), it could refer to the higher reaches of the Nahua nobility rather than just those who were eligible to become rulers of an *altepetl* (see AZTECS).

The position of *tlatoani* in Nahua society is best understood in relationship to the *altepetl*. A *tlatoani* headed his own CALPULLI (or *tlaxilacalli*), but he could also become the overall leader of the *altepetl*, a "first among equals." This ambiguity within a Nahua framework has often been ignored in favor of the popular notion that a *tlatoani*, especially one as famous as Montezuma, was an absolute ruler in some idealized European sense. From colonial times to the present, this misunderstanding has been reinforced by the use of such terms as *rey* (king) or *emperador* (emperor). Scholars have increasingly used the Nahuatl term as a way to focus on the Nahua, rather than European, dimensions and limitations of the position. Use of the Nahuatl term also stresses its importance as one of the defining characteristics of the *altepetl*. A community that had lost its *tlatoani* would be spoken of as being left in silence and darkness, with its people plunged into sorrow and weeping.

The *tlatoani* carried out a wide range of civil and religious functions and enjoyed privileges specific to his office. One of the most dramatic changes after the CONQUEST was his replacement at the apex of religious authority by the Spanish priests of the CATHOLIC CHURCH.

—Barry D. Sell

Further reading:
Rebecca Horn. *Postconquest Coyoacan: Nahua-Spanish Relations in Central Mexico, 1519–1650* (Stanford, Calif.: Stanford University Press, 1997).
James Lockhart. *The Nahuas after the Conquest: A Social and Cultural History of the Indians of Central Mexico, Sixteenth through Eighteenth Centuries* (Stanford, Calif.: Stanford University Press, 1992).

Tlaxcala This is the name of a state and its capital in Central MEXICO, located just east of present-day MEXICO CITY. Both are roughly coterminous with a late pre-Hispanic area and its leading *ALTEPETL* known in NAHUATL as Tlaxcallan (Place of Tortillas, or, more generically, Place of Bread). Tlaxcala continues to be famous for two main reasons. First, before the Spanish CONQUEST, it was one of two major states (the Tarascans of modern Michoacán were the other) to resist the expanding TRIPLE ALLIANCE (Aztec Empire) led by TENOCHTITLÁN. Second, the Tlaxcalans were early and valuable allies to HERNANDO CORTÉS; arguably, the conquest of Mexico could not have occurred without their assistance.

The Tlaxcalans faced an increasingly grim situation when the Spaniards arrived in 1519. Over a period of decades, forces from the Triple Alliance had gradually encircled their territory. This was accomplished through "FLOWER WARS," in which Aztec military might was applied in calculated military engagements of varying intensity and size. This measured approach achieved many victories with minimal cost. Over time, it sapped the strength of the Tlaxcalans, who continually lost both essential allies and vital TRADE routes. If not for the arrival of the Spanish, isolation and final defeat loomed.

The Spanish arrived in Tlaxcala in the first days of September 1519. From the Tlaxcalan perspective, the newcomers were an unknown quantity in terms of their military prowess and political allegiances. They tested both in a series of hard-fought battles and negotiations. Before the end of the month, these confrontations had culminated in an alliance that would soon send 6,000 Tlaxcalans with Cortés into the heartland of enemy territory. During the fall of 1521, as many as 20,000 Tlaxcalans participated in the final siege and conquest of the capital of the AZTECS, Tenochtitlán. For the Spanish, the encounter with some of the most adept fighters of Central Mexico was a rude awakening. Earlier victories over mainly commoners fulfilling their tribute duty as soldiers left them ill prepared to deal with the armies of disciplined and well-trained warriors that followed. The Spanish now had to contend with their first real losses in terms of men, horses, and equipment. This proved a salutary lesson for the battles ahead.

The aftermath of victory over their traditional enemies could not have been foreseen by the Tlaxcalans. Well before the end of the 16th century, epidemic DISEASE and heavy emigration from Europe to the New World had drastically changed the balance of power between local peoples and the colonizers. Indeed, one dominant power had been substituted for another.

Among the thousands of pages of NAHUATL-language documents from the colonial period is a set of Tlaxcalan CABILDO (town council) minutes from 1547–67. No other indigenous community of colonial Mexico has such an abundance of early *cabildo* records. They offer unique insights into indigenous governance just decades after the conquest.

—Barry D. Sell

Further reading:
Charles Gibson. *Tlaxcala in the Sixteenth Century* (New Haven, Conn.: Yale University Press, 1952).
Ross Hassig. *Mexico and the Spanish Conquest* (Norman: University of Oklahoma Press, 2006).

tobacco Tobacco has been important to indigenous societies throughout Latin America since ancient times. Several species of tobacco plants are indigenous to the Americas, with *Nicotiana rustica* and *N. tabacum* being common varieties that were domesticated in tropical Mesoamerica and South America, respectively.

Detail of Maya noble smoking a cigar from a Classic Maya incised shell (600–800) *(Redrawn from Schele and Miller 1986: 155, plate 59a; courtesy of Joel Palka)*

Archaeological evidence of tobacco use before European contact includes North American and Mesoamerican pipes and depictions of people smoking in Classic MAYA ART, with designs on ancient Maya murals at CALAKMUL indicating that tobacco was consumed as a paste or powder. Additionally, ancient Maya glyphs for tobacco snuff or paste label small ceramic bottles excavated in HONDURAS (see CERAMICS). Tobacco seeds were found in volcanic ash at the 1,500-year-old site of Cerén, EL SALVADOR.

CHRISTOPHER COLUMBUS noted the use of tobacco among indigenous populations in the Caribbean on his first voyage. Early European illustrations of NATIVE AMERICANS often show Indians smoking, indicating the newcomers' initial fascination and disgust with the practice. Tobacco was grown in gardens and fields that received adequate sun, warmth, and moisture (see AGRICULTURE). The leaves were cut, hung under roofs, and dried before being rolled, packaged, or ground up. The TAINO of the Antilles, like other Amerindians, smoked rolled dried leaves in their mouths or nostrils, or in bone, stone, and ceramic tubes. In addition to smoking, they used tobacco snuff and chew for therapeutic purposes or

to become intoxicated. Furthermore, indigenous peoples used tobacco for enemas, body paint (for decorative and medicinal purposes and to repel insects), and insecticide, and in religious ceremonies and TRADE (see MEDICINE; RELIGION). The Spanish word *tabaco* probably derived from the Taino or Arawak term for the dried leaves smoked as a cigar or in a tube. The Taino used the term *cohiba* for the tobacco plant and leaves. The Spanish terms *puro* (cigar) and *cigarro/cigarillo* (cigarette) may also have been taken from indigenous Latin American words for tobacco.

Indigenous people continued to use tobacco for ceremonial, curative, and everyday uses during the colonial period. They took tobacco with ALCOHOL and narcotics and added leaves or ground plants for flavoring. They offered tobacco to the deities, who were believed to prepare and consume the plant as people did. Colonial documents record that the inhabitants of colonial towns sometimes maintained trade relations with unconquered lowland indigenous groups, such as the Lacandón Maya, in order to acquire high-quality tobacco. This highlights not only the domestic importance of the plant but its great commercial value in the Americas and growing value in Europe. The importation of tobacco to Europe for pipe smoking was common after the 1550s, especially in Spain, England, and Holland. Later, tobacco for snuff and drink was taken for pleasure and as a stimulant, although it was believed to have medicinal purposes as well. Jean Nicot's experiments with growing tobacco in 16th-century Europe led to naming the plant's addictive component, nicotine, after him.

See also TOBACCO (Vols. II, III).

—Joel Palka

Further reading:
Iain Gately. *Tobacco: A Culture History of How an Exotic Plant Seduced Civilization* (New York: Grove Press, 2001).
Francis Robicsek. *The Smoking Gods: Tobacco in Maya Art, History, and Religion* (Norman: University of Oklahoma Press, 1978).

Toltecs The Toltecs ruled Central MEXICO during the Early Postclassic period (900–1200) and were the first group to integrate the region after the seventh-century fall of TEOTIHUACÁN. Much of what we know about the Toltecs comes from 16th-century Aztec descriptions; the AZTECS viewed the Toltecs as highly artistic, civilized, and urban people. This image, although idealized, is now partially supported by archaeological evidence and Postclassic iconography and inscriptions. The Toltecs' immediate ancestors might have been Chichimecas from northwestern Mesoamerica, who together with the Nonoalca of the Gulf coast settled in the Basin of Mexico, where cultural antecedents can be found in the Coyotlatelco culture dated to 700 C.E. According to Aztec traditions, these people were led by their hero Mixcoatl, whose son, Topiltzin QUETZALCÓATL, later became the legendary founder of the theocratic capital city of Tollan (although some sources place him as one of its last rulers). This Toltec ruler-priest was eventually banished by his rival, Tezcatlipoca, the same figure who also transformed Tollan into an expansionist WARFARE state.

The Toltec capital has been identified with the archaeological site of TULA in the modern Mexican state of Hidalgo. During its apogee (900–1150), Tula was one of the largest CITIES of its time, with a population composed of NAHUATL and Otomi speakers. Like Teotihuacán before it, Tula influenced a vast region through TRADE networks from COSTA RICA to the U.S. Southwest (probably using *POCHTECA*-like merchants) combined with military force, the last seen in the site's extensive warfare iconography. Toltec rulers further broadened their influence through MIGRATIONS and marital alliances. Even though their domain was not as vast as that of the later Aztec Empire, the Toltecs reached areas that the TRIPLE ALLIANCE did not, and their political control extended over Central Mexico, the northern Mesoamerican periphery, the Gulf coast, Soconusco, and parts of the Huasteca and Michoacán. Early Postclassic sites in EL SALVADOR might have been Toltec colonies established by Pipil migrants from Tula. Luxury goods from these regions have been found at Tula and might have been tribute items. The Toltecs also exported green OBSIDIAN from the Pachuca Mountains; it has been found at sites all the way down to Central America.

At CHICHÉN ITZÁ, an important MAYA site in Yucatán, striking similarities in ARCHITECTURE and iconography to that of Tula point to a Toltec presence. While the direction of these cultural influences is still debated, it is a clear that a pan-Mesoamerican religious transformation spread from Tula. This was associated with the cult of Quetzalcóatl (the "feathered serpent" god), as well as other Central Mexico deities such as Xipe Totec, Tlaloc, and Tezcatlipoca. The decline of Tula and gradual dispersal of the Toltecs might have been associated with new waves of Chichimec migrants (such as the Mexica) or with climatic change in the area. Still, many Late Postclassic lineages in Central Mexico and the Maya region claimed to be descendants of the Toltec dynasties, as symbols of prestige and ancestral status. Indeed, the Aztecs revered the Toltecs to the point of excavating in the already abandoned site of Tula in order to extract artifacts that they transferred to their temple in TENOCHTITLÁN.

—Danny Zborover

Further reading:
Alba Guadalupe Mastache, Robert H. Cobean, and Dan M. Healan. *Ancient Tollan: A Regional Perspective of the Toltec State* (Boulder: University Press of Colorado, 2002).

Tordesillas, Treaty of (1494)
The Treaty of Tordesillas was reached by Spain and Portugal in 1494 to resolve their competing claims regarding overseas territories. Earlier in the 15th century, papal decrees had given the Portuguese title to lands they had discovered during their explorations along the west coast of Africa, including the Azores and Cape Verde Islands. CHRISTOPHER COLUMBUS's Castilian-sponsored voyage in 1492 led to the discovery of lands that the Portuguese claimed lay within their jurisdiction. However, in a series of bulls issued in 1493, the Spanish-born pope Alexander VI granted to Spain a broad swath of lands in the Atlantic that conflicted with Portugal's claims. Alexander VI established a line of demarcation, giving Spain the lands lying 100 leagues west of the Azores and Cape Verde Islands. The line was so vague (it did not specify the length of the league or the precise point in the far-flung islands from which the measurement was to be taken) that it did little to settle the dispute.

Therefore, Portuguese and Castilian representatives met at the Spanish town of Tordesillas to negotiate an end to the conflict. The Spaniards agreed to extend the line 370 leagues west, instead of 100, and in turn, the Portuguese recognized Castilian claim to the lands Columbus had discovered. On June 7, 1494, the two monarchies ratified the accord in the Treaty of Tordesillas. The treaty line gave Portugal claim to BRAZIL when it was discovered by PEDRO ÁLVARES CABRAL in 1500. Spain used the papal bulls and the Treaty of Tordesillas to claim sovereignty over Spanish America and to justify its occupation of indigenous lands.

—Kendall Brown

Further reading:
Lyle N. McAlister. *Spain and Portugal in the New World, 1492–1700* (Minneapolis: University of Minnesota Press, 1984).

Totonacs
The Totonac civilization occupied various parts of eastern MEXICO at its peak, which coincided with the peak of AZTEC imperial expansion. The Totonacs were named such by the Aztecs and lived in what was then known as Totonacapan, which stretched between Patantla in the northeast to Cempoala in the south. In addition to cultivating the typical Mesoamerican foodstuffs of beans, MAIZE, and squash, by the 15th century, the Totonacs were also significant producers of liquid amber and COTTON. Their agricultural prowess enabled them to weather a massive famine that struck Mexico between 1450 and 1454 (see AGRICULTURE; FOOD). Indeed, during this period, the Totonacs became significant owners of Aztec slaves, as the Aztecs were desperate and willing to sell slaves in exchange for maize (see SLAVERY). The Totonacs were also recognized for their rich regalia and refined dress; early Spanish accounts of the Totonacs

are rife with references to their stateliness and elegance. This was due chiefly to the work of Totonac WOMEN, who excelled at weaving and embroidery (see CLOTHING; TEXTILES).

Having been at war with the Aztecs for much of the preceding century, the Totonacs were a natural ally for HERNANDO CORTÉS. The Totonac city of Cempoala was the first indigenous city that Cortés visited on his march inland toward the Aztec capital of TENOCHTITLÁN. Having joined forces with Cortés, the Totonacs, along with the Tlaxcalans (see TLAXCALA), played an instrumental role in the ultimate destruction of the Aztec Empire and the success of the Spanish CONQUEST. The Totonac community was annexed to the Spanish Empire with relatively little violence; however, the vibrancy of the Totonacs was destroyed as a result of epidemic DISEASE. Although greatly reduced in number, the Totonacs remained noteworthy on the world stage as the chief producers of vanilla until the mid-19th century. Today, some 90,000 Totonac speakers remain in the Mexican states of Hidalgo, Puebla, and Veracruz. Their language is isolated in its origins from other indigenous languages.

—Sean H. Goforth

trade

MESOAMERICA BEFORE 1492

Before the arrival of Europeans, trade was an important element of all ancient Mesoamerican cultures—the OLMECS, MAYA, MIXTECS, ZAPOTECS, Teotihuacanos (see TEOTIHUACÁN), and AZTECS. Beginning as early as the Preclassic period, marketplace systems were among the most sophisticated forms of exchange in Mesoamerica. Over time, these developed into elaborate networks of markets, dispersed throughout various regions.

Mesoamerican topography ranges from jungle-covered lowlands to mountainous terrain, and this remarkable diversity allowed for the cultivation and use of a wide range of products. Basic FOOD and other materials, such as MAIZE, beans, squash, CERAMICS, ground stone, and construction materials, were usually transported no more than a two-day walk by commercial traders (see TRANSPORTATION).

Luxury items, such as metals, semiprecious stones, feathers, salt, and OBSIDIAN, were transported in volume over much longer distances. Long-distance trade was an old practice and was devoted primarily to the exchange of elite items. Archaeological evidence suggests that long-distance trade was important to the development and subsistence of complex societies throughout Mesoamerica.

As a region, Mesoamerica was unified by a complex trade network, which provided markets with both raw and manufactured goods. Mesoamericans depended on local and regional markets as well as long-distance trading networks. As a result, commerce and trading routes were numerous and an essential part of Mesoamerican society.

Olmecs

Mesoamerican trade and exchange were important aspects of the early Gulf Coast Olmec civilization, located in the modern Mexican states of Tabasco and southern Veracruz (see MEXICO). During the Preclassic period, the Olmecs were part of an extensive long-distance trade network thought to spread throughout Mesoamerica. At the time, the major routes were land based, radiating from the Gulf coast west to the Mexican highlands and southeast along the Pacific coastal plain. The trade was mostly in luxury goods such as jade; however, it also included some utilitarian goods, such as obsidian from the Maya highlands. Olmec merchants traveled throughout Mesoamerica to acquire jades, jadeites, and serpentines.

Both utilitarian and nonutilitarian resources were traded into the Olmec heartland from as far away as Oaxaca and Guerrero. Archaeological excavations have uncovered trade goods associated with the Olmec ritual context. Several thousand tons of metamorphic stone were placed in the southwest platform at La Venta. This material was mined more than 60 miles (96.5 km) south of the site, across the Isthmus of Tehuantepec (see MINING). Obsidian found in the Olmec area was thought to be the result of trade from as far away as the Valley of Mexico, Oaxaca, and GUATEMALA.

Long-distance exchange was carried out on a large scale during the period of the Olmec civilization. The Olmec style has been found in objects distributed throughout Mesoamerica; these objects include portable artifacts such as figurines, personal ornaments, and ceramics, as well as monumental sculptures. Objects made out of material from other parts of Mesoamerica have also been found at Olmec sites. Most of this material consists of imported obsidian, and artifacts made out of limonite, jadeite, serpentine, turquoise, iron pigments, mica, mollusk shell, turtle shell, stingray spines, and shark teeth.

Maya

During the Preclassic period, the Maya utilized three different types of trade: local, regional, and long distance. Local trade consisted of exchanges made within a community. Regional trade occurred within major environmental areas, including the Pacific coastal plain, the southern mountainous and volcanic highlands, the central lowlands with tropical rain forest, and the northern lowlands with tropical vegetation. Under this system, one community would trade with neighboring communities to acquire goods not available locally within a specific area.

Long-distance trade was characterized by the exchange between major environmental areas and involved a far greater diversity of raw materials and products. For example, three major sources of obsidian used by the Maya have been found in the southern highlands, at El Chayal, Ixtepeque, and San Martín Jilotepeque. Obsidian found from 23 sites can be identified from these southern highland regions. Obsidian from all three sources was distributed northward from the highlands to the lowlands.

The Maya desired obsidian for both utilitarian and ritual purposes. Evidence of obsidian tools in Maya lowland areas indicates that utilitarian goods were part of long-distance trade. Increasing amounts of utilitarian goods such as obsidian and salt were traded through bulk transport by sea, from the Maya area to other parts of Mesoamerica and vice versa. Utilitarian goods exchanged in local, regional, and in some cases in long-distance trade included agricultural products (various areas); balsam (Pacific coast); bark cloth (Pacific coast and lowlands); basketry (various areas); COTTON (lowlands, Pacific coast, and the Yucatán); dyes and pigments (various areas); fish and sea products (coastal areas and lakes); flint and cert (lowlands); wild game (various areas); henequen and maguey (northern lowlands); lime (lowlands); *manos* and *METATES* (southern highlands); obsidian (southern highlands); ocote, or pitch pine (highlands); ceramics (various areas); salt (northern coastal lowlands); sugar, honey, and wax (northern lowlands from the Caribbean coast); TEXTILES (various areas); TOBACCO (lowlands); tortoiseshell (coastal areas); and volcanic ash (southern highlands) (see DYES AND DYEWOOD).

Markets in the plazas of major and minor ceremonial sites were the primary centers of trade. The ancient Maya included both part-time traders and full-time merchants. Families had to obtain some basic products at local or regional markets (see FAMILY). Ruling families and members of the royal court were supported by taxes and tribute, supplemented by trade in local markets. Craft specialists not attached to the elite would obtain their food at local markets. Even full-time farming families, who were the vast majority of the population, relied on trade for pottery, salt, CACAO, and stone tools and to add variety to their diet.

Long-distance trade was undertaken by a small group of wealthy, elite merchants. These merchants controlled foreign exchanges, including most of the commerce that passed through the Maya areas between Mexico and Central America. Long-distance trade played a major role in the wealth and power of the lowland Maya elite. The lowland Maya elite required important utilitarian goods to manage these complex societies such as salt, obsidian, and grinding stones. These goods were found throughout the lowlands but not enough to sustain a large populated society; however, the elite managed and controlled long-distance trade in order to have more access to these goods.

Long-distance trade materials were part of the costuming and regalia of Maya kings, queens, nobles, and priests; without these lavish costumes, they could not carry out the public rituals that were their principal duties. These materials were crafted into mosaic headdresses, shields, scepters, mirrors, and other regalia. Other elite long-distance goods traded within the Maya area included amber (Chiapas), cacao (lowlands, Caribbean,

and Gulf and Pacific coasts), cinnabar (southern highlands), copal and *pom* (lowlands), quetzal feathers (northern highlands), hematite (southern highlands), jadeite (northern highlands), jaguar pelts and teeth (southern and central highlands), pyrite (highlands), serpentine (highlands), albite (highlands), diorite (highlands), shark teeth (coastal area), shell (coastal area), coral and stingray spines (coastal area), polychrome ceramics (lowland area), and imported ceramics or artifacts from other Maya regions and from different regions in Mexico.

Long-distance goods and materials brought into the Maya realm from Mexico included kaolin, magnetite, metals (copper), pelts (rabbit), pottery, textiles, and turquoise. Goods and materials brought into the Maya area from other parts of Central America included chalcedony, cotton, feathers, metals (GOLD, silver, copper, and alloys), pottery, and rubber.

Mixtecs and Zapotecs

The Maya were also linked to western Mesoamerica through trade with the Zapotecs. The Zapotecs resided in the Valley of Oaxaca, along the Pacific coast. Their center was MONTE ALBÁN. The rich gold-bearing lands of the Mixtec and Zapotec civilizations lay across the Puebla border in Oaxaca. One of the largest Mesoamerican trading centers was Coixtlahuaca in Oaxaca. *POCHTECAS* (guild merchants) from all over southern Mexico met there to trade with their northern counterparts.

Teotihuacanos

During the Early Classic period, a substantial part of eastern Central Mexico was dominated by the great urban Center of Teotihuacán. Indeed, Teotihuacán's influence stretched all the way to Maya territory in Guatemala and HONDURAS. Long-distance trade was one of the important bases for the development of Teotihuacán civilization and the diffusion of Teotihuacán style. Stylistic links between Teotihuacán and virtually every part of Mesoamerica are often noted. Long-distance exchange was controlled by the elite Teotihuacán traders, or *pochtecas*, who moved goods in large caravans.

Most of the long-distance exchange focused on obsidian. There were several kinds of obsidian workshops at Teotihuacán: local, precinct, and regional. The products from regional workshops were distributed throughout the Basin of Mexico and beyond. The industry met the needs of literally millions of consumers.

A large proportion of the obsidian processed at Teotihuacán came from the Pachuca source complex. This material has a distinctive golden-green color and is exceptionally well suited to manufacturing fine prismatic blades. Teotihuacán controlled the Pachuca source of superior green obsidian. Much of it was used in the city itself, but small amounts have been found throughout Mesoamerica. Green obsidian was the only locally obtained valuable raw material.

Aztecs

In the Postclassic period, from their capital city of TENOCHTITLÁN in the Basin of Mexico, the Aztecs controlled an empire that stretched from Veracruz to the Pacific coast and from Central Mexico to Guatemala. Within the Aztec Empire, exchange was conducted in three major forms: marketplace transactions, state-sponsored foreign trade, and tribute and taxation. The trade and tribute systems provided resources essential to the maintenance of Tenochtitlán, its large population, and the Aztec ECONOMY in general.

Marketplace transactions were carried out by the common majority, such as farmers and part-time small-scale producers, who sold their goods locally. Most vendors of this type dealt in subsistence goods, ceramics, ground-stone tools, charcoal, and other basic items. In addition, there were regional merchants who served major markets in the provinces. Although they also dealt in subsistence goods, these middlemen concentrated on buying and selling high bulk, medium-value products, such as salt, cotton, and cacao. They transported these goods from market to market, often across political borders. These traders were independent entrepreneurs.

At the very top of the trader hierarchy were the *pochtecas*. These professional merchants were organized into hereditary guilds and lived in specific neighborhoods. In fact, there were seven different merchant areas, or wards, in Tenochtitlán and Tlatelolco. The most important was Pochtlán. The other important long-distance trading communities were Tepetitlán, Tzonmolco, Atlauhco, Amachtlán, and Itztotolco. These names appear in areas far beyond the Valley of Mexico, and it has been suggested that these sites may have been trading centers as far back as Toltec times (see TOLTECS). Most long-distance trade outside the empire was managed by *pochtecas*. The *pochtecas* traded in volume mainly luxury goods, as well as salt and obsidian. Long-distance trade had a major impact on craft specialization at Tenochtitlán.

Long-distance exchange gave the Aztecs better access to raw materials; as a result, skilled artisans moved to Tenochtitlán in large numbers, and specialization in the production of certain goods became increasingly centralized in the city. Raw materials imported by the *pochtecas* included feathers, cotton, cloth, jade, metal ornaments, and rubber balls. Featherworkers, lapidaries, and metalworkers were organized into guilds; moreover, these artisans held a special rank in Aztec society. They produced luxury goods both for local consumption and for export. Goods were traded to regional merchants for sale in local markets or were exchanged to the *pochtecas* to trade long distance.

In addition, Aztec tribute collectors, or *calpixque*, gathered tribute payments and taxes. The Aztecs collected tribute and taxes as revenue from conquered regions. Provinces in close proximity to Tenochtitlán gave goods such as foodstuffs, warrior garb, and a variety of textiles, wood, bowls, paper, and mats. More distant provinces from different ecological areas provided luxury goods such as precious feathers, jade, turquoise, gold, cacao, cotton, decorated cloaks, women's tunics, warrior garb and shields, gold shields, animal skins, feathers standards, gold diadems, gold headbands, and strings of gold beads (see CLOTHING).

Long-distance trade in the U.S. Southwest with northwestern Mesoamerica is shown through the presence of copper bells, iron pyrite mirrors, and macaws found among the Hokoham. Mesoamerica had a variety of cultures that not only conducted a vibrant regional trade but also exchanged goods well beyond their boundaries into the U.S. Southwest, Oklahoma, and the Mississippi Valley.

SOUTH AMERICA BEFORE 1492

There are many gaps in the archaeological record concerning trade in preconquest South America, and even in the late pre-European period, there were different systems by which goods circulated and people and societies met their needs. Nevertheless, at the most basic level, what can be said is that goods that were essential for subsistence, such as food, were circulated, and that this circulation frequently involved reciprocity. For example, in the highlands of the central Andes, households and lineages grew crops at different altitudes: POTATOES and other tubers were grown on the highest fields; maize and other crops on the temperate mid-level lands; and cotton, hot peppers, and COCA in the lowest, warmest fields. The farmers of an *AYLLU* either had fields at different altitudes or exchanged these goods among themselves, giving them all access to each type. The circulation of goods beyond this level, however, involved more distant groups. The people who carried out these exchanges were often individual traders, and they frequently had trading partners with whom they regularly exchanged goods. These relationships tended to be inherited from father to son and did not necessarily involve higher authorities. On the north coast of PERU, for example, fishermen were specialized and often lived at a distance from cultivated land. They obtained produce from farmers inland in exchange for fish and other marine products. It is not clear, however, whether these exchanges were between trading partners or took place in a more generalized market setting under the jurisdiction of a single political ruler.

The movement of essential foods within a household, lineage, or small polity did not generally involve travel over long distances. In contrast, luxury goods, ritual items, exotic items, and even lore or esoteric knowledge were frequently exchanged over greater distances by specialists. Such individuals may have had trading partners or may have attended pilgrimage fairs. Part of this trade was undoubtedly at the behest of their chief or ruler. These exchanges were often very important. For example, the highlanders of northern Peru received salt and hot peppers from Túcume farmers in exchange for water from their rivers, which the Túcume farmers used to irrigate their crops. While there was in fact no way to withhold this water, the exchange set up mutual relations of obligation that gave the highlanders access to lowland products and Túcume farmers rights of refuge in the highlands in times of drought or floods. Esoteric knowledge seems to have been an important type of exchange. Unlike material items, this exchange does not show up directly in the archaeological record; however, it can be seen in the expansion of religious cults and the use of particular healing practices (see RELIGION). Many of these exchanges also involved the use of fictive equivalences, which did not necessarily have to be logical or even roughly equal. Finally, in some exchange systems, particularly on the northern coast of Peru into Mesoamerica, the use of proto-monies had begun to emerge at the time of the arrival of the Spanish.

There has been much scholarly debate about whether there were markets in the Andean region. It appears that both sides are right, at least in part. It is known that very early on exchanges took place at religious festivals. These were either by barter or fixed equivalences. In the Andes of BOLIVIA and southern Peru, there was a tradition of long-distance trade involving coca and hot peppers from the warm eastern slopes of the Andes; llama meat and the wool of llamas and alpacas from the high puna region; dried potatoes, metals, and esoteric lore and religious beliefs from the altiplano around Lake Titicaca; and maize, cotton, hot peppers, and salt from the warmer valleys of the western slopes and the coastal valleys. Goods were circulated in a number of ways. By pre-Inca times, the large polities of the altiplano around Lake Titicaca had established colonies in the warm coca lands to the east and the maize-producing valleys of the coast to give them direct access to those products (see INCAS). Their core areas already included potato fields, high pastures for llamas and alpacas, access to the aquatic resources of Lake Titicaca, and access to ores and metals. Llamas were key. While they were important for their fiber and meat, they were also indispensable for the transport of bulky items over long distances. Thus, the specialists in this long-distance trade came from groups with access to llamas, though not all herders engaged in exchange.

Subsistence goods appear to have been exchanged on the basis of established equivalences. According to Spanish accounts, highland traders who came to Chincha on the southern Peruvian coast used small copper sheets as tokens, although this has not been established archaeologically. The trade routes from the coast to the altiplano appear to have been important in the diffusion of the Aymara language to the Titicaca Basin. The textiles, pottery, and other artifacts decorated in the style associated with the religion of the TIWANAKU culture also appear to have moved along these routes. In all these instances, exchanges were a means of establishing and maintaining relations between different groups. Later, the Inca state attempted to control all exchange, particularly that over long distances. Markets, where they existed, were highly circumscribed under the Incas.

There is considerable evidence for trade between the peoples of the AMAZON and those of the Andes. Lowland products included honey, the feathers of tropical birds, medicinal and hallucinogenic plants for ritual and curing, and esoteric lore (see MEDICINE). It is not clear what was exchanged in return, but it may have included gold or bronze objects, textiles, or stone for tools such as obsidian or chert. Exchange within Amazonia was carried out by individuals or small groups of men who traveled long distances, sometimes more than 600 miles (965.5 km). Items traded included stone axes, poison for arrows, pigments for decorating pottery, and esoteric lore. While such long trips were usually undertaken by canoe, frequently through hostile territory, there appears to have been a convention of respecting individuals on trading missions. Such expeditions frequently took many months because, while it was easy to travel downstream with high water, it was sometimes necessary to wait months for low water in order to return upstream. No archaeological evidence for markets or any item that might have functioned as money has been reported for Amazonia.

There appear to have been markets, long-distance trade, and even one or more systems of proto-money along the west coast of South America from the northern coast of Peru to Mesoamerica and beyond. One of the earliest trade items was the shell of the warm-water oyster (Spondylus), found off the Pacific coast of ECUADOR; these shells were traded southward to Peru beginning in the Initial period around 2000 B.C.E. The inhabitants of the central Andes associated Spondylus with abundant rainfall and thus considered it ritually essential for successful crops. The Spondylus recovered at the Initial-period temple of Kotosh and the later temple at CHAVÍN de Huántar probably entered Peru from Azuay and Loja in Ecuador along overland trade routes. Trade in MOCHE times, in the first millennium C.E., may also have been primarily conducted over land, since there is abundant evidence for large llama caravans at religious centers, and these are also depicted on Moche pottery. There is also archaeological evidence for large Moche watercraft made of bundled reeds, as well as evidence that the Moche sailed to the guano islands across the open sea.

It is the traders of Lambayeque, however, who exemplify trading by sea for the central Andes. The Lambayeque were not expansionist, but their pottery (and presumably Lambayeque traders) were found in LIMA and as far south as Chincha, in Peru. It is probable that some trade items were carried by llama caravans, but the Lambayeque also used rafts of balsa logs, guided by a system of movable centerboards, which allowed their vessels to sail against adverse currents. These rafts included a "hold" for cargo and masts with square-rigged or crescent sails. Lambayeque polities appear to have been the southern terminus of a network of marine trade that extended north along the Pacific coast of Ecuador. The inventory of the cargo recovered off the coast of northern Ecuador during FRANCISCO PIZARRO's second voyage to Peru included elaborate gold ornaments, EMERALDS, objects of green stone, textiles, and a large quantity of *Spondylus* shell and beads. The gold ornaments were worn by the chiefs of the region to indicate their status. The cloth may also have come from Lambayeque or from ports in southern Ecuador, while the green stone figures may have been traveling south. Copper and bronze objects were also traded. Two classes of goods seem to have had quasi-monetary status: beads made of *Spondylus* shell, called *chaquira*, and thin copper sheets in the form of I bars and axes. Of the two, *chaquira* appear to have been used more widely. The status of traders is not entirely clear. They seem to have been a privileged occupational group under the jurisdiction of their regional rulers, but it is not known if they made up a particular social group or came from particular ethnic groups, or whether they were present in all major polities but were directly dependent on the paramount rulers.

See also ECONOMY (Vols. II, III, IV); TRADE (Vols. II, III, IV).

—Stephanie Lozano
Patricia J. Netherly

Further reading:
Manuel Aguilar-Moreno. *Handbook to Life in the Aztec World.* (New York: Facts On File, 2006).
Terence N. D'Altroy. *The Incas* (Malden, Mass.: Blackwell Publishing, 2002).
Robert Sharer. *The Ancient Maya* (Stanford, Calif.: Stanford University Press, 2006).

transportation

THE AMERICAS BEFORE 1492

Ancient roads and transport networks in the Americas have drawn considerable scholarly attention and public interest in recent years. Whereas the use and deployment of waterborne craft, such as balsa and reed boats and rafts along the Peruvian coast and large dugout canoes in Mesoamerica and North America, were clearly instrumental in the growth of such transport networks, their documented use is limited mainly to ethnohistorical and contact-era accounts and journals. Archaeological information on waterborne TRADE and interaction is therefore largely inferred from secondary forms of evidence. Ancient road networks serve as key indicators of early human social, political, and economic interaction and trade in the Americas, and ancient ports along such rivers as the Mississippi, Rio Grande (Río Bravo), Usumacinta, Pasión, Lerma-Santiago, Motagua, and AMAZON provide indirect indications of pre-Hispanic interaction (see ECONOMY).

By extension, the celebrated *POCHTECA* merchants of the Aztec era (ca. 1250–1521) maintained legions of human burden bearers, who from childhood had been trained within *pochteca* guilds for the purpose of transporting goods (see AZTECS). Because both North and Middle America

were largely devoid of domestic draft animals, human burden bearers were the primary source of overland transport; only in western South America and Peru did llamas (camelids) serve as pack animals for negotiating those regions' treacherous mountain climes. However, while Peruvian llamas could carry upward of two 66-pound (30-kg) loads of goods (rotated between three adult camelid males) at the rate of about 12 miles (19 km) per day, llamas tire easily and become uncooperative when tired. By contrast, male and female *tlameme* (human burden bearers) could carry the equivalent of 65 or more pounds of cargo for distances of between 12 and 15 miles per day, all with little more than a tumpline or strap, known as a *mecapal*.

Of course, while they were more reliable and could bear larger loads, *tlamemes* needed to be fed from local supplies or from goods ported in transit. To ameliorate this drawback, Peruvian porters often carried supplies from one end of an assigned territory to the next; from there, neighboring porters conducted the load through the next territory. Nevertheless, it is to the credit of such human burden bearers that commerce, communication, and other forms of early human interaction were made viable in the Americas.

Early European exploration and recent scientific discoveries have identified major transport network systems and ancient roads in such diverse areas of the Americas as the U.S. Southwest; the Mississippian complex of eastern North America; Casas Grandes, in Chihuahua, MEXICO; La Quemada, Zacatecas; TEOTIHUACÁN and the Teotihuacán Corridor, in TLAXCALA; the Sierra de Puebla; MONTE ALBÁN and the Valley of Oaxaca; the *sacbé* (road) systems of the northern MAYA lowlands and Yucatán Peninsula; the southern Maya lowlands in GUATEMALA and HONDURAS; the Llanos of Barinas, in VENEZUELA; and the Andean cordilleras of PERU, BOLIVIA, CHILE, and ARGENTINA. Significantly, the Andean achievement alone served to integrate an ancient road system and transnational transport network consisting of major highways and trunk lines over some 20,000 to 25,000 miles (32,187–40,234 km). This latticelike network extended over a vast area by way of tandem coastal and highland routes that stretch from Quito, ECUADOR, in the north, through Peru, Chile, Bolivia, and Argentina in the south; this network consisted of at least 14,000 miles (22,531 km) of built roads and road-related features (such as rope-cable suspension bridges) that traversed some of the most inhospitable and rugged terrain imaginable. The growing body of archaeological and historical evidence now invites investigators to visualize the deployment of extensive and sophisticated transport networks and ancient road systems that once teemed with people, including the elite, commoners, traders, farmers, and soldiers.

By contrast with the well-documented roads of the Inca Empire (see INCAS), the long abandoned roads of the ancestral Pueblo, Chaco, or Anasazi peoples of the U.S. Southwest made up an integrated system of some 500 miles (805 km) of known masonry and paved and unpaved segments; this vast network connected major Pueblo towns and settlements throughout the U.S. states of New Mexico, Colorado, Arizona, and Utah. Unlike the Andean system, archaeologists continue to speculate on the probable functions of the roads and road-related features identified with the Chaco and Pueblo peoples.

Scholars have advanced a number of interpretations for the Chacoan roads, including their use as defensive networks for outlying Pueblo settlements and as trade routes, for ceremonial and political purposes, and for the transport of subsistence goods to and from rural communities. Among Pueblo peoples of the late 19th and early 20th centuries, scholars have noted the use of ceremonial circuits, or "Pueblo raceways" (replete with runners like the CHASQUI used by the Incas of Peru), that were intended to influence the movement of clouds, and thus rain, in the parched lands of the Southwest. American Indian beliefs and cosmologies regarding the importance and sanctity of such roads have yet to be fully considered.

Interestingly, while 16th-century Spanish accounts of the Mesoamerican road and highway systems of the Aztecs and their predecessors are readily available, only recently have scholars begun documenting these networks via ground verification studies, aerial (satellite) imagery, archaeological exploration, and ethnohistorical analysis. While Aztec-era transport network systems and roads were clearly instrumental in maintaining the Aztecs' massive tribute system, scholars continue to grapple with how earlier systems, such as those of the northern Maya lowlands, were used.

Accounts from the 16th and 17th centuries make clear that transport networks in Peru and Mesoamerica served both the sociopolitical and economic demands of the empires that designed, developed, and maintained them. And like the systems expanded on by the Incas of Peru, Aztec imperial interests drew on extant ancient road systems as the basis for the course of thoroughfares in their empire.

The Inca road system constituted "South America's largest contiguous archaeological remain." For the Incas, the *qhapaq ñan*, or *Inka ñan* (Inca road), was a complex sociopolitical and economic, managerial, ideological, symbolic, and otherworldly device for communicating the mandates, privileges, and prerogatives of the quadripartite Inca Empire, known as Tawantinsuyu. Given the vastness of the Peruvian transport networks, and those of Mesoamerica and North America, one is left to ponder the enormity of the achievement in question. The paucity of domestic draft animals, with the exception of llamas indigenous to the Andean cordilleras, clearly played a role in the rise and fall of cultures, technologies, and traditions in the Americas more broadly. The development of such networks ultimately fueled the rise, fall, and integration of communities, kingdoms, and empires wherever they were deployed.

Extant ancient road systems throughout the Peruvian highlands were integrated into the broader imperial network that was both upgraded and expanded by the Incas.

A massive LABOR force, predicated on the availability of MITA (conscripted) laborers, permitted the construction and ongoing maintenance of a vast interregional system that incorporated both formal and informal all-weather architectural features and pavements. While Inca engineers sought to minimize damage to the natural topography, they were nevertheless known for tunneling through precipitous rock formations or terracing hillsides to accommodate roadbeds. Moreover, they erected tall tapia-adobe walls and related earthworks, as well as wooden drawbridges, stone abutments, masonry bridges and culverts, dams, and rope-cable suspension bridges. Road construction ultimately varied according to local conditions, the available materials, topography, labor demands, public works projects, military mobilizations, ritual and cosmological associations, and religious processions.

Whereas pole-roads and tall tapia-adobe side walls were deployed along coastal routes, elsewhere broad thoroughfares, cut-stone stairways, masonry sidewalls, and related linear arrangements were used. High-elevation Andean road systems were engineered to withstand the harshest conditions, and their durability was legendary. The use of elaborate stone curbs and pavements, as well as masonry retaining walls and switchbacks, was a key characteristic of such roads. It was these latter roads that were ultimately best preserved and therefore testify to the sophistication of Andean road building. Elevated roadbeds and stone or adobe sidewalls lined or enclosed road features with an eye to protecting travelers from crosswinds, flooding, the encroachment of crops and livestock, and other related conditions in agricultural regions (see AGRICULTURE).

While Inca causeways typically were of rubble-core construction, earlier civilizations made use of a variety of masonry techniques, including sun-dried brick, puddled adobe, and rammed earth. Sun-dried brick construction, for instance, can be found at such sites as CHAN CHAN or the earlier MOCHE sites of the north coast of Peru. Such construction was often coordinated with stone retaining walls, rock-cut ramps, switchbacks, stairways, and related features, which were used to buffer ascent and descent in the precipitous rock topographies. Runners, or *chasquis*, were charged with carrying QUIPUS (knotted and colored cords used for record keeping), messages, and fresh fish and related products to and from the lowlands to the highlands. The speed with which a runner delivered a message was directly dependent on the plethora of trunk and feeder lines that constituted the all-weather highway system. Ultimately, the whole of the Inca Empire was integrated through a host of subsidiary installations and transport network features that amazed European observers. The soldier-chronicler PEDRO CIEZA DE LEÓN wrote in 1553 that "In human memory I believe that there is no account of a road as great as this, running through deep valleys, high mountains, banks of snow, torrents of water, living rock, and wild rivers . . . excavated into precipices and cut through rock in the mountains. . . . in all places it was clean and swept free of refuse, with lodgings, store-houses, Sun temples, and posts along the route."

TRAVEL TO THE AMERICAS

The European "discovery" of the Americas followed 15th-century maritime advances. Aided by new technology, including astrolabes and caravel ships, mariners advanced down the coast of Africa and then farther into the Atlantic, beyond the Canary Islands and the Azores. CHRISTOPHER COLUMBUS arrived in the Caribbean while searching for a sea route to Asia, and also sailing to Asia, albeit around the Cape of Good Hope, PEDRO ÁLVARES DE CABRAL landed in BRAZIL in 1499.

The early voyages yielded information about ocean currents and wind patterns that proved invaluable in establishing regular shipping routes. Subsequent voyages by FERDINAND MAGELLAN (1521–22), Miguel López de Legazpi (1564), and Friar Andrés de Urdaneta (1565) linked the Americas with Asia. The Americas thus came to serve as the critical link between transatlantic fleets and the Manila galleons (see FLEETS/FLEET SYSTEM). The Atlantic fleet initially sailed from Seville to Havana. From there, cargo ships continued on to destinations in Veracruz (Mexico), Nombre de Dios in PANAMA, and Cartagena in COLOMBIA. On the Pacific side, ships sailed between Acapulco (Mexico) and Manila (Philippines). LIMA's port of Callao linked the Andean ECONOMY with the rest of the Americas.

While regular oceanic transportation set in motion Spanish and Portuguese colonialism, it also facilitated the rise of a new mercantile economy. The Americas played a crucial role in this: American SILVER promoted commerce in European goods, African slaves, and Asian luxury products such as silk and spices (see SLAVERY). Lucrative trade inspired maritime rivalries and piracy, however, which resulted in the Spanish Crown developing a fleet system with an armed escort to provide greater security (see PIRATES AND PIRACY). Despite its initial success, the fleet, system did not make ships impervious to attack, nor was it entirely satisfactory to merchants. In 1628, Dutch vessels led by Piet Heyn captured the Spanish treasure fleet and during the second half of the 17th century, the fleet system became less profitable because of smuggling and increased trade within the Americas and with China.

TRAVEL WITHIN THE AMERICAS

Most European transport within the Americas followed overland routes, as there were few navigable rivers. One exception was the Río de la Plata (River Plate). In 1580, BUENOS AIRES was reestablished as a port to provide an Atlantic outlet to the silver mines of POTOSÍ, in Bolivia. Only in the late 18th century did Buenos Aires come to serve this purpose, although until then it occupied an important place in the transatlantic slave trade because of its proximity to Portuguese traders. For the most part, river transportation, and indeed most local transportation involving water systems, remained the preserve of NATIVE AMERICANS. Canoes figured prominently in

waterborne commerce in the Valley of Mexico, for example, where lakes and canals made canoes an efficient, inexpensive form of transportation. The largest canoes, more than 50 feet (15.25 km) long, were capable of carrying several tons of cargo to MEXICO CITY.

Before the CONQUEST, the Americas typically lacked draft animals for overland transportation, with the exception of alpacas and llamas in the Andes. In the absence of draft animals, Amerindians relied on people to carry goods. In Mexico, carriers known as *tamemes* were an integral part of the transport system. Spaniards even hired *tamemes* to carry them around town, notwithstanding government prohibitions. Before the arrival of Europeans, the indigenous people had made no use of the wheel. Afterward, mules were used to pull carts and wagons. In the Andes, where complex geography had previously made effective transportation essential to the integration of the Inca Empire, mules found a place alongside the traditional caravans, or *trajines*. The discovery of silver deposits in Potosí bolstered the use of *trajines* during the colonial period. Mules and horses became a mainstay of overland transport, sometimes with unforeseen consequences. Nonsedentary Native Americans, for instance in Chile and Mexico's north, soon adapted to horses and became sufficiently mobile to evade colonial control.

Spaniards followed Native American precedents in maintaining road networks. The Inca Empire had relied on trunk lines that ran from Quito through CUZCO and down to Chile. These lines were supplemented by feeder roads that traversed the diverse, mountainous topography. The overall Andean network stretched for thousands of miles, and many roads were paved with stone. With established trade routes there developed a wide range of facilities to support transportation, including inns, granaries, and storehouses, as well as customs houses. Where no previous roads existed, Spaniards built new ones to serve the silver mines and transcontinental trade. The royal road, or *camino real*, in Mexico connected Veracruz with the capital and Acapulco. The royal road thus played an integral part in connecting the Pacific and Atlantic economies.

See also TRANSPORTATION (Vols. II, III, IV).

—Richard Conway
Rubén G. Mendoza

Further reading:

Ross Hassig. *Trade, Tribute, and Transportation: The Sixteenth-Century Political Economy of the Valley of Mexico* (Norman: University of Oklahoma Press, 1985).

James Lockhart. "Trunk Lines and Feeder Lines." In *Of Things of the Indies: Essays Old and New in Early Latin American History*, 90–120 (Stanford, Calif.: Stanford University Press, 1999).

J. H. Parry. *The Age of Reconnaissance* (London: Weidenfeld & Nicholson, 1963).

Trent, Council of   See COUNCIL OF TRENT.

Triple Alliance (1428–1521)

Established in 1428 the Triple Alliance was a coalition established between the three largest polities in the Valley of MEXICO: the Mexicas (AZTECS) of TENOCHTITLÁN-Tlatelolco, the Acolhua of Texcoco, and the Tepanec of Tlacopan. Each of the alliance capitals was governed by its respective king (*TLATOANI*), who further ruled several domains and lesser kingdoms in his area. Nevertheless, since Tenochtitlán was commanding the CONQUEST wars, it soon became the most prominent of the three; indeed, *Aztec Empire* is often used as an equivalent term for the *Triple Alliance*.

In less than a century after its formation, the Triple Alliance ruled over the largest recorded territory of any indigenous polity in Mesoamerican history. Stretching from the Gulf coast to the Pacific Ocean, this noncontiguous empire was further divided into tributary provinces, each consisting of different ethnic groups. Towns that submitted peacefully were considered allies to the empire and thus their internal organization remained relatively unchanged; however, those groups that had to be subdued by military force were obligated to pay tribute, and their rulers often were replaced by Aztec emissaries. The tribute, which included FOOD supplies, raw materials, and exotic goods, was essential to the political economy of the Triple Alliance and was distributed unequally among the three capitals, with Tlacopan receiving the smallest portion. In addition, the Triple Alliance established military garrisons and enclaves in strategic provinces, which were populated by migrants from the Valley of Mexico. Still, some groups strongly resisted the marching armies of the empire, such as the Tlaxcalans and the Tarascans (see TLAXCALA).

The Triple Alliance dissolved soon after the Spanish conquest, although the colonial administration largely followed pre-Columbian territorial divisions and even took advantage of its provincial political and economic organization.

—Danny Zborover

Further reading:
Pedro Carrasco. *The Tenochca Empire of Ancient Mexico: The Triple Alliance of Tenochtitlán, Tezcoco and Tlacopan* (Norman: University of Oklahoma Press, 1999).

Tula (Tollan)

The Postclassic-period (ca. 650–1150) center of Tula served as the capital of the Mexican ethnic group known as the TOLTECS; the site lies in the Mexican state of Hidalgo, some 90 minutes north of MEXICO CITY. The city apparently grew from TRADE relations with the far larger TEOTIHUACÁN, located 40 miles (64 km) to the southeast. Tula entered its period of apogee sometime around 900. This was a time of political fragmentation and constant WARFARE, the latter evident in the glorification of soldiers in Tula ART. Indeed, the culture's most famous material artifacts are the so-called Atlantes, a series of iconic warrior statues measuring 15 feet (4.5 m) in height. The center's location undoubtedly related to nearby deposits of OBSIDIAN, the glassy black volcanic rock used in the manufacture of pre-Columbian knives and arrowheads. At its height, Tula controlled a vast trade empire that extended as far north as New Mexico.

Tula's relationship with the MAYA city of CHICHÉN ITZÁ in MEXICO's Yucatán Peninsula remains a subject of ongoing controversy. Scholars have long noted key similarities between the two sites and for many years believed that Tula had conquered Chichén Itzá. However, the supposed political links may have been more apparent than real, instead reflecting a common source of symbols and ideas current throughout Mesoamerica in the Early Postclassic era. The resemblances between the two centers may also have resulted from close economic relations, through which Tula provided obsidian in exchange for Chichén Itzá's salt.

After 1100, the city entered a severe decline, the reasons for which include a prolonged drought that scourged northern and Central Mexico, as well as the rise of peripheral cultures that had grown wealthy and powerful under Tula's wing. Sometime around 1150, Tula was burned and abandoned, giving rise to a period of Central Mexico political instability that ended only with the establishment of Aztec hegemony (see AZTECS). To this day, much of Tula and Toltec history remains elusive. Aztec legends of a mighty culture seated in a place called Tollan may have been more mythological than real. Modern archaeology was late in positively identifying Tula as the seat of Toltec power.

—Terry Rugeley

Tulum

Located approximately 80 miles (129 km) south of Cancún in MEXICO's Yucatán Peninsula and situated on a cliff overlooking the coast, the MAYA site of Tulum probably functioned as the port and lookout for the neighboring site of Cobá, located 26 miles (42 km) into the interior. Tulum's original name was apparently *Samá*, meaning "dawn," in reference to the striking sunrises visible from its coastal heights. The name *Tulum* means "wall" and refers to the fact that the original city was surrounded by walls, the remnants of which are still visible today.

Although the structures seen today date mostly from the Late Postclassic period (1250–1520), Tulum was inhabited as early as 400 or 500 C.E., in fact, it may have been a city of considerable importance in the 13th and 14th centuries. Its wealth and influence doubtless grew from its connection to maritime TRADE. The city appears to have functioned as an independent political jurisdiction at the time of European contact in the early 16th century. Tulum's most visible structure is notable for the presence of the so-called Descending God, who appears to be diving headfirst into unseen water. Its picturesque Castillo, which overlooks the Caribbean from a cliff high above the sea, has become an icon of Yucatec Maya archaeology.

—Terry Rugeley

Tupinambá A subgroup of the Tupí people of northeastern Brazilian territory, the Tupinambá were seminomadic forest dwellers encountered by Portuguese settlers in the early 16th century (see BRAZIL). Initially, Portuguese merchants engaged in TRADE with the Tupinambá; however, as SUGAR emerged as a major cash crop for Portuguese imperialists, the demand for Tupí land increased dramatically. Naturally, a confrontation resulted, as the Tupí felt no obligation to turn over their ancestral lands to the foreigners.

Another source of confrontation between the Portuguese and the Tupinambá was the practice of CANNIBALISM. An essential part of Tupí culture, the ritual of holding prisoners of war for several months only to fatten them up for a village feast horrified Portuguese settlers, as well as Jesuit missionaries who had been sent to Brazil to convert the Indians to Christianity (see RELIGION; RELIGIOUS ORDERS).

As the demand for sugar grew in Europe, the Portuguese in Brazil increasingly used force to clear the lands, forcing any remaining indigenous persons to work on the plantations (see SLAVERY). However, around 1547 at the Bay of All Saints, one of the most productive sites of sugarcane at the time, the Tupinambá revolted; they destroyed one of Brazil's Portuguese settlements and killed all of its inhabitants.

For the next half of the 16th century, the Portuguese Crown instituted a royal governor and constructed a capital city on that very site, as a means to formally establish authority over rebellious groups. As the Portuguese presence grew, the Tupinambá were absorbed into the settlement as slaves. Due to the unsanitary conditions and overcrowding in the slave quarters, fatal European DISEASES quickly worked their way through the indigenous populations, killing off many of the Tupí. In addition, the Tupinambá intermarried with members of other indigenous groups, until they finally ceased to exist as an identifiable group.

See also JESUITS (Vol. II).

—Christina Hawkins

Further reading:

John Charles Chasteen. *Born in Blood and Fire: A Concise History of Latin America* (New York: W. W. Norton & Co., 2001).

U

universities See EDUCATION.

Uruguay Uruguay is a small South American nation located on the South Atlantic Ocean between ARGENTINA and BRAZIL. During most of the colonial period, the region was referred to as the "Banda Oriental" (Eastern Band) of the Río de la Plata (River Plate). The term *Uruguay* is a GUARANÍ word that likely is derived from *urú,* a small bird that inhabits the region. Before the Spanish CONQUEST, most of Uruguay was inhabited by members of the Charrúa language group, whose subgroups included the Yanó and the Chaná. The Charrúa's existence was similar to that of nomadic hunting societies of Argentina. They lived in loose FAMILY groups of 10 to 15, largely for the purposes of self-defense. They lived in rudimentary unroofed dwellings supported by wooden posts and hunted deer and rhea on foot with bows and arrows, bolas, and nets. Charrúa groups that resided close to a river also fished from dugout canoes.

The conquest of Uruguay began mainly as an extension of Spain's conquest of the Inca Empire in PERU (see INCAS). By pushing south into CHILE, and from the Atlantic side seeking the source of the Río de la Plata, the Spanish hoped to find more precious metals as well as ways to ship more efficiently the SILVER and GOLD they continued to seize from the Incas.

Juan Díaz de Solís landed on the Banda Oriental in 1516, 70 miles (113 km) from the future site of Montevideo; however, shortly after landfall, Díaz and all the members of his party were killed by local Querandí Indians. FERDINAND MAGELLAN also explored the estuary in 1520; he managed to avoid the Querandí before continuing along his southerly route to the Pacific.

Sebastian Cabot explored Uruguay's coast in 1527. He anchored near the modern town of Colonia and established a fort nearby. From there, Cabot dispatched Captain Juan Álvarez Ramón to explore the Uruguay River. Álvarez's ship soon ran aground, however, and he and his men were ambushed by the Charrúa while they marched back to the fort. Álvarez and most of his men were killed. Undeterred, Cabot sent another party of three men inland toward Peru. One of them, Francisco César, was able to recount his journey but did so with a great deal of hyperbole. He told of conquering immense kingdoms and thereby created the myth of the "Lost City of Caesars," which Spanish explorers continued to look for until the 19th century. Cabot eventually returned to Spain but not before founding the soon-to-be-abandoned town of Sancti Spiritus along the Paraná River.

Upon his return to Spain, Cabot helped convince Charles I to fund a force of 1,600 to accompany PEDRO DE MENDOZA in his attempt to settle the Río de la Plata. Mendoza founded BUENOS AIRES in 1536, across the river from modern-day Uruguay. His large contingent, however, proved difficult to feed. Spanish desperation at a lack of FOOD and supplies provoked new hostilities with the Querandí, and Mendoza soon abandoned his men; he later died on his way back to Spain. The remaining residents of Buenos Aires abandoned the town in 1541.

There was very little Spanish activity in the Río de la Plata region until after 1580, when Buenos Aires was resettled.

See also MONTEVIDEO (Vol. II); URUGUAY (Vols. III, IV).

—Eugene C. Berger

Further reading:
R. B. Cunninghame Graham. *The Conquest of the River Plate* (New York: Greenwood Press, 1968).
Jorge Hidalgo. "The Indians of Southern South America in the Middle of the Sixteenth Century." In *The Cambridge History of Latin America*, Vol. I: *Colonial Latin America*, 91–118 (Cambridge: Cambridge University Press, 1984).

V

Valdivia, Pedro de (b. ca. 1500–d. 1553) *Spanish conquistador of Peru and conqueror and governor of Chile* Pedro de Valdivia was born in the town of Badajoz in the Spanish province of Extremadura sometime in 1500. As a young man, he enlisted in the service of Charles I (Holy Roman Emperor Charles V) in his many wars in Flanders and Italy from 1520 to 1525. Returning to Spain in 1533, Valdivia married Marina Ortíz de Gaete. He soon tired of domestic life, however, and in 1535, he left his wife in Spain and embarked on an expedition to VENEZUELA.

After a few years of participating in various expeditions, Valdivia came to serve under FRANCISCO PIZARRO in 1537 during his civil war with DIEGO DE ALMAGRO (see CIVIL WARS IN PERU). As a lieutenant under Pizarro's brother HERNANDO PIZARRO, Valdivia participated in the important BATTLE OF LAS SALINAS near CUZCO on April 26, 1538. In reward for his services, Valdivia was named lieutenant governor of CHILE and given permission to conquer the southern parts of PERU and the region of Chile recently discovered by Almagro.

Valdivia began his expedition of CONQUEST in January 1540. In an effort to avoid the perilous route through the Andes that Almagro had followed earlier, Valdivia took a route through the Atacama Desert. After a series of battles with the indigenous peoples of Chile, the expedition reached the fertile valley that the native people called Mapocho. On February 12, 1541, Valdivia founded the city of Santiago, which was to serve as capital of the new colony. Appointed governor of the new territory by the members of Santiago's *CABILDO* (town council), news of Francisco Pizarro's assassination arrived.

Receiving only a few reinforcements from Peru, Valdivia was determined to subdue the native population. For several years, he engaged in WARFARE with the indigenous peoples until he received word in 1547 of the rebellion of GONZALO PIZARRO and the arrival of a royal commissioner, PEDRO DE LA GASCA. Valdivia, swearing off his old allegiance to the Pizarros, offered his services to the royal army. Commanding forces at the Battle of Sacsayhuamán, Valdivia aided in the victory won on April 9, 1548, against Gonzalo Pizarro's forces. In reward for his services, Valdivia was confirmed with the title of royal governor of Chile. With more reinforcements, he then renewed his conquest of southern Chile.

In March 1550, Valdivia founded the city of Concepción and, later, the towns of Valdivia and Villarica. After returning to Santiago, Valdivia received reports that forces led by the Araucanian (Mapuche) chieftain Caupolican had attacked and defeated the Spanish at the fortress of Tucapel on December 2, 1553. In response, Valdivia led another expedition against the Araucanians but took only 50 mounted Spaniards. The Araucanian armies, under the command of the famed native leader Lautaro, defeated the Spaniards and captured Valdivia at the Battle of Tucapel on January 1, 1554. After torturing Valdivia, the indigenous group killed him, reportedly by stuffing him full of molten GOLD.

See also ARAUCANIANS (Vol. II).

—John F. Chuchiak IV

Further reading:
Ida Stevenson Weldon Vernon. *Pedro de Valdivia, Conquistador of Chile* (New York: Greenwood Press, 1969).

303

Vásquez de Coronado, Francisco   See CORONADO, FRANCISCO VÁSQUEZ DE.

Velázquez de Cuéllar, Diego (b. 1465–d. 1524)

Spanish conquistador and governor of Cuba   Diego Velázquez was born into a prominent Spanish family from Cuéllar, in Segovia. He first ventured to the Americas in 1493 on CHRISTOPHER COLUMBUS's second voyage, during which Velázquez traveled around much of CUBA, the island that he would later conquer and govern. During the 1490s, he participated in the CONQUEST and initial settlement of the island of HISPANIOLA. After the removal of Columbus as governor of the Indies, Velázquez was named lieutenant governor under the new royal appointee, Nicolás de Ovando. During this time, Velázquez became one of the wealthiest *encomenderos* on the island (see ENCOMIENDA).

Upset by the appointment of Diego Columbus as governor of the colony, in 1511, Velázquez organized an expedition to conquer Cuba. Members of this expedition included HERNANDO CORTÉS as his secretary, as well as BARTOLOMÉ DE LAS CASAS, PEDRO DE ALVARADO, Cristóbal de Olid, and BERNAL DÍAZ DEL CASTILLO, among others. Technically, this expedition was in violation of Diego Columbus's prerogatives as governor. Nonetheless, after successfully conquering the island and founding several towns, the Crown recognized Velázquez as governor of Cuba.

Beginning in 1517, Velázquez sought to expand his jurisdiction by organizing a series of expeditions to explore the mainland. In 1519, he sent Cortés on a voyage of exploration along the coast of Yucatán and MEXICO. Following Velázquez's example, Cortés sought to free himself from his superior's control. After the founding of Veracruz, Cortés led his forces into the Mexican interior, initiating the conquest of the Aztec Empire, and eventually, Cortés was successful in gaining royal acceptance of this action (see AZTECS). Velázquez had tried to forcibly stop Cortés by sending an expedition to Mexico under the command of PÁNFILO DE NARVÁEZ. Unfortunately for Velázquez, Narváez was defeated and his men incorporated into Cortés's company. In 1524, shortly after Cortés's successful conquest, Diego Velázquez de Cuéllar died in Cuba.

—Robert Schwaller

Venezuela   First encountered by CHRISTOPHER COLUMBUS on his third voyage in 1498, Venezuela is a land of diverse geography and rich history. Four distinct geographical regions make up the physical landscape, which covers just over 350,000 square miles (906,496 km²). The first region settled by European explorers was the coast. Consisting of low sandy beaches and rolling fertile hills inland, the coast stretches more than 1,700 miles (2,736 km), from the Gulf of Venezuela and Lake

Maracaibo on the western border to the Orinoco River Delta to the east. Lake Maracaibo, formed 36 million years ago, is the oldest and largest lake in South America; and the Orinoco River is one of the longest on the continent, extending west to east for more than 1,300 miles (2,092 km) before spreading into a 250-mile- (402-km-) long delta along the east coast.

South of Lake Maracaibo is the second region, the Andes and Segovia Highlands. A chain of the Andes rises more than 16,000 feet (4,877 m) from the south before dropping into the diverse ecosystem of semidesert, plains, and low mountains east of the great lake.

The Orinoco River, with its 200 tributaries, divides the final two regions of Venezuela. To the north, the Llanos (plains) and river valleys provide the country with vast grasslands that are ideal for raising livestock. South of the river and making up more than 45 percent of Venezuela's total landmass is the Guayana region. Mineral-rich, rocky highlands form the bulk of the area, which also claims the world's highest waterfall, Angel Falls.

The history of Venezuela's early inhabitants is even more diverse than the landscape they settled. While the first residents most likely came from Asia via the Bering Strait and then south through PANAMA, some scholars believe they came south from the chain of islands in the Caribbean (see MIGRATION). While their precise origins remain unclear, the archaeological evidence suggests that these first inhabitants, known as Paleoindians, had settled the region by about 20,000 B.C.E. The Paleoindians lived in hunter-gatherer groups, crafting stone tools and weapons.

From 5000 B.C.E. to 1000 C.E., another group, known as Meso-Indians, emerged. Settling along Venezuela's coast, the Meso-Indians crafted bone and shell tools. They became skilled navigators of the rivers and coastal areas. They also gathered edible and medicinal plants from among the diverse vegetation along the waterways (see MEDICINE).

Beginning around 1000 and lasting until the time of European exploration, the Neo-Indians settled along the Caribbean coast and Orinoco River. Composed of seminomadic and settled peoples, the Neo-Indians formed two separate but similar cultures; pottery styles and mortuary rituals were the main differences (see CERAMICS). The Neo-Indians spoke a variety of languages, including Arawak and Carib. Before the arrival of Europeans in the early 16th century, the Neo-Indians consisted of various groups, with an overall population of roughly 350,000 to 500,000.

Along the shores of Lake Maracaibo, the Guajiro, descendants of early Arawak cultures, operated a series of intricate canals and waterways, which to European explorers resembled those of the city of Venice. "Little Venice," or *Venezuela*, astounded early explorers. Other groups included the Timoto-Cuicas, the most agriculturally advanced group in Venezuela, and the Caquetíos, whose cave paintings and artwork still exist in areas west of the Andes (see AGRICULTURE). In the central and eastern regions of Venezuela, the CARIBS flourished.

Mastering basic agricultural methods and astronomy and developing a farming calendar, the Caribs were the first to make contact with European explorers.

By 1500, the Spanish had organized large pearl-fishing expeditions along Venezuela's northern coast, which they called "Terra Firme." Considered of nominal value by the local peoples, the Spanish originally obtained permission to exploit the large oyster beds. The Spanish enslaved indigenous people to find the pearls, which not only led to a rapid decrease in pearls but also sparked a dramatic decline in the native population (see SLAVERY). Within a few years, most of the pearl fisheries were barren. Still, the Spanish found other economic resources along the central coast: They gathered Amerindians in slave raids.

In 1528, the King Charles I of Spain (Holy Roman Emperor Charles V) issued the rights to settle Venezuela to a German banking firm. This firm, the Welsers, occupied Venezuela's western coast, where it established several small settlements. Searching for mineral deposits, slaves, and GOLD, the Germans embarked on several expeditions to the Andes and around the Maracaibo region. Numerous expeditions, under the leadership of men such as Ambrosius Alfinguer, NIKOLAUS FEDERMANN, and Georg von Speyer, led to nothing more than numerous legal and financial difficulties for the Crown. During the 1550s, the Welser firm returned administrative power to the Spanish. Although the Spanish and Germans did not find an Indian civilization comparable to the INCAS or AZTECS, early Spanish settlers profited through the exploitation of Venezuela's fertile valleys and grasslands.

See also CARACAS (Vols. II, III, IV); NEW GRANADA, VICEROYALTY OF (Vol. II); VENEZUELA (Vols. II, III, IV).

—Spencer Tyce

Further reading:
H. Michael Tarver and Julia C. Frederick. *The History of Venezuela* (Westport, Conn.: Greenwood Press, 2005).

Vespucci, Amerigo (b. 1454–d. 1512) *Italian explorer and cartographer*

Amerigo Vespucci was born and educated in Florence, Italy. His early career was shaped by the powerful de' Medici family, who dispatched him to their offices in Seville, Spain, in 1492. Vespucci first sailed to the Americas in 1497 under the sanction of King Ferdinand of Spain, who sought clarification on the nature of the mainland and island masses that had been discovered by CHRISTOPHER COLUMBUS. Between 1497 and 1504, Vespucci participated in at least two and possibly as many as four expeditions to the Americas, sailing first under the Spanish and later the Portuguese flag. His successive voyages to the New World took Vespucci to numerous destinations, including BRAZIL, GUYANA, HISPANIOLA, and, by some indications, Patagonia. These experiences, combined with his significant skills as an

astronomer, cartographer, and navigator, led Vespucci to conclude that these areas were too varied and large to be a part of Asia but instead constituted whole new continents (see MAPS).

In 1507, Martin Waldseemüller composed a world map, bestowing a Latin form of Vespucci's first name on the new continents, actually labeling just the southern portion *America*. By 1538, another map was published in Europe applying *America* to both continents, and the name stuck. Waldseemüller's map, along with two letters attributed to Vespucci (now widely believed to be forgeries), created a sense in Europe that Vespucci was trying to enhance his image at the expense of Columbus. Regardless, in 1508, the Spanish Crown created a special post for Vespucci, chief navigator of Spain. From Seville, Vespucci was paid a prodigious sum to streamline navigational EDUCATION and practices and plan future voyages. He died of malaria a wealthy man on February 22, 1512, with the knowledge that all of Europe considered the Americas a New World.

—Sean H. Goforth

Further reading:
Felipe Fernández-Armesto. *Amerigo: The Man Who Gave His Name to America* (London: Weidenfeld & Nicolson, 2006).

viceroy/viceroyalty

In the 15th and 16th centuries, the number of Spanish territorial possessions grew through dynastic acquisitions and overseas expansion. To more effectively manage these territories, the MONARCHS OF SPAIN appointed viceroys to govern specific regions. The political jurisdictions governed by viceroys are called viceroyalties. The first viceroy of the Americas was appointed prior to their discovery. In the contract between CHRISTOPHER COLUMBUS and the monarchs Ferdinand and Isabella, Columbus was promised the title of viceroy of any lands he discovered (see CAPITULATIONS OF SANTA FE). While Columbus and his son Diego both briefly ruled as viceroys, the appointment of future viceroys lapsed until after the discovery and CONQUEST of the Aztec and Inca Empires in the 1520s and 1530s (see AZTECS; INCAS). In both MEXICO and PERU, the Crown feared that the conquistadores who governed following their conquests might revolt against royal power.

In order to maintain better control over these newly acquired territories and to help restrain the excesses of the conquistador-settlers, the Spanish Crown divided the Americas into two viceroyalties. The Viceroyalty of New Spain was founded in 1535 with the appointment of ANTONIO DE MENDOZA as viceroy. The seat of this viceroyalty was based in the former Mexica capital of TENOCHTITLÁN, renamed MEXICO CITY. New Spain eventually encompassed all of modern-day Mexico, Central America, most of the Caribbean, parts of the U.S.

Southwest, California, FLORIDA, and the Philippines. After a devastating civil war between conquistadores in South America, in 1542, the Crown appointed Blasco Núñez Vela to govern the Viceroyalty of Peru from its capital, LIMA (see CIVIL WARS IN PERU). The Viceroyalty of Peru contained all of Spanish South America and some islands in the southern Caribbean. Viceroyalties were divided into provinces and smaller districts corresponding to various judicial and ecclesiastical officials. Each viceroyalty also held a high court, called an *AUDIENCIA*, over which the viceroy presided as president.

See also NEW GRANADA, VICEROYALTY OF (Vol. II); NEW SPAIN, VICEROYALTY OF (Vol. II); PERU, VICEROYALTY OF (Vol. II); RÍO DE LA PLATA, VICEROYALTY OF (Vol. II); VICEROY/VICEROYALTY (Vol. II).

—Robert Schwaller

Virgin of Guadalupe

The worship of the Virgin of Guadalupe is one of the best known and visually attested elements of Mexican culture. When the Spaniards first arrived in New Spain (see MEXICO), they brought with them many things from home, including a strong devotion to Marian cults. Two of the most popular Marian devotions transported to the New World were those of Our Lady of Guadalupe of Extremadura and the Virgin of los Remedios.

Brought to New Spain by one of HERNANDO CORTÉS's soldiers, the Virgin of los Remedios became associated with the CONQUEST and with the *peninsulares*, or those born on the Iberian Peninsula. Guadalupe of Extremadura, however, became closely linked to the Mexican Guadalupe.

The most well-known version of the Mexican legend states that in 1531 the Virgin of Guadalupe appeared before a Nahua man named Juan Diego and commanded him to tell the bishop of Mexico to build a shrine to her on the hill of Tepeyac. As lasting proof of the apparition, the Virgin's image was imprinted on Juan's cloak. Recent studies, however, strongly suggest that this event did not actually occur but rather was the creation of two 17th-century authors. Miguel Sánchez, in his Spanish account *Imagen de la Virgen María, madre de Dios de Guadalupe* (1648), and Luis Laso de la Vega, in his NAHUATL account *Huei tlamahuiçoltica* (1649), both describe the Virgin's appearance to Juan Diego. There are no 16th-century written accounts that relate such an apparition; thus, it is believed that the devotion does not stem from an actual event.

Prior to the legend of her apparition to Juan Diego, the Virgin was associated with an *ermita* (hermitage) at Tepeyac. The origins of the *ermita* are ambiguous at best, but most evidence indicates that it was founded by Archbishop Alonso de Montúfar around 1555 or 1556. Originally dedicated to the Nativity of the Virgin Mary, the *ermita* venerated an image that closely resembled an image of the Guadalupe of Extremadura in Spain.

Because the two images looked alike, the *ermita* began to take on the popular, unofficial name of Guadalupe.

It is widely believed that the indigenous population readily adopted the Virgin of Guadalupe as an object of devotion. The Nahua protagonist of the legend, Juan Diego, and Fray BERNARDINO DE SAHAGÚN's claim that the indigenous associated Guadalupe's shrine at Tepeyac with the Nahua mother deity Tonantzin, whose pre-Columbian worship was claimed to have also taken place on Tepeyac, certainly contributed to the assumption that native people widely supported the Virgin. Yet, the assumption pales under close examination. While Juan Diego was a creation of 17th-century authors, the lack of sources independent of Sahagún and the mendicant's overall rejection of the Tepeyac shrine as neo-idolatry until 1648, make an indigenous following doubtful. Indeed, there is no evidence to suggest that the 16th-century devotion to Guadalupe was ever popular among indigenous peoples. Prior to 1648, the Virgin of Guadalupe had only a modest, largely Spanish following.

See also GUADALUPE, OUR LADY OF (Vol. II); VIRGIN OF GUADALUPE (Vol. II, III).

—Mark Christensen

Further reading:

C. M. Stafford Poole. *Our Lady of Guadalupe: The Origins and Sources of a Mexican National Symbol, 1531–1797* (Tucson: University of Arizona Press, 1995).

Vitoria, Francisco de (b. ca. 1486–d. 1546)

Spanish theologian and founder of international law Francisco de Vitoria was born around 1486 in Vitoria, in the Basque province of Avala. He joined the Dominican order, which sent him to France to study at the University of Paris (see RELIGIOUS ORDERS). Vitoria returned to Spain in 1523 and three years later gained the prestigious Prime (*prima*) Chair of Theology at the University of Salamanca (see SALAMANCA, SCHOOL OF). Responding to the threat posed by the Protestant Reformation to Catholicism, Vitoria reinvigorated scholasticism at Salamanca and in other Spanish universities.

Vitoria was also deeply engaged in the debates over laws governing Spanish treatment of the Amerindians. He rejected Spain's claim to sovereignty over the Americas based on the papal donation of 1493 and the TREATY OF TORDESILLAS. Instead, he argued that Amerindians were rational beings in a world community subject to natural law and the law of nations. Thus, Vitoria held that they retained their natural right to their lands and LABOR. He conceded that Spaniards had the right to preach Christianity in the New World and to seek indigenous converts, although the missionaries could not coerce the Amerindians into baptism (see RELIGION). Only if the indigenous peoples prevented such teaching were the Spaniards justified in making war against them or deposing their leaders. Indigenous practices such as CANNIBALISM, he held, might warrant the Spaniards' holding them in temporary tutelage.

Vitoria's students and disciples published his lectures posthumously. They include *De Indis* and *De Jure belli Hispanorum in barbaros*. The Spanish monarch Charles I often consulted with Vitoria on important legal matters. Vitoria and his students influenced thought on the law of nations (*jus gentium*), and Vitoria has thus been called the founder of international law. His students included Melchor Cano, Bartolomé Medina, and Domingo de Soto. Vitoria died in 1546.

—Kendall Brown

Further reading:

Bernice Hamilton. *Political Thought in Sixteenth-Century Spain* (Oxford: Clarendon Press, 1963).

Francisco de Vitoria. *Political Writings*, edited by Anthony Pagden and Jeremy Lawrance (New York: Cambridge University Press, 1991).

warfare

CARIBBEAN

The early European chroniclers generally described the Taino inhabitants of the Greater Antilles as peaceful, in contrast with the warlike Carib who lived on the Lesser Antilles to the east and on the coastal mainland of South America. However, both Taino and Carib warriors proved to be skillful fighters, as well as resourceful and brave defenders of their lands.

Among able-bodied Taino males, warfare was a secondary activity to farming, fishing, and hunting. There is little evidence of internal conflict among Taino bands or even against the archaic indigenous inhabitants of the islands, who survived in areas of Cuba and Hispaniola until the European conquest. However, raids by the aggressive Carib launched from South America displaced the Taino from the eastern Caribbean and from as far as the Virgin Islands by 1492. This threat led to a corresponding militarization of Taino culture in Puerto Rico and Hispaniola, whose inhabitants were the most vulnerable due to their proximity to the Carib-held islands.

Taino men were physically fit and were expert swimmers. Because they were defending their home islands and villages, they also enjoyed the advantage over their enemies of knowing the terrain. They were skilled in the use of their traditional weapons, which evolved from modified tools. For hand-to-hand combat, the weapon of choice was the *macana*, a paddlelike sword made from especially dense hardwood; *macanas* measured about three feet (1 m) long. The wood was highly polished and sometimes embellished with carvings or paint. Other close-quarter weapons included axes and knives made from highly pol-ished and sharpened stones. Defensive equipment such as shields, helmets, and body armor were unknown.

The Taino arsenal also included missile weapons such as bows and arrows, several examples of which have been recovered in Cuba. Bows tended to be about five feet (1.5 m) tall and crafted from a single piece of wood. Arrows were about three feet (1 m) long, with feathers (fletches) fixed at the base of the shaft to help ensure accuracy. Arrowheads were made from diverse materials, including stone (chert and flint), shell, fire-hardened wood, stingray spines, and fish teeth used both as points and as barbs. Taino warriors also used light spears or javelins of about six feet (1.8 m) in length and dart throwers (similar to the *atlatl* used in Mesoamerica); the latter were used to launch darts, four to five feet (1.2–1.5 m) in length, which had great penetrating power at close range.

A toxic coating of *ají* (chili) paste or poisonous tree sap was added to all of these missiles. A version of tear gas was also sometimes used; perforated gourds were filled with ground chilies mixed with ashes and flung, creating a cloud of irritating dust. Before and after combat, Taino warriors would join the rest of village in a spiritual ceremony, or *areyto*, which required the purging of the body, inhalation of *cohoba* (a hallucinogenic herbal mixture) and tobacco smoke, dancing and offerings to the *cemíes*, or ancestral spirits. These ceremonies provided psychological support and enhanced warrior morale. Afterward, the cacique, or chieftain, would address the men to make sure they understood the goals of the operation and shared any available information about the enemy. The typical Taino force could range from a few dozen to a few hundred warriors; however, Spanish chroniclers indicate that they faced large armies numbering in the thousands in both Hispaniola and Puerto Rico.

Logistical support was minimal, usually consisting of a water bottle made from a gourd and *casabe* (yucca bread), since the Taino as a rule always operated in their home territory, close to FOOD and other supplies. While the local cacique was in command of the warriors from his own village, overall command of larger forces was held by a designated supreme cacique.

In terms of military tactics, the Taino favored surprise and stealth, such as ambush, using the thick tropical vegetation as cover, and predawn attacks on enemy encampments or villages. After hitting the enemy with missiles, the warriors would dash in to engage in hand-to-hand combat. Once the battle started, warriors would engage in single combat with the closest enemy, with the caciques shouting encouragement but having little overall control of the fight. The caciques would also lead the chase if the enemy broke or direct the retreat if the Taino were forced to withdraw. Since killing or driving off raiders and recovering any captives were the main purposes of military expeditions, there was little emphasis on taking prisoners. There are some accounts of combat at sea between Taino and Carib raiders, although this seems to have been the result of chance encounters rather than planned naval battles.

For Carib males, to be a man was to be a warrior. The Caribs thus developed a fearsome reputation not only because of their deadly seaborne raids but also because they practiced CANNIBALISM. Men achieved prestige and honor by obtaining captives to serve as laborers or concubines or to be ritually eaten. Carib villages did not have a clearly defined social hierarchy; rather, a well-respected and successful warrior leader, or *ubutu*, would approach the village warriors and convince them to launch a raid. Other villages might also join in the expedition. These were launched during favorable seasons when the seas were relatively calm. The typical Carib raid involved eight to 10 *piraguas*, or large canoes, with about 500 warriors and several dozen WOMEN to serve and cook.

The typical Carib raider was a seasoned sailor and warrior. His weapons were almost identical to those used by the Taino, such as the *butu*, or hardwood war club, akin to the *macana*, two to three feet (0.6–1 m) in length, three inches (7.6 cm) thick, and elaborately carved. The Carib also excelled as archers; their bows were described as similar to the English longbow; they were roughly six feet (1.8 m) long and fired poisoned barbed arrows. The Carib also used blowguns, but apparently only for hunting.

Because their raids could often take them hundreds of miles into enemy lands, Carib warriors had to carry some provisions with them, usually *casabe* bread and smoked fish. Upon reaching enemy territory, the Carib would send scouts to determine the location of villages and other useful information. Once ready, the Carib would wait until dawn to attack; night attacks typically occurred when there was a full moon. The warriors would paint their bodies with black dye and would surge into the unsuspecting village amid loud cries and shouts aimed at terrifying the inhabitants. If the element of surprise was lost, the Carib

would shoot incendiary arrows into the village, setting the huts on fire and forcing the defenders into the open. They would capture men, women, and children, as well as provisions for the return voyage. The Carib would also take with them the bodies of fallen comrades.

Upon arriving to their home island, the captives would be divided among the warriors and a feast would take place, in which selected enemy males would be cooked and eaten as part of the victory ritual. Other captives would be traded with neighboring Carib villages or to other ethnic groups along the South American mainland (see TRADE).

MESOAMERICA

The history of pre-Columbian Mesoamerica was one of violence, though no more so than that of any other region of the ancient world. It was a universe of shifting alliances and mutual antagonisms, in which increasingly strong political entities forged themselves and then broke apart. Indigenous peoples throughout the Americas lived in bands that sometimes came together to form chieftaincies, from which occasionally emerged paramount chieftaincies or confederacies. These in turn occasionally became centralized enough to constitute states, and twice in the Americas—in the case of the AZTECS and the INCAS—states expanded their power over others to form empires, though even in these cases the leading city-state (or ethnic state) did not have an unshakable grasp on power. Mesoamerica had the oldest tradition of AGRICULTURE in the hemisphere. Populations there were thus denser and accumulations of wealth greater than in most other regions. The stakes in warfare were therefore higher: States came to power and ultimately crumbled, leading to widespread dislocation.

The OLMECS were the first Mesoamerican group to expand their influence. Although they developed a military force, they seem to have done so only to protect the trade on which they depended, rather than to conquer new territory. By contrast, TEOTIHUACÁN is considered the first center of military expansion in the Mesoamerican world, dominating the central valley of MEXICO and surrounding area (perhaps even dispatching military expeditions as far as MAYA territory) from about 100 to about 750 C.E. After its decline, other powerful entities emerged. From 950 to 1150, the TOLTECS and their allies dominated Central Mexico. Toward the end of the Toltec domination, nomads (called Chichimecas by their descendants) began to come down from the north, disrupting the settled peoples of Central Mexico. In the early 15th century, the Mexica-Tenochca (now often called the AZTECS) emerged as the dominant Chichimec group, establishing a tight alliance with Texcoco, Tlacopan, and other smaller groups (see TRIPLE ALLIANCE).

Until the 1970s, many scholars believed that the Maya were unique among Mesoamericans and did not actively participate in the cycles of alliance building and warfare. The now largely decoded Maya glyphs tell us otherwise, however. The Maya made war as readily as all others and saw many of their own states rise and fall. Nonetheless, the most detailed information on war relates to the Aztecs. Historical annals written in NAHUATL in the 16th century, when there were still people alive who remembered the old oral histories, include many details and even the Aztecs' thought processes regarding warfare.

Some recurrent myths are associated with Aztec warfare, such as that the warriors did not fight to kill but only to take captives to be used as sacrificial victims (see HUMAN SACRIFICE). While it is true that most Mesoamerican war parties wished to return home with prisoners suitable for sacrifice, there was almost always a wider political purpose for war, and this determined the nature of the fighting. One ethnic state might attack another merely to remind disgruntled tribute payers who had the upper hand, and thus take only a few prisoners. A state might also launch a war against another people who had long prevented them from dominating a region and for that reason might kill thousands. Aztec annals record, for example, that when the Mexica and their allies attacked the Huastecs, it had been their goal to wipe the Huastec nation from the face of the earth. Such an agenda was quite rare in the history of Mesoamerican warfare, however; most of the time, no single state had sufficient power to eliminate all its enemies.

It is also true that Aztec understandings and representations of warfare revolved around the religious practice of human sacrifice (see RELIGION). Warriors rose through the ranks to attain fame and glory, which was based on the number of captives they acquired and the circumstances of their capture. To go to battle was to accept the possibility of oneself's being sacrificed to the gods. Women also partook of the honor associated with war. When they gave birth, it was said that they had seized a human soul from the cosmos; if they died in the process, they went to the same heaven reserved for men who died in battle. Again, however, wars were rarely undertaken for spiritual reasons alone but rather to gain control over chiefly lines and thus over resources. When the Aztecs fought the people of Cuauhnáhuac (Cuernavaca), for example, they took home not only prisoners to sacrifice but also a woman of the ruling Tlahuica line to marry their king so that her children would be Aztecs as much as Tlahuicas. It was through such marriages that the Aztecs gained control over the majority of Mexican territory where COTTON was cultivated.

In Mesoamerica, as elsewhere, the mechanics of warfare changed over time. With farming came a settled, as opposed to a nomadic, existence, and fortifications were built to protect communities. Over time, a fort or cluster of forts might grow powerful enough to prevent potentially hostile peoples from passing through an area. This was a significant step toward being able to farm more intensively, which led to better food supply and thus population growth. Teotihuacán was the first to amass a group of men large enough to be classified as a true "army." Because many men could go into battle, projectile weapons such

as slings, spears, and dart throwers were developed, and padded cotton armor was invented. On the other hand, the Maya states that dominated their surrounding regions had smaller populations and continued to rely principally on hand-to-hand combat. Later, the Toltecs invented a short sword, which was both lighter than previous blades and more efficient; the same man could now carry a dart thrower with shield and quiver as well as a lethal blade. When the Chichimecas migrated to Central Mexico from the north, they brought with them the bow and arrow (see MIGRATION). This weapon made small, lightly loaded forces more powerful than before as they could inflict more damage from hidden vantage points.

The Aztecs appropriated the best weapons from both the ancient Mesoamerican and invading Chichimec peoples. They used darts and dart throwers (*atlatl*), bows and arrows (*mitl*), stones and slings, long spears, bladed and knobbed clubs, and, especially, a newly invented sword (*macuahuitl*) that contained several projecting OBSIDIAN blades and delivered a deadly, slashing blow. (It rapidly became the weapon of choice throughout much of Mesoamerica.) The Aztecs also improved cotton armor and developed a lighter shield made, not from wood, but other fire-hardened plant materials. The Aztec army was highly organized at all levels, from generals to novice foot soldiers. All Aztec boys went to school to learn the arts of war. Most of the time, men lived as farmers and/or artisans, but when they were called to go on a military expedition, they knew what to do. On taking his first captive, a novice attained a higher status, was given certain prizes, and was grouped differently the next time he went to war. The same process occurred after the second, third, and fourth captives were taken. Few men, apparently, ever captured more than that. If they did, however, and if they took them from a particularly fearsome set of enemies, such as the Huexotzinco, they became commanders.

Aztec society was so deeply committed to warfare that it spawned the notion of staged battles, called "FLOWER WARS," or *xochiyaoyotl*, with rival states. In these prearranged conflicts, Aztec forces frequently faced off against the unconquered people of TLAXCALA, for example. Although the wars were prearranged, the losers still faced death on the field or sacrifice afterward. Whether these wars were designed to keep the population of young men on their toes or for some other reason is not certain. One theory suggests that the flower wars were a long-term military strategy designed to weaken powerful polities over time and thus avoid the heavy casualties that would result from a single conquest campaign.

Once a group began to attain power over its neighbors, a "snowball effect" was often seen, with more and more communities succumbing to the dominant power. However, large territories of subject peoples were difficult to control in an era before rapid communication was possible, thus power was always somewhat tenuous. The Aztec state famously crumbled when the Spanish appeared on the scene, and this was not a new phenomenon.

Priest who captured an enemy in battle

The same priest as before, for capturing two enemies in battle, was given the style of warrior costume that he wears.

The same priest as before, for having captured three enemies in battle, was given for his bravery the style of warrior costume that he wears.

Captive

The same priest as those drawn above, for having captured four enemies in battle, was given as a sign of his style of warrior he wears.

was given as bravery the costume that

The same priest as drawn previously, for having captured five enemies in battle, was given as a sign of his bravery the style of warrior costume that he wears.

The same priest as drawn previously, for having captured six enemies in battle, as a sign of his courage and valor was given by the lord of Mexico the style of warrior costume that he wears.

Captive

Quauhnochtli. officer

Tlilancalqui. officer

Atenpanecatl. officer

Ezguaguacatl. officer

These four in this row served as commanders and officers for whatever the lords of Mexico ordered and decided

Tlacochcalcatl.

Tezcacoacatl.

Ticocyahuacatl.

Tocuiltecatl.

These four in this row are valiant warriors and captains in the Mexican army, and persons who serve as generals in the Mexican army.[1]

Named after the Spanish viceroy of Mexico Antonio de Mendoza, the Codex Mendoza was compiled roughly two decades after the conquest of the Aztec Empire. The information contained in this remarkable work was gathered from indigenous scribes and interpreters who had firsthand knowledge of the Aztec Empire before the arrival of Europeans. This image shows various Aztec priests and their captives, as well as the assorted regalia they wore as signs of their military achievements. (Codex Mendoza, Courtesy of Frances F. Berdan and Patricia Reiff Anawalt)

Long before, Teotihuacán, Tula, and the Classic Maya city-states had met a similar fate.

SOUTH AMERICA

Warfare, rebellion, and other forms of interregional conflict and violence were once so prevalent in ancient Peru that archaeologists subdivided the region's primary cultural and temporal developments on the basis of conquest events and periods of political and social consolidation, instability, and fragmentation. Organized violence and the use of coercive force arose in tandem with the evolution of state-level societies and complex civilizations the world over. Patterns of warfare and social violence initially surfaced in Peru with the advent of the Initial period (ca. 1800 B.C.E.) and soon proliferated with the expansion of the Chavín Horizon at 800 B.C.E. These patterns were soon institutionalized with the rise of Wari and Tiwanaku in the highlands around 600 to 1000 C.E. The Late Horizon (1450–1532), in turn, corresponded with the dynamics of Inca conquest, expansionist warfare, the violent suppression of ethnic rebellion, and the rise and fall of empire (see Incas). Because the Incas were ultimately toppled through the coincidence of a protracted civil war, pandemic disease, and the violent and the direct onslaught of Spanish forces and their indigenous allies, Inca imperial warfare and military institutions are among the most thoroughly documented contact-era forms of organized (state-level) violence in all of South America.

The complexities of the chronological subdivisions in question should therefore provide some sense of the many groups, cultures, and civilizations that rose to prominence and statehood on the basis of protracted episodes of conflict, the deployment of coercive force, and the escalation of ritualized forms of violence that culminated in the pre-Hispanic era, with the fall of the Inca Empire in 1532. The emergence of complex states is largely identified with the harnessing of coercive force and the use of organized violence for political ends, and in ancient Peru, such forms of conflict and violence are seen to coincide with the emergence of the Initial period in 1800 B.C.E. While interregional conflict and violence can be traced to far earlier periods in Peru and South America more generally, it was only with the advent of intensive farming, irrigation systems, public works, and the growth of large towns and cities that scholars see an escalation in the ubiquity of human trophies, cranial trauma, and the portrayal of militaristic themes and the iconography of violence in art.

Early evidence for the bloody aftermath of early forms of interethnic conflict and warfare has been identified on Peru's north coast, at the site of Cerro Sechín within the Sechín Alto platform complex. Touted as the largest early monument complex in the Americas, archaeologists recovered a "macabre megalithic wall" composed of sculpted monoliths dating to 1200 B.C.E. The megalithic wall depicts dismembered human remains, decapitated heads, stacked skulls, severed limbs, torsos, and viscera interspersed with helmeted and armed warriors brandishing shock weapons such as pikelike clubs or stone maces. At the nearby highland settlement of Chavín de Huántar (dated by radiocarbon assay to ca. 800 B.C.E.), a constellation of particularly graphic and supernaturally inspired iconography devoted to the depiction of mutilated enemies and human trophies has similarly been identified. Such depictions were but one of the many technologies of terror that were refined over the course of Peruvian prehistory to exalt the exploits of the victors, intimidate enemies, perpetuate fear in subject populations, and reify the status of warrior elites and the patrons of war.

The Moche civilization of Peru redefined the art of war and ritual violence by fabricating a massive corpus of particularly graphic depictions of warfare in ceramics, paint, and related works of art. The multitude of finely detailed ceramic depictions of pitched battles, elaborately dressed warriors, weaponry, competing elites and warlords, and supernaturals provides a major resource for the study and interpretation of Peruvian warfare and ritual violence; it also reflects the growing importance of militarism and the martial arts with the emergence of the Moche state in the Early Intermediate period (ca. 200 B.C.E.–600 C.E.).

The rise of the early highland expansionist states of the Wari (Peru) and Tiwanaku (Bolivia) serve to define those forms of Andean warfare and attendant forms of social violence and bloodshed; these forms prevailed well into the Late Horizon period (1450–1532) and culminated with the collapse of the Inca Empire in 1532. Middle Horizon (600–1000 C.E.) patterns of warfare specific to the Wari and Tiwanaku coincide with the emergence of elaborate militaristic displays at major centers and Wari colonies in the Cuzco and Moquegua regions, albeit with initially limited evidence for violent conflict, conquest, or provincial resistance. A recent forensic study of drilled, perforated, and suspended human trophy heads from the Wari site of Conchopata (600–1000 C.E.) suggests that the taking of heads largely took place among fresh kills or freshly dispatched war captives, primarily men and children.

Wari rule from 650 to 800 was specifically correlated with high levels of violence and cranial trauma, with upward of 33 percent of the adult samples from Beringa, 26 percent from Conchopata, and 31 percent from La Real exhibiting such trauma. Interestingly, wound patterning in females differs from that of males, with females bearing wounds primarily on the posterior of the cranium and males on the anterior. This may indicate that the females were dispatched or executed with blows to the back of the head, whereas males tended to be felled during hand-to-hand combat.

During this same period, Wari influence became widespread in highland contexts; Wari centers emerged in regions once thought to constitute the exclusive domain of the Tiwanaku state. While Wari sites in the core area are only marginally retrofitted or strategically located with defensive consideration in mind, Wari provincial or frontier centers exhibit elaborate defensive features. The frontier hill fort at Pikillacta consists of a large walled complex with a supporting suite of regional settlements and strategically situated hilltop emplacements located over mountain passes within striking distance of key exchange routes in the highlands.

With the emergence of the Late Intermediate period (ca. 1000–1450), much of Peru and the Andean highlands was dominated by fragmented regional polities and pervasive warfare. At the same time, little in the way of militaristic iconography or martial themes prevails in any given region, despite the intensification of warfare and other forms of social violence. Despite this fact, indigenous informants recalled the period as that of the *auca runa*, or the "time of warriors," fragmented polities, and constant warfare. With the exception of the Chimú state of north coastal Peru, the highlands were dominated by *pukaras*, or hilltop forts and redoubts, with extensive evidence of violence and conflict.

The Ecuadorean highlands, for example, saw the proliferation of hilltop sites and fortifications and significant quantities of stone and bronze mace heads, axes, and related shock weapons (see Ecuador). Other highland regions witnessed the development of fortified hilltop settlements or forts, replete with walls, ditches, towers, and defensive terrace systems. The escalation of conflict corresponded with the growing deployment of *bolas* (sling stones), stone and bronze mace heads, and an increase in craniofacial trauma borne in the skeletal remains of period populations. Scholars interpret these findings as reflections of the tandem emergence and proliferation of small, fragmented, raiding polities and the occasional expansion of the conquest state in the wake of the decline of both the Wari and Tiwanaku ca. 1000 c.e. This, in turn, coincided with the emergence of *kuraka* lords, hereditary warlords, and *sinchi* war leaders; the proliferation of hill forts or *pukaras* with concentric fieldstone walls, parapets, and baffled or staggered gates; the proliferation of stone mace heads, projectile points, and sling stones; and the coincident balkanization, or fragmentation, of the former political and economic integrity of the Titicaca Basin in the period from 1000 to 1450.

The fractious polities and wars of the Late Intermediate period were quelled with the emergence of the Incas as a formidable sociopolitical and economic bulwark of highland Andean civilization in the mid- to late 15th century. While the preceding Late Intermediate period was one of political and economic fragmentation and internecine warfare, the Inca juggernaut fashioned order out of chaos, all through an ambitious and determined program of conquest and consolidation. Archaeological evidence and historical accounts indicate that target groups that readily surrendered or submitted to Inca authority were treated with considerable lenience; however, groups that resisted Inca control were systematically eliminated through outright conquest, genocide, and deportation. Resettlement programs were undertaken to assuage or minimize the potential for ethnic rebellions within the empire, a preoccupation that appears to have weighed heavily on the nature of Inca military strategy (see Mitmaq).

Significantly, period accounts make clear the Incas' ability to rapidly mobilize and deploy vast armies of citizen-soldiers, mita (labor service or tax) conscripts and auxiliaries, porters, women, llama pack trains, and related support personnel often numbering into the tens of thousands, and in some cases, the hundreds of thousands. Spanish victories over the massive Inca forces make clear that the Incas were predisposed to traditional military deployments that relied on massing, or the concentration of armed forces in overwhelming numbers, a command structure that relied on the physical leadership of officers at the helm of major engagements, and the deployment of flanking movements and the three-pronged attack.

In addition to the aforementioned command orientation and numbers, Inca armies drew heavily on highland and coastal resources and access, including the vast road and transport networks, distant storage facilities numbering into the thousands, ancient Wari civic-ceremonial and military installations, an effective organizational and bureaucratic framework, and the creation and mobilization of a host of allies across the length and breadth of the Andean cordilleras. In this way, the Incas launched an effective and overwhelming program of conquest. Through intermarriage, they established a complex network of alliances. Together, these strategies characterized the expansion and consolidation of the Inca Empire, the largest empire ever forged in the Americas prior to European contact.

See also military (Vols. II, III, IV); presidio (Vol. II); riots and rebellions (Vol. II); war (Vol. II).

—Francisco J. González
Rubén G. Mendoza
Camilla Townsend

Further reading:
Elizabeth N. Arkush. "Collapse, Conflict, Conquest: The Transformation of Warfare in the Late Prehispanic Andean Highlands." In *The Archaeology of Warfare: Prehistories of Raiding and Conquest*, edited by Elizabeth N. Arkush and Mark W. Allen, 286–335 (Gainesville: University Press of Florida, 2006).
Richard J. Chacon and Rubén G. Mendoza, eds. *Latin American Indigenous Warfare and Ritual Violence* (Tucson: University of Arizona Press, 2007).
Inga Clendinnen. *Aztecs: An Interpretation* (Cambridge: Cambridge University Press, 1992).
Terence N. D'Altroy. *The Incas* (Malden, Mass.: Blackwell Publishers, 2002).
Ross Hassig. *Aztec Warfare: Imperial Expansion and Political Control* (Norman: University of Oklahoma Press, 1988).
———. *War and Society in Ancient Mesoamerica* (Berkeley: University of California, 1992).
Peter Hulme and Neil L. Whitehead, eds. *Wild Majesty: Encounters with Caribs from Columbus to the Present Day* (Oxford: Clarendon Press, 1992).

Irving Rouse. *The Tainos: Rise and Decline of the People Who Greeted Columbus* (New Haven, Conn.: Yale University Press, 1992).

Linda Schele and David Freidel. *A Forest of Kings: The Untold Story of the Ancient Maya* (New York: Morrow, 1990).

Samuel L. Wilson, ed. *The Indigenous People of the Caribbean* (Gainesville: University Press of Florida, 1997).

Wari (Huari)

Between 600 and 1000 C.E., the largest Andean power was the Wari Empire. Its capital city, Huari, located near the modern city of Ayacucho, was a dense urban settlement that covered more than 1.5 square miles (3.9 km²). At its height, the Wari Empire controlled some 800 miles (1,287.5 km) of the Peruvian Andes, from Cajamarca to Moquegua. Before the rise of the INCAS, the Wari built a vast network of roads to connect administrators in different areas to the central capital and facilitate the movement of goods and information (see TRADE). The Wari Empire coexisted with the north coast MOCHE civilization and the TIWANAKU state to the south in BOLIVIA. Wari society was characterized by its unique standardized ARCHITECTURE, agricultural innovations, and lavish imperial goods (see AGRICULTURE).

The Wari built administrative centers in many highland regions, such as Azangaro and Jincamocco in Ayacucho, Pikillacta in Cuzco, Cerro Baúl in Moquegua, and Viracochapampa in Huamanchuco. Smaller centers have been uncovered in the coastal Nazca and Majes Valleys. While no Wari installations have been found in the coastal areas between the Moche and Nazca drainages, societies living in this area imitated Wari-style goods and obtained a few high-quality imports made in the imperial capital. It remains unclear if the Wari Empire ever conquered or controlled these groups.

Wari centers of administration are easily identified in aerial photographs because they used a unified spatial design. Large walled complexes were subdivided into smaller rectilinear compounds that consisted of lateral halls built around a central open patio space called a "patio group." Such units were sometimes adjoined to open plazas or clusters of small irregular rooms. Some Wari sites had D-shaped temples; others had large rectangular buildings with a series of interior wall niches. Both were related to ancestor worship or the dedication of offerings (see RELIGION). Wari imperial architecture contrasts with that of Moche and Tiwanaku because it does not include pyramidal monuments.

Wari installations were often affiliated with subsidiary settlements and a sophisticated system of agriculture. Since Wari colonies occupied areas that required irrigation to grow crops, some scholars have suggested that they developed the technology to build canals across rugged terrain and perhaps were the first to terrace steep hills below the altitude of seasonal rainfall. Irrigation technology allowed more land to be used for agriculture in areas with warmer climates that were favorable for growing

Large Wari drinking vessels, called *k'ero*, were used at ceremonial events to drink *chicha*. Ritually smashed in the Wari brewery at Cerro Baúl, this example depicts the head of the front-face deity, with surrounding decorative animal heads drawn in a similar manner to the Tiwanaku style. Such Wari-Tiwanaku hybrids provide evidence of the frontier interaction between the Wari and Tiwanaku people in the Moquegua Valley of southern Peru. *(Courtesy of Donna Nash/Photo credit Ryan Williams)*

MAIZE. During Inca times, maize was valued because it was made into a fermented drink called *CHICHA*. The brewing of *chicha* at Wari sites, depictions in Wari ART, and elaborate decorated drinking vessels show that *chicha* was equally important in Wari society (see ALCOHOL).

Wari ritual and luxury items shared several features with Tiwanaku art, such as the icon of the "staff god," a human or supernatural person grasping a staff in each hand. The staff god is depicted on both Wari and Tiwanaku TEXTILES, as well as other kinds of goods. Wari designs are highly variable and reflective of multiethnic interactions within the empire; however, some goods, such as the "face neck jar," appeared throughout the empire (see CERAMICS). Decorated as persons of different ages wearing diverse CLOTHING, these jars came in various sizes, and some were life size. Face neck jars were used to serve *chicha* and often bore intricate designs. Depictions of Wari elites show that WOMEN wore long dresses overlaid by a cloak or long shawl, while men wore thigh-long shirts along with a loincloth and some form of hat or headdress.

—Donna Nash

Further reading:
Gordon F. McEwan. *Pikillacta: The Wari Empire in Cuzco* (Iowa City: University of Iowa Press, 2005).

wheat Wheat was brought to the Americas by Europeans; before their arrival, most indigenous populations cultivated MAIZE, other native cereals, or tubers as staples. Because wheat flour, along with WINE and olive oil, was an essential part of the "Mediterranean trinity," Spaniards in the New World attempted to introduce wheat into native agricultural production (see AGRICULTURE). This met with varying degrees of success, but most indigenous people initially rejected wheat for a variety of reasons, the principal being, simply put, that they considered wheat to be inferior to maize. For an equal measure of seed, maize yielded 10 times more FOOD than wheat. Maize also produced more with less LABOR and less land. Maize, then, was cheaper both to produce and to buy. Additionally, wheat grown on land larger than a garden plot required costly European equipment such as a plows, as well as draft animals. And because indigenous peoples were required to pay tithes on transactions involving Spanish goods and lands, wheat was subject to the tithe, whereas maize was not. Finally, the processes of threshing by treading—by running animals over the sheaves—and milling were unfamiliar to New World populations.

By the mid-16th century, however, wheat was being grown on small farms that were usually owned by Spaniards and worked by native laborers. Andean indigenous populations, in particular, were more willing than other NATIVE AMERICANS to accept wheat as a food crop. The reasons for this might have included the fact that colder, higher elevations are more suitable for growing wheat than maize or other local cereals; moreover, Andeans were familiar with quinoa, which is similar to wheat. In any event, wheat production was more prevalent early on in PERU than anywhere else in the Americas; indeed, by the late 16th century, the Peruvian region of Huamanga produced approximately 75,000 bushels of wheat annually. Overall, by the mid-16th century, wheat was available in local markets throughout the Americas, largely for a Spanish clientele (see TRADE).

The Spaniards' introduction of and demand for wheat immediately imbued the cereal with defining capabilities. For Spaniards, wheat was a "civilized" cereal that helped to draw the line between them and the native, maize-eating populations. Throughout the colonial period, the social implications of wheat continued to evolve, especially in the presence of a growing mestizo population that increasingly chose wheat over maize (see *MESTIZAJE/MESTIZO*). This choice was not one of prudence (wheat could be up to 10 times more expensive than maize) but of preference

and status. In addition, the flow of European immigrant workers into the growing MINING industry and the local ECONOMY contributed to an increased demand for wheat as a staple cereal. Nevertheless, indigenous peoples continued to prefer maize, thus Spaniards and their mestizo offspring—familiar with Old World techniques and relying heavily on native labor—dominated the wheat market.
See also WHEAT (Vols. II, III).

—Mark Christensen

Further reading:
Arnold J. Bauer. *Goods, Power, History: Latin America's Material Culture* (Cambridge: Cambridge University Press, 2001).

wine Viniculture, or wine production, in the Americas dates back to the 16th century. Although several wild species of grapes (*vitis*) existed in the Americas before 1492, there is no evidence that NATIVE AMERICANS ever produced wine. Spanish colonists introduced European vines after the CONQUEST OF MEXICO in 1521, and thereafter, European vines and wine production spread rapidly. By the 1530s, the New World was producing its own wine from locally cultivated vines.

Wine formed part of what one scholar characterized as the "essential triad" of necessities (the others being WHEAT and olive oil) for all Iberian colonists. Wine was not just a central part of the Iberian diet; it was an essential ingredient in the celebration of Catholic Mass. The religious significance of wine made it necessary to ship vast quantities across the Atlantic. This posed a series of problems. For one, the vast distances between Spain and its overseas possessions made it difficult to supply the entire colony. Not only that, but it was not uncommon for wine shipments to spoil en route. The cost of TRANSPORTATION also meant that Spanish wine was expensive for colonists to purchase. For these reasons, policies were introduced both in Spain and the colonies to promote the development of local viticulture. For example, in 1519, Spain's Board of Trade (CASA DE CONTRATACIÓN) ordered that each ship bound for the Indies carry vines for the establishment of vineyards.

The introduction of Old World vines met with mixed results. Attempts to grow European vines in Mexico failed miserably, mainly because of the environmental differences between Mexico and Spain. Conditions in PERU, CHILE, and ARGENTINA proved far more propitious, however. Given the importance of wine in Catholic sacraments, it is hardly surprising that the Jesuit order emerged as one of the most important wine producers in the early colonial period (see RELIGIOUS ORDERS).

Most of early colonial Latin America's wine production supplied local markets. Increasingly, however, wines produced in South America found their way to other parts of the Americas, where they could be purchased for less than Spanish wines. By the 17th century, in response to protests from viticulturalists in Spain that American wines represented a serious threat to their economic well-being, the Spanish Crown began to issue bans on the expansion of New World vineyards.

See also JESUITS (Vol. II); WINE (Vol. II).

—J. Michael Francis

Further reading:

John Dickenson and Tim Unwin. *Viticulture in Colonial Latin America: Essays on Alcohol, the Vine, and Wine in Spanish America and Brazil* (Liverpool, U.K.: University of Liverpool, Institute of Latin American Studies, 1992).

witchcraft   The defining characteristic of witchcraft in the belief of early modern Christendom was a pact with the devil (see DIABOLISM IN THE NEW WORLD). The witch acquired supernatural powers from the devil through such a pact. The next most notable characteristic was that the witch was most often a woman, consistent with the medieval Christian notion that WOMEN were weak willed and thus more susceptible to the devil's temptations. These two characteristics were less prevalent in the witchcraft of 16th-century Latin America, but over time, they became increasingly associated with ideas about witchcraft in the New World. By the 17th century, as the associations among witchcraft, women, and the devil gradually disseminated in Latin America, other standard features of witchcraft beliefs were elaborated, although not to the extent that they were in Europe. These included flight (transvection), often to gatherings known as witches' sabbaths where Christian rites were inverted and mocked; sexual relations with demons or the devil himself; the use of animal familiars as mediators between the demonic and terrestrial realms; and the use of talismans, potions, powders, and salves to achieve supernatural and usually harmful ends.

In the 16th century, Spaniards in the Americas tended to see the hand of the devil nearly everywhere, in otherwise seemingly inexplicable misfortunes or in anything heterodox, especially among the indigenous populations. Thus, colonial officials often were warned about diabolical influence. The written instructions given to VICEROYS at the time of their appointment cautioned them to be mindful of the workings of the devil and to work to prevent the public practice of sorcery (*hechicería*). Parish priests conceded that witchcraft (*brujería*) was widely practiced among the indigenous populations. But for most of the century, what Spaniards interpreted as diabolical witchcraft is more accurately described as an assortment of native pagan rites and shamanistic practices (see RELIGION).

Strictly speaking, there was a distinction between the early modern Christian concepts of witchcraft and sorcery as understood by learned authorities, although the two were often conflated in the popular understanding. As noted, the witch acquired her supernatural powers from the devil or a demon through a pact, while the sorcerer was skilled at using things such as spells, incantations, rituals, and recipes based on ingredients with supposed supernatural properties, all of which were the source of his power. For 16th-century Latin America, there is a further distinction between indigenous and European sorcerers: The former marshaled their powers primarily as a means to influence natural or divine forces, while the latter applied their powers to the practice of maleficent magic, or sometimes to counter the magic of other sorcerers or the harm done by witches.

The great witch hunts of 16th- and 17th-century Europe were in large part the result of a complex of confessions obtained by coercion, often under torture or the threat of torture, combined with denunciations from confessed witches who were obliged to identify all others whom they knew to be witches. The early modern conceptualization of witchcraft was that it was a collective activity, culminating in the witches' sabbath, and therefore, it was impossible that a confessed witch did not personally know any other witches. Thus, a witch who refused to name accomplices would be interrogated repeatedly over a long period of time, often in conjunction with further torture, until authorities were satisfied that she had identified all her accomplices. This probably helps to explain why in 16th-century Latin America, accusations of sorcery were much more frequent than accusations of witchcraft. Until the ecclesiastical and civil apparatuses for the prosecution of witchcraft were in place, and until authorities came to believe witchcraft posed a substantial threat, conditions did not favor mass hysteria over witches on a scale seen in Europe.

Nevertheless, there was still great concern in Latin America over the wide variety of heterodox practices that Spaniards considered superstitious. During the period ending about 1560, there were numerous prosecutions for the practice of sorcery in MEXICO, while the problem did not appear in most of the rest of Latin America until the 17th century. The first accusations of sorcery in Mexico were made against indigenous people for pagan practices that more closely resembled what the Spanish referred to as native idolatry. This helps explain the lack of correspondence between European ideas about witchcraft and sorcery or witchcraft cases in the New World during the first decades after the CONQUEST. Spaniards often recognized that Indian heterodox practices had their origins in preconquest religions, but because they associated native religions with the devil and demons, it was a short leap for them to connect idolatry and witchcraft. And as the decades progressed, the cases gradually came to have more in common with standard European notions about witchcraft.

The Holy Office of the Inquisition was not established as an independent tribunal in Mexico until 1571, but the first friars of the postconquest period had the authority to exercise inquisitorial powers; Mexico's first bishop, Fray Juan de Zumárraga, had inquisitorial authority as ecclesiastical judge ordinary beginning in 1532 and later under the title of apostolic inquisitor. Zumárraga believed it was important that he prosecute idolatry and maleficent magic among the indigenous people, although he also tried a relatively small number of cases against Spaniards, Amerindians, and Africans during his brief career (d. 1548). These included offenses such as the use of love magic, divination, invocation of the devil, quackery, and even the exercise of maleficent magic by a Spanish parish priest in 1540. Many of the charges against the priest resembled those made against witches in Europe, including the power to make himself invisible, transvection, calling on the devil in hell, and possession of a book containing the devil's signature.

After Zumárraga's death, subsequent inquisitors continued to prosecute cases of dealings with the devil and maleficent magic in general, and the details of these cases gradually came to conform more closely to European ideas about witchcraft. For example, in 1558, a NAHUATL-speaking individual who was accused of the hanging death of his wife argued in his defense that he had been tricked by the devil into committing the offense. As Christian ideas took firmer root in the belief systems of indigenous peoples, there was a blending of Christian and native spiritual discourse, in which both Amerindians and Spaniards came to associate preconquest gods more closely with the Christian devil, and thus associated native pagan practices more closely with witchcraft (see SYNCRETISM).

See also INQUISITION (Vol. II).

—Michael S. Cole

women

MESOAMERICA

Women are depicted on the ancient ruins of Mesoamerica and figure in the histories recorded in the Mayan glyphs (see MAYA). From these sources, archaeologists have gained insights into the lives of women in Mesoamerica before 1492. Beyond this, the lives of Nahua women are discussed in myriad contexts and described from a variety of viewpoints in 16th-century texts written in NAHUATL by indigenous men who had mastered the Roman alphabet (see AZTECS; CODICES). All scholars now agree on a central truth regarding Mesoamerican women: They were not marginalized or disparaged but rather played central roles in society that were understood to be complementary to those of men. These roles were in general consistent throughout the region, though there were of course variations.

Women worked in the household. While their lives centered on the home, they also moved freely in the streets, markets, and fields. The four-cornered house held spiritual significance in that it mirrored the universe. Women's work keeping house—sweeping, washing, keeping order—was therefore considered sacred. It was the job of humans in general to maintain order in the universe

and stave off pandemonium, and ordinary women were central in this regard, as were priestesses and priests. In the Maya world and in a number of other Mesoamerican cultures, weaving was considered a holy act, reminiscent of a godly act of creation (see RELIGION; TEXTILES).

Women's most important contribution was understood to be as bearers of the next generation; they would keep the FAMILY line from being extinguished, hold to traditions, and ensure that future years unfolded as they should. Children were "precious" in Nahuatl terminology and were likened to the green shoots of a tree, chips of stone from a mother rock, and hair growing. When a woman gave birth, she was thanked by all the family for making the future possible. Her courage was likened to that of a warrior: She had gone into battle and seized a soul out of the universe and brought it home to help worship the gods. If a woman died in childbirth, she went to the same heaven reserved for men who had died in battle (see WARFARE). This tradition stood in stark contrast to the Judeo-Christian concept that the Spanish would later introduce to the indigenous world, namely, that childbirth was woman's punishment for her essential evil.

Nevertheless, successful warriors and noblemen often had numerous wives, and the inequality bred by that situation had repercussions in women's daily lives. Polygyny brought some advantages for women; for example, as a woman aged, she was likely freed from much of the harder LABOR as younger women took over the work. However, for the least powerful women in a household, and especially those taken as prisoners of war, life was likely very difficult. Additionally, except for the women of the most powerful states, women in ancient Mesoamerica lived with the constant threat of war. A woman who was taken from her people and brought to live with her conquerors generally was not abused, her labor was valued, and her children were not considered slaves. She had, nonetheless, lost the opportunity to mother the children that would carry her own family line forward, and she had lost her place in her kinship group and thus much of her identity.

Women's value to society and their vulnerability are especially evident in the lives of noblewomen, about whom the most is known. Archaeological and documentary sources all support the notion that women played crucial roles in establishing a ruling chief's lineage and, thus, in giving him authority; that is, who a man's mother was mattered if he wanted people to believe that he had a legitimate right to rule. The entire family tree created legitimacy. The other side of this picture, however, was that a noblewoman's marriage and the fate of her children might be bound up with politics and with violence. A woman might be married off to prevent or end a war. She might marry into an allied state but in later years find her husband's state at war with her own. In that case, her sons' status as heirs would be threatened. These permutations were often very tricky. For example, Nezahualpilli, king of Texcoco, was only seven years old when his father, Nezahualcóyotl, died in his 70s. Nezahualpilli had much older half brothers, born to a wife whose lineage had lost power since her marriage, and many of them were killed in their father's old age. Some of them had escaped that fate, however, and began a civil war when Nezahualpilli was crowned as king. Such a narrative was not uncommon in the Mesoamerican context.

Women's public roles varied considerably between regions. Among the MIXTECS, women and men inherited power in parallel descent, thus women were often rulers. Among the Nahuas, it was rare for women to rule, though this did occur. Women also sometimes spoke publicly, and public speech was integral to power. Priestesses spoke publicly, though it is not certain whether they spoke before mixed audiences. Likewise, female poets sometimes intoned their songs, though it is unclear if they did so only within a closed circle where high nobles were being entertained. After the Spanish CONQUEST, women often addressed Spanish or indigenous authorities on behalf of their families, which may have been an ancient tradition. The evidence suggests that the strongest variant of patriarchy in Mesoamerica was among the Maya, though even here it was far from rigid. This may have been because the Maya were engaged in almost constant warfare. Limitations on women may have been increasing among the Aztecs before the arrival of the Spanish for the same reason. It seems logical to assume that masculinity was deemed more important than femininity in those places most dependent on the success of male warriors for their survival, but even this would not be a universal truth.

Archaeologists have more information about certain subgroups of women in the Nahua world than elsewhere. Aztec merchants, for example, seem to have formed almost a clan apart, and their wives played unusual roles by Mesoamerican standards. People were born into merchant families, and merchants married within their group. Women worked in partnership with their husbands, trading goods in their husbands' absence and selling in the marketplace (see TRADE). Midwives, doctors, girls' teachers, and priestesses (categories that overlapped to an unknown degree) also had somewhat unusual roles, in that they dedicated more of their time to what might be termed their professional activities than to work in the home. It is not known how these women attained their positions. They, too, might have been born into them, or certain inclinations and talents may have come into play. Most likely, both these factors were true to differing extents.

Women's lives in pre-Columbian Mesoamerica had much in common, though there was variability between regions and subgroups. Although they often lived with the danger of warfare and of becoming concubines to the enemy, they generally enjoyed roles complementary to those of men.

SOUTH AMERICA

South America is a vast continent with several distinct cultural regions and in the past was home to many diverse societies. Each of these societies had its own idea of the roles women and men were to play in the family and in the wider community. The only "written" indigenous records for pre-Columbian South American history consist of the Inca QUIPU, but these have not yet been deciphered (see INCAS). Thus, scholars must rely mainly on the accounts of European conquistadores and clergy to understand the lives of women and men at the time of colonial contact.

Accounts written by European peoples are highly problematic, and many ignore the roles of women in South American societies; however, a few provide glimpses of women's importance and power in colonial contexts. Understanding the lives of women in precontact New World societies is even more difficult because archaeology rarely provides information about individual people and daily life. Many historical narratives of prehistoric South American peoples are merely projections of Victorian ideals that place women in the home and men in the public sphere. A close examination of New World communities, however, paints a very different picture. Depictions of people, mythical and otherwise, as well as human burials, provide evidence that aids in the understanding of the real or ideal roles of women and their relationship to men. The following examples convey the diversity of women in South America before 1532.

Based on the accounts of Spanish CHRONICLERS, the Incas had clear ideas about the roles of women in Andean society. Women were responsible for making clothes for their families, and many also paid tax to the Inca state with their weaving labor. Some girls between the ages of eight and 10 were selected to become AQLLAKUNA; these "chosen women" were kept secluded and received special training to make high-quality CLOTHING, FOOD, corn beer (called CHICHA), and many other products specifically for the Inca ruler, or Sapa Inca (see ACLLA). Upon reaching maturity, these educated women, called *mamaconas*, served many important roles in the Inca Empire. Some *mamaconas* continued to live in these educational and productive female enclaves, called *aqllawasi*. Every provincial capital in the Inca Empire had an *aqllawasi*, and each compound had its own female administrators who managed land and large stores of corn, wool, and other materials. These administrators were also charged with the EDUCATION of young *aclla* students.

Mamaconas of high status served in temples as priestesses and were charged with the care of important shrines or served as deity impersonators. The earth and the Moon were powerful female deities throughout the Andean region. Distinctively female deities are represented on stone sculptures at the early highland monumental site of CHAVÍN de Huántar and appear on large, elaborately painted ceramic urns from the WARI south coastal center of Pacheco (600–1000 C.E.). Sacred mountain peaks, highland lakes, and springs took on both male and female personas and were worshipped in their respective regions with festivals and offerings. During Inca times (1400–1532), both boys and girls were interred as HUMAN SACRIFICES in mountaintop offerings.

Perhaps the most famous of these sacrificial victims, called Juanita, was recovered by Johan Reinhard and his research team from Mount Ampato 20,932 feet (6,380 m) above sea level near Arequipa, PERU. Juanita was dressed in the clothing of a *mamacona*.

Women were highly valued in many Andean societies because of the importance of the textiles they produced and the food and *chicha* they prepared; these items were all important items in Inca political encounters. In many ways, the labor and knowledge of skilled *mamaconas* were key sources of the Sapa Inca's wealth and power and were crucial to Andean politics during Inca times. Women's production of textiles and food preparation was widespread in the Andes; however, it should be noted that there are known instances of men fulfilling these roles among some prehistoric groups.

Archaeological investigations of ancient tombs and human remains are important sources of information about individuals and the different sorts of people who lived in towns and communities throughout South America. Because of the excellent preservation on the western desert coast of Peru and CHILE, most archaeological evidence that can be linked specifically to women comes from the graves uncovered in these countries.

Going back to the earliest mummies in the world, of the Chinchorro of northern Chile (ca. 5000–1700 B.C.E.), women received parallel treatment in burial to men. Some scholars believe that the elaborate mummification practices of the Chinchorro demonstrate that South Americans revered and perhaps worshipped their ancestors. As both women and men were buried in a laborious fashion, it appears that they were equally valued ancestors among the coastal Chinchorro.

Human skeletons can reveal the effects of daily life on the body. In general, early burial populations that permit comparisons between females and males are few, but some groups of fisher/hunter-gatherers (ca. 6600–3600 B.C.E.) exhibit similar patterns of stress on the skeletons of both sexes, suggesting that women and men may have shared work tasks, whereas other groups show disparities in health and nutrition between the sexes. The difference between early groups is not surprising given the variety encountered by Spanish explorers at the time of first contact with South American groups.

A great deal more information exists for groups later in time. As large settlements appeared and individuals were given special burials for religious reasons or because of their status, women were among those buried in monuments or to be accompanied by numerous or elaborate goods. For instance, the site of La Galgada (ca. 1950–1550 B.C.E.) included the burials of elite women alongside those of men in successive phases of the monumental constructions. Indeed, the interments at La Galgada exhibit early evidence for typical elite female dress, including the use of *tupu* pins as clothing accessories.

The goods buried with female and male persons can provide information about the real or ideal roles of

women and men in a society. In many coastal cemeteries, women were buried with spinning and weaving implements. Interestingly, it is in the graves of Paracas-period women located in the Ica Valley (Peru) that the earliest known form of the *quipu* has been found.

Women who were members of families engaged in ceramic production also seem to have held high status, perhaps because of their crafting skill. High-status female burials associated with pottery making have been uncovered at the Wari site of Conchopata in Ayacucho and in the urban sector of the MOCHE capital between the two pyramidal monuments, Huaca de la Luna and Huaca del Sol.

Forensic examinations of human skeletons can reveal details about the general health and well-being of women in the past. For instance, some Wari burials exhibit evidence of domestic violence, while many Nazca trophy heads, presumed to be warriors captured in battle, are now known to be the skulls of women. Inca mountaintop sacrifice victims, interpreted as noble children, include both male and females of different ages. Elements of these sacrifices are similar: The victims are finely dressed and

Felipe Guamán Poma de Ayala's illustration of men and women from the Inca nobility preparing the soil for planting, which occurred during the month of August. *(The Royal Library, Copenhagen, Denmark)*

are accompanied by extra clothing and dressed human statuettes in GOLD, SILVER, and *Spondylus* of the same sex as the interment; yet boys also have llama figurines, whereas the girls are associated with ceramic vessels. Thus, burial evidence suggests that even within the same society, women had a variety of experiences based on class, occupation, personal accomplishments, or life histories; moreover, women and men might have had equitable value, but they also had particular symbolic associations based on their ideal roles within the larger society.

Women's contribution to daily household activities is not surprising, but Andean women were active in community affairs and participated in most of the same jobs as men. Couples often worked together, and there were few instances in which men were separated from their wives. For instance, during the Inca period, women accompanied soldiers on military campaigns, carrying men's gear, preparing food, and caring for the injured. Women participated equally in agriculture, pastoralism, and craft production. A representational mold-made Moche ceramic vessel shows a man and women working together to brew *chicha*. There is little to no evidence to suggest that there were restrictions on women owning goods or having access to land. Historical accounts describe how the mothers and favored wives of Inca emperors had their own country estates, supplied with dedicated servants to work their fields and maintain their palaces. Inca queens were mummified and venerated after death in the same manner as male Inca rulers. Likewise, on the northern coast during the early contact period, Spanish conquistadores encountered small polities that were ruled by women.

This same pattern of equality in access to resources and relative political power also seems to apply to other regions of South America. Metal votive figurines from the Quimbaya culture of COLOMBIA show both men and women holding the same objects, such as cigar holders and fine green stone adzes, which have been interpreted as items of prestige.

Information about women's lives in the prehistoric societies of South America is limited and remains an underexplored theme in archaeological research. Future research examining human skeletal populations and representations of people in art holds promise for understanding the roles of women in the diverse communities that occupied the South American continent before 1532.

EARLY COLONIAL

The Spanish introduced to the New World ideals of society, government, and religion that were highly patriarchal and that often conflicted with the gender roles of indigenous populations. Indigenous gender roles were based largely on different, yet equally important roles for men and women. Although this "gender parallelism" should not be mistaken for equality—men dominated the apex of the precontact social hierarchy—difference did not mean devaluation. However, the development of colonial

society included the adoption of Spanish forms of gender relations, which took some 50 to 70 years to emerge fully in Central Mexico, and longer in other regions. This delay, coupled with a demographic imbalance that favored women due to the wars of conquest, allowed indigenous women to maintain their traditional status and power in the years immediately following the conquest.

The CATHOLIC CHURCH believed that the home provided safety in which women could perform their duties free from the temptations of the outside world, which ostensibly could corrupt a woman's fragile and weak nature. European women received strict counsel to avoid the public sphere. Indeed, women were to remain in the "private" sphere, while men attended to the "public" one. Thus, in Spanish society, women were prohibited from participating in politics. Although they had some legal rights, most laws supported the power and authority of men.

In contrast, early colonial society in New Spain saw indigenous women playing a significant and active role in the courts. Women made wills and served as witnesses for wills; they initiated and defended in litigation at rates comparable to those of men. Moreover, they sold, bought, and inherited property. The extent of women's legal participation even inspired one 16th-century Spanish jurist to comment that an indigenous man with a legal dispute to settle "will not appear before the court without bringing his wife with him."

Furthermore, Spaniards' toleration and reinforcement of indigenous rulers' political authority and landholdings worked to the advantage of many noble Mixtec women. In Mixtec culture, marriage alliances were necessary to form the *yuhuitayu* sociopolitical unit. If the male ruler died, the female ruler, or *cacica*, could continue to rule alone, without remarrying (see CACIQUE). Native people, Spaniards, and the church alike recognized the status of *cacicas*. Mixtec *cacicas* owned large houses, the best lands, large herds of sheep, saltworks, and many other material possessions.

Although Mixtec *cacicas* seemed to fare better than most, indigenous noblewomen responded to the opportunities the conquest provided. In the Andes, Spanish definitions of "private property" were largely absent prior to the conquest. Yet, as Spaniards began to enforce their understandings of property to usurp land, Andean noblewomen often joined in the land grab, manipulating the new property forms for their own benefit. In Central Mexico, many native noblewomen married Spaniards, thus aligning themselves with the ruling party, and this was made easier by the shortage of Spanish women. This strategy not only secured the status of a noblewoman and her family but provided her offspring with a more financially and socially secure position in society. Whereas native men had much more difficulty in marrying Spanish women, 16th-century indigenous noblewomen throughout New Spain increasingly married Spanish men.

Spanish perceptions of the public and private spheres discouraged women from participating in labor outside the home. In the years immediately after the conquest, however, indigenous women continued to fulfill many public roles. Although the Spanish prohibited specific vocations—such as priestess, female market official, and female confessor—most women went about their work much as they had before the conquest. Indeed, colonial society (and especially Spanish settlers) greatly depended on women's labor to supply foodstuffs and other goods. Thus, indigenous women labored daily in their homes and in the local colonial ECONOMY as craft producers, members of artisan guilds, spinners, embroiderers, featherworkers, and preparers of food. Every day, significant numbers of women left their homes to sell the products of their labor in the markets. Others served city-dwellers as wet nurses, weavers, flour grinders, and maids. Overall, the documentary evidence suggests that colonial indigenous women participated in politics and society much as they had in precontact times. As a result, their household labor for and marriage to Spanish colonists enabled women to become key figures in transmitting indigenous culture to colonial society.

Although many indigenous women exploited the opportunities the conquest afforded, or managed to get along in colonial society without being overrun by it, some women were affected much more negatively. Female slaves made up a large proportion of the female population in early colonial society (see SLAVERY). Representing 30 to 40 percent of all enslaved Africans transported to the Americas, female slaves were put to work everywhere, from rural SUGAR plantations to urban Spanish homes. These women had minimal legal rights. Uprooted from their country and deprived of their freedom, slave women faced the greatest challenges of all women in the New World.

Due to their utility, female slaves outnumbered male slaves in nearly every city of colonial Latin America. Urban slave women were typically domestics serving as cooks, household servants, wet nurses, laundresses, and seamstresses. Many owners, particularly widows, hired out their female slaves to provide themselves with a fixed monthly income. Although subject to many abuses, particularly the sexual advances of their owners, urban slave women fared better than rural slave women. Slave women assigned to the fields worked alongside male slaves, performed the same tasks, and received the same punishments. Women cut and ground sugarcane, chopped firewood, worked inside the dangerous mills, and drove animals. Plantation owners knew no gender differentiation in physical tasks, but they did reserve the more skilled jobs and supervisory roles for men.

While some Spanish women were present in the early years—some even participated in the wars of conquest—they represented only 16.5 percent of all immigrants by 1560. Many came as wives, others as prospective wives, and still others as common laborers. Spanish women also came in religious capacities. In 1530, six Spanish nuns came to the New World to establish a school for young indigenous girls. Convents emerged within two decades of the conquest and continued proliferating throughout the colonial period. These institutions provided a respectable option for unmarried elite women and wealthy widows, while finding a place for those socially incongruent. Indeed, the Santa Clara convent in CUZCO was intended to house orphaned mestiza girls Spanish society deemed too anomalous (see MESTIZAJE/MESTIZO).

The paucity of Spanish women in early colonial society meant that indigenous and black women experienced the brunt of Spaniards' sexual desires—a large number were raped or otherwise sexually abused. ENCOMIENDA labor demands commonly forced women into the households of Spanish men, and the archives are replete with court cases concerning *encomenderos* or other Spanish men raping or otherwise abusing their indigenous servants. Domestic female slaves shared a similar fate. Moreover, the *encomienda*'s tribute quota of goods, commonly cotton cloth or other textiles, fell heaviest on indigenous women producers and continued to grow as the indigenous population declined. And as the colonial period progressed, native women were frequently forced to work in sweatshops, or *obrajes*.

Despite widespread abuses, 16th-century women were not all passive victims. Admittedly, the colonial experience of a native elite was unlike that of a commoner or a slave. Yet all strata provide numerous examples of women who actively manipulated Spanish laws and culture, within set parameters, to accommodate and adapt to a nascent colonial society.

See also DOWRY (Vol. II); WOMEN (Vols. II, III, IV).

—Mark Christensen
Donna Nash
Camilla Townsend

Further reading:

Karen Bruhns and Karen Stothert. *Women in Ancient America* (Norman: University of Oklahoma Press, 1999).

Louise Burkhart. "Mexica Women on the Home Front: Housework and Religion in Aztec Mexico." In *Indian Women of Early Mexico*, edited by Susan Schroeder, Stephanie Wood, and Robert Haskett, 25–54 (Norman: University of Oklahoma Press, 1997).

Rosemary Joyce. *Gender and Power in Prehispanic Mesoamerica* (Austin: University of Texas Press, 2000).

Susan Kellogg. *Weaving the Past: A History of Latin America's Indigenous Women from the Prehispanic Period to the Present* (Oxford: Oxford University Press, 2005).

Alida Metcalf. "Women as Go-Betweens? Patterns in Sixteenth-Century Brazil." In *Gender, Race and Religion in the Colonization of the Americas*, edited by Nora E. Jaffary, 15–28 (Burlington, Vt.: Ashgate, 2007).

Susan Socolow. *The Women of Colonial Latin America* (Cambridge: Cambridge University Press, 2000).

X

Xerez, Francisco de (b. 1497–d. ca. 1565) *secretary to Francisco Pizarro and Spanish chronicler* Born in Seville in 1497, Xerez came to the New World in 1514. In 1524, he sailed on FRANCISCO PIZARRO's first voyage of exploration as his secretary, responsible for a complete account of the expedition. Unfortunately, this account has not survived. Xerez also embarked on Pizarro's second voyage in 1526, again as secretary. The account of this journey was long attributed to Juan de Sámano, secretary to the COUNCIL OF THE INDIES, who had it copied for a member of the royal family and signed the copy. However, internal evidence and comparison with Xerez's later account make it clear that Xerez was the author of this earlier text, which is known now as *La relación Sámano-Xerez* (see CHRONICLERS). The account describes the geography and the indigenous peoples encountered, as well as the capture of a native trading vessel from Salango by the pilot Bartolomé Ruiz (see TRADE). The work describes the vessel and its crew and provides a meticulous inventory of the GOLD and other precious artifacts it carried.

Xerez embarked again on Pizarro's third voyage to PERU, in 1532, describing Tumbes, the journey to Cajamarca, and the events that led to the capture and seizure of the Inca ruler ATAHUALPA. Xerez broke his leg the day the Sapa Inca was captured and was bedridden for months (see CONQUEST; INCAS). During this period, he completed his account. Xerez received his share of the spoils of Cajamarca and returned to Seville in June 1534. The following month, he published his *Verdadera relación de la conquista del Perú* (*True Account of the Conquest of Peru*); in part, Xerez's work aimed to correct an account published months earlier by Cristóbal de Mena. The *Verdadera relación* was an instant success and was trans-lated into every major European language. It remains the definitive source for the events of the period it covers, a tribute to the precision and impartiality Xerez brought to his task.

—Patricia J. Netherly

Further reading:

Raúl Porras Barrenechea. *Los cronistas del Perú (1528–1650) y otros ensayos*, edited by G. Y. Franklin Pease (Lima: Banco de Crédito del Perú, 1986).

Xibalbá Xibalbá refers to the pre-Columbian MAYA underworld. The most extensive treatment of the term comes from the POPOL VUH, or "Council Book," a compilation of myth, history, and genealogy composed in the Postclassic K'iche' (Quiché) language of western GUATEMALA but written in the Roman alphabet and shown to friar Francisco Ximénez sometime between 1701 and 1703. Ximénez copied the manuscript, which eventually made its way into Guatemala's University of San Carlos library, where it was rediscovered in the 1850s. Xibalbá stories come from the first half of the Popol Vuh, the section most closely identified with Classic-era mythology (250–1000 C.E.) and hence is pre-K'iche' in origin.

The term *Xibalbá* probably means "place of fright." It was the subterranean home of the Death Gods, hideous, insectlike beings that ruled the world before the creation of human beings. However, as the Popol Vuh relates, through a series of tricks, the Hero Twins Hunahpu and Xbalanque descended to the underworld to avenge the death of their father and uncle. Disguised as traveling magicians, Hunahpu cut Xbalanque into many pieces, then reassembled him alive. When the Death Gods asked Hunahpu to work the same magic on them, he obliged, but after cutting them up refused to bring them back to life. The Hero Twins thus vanquished the Death Gods and limited their power to Xibalbá, whence they could no longer demand sacrifice of the living (see HUMAN SAC-RIFICE). Only at this juncture was the world safe for the creation of human beings.

Exactly how universal the concept of Xibalbá was remains uncertain. The Maya were and are a fragmented peoples, whose language and cultural constructs differed significantly from place to place. Contemporary Yucatec Maya use the term *metnal* to refer to the underworld, and their concept of its ways and means bears a heavy imprint of Spanish Catholicism (see CATHOLIC CHURCH; SYNCRETISM).

—Terry Rugeley

Further reading:
Allen J. Christenson. *Popol Vuh: The Sacred Book of the Maya* (Norman: University of Oklahoma Press, 2007).

Y

yana Long before the rise of the Inca state in the Andes, local and regional leaders, or KURAKAS, obtained LABOR through the institution of *yana* (plural *yanakuna*, *yanacona*), meaning "he who serves me" (see INCAS). The *yanakuna* were men who had been given to the *kuraka* either as children or adults by their AYLLU, or group of origin. Such individuals were no longer counted as members of their *ayllu*; rather, they were counted among the *yanakuna* of their *kuraka*, which was a separate category.

Yana was a permanent status. In most cases, one of the sons of a *yana* would take his place when he died. In other cases, the other sons returned to their father's group of origin; however, in the case of distant farmers or herders, they stayed on and were counted as *yanakuna*. *Yanakuna* married WOMEN given or designated by their *kuraka* or the Sapa Inca (see FAMILY). Andean polities were composed of groups of nested corporate groups called *ayllus*, which were in turn grouped into moiety divisions. At each level, the farming households cultivated the fields of their *kurakas* and provided, on a rotating basis, a service that was apportioned to their group or *ayllu* and carried out over short periods each year. This system was known as the MITA.

Andean rulers needed access to full-time service for their own households, however, in order to cultivate their personal fields of specialized crops such as COCA or to look after their personal herds in distant ecological zones; likewise, they required specialized artisans. The *yanakuna* who were assigned to work at a distance, either farming, herding, or as craftsmen, were probably selected as young adults. Those who were chosen to serve in the household of the *kuraka*, or who assisted in administration or diplomatic missions, were likely chosen as children from among the best and brightest; these children were raised in the household of their *kuraka*, where they received the necessary training. They were also supported by their *kuraka*, which is why early Spanish observers referred to them as "*criados*," a term applied to individual servants who had been raised in a Spanish noble's household to provide confidential service. It should be noted that these *yanakuna* were not "servants," as the term is sometimes translated.

Yanakuna may have made up between 1 and 5 percent of the workforce. Women of high rank were "given" women on a permanent basis from the *ayllus* subordinate to their fathers or husbands; these women provided personal service and served as weavers. While they were not called *yanakuna*, clearly the levy was similar. The Incas used this long-standing Andean institution in new ways to increase their direct access to resources. For example, the Inca HUAYNA CÁPAC had personal herds of camelids, distinct from state herds, in the altiplano near Cochabamba; these herds were tended by *yanakuna*, who also transported the MAIZE grown by the MITMAQKUNA of Cochabamba to Cuzco by llama caravan (see TRANSPORTATION). Some high-ranking *yanakuna* were placed by the Inca as *kurakas* over regional polities; this happened at Collique in the Chillón Valley, on the central coast of PERU.

See also *YANACONAJE* (Vol. II).

—Patricia J. Netherly

Z

Zapotecs The term *Zapotec* refers to a linguistic and ethnic group who designate themselves as the Benizaa, or "people of the cloud." Located in central and southern Oaxaca, MEXICO, the Zapotecs occupy four distinct ecological zones—valley, highland, isthmus, and the Miahuatlán region—and speak no fewer than six mutually unintelligible dialects. Around 1500 to 1100 B.C.E., several Zapotec egalitarian families first settled in the Valley of Oaxaca, an area that remains the central hub for Zapotecs to this day. In 900 B.C.E., a ranked authority had formalized in San José Mogote, a village in the valley's upper arm; there, archaeologists have discovered the earliest known "public structure" in Oaxaca and signs of economic, artistic, and religious contact with the OLMECS. The earliest evidence for glyphic writing and the sacred calendar anywhere in Mesoamerica was also found at this site and dates to about 600 B.C.E.

Zapotec society was composed of two endogamous strata, the hereditary nobility and the commoners, each further divided into several social ranks. State affairs were headed by the male ruler (*coqui*), together with his wife (*xonaxi*); priests were chosen from among their relatives (see FAMILY). Although no Zapotec CODICES have survived from pre-Columbian times, the Zapotecs left numerous carved and inscribed stone monuments that depict the rulers involved in ceremonial activities and often their genealogies. Many of these monuments have been found in decorated tombs, since the Zapotecs practiced ancestor worship and often revisited burial sites. The Zapotecs further believed that the cosmos was partitioned between the forces of the "Lightning" and those of the "Earthquake," and they venerated the supreme creator god Coquixee and the god of lightning and rain,

Cocijo. The vital force that breathed life into everything was called *pi* (see RELIGION).

Between 900 and 500 B.C.E., other minor Zapotec centers appeared in each of the three arms of the Valley of Oaxaca, and there is evidence for intercommunity conflict and raiding. In 500 B.C.E., the central site of MONTE ALBÁN was established by a Zapotec confederation and became Mesoamerica's first imperialist kingdom. At this period, the Zapotec people had a strong connection with TEOTIHUACÁN and established an enclave in this important city. The Zapotecs excelled in the manufacture of a specialized gray pottery, and its presence outside of the Valley of Oaxaca is often a good indicator of their presence (see CERAMICS).

After the fall of Monte Albán around 800 B.C.E., the valley's political organization fragmented into smaller Zapotec kingdoms, among which were those of Zaachila and Mitla. The latter became an important religious center, and today stands out for its ornate architecture. There is further evidence for a Mixtec presence at this site and others in the valley and probably even encroachment over ancestral Zapotec lands (see MIXTECS). In the late 15th century C.E., Cociyopij, a ruler from the Zaachila royal house, established a new Zapotec capital in the Isthmus of Tehuantepec, close to Oaxaca's Pacific coast. This kingdom fought fiercely against the advancing armies of the AZTECS but eventually cooperated after a political marital alliance. The Aztecs established the city of Oaxaca as a tributary province to their empire, and it was the Aztecs who coined the appellation *Zapotec*, meaning "people of the zapote tree." Today there are about 300,000 Zapotec speakers who live mostly in nucleated villages throughout Oaxaca.

—Danny Zborover

Further reading:
Joyce Marcus and Kent Flannery. *Zapotec Civilization: How Urban Society Evolved in Mexico's Oaxaca Valley* (London: Thames & Hudson, 1996).

zeque system (*ceque* system)

The *zeque* system was one of the most elaborate ceremonial schemes in ancient America. It functioned between the 15th and 16th centuries in the Inca capital city of Cuzco and probably also in other provincial centers (see INCAS). Much of the present knowledge of the system comes from the 17th-century description of Father Bernabé Cobo, who likely derived his information from the writings of the Spanish chronicler Polo de Ondegardo, which date back to the late 1550s (see CHRONICLERS). Archaeological investigations in and around Cuzco have confirmed and expanded on these historical descriptions and have further linked the *zeque* to similar Andean cultural phenomena, such as the NAZCA LINES.

The *zeque* system was composed of an articulated system of HUACAS, or shrines, which Cobo numbered at 328 but which originally might have reached 400. *Huacas* consisted of buildings and tombs, as well as natural or modified landscape features such as springs, stones, hills, fields, caves, trees, and roads. These shrines were positioned on a radial system of 41 or 42 abstract lines, or *zeques*, that stretched out from the center of Cuzco. Although the lines were not physically marked on the landscape, the *huacas* were connected through a network of visible trails. The lines were further distributed between the four territorial divisions that constituted Tawantinsuyu, or the Inca Empire: Chinchaysuyu, Antisuyu, and Collasuyu had nine lines each, while Cuntisuyu had 14 or 15. The lines' length measured between three and 28 miles (4.8 and 45 km), and each included three to 15 *huacas*. The first *huaca* in a line was within the Cuzco city limits (in or close to Coricancha, the Temple of the Sun), while the last was usually located at the edge of the Cuzco Valley. The system was not symmetrical, nor were the lines straight, often being skewed to accommodate certain shrines.

This complex system had both a social and ritualistic function. Some of the *huacas* served as horizon markers for astronomical observations in the ritual calendar, while others were tied to the irrigation system and water distribution in the valley. Certain *huacas* served as boundary markers between social groups (see AYLLU). Each cluster of lines was further divided into groups of three, which were assigned a rank according to the Inca kinship hierarchy of moieties. Individual lines were also assigned a rank, usually one to a royal kin group (*panaga*) and the others to nonroyal groups. Each group performed ceremonies at their respective *huacas*, during which they offered seashells, COCA, GOLD, and SILVER, and sacrified llamas, GUINEA PIGS, and even children (see HUMAN SACRIFICE). According to Cobo, more than 1,000 people were required to record the history and rituals associated with each of the *huacas*, and the resemblance of the *zeque* system to a spread-out QUIPU is often noted. The *zeque* system, however, was not static and probably developed through time to adapt to new social realities, such as the addition of royal kin groups. It came to an end by the late 16th century, when most of the *huacas* were destroyed by the Spaniards and the Inca kinship system became fragmented.

—Danny Zborover

Further reading:
Brian S. Bauer. *The Scared Landscape of the Inca: The Cusco Ceque System* (Austin: University of Texas Press, 1998).

APPENDIX
PRIMARY SOURCE DOCUMENTS

The following section contains more than a dozen primary documents designed to give readers firsthand accounts of the indigenous world and the encounter between Native Americans and Europeans. Each primary source is preceded by a brief introduction, designed to provide readers with a general framework from which to begin a deeper analysis of the document. It is important to recognize that the introductions are not meant to serve as the final word on these complicated and, in some instances, contradictory texts; instead, readers should be encouraged to think critically about the sources that follow. Why were they written? Who is the intended audience? What do these sources tell about the pre-Columbian period and the nature of the conquest and early colonization of the Americas? What do they ignore? How trustworthy are these documents, and how should historians interpret them?

The texts that follow provide broad geographical coverage and introduce readers to a wide range of topics and themes. The sources are divided into five different sections. Wherever possible, I have selected texts that provide insight into the indigenous worlds that Europeans encountered after 1492. While some of these accounts were written by Europeans, several of the selections that follow were composed by Native American authors, written in native languages.

Two Native Texts from Mesoamerica

The following two documents provide a unique window into the indigenous world of Mesoamerica. The first selection is a brief excerpt from one of the most remarkable texts ever produced in the Americas, known as the Popol Vuh (Council Book). Written by the K'iche' Maya of western Guatemala, the Popol Vuh tells the story of creation, and the excerpt here records the beginning, from the primordial world to the creation of the earth and the animals.

The second document is a little-known Nahuatl-language poem, entitled "Chalcacihuacuicatl," which is filled with humor and evocative emotion.

"The Primordial World," Popol Vuh, Date Unknown (Excerpt)

The Popol Vuh is the single most important example of Maya text to have survived the Spanish conquest. It is also one of the world's great works of literature, containing extensive sections on the creation of the world, the formation of animals, the creation of the first human beings out of maize, the actions of gods in the otherworld, and the relationship between deity and humankind in Maya theology.

Most previous translations have relied on inaccurate Spanish versions rather than the original K'iche' (Quiché) Mayan text. Based on nearly 30 years of research by a leading scholar of Mayan literature, this translation with extensive notes is uniquely faithful to the original language of its authors. Retaining the syntax and style of the text, the reader is provided with a window into the worldview of the ancient Maya. Nevertheless, the clarity and eloquent narrative of the text is also remarkably accessible to nonspecialists with an interest in world religions and literature.

The Popol Vuh was written by anonymous noble members of the K'iche', a branch of the Maya that dominated the highlands of western Guatemala prior to the arrival of Spanish conquerors in 1524. The anonymity of the authors is unusual since most colonial-period highland Mayan documents were prepared for some official purpose, such as land titles, and were duly signed by their authors as testimony of their veracity. It is likely that those who were responsible for compiling the Popol

Vuh did not wish their identities to be known for fear of persecution by Spanish authorities.

The authors of the Popol Vuh were traditionalists in the sense that they recorded the history and theology of the ancient highland Maya people without adding material from European sources. The text thus contains very little direct Christian influence. By its own account, it is a faithful record of the contents of a much older pre-Columbian book that could no longer be seen. The K'iche' authors venerated their traditional Maya gods as "luminous, wise beings who brought life and light" to the world through their creative works and who "accomplished their purpose in purity of being and in truth" long before the arrival of the Christian God to their lands. Thus, the Popol Vuh contrasts its "ancient word" with that of the more recent voice of Christianity.

Such unapologetic reverence for the ancient Maya gods would have been offensive to the Spanish missionaries who, in the early decades of the Spanish conquest, sought to destroy the most overt expressions of Maya religion and literature. Nearly two centuries after the arrival of the Europeans in Guatemala, a Dominican priest named Francisco Ximénez wrote that many ancient books were still kept in secret by the K'iche's so that the Spanish authorities would not learn of them. It was the loss of such precious books as the glyphic Popol Vuh that may have prompted K'iche' scribes to preserve what they could of their literature by transcribing their contents into a form that would make them safer from the fiery purges of Christian authorities.

Although the Popol Vuh is undated, internal evidence points to the work being completed within a few decades of the Spanish conquest, sometime between 1554 and 1558. The fate of the 16th-century transcription of the Popol Vuh is unknown for the next 150 years, until 1701, when Ximénez became aware of the existence of the manuscript and borrowed it long enough to make a copy of the Maya text. Ximénez's copy is the oldest known version of the text, as the original was apparently returned to the Maya and has not been seen since. There must have been hundreds, if not thousands, of texts destroyed in the purges of the Spanish conquest. The survival of the Popol Vuh is therefore a fortuitous accident that allows the reader to hear the authentic voice of its Maya authors speaking centuries after their passing.

༄༅

THE PRIMORDIAL WORLD

THIS IS THE ACCOUNT of when all is still silent and placid. All is silent and calm. Hushed and empty is the womb of the sky.

THESE, then, are the first words, the first speech. There is not yet one person, one animal, bird, fish, crab, tree, rock, hollow, canyon, meadow, or forest. All alone the sky exists. The face of the earth has not yet appeared. Alone lies the expanse of the sea, along with the womb of all the sky. There is not yet anything gathered together. All is at rest. Nothing stirs. All is languid, at rest in the sky. There is not yet anything standing erect. Only the expanse of the water, only the tranquil sea lies alone. There is not yet anything that might exist. All lies placid and silent in the darkness, in the night.

All alone are the Framer and the Shaper, Sovereign and Quetzal Serpent, They Who Have Borne Children and They Who Have Begotten Sons. Luminous they are in the water, wrapped in quetzal feathers and cotinga feathers. Thus they are called Quetzal Serpent. In their essence, they are great sages, great possessors of knowledge. Thus surely there is the sky. There is also Heart of Sky, which is said to be the name of the god.

THE CREATION OF THE EARTH

THEN came his word. Heart of Sky arrived here with Sovereign and Quetzal Serpent in the darkness, in the night. He spoke with Sovereign and Quetzal Serpent. They talked together then. They thought and they pondered. They reached an accord, bringing together their words and their thoughts. Then they gave birth, heartening one another. Beneath the light, they gave birth to humanity. Then they arranged for the germination and creation of the trees and the bushes, the germination of all life and creation, in the darkness and in the night, by Heart of Sky, who is called Huracan.

First is Thunderbolt Huracan, second is Youngest Thunderbolt, and third is Sudden Thunderbolt. These three together are Heart of Sky. Then they came together with Sovereign and Quetzal Serpent. Together they conceived light and life:

"How shall it be sown? When shall there be a dawn for anyone? Who shall be a provider? Who shall be a sustainer?

"Then be it so. You are conceived. May the water be taken away, emptied out, so that the plate of the earth may be created—may it be gathered and become level. Then may it be sown; then may dawn the sky and the earth. There can be no worship, no reverence given by what we have framed and what we have shaped, until humanity has been created, until people have been made," they said.

Then the earth was created by them. Merely their word brought about the creation of it. In order to create the earth, they said, "Earth," and immediately it was created. Just like a cloud, like a mist, was the creation and formation of it.

Then they called forth the mountains from the water. Straightaway the great mountains came to be. It was merely their spirit essence, their miraculous power, that brought about the conception of the mountains and the valleys. Straightaway were created cypress groves and pine forests to cover the face of the earth.

Thus Quetzal Serpent rejoiced:

"It is good that you have come, Heart of Sky—you, Huracan, and you as well, Youngest Thunderbolt and Sudden Thunderbolt. That which we have framed and shaped shall turn out well," they said.

First of earth was created, the mountains and the valleys. The waterways were divided, their branches coursing among the mountains. Thus the waters were divided, revealing the great mountains. For thus was the creation of the earth, created then by Heart of Sky and Heart of Earth, as they are called. They were the first to conceive it. The sky was set apart. The earth also was set apart within the waters. Thus was conceived the successful completion of the work when they thought and pondered.

THE CREATION OF THE ANIMALS

THEN were conceived the animals of the mountains, the guardians of the forest, and all that populate the mountains—the deer and the birds, the puma and the jaguar, the serpent and the rattlesnake, the pit viper and the guardian of the bushes.

She Who Has Borne Children and He Who Has Begotten Sons then asked:

"Shall it be merely solitary, merely silent beneath the trees and the bushes? It is well that there should be guardians for them," they said.

Thus they considered and spoke together, and immediately were created the deer and the birds. Having done this, they then provided homes for the deer and the birds:

"You, deer, will sleep along the courses of rivers and in the canyons. Here you will be in the meadows and in the orchards. In the forests you shall multiply. You shall walk on all fours, and thus you will be able to stand," they were told.

Then they established the homes of the birds, both small and great.

"You, birds, you will make your homes and your houses in the tops of trees, and in the tops of bushes. There you will multiply and increase in numbers in the branches of the trees and the bushes," the deer and the birds were told.

When this had been done, all of them received their places to sleep and their places to rest. Homes were provided for the animals on the earth by She Who Has Borne Children and He Who Has Begotten Sons. Thus all was completed for the deer and the birds.

Source: Allen J. Christenson. *Popol Vuh: The Sacred Book of the Maya*, 67–75 (Norman: University of Oklahoma Press, 2007).

"Chalcacihuacuicatl" ("Chalca Woman's Song"), Date Unknown

The tradition of singing poems aloud in public settings was an important part of the Nahua world. These songs were passed from generation to generation, changing with the times. Many of them were written down in the second half of the 16th century with the encouragement of the Franciscans. Within the song tradition, there existed a subgenre that centered on the persona of the concubine. There is evidence that the song below—or a version very close to it—was used as a political protest by the Chalca people after they had been conquered by the Mexica (Aztecs) and wanted their chiefly lines reinstated. The life of a concubine taken in war is likened to the life of a conquered city-state. The sexual imagery and the evocation of a woman's sphere through references to spinning and weaving are typical enough in the Nahua world for us to assume that such metaphors appeared in other common versions of the song as well.

Here, the character who sings veers between trying to make the best of her life with her new lord (even making sexual overtures) and expressing agonizing pain and regret (especially about her lost ability to become the respected mother

of a recognized clan). In the end, she is an old woman, lamenting her life, yet asking for peace. Such mixed reactions were undoubtedly typical of women in her situation.

Readers should remember that in Nahuatl, the song is very funny and erotic in certain sections and very beautiful and tragic in others. Most probably the song was performed by a man, but we cannot be certain of the conventions surrounding performance. Certainly, the song is saturated with images that would have been familiar to the audiences of that day, though they are entirely unfamiliar to us. To sing "Tocuilan style," for example, seems to have had to do with singing exuberantly. Flowers represented the fragility and beauty of life. To call a king or any other social superior "a little boy" was actually an accepted form of expressing the opposite, that is, of deference. A king might do the reverse, addressing his social inferiors as his grandfathers. Undoubtedly other aspects of the song that still seem mysterious today will one day be translated more effectively.

"This is a composition of the Chalca, with which they came to entertain King Axayácatl because he had conquered them as if they were just women."

Stand up [or, Stop!], you who are
my little sisters! Let's go, let's go,
we will look for flowers. Let's go,
let's go, we will pick some flowers.
They were here, they were here,
scorched flowers, shield-flowers.
It is enticing, it is enjoyable, in the
flower garden of war.

Good are the flowers. Let them be
my wreath. In these my various
flowers let me wrap myself. I am a
Chalca woman.

I long for the flowers, I long for
the songs. In our spinning place,
our customary place [our womanly
sphere], I am intoning the songs of
the king, little Axayácatl. I twirl
them together [into a strand] like
flowers; I twist them forth as a
flower.

Their songs are like paintings, they
are good, like fragrant [pleasant]
flowers. My heart imbibes the
sweet smell of the earth.

What in the world am I to think
of what you say, my lover [sexual
partner], you, little Axayácatl?
What if I were to pleasure him . . .

I just sing Tocuilan style, I whistle
to him. What if I were to pleasure
him . . .

Boy, little servant boy, you who are
king, little Axayácatl, are you truly
a man? Though it may be you are
someone spoken of [well-known,
chosen], is it true you no longer go
to cut firewood? Ay, go stoke the
pot and light a big fire!

Come and bring it, come bring
what is there! Come give it to me!
O child! You! Lay out the things
[the mats]. You and I will lie
together. You will be happy, you
will be happy, will be happy. And
I will do it peacefully, gently.

Let it not be, please don't stick
your hand in my skirts, little boy,
you who are king, little Axayácatl.
Maybe I am painted, my little hand
is itching. Again and again you
want to seize my breast, even my heart.

Now perhaps you yourself will
ruin my body-painting. You
will lie watching what comes to
be a green quechol bird flower.
I will put you inside me. Your
tenchalohtli lies there. I will rock
you in my arms.

It is a quetzal popcorn flower, a
flamingo raven flower. You lie on
your flower-mantled mat. It lies
there inside . . . No longer.

You lie on your golden reed mat.
It lies in the [precious] feathered
cavern house, inside the painted
house . . . No longer.

. . . this is the home. I am
distraught. O mother, maybe I
can spin. Maybe I even used to be
able to weave—but it was all for
naught. As a noble girl-child, I was
spoken of in connection with my
[future] marriage.

It is infuriating. It is heartrending,
here on earth. Sometimes I worry

and fret. I consume myself in rage.
In my desperation, I suddenly say,
hey, child, I would as soon die.

Hey mother, I am dying of sadness
here in my life with a man. I can't
make the spindle dance. I can't
throw my weaver's stick. You cheat
me, my child.

What in the world can I do? Am
I to go along sacrificing myself,
just as people are offered on their
shields in the fields [of war]? You
cheat me, my child.

Little boy, my child, you who are
king, little Axayácatl, you just
ignore me [are negligent toward
me]. You used to sacrifice yourself.

You say you are manly [you
consider yourself a man]. Do I [a
woman] know my way in war? I
know your enemies, my child. And
you just ignore me.

I wish you yourself had been a
woman. Perhaps then you would
not sample [use sexually] she who
is like the blossom and song of
concubinage, my child.

Ah manly nobleman, my lord,
you who are king, little Axayácatl.
Instead you've taken off. You're
angry, little boy. My child, I'm
about to go home, too.

Perhaps thus you took me with
sorcery. You spoke the right words.
Behold now the drunkard, maybe
you yourself are drunk. Are there
social rules in our home?

Did you buy me anywhere? Did
you buy me for yourself, my child?
Did my aunts and uncles come
to trade? Yet you do it heedlessly
[impetuously, without restraint]
and you get angry, little boy. I'm
going home, my child.

You who are my little sister,
woman priest, please look! Many

songs were offered in Cohautepec, at the wooden [or eagle] circling wall, where they came down upon us at Panohuayan.

I make [live] my womanhood. My heart suffers. I don't know what in the world I am to do. I will become a man like [together with] him— howsoever it was that the skirts and blouses of our men, our lovers, were many and full [literally "more," "plentiful"].

Hand me my softened maize, you who are king, little Axayácatl. Let me just pat one [tortilla] out for you. *Neoc*, my child, *neoc*, my child. Pleasure him. Sing to him. Tocuilan style.

Do you call yourself an eagle, an ocelot, my child? Do you boast before your enemies? *Neoc*, my child. Pleasure him . . .

I, a woman, don't yet have a skirt, a blouse [I have not yet attained true womanhood.] He's the one who came here to offer their beautiful songs; he came here to offer shield-flowers [war]. What is to become of us? I'm a Chalca woman and I'm Ayocuan.

I crave my fellow women, the Acolhuaque. I crave my fellow women, the Tepaneca. What is to become of us? I'm a Chalca woman and I'm Ayocuan.

They are ashamed to be made concubines, my child. Are you going to do to me what you did to the poor little Cuauhtlatoa? Peacefully take off your skirts, spread your legs, you the Tlatelolca, you who stink. Come take a look here in Chalco!

Let me have my plumes, mother! Paint me up! What will my lover think of me? You pass before them [her lover and his men] as you leave. Won't he be greedy,

rapacious in Huexotzinco, in Xayacamachan?

How is the song sung, how did people used to sing? He is an eagle *quecholli*. Won't he be greedy, rapacious in Huexotzinco, in Xayacamachan?

In Tetzmolocan I, a woman, anoint my hands and feet with oil. I came to get my maguey skirt and blouse, and I'm going to go use them up.

I desire the Xaltepetlapan Huexotzinca, their leather ropes, their leather thongs. I'm going to go use them up.

He jests [or deceives, or knows] a bit more. He demands me, the child, the king, little Axayácatl. Hey! What comes of it that it seems he makes me live as a concubine in the home of [dependent upon] others? Because of me, you will have twice the kingdom [or family] to keep, my child. Maybe that's the way your heart wants it. Though it should be so . . .

Is it not wholeheartedly, my child, that you bring in concubinage, since it is your home? Maybe that's the way your heart wants it.

What in the world have you done to me, my lover? Don't adorn yourself thus any longer—you are really a bad man. What have you confused [disordered]? It is my heart. You flower-twist your words.

In my spinning place, I speak of you. In my weaving place, I remember you. Little boy, what have you confused? It is my heart.

I am an old courtesan. I am your [plural] mother. I become a rejected old woman, an old maiden lady. I am a Chalcan person. I have

come to pleasure you, my flower
doll, my purple flower doll.

Little king Axayácatl also wants
it. Come see my flowery painted
hands, come see my flowery
painted breasts.

Don't go let your heart take a
needless tumble somewhere, little
Axayácatl. Here is your hand. Go
along holding me by my hand. Be
content.

On your flowery reed mat, in your
sitting place, little boy, peacefully
go to sleep. Relax, my child, you
who are King Axayácatl.

Source: Camilla Townsend. *Malintzin's Choices: An Indian Woman in the Conquest of Mexico*, 216–226 (Albuquerque: University of New Mexico Press, 2006).

Christopher Columbus and the Early Conquest of the Americas

The three short documents that follow are all well known to scholars of the early colonial period. This section includes the two 1492 contracts between Christopher Columbus and the Crown of Castile. These documents are then followed by one of the most controversial and often ridiculed texts of the early colonial period, the Requirement, or Requerimiento.

The Capitulations of Santa Fe, April 17, 1492

After many years trying to secure royal support to sponsor his expedition across the Atlantic, Christopher Columbus finally reached an accord with Queen Isabella and King Ferdinand in mid-April 1492. The formal contract, known as the Capitulations of Santa Fe, came just four months after the fall of Granada, the last Moorish kingdom on the Iberian Peninsula. Juan de Coloma, the royal secretary, represented the Crown in the negotiations with Columbus. The overall cost of the initial voyage, including three ships, crews, and supplies, was relatively modest. However, if the venture proved successful, Columbus stood to gain handsome rewards, both in titles and in material goods. As compensation for his services, Isabella and Ferdinand offered Columbus five significant concessions. They appointed him admiral of all the territories he discovered

and promised that the title would pass to his heirs in perpetuity. Secondly, Columbus was granted the commission of viceroy and governor general. He was also given the right to one-tenth of all merchandise, including gold and silver, acquired in any territory he discovered. Moreover, the monarchs granted Columbus jurisdiction over whatever legal disputes arose in his jurisdiction. Finally, Isabella and Ferdinand authorized Columbus the right to invest up to one-eighth of the costs of all merchant vessels in his admiralty and to keep for himself up to one-eighth of all profits generated from that commerce.

Readers will note that the agreement makes no mention of Asia, an omission that has led some scholars to conclude that Columbus's intentions were to discover new lands and not an Atlantic passage to Asia. However, the absence of any specific reference to Asia does not necessarily mean that Columbus had no intention of discovering a western route to the continent. In fact, it is worth noting that King Ferdinand and Queen Isabella gave Columbus a letter of introduction to the great khan; moreover, one of the crewmembers on Columbus's 1492 voyage was an interpreter who spoke some Arabic, a language that was understood in many parts of India and one that Europeans believed would be understood in East Asia.

∞◇∞

The things requested and that Your Highnesses give and grant to Sir Christopher Columbus in partial reward for what he will discover on the voyage that now, with the help of God, he is to make on the Ocean Seas in the service of Your Highnesses, are the following:

First, Your Highnesses, as the lords you are of the Ocean Seas, appoint Sir Christopher Columbus from now on as your admiral on all those islands and mainland discovered or acquired by his command and expertise in the Ocean Seas during his lifetime and, after his death, by his heirs and successors one after the other in perpetuity, with privileges and prerogatives equal to those that Sir Alfonso Enríquez, your high admiral of Castile, and his other predecessors in the office held in their districts.

It pleases Their Highnesses. Juan de Coloma.

Also, Your Highnesses appoint Sir Christopher your viceroy and governor general in all those islands and any mainland and islands that he may discover and acquire in the seas. For the governance of each and every one of them, he will nominate three persons for each office, and Your Highnesses will select and appoint the one most beneficial to your service, and thus the lands that our Lord permits him to find and acquire will be best governed to the service of Your Highnesses.

It pleases Their Highnesses. Juan de Coloma.

You wish him to have and take for himself one-tenth of all and any merchandise, whether pearls, precious stones, gold, silver, spices, and any other things and merchandise of whatever kind, name, or sort it may be, that is bought, exchanged, found, acquired, and obtained within the limits of the admiralty that Your Highnesses from now on bestow on Sir Christopher, deducting all the relevant expenses incurred, so that, of what remains clear and free, he may take and keep one-tenth for himself and do with it as he pleases, reserving the other nine-tenths for Your Highnesses.

It pleases Their Highnesses. Juan de Coloma.

Should any lawsuits arise on account of the merchandise that he brings back from the islands and mainland acquired or discovered, or over merchandise taken in exchange from other merchants there in the place where this commerce and trade is held and done, and if taking cognizance of such suits belongs to him by virtue of the privileges pertaining to his office of admiral, may it please Your Highnesses that he or his deputy, and no other judge, shall be authorized to take cognizance of and give judgment on it from now on.

It pleases Their Highnesses, if it pertains to the office of admiral and conforms to what the admiral Sir Alfonso Enríquez and his other predecessors had in their districts, and if it be just. Juan de Coloma.

On all vessels outfitted for trade and business, each time, whenever, and as often as they are outfitted, Sir Christopher Columbus, if he wishes, may contribute and pay one-eighth of all that is spent on the outfitting and likewise he may have and take one-eighth of the profits that result from such outfitting.

It pleases Their Highnesses. Juan de Coloma.

These are authorized and dispatched with the replies from Your Highnesses at the end of each article. In the town of Santa Fe de la Vega de Granada, on the seventeenth day of April in the year of the birth of our savior Jesus Christ one thousand four hundred and ninety-two.

I, the Queen. By command of the king and queen.
Juan de Coloma.

Source: Helen Nader, ed. and trans., and Luciano Formisano, ed. *The Book of Privileges Issued to Christopher Columbus by King Fernando and Queen Isabel, 1492–1502*, 63–66 (Berkeley: University of California Press, 1996).

The Capitulations of Granada, April 30, 1492

Just two weeks after signing the Capitulations of Santa Fe, King Ferdinand and Queen Isabella issued a writ, known as the Capitulations of Granada. This agreement formally conferred on Columbus the offices of admiral, viceroy, and governor of the islands and mainland he might discover. The agreement also formalized Columbus's title of nobility (which would be passed on to his heirs).

∽∾

Granada, 30 April 1492

Sir Fernando and Lady Isabel, by the grace of God king and queen of Castile, León, Aragón, Sicily, Granada, Toledo, Valencia, Galicia, the Belearics, Seville, Sardinia, Córdoba, Corsica, Murcia, Jaén, the Algarve, Algeciras, Gibraltar and the Canary Islands, count and countess of Barcelona, lords of Vizcaya and Molina, dukes of Athens and Neopatria, counts of Rousillon and Cerdagne, marquises of Oristano and Goceano.

Because you, Christopher Columbus, are going at our command with some of your ships and personnel to discover and acquire certain islands and mainland in the Ocean Sea, and it is hoped that, with the help of God, some of the islands and mainland in the Ocean Sea will be discovered and acquired by your command and expertise, it is just and reasonable that you should be remunerated for placing yourself in danger for our service.

Wanting to honor and bestow favor for these reasons, it is our grace and wish that you, Christopher Columbus, after having discovered and acquired these islands and mainland in the Ocean Sea, will be our admiral of the islands that you discover and acquire and will be our admiral, viceroy, and governor of them. You will be empowered from that time forward to call yourself Sir Christopher Columbus, and thus your sons and successors in this office and post may entitle themselves sir, admiral, viceroy, and governor of them.

You and your proxies will have the authority to exercise the office of admiral together with the offices of viceroy and governor of the islands and mainland that you discover and acquire. You will have the power to hear and dispose of all the lawsuits and cases, civil and criminal, related to the offices of admiral, viceroy, and governor, as you determine according to the law, and as the admirals of our kingdom are accustomed to administer it. You and your proxies will have the power to punish and penalize delinquents as well as exercising the offices of admiral, viceroy, and governor in all matters pertaining to these offices. You will enjoy and benefit from the fees and salaries attached, belonging, and corresponding to these offices, just as our high admiral enjoys and is accustomed to them in the admiralty of our kingdoms.

With this our writ or its transcript certified by a public clerk, we order Prince Sir Juan, our most dear and beloved son, and the princes, dukes, prelates, marquises, counts, masters, priors, and commanders of the orders; royal councilors, judges of our appellate court, and judges and any other justices of our household, court, and chancery; subcommanders and commanders of our castles, forts and buildings; all municipal councils, royal judges, corregidores, municipal judges, sheriffs, appeals judges, councilmen, parish delegates, commissioned and noncommissioned officers, municipal officials, and voting citizens of all cities, towns, and villages of these our kingdoms and domains and of those that you may conquer and acquire; captains, masters, mates, warrant officers, sailors and ship's crews; and each and every one of your subjects and citizens now and in the future, that, having discovered and acquired any islands and mainland in the Ocean Sea, once you and your designated representative have performed the oath and formalities required in such cases, from then on you shall be accepted and regarded for the rest of your life, and your sons and successors after you forevermore, as our admiral of the Ocean Sea and viceroy and governor of the islands and mainland that you, Sir Christopher Columbus, discover and acquire.

[All the officials and people] shall put into effect everything pertaining to these offices, together with you and the proxies you appoint to the offices of admiral, viceroy, and governor. They shall pay and cause to be paid to you the salary, fees, and other perquisites of these offices. They shall observe and cause to be observed for you all the honors, gifts, favors, liberties, privileges, prerogatives, exemptions, immunities, and each and all of the things that, by virtue of the offices of admiral, viceroy, and governor, you should receive and that should be paid to you fully and completely, in such a way that nothing will be withheld from you. They shall not place of consent to place hindrance or obstacle against you in any way.

For with this writ we grant to you from now on the offices of admiral, viceroy, and governor as a hereditary right forevermore, and we grant you actual and prospective possession of them, as well as the authority to administer them and collect the dues and salaries attached and pertaining to each of them.

If it should be necessary for you, and you should request it of them, we command our chancellor, notaries, and other officials who preside over the table with our seals to give, issue, forward, and seal our letter of privilege with the circle of signatures, in the strongest, firmest, and most sufficient manner that you may request and find necessary. None of you or them shall do otherwise in any way concerning this, under penalty of our displeasure and a fine of 10,000 maravedís for our treasury on each person who does the contrary.

Furthermore, we command the man who shows you this writ to summon you to appear before us in our court, wherever we may be, within fifteen days of having been cited, under the same penalty. Under this same penalty, we command every public clerk who may be summoned for this purpose to give the person showing this writ to him a certificate to that effect, inscribed with his rubric, so that we may know how well our command is obeyed.

Given in our city of Granada on the thirtieth day of the month of April in the year of the birth of our Lord Jesus Christ one thousand four hundred and ninety-two.

> I, the King
> I, the Queen
> I, Juan de Coloma, secretary of the king and queen or lords, had this written at their command.
> Approved in form: Rodericus, doctor.
> Registered: Sebastián de Olano. Francisco de Madrid, chancellor.

Source: Helen Nader, ed. and trans., and Luciano Formisano, ed. *The Book of Privileges Issued to Christopher Columbus by King Fernando and Queen Isabel, 1492–1502*, 66–67, 69 (Berkeley: University of California Press, 1996).

The Requerimiento, 1513

Drafted by the Spanish jurist and university professor Juan López de Palacios Rubios (1450–1524) the requerimiento, *or "requirement," was a legal document that constituted, in the words of historian Patricia Seed, a "protocol for conquest." In 1512, Spain's king Ferdinand convened a meeting of prominent jurists and theologians, including Palacios Rubios, to address charges of Spanish cruelty and exploitation of the indigenous peoples of the Caribbean. Palacios Rubios defended the legality of Spain's overseas empire, as well as the authority they had to enslave the native population. From these deliberations, Palacios*

Rubios provided the text for the requirement. This legal document was used by the Spanish to legitimize their conquests in the Americas and justify the enslavement of Amerindians who rejected Spanish rule. Influenced by medieval Spanish legal traditions, the requerimiento *provided an outline of the hierarchy of Spanish colonial authority. It traced how God had granted the popes not only spiritual but also temporal authority over all peoples of the world, descendants of Adam and Eve.*

As a legal document, the requerimiento *named indigenous peoples as vassals of the Crown and demanded that they submit to the pope and Spanish authority and allow Christian missionaries to preach freely. In return for their submission, the document promised them protection and royal privilege. However, if they rejected these terms, the Spanish could justifiably wage war upon and enslave them. The* requerimiento *was intended to be read aloud to indigenous peoples in the presence of a notary and an interpreter. Of course, even if the document were read before the start of any hostilities, the Native Americans who heard its content would not have understood what it conveyed. Not surprisingly, many Spanish contemporaries, including the Dominican friar Bartolomé de Las Casas denounced the document and its usage in the conquest campaigns. One 16th-century chronicler writing about the early phases of the Caribbean conquests asserted that the Indians would hear the requirement (in a language they did not understand) only after they had been captured and enslaved.*

∽∞∽

On the part of the King, don Fernando, and of doña Juana, his daughter, Queen of Castille and León, subduers of the barbarous nations, we their servants notify and make known to you, as best we can, that the Lord our God, Living and Eternal, created the Heaven and the Earth, and one man and one woman, of whom you and we, all the men of the world, were and are descendants, and all those who came after us. But, on account of the multitude which has sprung from this man and woman in the five thousand years since the world was created, it was necessary that some men should go one way and some another, and that they should be divided into many kingdoms and provinces, for in one alone they could not be sustained.

Of all these nations God our Lord gave charge to one man, called St. Peter, that he should be Lord and Superior of all the men in the world, that all should obey him, and that he should be the head of the whole human race, wherever men should live, and under whatever law, sect, or belief they should be; and he gave him the world for his kingdom and jurisdiction.

And he commanded him to place his seat in Rome, as the spot most fitting to rule the world from; but also he permitted him to have his seat in any other part of the world, and to judge and govern all Christians, Moors, Jews, Gentiles, and all other sects. This man was called Pope, as if to say, Admirable Great Father and Governor of men. The men who lived in that time obeyed that St. Peter, and took him for Lord, King, and Superior of the universe; so also they have regarded the others who after him have been elected to the pontificate, and so has it been continued even till now, and will continue till the end of the world.

One of these Pontiffs, who succeeded that St. Peter as Lord of the world, in the dignity and seat which I have before mentioned, made donation of these isles and Tierra-firme to the aforesaid King and Queen and to their successors, our lords, with all that there are in these territories, as is contained in certain writings which passed upon the subject as aforesaid, which you can see if you wish.

So their Highnesses are kings and lords of these islands and land of Tierra-firme by virtue of this donation: and some islands, and indeed almost all those to whom this has been notified, have received and served their Highnesses, as lords and kings, in the way that subjects ought to do, with good will, without any resistance, immediately, without delay, when they were informed of the aforesaid facts. And also they received and obeyed the priests whom their Highnesses sent to preach to them and to teach them our Holy Faith; and all these, of their own free will, without any reward or condition, have become Christians, and are so, and their Highnesses have joyfully and benignantly received them, and also have commanded them to be treated as their subjects and vassals; and you too are held and obliged to do the same. Wherefore, as best we can, we ask and require you that you consider what we have said to you, and that you take the time that shall be necessary to understand and deliberate upon it, and that you acknowledge the Church as the Ruler and Superior of the whole world, and the high priest called Pope, and in his name the King and Queen Doña Juana our lords, in his place, as superiors and lords and kings of these islands and this Tierra-firme by virtue of the said donation, and that you consent and give place that these religious fathers should declare and preach to you the aforesaid.

If you do so, you will do well, and that which you are obliged to do to their Highnesses, and we in their name shall receive you in all love and charity, and shall leave you, your wives, and your children, and your lands, free without servitude, that you may do with them and with yourselves freely that which you like and think best, and they shall not compel you to turn Christians, unless you yourselves, when informed of the truth, should wish to be converted to our Holy Catholic Faith, as almost all the inhabitants of the rest of the islands have done. And, besides this, their Highnesses award you many privileges and exemptions and will grant you many benefits.

But, if you do not do this, and maliciously make delay in it, I certify to you that, with the help of God, we shall powerfully enter into your country, and shall make war against you in all ways and manners that we can, and shall subject you to the yoke and obedience of the Church and of their Highnesses; we shall take you and your wives and your children, and shall make slaves of them, and as such shall sell and dispose of them as their Highnesses may command; and we shall take away your goods, and shall do you all the mischief and damage that we can, as to vassals who do not obey, and refuse to receive their lord, and resist and contradict him; and we protest that the deaths and losses which shall accrue from this are your fault, and not that of their Highnesses, or ours, nor of these cavaliers who come with us. And that we have said this to you and made this Requisition, we request the notary here present to give us his testimony in writing, and we ask the rest who are present that they should be witnesses of this Requisition.

Source: Arthur Helps. *The Spanish Conquest in America and Its Relation to the History of Slavery and to the Government of the Colonies*, vol. 1, 264–267 (London: J. W. Parker & Sons, 1855–1861).

Spanish and Indigenous Voices in the Conquest of Mexico

What follows are a series of brief vignettes from one of the most dramatic episodes of the 16th century, the conquest of Mexico. The first three documents are taken from Spanish sources, two of which are drawn from eyewitness accounts of the conquest. However, unlike many regions of the Americas where the conquest narrative is told only from the perspective of the Spanish participants, Mexico's story has also been told from the perspective of the vanquished. Thus, the Spanish accounts are then followed by three indigenous accounts of the conquest, originally written in the Nahuatl language just decades after the events they describe and appearing in the Florentine Codex.

Hernando Cortés, Third Letter to King Charles I, May 15, 1522 (Excerpt)

In 1519, Cuba's governor, Diego Velázquez de Cuéllar, appointed Hernando Cortés to lead an exploratory expedition to the Mexican coastline. However, Cortés had other plans. Cuba's governor had granted Cortés license to explore and trade along the Gulf coast of Mexico, but he was not granted authorization to conquer or colonize. Nevertheless, Cortés ignored those instructions (and restrictions) and instead transformed the exploration into a two-year war of conquest against the Aztec Empire. In order to gain the favor of King Charles of Spain, Cortés wrote a series of letters, justifying his actions and outlining his services to the Crown. Below is an excerpt from Cortés's third letter to the king, dated May 15, 1522. The letter records the lengthy siege of the city of Tenochtitlán and its final capture on August 13, 1521.

That evening I arranged that when we entered the city on the following day three heavy guns should be prepared and taken into the city with us, for I feared that the enemy, who were so massed together that they had no room to turn around, might crush us as we attacked, without actually fighting. I wished, therefore, to do them some harm with the guns, and so induce them to come out to meet us. I also ordered the *alguacil mayor* (chief constable) to make ready the brigantines, so that they might sail into a large lake between the houses, where all the canoes had gathered; for they now had so few houses left that the lord of the city lived in a canoe with certain of his chieftains, not knowing where else to go. Thus we made our plans for the morrow.

When it was light I had all the men made ready and the guns brought out. On the previous day I had ordered Pedro de Alvarado to wait for me in the market square and not to attack before I arrived. When all the men were mustered and all the brigantines were lying in wait behind those houses where the enemy was gathered, I gave orders that when a harquebus was fired they should enter the little of the city that was still left to win and drive the defenders into the water where the brigantines were waiting. I warned them, however, to look with care for Guatimucín [Cuauhtémoc], and to make every effort to take him alive, for once that had been done the war would cease. I myself climbed onto a roof top, and before the fight began I spoke with certain chieftains of the city whom I knew, and asked them for what reason their lord would not appear before me; for, although they were in the direst straits, they need not all perish; I asked them to call him, for he had no cause to be afraid. Two of those chieftains then appeared to go to speak with him. After a while they returned, bringing with them one of the most important persons in the city, whose name was Ciguacoacin, and he was captain and governor of them all and directed all matters concerning the war. I welcomed him openly, so that he should not be afraid; but at last he told me that his sovereign would prefer to die where he was rather than on any account appear before me, and that he personally was much grieved by this, but now I might do as I pleased. I now saw by this how determined he was, and so I told him to return to his people and to prepare them, for I intended to attack and slay them all; and so he departed after having spent five hours in such discussions.

The people of the city had to walk upon their dead while others swam or drowned in the waters of that wide lake where they had their canoes; indeed, so great was their suffering that it was beyond our understanding how they could endure it. Countless numbers of men, women and children came out toward us, and in their eagerness to escape many were pushed into the water where they drowned amid that multitude of corpses; and it seemed that more than fifty thousand had perished from the salt water they had drunk, their hunger and the vile stench. So that we should not discover the plight in which they were in, they dared neither throw these bodies into the water where the brigantines might find them nor throw them beyond their boundaries where the soldiers might see them; and so in those streets where they were we came across such piles of the dead that we were forced to walk upon them. I had posted Spaniards in every street, so that when the people began to come out they might prevent our allies from killing those wretched people, whose number was uncountable. I also told the captains of our allies that on no account should any of those people be slain; but they were so many that we could not prevent more than fifteen thousand being killed and sacrificed that day. But still their warriors and chieftains were hiding in corners, on roof tops, in their houses or in canoes on the lake, but neither their dissimulations or anything else availed them anything, for we could clearly see their weakness and their suf-

fering. When I saw that it was growing late and that they were not going to surrender or attack I ordered the two guns to be fired at them, for although these did some harm it was less than our allies would have done had I granted them license to attack. But when I saw that this was of no avail I ordered the harquebus to be discharged, whereupon that corner which they still held was taken and its defenders driven into the water, those who remained surrendering without a fight.

Then the brigantines swept into the inner lake and broke through the fleet of canoes; but the warriors in them no longer dared fight. God willed that Garci Holguín, a captain of one of the brigantines, should pursue a canoe which appeared to be carrying persons of rank; and as there were two or three crossbowmen in the bows who were preparing to fire, the occupants of the canoe signaled to the brigantine not to shoot, because the lord of the city was with them. When they heard this our men leapt aboard and captured Guatimucín and the lord of Tacuba and the other chieftains with them. These they then brought to the roof close to the lake where I was standing, and, as I had no desire to treat Guatimucín harshly, I asked him to be seated, whereupon he came up to me and, speaking in his language, said that he had done all he was bound to do to defend his own person and his people, so that now they were reduced to this sad state, and I might do with him as I pleased. Then he placed his hand upon a dagger of mine and asked me to kill him with it; but I reassured him saying that he need fear nothing. Thus, with this lord as prisoner, it pleased God that the war should cease, and the day it ended was Tuesday, the feast of Saint Hippolytus, the thirteenth of August, in the year 1521. Thus from the day we laid siege to the city, which was on the thirtieth of May of that same year, until it fell, there passed seventy-five days, during which time Your Majesty will have seen the dangers, hardships and misfortunes which these, Your vassals, endured, and in which they ventured their lives. To this, their achievements will bear testimony.

Of all those seventy-five days not one passed without our being engaged in some manner with the enemy. On the day that Guatimucín was captured and the city taken, we gathered up all the spoils we could find and returned to our camp, giving thanks to Our Lord for such a favor and the much desired victory which He had granted us.

Source: Hernando Cortés. *Letters from Mexico*, rev. ed., translated and edited by Anthony Pagden, 262–265 (New Haven, Conn.: Yale University Press, 1986).

Francisco López de Gómara, *Istoria de la conquista de México*, 1552 (Excerpt)

In 1552, roughly three decades after the Spanish conquest of Tenochtitlán, Hernando Cortés's private secretary, Francisco López de Gómara, published a history of the conquest of Mexico (Istoria de la conquista de México). Gómara himself was not a participant in the conquest; however, he had access to Cortés's papers, and he likely interviewed some of the participants. Gómara's work celebrated and glorified Cortés's role in the conquest of Mexico, ignoring the contributions of other conquistadores. This omission irritated many of the other Spanish participants in the conquest, and Gómara's publication certainly influenced Bernal Díaz del Castillo to complete his True History of the Conquest of Mexico.

The excerpt below describes an event that occurred during the late spring of 1520 in the Aztec capital city of Tenochtitlán. Cortés and his men had arrived in Tenochtitlán in early November 1519. Within the first week, Cortés had taken Montezuma captive and placed the Aztec ruler under house arrest. Meanwhile, Cuba's governor Diego de Velázquez de Cuéllar had dispatched a group of 800 men led by Pánfilo de Narváez to capture Cortés—who had disobeyed the governor's orders by sailing to Mexico—and take him back to Cuba as prisoner. Narváez's party landed on the Mexican coast on April 20, 1520. When Cortés learned of their arrival, he quickly assembled 266 men and set off from Tenochtitlán for the coast. On arrival, he launched a surprise nighttime attacked during which he captured Narváez; not only that, but he also managed to persuade most of Narváez's men to accompany him back to Tenochtitlán to assist in the conquest.

However, when Cortés returned to the capital, he quickly discovered that all had not gone well during his absence. When Cortés had left Tenochtitlán for Veracruz two months earlier, he appointed Pedro de Alvarado to be in charge of the 80 Spaniards left behind in the city. In Cortés's absence, Alvarado ordered the massacre of a large number of indigenous nobles during the Aztec festival of Tóxcatl, the celebration to honor the god Huitzilopochtli. The killings provoked Tenochtitlán's residents to attack the Spaniards, and the fighting forced the Spaniards to retreat into the city's fortified palace compound.

Below is Gómara's account of the Tóxcatl massacre. Readers should compare Gómara's rendering of this event with the Nahua version of the same incident, which is also included in the following pages.

❧❦❧

Cortés wanted to get at the root of the rebellion of the Mexicans. He interrogated all the Spaniards together, and some said it was caused by the message sent by Narváez; others, by the desire of the people to drive them out of Mexico, as had been planned, as soon as there were ships in which to sail, for during the fighting they kept shouting "Get out!" Others said it was to liberate Montezuma, because the Indians said "Free our god and king if you wish to live!" Still others said it was because the Indians wanted to steal the gold, silver, and jewels of the Spaniards, for they heard the Indians say: "Here you shall leave the gold you took from us!" Again, some said it was to keep the Tlaxcalans and other mortal enemies out of Mexico. Many, finally, believed it was because the images of the gods had been cast down and [the Indians] wished to give themselves to the devil.

Any of these things could have caused the rebellion, let alone all of them together; but the principal one was this: A few days after Cortés had left to encounter Narváez, there was

a solemn festival, which the Mexicans wished to celebrate in their traditional fashion. They begged Pedro de Alvarado (who had stayed behind to act as warden and Cortés' lieutenant) to give his permission, so that he would not think they were gathering to massacre the Spaniards. Alvarado consented, with the proviso that they were not to kill men in sacrifice or bear arms. More than six hundred (some say more than a thousand) gentlemen, and even several lords, assembled in the yard of the main temple, where that night they made a great hubbub with their drums, conches, trumpets, and bone fifes, which emit a loud whistle. They were naked, but covered with precious stones, pearls, necklaces, belts, bracelets, jewels of gold, silver, and mother-or-pearl, wearing many rich plumes on their heads. They performed the dance called macehualixtli, which means "reward through work" (from macehualli, a farmer).

. . . [T]hey spread mats in the temple yard and placed drums upon them. They danced in rings, grasping hands, to the music of the singers, to which they responded. The songs were sacred, not profane, and were sung to praise the god whose feast was being celebrated, to induce him to give them water or grain, health or victory, or to thank him for giving them peace, children, health, and the like. Those who knew the language and these ceremonial rites said that, when the people dance in the temple [on this occasion], they performed very differently from those who danced the netotelixtli, in voice, movement of the body, head, arms, and feet, by which they manifest their concepts of good and evil. The Spaniards called this dance an areyto, a word they brought from the islands of Cuba and Santo Domingo.

While the Mexican gentlemen were dancing in the temple yard of Huitzilopochtli, Pedro de Alvarado went there, whether of his own notion or following the decision of the rest, I cannot say. Some say he had been warned that the Indian nobles of the city had assembled to plot the mutiny and rebellion which they later carried out; others, that [the Spaniards] went to see them perform this much-praised and famous dance, and, seeing them so rich, they coveted the gold the Indians were wearing, so he [Alvarado] blocked the entrances with ten or twelve Spaniards at each one, himself went in with more than fifty, and cruelly and pitilessly stabbed and killed the Indians, and took what they were wearing. Cortés, who must have felt badly about the affair, dissembled his feelings so as not to irritate the perpetrators, for it happened at a time when he had need of them, either against the Indians, or to put down trouble among his own men.

Source: Francisco López de Gómara. Istoria de la conquista de Mexico. In Cortés: The Life of the Conqueror, translated and edited by Lesley B. Simpson, 206–208 (Berkeley: University of California Press, 1964).

Bernal Díaz del Castillo, The True History of the Conquest of Mexico, ca. 1567 (Excerpt)

This excerpt comes from the firsthand account of the Spanish conquistador Bernal Díaz del Castillo, who was an eyewitness to one of the most defining moments in history, the Spanish conquest of Mexico. Díaz is best known today for his detailed chronicle Historia verdadera de la conquista de la Nueva

España (The True History of the Conquest of New Spain). *He was born in the Spanish town of Medina del Campo in 1495, and he arrived in the New World as a young man in 1514. Before participating in Hernando Cortés's fateful voyage in 1519, Díaz had participated in other expeditions as a foot soldier in Cuba and Yucatán. Nonetheless, while his chronicle covers the general period from 1517 to 1568, its primary focus is the events from 1519 to 1521: the downfall of Tenochtitlán and the Aztec Empire.*

He began writing his retrospective account in 1551 and used Cortés's own letters to the Spanish king and Francisco López de Gómara's biographic chronicle, often by taking a strong position against the latter. Many of the inaccuracies pointed out in Díaz's chronicle are probably due to the fact he was writing three decades after the events he described. Furthermore, Díaz was attempting to morally justify the Spaniards' actions during the conquest, depicting the conquistadores as the Christian liberators of New Spain, both from the devil's influence as well as the brutal Aztecs; he further emphasized his own poverty and the small return the conquistadores had received and thus hoped that his chronicle would guarantee a future prosperity for his heirs. A copy he sent to Spain in 1575 was not published until 1632. Díaz kept working on another version until his death in Guatemala in 1584. This latter manuscript was not published until the early 20th century and is considered today as one of the most detailed chronicles of the conquest of Mexico.

In the excerpt below, Díaz describes the moment when the Spaniards, led by Cortés, first caught glimpse of the Mexica city of Tenochtitlán, capital of the Aztec Empire. Not only does Díaz marvel at the site of the city, its natural setting, its architecture and beauty, but he also laments its destruction. Of course, it is worth noting that Díaz neglects to mention the thousands of Indian allies who had accompanied Cortés and his men to Tenochtitlán.

⤜∾⤛

During the morning, we arrived at a broad Causeway and continued our march towards Iztapalapa, and when we saw so many cities and villages built in the water and other great towns on dry land and that straight and level Causeway going towards Mexico, we were amazed and said that it was like the enchantments they tell of in the legend of Amadis, on account of the great towers and cues and buildings rising from the water, and all built of masonry. And some of our soldiers even asked whether the things that we saw were not a dream. It is not to be wondered at that I here write it down in this manner, for there is so much to think over that I do not know how to describe it, seeing things as we did that had never been heard of or seen before, not even dreamed about.

Thus, we arrived near Iztapalapa, to behold the splendour of the other Caciques who came out to meet us, who were the Lord of the town named Cuitlahuac, and the Lord of Culhuacan, both of them near relations of Montezuma.

And then when we entered the city of Iztapalapa, the appearances of the palaces in which they lodged us! How spacious and well built they were, of beautiful stone work and cedar wood, and the wood of other sweet scented trees, with great rooms and courts, wonderful to behold, covered with awnings of cotton cloth.

When we had looked well at all of this, we went to the orchard and garden, which was such a wonderful thing to see and walk in, that I was never tired of looking at the diversity of the trees, and noting the scent which each one had, and the paths full of roses and flowers, and the many fruit trees and native roses, and the pond of fresh water. There was another thing to observe, that great canoes were able to pass into the garden from the lake through an opening that had been made so that there was no need for their occupants to land. And all was cemented and very splendid with many kinds of stone [monuments] with pictures on them, which gave much to think about. Then the birds of many kinds and breeds which came into the pond. I say again that I stood looking at it and thought that never in the world would there be discovered other lands such as these, for at the time there was no Peru, nor any thought of it. Of all these wonders that I then beheld today all is overthrown and lost, nothing left standing. Let us go on, and I will relate that the Caciques of that town and of Coyoacan brought us a present of gold, worth more than two thousand pesos.

Early next day we left Iztapalapa with a large escort of those great Caciques whom I have already mentioned. We proceeded along the Causeway which is here eight paces in width and runs so straight to the city of Mexico that it does not seem to me to turn either much or little, but, broad as it is, it was so crowded with people that there was hardly room for them all, some of them going to and others returning from Mexico, besides those who had come out to see us, so that we were hardly able to pass by the crowds of them that came; and the towers and cues were full of people as well as the canoes from all parts of the lake. It was not to be wondered at, for they had never before seen horses or men such as we are.

Gazing on such wonderful sights, we did not know what to say, or whether what appeared before us was real, for on one side, on the land, there were great cities, and in the lake ever so many more, and the lake itself was crowded with canoes, and in the Causeway were many bridges at intervals, and in front of us stood the great City of Mexico, and we—we did not even number four hundred soldiers! and we well remembered the words and warnings given us by the people of Huexotzingo and Tlaxcala, and the many other warnings that had been given that we should beware of entering Mexico, where they would kill us, as soon as they had us inside.

Let the curious readers consider whether there is not much to ponder over in this that I am writing. What men have there been in the world who have shown such daring?

Source: Bernal Díaz del Castillo. *The Discovery and Conquest of Mexico,* 2d ed., translated by A. P. Maudslay, 190–192 (Cambridge: Da Capo Press, 2003).

A Nahua Account of the Tóxcatl Massacre, Florentine Codex, ca. 1550s (Excerpt)

The three brief excerpts that follow are all taken from the Florentine Codex, one of the most remarkable texts ever produced in the New World. This monumental work, written in Nahuatl and Spanish, was completed under the direction of the famed Franciscan friar Bernardino de Sahagún. It is bound in three volumes, divided into 12 parts called "books." Sahagún conceived the work as something akin to an encyclopedic history of traditional Nahua (Aztec) life and culture (the first 11 books), culminating in a Nahua account of the conquest of Mexico (book 12).

The Florentine Codex is unique in its size, coverage, sophistication, and depth; its hundreds of folios are beautifully written in parallel Nahuatl and Spanish columns and copiously illustrated. Sahagún began to compile material for the manuscript in the late 1540s, almost three decades after the conquest, and he continued to work on it throughout the 1550s and 1560s. However, the final product was very much a collaborative effort. Sahagún employed numerous Nahua aides to gather information, interview witnesses, and compose the text in their own language (Nahuatl). For example, much of the information used to write about the Spanish conquest likely was based on testimonies gathered from individuals who witnessed the events firsthand.

Still, it is important to recognize that the entire work was completed under Sahagún's careful supervision, even if the extent of Sahagún's influence remains difficult to quantify. However, despite the friar's involvement in the creation and organization of the Florentine Codex, recent scholarship (in particular the magisterial work of James Lockhart) has convincingly demonstrated that the work contains numerous elements, both in form and content, that derived from Nahua oral traditions. It is therefore highly likely that the views of the Spanish conquest in the three excerpts that follow represent authentic Indian voices, told by survivors who witnessed firsthand the fall the Aztec capital city of Tenochtitlán.

Chapter 20 of book 12 presents a Nahua version of the Tóxcatl massacre of 1520. Readers should compare the Nahua version of this event with the Spanish account of Francisco López de Gómara (included in previous pages).

∽∞∾

Twentieth chapter, where it is said how the Spaniards killed and annihilated the Mexica who were celebrating the feast of Huitzilopochtli at what they call the Teoithualco [Divine Courtyard, Courtyard of Gods, temple courtyard].

When things were already going on, when the festivity was being observed and there was dancing and singing, with voices raised in song, the singing was like the noise of waves breaking against the rocks.

When it was time, when the moment had come for the Spaniards to do the killing, they came out equipped for battle.

They came and closed off each of the places where the people went in and out: Quauhquiahuac, Tecpantzinco, Acatliyacapan, and Tezcacoac. And when they had closed these exits, they stationed themselves in each, and no one could come out any more.

When this had been done, they went into the temple courtyard to kill people. Those whose assignment it was to do the killing just went on foot, each with his metal sword and his leather shield, some of them iron-studded. Then they surrounded those who were dancing, going among the cylindrical drums. They struck a drummer's arms; both of his hands were severed. Then they struck his neck; his head landed far away. Then they stabbed everyone with iron lances and struck them with iron swords. They stuck some in the belly, and then their entrails came spilling out. They split open the heads of some, they really cut their skulls to pieces, their skulls were cut up into little bits. And some they hit on the shoulders; their bodies broke open and ripped. Some they hacked on the calves, some on the thighs, some on their bellies, and then all their entrails would spill out. And if someone still tried to run it was useless; he just dragged his intestines along. There was a stench as if of sulfur. Those who tried to escape could go nowhere. When anyone tried to go out, at the entryways they struck and stabbed him.

But some climbed up the wall and were able to escape. Some went into the various calpulli temples and took refuge there. Some took refuge among, entered among those who had really died, feigning death, and they were able to escape. But if someone took a breath and they saw him, they stabbed him. The blood of the warriors ran like water; the ground was almost slippery with blood, and the stench of it rose, and the entrails were lying dragged out. And the Spaniards went everywhere searching in the calpulli temples, stabbing in the places where they searched in case someone was taking shelter there. They went everywhere, scratching about in all the calpulli temples in searching.

And when it became known [what was happening], everyone cried out, "Mexica warriors, come running, get outfitted with devices, shields, and arrows, hurry, come running, the warriors are dying; they have died, perished, been annihilated, o Mexica warriors!" Thereupon there were war cries, shouting, and beating of hands against lips. The warriors quickly came outfitted, bunched together, carrying arrows and shields. Then the fighting began; they shot at them with barbed darts, spears, and tridents, and they hurled darts with broad obsidian points at them. A cloud of yellow reeds spread over the Spaniards.

Source: James Lockhart, ed. and trans. *We People Here: Nahuatl Accounts of the Conquest of Mexico*, 132–136 (Berkeley: University of California Press, 1993).

A Nahua Account of the Noche Triste, Florentine Codex, ca. 1550s (Excerpt)

Following the 1520 Tóxcatl massacre, Pedro de Alvarado and his small Spanish force came under siege in Tenochtitlán. Hernando Cortés and 266 of his men were absent, having left the city to engage the forces of Pánfilo de Narváez, who had been sent from Cuba to arrest Cortés. However, Cortés managed to capture Narváez in a surprise attack, and he convinced most of Narváez's men to return with him to Tenochtitlán to resume the conquest. With his forces replenished (1,300 Spaniards and 200 Tlaxcalans), Cortés was permitted to reenter Tenochtitlán unimpeded. However, he and his men soon found themselves trapped and under attack. Unable to withstand the siege, the Spaniards attempted to escape the city during a strong rainstorm, late at night on June 30, 1520. The Mexica (Aztecs) discovered them, however, and attacked them as they fled on the causeway. Only a portion of the group—which included Cortés—was able to reach the western shore of the lake alive. In total, 860 Spaniards and at least 1,000 Tlaxcalans were killed before the survivors finally reached Tlaxcala five days later. Spanish chroniclers would later refer to this event as the Noche Triste, or "night of sorrows."

Twenty-fourth chapter, where it is said how the Spaniards and Tlaxcalans came out and fled from Mexico by night.

When night had fallen and midnight had come, the Spaniards came out. They formed up, along with all the Tlaxcalans. The Spaniards went ahead, and the Tlaxcalans were following, bringing up the rear, like their wall of protection. [The Spaniards] went carrying a wooden platform [or platforms]; they laid it down at a canal and crossed over on it.

At this time it was drizzling and sprinkling, the rain was gently dripping down. They were able to cross some other canals, at Tecpantzinco, Tzapotla, and Atenchicalco. But when they got to Mixcoatechialtitlan, at the fourth canal, there they were seen coming out. It was a woman fetching water who saw them; then she shouted, saying, "O Mexica, come running, your enemies have come out, they have emerged secretly!" Then another person shouted, on top of [the temple of] Huitzilopochtli; his crying spread everywhere, everyone heard it. He said, "O warriors, o Mexica, your enemies are coming out, let everyone hasten with the war boats and on the roads!"

When it was heard, there was a clamor. Everyone scrambled; the operators of the war boats hastened and paddled hard, hitting one another's boats as they went in the direction of Mictlantonco and Macuilcuitlapilco. The war boats came upon them from both directions; the war boats of the Tenochca and the war boats of the Tlatelolca converged on them. And some people went on foot, going straight to Nonoalco, heading toward Tlacopan to try to cut them off there. Then the war-boat people hurled barbed darts at the Spaniards; from both sides the darts fell on them. But the Spaniards also shot at the Mexica, shooting back with iron bolts and guns. There were deaths on both sides. Spaniards and Tlaxcalans were hit, and Mexica were hit.

When the Spaniards reached Tlaltecayoacan, where the Tolteca canal is, it was as though they had fallen off a precipice; they all fell and dropped in, the Tlaxcalans, the people of Tliliuhquitepec, and the Spaniards, along with the horses, and some women. The canal was completely full of them, full to the very top. And those who came last just passed and crossed over on people, on bodies.

When they reached Petlacalco, where there was yet another canal, they passed gently, slowly, gradually, with caution, on the wooden platform. There they restored themselves, took their breath, regained their vigor. When they reached Popotlan, it dawned, light came. They began to go along with spirit, they went heading into the distance.

Then the Mexica went shouting at them, surrounding them, hovering about them. They captured some Tlaxcalans as they went, and some Spaniards died. Also Mexica and Tlatelolca were killed; there was death on both sides. They drove and pursued [the Spaniards] to Tlacopan. And when they had driven them to Tiliuhcan, to Xocotliiyohuican, at Xoxocotla, Chimalpopoca, son of Moteucçoma, died in battle. They came upon him lying hit by a barbed dart and struck [by some hand weapon]. At the same place died Tlaltecatzin, a Tepaneca lord who had been guiding the Spaniard, pointing out the way for them, conducting them, showing them the road.

Then they crossed the Tepçolatl (a small river); they forded and went over the water at Tepçolac. Then they went up to Acueco and stopped at Otoncalpolco, [where] wooden walls or barricades were in the courtyard. There they all took a rest and caught their breath, there they restored themselves. There the people of Teocalhueyacan came to meet them and guide them.

Source: James Lockhart, ed. and trans. *We People Here: Nahuatl Accounts of the Conquest of Mexico*, 154–156 (Berkeley: University of California Press, 1993).

A Nahua Account of the Smallpox Epidemic, Florentine Codex, ca. 1550s (Excerpt)

The following document, from chapter 29 of book 12 of the Florentine Codex, records the spread of a smallpox epidemic that struck Central Mexico between October and December of 1520. Among the many victims (some have suggested that the epidemic claimed 40 percent of Central Mexico's population in just one year) was the new Aztec ruler who followed Montezuma, Cuitláhuac.

Twenty-ninth chapter, where it is said how, at the time the Spaniards left Mexico, there came an illness of pustules of which many local people died; it was called "the great rash" [smallpox].

Before the Spaniards appeared to us, first an epidemic broke out, a sickness of pustules. It began in Tepeilhuitl. Large bumps spread on people; some were entirely covered. They spread everywhere, on the face, the head, the chest, etc. [The disease] brought great desolation; a great many died of it. They could no longer walk about, but lay in their dwellings and sleeping places, no longer able to move or stir. They were unable to change position, to stretch out on their sides or face down, or raise their heads. And when they made a motion, they called out loudly. The pustules that covered people caused great desolation; very many people died of them, and many just starved to death; starvation reigned, and no one took care of others any longer.

On some people, the pustules appeared only far apart, and they did not suffer greatly, nor did many of them die of it. But many people's faces were spoiled by it, their faces and noses were made rough. Some lost an eye or were blinded.

This disease of pustules lasted a full sixty days; after sixty days it abated and ended. When people were convalescing and reviving, the pustules disease began to move in the direction of Chalco. And many were disabled or paralyzed by it, but they were not disabled forever. It broke out in Teotl eco, and it abated in Panquetzaliztli. The Mexica warriors were greatly weakened by it.

And when things were in this state, the Spaniards came, moving toward us from Tetzcoco. They appeared in the direction of Quauhtitlan and made a halt at Tlacopan. There they gave one another assignments and divided themselves. Pedro de Alvarado was made responsible for the road coming to Tlatelolco. The Marqués [Cortés] went and established himself in Coyoacan, which became his responsibility, along with the road coming from Acachinanco to Tenochtitlán, for the Marqués considered the Tenochca great and valiant warriors.

And it was right in Nextlatilco, or in Ilyacac, that war first began. Then [the Spaniards] quickly reached Nonoalco, and the warriors came pursuing them. None of the Mexica died; then the Spaniards retreated. The warriors fought in boats; the war-boat people shot at the Spaniards, and their arrows sprinkled down on them. Then [the main force of the Mexica] entered [Nonoalco]. Thereupon the Marqués sent [his men] toward the Tenochca, following the Acachinanco road. Many times they skirmished, and the Mexica went out to face them.

Source: James Lockhart, ed. and trans. *We People Here: Nahuatl Accounts of the Conquest of Mexico*, 180–184 (Berkeley: University of California Press, 1993).

Spanish and Indigenous Voices in the Conquest of Peru

The first document in this section records one of the most dramatic episodes in the conquest of the Inca Empire, namely the capture of the Inca ruler Atahualpa. It is told from the perspective of the Spanish soldier-chronicler Pedro de Cieza de León. Cieza was not present at the time of Atahualpa's capture, but his account, written more than three decades after the events it describes, is still one of the most important texts for early colonial Peru.

Cieza's account is then followed by a remarkable indigenous text, written by Titu Cusi Yupanqui, the eldest of Manco Inca, the ruler installed by the Spanish after Atahualpa's execution. In this excerpt, Tuti Cusi records two speeches that he claimed his father delivered before his death.

The final document in this section is an incredible letter written by a disgruntled conquistador to Spain's King Philip II. The letter's author, Lope de Aguirre, condemns King Philip for not rewarding those who fought and suffered in His Majesty's service. Aguirre then explains his reasons for rebelling against the Crown and his intentions to conquer Peru for himself and his followers.

Pedro de Cieza de León, *Crónica del Perú*, ca. 1554 (Excerpt)

Born in Llerena, Spain, sometime between 1518 and 1522, Pedro de Cieza de León was still a young boy when he left his family in early June 1535 and journeyed across the Atlantic. After a brief stay on the island of Hispaniola, Cieza de León sailed to Cartagena (present-day Colombia). From 1535 until his return to Llerena in 1552, Cieza de León traveled extensively throughout Colombia, Ecuador, Peru, and Bolivia. He took copious notes on his journeys and interviewed Spanish veterans of the initial conquest campaigns, as well as Inca lords and indigenous informants who survived the initial conquest of Peru. From his personal experiences and his detailed interviews, Cieza de León drafted one of the finest chronicles of the 16th century, Crónica del Perú. *Initially, Cieza planned to write a four-part history of Peru; however, his death in 1554 prevented him from completing the entire chronicle. Nevertheless, Cieza's remarkable history remains one of the most important accounts of the conquest and early settlement of the Andean region of South America.*

In the brief excerpt below, Cieza records one of the most dramatic episodes in the conquest of Peru, the capture of the Inca Atahualpa. In November 1532, a small band of 168 Spanish conquistadores, led by Francisco Pizarro, marched into the northern Andes of Peru, thus initiating the conquest of the Inca Empire. After reaching the city of Cajamarca, Pizarro sent two squads, headed by Hernando de Soto and Hernando Pizarro, to the camp where the Inca Atahualpa and his army rested. Atahualpa and his forces had just emerged victorious in a lengthy and brutal civil war between Atahualpa and his half brother Huáscar. Using Indian translators who had been seized during one of Pizarro's earlier expeditions to Peru, the emissaries conversed with Atahualpa, who agreed to visit the Spaniards in Cajamarca.

The following afternoon, November 16, Atahualpa went down into the town, carried on a litter and accompanied by several thousand bodyguards. Pizarro sent out Father Vicente de Valverde, who explained to Atahualpa (through the indigenous translator named Felipillo by the Spaniards) the requerimiento, *a legalism that asserted Spain's sovereignty over the New World by way of papal donation and that encouraged the indigenous peoples to become Christians. Never having seen a book, Atahualpa asked to see a Bible carried by the priest but haughtily threw it on the ground when he could make nothing of it. At that point, the priest ran toward the*

Spaniards, who were hidden in buildings around the square. They fired upon Atahualpa's men and then stormed out, the horses trampling the Inca's escort. Terrified Indians tried desperately to escape from the walled square but were cut down. In the end, Pizarro himself captured Atahualpa and placed the Inca ruler under house arrest. Thus began the conquest of the Incas.

☙❧

CHAPTER XLV
About how Atahualpa entered the plaza where the Christians were, and how he was seized and many of his people were killed and wounded

Don Francisco Pizarro had ordered that General Hernando Pizarro and the captains Soto, Mena and Belalcázar and the Spaniards on horseback ready for battle should be prepared to charge at the enemy because Atahualpa had sent word that they should be hidden and even the horses tied up. They put some small guns in a high place designated for watching games or making sacrifices, so that Pedro de Candia could discharge them when a certain signal, agreed upon by all of them, was given. At that [signal], the horsemen and footmen were to boldly charge, and about only fifteen shield bearers would stay with the governor. They would prudently allow some squadrons and Atahualpa to enter the plaza, but then they would take the two gates, and if [the Indians] wanted war, they would lance and capture those that they could. But they also discussed that if Atahualpa came in peace, they would uphold it.

[Atahualpa] began to depart from where he had halted; in a short time all the tents were raised, and the people kept the order and arrangement of their squadrons, many with hidden arms, as has been written. They carried large drums, many trumpets, and their banners were raised; it certainly was a marvelous sight to see such an army mobilized for so few. Every so often an Indian came to survey the condition of the Spaniards. Each one would return joyfully, [saying] that they all hid out of fear in the houses, and only their captain with very few men were visible. When Atahualpa heard this, his pride grew further, and he seemed fiercer than he later appeared. Most of his men urged him to go or give them permission to go and tie up the Christians, who did not emerge, already fearful because they saw their strength. When [Atahualpa] arrived within a crossbow shot of the lodgings, some Indians went ahead, surveying more carefully how our men were. They saw what they had heard: not a horse or a Christian other than the governor with those few could be seen. They talked about [the Christians] as if they already were prisoners in their power.

They began to enter the plaza. When the squadrons reached the center of it, they formed a very large circle. Atahualpa entered after many of his captains and their people had done so. He passed all of them before his litter was set down. Because he was in the middle of the people, he stood up on top of the platform. He spoke loudly that they should be brave, that they should take care that no Christian escape them, or any horse, and that they should know that [the Christians] were hiding in fear. He reminded them how they had always

vanquished many people and nations, serving under his and his father's banners. He assured them that if because of their sins the Christians should prevail against them, it would be the end of their pleasures and religious beliefs because they would do with them what they had heard had been done with those of Coaque and Puná. He took one banner in his hand and vigorously waved it.

When Pizarro saw that Atahualpa had halted in the plaza, he ordered Friar Vicente de Valverde, a Dominican, to go to Atahualpa and prod him to come because it was already so late that the sun was about to set and to admonish him to put down the weapons and come in peace. The friar took along Felipillo so that his cause would be understood by Atahualpa. When he reached him, he told him what has been said and that he was a priest of God who preached His law and strove whenever possible for peace rather than war because that pleased God very much. While he was saying this, he held his breviary in his hands. Atahualpa listened to this as something of a mockery. Through the interpreter he understood everything well. He asked Friar Valverde for his breviary. He placed it in his hands, somewhat disconcerted from finding himself among such people. Atahualpa looked at it and looked at it again, and he leafed through it once or twice. Annoyed with so many pages, he flung it into the air without knowing what it was because to have understood it, they should have told him in another way, but the friars never preach around here, except where there is no danger or raised lances. And looking at Friar Vicente and Felipillo, [Atahualpa] said to tell Pizarro that he would not move from the place where he was until they return and restitute to him all the gold, silver, stones, cloth, Indian men and women, and everything else that they had stolen. With this answer, having collected the breviary, the skirts of his habit flying high, [the friar] rushed back to Pizarro, telling him that this tyrant Atahualpa was like a wounded dog and that they should attack him.

When the friar left, according to what they tell us now, in order to provoke his people's anger Atahualpa told them that the Christians—in contempt of him and after having raped so many women and killed so many men and pillaged whatever they could without shame or fear—were asking for peace with the intention to gain supremacy. They let out loud cries and sounded their instruments. The rest of the squadrons had arrived, but they did not enter the plaza because it was so full; they remained next to it on another plain. When Pizarro learned what had happened to Friar Vicente with Atahualpa, and realizing that there was no time to spare, he raised a towel, the signal to move against the Indians. Candia fired the shots, a novelty for them and frightening, but even more so were the horses and the horsemen who loudly shouting "Santiago, Santiago!" came charging out of the lodgings against the enemies, who were stunned and did not make use of the artifices they had planned. They did not fight; rather, they looked where they could flee. The horsemen entered among them, quickly defeating them. Many were killed and wounded.

With the footmen, who fought with buckler and sword, the governor pushed toward the litter where there was a group of lords. They gave them some slashes that would sever the hand or arm of those who held the litter, who then with great courage would hold it with the other, wishing to protect their Inca from death or prison. A foot soldier, Miguel Estete, native of Santo Domingo de la Calzada, arrived—the first one to lay a hand on Atahualpa in order to seize him. Then Alonso de Mesa arrived. Pizarro, shouting that they should not kill [Atahualpa], came next to the litter. Because there were so many Indians, they hurt each other more; the horses fell between them everywhere, and they had neither the spirit nor the inclination to fight; they were found wanting that day, or God wished to blind them. They wanted to leave the plaza, but could not because so many filled it. They did a deed never seen or heard; in one furious throng they went for one part of the bulwark that surrounded the plaza, and because the wall was wide, they forced it with such vehemence that they broke it and made way to flee.

They wailed loudly. They were shocked by what they were seeing. They asked each other if it was real or if they were dreaming. And the Inca, where was he? More than two thousand Indians died, and many were wounded. [The Spaniards] went out of the plaza in pursuit to where Atahualpa's camp was. A heavy rain came, which was sufficient relief for the Indians. The Lord Atahualpa was taken by the governor to the lodging, and he ordered that he should be given full honors and good treatment. Some of the Christians shouted to the Indians to come and see Atahualpa because they would find him alive and well and without any wounds—a joyous news for all of them. Thus, more than five thousand Indians without weapons were collected that night; the others dispersed throughout the district of Cajamarca, proclaiming the great misfortune that befell them and shedding many tears for the capture of the lord whom they loved so much.

All the Christians came together and assembled, and Pizarro ordered that they should fire a shot so they could hear what he wanted. There were great spoils of gold and silver vessels, cups of thousands of shapes, cloth of great value, and other jewels of gold and precious stones. Many principal ladies of royal lineage or of *caciques* of the kingdom became captives—some very lovely and beautiful, with long hair, dressed according to their fashion, which is of an elegant style. They also held many *mamaconas*, who are the virgins in their temples. The loot that these 160 men could have had was so great that if they had learned about it without killing Atahualpa and had asked him for more gold and silver, although what he gave was a lot, there would not have been in the world anyone who could equal them. None of the Spaniards had been in danger. They all believed it was a miracle that God allowed it to transpire as it did, and therefore they gave Him many thanks for it. The defeat and capture of Atahualpa took place in the province of Cajamarca, in the jurisdiction of what is today the city of Trujillo, on Friday, the day of the Holy Cross of May of the year of the Lord fifteen hundred and thirty-three years.

Source: Pedro de Cieza de León. *The Discovery and Conquest of Peru*, edited and translated by Alexandra Parma Cook and Noble David Cook, 209–213 (Durham, N.C.: Duke University Press, 1998).

Titu Cusi Yupanqui, *History of How the Spaniards Arrived in Peru*, 1570 (Excerpt)

The following account is a brief excerpt from a 1570 manuscript entitled Relación de cómo los españoles entraron en Pirú (History of How the Spaniards Arrived in Peru). *The account, written by Titu Cusi Yupanqui, is one of only a few colonial texts authored by a native Andean. Titu Cusi was born around the time that Francisco Pizarro initiated the conquest of the Inca Empire in 1532. He was the eldest son of Manco Inca, whom Spanish conquistadores installed as a puppet ruler after they executed Atahualpa in 1533. At the time, Manco Inca was about 20 years old. Manco was a son of the great Inca ruler Huayna Cápac, whose death had touched off a civil war within the Inca Empire between two of Manco's half brothers, Atahualpa and Huáscar.*

Initially, Manco struggled to win the support of his own people. They knew the Spaniards controlled him, and some wondered if another of Huayna Cápac's sons might better defend the people. A few conspired against him, and Manco persuaded Diego de Almagro, one of the Spanish leaders, to have them murdered. However, despite his initial alliance with the Spanish, Manco soon began to resent the Spaniards' abuse of the Indians and particularly of himself. He therefore conspired to overthrow and expel the Spaniards. On April 18, 1536, Manco Inca escaped from Cuzco and raised a huge army. The Incas besieged Cuzco and ambushed Spanish relief expeditions that had been sent from Lima.

Although Manco nearly captured Cuzco, the siege ultimately failed, and his army disintegrated. He withdrew with several thousand followers northwest of Cuzco to Vilcabamba, where he established a new Inca state. On occasion, Manco negotiated with the Spaniards; he even allowed several Spaniards to take refuge at Vilcabamba after they had murdered Francisco Pizarro in revenge for the execution of Diego de Almagro. In 1544, hoping to please the new Spanish viceroy, Blasco Núñez de Vela, the Almagristas murdered Manco while playing quoits.

It is unclear why Titu Cusi wrote this account, but he may have been negotiating with Spanish officials to be recognized as the head of the Inca dynasty. Much of the account chronicles the breakdown of the initial alliance between Francisco Pizarro and Manco Inca. Below, Titu Cusi records the speech that Manco Inca allegedly delivered to his captains shortly before his death. It is followed by Titu Cusi's account of the speech his father gave him shortly before his death.

Speech that Manco Inca made to his captains when he was near death. He said:

"Sons, you see me in this way because I trusted these Spanish people, especially the seven who guarded me for so long and whom I treated like sons, as you have seen. And they have repaid my good treatment by doing this to me! I do not think that I will escape from this. By your very lives, remember what I have told you and admonished you about so many times in Cusco, in Tambo, and in all of the other places where you have been gathered together in response to my call and in all the places where you have gone with me. I do not want to go into it now, since I know that you all remember what I have said. The pain will not permit it and there is no reason to bother you with it.

"I charge you with looking after my son Titu Cusi Yupanqui. You know he is the light of my eyes and that I consider this boy not just a son, but also a brother because of his great capacity for understanding. So I have charged him to look after, and be responsible for, all of you and any children I have. I beg you to treat him in the same way that you have treated me. I am so impressed with him that I know he will thank you and pay you well for it. Therefore, call him to me here so that I can give him my blessing and tell him what he must do."

Speech that Manco Inca made to his son at the moment of his death

"My beloved son, you can see how I am, and so I do not have to say any more about my pain in words since deeds have already told the tale. Do not cry. If someone should cry, it should be me, if I could, for having gotten myself into this fix, for believing so firmly in such people as this and treating them so well, even though they were undeserving. As you know, those men came here fleeing from their companions because of crimes they must have committed where they had come from. I took them in and favored them with the heart of a father. Look well: I order you never, ever, to enter into any kind of accord with people such as this, so that what happened to me will not happen to you. Do not allow them to enter your land, even if they approach you with sweet words. Their words deceived me and will deceive you, too, if you believe them.

"I commend your brothers and sisters and your mother to your care, so that you will look after them and take care of them and favor them in the same way I would treat you. See that you do not make my bones suffer by treating your siblings and mother badly, because you know that they will feel it greatly if you do.

"I commend these poor Indians to your care as well. Look after them so far as is reasonable. Remember that they have followed me and protected me and helped me in all my times of need, leaving their lands and environs out of love for me. So do not work them too hard, or harass them, or scold or punish them without reason, because in doing so you will anger the Viracochan. I have ordered them to respect you and honor you as lord in my place, since you are my firstborn son and heir to my kingdom and this is my last wish. I rely on their goodness, and expect them to honor and respect you as their lord and not to do anything other than what I have ordered them or what you would tell them." Then my father died and left me in the town of Vitcos. . . .

Source: Titu Cusi Yupanqui. *History of How the Spaniards Arrived in Peru*, edited and translated by Catherine Julien, 141–143 (Indianapolis, Ind.: Hackett Publishing Co., 2006).

Lope de Aguirre, Letter to King Philip II of Spain, 1561

Born in the Basque town of Oñate ca. 1514, Lope de Aguirre was one of thousands of early 16th-century Spaniards who journeyed to the Americas in search of fame and fortune; however, Aguirre's story is one of frustration, bitterness, and anger. In 1560, an aging Aguirre joined Pedro de Ursúa's ill-fated expedition to search for the land of El Dorado, a kingdom east of Peru rumored to be filled with unimaginable riches. Aguirre joined a force of more than 300 Spaniards and scores of African slaves and indigenous carriers. After months of suffering in the Amazon's blistering heat, the party found no evidence of El Dorado. Then on New Year's Day of 1561, as frustrations mounted, Aguirre joined with a dozen other armed men and stormed Ursúa's tent and murdered the expedition leader. Aguirre's revolt against the Crown had begun, and over the next six months, another 60 members of the expedition were killed. The survivors sailed down the Amazon River and eventually reached the island of Margarita on July 20, 1561. There, Aguirre and his close followers plotted to return to Peru and conquer it for themselves.

Aguirre never reached Peru, however. With his rebellion collapsing from within and Spanish forces closing in to capture him, Aguirre drafted a remarkable letter to King Phillip II, in which he denounced the Spanish ruler for failing to recognize and reward those who had suffered so greatly in the service to the Crown and who never received their due compensation. The document that follows is a translation of Aguirre's letter to the king.

Shortly before his death, Aguirre murdered his mestiza daughter, Elvira, an act he justified as merciful to spare her from the abuse she would endure as the daughter of a rebel. Soon thereafter, on October 27, 1561, Aguirre was shot; his corpse was beheaded, quartered, and put on public display as a warning to other potential rebels.

∽∾∽

To King Philip, the Spaniard, son of Charles the Invincible: From Lope de Aguirre, your lesser vassal, old Christian, of middling parents but fortunately of noble blood, native of the Basque country of the kingdom of Spain, citizen of the town of Onate.

In my youth I crossed the sea to the land of Peru to gain fame, lance in hand, and to fulfill the obligation of all good men. In 24 years I have done you great service in Peru, in conquests of the Indians, in founding towns, and especially in battles and encounters fought in your name, always to the best of my power and ability, without requesting of your officials pay nor assistance, as can be seen in your royal records.

I firmly believe, most excellent King and lord, that to me and my companions you have been nothing but cruel and ungrateful. I also believe that those who write to you from this land deceive you, because of the great distance.

I demand of you, King, that you do justice and right by the good vassals you have in this land, even though I and my companions (whose names I will give later), unable to suffer further the cruelties of your judges, viceroy, and governors, have resolved to obey you no longer. Denaturalizing ourselves from our land, Spain, we make the most cruel war against you that our power can sustain and endure. Believe, King and lord, we have done this because we can no longer tolerate the great oppression and unjust punishments of your ministers who, to make places for their sons and dependents have usurped and robbed our fame, life, and honor. It is a pity, King, the bad treatment you have given us.

I am lame in the right leg from the arquebus wounds I received in the battle of Chuquinga, fighting with marshall Alonzo de Alvarado, answering your call against Francisco Hernandez Girón, rebel from your service as I and my companions are presently and will be until death, because we in this land now know how cruel you are, how you break your faith and your word, and thus we in this land give your promises less credence than to the books of Martin Luther.

Your viceroy the marquis of Canete hanged Martin de Robles, a man distinguished in your service; and the brave Tomas Vasquez, conquistador of Peru; and the ill fated Alonso Dias, who worked more in the discoveries of this kingdom than the scouts of Moses in the desert; and Piedrahita, a good captain who fought many battles in your service. In Pucara they gave you victory, and if they had not, Francisco Hernandez would now be the king of Peru. Do not give much credence to the claims your judges make of services performed, because it is a great myth, unless they call having spent 800,000 pesos of your royal treasury for their vices and evil deeds, a service. Punish them as evildoers, as such they certainly are.

Look here, King of Spain! Do not be cruel and ungrateful to your vassals, because while your father and you stayed in Spain without the slightest bother, your vassals, at the price of their blood and fortune, have given you all the kingdoms and holding you have in these parts. Beware, King and lord, that you cannot take, under the title of legitimate king, any benefit from this land where you risked nothing, without first giving due gratification to those who have labored and sweated in it.

I am certain there are few kings in hell because there are few kings, but if there were many none would go to heaven. Even in hell you would be worse than Lucifer, because you all thirst after human blood. But I don't marvel nor make much of you. For certain, I and my 200 arquebus-bearing Marañones, conquistadores and *hidalgos*, swear solemnly to God that we will not leave a minister of yours alive, because I already know how far your clemency reaches. Today we consider ourselves the luckiest men alive, because we are in these parts of the Indies, with faith in God's commandments full and uncorrupted as Christians, maintaining all that is preached by the holy mother church of Rome, and we intend, though sinners in life, to achieve martyrdom through God's commandments.

Upon leaving the Amazon river, called the Maranon, on an island inhabited by Christians called Margarita, I saw some reports from Spain regarding the great schism of Lutherans there, which caused us to be frightened and surprised. In our company there was a German named Monteverde, and I ordered him cut to pieces. Destiny rewards the prudent. Believe this, excellent Prince: Wherever we are we ensure that all live perfectly in the Christian faith.

The dissolution of the priests is so great in these parts that I think it would be well that they feel your wrath and punishment, because there is now none among them who sees himself as less than governor. Look here, King, do not believe what they might tell you, because the tears that they shed before your royal person is so that they can come here to command. If you want to know the life they lead here, it is to deal in merchandise, seek and acquire temporal goods, and sell the Sacraments of the Church for a price. They are enemies of the poor, uncharitable, ambitious, gluttonous, and arrogant, so that even the lowest of the priests tries to command and govern all these lands. Correct this, King and lord, because from these things and bad examples faith is not impressed upon the natives. Furthermore, if this dissolution of the priests is not stopped, there will be no shortage of scandal.

If I and my companions, by the correct position we have taken, are determined to die, for this and for other things that have happened, singular King, you are to blame, for not duly considering the labor of your vassals and for not thinking of what you owe them. If you do not look out for your vassals, and your judges do not take care of this, you certainly will fail in government. Certainly there is no need to present witnesses, but simply to point out that each of your judges has 4,000 pesos of salary, 8,000 pesos in expenses, and after three years in office each has 60,000 pesos saved, along with properties and possessions! Despite all this we would be willing to serve them as we do, except that for our sins they want us to drop to our knees wherever we are and worship them like Nebuchadnezzar. This is insufferable. Just because I am an unfortunate man made lame in your service (and my companions long and weary in the same) I should not fail to advise you never to trust your conscience to these learned persons. It is in your royal interest to watch out for them, as they spend all their time planning the marriages of their children, and care for nothing else. The common refrain among them is: "To the left and to the right, I possess all in my sight."

The friars do not want to bury poor Indians, and they are lodged in the best estates in Peru. The life they lead is bitter and burdensome, as each one has as a penance a dozen young women in his kitchen, and as many boys engaged in fishing, hunting partridges, and bringing fruit! They get a share of everything. In Christian faith I swear, King and lord, that if you do not remedy the evils of this land, divine punishment will come upon you. I tell you this to let you know the truth, even though I and mine neither expect nor want mercy from you.

Oh, how sad that a great Caesar and Emperor, your father, should conquer with the power of Spain the great Germany, and should spend so much money from these Indies discovered by us, and that you should not concern yourself with our old age and weariness enough to provide for our daily bread.

You know that we know in these parts, excellent King and lord, that you conquered Germany with arms, and Germany has conquered Spain with vices. We over here are happier with just corn and water, to be removed from such a bad irony. Let those who suffer such an irony keep their reward. Let wars spread where they may, and where men take them. Never, no matter what adversity might come upon us, will we cease to be subject to the teachings of the Holy Mother Church of Rome.

We cannot believe, excellent King and lord, that you would be so cruel to such good vassals as you have in these parts. Your judges must be acting this way without your consent. I say this, excellent King, because two leagues from the city of Kings [Lima], there was discovered near the sea a lake where there were some fish God permitted to exist there. Your evil judges and officials, to profit from the fish for their pleasures and vices, leased them in your name, giving us to understand, as though we were fools, that this was done by your will. If this is so, master, let us catch some of the fish, because we worked to discover it, and because the King of Castile has no need for the 400 pesos they leased it for. Illustrious King, we do not ask for grants in Cordoba or Valladolid, nor in any part of Spain, which is your patrimony. Deign to feed the weary and poor with the fruits and proceeds from this land. Remember, King and lord, that God is the same for all, and the same justice, reward, heaven, and hell.

In the year 1559 the marquis of Canete entrusted the expedition of the river of the Amazons to Pedro de Ursua, Navarrese, or rather, a Frenchman. He delayed the building of the boats until the year 1560 in the province of the Motilones, in Peru. The Indians are called Motilones because they wear their head shaved. These boats were made in the wet country, and upon launching most of them came to pieces. We made rafts, left the horses and supplies, and took off down the river at great risk to our persons. We then encountered the most powerful rivers of Peru, and it seemed to us to be a fresh water sea. We traveled 300 leagues from the point of launching.

This bad governor was so perverse and vicious and miserable that we could not tolerate it, and it was impossible to put up with his evil ways. Since I have a stake in the matter, excellent King and lord, I will say only that we killed him; certainly a very serious thing. We then raised a young gentleman of Seville named Don Fernando de Guzman to be our king, and we made an oath to him as such, as your royal person will see from the signatures of all those who were in this, who remain in the island of Margarita, in these Indies. They appointed me their field commander, and because I did not consent to their insults and evil deeds they tried to kill me, and I killed the new king, the captain of his guard, the lieutenant-general, his majordomo, his chaplain, a woman in league against me, a knight of Rhodes, an admiral, two ensigns, and six other of his allies. It was my intention to carry this war through and die in it, for the cruelties your ministers practice on us, and I again appointed captains and a sergeant major. They tried to kill me, and I hung them all.

We went along our route down the Maranon river while all these killings and bad events were taking place. It took us ten and a half months to reach the mouth of the river, where it enters the sea. We traveled a good hundred days, and traveled 1,500 leagues. It is a large and fearsome river, with 80 leagues of fresh water at the mouth. It is very deep, and for 800 leagues along its banks it is deserted, with no towns, as your majesty will see from the true report we have made. Along the route we took there are more than 6,000 islands. God only knows how we escaped from such a fearsome lake! I advise you, King and lord, not to attempt nor allow a fleet to be sent to this ill-fated river, because in Christian faith I swear, King and lord, that if a hundred thousand men come none will escape, because the stories are false and in this river there is nothing but despair, especially for those newly arrive from Spain.

The captains and officers with me at present, and who promise to die in this demand like pitiful men are: Juan Jeronimo de Espinola Ginoves, admiral; Juan Gomez, Cristobal Garcia, captain of infantry, both Andaluz; mounted captain Diego Tirado, Andaluz, from whom your judges, King and lord, with great injury, took Indians he had earned with his lance; captain of my guard Roberto de Sosaya and his ensign Nuflo Hernandez, Valencian; Juan Lopez de Ayala, from Cuenca, our paymaster; general ensign Blas Gutierrez, conquistador for 27 years; Juan Ponce, ensign, native of Seville; Custodio Hernandez, ensign, Portuguese; Diego de Torres, ensign, Navarre; sergeant Pedro Gutierrez Viso and Diego de Figueroa; Cristobal de Rivas, conquistador, Pedro de Rojas, Andaluz; Juan de Saucedo, mounted ensign; Bartolome Sanchez Paniagua, our lawyer; Diego Sanchez Bilbao, supply; Garcia Navarro, inspector general, and many other hidalgos of this league. We pray to God our Lord that your fortune ever be increased against the Turk and the Frenchman, and all others who wish to make war on you in those parts. In these, God grant that we might obtain with our arms the reward by right due us, but which you have denied.

Son of your loyal Basque vassals, and I, rebel until death against you for your ingratitude.

Lope de Aguirre, the Wanderer

Source: Thomas H. Holloway. "Whose Conquest Is This Anyway? *Aguirre, the Wrath of God*." In *Based on a True Story: Latin American History at the Movies*, edited by Donald F. Stevens, 39–44 (Wilmington, Del.: Scholarly Resources, 1997).

Views from Colombia and Brazil

The final two documents provide a brief look at two regions often ignored in studies of the early colonial period. The first document is a translation of a formal contract (capitulación) between the Spanish Crown and Don Pedro Fernández de Lugo. This contract granted Lugo the rights to explore and conquer Colombia's interior. Lugo's contract initiated one of the last major conquest expeditions in 16th-century South America, which was led by Gonzalo Jiménez de Quesada.

Finally, the primary source section ends with a remarkable text, originally written in French, about Brazil's Tupinambá Indians. The excerpt is taken from Jean de Léry's History of a Voyage to the Land of Brazil, *and records the nature of Tupinambá marriage rituals and practices, as well as the treatment of their children.*

Contract between Pedro Fernández de Lugo and the Spanish Crown, January 22, 1535

It is important to recognize that the Spanish Crown never possessed the resources to fund the exploration, conquest, or settlement of the New World; instead, it negotiated private agreements with individuals or corporations, offering financial rewards, offices, and titles to those who organized, equipped, and funded these early ventures. Over the course of the 16th century, the Crown entered into more than 70 of these private agreements, known in Spanish as capitulaciones. *Such private contracts helped push the boundaries of Spain's American possessions and, at the same time, mitigate the threat of Portuguese, French, and English expansion in the New World.*

Below is an example of one such contract, a 1535 agreement between the Spanish Crown and the governor of the Canary Islands, Pedro Fernández de Lugo. The agreement reveals a great deal about the expectations and motivations of Fernández de Lugo, his son, and the Crown. However, it must also be read with caution. In spite of his position as governor of the Canary Islands, Fernández de Lugo was not in a position to fund the entire armada on his own. In order to finance this ambitious venture, he needed partners. Thus, while Alonso de Lugo traveled to Seville to recruit men, gather equipment, and negotiate the armada's costly transportation across the Atlantic, Pedro Fernández de Lugo worked to secure additional financing. In May 1535, he reached an agreement with two Italian merchants, both residents of Tenerife, to split the costs of the armada. Juan Alberto Gerardini and Cristóbal Francesquini agreed to divide equally the expenses of the Lugo venture, in return for an equal share of future profits over the next three years in the Santa María region (in modern-day Colombia).

At the end of November 1535, after more than seven months of careful and costly preparations, Pedro Fernández de Lugo's armada departed from the port of Santa Cruz, on the island of Tenerife. In total, the armada consisted of no fewer than 10 ships, which together carried somewhere between 1,000 and 1,200 passengers (among them a small number of women and black slaves). After a brief stop on the island of Hispaniola to gather additional supplies, the armada continued to Santa Marta, where it arrived to great fanfare and celebration on January 2, 1536. The new governor wasted no time in his effort to recoup the expenses he had incurred over the previous months. After several moderately profitable campaigns into nearby provinces, Fernández de Lugo selected his lieutenant general, Gonzalo Jiménez de Quesada, to command an expedition up the Magdalena River. In early April, just three months after his armada had arrived in Santa Marta, Fernández de Lugo sent the Jiménez expedition into the Colombian interior to search for an overland route to Peru, rich new lands to conquer, and a route to the South Sea (Pacific Ocean).

Unfortunately for Fernández de Lugo, most of the spoils of the conquest of Santa Marta found their way to other pockets. In fact, Fernández de Lugo never even learned the fate of the expedition he had worked so hard to organize and fund. On October 15, 1536, just six months after the Jiménez expedition had departed, Santa Marta's elderly governor was dead.

⌒⌒⌒

First, I hereby grant license and authority to don Pedro Fernández de Lugo, *adelantado* of the Canary Islands, on our behalf and in our name and in the name of the Royal Crown of Castile, to conquer, pacify and colonize the lands and provinces still left to be conquered, pacified and colonized in the Province of Santa Marta. The Province of Santa Marta extends westward to the borders of the Province of Cartagena, whose conquest and governorship we have entrusted to Pedro de Heredia, and eastward to the borders of the Province of Venezuela, whose conquest and governorship has been entrusted to the Germans Bartolomé and Antonio Welser. From there, the Province of Santa Marta extends south all the way to the South Sea, provided that you do not enter the boundaries or jurisdictions of any other province that has been granted to any other governor.

In recognition of his obedient service on our behalf, and in order to pay him due honor, we promise to make the said *adelantado* our governor and captain general of Santa Marta and the towns within its borders for all the days of his life, with an annual salary of one million *maravedíes*, which he is to enjoy from the day he and his people set sail from one of the ports in the Canary Islands to carry out the conquest. The salary is to be paid from our royal revenues and taxes generated in the province. During his tenure as governor and captain general he is to colonize and conquer the territory; if this should not occur, we are not obligated to pay him anything whatsoever.

We want and we order that when it is our lord God's pleasure to take the *adelantado* don Pedro Fernández de Lugo from this present life, that you, Alonso Luis de Lugo should inherit the governorship and Captaincy General of the province for all the days of your life, with the annual salary of one million *maravedíes* in accordance with the same terms, and in the same manner, in which your father, the *adelantado*, holds it.

Furthermore, we grant the *adelantado* don Pedro Fernández de Lugo the title of our *adelantado* of the lands and provinces that are discovered and populated. Upon your father's death, you, don Alonso Luis de Lugo, are to inherit this title.

Furthermore, I give him license to construct, in accordance and agreement with our officials in the province, two fortresses within the borders of the territories discovered and colonized. These fortresses are to be built in locations that he and our royal officials consider necessary for the defense and pacification of the lands and provinces. And we grant him an annual salary of 75,000 *maravedíes* for the maintenance and occupancy of each fortress. These fortresses are to be built at his own expense; we are not obliged to pay for them, nor are any of the monarchs who follow us. Once our royal officials deem them fully operational, the salary for each fortress is to be paid from the fruits of the land.

Furthermore, you, don Alonso Luis de Lugo, on behalf of your father don Pedro Fernández de Lugo, have requested that we grant you a certain number of Indian vassals from the new lands and provinces that you happen to discover and pacify. As far as this request is concerned, we have decided to wait until we receive detailed reports about the nature of the new lands that you discover and colonize. In the meantime, in order to compensate you for your hardships and your services, we decree that you are to receive an annual share of one-twelfth of all benefits that pertain to the Crown, excluding revenues from lands already discovered and pacified. However, before you receive your share, you are to pay all the expenses and salaries incurred by our royal officials in the conquest.

Furthermore, in order to assist you with the costs of transporting the people necessary for the conquest, we will reward you with a payment of four thousand gold *ducados*, to be paid by our officials from the taxes and benefits that we receive from the lands and provinces conquered.

We give you permission to issue land grants to the residents and settlers of the lands and provinces that are conquered and colonized, in the same manner as our governors in other provinces of our Indies have done before, and continue to do.

We give license so that Lugo, or anyone else to whom he gives authority, can transport one hundred black slaves from our kingdom, or from the Kingdom of Portugal and Cape Verde Islands, to Santa Marta. At least one-third of these slaves must be females; and you shall be exempt from all applicable taxes that belong to us in such circumstances. However, should you sell them all, or even some of them, on the islands of Hispaniola, San Juan, or Cuba, or anywhere else for that matter, you will forfeit these tax exemptions, which then must be paid to our royal treasury.

We will send orders to grant *adelantado* Lugo permission, as is customary, to take as many as three ships currently docked in the Canary Islands. These ships, and their captains, must have some familiarity and knowledge of the Indies; and/or they must be willing to sail there. Furthermore, these vessels must be free of commitments to any other armada. And the owners of these vessels are to be paid a just fee.

One of the conditions of this agreement is that, as far as the pacification, conquest, settlement, and treatment of the Indians is concerned, your father, the *adelantado*, is required to follow and obey to the letter, all that is proclaimed in the laws and instructions that we have issued, and anything else that we decree in the future.

This agreement is made with your father, the said *adelantado*, on the condition that when he departs from the Canary Islands on this conquest and colonization, he takes with him any and all religious clergy that we assign to the task of instructing the native Indians of those lands in Our Holy Catholic Faith. He is not to carry out the conquest without them. And he is to pay the costs of their passage, their provisions, and all other necessary maintenance costs, in accordance with their character. He is to incur all of these expenses over the course of the entire voyage, without taking from them anything whatsoever. We entrust that he will do this and comply with our orders, as it serves both God and us; should he do differently, we will consider it a great disservice.

In accordance with the rights and laws of our kingdoms, when our subjects and the captains of our armies happen to capture some prince or lord from the lands where, under our orders, they are at war, the ransom collected from that lord or *cacique*, as well as all of his private possessions, belong to us. However, in consideration of the great hardships and difficulties that our subjects endure in the conquests of the Indies, and in order to reward them for their services and offer them some compensation, we declare and order that should you happen to take some cacique or lord captive, then his treasures of gold, silver, precious stones, and pearls that you acquire, either through ransom or in any other manner, that you give us a share of one-sixth. The remainder should be divided amongst the conquistadors, having first paid the royal-fifth tax. In the event that the said cacique or principal lord should die in battle, or later through the legal process, that we be given half of his belongings. This payment shall be issued before any of the costs incurred by our royal officials are reimbursed. The other half shall be divided amongst the conquistadors, once again after the royal-fifth is paid.

In the Villa de Madrid, 22-01-1535.

Source: J. Michael Francis. *Invading Colombia: Spanish Accounts of the Gonzalo Jiménez de Quesada Expedition of Conquest*, 29–33 (University Park: Pennsylvania State University Press, 2007).

Jean de Léry, *History of a Voyage to the Land of Brazil*, 1578 (Excerpt)

The 1494 Treaty of Tordesillas, which divided the New World between Spain and Portugal, certainly did not prevent other European powers from attempting to establish permanent footholds in the New World. For example, beginning early in the 16th century, French sailors and merchants actively engaged in trade up and down the Brazilian coast, where they exchanged European goods for brazilwood, highly valued in Europe for the red dye it produced. In 1555, after decades of trading ventures along the Brazilian coast, the French attempted to establish a permanent settlement in Brazil. A year later, a young Calvinist minister named Jean de Léry arrived in the French colony to preach the new faith to Brazil's Tupinambá Indians.

Jean de Léry was born in Burgandy, France, in 1534. In 1556, Léry was one of 14 Calvinist ministers who left Europe for Brazil to establish what became the first Protestant mission in the New World. His History of a Voyage to the Land of Brazil *was not completed and published until 1578, 20 years after Léry had returned from Brazil. At times fanciful and romantic, Léry's rich descriptions and keen observations about*

Tupinambá society make his chronicle among the most important and valuable primary accounts of Brazil's indigenous peoples in the 16th century. The lengthy chronicle, consisting of 22 chapters, addresses a wide range of subjects and themes, from geography, flora, and fauna to Tupinambá religious practices, warfare techniques and weapons, the treatment of military captives, as well as the practice of cannibalism. In the section that follows, Léry describes Tupinambá marriage practices, polygamy, adultery, and childhood. Léry died of the plague in France in 1613.

∽∞∽

CHAPTER XVII:
Of Marriage, Polygamy, and Degrees of Consanguinity Observed by the Savages; and of the Treatment of Their Little Children.

Now to touch on the marriage customs of our Americans. They observe only these three degrees of consanguinity: no one takes his mother, his sister, or his daughter as a wife, but an uncle may take his niece; aside from this, all the other degrees are of no concern to them. As for ceremonies, they have none, except that he who wants to take a wife, whether widow or maiden, after having ascertained that she is willing, will address himself to the father (or, if that is not possible, the nearest kinsman) and ask that she be given to him in marriage. If the answer is "Yes," then without further contract (for there is no profit in it for notaries) he will take her to wife. If, on the contrary, he is refused, he will desist without further ado. But note that since polygamy, that is, a plurality of wives, is common in their region, men may have as many as they please; in fact, they make a virtue out of a vice, so that those who have the greatest number are deemed the most valiant and bold. I have seen one who had eight, about whom he told tales in his own praise.

And what makes one marvel in this multitude of women is that while there is always one who is the husband's favorite, the others are not at all jealous and do not complain, or at least show no signs of it; all of them, busy with the housework, weaving their cotton beds, tending their gardens, and planting their roots, live together in an incomparable peace. On that point I will let each of you consider whether (even if it were not forbidden by God to take more than one wife) it would be possible for our women over here to live in such harmony. Better to send a man to the galleys than to put him in the midst of such a tumult and uproar as undoubtedly there would be; witness what happened to Jacob for having taken Leah and Rachel, even though they were sisters. How could several of our women live together, considering how often she who was especially ordained of God to be man's helpmeet and delight, is instead like a familiar demon in his house? In saying this, by no means do I intend to censure in any way those who behave otherwise: that is, who render the honor and obedience that they rightfully owe their husbands; on the contrary, when they are dutiful, thus bringing honor upon themselves first of all, I consider them as praiseworthy as I deem the others deserving of all blame.

To return, then, to the marriage customs of our Americans. Adultery on the women's part is held in such horror that, even though they have no other law than that of nature, if a married woman abandons herself to anyone other than her husband, the husband is empowered to kill her, or at least to repudiate her and send her away in shame. It is true that before they marry off their daughters, the fathers and relatives have no great scruples about prostituting them to the first comer; as I have already mentioned elsewhere, although the Norman interpreters had already, before our arrival, taken advantage of them in several villages, nonetheless their reputations were not ruined. But, as I said, once they are married they take care not to stumble, under pain of being beaten to death or sent away in shame.

I will add that, considering the hot region they inhabit, and in spite of what is said of Orientals, the marriageable young people of that land, boys as well as girls, are not so much given over to lust as one might think; and would to God it held no more sway over here. Nevertheless (for I would not make them out to be more virtuous than they are), sometimes when they are greatly vexed with each other they call each other *tyvire*, which is to say "bugger"; one can conjecture from this (for I affirm nothing) that this abominable sin is committed among them.

When a woman is with child, she avoids carrying heavy burdens, but does not abandon her ordinary tasks. Indeed, the women of our Tupinamba work far and away more than the men; for except for a few mornings (and not in the heat of day) when they cut wood to make gardens, the men do nothing except go to war, hunt, fish, and make their wooden swords, bows, arrows, feather garments, and the other things I have specified elsewhere, with which they adorn their bodies.

Concerning childbearing, here is what I can say as an eyewitness. Another Frenchman and I had bedded ourselves down one night in a village. Around midnight we heard a woman scream; thinking that is was that ravaging beast *Jan-ou-are* [jaguar] (which, as I have said elsewhere, preys on the savages) trying to devour her, we ran to her immediately. We found it was not that, but rather that her labor pains were making her cry out. So I myself saw the father receive the child in his arms, tie off the umbilical cord, and cut it with his teeth. Continuing to serve as midwife, but unlike ours over here, who pull on the noses of newborn infants to make them more beautiful, he, on the contrary, pushed in his son's nose and crushed it with his thumb; this is done over there with all children, who are thought to be prettier when they are snub-nosed.

As soon as the baby has come out of his mother's womb, he is washed clean and immediately painted all over with red and black by the father, who then lays him down, without swaddling him, in a cotton bed hung in the air. If the child is a male, the father makes him a little wooden sword, a little bow, and little arrows feathered with parrot plumes; then, placing it all beside the infant, and kissing him, he will say to him, his face beaming, "My son, when you come of age, be skilled in arms, strong, valiant, and warlike, so that you can take vengeance on your enemies." The father of the child I saw born named him *Orapacen*, that is, the bow and the string: for this word is composed of *orapat*, which is bow, and *cen*, which means its string. And that is how they name all their children, randomly giving them names of familiar things, just as we do to dogs and other animals over here: *Sarigoy* [opossum], a four-footed animal; *Arignan*, a hen; *Arabouten*, the brazilwood tree; *Pindo*, a tall grass, and so on.

As for nourishment, it will be some chewed flour, and other soft foods, along with the mother's milk. The mother stays in bed only a day or two, and then takes her baby, suspended from her neck in a cotton scarf made for the purpose, and goes off to the garden or to her other tasks. This is not to disparage the customs of the ladies over here, who, on account of our bad air, stay in bed for two or three weeks, and are for the most part so delicate that, although they have no illness that would prevent them from nurturing their infants as the American women do, as soon as they are delivered of them they are inhuman enough to send them away; so that if the children do not die without their mothers' knowing anything about it, in any case they must be partly grown and old enough to provide some pastime before their mothers will endure their presence.

Now if there are some dainty ladies here who think I do them wrong in comparing them to these savage women, whose rural fashioning (they will say) has nothing to do with their own tender and delicate bodies, I am content, so as to sweeten this bitter pill, to send them school to the brute beasts, which, even down to the smallest birds, will reach them this lesson: that it is up to each species to take care—indeed, to be at pains—to raise the progeny itself. But to cut short all their retorts, let me ask whether they would be more coddled than a former queen of France (as we read in the histories) was impelled by a true maternal passion: when she learned that her child had been suckled by another woman, she was so jealous that nothing would do but that she would make him vomit the milk that he had taken elsewhere than from his mother's breasts.

Now to return to my subject. It is commonly believed over here that if children in their tender and early infancy were not tightly swaddled, they would be deformed and bow-legged. Although that custom is by no means observed for American children (who, as I have said, are from their birth held and laid down without being swaddled), nevertheless you could not find children who walk straighter than they do. I admit that the gentle air and moderate temperature of that land are in part the cause, and I grant that in the winter it is good to keep our children well wrapped, covered, and tucked into their cradles, because otherwise they could not withstand the cold; but in the summer, and even in the temperate seasons, especially when it is not freezing, it seems to me from what I have seen (if I am not mistaken) that it would be better to let the little children caper about freely on some kind of bed one could devise, from which they could not fall, than to keep them so confined. And in fact, it is my opinion that it does great harm to these poor tender little creatures to be sweltering and half-roasted during the hot season in these swaddling clothes where they are bound as if for torture.

In any case, lest you tell me that I meddle in too many things, I will leave the raising of children over here to their fathers, mothers, and nurses, and add the following to what I have already said of American children. Although the women of that country have no clothes to wipe the behinds of their children, and do not even use the leaves of trees and grasses,

which they have in such abundance, nevertheless they are so careful that simply by using small sticks of wood that they break off, like little dowels, they clean their children so well that you never see them dirty. This is also what the adults do; of them, however (I digress to treat this foul subject), I will merely say that they ordinarily make water in their houses (since the ground is strewn with sand, and since there are fires burning throughout, there is no bad smell), but go off a long distance to get rid of their excrement.

The savages take care of all their children, which they have in swarms (although you will not find that any single father among our Brazilians will have six hundred sons, as has been written of a king of the Moluccan islands, which must be counted as a prodigy); still, because of their wars, in which it is only the men who fight and seek vengeance on their enemies, the males are more cherished than the females. You may ask what station of life the children are prepared for, and what they are taught when they are grown. In Chapters VIII, XIV, and XV, and elsewhere in this history, I have spoken of their natural state, their wars, and their eating of their enemies; you can easily imagine, since they have neither schools nor any other means of acquiring the learning of cultivated people—even less the liberal arts—, that their ordinary occupation, both as adults and as children, is to be not only hunters and warriors (true successors of Lamech, Nimrod, and Esau), but also killers and eaters of men.

Taking the discussion of the marriage customs of the Tupinamba as far as one decently can: contrary to what some people have imagined, the men preserve the modesty of nature by never consorting with their wives in public. In that respect, I maintain that they are preferable to that base Cynic philosopher who, caught in the act, instead of being ashamed said that he was planting a man; and surely those stinking billygoats that one sees in our time over here, who have not hidden themselves when committing their lustful acts, are incomparably more disgusting than they are.

To which I will add that during the space of about a year that we lived in that country and spent time in their company, we never saw in the women any signs of their monthly flux. I am of the opinion that they divert that flow, and have another way of purging themselves than that of the women over here. For I have seen young girls, twelve to fourteen years of age, whose mothers or female relatives would stand them up, feet together on a stone, and incise them with an animal's tooth as sharp as a knife, deep enough to draw blood, from the armpit down along the side and thigh, all the way to the knee. The girls, gritting their teeth in great pain, bled for some time. I think, as I have said, that from the beginning they use this remedy to hide the signs of their flow. Physicians or others more learned than I in such matters may reply, "How can you reconcile this with what you said earlier, that when they are married they are very fertile, seeing that when women cease to have their monthly flow they cannot conceive?" I reply that my intention is neither to resolve this question, nor to say any more about it.

Source: Jean de Léry. *History of a Voyage to the Land of Brazil*, translated by and with introduction by Janet Whatley, 152–157 (Berkeley: University of California Press, 1990).

GLOSSARY

adelantado Military title awarded to some Spanish conquistadores

adobe Mudbrick

aguada Artificial water reservoir

ají Chili pepper

aj pitzal Maya term for ball player

alcalde mayor Spanish official in charge of a certain district

aldeia Mission village in colonial Brazil

alguacil mayor Policeman and officer in a Spanish town council

alpaca Domesticated camelid in South America. Alpaca wool was used in textile production.

Antisuyu One of the four quarters of the Inca empire, located in the eastern section

apo In Inca Empire, a great lord or person of high status

arroba Spanish weight measure, roughly equivalent to 25 pounds (11.36 kg)

aryballus Double-handed storage vessel used by the Incas

atl Nahuatl word meaning "water"

atlatl Nahuatl word for spear or dart thrower

Aztlán Mythical homeland of the Mexica (Aztecs) before they migrated to the Central Valley of Mexico in the 13th century

Bakamo Carib deity, the Sky Serpent

baktun Largest unit of time in the Maya calendar, measuring a period of 400 years

balche Potent alcoholic beverage made from bark

barrio Spanish term for neighborhood or district

bohío Small hut or dwelling

boyez Carib shaman

brujería Spanish term for witchcraft

butu Hardwood war club used by Carib warriors

cactli Nahuatl word for "sandals"

Calendar Round Combination of the 365-day solar calendar (*haab*) and the 260-day sacred calendar (*tzolkin*). A total of 52 years has to pass before the same calendar combination repeats.

calli Nahuatl word meaning "house"

calmecac Aztec schools where young nobles were trained to become priests or warriors

calpixqui Tribute collector in Aztec Empire

capitulación Formal contract between the Crown of Castile and a private individual, outlining the obligations between the parties

casta Person of mixed race

cédula Spanish term for royal decree or order

cenote Maya term for sinkhole

Chaak Maya rain deity

Chac-Mool Meaning "red tiger," a stone sculpture of a reclining human figure with an offering bowl or plate on its stomach

charqui Quechua word for freeze-dried meat

chibal Maya term for a "patronym group"

chicle Sticky sap from the *zapote* tree, later used to make chewing gum

chimalli Nahuatl word for the shield used by Aztec warriors

Chinchaysuyu One of the four quarters of the Inca Empire, located in the northern quarter of the empire

chuño Quechua word for freeze-dried potato

cihuacóatl The Aztec ruler's closest adviser. In spite of its name, which means "snake woman," for an Aztec goddess, the office was held by a male.

Coatepec "Serpent Mountain" in Nahuatl; the place where the Mexica god Huitzilopochtli was born

coatequitl Aztec draft labor system

Coatlicue The name translates as "Lady of the Serpent Skirt." She was Huitzilopochtli's mother.

cofradía Spanish term for a lay religious brotherhood

cohiba Taino term for tobacco plant and leaves

colca Inca storehouse

Collasuyu One of the four quarters of the Inca Empire, located in the western quarter of the empire

conopa Andean domestic god, often made from stone

consulado Spanish merchant guild

copal Maya incense made from pine resin

Coricancha Incan Temple of the Sun in Cuzco

Coyolxauhqui   "Lady of the Bells" in Nahuatl, the moon goddess who was killed and dismembered by her brother Huitzilopochtli

creole   Person born in the New World to Spanish parents

cue   Aztec temple

Cuntisuyu   One of the four quarters of the Inca Empire, located in the northern quarter of the empire

doctrina   Rural parish in colonial Spanish America

domesticated   Of the reproduction of a plant or animal species, controlled by human intervention

encomendero   Individual who holds an *encomienda*

engenho   Sugar mill in colonial Brazil

entrada   Spanish term for military invasion

epigraphy   The study of ancient inscriptions, such as the Mayan glyphs

fanega   Spanish measure of volume, equivalent to about 15 bushels

geoglyph   Drawing etched on the surface of the ground

haab   The 365-day Maya solar calendar

hacienda   Landed estate for farming and ranching

hanan   Term used to designate the upper half of the two units (moieties) that divided Inca sociopolitical organization. The other half was the *hurin*.

hatun runa   Quechua term, meaning "adult, married male," or head of household

hechicería   Spanish term for sorcery

hidalgo   Spanish nobleman

horizon   Archaeological term used to designate a particular period in time when vast regions shared a series of common traits

huey tlatoani   The supreme Aztec ruler

Huitzilopochtli   "Hummingbird of the South," in Nahuatl; Mexica patron deity, associated with the Sun and with warfare

Hunahpu   One of the Hero Twins in the Maya story of creation (Popol Vuh)

hurin   Term used to designate the lower half of the two units (moieties) that divided Inca sociopolitical organization. The other half was the *hanan*.

huunal   Maya jester god

Illapa   Inca god of thunder or weather

Inti   Inca Sun God

Itzamnaaj   Maya Sky God

Ixchel   Maya Moon Goddess

ixcuahuac   Aztec sacrificial knife

kaloomte   Title assigned to the most powerful Maya rulers

katun   Maya unit of time, representing a period of 20 years

k'awiil   Maya god

kin   Maya unit of time, representing one day

K'inich   Maya Sun God, also known as God G

K'ujul Ajaw   Maya holy lord

limpieza de sangre   Spanish term for blood purity, or the absence of Jewish or Moorish ancestry

lintel   A wooden or stone beam that supports the wall above a doorway

llama   Domesticated camelid in South America. Llama wool was used in textile production, and llamas also served as beasts of burden.

macuahuitl   Mesoamerican sword, lined with sharp obsidian blades

maguey   Mexican plant used to make pulque

malqui   Quechua word for ancestor mummy

mameluco   In Brazil, the offspring of Portuguese and Indian parents

mano   Cylindrical stone used to grind maize, cacao beans, and chiles on the *metate* stone

masato   Fermented beer made from manioc

Mesoamerica   A region that covers 392,000 square miles (1.015 million km²) and includes all of modern Guatemala and Belize, two-thirds of Mexico, western Honduras, most of El Salvador, and northwestern Costa Rica

midden   Garbage heap that contains household or community artifacts

mitayo   An indigenous person forced to serve in a rotating labor draft called the *mita*

moiety   A division of society into two parts

obraje   Spanish term for textile workshop or factory

oca   A domesticated tuber grown in the high Andes

oidor   A Spanish judge in the high court, or *audiencia*

orejón   Literally, "long ear," in Spanish. Term applied to the Inca nobility, who were recognized by the large earspools they wore

oro   Spanish word for "gold"

pampa   Extensive grasslands region that extends over much of southern Argentina

patio process   Process by which silver is refined through the amalgamation with mercury

peso   Spanish coin and monetary unit. In Spanish America, one peso was worth eight reals of silver

piragua   Large canoe

plata   Spanish word for "silver"

pre-Columbian period   Term used to designate the period of the history of the Americas before the arrival of Christopher Columbus

quinoa   A domesticated grain grown in the Andean highlands of South America

relación   Spanish word for an "account" or "report"

repartimiento   The allocation of a group of indigenous people to a Spaniard to provide labor

residencia   Judicial review of a royal official's tenure in office *sacbé*   Raised paved road or causeway built by the Maya

Sapa Inca   The supreme Inca ruler

shaman   Priest or priestess who uses magic in curing or other divinatory practices

stela   Carved stone slab erected in front of Maya temples and altars, often with carved images and glyphic inscriptions

swidden   Synonymous with slash-and-burn agriculture

talud-tablero   Architectural style consisting of a platform structure, or *tablero*, on top of an inward-sloping surface or panel, or *talud*

tambo   Inca lodge or inn to house travelers

tameme   Nahuatl term for porter or carrier

Tawantinsuyu   Quechua word meaning "Land of Four Quarters." It was the name that the Incas used for their empire.

techcatl   Nahuatl word for sacrificial stone

tecpatl   Nahautl word for a flint knife used in ritual sacrifices

tematlatl   Aztec sling

Templo Mayor   The Great Temple in the Aztec capital of Tenochtitlán

teotl   Nahuatl term that describes a divine power or essence, found both in the natural world and in human beings

tepache   Fermented beverage of low alcohol content; common in many parts of Mexico

tepetl   Nahuatl word for mountain, hill

teuctli   Nahuatl word for lord

Tezcatlipoca   One of the four main creator gods of the Aztecs; his name translates as "Smoking Mirror"

tlacohtli   Nahuatl word for slave

tlacuiloque   Nahuatl term for scribe

Tlaloc   Aztec Rain God associated with fertility. His name translates as "He Who Makes the Plants Spring Up."

tlamani   Nahuatl word for captor

Tlatelolco   Tenochtitlán's sister city, located on the northern part of the island. It was the site of a great market.

tlatoani   An Aztec ruler, including the supreme ruler of the empire

tokrikoq   Provincial governor in Inca Empire

Tonatiuh   Aztec solar deity

tun   Maya unit of time, representing one year

tzolkin   The 260-day Maya sacred calendar

tzompantli   Nahuatl term for skull rack

uayeb   The unlucky last five days of the Maya solar calendar (*haab*)

uinal   Maya unit of time, representing 20 days, or one month in the 18-month Maya solar year

Virachocha   Inca Creator God

visita   Official visitation or inspection conducted by Spanish royal official or ecclesiastical authority

Xbalanque   One of the Hero Twins in the Maya story of creation (Popol Vuh)

Xipe Totec   Aztec god whose name translates as "Our Lord the Flayed One," closely associated with the practice of human sacrifice

zócalo   Open plaza

SUGGESTED READINGS FOR THIS VOLUME

Adams, Richard E. W. *Ancient Civilizations of the New World.* Boulder, Colo.: Westview Press, 1997.

——. *The Cambridge History of the Native Peoples of the Americas.* Vol. 2. Cambridge: Cambridge University Press, 2000.

——. *Prehistoric Mesoamerica.* 3d ed. Norman: University of Oklahoma Press, 2005.

Asselbergs, Florine. *Conquered Conquistadors: The Lienzo de Quauhquechollan, a Nahua Vision of the Conquest of Guatemala.* Leiden, Netherlands: Research School CNWS, 2004.

Baker, Geoffrey. *Imposing Harmony: Music and Society in Colonial Cuzco.* Durham, N.C.: Duke University Press, 2008.

Bakewell, P. J. *A History of Latin America: Empires and Sequels, 1450–1930.* Malden, Mass.: Blackwell Publishers, 1998.

Beckerman, Stephen, and Paul Valentine, eds. *Revenge in the Cultures of Lowland South America.* Gainesville: University Press of Florida, 2008.

Berdan, Frances. *The Aztecs of Central Mexico: An Imperial Society.* Fort Worth, Tex.: Harcourt Brace Jovanovich, 1982.

Blomster, Jeffrey P., ed. *After Monte Albán: Transformation and Negotiation in Oaxaca, Mexico.* Boulder: University Press of Colorado, 2008.

Brading, D. A. *The First America: The Spanish Monarchy, Creole Patriots, and the Liberal State, 1492–1867.* Cambridge: Cambridge University Press, 1993.

Brady, James E., and Keith M. Prufer. *In the Maw of the Earth Monster: Mesoamerican Ritual Cave Use.* Austin: University of Texas Press, 2005.

Breton, Alain, ed. *Rabinal Achi: A Fifteenth-Century Maya Dynastic Drama.* Translated by Teresa Lavender Fagan and Robert Schneider. Boulder: University Press of Colorado, 2007.

Bruhns, Karen Olsen. *Ancient South America.* Cambridge: Cambridge University Press, 1994.

Bruhns, Karen Olsen, and Karen E. Stothert. *Women in Ancient America.* Norman: University of Oklahoma Press, 1999.

Burkholder, Mark A., and Lyman L. Johnson. *Colonial Latin America.* New York: Oxford University Press, 2008.

Carmack, Robert M., Janine Gasco, and Gary H. Gossen. *The Legacy of Mesoamerica: History and Culture of a Native American Civilization.* Upper Saddle River, N.J.: Prentice Hall, 1996.

Carr, Raymond, ed. *Spain: A History.* Oxford: Oxford University Press, 2000.

Carrasco, Davíd, Lindsay Jones, and Scott Sessions. *Mesoamerica's Classic Heritage: From Teotihuacán to the Aztecs.* Boulder: University Press of Colorado, 2002.

Carrasco, Davíd, with Scott Sessions. *Daily Life in the Aztecs: People of the Sun and Earth.* Indianapolis, Ind.: Hackett Publishing, 2008.

Carrasco, Pedro. *The Tenochca Empire of Ancient Mexico: The Triple Alliance of Tenochtitlán, Tetzcoco, and Tlacopan.* Norman: University of Oklahoma Press, 1999.

Chasteen, John Charles. *Born in Blood and Fire: A Concise History of Latin America.* New York: W. W. Norton & Co., 2006.

Christenson, Allen J. *Popol Vuh: The Sacred Book of the Maya.* Norman: University of Oklahoma Press, 2007.

Cieza de León, Pedro de, Alexandra Parma Cook, and Noble David Cook. *The Discovery and Conquest of Peru: Chronicles of the New World Encounter.* Durham, N.C.: Duke University Press, 1998.

Clendinnen, Inga. *Ambivalent Conquests: Maya and Spaniard in Yucatan, 1517–1570.* New York: Cambridge University Press, 2003.

——. *Aztecs: An Interpretation.* Cambridge: Cambridge University Press, 1991.

Coe, Michael D. *Breaking the Maya Code.* New York: Thames & Hudson, 1999.

——. *The Maya.* 6th edition. New York: Thames & Hudson, 1999.

——. *Mexico: From the Olmecs to the Aztecs.* 4th ed. New York: Thames & Hudson, 1994.

Cushner, Nicholas P. *Why Have You Come Here? The Jesuits and the First Evangelization of Native America*. New York: Oxford University Press, 2006.

D'Altroy, Terence N. *The Incas*. Malden, Mass.: Blackwell Publishing, 2003.

Demarest, Arthur Andrew. *Ancient Maya: The Rise and Fall of a Rainforest Civilization*. Cambridge: Cambridge University Press, 2004.

Demarest, Arthur Andrew, Prudence M. Rice, and Don Stephen Rice. *The Terminal Classic in the Maya Lowlands Collapse, Transition, and Transformation*. Boulder: University Press of Colorado, 2004.

Díaz del Castillo, Bernal. *The Discovery and Conquest of Mexico, 1517–1521*. Cambridge, Mass.: Da Capo Press, 2003.

Donahue-Wallace, Kelly. *Art and Architecture of Viceregal Latin America, 1521–1821*. Albuquerque: University of New Mexico Press, 2008.

Durán, Diego. *The History of the Indies of New Spain*. Norman: University of Oklahoma Press, 1994.

Eakin, Marshall C. *The History of Latin America: Collision of Cultures*. New York: Palgrave Macmillan, 2007.

Elliott, J. H. *Empires of the Atlantic World: Britain and Spain in America, 1492–1830*. New Haven, Conn.: Yale University Press, 2006.

———. *Spain and Its World, 1500–1700: Selected Essays*. New Haven, Conn.: Yale University Press, 1989.

Farriss, Nancy M. *Maya Society under Colonial Rule: The Collective Enterprise of Survival*. Princeton, N.J.: Princeton University Press, 1984.

Ferguson, William M., and Richard E. W. Adams. *Mesoamerica's Ancient Cities*. Rev. ed. Albuquerque: University of New Mexico Press, 2001.

Fitzsimmons, James L. *Death and the Classic Maya Kings*. Austin: University of Texas Press, 2009.

Francis, J. Michael, ed. *Iberia and the Americas: Culture, Politics, and History*. 3 vols. Santa Barbara, Calif.: ABC-CLIO, 2006.

Gill, Richardson B. *The Great Maya Droughts: Water, Life, and Death*. Albuquerque: University of New Mexico Press, 2000.

Gonlin, Nancy, and Jon C. Lohse, eds. *Commoner Ritual and Ideology in Ancient Mesoamerica*. Boulder: University Press of Colorado, 2007.

Haring, C. H. *The Spanish Empire in America*. San Diego, Calif.: Harcourt Brace Jovanovich, 1947.

Hassig, Ross. *Mexico and the Spanish Conquest*. 2d ed. Norman: University of Oklahoma Press, 2006.

Hemming, John. *The Conquest of the Incas*. London: Macmillan, 1970.

Hill, Jonathan D., and Fernando Santos-Granero. *Comparative Arawakan Histories: Rethinking Language Family and Culture Area in Amazonia*. Urbana: University of Illinois Press, 2002.

Janusek, John Wayne. *Ancient Tiwanaku*. Cambridge: Cambridge University Press, 2008.

Julien, Catherine J. *Reading Inca History*. Iowa City: University of Iowa Press, 2000.

Kamen, Henry. *How Spain Became a World Power*. New York: HarperCollins, 2003.

Keatinge, Richard W. *Peruvian Prehistory*. Cambridge: Cambridge University Press, 1988.

Keegan, William F. *Taíno Indian Myth and Practice: The Arrival of the Stranger King*. Gainesville: University Press of Florida, 2007.

Kepecs, Susan, and Rani T. Alexander, eds. *The Postclassic to Spanish-Era Transition in Mesoamerica: Archaeological Perspectives*. Albuquerque: University of New Mexico Press, 2005.

Kiple, Kenneth F., and Kriemhild C. Ornelas, eds. *The Cambridge World History of Food*. 2 vols. Cambridge: Cambridge University Press, 2000.

Lathrop, Jacqueline Phillips. *Ancient Mexico: Cultural Traditions in the Land of the Feathered Serpent*. Dubuque, Iowa: Kendall/Hunt Publication Co., 1998.

Lee, Jongsoo. *The Allure of Nezahualcoyotl: Pre-Hispanic History, Religion, and Nahua Poetics*. Albuquerque: University of New Mexico Press, 2008.

León Portilla, Miguel. *The Broken Spears: The Aztec Account of the Conquest of Mexico*. Boston: Beacon Press, 1992.

Léry, Jean de. *History of a Voyage to the Land of Brazil, Otherwise Called America*. Berkeley: University of California Press, 1990.

Lockhart, James. *The Nahuas after the Conquest*. Stanford, Calif.: Stanford University Press, 1992.

———. *We People Here: Nahuatl Accounts of the Conquest of Mexico*. Berkeley: University of California Press, 1993.

Lockhart, James, and Stuart B. Schwartz. *Early Latin America: A History of Colonial Spanish America and Brazil*. Cambridge: Cambridge University Press, 1983.

Lohse, Jon C., and Fred Valdez Jr., eds. *Ancient Maya Commoners*. Austin: University of Texas Press, 2004.

Lucero, Lisa J. *Water and Ritual: The Rise and Fall of Classic Maya Rulers*. Austin: University of Texas Press, 2006.

Lynch, John. *Spain, 1516–1598: From Nation State to World Empire*. Oxford: Blackwell, 1991.

Malpass, Michael A. *Daily Life in the Inca Empire*. Indianapolis, Ind.: Hackett Publishing, 2008.

Mann, Charles C. *1491: New Revelations of the Americas before Columbus*. New York: Knopf, 2005.

Martin, Simon, and Nikolai Grube. *Chronicle of the Maya Kings and Queens: Deciphering the Dynasties of the Ancient Maya*. London: Thames & Hudson, 2000.

Matthew, Laura E., and Michael R. Oudijk. *Indian Conquistadors: Indigenous Allies in the Conquest of Mesoamerica*. Norman: University of Oklahoma Press, 2007.

McKillop, Heather. *The Ancient Maya: New Perspectives*. New York: W. W. Norton & Co., 2004.

McNeil, Cameron L., ed. *Chocolate in Mesoamerica: A Cultural History of Cacao*. Gainesville: University Press of Florida, 2006.

Meyer, Michael C., William L. Sherman, and Susan Deeds. *The Course of Mexican History*. 8th ed. New York: Oxford University Press, 2007.

Mills, Kenneth, and William B. Taylor. *Colonial Latin America: A Documentary History.* Wilmington, Del.: Scholarly Resources, 2002.

Minelli, Laura Laurencich. *The Inca World: The Development of Pre-Columbian Peru, A.D. 1000–1534.* Norman: University of Oklahoma Press, 2000.

Moseley, Michael E. *The Incas and Their Ancestors.* London: Thames & Hudson, 1992.

Nesvig, Martin Austin. *Local Religion in Colonial Mexico.* Albuquerque: University of New Mexico Press, 2006.

Norton, Marcy. *Sacred Gifts, Profane Pleasures: A History of Tobacco and Chocolate in the Atlantic World.* Ithaca, N.Y.: Cornell University Press, 2008.

Pasztory, Esther. *Teotihuacán: An Experiment in Living.* Norman: University of Oklahoma Press, 1997.

Patterson, Thomas Carl. *The Inca Empire: The Formation and Disintegration of a Pre-Capitalist State.* Oxford: Berg, 1997.

Quilter, Jeffrey, and Mary Ellen Miller. *A Pre-Columbian World.* Washington, D.C.: Dumbarton Oaks, 2006.

Restall, Matthew. *The Maya World: Yucatec Culture and Society, 1550–1850.* Stanford, Calif.: Stanford University Press, 1997.

———. *Seven Myths of the Spanish Conquest.* Oxford: Oxford University Press, 2003.

Rostworowski de Diez Canseco, María. *History of the Inca Realm.* Cambridge: Cambridge University Press, 1999.

Sabloff, Jeremy A. *The Cities of Ancient Mexico: Reconstructing a Lost World.* New York: Thames & Hudson, 1997.

Safford, Frank, and Marco Palacios. *Colombia: Fragmented Land, Divided Society.* New York: Oxford University Press, 2002.

Salomon, Frank, and Stuart B. Schwartz. *The Cambridge History of the Native Peoples of the Americas.* Vol. 3: *South America.* Cambridge: Cambridge University Press, 1999.

Sandstrom, Alan R., and E. Hugo García Valencia, eds. *Native Peoples of the Gulf Coast of Mexico.* Tucson: University of Arizona Press, 2005.

Schroeder, Susan, Stephanie Wood, and Robert Haskett, eds. *Indian Women of Early Mexico.* Norman: University of Oklahoma Press, 1997.

Schwartz, Stuart B. *Victors and Vanquished: Spanish and Nahua Views of the Conquest of Mexico.* Boston: Bedford/ St. Martin's, 2000.

Silverblatt, Irene. *Moon, Sun, and Witches: Gender Ideologies and Class in Inca and Colonial Peru.* Princeton, N.J.: Princeton University Press, 1987.

Smith, Michael E. *Aztec City-State Capitals.* Gainesville: University Press of Florida, 2008.

———. *The Aztecs.* Oxford: Blackwell, 1996.

Socolow, Susan Migden. *The Women of Colonial Latin America.* Cambridge: Cambridge University Press, 2000.

Staden, Hans. *Hans Staden's True History: An Account of Cannibal Captivity in Brazil.* Edited by Neil L. Whitehead. Durham, N.C.: Duke University Press, 2008.

Stein, Gil J. *The Archaeology of Colonial Encounters: Comparative Perspectives.* Santa Fe, N.Mex.: School of American Research Press, 2005.

Sugiyama, Saburo. *Human Sacrifice, Militarism, and Rulership: Materialization of the State Ideology at the Feathered Serpent Pyramid, Teotihuacán.* Cambridge: Cambridge University Press, 2005.

Tenenbaum, Barbara A., and Georgette M. Dorn. *Encyclopedia of Latin American History and Culture.* New York: C. Scribner's Sons, 1996.

Todorov, Tzvetan. *The Conquest of America: The Question of the Other.* Norman: University of Oklahoma Press, 1999.

Trigger, Bruce G., and Wilcomb E. Washburn. *The Cambridge History of the Native Peoples of the Americas.* Vol. 1: *North America.* Cambridge: Cambridge University Press, 1996.

Van Tuerenhout, Dirk R. *The Aztecs: New Perspectives.* Santa Barbara, Calif.: ABC-CLIO, 2005.

Webster, David L. *The Fall of the Ancient Maya: Solving the Mystery of the Maya Collapse.* London: Thames & Hudson, 2002.

Wells, E. Christian, and Karla L. Davis-Salazar, eds. *Mesoamerican Ritual Economy: Archaeological and Ethnological Perspectives.* Boulder: University Press of Colorado, 2007.

Wood, Michael. *Conquistadors.* Berkeley: University of California Press, 2000.

Yannakakis, Yanna. *The Art of Being In-Between: Native Intermediaries, Indian Identity, and Local Rule in Colonial Oaxaca.* Durham, N.C.: Duke University Press, 2008.

⊰ INDEX ⊱

Italic page numbers indicate illustrations; **boldface** page numbers indicate main headings; page numbers followed by g indicate glossary entries; page numbers followed by m indicate maps.